RELIGION IN THE ANDES

Religion in the Andes

VISION
AND IMAGINATION IN
EARLY COLONIAL
PERU

SABINE MACCORMACK

PRINCETON UNIVERSITY PRESS

PRINCETON, NEW JERSEY

LIBRARY OF CONGRESS CATALOGING-IN-PUBLICATION DATA
MacCormack, Sabine.
Religion in the Andes : vision and imagination in early
colonial Peru / Sabine MacCormack.
p.   cm.
Includes bibliographical references and index.
ISBN 0-691-09468-3 (alk. paper)
1. Incas—Religion and mythology. 2. Incas—Historiography.
3. Peru—History—Conquest, 1522–1548. 4. Indians of
South America—Andes Region—Religion and mythology.
5. Indians of South America—Andes Region—History—
17th century. 6. Catholic Church—Missions—
Andes Region—History. I. Title.
F3429.3.R3M278   1991
299'.895—dc20   91-15441

This book has been composed in Linotron Bembo

Princeton University Press books are printed on
acid-free paper, and meet the guidelines for permanence
and durability of the Committee on
Production Guidelines for Book Longevity
of the Council on Library Resources

Printed in the United States of America

2   4   6   8   10   9   7   5   3

FOR CATHERINE

Homo liber de nulla re minus quam de morte cogitat, et eius sapientia non mortis sed vitae meditatio est.

Spinoza, *Ethica* IV, prop. LXVII

CONTENTS

CONTENTS

GRATIARUM ACTIO

WORK ON this book has brought with it many felicitous encounters and friendships that I record with gratitude now that the book is going on its way. The early years of my research were blessed by Nigel Glendinning's support and encouragement. He helped me feel at home in Spanish libraries and archives and encouraged me to grow confident about moving so far away from the study of the late antique Mediterranean, the field in which I was originally trained.

The welcome I received from colleagues in the United States far exceeded my hopes when I first came here some eleven years ago. I am moved both by the generosity of the scholars whom I have been privileged to know and by the affection and sheer human proximity of friends, scattered though most of them are across the length and breadth of the country. At the University of Texas at Austin, Janet Meisel's company and conversation deep into many nights and on those wonderfully hot and sunny Texas afternoons sustained the isolation of other times spent over books and papers. Hours of talk about the Andes with Elayne Zorn and Linda Seligmann and evenings of listening to Tom Torino's music come back now, as I recall them, with all the intense aliveness of interests and loves that are deeply shared.

Inés Sanchez Ochoa guided my steps when I first arrived in Madrid, eager to learn but speaking almost no Spanish. Later, in Madrid, Ithaca, and elsewhere, John Murra helped my inquiries and told wonderful stories, both historical and other. Franklin Pease in Lima gave me a lovely glimpse into the world of learning and of books as it was in the City of the Kings, and thanks to conversations with Maria Rostworowski I thought much more carefully about Garcilaso de la Vega the Inca than I would have done otherwise. In Seville I learned about the world of Fernando de Avendaño from Antonio Acosta, and in Madrid Fermin del Pino Diaz, with his students Lorencio Lopez-Ocon Cabrera and Jesus Bustamante, produced information and arguments that led me to reconsider my ideas about sixteenth century Spanish historians.

Travel for research in Spain and Peru was in part funded by the American Philosophical Society, and by the Center of Latin American Studies and the Pew Trust, both at Stanford University. I am very grateful to these institutions for supporting my work. My very special gratitude goes to the staff of the Biblioteca Nacional in Madrid. Throughout the years of working on this book and on related projects, I have never left the Library without a deep sense of peace and of having found a home there to which I will always be glad to return. Another environment of quiet reflection where I learned a great deal was the bookshop of Luis Bardón Lopez in Madrid, and I thank him for allowing me to spend so much time reading in his books and browsing along his shelves. Long hours in Green Library at Stanford University come back now with a sunny richness which I wish might be reflected back to the librarians who made it possible.

At the Wilson Center in Washington, D.C., thoughts about this book first acquired concrete form, and I would like to thank Richard Morse and Ann Sheffield for fostering my pursuits with their amiable mingling of interest and benevolence. Dumbarton Oaks was beautiful, and it was there that old work on late antiquity finally became continuous with new work on Spain and Peru. This would not have occurred so happily without Elizabeth Boone's most generous support and without the conversation and friendship of Robert Edwards.

Talking with John Rowe helped clarify ideas about Inca history, festivals, and sacred places, and Enrique Mayer's comments about Andean agriculture made those ideas more concrete. Bruce Mannheim, Tristan Platt, Frank Salomon, and Tom Abercrombie have shared their knowledge and thoughts with me. And I remember some wonderful hours talking with Tom Zuidema and teaching in one of his classes.

At Stanford, Amos Funkenstein confirmed by word and example the proposition that thinking is natural to human beings thus opening the door to many fine conversations relating to this book and to other matters. Michael Ryan believed that the book I had in mind to write could actually be written, thus leading me to make a start. Paul Robinson looked over my shoulder as I wrote the first chapters, read them, and encouraged me to continue. His presence was instrumental in finding the sequences and shapes in which to order my ideas. Cornell Fleischer also read those beginning chapters and reminded me, at times when it was important, of the proper direction of thoughts and arguments. I thank Rolena Adorno for reading part of the first, and all of the second, draft of the book. Another early reader was Peggy Liss, who asked a variety of useful questions, in addition to giving me her copy of Las Casas' *Apologética*, a present that I very much cherish. Catherine MacCormack's suggestions for rewriting the first chapter were crucial, and I also thank her for being a lovely companion on our many journeys.

It was a delight to share with Vincent Gilliam my early explorations of Leone Ebreo and Aristotle's *De anima*; to talk about sixteenth-century Spain with Gladys White; and to be kept up to date in late antiquity by

Nora Chapman and Rachel Stocking. Trials of acquiring pictures for this book have become associated with the sound of Laura Downs laughing and with sitting on a rooftop with her overlooking New York at dusk. John Hyslop gave me two wonderful days in the American Museum of Natural History in New York. Costanza di Capua most generously obtained for me the photograph that is reproduced in figure 49. When at last the manuscript was ready for editing, Victoria Wilson-Schwartz asked a very large number of useful questions by way of chasing down obscurities, inconsistencies, and errors. I thank her warmly.

I would have dearly liked to have placed this book into the hands of Arnaldo Momigliano. Indeed, when I saw him last, he asked me about the book, but at that time I had little to say. Thus, by way of responding to his question, I fell silent and followed my thoughts as I stood next to his hospital bed. "But you are reflecting on it," he said after a long while, and hesitating just a moment, I concurred. When I heard of Arnaldo Momigliano next, not long afterward, it was that he had died. At that time, I was reading Spinoza. From missionary treatises and catechisms I was familiar with the precept that one should live bearing in mind the day of one's death and was thus struck by Spinoza's statement, in the *Ethics*, that "a free man thinks of nothing less than of death and his wisdom is a meditation not of death, but of life." This was one of the passages, as it turned out, that Arnaldo Momigliano had chosen to be read at the service to remember him, and it is in this way that I do remember him and thank him for his friendship.

ILLUSTRATIONS

ILLUSTRATIONS

Pasto

E Q U A T O R

Quito

Manta
Puerto Viejo
▲ Chimborazo
Riobamba
Tumebamba

Tumbez

Paita

Río Marañón

Chachapoyas

Cajamarca

Huamachuco

Río Ucayali

Trujillo

Huaylas

Recuay
Huánuco
Ocros
Cajatambo

Chilón
Xauxa
Canta
Lima
Huarochiri
Pachacamac
Huamanga

Río Apurímac

Vilcas
Calca
Chincha
Andahuaylas
Cuzco
Urcos
Ica

Nasca

Ayaviri
Lampaz E L   C O L L A O
Chucuito LAKE TITICACA
Arequipa
Copacabana La Paz (Chuquiabo)

Sicasica
Cochabamba

PACIFIC OCEAN

Arica
La Plata
(Chuqisaca)

C H A R C A S
Potosí

MAP
LOCATION

0   200 miles
0   200 km

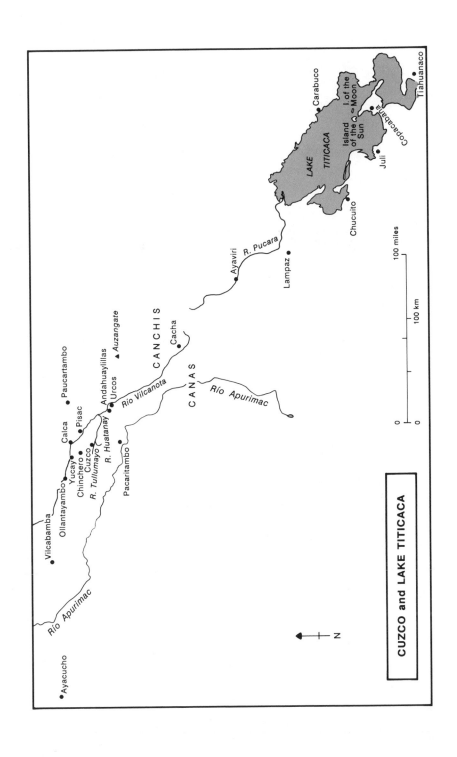

CUZCO and LAKE TITICACA

RELIGION IN THE ANDES

PROLOGUE:
THEMES AND ARGUMENTS

THIS BOOK is the first of two volumes studying Inca and Andean culture as they were understood in the sixteenth and seventeenth centuries. It focuses on religious experience in the Andes, while the second volume will have as its main theme Inca and Andean perceptions of myth and history.

Between 1524 and 1532, a band of Spanish soldiers of fortune led by Francisco Pizarro, planned, and then implemented, an invasion of the Inca empire that resulted in the capture and execution of its ruler, the Inca Atahualpa, in 1533. At that time, this empire comprised most of contemporary Peru and Bolivia, the southern part of Ecuador, and the northern part of Chile. The empire's heartland lay around the capital of Cuzco. The expansion of the Incas from Cuzco had been recent, beginning in the mid-fifteenth century. The Spanish invaders, arriving some eighty years later, also worked fast, for the conquest and reorganization of Atahualpa's far-flung dominions as the viceroyalty of Peru can be said to have been completed by 1581, when the fifth viceroy, Francisco de Toledo, ended his term.

Inca religion in the narrow sense consists of the beliefs and rituals that the Incas practiced in their homeland, in and around Cuzco. The beliefs and rituals they brought to their subjects and allies arose from what was done in Cuzco. But the Inca empire comprised a variety of regional polities that succeeded to a certain extent in maintaining separate identities. The degree to which Inca religious belief and practice were absorbed by those polities varied greatly, so that, overall, the religious beliefs and practices of Cuzco varied from their counterparts elsewhere. When, thus, I write of Inca religion, it is the imperial religion of Cuzco and its direct offshoots that I refer to. This religion came to an end with the fall of the Inca empire. But vestiges and memories of it lived on for many generations in different parts of the Andes. Indeed, some Inca religious ideas and practices are still adhered to. But for the most part, the non-Inca, nonimperial cults and myths of the Andes proved much more tenacious and resilient than those of imperial Cuzco. Although it is hard to overestimate the destructive effect that throughout the Andes the Spanish invasion brought with it, the fact remains that outside the city and region of Cuzco, religious life was in general more continuous. Given this continuity, I use the term Andean religion to refer both to non-Inca beliefs and practices as followed in Inca times, and to the non-Christian beliefs and practices of Andeans living in Spanish Peru. After describing the cognitive and theological preconceptions of sixteenth-century Spaniards as relevant to their understanding of Inca and Andean religion (chapter I), I turn to those aspects of Inca religion that the invaders actually observed before the collapse of the Inca empire (chapter II). I then go on to deal with what was remembered about Inca religion after 1533 and with the conglomerate, which endured long after the Incas were gone, of Inca, fused with regional Andean, beliefs and cults. While realizing that Inca and Andean religion are not identical, I study them in this book as converging, not as rigidly separate entities.

We know about Inca and Andean religion for the most part from Spaniards. We have not learned how to "read" the *quipus*, bundles of knotted strings, on which the Incas recorded both numerical and narrative information. Indeed, only a very small proportion of the quipus that must once have existed now survive. What can be learned about the Incas must thus be searched for in colonial documents, in the writings of the early Spanish historians of Peru, and in a small group of texts composed by Andeans during the early colonial period. In addition, archival research is adding an ever-increasing number of documents to the existing inventory, and Andean archeology and ethnography are growing in volume and refinement. A little over a century ago, there existed only a handful of cultured individuals for whom the Inca empire was more than a name to which a small oddment of facts could be attached. This situation has changed almost beyond recognition. We have learned so much that bibliographical guides, which would have been superfluous a hundred years ago, are becoming indispensable. In addition, we have learned that however unpromising, biased, or incomplete our sources may be, they can be dissected in such a way as to reveal information the very existence of which it had earlier been next to impossible even to imagine.

The present book could not have been so much as thought of without the path-breaking research of other Andean scholars, both past and present. Nonetheless, its central themes lie to one side of the mainstream of Andean research as it stands today.

I begin my account of Inca and Andean religion with the year of the Spanish invasion, 1532, and I end it in around the year 1660. By this time, so I seek to show, such vestiges as remained of Inca religion had been so firmly incorporated into regional Andean cults that the two components, always difficult to distinguish in any absolute sense, had fused almost completely. It was not to imitate the Incas that Andeans still addressed prayers to the divine Sun in the 1660s, but because their fathers and fathers' ancestors had prayed to the Sun from time immemorial. In short, the Inca cult of the Sun was no longer remembered in its own right but only as part of the ancient ancestral religion. The other consideration that leads me to end my account in the 1660s is that by that time, although colonial government allied with Christian missionary efforts had in part transformed, and in part destroyed, Andean religious practice and sensibility, some aspects of Andean religion lived on relatively unchanged. This was no longer the case by the early eighteenth century. Taking the 1660s as a watershed, I examine in the last chapter what was old and what was new in Andean religion at that time (IX.2).

Both the structure and the argument of the book arise from the inescapable fact that whatever understanding it may now be possible to gain of Inca and Andean religion must be channeled through the writings of men who in one way or another were outsiders to that religion.[1] No one, not even the handful of Andeans who in the sixteenth and seventeenth centuries set pen to paper, wrote explicitly as adherents of the ancient religious beliefs and practices of the Andes. And the majority of Spaniards and criollos who wrote about Andean religion from personal observation wrote with the intention of assisting Christian missionary endeavor. As time went on, missionaries increasingly allied themselves with the secular government so as to destroy or "extirpate" Andean religion, hoping thereby to make Andeans more willing listeners to their message. Put differently, a vital component of our information about Inca and Andean religious practice comes from men committed to its destruction (chapters II, IV, VI, IX).

At the same time, not all Spanish observers of the Incas and their empire, whether they wrote as missionaries, administrators, or independently as historians, advocated the violent destruction of Andean religion and of its cultural and economic underpinnings. They did, however, agree with their more aggressive colleagues that the people of the Andes ought to convert to Christianity. What was not agreed upon was the most appropriate method of achieving this end (chapters V, VIII).

I show that, inevitably, the divergent theological and political programs these authors stood for conditioned not only their interpretation of Andean data, but also the way in which they selected those data. Were this not the case, the sources that come to us from the Andes during the sixteenth and seventeenth centuries would be very different—perhaps not better, but certainly different.

Given that everything we know about Inca and Andean religion arises

[1] On the strengths and limitations of outsiders as faithful observers, see A. Momigliano, *Alien Wisdom: The Limits of Hellenization* (Cambridge, 1975), a work I have resorted to at many times in writing this book.

PROLOGUE

from the Spanish invasion of the Inca empire and from continuing tension and conflict between Andeans and invaders, I examine Inca and Andean religion in the light of this reality, rather than endeavoring to peer behind it. What, therefore, I seek to describe and explain is not Inca and Andean religion in isolation, but Inca and Andean religion as it was practiced, observed, and remembered during the sixteenth and seventeenth centuries.

It was in the first years after the invasion that a beginning was made of devising the terminology with which to describe Inca and Andean religion by transferring to the Andes the differentiations between true and false religion that had been used in Christian Spain and Europe for centuries. As used in the Andes, this terminology changed, because Spanish perceptions of Inca and Andean religion changed and became more knowledgeable. The first invaders had little interest in religion and described without prolonged reflection what came before their eyes. When Atahualpa was dead and after the first wave of Inca resistance had been quelled, opportunity arose for more sustained observation and reflection. Once the missionaries and some of the conquerors had begun to learn Quechua, it was possible to go beyond the all too primitive mediation that the interpreters whom the first invaders had pressed into service were able to supply. At the same time, however, while Spanish understanding of the Andes changed, so did Andean religious thought and observance. Moreover, in due course, Andeans themselves addressed the invaders on the subject of religion. In studying Inca and Andean religion, therefore, we study a series of distinct phases and layers both in Andean reality and in different perceptions of this reality. The chapters of this book thus move not only through a chronological sequence, but also through a sequence of phases of change in Inca and Andean religion, and through distinct and changing layers of perception expressed by those who wrote about religion in the Andes.

As a result, I am as interested in the mental furniture, thoughts, and doings of the invaders as I am in those of Incas and Andeans. Indeed, because the earliest information, and also the most continuous and consistent strands of information, about Inca and Andean religion come to us from the invaders, I begin with them. Confrontations with adherents of alternative or deviant systems of religious belief and practice were nothing new for Spanish Catholics in the sixteenth century (chapter I). Strategies of observing, describing, and suppressing Inca and Andean religion were thus adapted from earlier experience in Spain. That experience was of more than practical and political importance, for it reached into every recess of thinking and feeling. I thus show that what the invaders, be they simple soldiers and administrators or men of learning and reflection, saw in the Andes arose in part from what was actually there to be seen, and in part from what these men regarded as perceptible, and thus knowable, in the first place. For example, the devil will be neither seen nor known by those who do not think he exists. Spaniards did, however, see and hear the devil quite regularly in Spain and even more regularly in the Andes (chapter II.1). This tells us much about their conceptions of cosmic and social order and about what they believed could be known, and how.

During the sixteenth and seventeenth centuries, authors writing about the Andes who occupied themselves with this issue, whether directly or by implication, conceptualized cognition in terms that derived, in the last resort, from Aristotle's discussion of the faculties of the soul, in particular intellect, sense perceptions, and imagination. They thought of imagination as the faculty that distilled phantasms or imaged concepts from sense perception. These phantasms were then processed by the intellect into reasoned thought. On the one hand, imagination was therefore the necessary mediator between the mind and what sense perception gathered about the world external to the mind. But on the other hand, imagination was regarded as being constantly in danger of forming random or illusory phantasms not strictly based on sense perceptions, as happens in dreams. Equally, theologians reasoned, imagination could open itself to demonic illusions. From the beginning, Spaniards in the Andes considered the Andean imagination to be particularly vulnerable in this respect (chapters III.1; IV.3). However, given the prevalence of such ideas, one can also ask, what specifically occasioned the Spanish conviction that the devil was so exceptionally active in Peru?

The resolution of these issues constitutes one thematic strand in this book. This strand has two aspects. First, Spanish perceptions of the devil's ubiquity in Peru point to the vital importance of Inca and Andean divinatory cults. For, as Spaniards understood it, it was the devil who spoke in Andean oracles (chapter II.1). This fact has led scholars, few of whom believe in the devil's existence, to give short shrift to information about Andean divination, demonically inspired as it was alleged to have been. If, however, one separates Spanish preconception from Andean reality, it is possible not only to reveal something of the political workings of Andean oracles, but also to understand one of the several ways Andean deities had of touching and entering into the hearts of human beings (chapters II.1; cf. IV.3; VII; IX.2).

Second, however, this issue of how a deity may touch a human being requires that we explain how such touching was perceived. Christian theologians in medieval and Renaissance Europe gave much thought to the question of how God touched human beings, and how he might, however indirectly, be perceived and known by them. Their answers focused, precisely, on the indirect nature of the touching, perceiving, and knowing. Man cannot know God directly through either intellect or the senses. Rather, one of the ways God had of touching man was by placing into the imagination some vision or phantasm conducive to perceiving, knowing, and approaching him (chapter I). It was taken for granted that such phantasms and visions would be beyond all doubt recognizable. The crucified Christ, for instance, would be recognizable by his wounds and the instruments of his passion (chapter I.1). And yet, this faith in the recognizability of visions and phantasms of a religious nature was a fragile one. For both in Spain and in colonial Peru it was hedged about by a barrage of regulations designed to authenticate genuine visions and phantasms and to discredit erroneous or demonic ones (chapter I; cf. VII; VIII.2).

To investigate the demonic visions and phantasms that interested theologians and philosophers of the sixteenth and seventeenth centuries can easily lead one to overlook the fact that this apparently theological issue had a vital cultural and political dimension. For what made visions recognizable as divine or demonic was culturally specific. It was thus for cultural and political reasons, not only for theological and philosophic ones, that in Europe, certain visions and phantasms seen in the imagination were defined as demonic. This is why no philosophical and cognitive vocabulary was available to evaluate Andean oracles in any terms other than those of European culture and politics. Spaniards in Peru had no choice but to describe those oracles as demonic (chapters V; VI; IX.1–2).

Up to the early seventeenth century or slightly beyond, individuals of theological and philosophical refinement living in Spain, and in Europe at large, shared a common vocabulary with their fellows in Peru. But this ceased to be the case after the early seventeenth century. In the Andes, the rift between Andean religion and Christianity was growing ever more profound (chapter IX). Andean religion came to be seen no longer as an approach, however limited, to religious understanding, but as a set of superstitions the Indians were unable to shed because, thanks to their perceived cultural backwardness and lack of intellectual talent, they were and remained victims of demonic frauds and delusions. If ever Andeans had been considered as partners in a religious and cultural discourse, as they indeed had been by, among others, Bartolomé de Las Casas (chapter V) and Garcilaso de la Vega (chapter VIII), they were no longer considered thus in the mid-seventeenth century (chapter IX.1). This happened not only because the colonial church came increasingly to rely on coercion rather than persuasion (chapter VI), but also because the political and economic program of the colonial state entailed an ever deepening rift between conquerors and conquered.

In Europe, meanwhile, it was Spinoza who conceptualized an imaginative faculty that was not dependent on culturally specific visions and mental images and was not enticeable by the devil (Epilogue). Indeed, one of the reasons why Spinoza's philosophy and theology required no demons was that he regarded the cultural and religious traditions that were at the same time vehicles for religious exclusivity and intolerance as irrelevant to the true knowledge of God and man. But by Spinoza's time the colonial church in Peru had settled into its own fixed patterns, and philosophical and theological breakthroughs in Europe had no repercussions on Peruvian clerical thinking. In any case, Spinoza's philosophy was not widely influential during his own lifetime. Spinoza does, however, highlight the nature and intractability of the theological predicaments with which missionaries and other European newcomers were confronted in Peru.

I thus use sixteenth-century concepts of the imagination and of the devil, who is so prevalent in the Andean sources, as instruments that allow me to catch some glimpses of Andean religious experience. At the same time, it is the prevalence of the devil in the sources that makes it possible to describe the religious mentalities of Spanish missionaries and officials in a new way. These men have left a set of unflattering portraits of themselves in the documents they generated. They are, however, portraits we can endeavor to understand. The officials and missionaries of colonial Peru acted from within their own culture and from within the constraints that this culture imposed on them. Although there did exist certain choices as to how, specifically, the values of that culture could be accommodated in the Andes, these choices were limited. Much has been written regarding Peru and other colonial societies about the constraints of violence and economic exploitation that are the upshot of colonial government. Cultural constraints—which comprise also the constraints of religious belief—have in general been overlooked. I have sought, for Peru, to redress this imbalance in our understanding of colonial societies. Cultural constraints were operative for all participants in the story I tell. This story is therefore not simply about Andean responses to missionary initiative and coercion. Rather, it is about violent confrontations between representatives of opposing religious traditions, who all acted, to a greater or lesser degree, within the constraints imposed by those traditions. To consider what the constraints that pressed on the missionaries actually were makes it possible to avail ourselves of their perceptions in order to comprehend more clearly the Andean beliefs and cults that they combated so bitterly, rather than seeking to impose our own vision on what we feel they ought to have seen but did not see.

Within this framework of theme and argument, the structure of the present study is guided by a further consideration. It is that the Andeans and Spaniards on whose writings I draw understood what they understood and wrote what they wrote within a specific framework of space and time. My chapters are thus composed from clusters of information that, in so far as the sources permit, cohere with regard to their time and place of origin.

I open my account of Inca religion with a detailed description by a Spanish eyewitness of the celebration of the maize harvest in Cuzco in 1535 (chapter II.2). It is a unique document, written at the very moment when the imperial religious edifice was beginning to collapse. Nonetheless, information about these festivals continued to accumulate, but it was information of a different kind (chapters III.2–3; IV.1–3). During the generation or so after the invasion, officials, historians, and missionaries sought to learn how the Inca empire had been organized and how it was administered. Most of their inquiries were conditioned by the practical concerns of government and Christian mission. These inquiries thus focused on the ritual calendar, on landed and other properties of the Incas and of Andean deities, and on the organization of labor. The finer points of ritual, belief, and myth were of less interest, although one of the invaders, Juan de Betanzos, who had married the Inca Atahualpa's consort, wrote a careful account of what this lady's kinsfolk told him about such matters (chapter III.2–3). Most of what we know about Inca imperial festivals and related questions comes from texts composed before 1581, when the viceroy Toledo, having governed Peru since 1569, returned to Spain. These were years of great upheaval in the Andes, when Toledo eliminated what remained of Inca resistance, created a colonial tax structure, and moved large sectors of the Andean population from their original settlements to Spanish-style villages. He also organized a series of inquiries into the Inca past. The historical and historiographical issues arising from Toledo's inquiries and related documents will be central themes in the volume that is to follow about myth and history in the Andes. Here, I will only consider the ecclesiastical response to what had been learned during Toledo's period as viceroy; this response is contained in the acts of the Third Council of Lima in 1583 (cf. chapter VI). The years between the invasion and 1583 form a unit and possess a certain continuity, which I have used to formulate my choice of themes in the first part of the book (chapters II, III, IV).

The missionary and theologian who in the sixteenth century reflected most deeply and extensively on imagination and demonic illusion among the inhabitants of the New World was Bartolomé de Las Casas. He devoted most of his adult life to fighting for just government in the New World and was exceptionally well informed about Indian civilizations. Las Casas produced a sharp, passionate, and detailed account of what he considered to be at issue in converting Indians to Christianity without coercion—this being the only mode of conversion he countenanced. Las Casas' stance on conversion conditioned his positive interpretation of Andean and Inca religious history. It also highlights the extent to which approaches to the study of Andean religion were inevitably influenced by considerations extraneous to it, as indeed they still are. The missionaries understood the Andes in the light of their own culture. Similarly, the culture of the later twentieth century informs our evaluations of what the missionaries wrote. But because we are often blind to the constraints imposed on us by our own culture, we are liable to exaggerate the freedom afforded to others by theirs. The work of Las Casas on Andean religion and on the religions of the New World in general is thus all too easily read as mere propaganda for his views, and not as religious history (chapter v).

Much debated though the opinions of Las Casas were in the mid-sixteenth century, they were not the opinions that prevailed in the Andes, as is revealed by the career and writings of the Jesuit missionary José de Acosta, who was in Peru from 1569 to 1583 and knew the viceroy Toledo (chapter vi). Acosta's career in Peru bridges the watershed between the time when the Incas were still a living memory and the time when they began receding into history on the one hand and into myth on the other. This process of change can be traced at the turn of the sixteenth to the seventeenth century through the writings and memories of Andeans, not Spaniards (chapter vii). The duress of colonial rule had forced these Andeans to accept Christianity as the true and superior religion. They accepted it, they wrote, voluntarily and eagerly. But this did not mean that their Andean religious sensibility simply disappeared. Instead, these Andeans reformulated the religious history of their ancestors, whether Inca or non-Inca, so as to make the new religion their own. But this could only be done in the light of the non-Christian cognitive categories within which Andeans thought and felt. Andean conversions to Christianity should thus be understood as a chapter in the history not only of Christianity but also of Andean religion.

Like colonial Christianity elsewhere, Andean Christianity has been described as syncretistic, as a mixture of old and new, indigenous and alien elements. I show instead that in order to understand why these Andeans of the turn of the sixteenth to the seventeenth century and their descendants at later times have described themselves as Christians, we must delineate the concepts and values that these converts and their heirs sustained in their thoughts and feelings. These concepts and values were more often in tension and conflict with each other than in harmony. If there is a European analogy to the Andes around 1600, it is not early medieval Europe, where Christianity could be taken for granted. Rather it is the late antique Mediterranean, where even Christians were deeply divided as to how much of their pagan past could permissibly be salvaged and how much of it simply had to be salvaged if meaningful existence was to continue. As regards the Andes, accounting for the period around

1600 amounts to realizing that Andean religion, or even the religion of the Incas before the invasion, cannot be fully comprehended without considering the impact of conversion. For it was their conversion to Christianity that led the Andean historians Guaman Poma de Ayala and Joan Santa Cruz Pachacuti Yamqui to ponder and review both the religion of the Incas and Andean religion in general (chapter VII). Put differently, understanding Inca religion means that we must not seal it off hermetically in 1532 by refusing to consider what happened later. For were we to do this, we would be left without evidence other than what archeology affords us.

The dilemma of late antiquity, experienced anew as it was in the Andes, that there could be no Christian present if there was not at the same time a valued pagan past, also lies at the root of Garcilaso de la Vega's concern with the Incas, his maternal ancestors (chapter VIII). Garcilaso lived all his adult life in Spain, and among his friends were some eminent Andalucian eruditi. Where, accordingly, Garcilaso's Andean contemporaries retold Andean myths and histories, sometimes with a cultic context, so as to locate themselves in their Christian present, Garcilaso gave a more strictly historical account of the Andean religious past by way of achieving the same end. He did so, however, not in the familiar idiom of imagination and demonic illusion, but as a Platonist. Because, in a Platonic universe, concepts of deity are innate in man, the vagaries of imagination are not central to the question of how god can be known. Garcilaso thus insisted that Inca religion must be understood as a necessary step toward Christianity in much more emphatic terms than Las Casas had done. It has frequently been argued that this led him to misrepresent Inca religion beyond recognition. But I show here that precisely because, like Las Casas, Garcilaso wrote with a declared apologetic purpose, he was able to explain fundamental aspects of Andean religious cognition better than any of his predecessors or contemporaries. The reason is that Garcilaso understood clearly which Andean religious concepts Europeans had difficulty in comprehending and therefore explained those concepts with especial care (chapter VIII).

Yet horizons were narrowing in the Peru of Garcilaso's old age. Andeans, formerly the subjects of the Incas, had been turned into despised, tribute-paying Indians. This meant, inter alia, that historians and scholars no longer consulted Andeans about their past but instead reviewed the writings of earlier Spanish students of the Andes. At the same time, extirpation of idolatries became established as a regular component of missionary policy. Massive destruction of Andean objects of worship and of *mallquis*, the bodies of revered ancestors, brought with it an ever-growing contempt for Andean culture and religion on the part of the Peruvian elite living in colonial Lima (chapter IX.1).

The proceedings of campaigns of extirpation undertaken during the early and mid-seventeenth century were recorded in meticulous detail, including, in many cases, verbatim transcripts of statements by Andean witnesses. In a set of such documents from Cajatambo, witnesses speak of every particular of their religious lives. Over a century after the invasion, and despite intensive missionary endeavor, Christianity had made little impression. At the same time, Inca deities and cults had receded into the past or had fused with those pre-Inca observances that still endured: cults punctuating the agricultural calendar, and cults of ancestors, of mythic founders, of the Sun, and of the atmospheric deities. The extirpators destroyed whatever objects of worship could be found and imposed ferocious penalties on religious leaders and many of their followers. The story of the first missionaries, who inquired into Inca religious observance in order to preach against it, was thus repeated, and in a much grimmer tone (chapters III.1; IV.1, 3; X.2). But this was not the end of the story.

In many parts of the Inca empire, the myths and cults that the Incas brought with them constituted little more than a veneer that disappeared within a generation of the Spanish invasion. What endured were pre-Inca myths and cults, along with the conceptions of deity, of human society, and of cosmic order and disorder that these myths and cults articulated. Although policies of extirpation destroyed the cults and disrupted or changed the myths, many of the guiding religious ideas that speak through the documents recording campaigns of extirpation continue to be expressed by contemporary Andeans. Moreover, not infrequently, these contemporary ideas echo or shed light on what may be learned about Inca religion from a sixteenth-century source.

I study Inca and Andean religion as the focal point of a dialogue between Andeans and invaders, violent and full of conflicts though this dialogue usually was. Scholars whose main interest is the Incas and the Andes incline to think that this dialogue between Andeans and aliens has blurred and confused Andean realities. Similarly, students of the Spanish Golden Age and of colonial culture are prone to overlook the role of Andeans in this age and this culture. Therefore, instead of investigating either one of these fields in isolation, I have tried to show that the confrontation between Andeans and invaders activated for both sides a particular range of religious action and experience through which it is possible to gain a more intimate understanding not only of Andean but also of Spanish and Christian religion and culture. For this confrontation formed and conditioned Andean memories of the pre-Hispanic past while at the same time giving shape to Spanish and colonial historical writing about the Andes.

One might want to ask for an authentic description of Inca and Andean religion: objective, balanced, truthful. Some scholars suggest that such a thing cannot be had, and perhaps they are right. Nonetheless, I have endeavored to address this question of objectivity, albeit from a new angle. I have described Inca and Andean religion as understood by the invaders. With changing circumstances both in Spain and in colonial Peru, this understanding shifted and changed. Simultaneously, I have described Inca and Andean religion both as understood and practiced by the people of the Andes and as remembered by them once they had become Christians. We perhaps cannot really understand how deity touches human beings. But at times, human beings do speak about this touching. What I have sought to do is to construct a framework in which Spanish and Christian ideas on this subject are rendered intelligible and can engage our sympathy, a framework also where the voices of those Andean people of so long ago can be heard speaking about the divine powers of their majestic land.

 I

REALITY REPRESENTED IN
THE IMAGINATION

THE LATTER months of the year 1435 found the scholar, statesman, and courtier Don Iñigo López de Mendoza, Marqués de Santillana, contemplating the vicissitudes of fortune and composing a poem about them. For in August of that year, King Alfonso V of Aragon and his two brothers, Don Juan, king of Navarre, and Don Enrique, master of the Order of Santiago, had been defeated in a naval battle and had been made prisoners by the Genoese. Not long afterward Queen Leonore, the mother of the three prisoners, died. In Santillana's poem, this lady recounted a prophetic dream, full of foreboding of the adverse fortune that was to befall her sons. "In my chamber," she said, "overcome by sleep, I know not whether in phantasm or vision, a revelation was shown to me such as has never been seen or conceived of." The revelation was of a terrifying storm at sea, and when the Queen awoke, news had already arrived of her sons' captivity.[1]

Dreams, phantasms, and visions were a frequent theme of Spanish fifteenth-century poets,[2] and the Marques de Santillana himself wrote about them repeatedly. Did dreams adumbrate some reality, or did they not? he asked himself in one poem, and answered his question in the affirmative by citing prophetic dreams outlined by the Roman encyclopedist Valerius Maximus.[3] Another of Santillana's sources was Dante, on whose *Inferno* he modeled a didactic visionary journey of his own.[4] Else-

---

[1] Marqués de Santillana, *Comedieta de Ponça* (1987), stanza 50. For the battle, see J. N. Hillgarth, *The Spanish Kingdoms 1250–1516* (Oxford, 1978), 2: 251.

[2] Goldberg, "The Dream Report," *Hispania* 66 (1983): 21–31.

[3] Marqués de Santillana, "El Sueño," in his *Canciones y Decires,* ed. V. Garcia de Diego, stanza 20; Valerius Maximus, *Factorum et dictorum memorabilium libri novem,* ed. C. Kempf (Stuttgart, 1965), 1.7.

[4] On the reception of Dante in Spain, see Schiff, "La première traduction," *Homenaje a Menendez y Pelayo* (1899), 1: 270; Schiff, *La bibliothèque* (1905), pp. 275–319; cf. Nader, *Mendoza Family* (1979), p. 93; Round, "Renaissance Culture," *Modern Language Review* 57 (1962): 204–215, and 64 (1969): 793–805. On Villena, the translator of Dante, see Cotarelo y Mori, *Don Enrique de Villena* (1896) and Enrique de Villena, *Tratado de la consolación,* ed. D. C. Carr (Madrid, 1976), p. xlixf. For more on Dante's influence in Spain, compare Juan de Mena, *Laberinto,* stanza 16, with Dante, *Inferno* 31.22ff.: both Dante and Mena see as towers what actually are giants; Mena, "Mi vista mi faze grand cuerpo de cuerpo no grande." Cf. Lida de Malkiel, *Juan de Mena* (1984), p. 15ff., 260. On the original passage in Dante, see P. Dronke, *Dante and Medieval Latin Traditions* (Cambridge, 1986), pp. 34–37;

where he extolled Fortitude, Loyalty, and Chastity in an allegorical vision.[5] But much more was at issue in Santillana's preoccupation with dreams and visions than the literary tastes of his Spanish contemporaries or the influence of Dante. For phantasms, images generated in the imagination, were not merely the substance of dreams, visions, and prophecies, they also conditioned the process of thinking. To think something was to form a mental image of it, and therefore, to understand a person's thought amounted to understanding the mental images that underlay it.

In the Americas, Spaniards accordingly asked themselves again and again how Indians formed mental images and how appropriately these images represented the reality from which they were derived. The vast religious and cultural differences between America and Europe tended to be perceived by the invaders in terms of mental process, and questions about historical change and evolution were secondary to the overarching interest in how human beings thought and reasoned. This was why sixteenth-century discussions of American cultures so regularly veered into, or took the form of, discussions of the human nature of Indians.[6] But the conceptions of mental process and in particular of mental images and imagination which figured in these discussions were far from forming a unitary body of doctrine.

The idea that imagination was the mental vehicle of prophetic or visionary experience was derived, in the last resort, from Plato,[7] although in Christian Europe this idea was defined and circumscribed by the more pragmatic and prosaic analysis of imagination by Plato's successor and critic, Aristotle. As Aristotle understood it, imagination mediated between intellect and sense perception, so that phantasms or mental images resulting from sense perception constituted a precondition for thought.

Aristotle's most influential Christian commentator was Thomas Aquinas. His commitment to Aristotle's conception of imagination was, however, conditioned by an issue in which Aristotle himself had expressed no interest. This was the immortality of the soul, posited by

---

also, Mena, *Laberinto*, stanza 19. On Dante's *Commedia* quoted by a Spaniard, see Gilly, *Buchdruck* (1985), p. 4; further, Peritore, "Studio di Dante," in *Dante nel Pensiero* (1975), pp. 423–432. On printing: Norton, *A Descriptive Catalogue* (1978), nos. 275, 888, 925; J.P.R. Lyell, *Early Book Illustration in Spain* (London, 1926; New York, 1976), p. 84; Bataillon, *Erasmo y España* (1950), p. 809. On Dante in Garcilaso's library: Durand, "Biblioteca del Inca," *Nueva Revista de Filología Hispánica* 3 (1948): 254.

[5] Marqués de Santillana, "Infierno" and "La Vision" (both in his *Canciones y Decires*).

[6] For an authoritative discussion of this subject, see A. Pagden, *The Fall of Natural Man* (1982).

[7] See in particular Plato, *Timaeus* 70d–72b.

Christian theology. By way of accomodating Aristotle's psychology to this requirement, Aquinas described the soul's thinking and reasoning faculty as immortal. But Aquinas agreed with Aristotle in regarding as mortal the faculty of the soul that experienced the perceptions registered by the five senses: as organs of the body, these are all, like the body itself, subject to death. So, according to Aquinas, was the imagination, which coordinated sense perceptions.[8] By drawing this distinction between the soul's mortal and immortal parts, Aquinas accomodated Aristotle's psychology to a Christian framework.[9]

A further divergence between Aristotle's psychology and that of Aquinas concerns visions and prophecies, to which Aristotle was indifferent: for Aquinas, by contrast, the visions and prophecies recounted in the Bible required explanation and exegesis. It was here that Aquinas modified Aristotle's view of imagination by recourse to Plato and to Plato's Christian successors.[10] As a result, Plato's and Aristotle's different approaches to imagination often coexisted or converged with each other in Christian writings, as they did for instance in the works of Dante and Santillana.[11]

At issue was not merely the interpretation of Scripture or the creation of poetic imagery for the benefit of a literate and learned minority. For in Spain, as elsewhere in Christian Europe, visionary and prophetic experience had not come to an end with biblical times. Rather, men and women of all walks of life continued imagining, thinking about, and sometimes participating in, visions and prophecies.[12] Jesus, the Virgin Mary, and the saints were present in the life of every day, and their interventions were hoped for and expected. In the Americas also, Spaniards felt themselves to be living under the protection of these supernatural companions, so that the Virgin who had first appeared to a herdsman near Guadalupe in Spanish Extremadura in due course was also seen in Mexico and in Peru.[13]

[8] Thomas Aquinas, *Summa* 1, q. 76, a.3; q. 78, a.4; q. 85, a.1; q. 89, a.1–8.

[9] Aquinas, *Summa* 2.2, q. 173, a.2. For some early and crucial steps in accommodating Aristotle's soul to Christian concepts of soul see Augustine, *De Musica*, ed. G. Marzi (Florence, 1969), 6.11.32; 6.13.39.

[10] On Plato and Aristotle, cf. E. R. Dodds, *The Greeks and the Irrational* (Berkeley, 1951), esp. chaps. 3–4; Bundy, *The Theory of Imagination* (1927), p. 226; Klein, "L'imagination," *Revue de Métaphysique et de Morale* 61 (1956): 18–39; Wolfson, "Internal Senses," *Harvard Theological Review* 28 (1935): 69–133.

[11] Bundy, *The Theory of Imagination*, chap. 11; on the patristic background, P. Hadot, "L'image de la Trinité," *Studia Patristica* 6 (1962): 409–442.

[12] Christian, *Local Religion* (1981) and *Apparitions* (1981). For a vision gone awry, at any rate in the eyes of the ecclesiastical authorities, see Nalle, "Popular Religion," in *Inquisition and Society*, ed. Haliczer (1987), pp. 67–87.

[13] R. Vargas Ugarte, *Historia del culto de Maria en Iberoamerica y de sus imagenes y santuarios mas celebrados* (Madrid, 1956), vol. 2, pp. 99ff. about the Virgin of Guadalupe in Pacasmayo;

I. REALITY REPRESENTED IN THE IMAGINATION

1. Philosophy and Theology

A short poem of the later sixteenth century, perhaps by the Carmelite mystic John of the Cross, spells out just how naturally and spontaneously a person could become involved in visionary experiences. The poet imagined encountering, around Christmas time, the pregnant Virgin Mary on the road he was walking:

Del Verbo divino	The wayfaring Virgin
La Virgen preñada	Word in her womb,
Viene de camino	Comes walking your way.
Si le dais posada.	Haven't you room?

These verses were recited in Carmelite monastic communities every Christmas by way of calling the monks and nuns to celebrate the festival as a present reality. Indeed, the verses perhaps allude to an occasion earlier in the sixteenth century, when a shepherd from Leon came upon an apparition of the Virgin. She was called by the name of Virgen del Camino, the Virgin of the Road, and a few years later, a shrine was built for her on the road where the shepherd had seen her.[1] Stories abounded in late medieval and Renaissance Spain of similar occurrences, impingements by supernatural beings into the ordinary doings of every day. In churches and even in some homes, the Virgin and the saints were represented as permanently present in earthly life through their statues. This imaged presence could in turn give rise to visionary apparitions of the sacred personage who was represented in the statue (fig. 1).[2]

In a different sense, Christ was present in the consecrated eucharistic host. His sacramental presence was made concrete in both sacred legend and daily experience. According to one legend, a woman in Pope Gregory's Rome had denied the real presence of Jesus in the eucharistic host because she recognized the host as the same bread that she herself had baked earlier. In response to this lack of faith, Christ appeared on the altar as the Man of Sorrows at the very moment when Pope Gregory pronounced the words of consecration. Such visions were shared in living reality by ordinary people[3] and figured

p. 299 about the Virgin of Guadalupe in Chuquisaca. This latter shrine was founded in 1601 by Fray Diego Ocaña, for whom see below, chap. VI at n. 147; Epilogue at n. 4.

[1] Christian, *Apparitions*, p. 150; John of the Cross, *The Poems of St. John of the Cross*, original Spanish texts with English Translations by John Frederick Nims (Chicago, 1979), p. 95, with p. 149.

[2] For Berruguete's painting of the Virgin appearing to a monastic community (fig. 1), see Museo del Prado, *Catalogo de las pinturas* (Madrid, 1986), inventory 615, p. 57.

[3] Cf. C. W. Bynum, *Holy Fast and Holy Feast* (Berkeley, 1987).

1. The twofold presence of the Virgin Mary as depicted by Pedro Berruguete: she appears to a community of Dominican friars, while the triptych
on the altar displays her seated statue with the Christ child on her lap.
Prado, Madrid.

regularly in late medieval and Renaissance devotional painting.[4] The painter Diego de la Cruz thus pictured the Man of Sorrows stepping out of his tomb which is located in the place of the tabernacle behind the altar, while the pope and his clerics genuflect reverently. The background to this dramatic event is crowded with the instruments of Christ's passion (fig. 2).[5] A more dignified, contemplative rendering of the legend by Hieronymus Bosch shows a tranquil and composed Jesus surrounded by nine small cherubim standing above the altar. The pope, his clerics, and the woman who had doubted that the consecrated host was indeed Christ's body quietly pray in their Lord's presence (fig. 3).[6] The legend of St. Gregory's vision had many parallels. One of them, which circulated in Spain, recounted how the doubts of a monk regarding the real presence of Christ in the Eucharist vanished when he saw the child Jesus on the altar in place of the consecrated host.[7] Similar stories were later told in Peru.[8]

These devotional paintings, legends, and accounts of actual apparitions of Jesus and the saints, in particular of the Virgin Mary, speak eloquently of many people's insistent yearning for some tangible contact with supernatural and divine presences in this terrestrial life. Theologians and ecclesiastical authorities, on the other hand, often expressed reserve and even criticism in the face of such experiences, and their attitudes were reiterated in manuals of spiritual guidance. John of the Cross himself echoed earlier writers on the spiritual life when he warned contemplatives not to pay too much attention to visionary experiences.[9] Some thorny questions were involved. Were visions seen by human eyes? Or were they merely assembled in the imagination out of disparate fragments of normal visual experience? Most problematic of all, how was one to ascertain whether a given vision had been sent by God or whether it had been some kind of demonic illusion designed to distract the visionary from single-mindedly focusing his attention on God? In the light of such difficulties,

[4] Borchgrave d'Altena, "La messe de Saint Grégoire," *Bulletin des Musées Royaux des Beaux Arts* (1959): 3–34; Post, *History of Spanish Painting*, vol. 14, pp. 55ff., with fig. 23 in that work. For an eerie but starkly realistic rendering of the miracle by Dürer, see E. Panofsky, *Albrecht Dürer* (Princeton, 1945), p. 137 and fig. 183.

[5] See de Bosque, *Quentin Metsys* (1975), pp. 130ff. for this and similar compositions.

[6] W. Fränger, *Hieronymus Bosch* (New York, 1983; German original, 1975), pp. 310f. For a note of caution on Fränger's overall interpretations of Bosch, see W. S. Gibson, *Hieronymus Bosch; An Annotated Bibliography* (Boston, 1983), pp. xxvff., 82f.

[7] Clemente Sanchez de Vercial, *Libro*, pp. 337f.

[8] E.g. *Relación verdadera de un niño hermosissimo que fue visto en la Hostia consagrada la vispera de la fiesta del Corpus a dos de Junio del año passado de 1649 en la iglesia del seraphico P.S. Francisco del pueblo de Etem Diocesis del Obispado de Truxillo del Perú* (Biblioteca Nacional, Madrid, MS. 2382), fol. 304.

[9] John of the Cross, *Subida del monte Carmelo*, in his *Vida y obras* 2: 16–32; Francisco de Osuna, *Third Spiritual Alphabet*, Seventh Treatise 4–5.

2. The Mass of Saint Gregory by Diego de la Cruz, later fifteenth century. The Pope flanked by his deacon and subdeacon kneels before the apparition of Jesus on the altar. Blood from the side of Jesus flows into the chalice containing the consecrated eucharistic wine. The background of the picture is filled with faces and objects evocative of the Passion. The lady donor, kneeling at the right, in front of her patron saints, is placed in the space occupied in other depictions of this episode by the Roman woman whose denial of the real presence gave rise to the miracle, cf. figure 3.
Colección Torelló, Barcelona.

it seemed best not to look for visions and to pass over them lightly if they did occur.

This was good practical advice, but it did not dispose of either the cognitive or the theological dilemmas that the possibility of visions entailed. Thomas Aquinas had been one of many theologians to reflect on what

3. Vision and tranquil devotion: Pope Gregory, having spoken the words of consecration, sees Jesus as Man of Sorrows, surrounded by nine cherubim. Epiphany triptych by Hieronymus Bosch, with wings closed. Prado, Madrid.

was at issue and had devoted a most carefully worded passage to eucharistic visions.[10] What did the visionary see, Aquinas asked, when instead of the host there seemed to be on the altar Christ as a child? Aquinas rejected the idea that the nature of Christ's presence in the eucharistic elements had in any way changed. Rather, he concluded that if many people saw such a vision at the same time, it was because "a miraculous mutation occurs in the accidents [of the host], for instance in its contours[11] and colour . . . so that a boy is seen." The mutation thus occurred outside, and independently of, the beholder. If, by contrast, a vision was seen by a single, isolated visionary, the change more probably lay in the visionary's eyes, which had been transformed in some way by divine intervention, that is, miraculously.[12] This miraculous aspect of visionary experience notwithstanding, Aquinas sought to avoid looking for miracles in the order of nature. He therefore insisted that phenomena be examined primarily in the light of sense perception and reason.[13] Yet, in the last analysis, a eucharistic vision did disrupt the natural order, because it did not come about by the normal production of phantasms from sense impressions. Rather, Aquinas wrote, "An appearance such [as that of Christ in the host] is divinely formed in the eye so as to represent a certain truth; to wit, it is made manifest that the true body of Christ is in this sacrament."[14] This divine forming of a vision in the beholder's eye was in some sense akin to the inspirational imagination or "high fantasy" which a generation later was to occupy Dante and subsequently his Spanish followers. Dante's earliest conscious experiences of imagination had been stimulated by sense perceptions, by seeing Beatrice, his beloved. But as he ascended into the higher reaches of the Mount of Purgatory, this sensory imagination was supplemented, and in due course supplanted, by a state of mind in which noncorporeal images "rain down" into "high fantasy" independently of the senses of the body.[15] One of Dante's Spanish readers felt that this high fantasy pervaded the *Commedia* to such an extent that he described the entire work in the Platonist sense as "maravillosa fanta-

[10] Aquinas, *Summa* 3, q. 76, a.8. Questions of vision, perception, and cognition are here discussed with reference to Aquinas and his Spanish followers only, but these questions were also examined, using the same Aristotelian vocabulary, by other philosophers. See K. H. Tachau, *Vision and Certitude in the Age of Ockham: Optics, Epistemology and the Foundations of Semantics, 1250–1345* (Leiden, 1988).

[11] The Latin term is *figura*.

[12] For another kind of eucharistic vision, where a donkey recognized the presence of Christ behind the accidents of the consecrated host, see Post, *History of Spanish Painting* 14: 48ff. and fig. 18 of that work, with Christian, *Apparitions*, p. 99.

[13] See Aquinas, *Summa* 3, q. 75, a.5 ad 2, regarding transubstantiation.

[14] Aquinas, *Summa* 3, q. 76, a.8 resp.

[15] Dante, *Purgatorio* 17.13, with C. Singleton, *The Divine Comedy: Translated with a Commentary* (Princeton, 1970–1975), ad loc.; cf. *Paradiso* 33.142, with Singleton.

sia."[16] Dante's high fantasy was independent of sense perception. Aquinas, by contrast, envisioned that God lodged the perception of the miraculous transformation of the eucharistic host in the visionary's eyes, that is, in the mortal organ of sense perception. Where, accordingly, Dante posited two different kinds of imagination, one arising from sense perception, the other not, Aquinas thought that the difference between ordinary and inspired imagination was to be sought in the object that generated imagination's phantasms.

Aquinas' reasoning on the functioning of reason, sense perception, and imagination was ultimately derived from Aristotle's discussion of these faculties in his treatise *On the Soul*. Aristotle differentiated imagination from both thought and sense perception. While being activated by sense perception, imagination was a separate faculty. Similarly, imagination differed from thought. For although the sense of sight could unambiguously declare that an object was white, reason, aided by imagination, could nonetheless draw erroneous inferences from this fact as to the object's true nature.[17] The point was that the intellect did not function directly on the basis of sense perceptions, but rather on the basis of mediating mental images, or phantasms, that were formed in the imagination. These phantasms were related to intellect as the external world made up of sensible objects was related to the five senses. It was because sense perception was mediated to intellect by imagination that intellect could not know anything without constantly "returning" or "bending back" to phantasms.[18] "The soul never thinks without a phantasm," a mental image formed by the imagination, Aristotle had therefore said, and Aquinas agreed.[19]

Phantasms in the imagination were composed of observations made by the five bodily senses. Aristotle had asked how the disparate data collected by the senses could be joined together,[20] and his medieval followers thought that the task was performed by a distinct faculty, that of common

[16] Schiff, *La bibliothèque* (1905), p. 304. Note also Enrique de Villena, *Tratado de la consolación*, ed. Carr, pp. 15–16: presentaronse las ymagines de Job, de Boecio . . . a la fantasía elevada. I.e., Villena experienced a truthful imaginative experience of the individuals in whose lives and writings he anchors his treatise. Contrast p. 113 on false hope: quantas vezes ymaginastes por la comun elevación de la fantasia que vuestros padres e abuelos subiesen a mayores riquezas e estado por vuestra ayuda; also p. 139, "ymaginación" forms dreams.

[17] Aristotle, *On the Soul* 425a23ff.; 428b21; cf. 428a12.

[18] See G. P. Klubertanz, "St. Thomas and the Knowledge of the Singular," *New Scholasticism* 26 (1952): 135–166; also Brennan, "Thomist Concept," *New Scholasticism* 15 (1941): 149–161; Kenny, "Intellect and Imagination," in *The Anatomy of the Soul* (1973), pp. 62–80; cf. Aristotle, *On the Soul* 428a13.

[19] Aristotle, *On the Soul* 431a16; "On Memory and Recollection" 450a1; Aquinas, *Summa* I, q. 84, a.7. For a most illuminating discussion of these issues, see V. Gilliam, *The Evolution of the Mystical Language of Love in San Juan de la Cruz* (Ph.D. dissertation, Department of Religious Studies, Stanford University, 1990), chap. 2, sec. 4.

[20] Aristotle, *On the Soul* 426b8–427a15.

sense (see fig. 24). The joining together resulted in a mixture or mean,[21] in which, ideally, the findings of all five bodily senses were appropriately represented. It was, however, in the composition of such a mean that error was prone to arise,[22] as for instance when an object was perceived indistinctly or misleadingly. Thus, wrote Aristotle, "The sun seems to measure a foot across, but is believed to be greater than the world."[23] As interpreted by Aristotle, this belief, anchored though it was in earlier Greek scientific thinking, rested on the highly complex set of relations among sense perceptions, phantasms, and opinions.[24] To arrive at correct beliefs on topics such as the size of the sun was thus a most difficult undertaking.

Aristotle saw additional occasions for error arising out of the very nature of mental images. He thus noted that images could be created in the mind independently of objects perceived by the senses. For instance, a person might form a memory system by mapping in the mind's "vast hall of memory" images to describe distinct conceptual spaces, where different types of information could be stored.[25] Such images were formed by choice and voluntarily, while the perceptions of the senses were involuntary. Aristotle described this activity of defining conceptual spaces in the mind in visual terms: the mind was "making images," which he termed "eidola," thus differentiating them from phantasms, images created in the imagination by sense perceptions derived from external objects. If these eidola were mistaken for sense perception, or were thought to derive from it, they resulted in error. This happened when a person was dreaming, sick, delirious, or overcome by an emotion, such as hope or fear.[26] At the same time, however, eidola appearing in dreams could arise from movements of matter touching the dormant senses indirectly, like gentle ripples of water caressing a lakeshore.[27] This tacit distinction Aristotle drew between phantasms and eidola was taken up by Aquinas, who dif-

[21] Ibid., 431a17–20, mesotes.

[22] Ibid., 428a12; 15ff.

[23] Ibid., 428b4. Regarding the size of the sun as no more than a foot across, see further, Heraclitus, frag. 57, in *Heraclitus: Greek Text with a Short Commentary*, ed. M. Marcovich (Menda, Venezuela, 1976), pp. 307f.

[24] Cf. Aristotle, *On the Soul* 425a14ff., on the senses and common sense.

[25] Such a system is described in Johannes Romberch, *Congestorium artificiose memorie . . . omnium de memoria preceptiones aggregatim complectens . . .* (Venice, 1533); this work was translated into Italian by Lodovico Dolce as *Dialogo . . . nel quale si ragiona del modo di accrescere et conservar La Memoria* (Venice, 1575). Dolce's illustrations are printed from the same blocks as those of Romberch. See fig. 26 of the present book for an image depicting the ordering of memory; also, F. Yates, *The Art of Memory* (London, 1966). The phrase "vast hall of memory" (*aula ingens memoriae*) is from Augustine's *Confessions* 10.8.14.

[26] Aristotle, *On the Soul* 429a5–9; see also Aquinas *Summa* 1, q. 84, a.7 resp.

[27] Aristotle, *On Prophecy in Sleep* 465a5 and 464b14, with Burkert, "Air-Imprints," *Illinois Classical Studies* 2 (1977): 107f. *On Prophecy in Sleep* is included among the treatises known as *Parva Naturalia*.

ferentiated from the other phantasms those mental images that did not arise directly out of waking sense perception. By way of doing so, he adduced an example that Aristotle had not used. "The passion of imagination," Aquinas wrote, "is in us when we will, because it is in our power to form something as though it appeared before our eyes, such as golden mountains or whatever else we want."[28] Golden mountains and other objects devoid of concrete existence could thus be imagined by drawing on the stock of images stored in memory and by combining different aspects of those images. Alternatively, images of golden mountains could arise in the imagination when the ripple effect of movements in the material world made its impact on the dormant senses.

For Aquinas, golden mountains served as one of many morally and intellectually neutral examples illustrating the workings of imagination. In the Americas, however, these arguments acquired a further dimension, because the workings of human imagination served to explain Amerindian cultural and religious difference. For missionaries in the later sixteenth century, therefore, the example of golden mountains helped to demonstrate that Indians were unable to draw the appropriate distinction between phantasms derived from physical reality and the fictions of their own disordered and undisciplined imaginations.[29] In being applied to non-Christian cultures, Christian European cognitive vocabulary was thus imperceptibly reformulated to explain not cognition but cultural hierarchy under the guise of cognition.[30]

Medieval philosophers referred to imagination, memory, and common sense as the internal senses. The term served to differentiate these three from the five bodily senses, while also making clear that they were only partially dependent on reality external to the individual. For, on the one hand, as Aristotle had already pointed out, imagination formed phantasms on the basis of data that were external to the person and were supplied by the five senses, but on the other hand, the formation of phantasms was also dependent on an individual's inner condition. Hence Aristotle observed that human beings when disturbed by emotion or passion acted according to the imagination's phantasms as though they were sense perceptions.[31] In addition, as both Aristotle and Aquinas noted repeatedly, the condition of the human body, its health or disease, its state of hunger or satiety, affected the functioning of the faculties of the soul in relation to each other. Intellect, imagination, and the other internal senses thus did not always harmonize with each other or with the bodily or ex-

[28] Aquinas, *In Aristotelis librum de anima commentarium* 3, Lectio 4, 633; see further below, chap. VIII.2 at n. 31.
[29] Gregorio Garcia, *Origen* 5.1; cf. Las Casas, *Apologética Historia* 96, p. 499.
[30] See below, chap. VI at n. 124.
[31] Aristotle, *On the Soul* 429a7.

ternal senses.[32] In women, for example, the balance of the faculties of the soul was thought to be constantly disrupted by menstruation, this being one of the reasons why women's intelligence was regarded as being inferior to that of males.[33] These tenets had far-reaching repercussions in European evaluations of Amerindian religions and cultures. Some sixteenth-century Spaniards argued, for example, that the climate of the New World had produced in the Indians a lesser breed of men whose imagination and intellect anchored as these were in the condition of the body, which depended on climate, were far outstripped by those of Europeans.[34]

Ordinary cognition was, therefore, considered to result from a delicate balance between intellect and the external and internal senses, between soul and body. Cognition derived from visionary experience, on the other hand, was more specifically anchored in imagination and the sense of sight. Another issue that figured in the functioning of cognition and visionary experience was the distinction that Aquinas, along with other medieval philosophers, drew between an object's accidents, or external appearance, and its substance, or true nature. This distinction underlies the explanation Aquinas and his followers offered of what the five bodily senses actually perceived as opposed to what the intellect learned from these perceptions. Regarding Aristotle's example of the sun measuring a foot across, for instance, Aquinas explained that it was the sense of sight that perceived the accidents of the sun's luminosity and apparent size, while intellect, aided by the internal senses, was capable of perceiving the sun's substance, that is, its true size.

At a more general level, the distinction between substance and accidents extended into the broader distinction between immaterial universals and material particulars. According to Aquinas, who here took issue with Plato's theory of ideas, human understanding of universals could in this life be achieved only through understanding particulars. One could not therefore expect to understand the nature of rocks without first understanding particular rocks. Similarly, one understood the substance of an object in the light of phantasms regarding size, color, shape, and other accidents discernible to the bodily senses. Common sense abstracted these into a mean that the imagination presented to the intellect as phantasms. Given therefore that humans could not comprehend objects without considering their accidents, an object's accidents were in relation to the five senses what its substance was in relation to the intellect.

This reasoning underlies not only Aquinas' explanation of visions but also his explanation of transubstantiation. Here, thanks to the words of

[32] Aquinas, *Summa* 1, q. 87, a.7.
[33] Aristotle, *On Dreams* 460a7ff. This treatise is included in *Parva Naturalia*.
[34] The issue is discussed by Las Casas, *Apologética Historia* 23–35; see below, chap. v.1.

consecration spoken by a priest, the substance of the eucharistic bread and wine changed into the body and blood of Christ, while the accidents remained those of bread and wine. This transformation was accessible to human intellect because the Christian faith itself was an object of intellect, not of imagination or sense perception. It was therefore not imagination and sense perception that contemplated the mutation of the eucharistic substance but intellect, moved by faith. Meanwhile, the senses perceived the unchanged aspect of the accidents of the eucharistic bread and wine, thus facilitating intellect's conclusion that the Eucharist was in effect consecrated by an act of divine power.[35] The consecration of the Eucharist and eucharistic visions, therefore, exemplified a specific natural order, in which intelligible statements could be made about accidents as distinct from substance and about substance as distinct from accidents. The distinction of accidents from substance was fundamental to explaining how people could see Christ as a child in place of the host, without there occurring a change in the nature of Christ's presence on the altar. Here, the accidents changed, but not the substance. The same distinction was also operative in explaining how, when the words of consecration were spoken over the eucharistic bread and wine, their accidents remained the same, while the substance changed into the body and blood of Christ.[36]

But if God could exploit this disjuncture between accidents and substance, appearance and reality, in the material universe, so could the devil. This is why Aquinas was careful to differentiate divine visions from illusions and demonic deceptions. The object of a eucharistic vision was placed into the visionary's eye by God himself, so that such a vision was distinguishable from illusions and demonic deceptions by reference to the object of perception, to what the five external senses actually took in, and hence by reference to the theological significance that the object of perception conveyed. It was thanks to the object of perception that eucharistic visions were in no sense comparable to "deceptions, such as occur in the illusions of sorcerers." Rather, because the object of perception delineated "some truth" regarding the divine nature, such visions were to be interpreted by sense perception and reason under the guidance of faith.[37]

Yet in practical terms these distinctions were hard to uphold. For quite apart from the difficulty of gathering the requisite information, especially regarding what exactly a visionary might have beheld, it was well known that the devil was prone to leading the faithful astray, as the apostle Paul had expressed it, in the guise of "an angel of light."[38] The nature of such fake angels was entirely comprehensible in view of the distinction between substance and accidents. The demonic substance was hidden be-

[35] Aquinas, *Summa* 3, q. 75, a.5 resp. and ad 1–3.
[36] See Aquinas, *Summa* 3, q. 75.
[37] Quotes are from Aquinas, *Summa* 3, q. 76, a.8 resp.; see also *Summa* 3, q. 75, a.5.
[38] 2 Cor. 11:14, quoted by Castañega, *Tratado de las supersticiones* 3, p. 29.

neath angelic accidents, beneath the external appearance of one of God's own ministers. From late antiquity onward, many Christians were accordingly convinced that demons dwelt in, and acted through, the statues of Greek and Roman deities. In Peru, their theories were reiterated by the band of Spanish invaders who in 1533 desecrated the temple of the prophetic deity Pachacamac,[39] and later by numerous missionaries who observed Andean religious practice at close quarters.[40]

This disjuncture between substance and accidents affected not only eucharistic visions and the doctrine of transubstantiation but also the configuration of the cosmos. As late as the seventeenth century, scientists and astronomers regarded the entire physical universe as being governed by angelic and demonic energies.[41] Angelic energies moved the stars in their celestial spheres, while much of the sublunary world was permeated by the negative impulses of devils and demons. For just as the substance of Christ's flesh and blood was hidden within the accidents of the eucharistic bread and wine, so the stellar bodies were vehicles for angelic powers, while here below demons disguised themselves in clouds and vapors. These demons caused tempests and earthquakes, polluted and corrupted the air, and spread diseases.[42] In the same way, demons manipulated matter so as to attract the attention of human sense perception to some configuration that disguised their presence. The demons were thus particularly fond of appearing in the guise, or under the accidents, of the dead,[43] as may have happened when King Saul asked the witch of Endor to bring before him the ghost of the prophet Samuel.[44] This much-discussed example of Old Testament necromancy acquired a new relevance when, in the first half of the sixteenth century, the soldier historian Pedro Cieza de León studied Andean burial customs. For Cieza, like many others, was convinced that the devil spoke to Andeans in the guise of their deceased ancestors.[45]

The cult of the dead, as the sixteenth-century missionary Acosta ex-

[39] For demons in statues of deities, see M. Camille, *Gothic Idol*, pp. 57ff.; on Pachacamac, see below, chap. II.1 at nn. 2ff.

[40] See below, chap. II.1 at n. 18; see also chap. IV.1 at nn. 25ff., chap. VI at nn. 104ff.

[41] H. A. Wolfson, "Souls," *Dumbarton Oaks Papers* 16 (1962): 65–93; D. P. Walker, *Spiritual and Demonic Magic* (1958); cf. Millas Vallicrosa, "El libro de Astrologia de Don Enrique de Villena," *Revista de Filología Española* 27 (1943): 25. For a general discussion, see W.P.D. Wightman, *Science and the Renaissance* (Aberdeen, 1962), pp. 284–302; but note Funkenstein, *Theology and the Scientific Imagination*, p. 314, with pp. 31–35.

[42] This theory that demons intervened in atmospheric phenomena was stated explicitly for the first time by Apuleius in *De deo Socratis*. Aquinas formulated the issue with some caution in *Summa* 1, q. 114, a.4; cf. q. 115, a.5, quoting Apuleius and Augustine. See also Kramer and Sprenger, *Malleus Maleficarum* 2, q. 1, chap. 15, pp. 247ff. Further, on the question of whether thunderstorms should be exorcised, Ciruelo, *Treatise* 3: 9, especially for present purposes sec. 7, p. 293, and Jofreu's commentary, pp. 301–303.

[43] Aquinas, *Summa* 1, q. 117, a.4 ad 2.

[44] Ibid., q. 89, a.8 ad 2; *Summa* 2.2, q. 95, a.4 ad 2; Castañega, *Tratado* 5, p. 38.

[45] See below, chap. III.1 and chap. V.2 at nn. 17ff.

pressed it, focused on objects that "truly were and are something,"[46] whether or not demons determined the exact nature of this cult. Other forms of erroneous belief and worship, by contrast, were anchored in fictions of the human imagination that, according to the same missionary, "neither are nor ever were anything" and that demons were capable of exploiting. For given that the imagination was capable of creating phantasms of mountains of gold and the like, the demons sometimes misled the senses by dangling before them the accidents of entities that had no real existence at all. Such, according to some theologians, were the centaurs, sirens, and nymphs of classical mythology,[47] and also certain Andean divinities.[48]

It was in the light of these theories that Flemish painters of the later fifteenth century depicted the workings of diverse demonic deceptions. Thus, in a painting by Juan de Flandes, who spent some of his life in Spain, the devil when tempting Jesus in the wilderness is dressed in the habit of a Franciscan friar (fig. 4). Holding his rosary in one hand and a stone in the other,[49] the Evil One suggests to Jesus, who has been fasting for forty days, that he should manifest his divinity by turning the stone into bread. Jesus, however, recognizes the substance of the devil behind the accidents of the Franciscan friar's habit and wearily lifts his hand by way of making a gesture of negation.

During the later part of the fifteenth century and throughout the sixteenth, Flemish paintings were in vogue among Spanish patrons. Among the pictures that entered Spanish collections at this time are renderings by Joachim Patinir and Hieronymus Bosch of the temptation of the hermit St. Anthony. In Patinir's painting, the saint is tempted by three lovely young ladies (fig. 5). He has slipped and is about to fall at the very moment when the ladies approach him. One of the three is thus shown in the act of arresting Anthony's fall, while another innocently holds out an apple toward him. Things are not as they appear, however, for behind the three ladies an ugly old hag emits a piercing scream, while the train of one young lady's gown terminates in a tiny devilish dragon. Anthony closes his eyes and turns away in anguish, as though knowing yet not knowing, what confronts him.[50] Hieronymus Bosch painted the temptations of St. Anthony several times. An early sixteenth-century copy of one panel, now lost, shows the saint with folded hands, looking out into some void, while to one side there appears a grotesque vision of a flooded house, its gable made up of the gigantic head of an elderly woman, be-

---

[46] Acosta, *Historia natural y moral de las Indias* 5.2; see below, chap. VI at nn. 81ff.

[47] Lope de Barrientos, *Tratado del dormir*, in his *Vida y obras*, pp. 39ff.

[48] See below chap. V.2 at nn. 62f.; chap. VIII.2 at n. 31.

[49] See Luke 4:3.

[50] Museo del Prado, *Catálogo de las pinturas*, inventory 1616.

4. Demonic disguise: the devil dressed as a Franciscan friar tempts Jesus to turn a stone into bread. In the background, right, Jesus is tempted to throw himself from a tower, while on the mountain at the left, the devil shows him the glory of this world (Matthew 4:8). Juan de Flandes. National Gallery of Art, Washington, D.C., Ailsa Mellon Bruce Fund.

5. Joachim Patinir, following long Christian tradition, depicts the hermit Anthony being tempted by demonic evil disguised as feminine beauty. The apple being offered to the hermit recalls the apple of Eve.
Prado, Madrid.

neath whom stands the figure of a naked girl—a demonic vision, perhaps, of the marital life Anthony has renounced.[51] Another painting by Bosch shows Anthony sheltered within a hollow tree, his faithful companion pig at his side (fig. 6).[52] Plants flower at his feet, and in front of him flows a small, tranquil brook. Yet all is not well, for the entire landscape is littered with aberrations of nature, both great and small. Behind the saint,

[51] Museo del Prado, *Catálogo de las pinturas*, inventory 2913; Bermejo Martinez, *Primitivos Flamencos* (1982), vol. 2, pp. 126f.

[52] Museo del Prado, *Catálogo de las pinturas*, inventory 2049, from the Escorial, not attributed to Bosch by Bermejo Martinez. But W. Fränger, *Hieronymus Bosch* (New-York, 1983), pp. 305–308, regards the painting as authentic. Fränger's interpretation of Anthony's mood differs from mine but does not rule out my main point, which concerns the nature of imagination.

6. The peace of hermit Anthony's solitude is disrupted by illusions: or are the phenomena surrounding him real? Hieronymus Bosch; Prado, Madrid.

a figure half-dragon and half-human carries a pitcher of water; out of the brook, a creature yells at Anthony while reaching up toward him with a clawlike hand; and in the distance, deformed humans play at war. Evidently, the sense perceptions cannot be trusted to collect from the environment usable data out of which imagination might present to the intellect phantasms fit for thought. Anthony is thus resting his chin on folded hands, resolved to endure the demonic visitation, but his face speaks of wordless dismay.

Anthony's ascetical training had enabled him to detect the cunning of demons, but the same could not be said of the people of the Andes. Some early illustrated histories of the Incas thus depict Andeans conversing with the devil, without, apparently, being aware of their interlocutor's identity (figs. 8, 9).[53] The philosophical tenet that an object's accidents, its external appearance, could conceptually be separated from its substance, from what the object really was, thus entailed consequences of profound ambivalence. For while this tenet lay at the root of the Thomist explanation of transubstantiation and eucharistic visions, it also explained only too graphically how the demons and the devil were capable of playing havoc with human sense perception by deluding it with illusory images.

Thomist opinions regarding the conditioning of the soul's faculties by both the body and the environment were thus interwoven at many levels with philosophical opinions regarding the nature of specific objects of sense perception and of the material universe at large. This state of affairs was exemplified in Aquinas' explanation of visions and transubstantiation by reference to an object's substance and accidents, and by reference to the faculties of the soul, in particular intellect, imagination, and the sense of sight. These doctrines, reiterated many times by Aquinas' followers, had profound religious and political repercussions in Spain and the Americas, because they formed part and parcel of an explanatory system regarding the nature of human experience and of the cosmos that reached far beyond universities and the retreats of monks and nuns. Visions, whether legendary or real, were isolated occurrences. The doctrine of transubstantiation, however, was brought into play whenever people gathered for the Mass, while the tempests and epidemics that demons were capable of mobilizing likewise affected everyone.

The consecration of the eucharistic elements exemplified God's power over the order of nature, for it was by his decree that the bread and wine were transubstantiated. But the agents and executors of God's power

---

[53] Depictions similar to the one from Zárate in fig. 8 may be found in Pedro Cieza de León, *Parte primera de la Crónica del Perú* (Seville, 1553); for reproductions, see the edition of this work by F. Pease (Lima, 1984), facing pp. 72 and 73. The 1554 Antwerp edition of Cieza, which is also illustrated, has similar pictures (see fig. 9 of the present work).

were the priests of the Catholic Church, who uttered the words of consecration. In examining this issue, we enter into the social and political ramifications of Aristotelian and Thomist interpretations of cognition and imagination.

Ordination, Aquinas explained, conferred on priests the power to consecrate the eucharistic elements. This power was institutional, not personal, because consecration occurred when the appropriate words were spoken, independently of the priest's intention.[54] Indeed, the intention of the priest when speaking the words was irrelevant, because the consecration was effected out of the person of Christ, not out of that of the priest, who "in accomplishing this sacrament merely repeats the words of Christ."[55] These were divine, not human, words, analogous in some way to the words God spoke at the creation. However, at the creation, God spoke in imperatives, as when he said, "Let there be light"; while in the Eucharist, when Christ said, "This is my body," he spoke "according to the power of signification."[56] In Christ's explanatory utterance, human and divine speech converged, just as human and divine nature converged in Christ's person. Although the priest himself was only human, he repeated Christ's words by virtue of his institutional power. Accordingly, the consecration of the Eucharist, and by implication eucharistic visions, exemplified a social order in which priests exercised divinely delegated functions in a hierarchy of authority that descended from god via the priesthood to laypeople. Theology, philosophy, and social order, religion and politics, went hand in hand.

2. RELIGION AND POLITICS

Unlike France, where Aquinas taught, and Flanders, the home of Bosch and Patinir, the Spanish kingdoms did not possess a uniformly Christian culture. Rather, significant minorities of Jews and Muslims, of converts from Judaism and Islam, and of country people still adhering to fragments of ancient pagan practices and beliefs constituted a constant challenge to the Christian establishment. In 1552 Francisco López de Gómara, historian of the Americas and of the conquest of Mexico, proudly proclaimed that non-Christian political power had been eliminated in the peninsula by the time Columbus found America, thus leaving Spain free to combat infidels elsewhere.[1] Even so, non-Christian religious observances of Islamic and Jewish, popular and pagan origin endured in the peninsula long past the time of Columbus.

[54] Aquinas, *Summa* 3, q. 74, a.2 ad 2.
[55] Aquinas, *Summa* 3, q. 78, a.1 resp.
[56] Aquinas, *Summa* 3, q. 78, a.2 ad 2.
[1] Gómara, *Historia general de las Indias*, Preface, addressed by the author to Charles V.

In the seventeenth century, medicinal plants were still collected on mid-summer morning in accord with the ancient belief that they were more potent if harvested at this time of year, during the summer solstice.[2] Near Seville and Madrid, people invoked the star of Diana,[3] and elsewhere in Spain other stars were called upon to give assistance in matters of love.[4] Divinatory and magical rituals were performed as a matter of course,[5] and beliefs at variance with official Christian doctrines were widely subscribed to.[6]

One of these beliefs in particular attracted the attention of ecclesiastical authorities. Country people in the Pyrenees and elsewhere in Spain believed that some of their number, usually women, were wont to fly through the air to attend periodic nocturnal meetings in honor of the lady Abundantia or Diana. The observance was to safeguard communal well-being and prosperity.[7] In the early fifteenth century, the Dominican Fray Lope de Barrientos, bishop of Cuenca, intimate counselor to Enrique II of Castile and tutor of the infante, commented on this phenomenon but rejected the idea that women could really fly through the air. Like the good Aristotelian and Thomist that he was, he felt that "such things do not happen bodily, but only in dreams and by the working of the imagination." Nonetheless, in 1529 the Franciscan friar Martín de Castañega was still interested in the issue, which was at this same time being investigated by the Inquisition.[8] Yet, however widespread pagan and popular beliefs and practices may have been in the peninsula, they did not pose nearly as serious a challenge to Christian authority as did the beliefs and practices of Jews and *conversos*. It was these latter that Fray Lope de Bar-

---

[2] Cirac Estopañán, *Procesos de hechicerias*, p. 40; J. G. Frazer, *The Golden Bough* (London, 1913; rpt. 1976), pt. 7, 2: 45–75.

[3] Cirac Estopañán, *Procesos de hechicerias*, pp. 110, 207.

[4] Cirac Estopañán, *Procesos de hechicerias*, pp. 106ff., 143f.

[5] E.g. Cirac Estopañán, *Procesos de hechicerias*, pp. 40ff. See also *Fontes Iudaeorum regni Castellae*, ed. Carrete Parrondo, vol. 2 (hereafter *FIRC* 2, cited by the numbered sections of the document), 171–175 passim.

[6] E.g. Cirac Estopañán, *Procesos de hechicerias*, pp. 66ff.; *FIRC* 2: 173, 194, 208. Note *FIRC* 2: 212: a cura claimed to possess jewels worn by the angels at the Nativity (cf. Fra Cipolla's feather from the wing of the angel Gabriel in Boccaccio, *Decameron*, day 6, novel 10). See further, *FIRC* 2: 227f.; cf. A. Castro Diaz, "Pecado, demonio y determinismo en *La Celestina*," in *Homenaje a José Antonio Maravall* (Madrid, 1985), 1: 383–396; J.-P. de Dieu, "The Inquisition," in S. Haliczer (1987), pp. 129–146.

[7] J. Caro Baroja, *World of the Witches*, p. 144 with p. 288, nn. 7–8; C. Ginzburg, *Night Battles* (1985), esp. pp. 40ff.; B. Levack, *Witch-Hunt*, pp. 40ff.; M. Camille, *The Gothic Idol* (1989), pp. 107ff.

[8] Barrientos, *Tratado de la adivinanza*, in his *Vida y obras*, p. 177; Castañega, *Tratado*, p. 44. Barrientos and Castañega both cited the "Canon Episcopi," unaware that it was a forgery. The "Canon" preoccupied them as much as did living unorthodox beliefs and practices. See also M. Menendez y Pelayo, *Historia de los heterodoxos españoles* (Santander, 1946–1947), vol. 1, chap. 6; vol. 2, chap. 7 and Kramer and Sprenger, *Malleus* 2, q. 1, chap. 3, p. 104, with Las Casas, *Apologética Historia* 97, p. 505. For Peru, see below, chap. IV.3 at n. 140.

rientos attempted to refute in his treatises on sleep, dreaming, and divination, which he wrote at the request of Enrique II of Castile.

Barrientos thus argued against books of secret wisdom of Jewish origin by claiming that, unlike the scriptures recognized by Catholic Christianity, they were forgeries. For instance, he contradicted the claim that the *Book of Raziel* had been given to a son of Adam by the angel who stood at the gate to the earthly paradise.[9] He also denied that this angel had planted on earth a branch of the tree of life from which, later, wood for the cross of Jesus was cut. These teachings, Barrientos asserted, conflicted with doctrines based on revealed Scripture. Furthermore, he claimed, much as Aquinas might have done, that the rituals recommended in the *Book of Raziel* for invoking the magical aid of angels so as to achieve cures and to predict the future conflicted with natural causation as commonly observed and therefore could only be inefficacious. Finally, he explained that supernatural power over diseases and demons was bestowed by God on the apostles and their successors, but on no one else. The authority claimed by writings such as the *Book of Raziel* was thus false in scientific terms because its recommendations contravened the observed natural order, and it was false in theological terms because it conflicted with the divinely sanctioned authority of the apostles and their successors, the Catholic clergy. What was at issue was not merely the beliefs of a Jewish minority. For the *Book of Raziel* and similar works, such as the *Key of Solomon*[10] and diverse manuals of divination[11] circulated widely. The copies of these works that Fray Lope de Barrientos read had thus belonged not to Jews but to Don Enrique de Villena, the translator of Dante and friend of the Marqués de Santillana, many of whose books were burned after his death in 1434 because of their heterodox content.[12]

The spread among Christians of heterodox opinions considered to be of Jewish origin occasioned ever-increasing official hostility in fifteenth-century Spain. Persecution and—in many cases—massacre of the Jews throughout the peninsula during the years 1391 and 1392 brought to an end the religious pluralism, *convivencia*, that had tended to prevail until then. Under pressure, many Jews converted to Christianity. But tensions and conflicts between these conversos and old Christians were ubiquitous, so that pleas for moderation[13] were rarely heeded. Instead, through-

[9] Barrientos, *Tratado de la adivinanza*, p. 122, pp. 116ff., respectively. See also, *Encyclopedia Judaica* s.v. Razim, sefer ha-.

[10] Cf. C. C. McCown, *The Testament of Solomon* (1922), pp. 100f.

[11] Barrientos, *Tratado de la adivinanza*, p. 122 mentions a work entitled *De arte notoria*; cf. Aquinas, *Summa* 2.2, q. 96, a.1.

[12] See Barrientos, *Tratado de la adivinanza*, p. 117; further, Cirac Estopañán, *Procesos de hechicerias*, pp. 11–38; *FIRC* 2: 13, 18, 72, 82, 96.

[13] E.g. Lope de Barrientos, *Contra algunos zizanadores*, in his *Vida y obras*, pp. 181–204; see also S. W. Baron, *A Social and Religious History of the Jews: Late Middle Ages and Era of*

out the peninsula, community rivalries focusing on both the real and the perceived social status and economic success of conversos were aggravated by royal debt and rising prices. The establishment in Spain of the Inquisition as an arm of royal government and the expulsion of the Jews in 1492 were the direct results of this evolution.[14]

Yet the rationale of inquisition and expulsion was not exclusively economic and political, but emerged from long-established habits of theological reasoning.[15] Arguments polarizing authority, knowledge, ritual, and religious belief between true and authentic on the one hand, erroneous and counterfeit on the other, had been discussed by theologians for generations. In the later fifteenth century, these arguments were coordinated and sharpened by being used to implement religious persecution and activate religious hatred. Since Christians worshiped holy images, Jews and conversos must needs desecrate them, just as they were alleged to flout the dietary rules of the church by observing those of Judaism.[16] Similarly, while Christians worshiped Jesus, Jews awaited their own Messiah, observed their own law, and read their own scriptures. In all these ways Jews were thought to challenge—at least by implication—the established political order.[17] Moreover, both representatives of the church and secular rulers were equally convinced that this challenge extended far beyond Jewish communities, to conversos and old Christians alike. And indeed, year after year, the inquisitors uncovered concrete evidence of this reality. Doubt as to the veracity of the tenets of Catholic theology was expressed by many people as a matter of routine. What endowed such doubt with coherence and weight was the maintenance—in however fragmentary a form—of Jewish beliefs and rituals.[18]

European Expansion, 1200–1650, vol. 10, *On the Empire's Periphery* (New York, 1965), 167–219; cf. F. Talmage, "Trauma at Tortosa: The Testimony of Abraham Rimoch," *Revue des Études Juives* 47 (1985): 379–415; A. A. Sicroff, *Los estatutos de limpieza de sange* (1985).

[14] See A. MacKay, "Popular Movements," in his *Society, Economy and Religion* (1987), no. 10; E. Peters, *Inquisition* (1988), pp. 81ff.

[15] See Kriegel, "La prise d'une décision," *Revue Historique* 260 (1978): 49–90; J. Edwards, "Elijah and the Inquisition," *Nottingham Medieval Studies* 28 (1984): 79–94. H. Beinart, "The *Converso* Community in 15th Century Spain," in *The Sephardi Heritage*, ed. R. D. Barnett (New York, 1971), pp. 425–456.

[16] H. Beinart, "The Spanish Inquisition," *Medieval Studies* 43 (1981): 459f.; Edwards, "Elijah and the Inquisition," p. 84; R. Levine-Melammed, "Sixteenth-Century Justice in Action: The Case of Isabel Lopez," *Revue des Études Juives* 145 (1986): 51–73.

[17] R. Elinor, "Messianic Expectation and Spiritualisation of Religious Life in the Sixteenth Century," *Revue des Études Juives* 145 (1986): 35–49; Edwards, "Elijah and the Inquisition." But note that at this same time more eirenic attitudes continued to be expressed: e.g., Columbus, *Libro de profecias* (1502), in C. de Lollis, *Autografi di Cristoforo Colombo con prefazione e trascrizione diplomatica* (Rome, 1892), p. 107, where the Holy Spirit is said to work among Christians, Jews, Muslims, and all other sects, and to inspire not only the wise but also the ignorant.

[18] See Castañega, *Tratado* 19, pp. 120f.; for a detailed study of *FIRC* 2 see J. Edwards, "Religious Faith and Doubt," *Past and Present* 120 (1988): 3–25. See also C. J. Somerville and J. Edwards, "Debate. Religious Faith, Doubt and Atheism," *Past and Present* 128 (1990): 152–161.

By the later fifteenth century, the systematic juxtaposition between true and false doctrine that pervaded the proceedings of the Inquisition had come to be spelled out in the realm of theology in an equally systematic contrast between god and devil. Aquinas and, after him, Lope de Barrientos and others had been cautious in their evaluation of the concrete reality of demonic phenomena. While allowing that the demonic could be real, these theologians also explained sin and deviance in the light of the errors and vagaries of human imagination: temptation was no less pressing for being imagined on the basis of dreams and phantasms not caused by demons. A much less subtle approach to these issues was propounded by Henry Kramer and James Sprenger in a book entitled *The Hammer of Witches*, which was first printed c. 1484, enjoyed great popularity throughout Europe, and was even quoted by Bartolomé de Las Casas, bishop of Chiapas in Mexico.[19] Where, for instance, Barrientos had considered it crucial to make clear that women did not physically ride through the air to worship Diana, however concretely such exploits might be imagined,[20] Kramer and Sprenger asserted the exact opposite, their declared purpose being to see to it that witches did not escape punishment.[21] In their view, witches and other ministers of the devil invariably wielded an actual and physical, not an imaginary, power.

In Spain, a similar reasoning speaks through two treatises on superstition and witchcraft of the early sixteenth century that were designed to counteract religious nonconformity in the Basque country and the foothills of the Pyrenees. The first treatise, by the Franciscan friar Martín de Castañega, was published in Logroño in 1529. The second, by Pedro Ciruelo, was published in the following year in Alcalá and was several times reprinted. Garcilaso de la Vega, the author of an important history of Inca and early colonial Peru, owned a copy of this work.[22] Castañega and Ciruelo both contrasted true and false beliefs, rituals, and religious authorities, although in terms not quite as crude as those deployed by Kramer and Sprenger. For example, Castañega felt that riding forth at night to honor Diana could be a physical event but also speculated that it might be an event in the imagination.[23] Similarly, Castañega and Ciruelo alike thought that tempests and hailstorms were natural phenomena, the causation of which was sufficiently explained by Aristotelian natural science.[24] Sprenger and Kramer on the other hand enumerated instances of tempests and hailstorms that they were convinced had been caused by

[19] Las Casas, *Apologética Historia* 95, p. 492; 98, p. 512.
[20] Barrientos, *Tratado de la adivinanza,* in his *Vida y obras,* p. 177.
[21] Kramer and Sprenger, *Malleus* 2, q. 1, chap. 3, p. 104, citing the "Canon Episcopi."
[22] J. Durand, "La biblioteca del Inca," *Nueva Revista de Filología Hispánica* 2 (1948): 253.
[23] Castañega, *Tratado* 6.
[24] Castañega, *Tratado* 19; but cf. 22; Ciruelo, *Treatise reproving superstitions* (1977) 3.9, pp. 288ff. See now C. Ginzburg's important work, *Ecstasies* (1991).

demons and witchcraft.[25] However, although Castañega and Ciruelo evaluated atmospheric phenomena and the movement of the stars, as well as health and disease,[26] in scientific terms, they nonetheless conceptualized the human world in terms of those polar opposites of God and devil, licit and illicit authority, that also speak in the program of the Inquisition.

Where the inquisitors might thus examine a Black Mass, the demonic counterfeit of the real Mass that had been instituted by Christ,[27] Castañega thought of the holy Catholic church of God confronting an unholy "church" of Jews and Moors, and of unholy "execraments" inspired by the devil mockingly imitating the holy sacraments of Catholic Christianity.[28] Similarly, Ciruelo's central concern was to combat beliefs held and rituals performed outside the institutional framework of the Catholic church. He thus began by differentiating the nature of these beliefs and rituals, which he described as idolatrous superstitions, from Catholic ones. The distinction rests on the twofold foundation that had already been expounded by Aquinas and Barrientos, that is, on the authority of Scripture and hence of priestly power, and on an Aristotelian philosophy and natural science. In a sense, these two branches of knowledge, the scriptural and the scientific, amounted to one and the same thing for Ciruelo, because he regarded the Decalogue as a statement of natural law,[29] that is, law binding on all human beings irrespective of promulgation. A person thus could not fail to know the principles of natural law, just as one could not fail to observe the workings of the fundamental laws of natural philosophy. Given that the Decalogue was natural law, Ciruelo viewed monotheism resulting in Christianity as humanity's original religion; departures from it constituted a perversion of man's original purity and righteousness. Like Castañega, Ciruelo therefore thought that such departures implied a pact with the devil.[30] The universe was thus polarized between god and devil, good and evil, and at the human level this polarization found expression in true religion on the one hand and in "idolatrous superstition" on the other. The same reasoning was later used in Peru to combat Inca and Andean religion. Confession to Andean priests was viewed as a travesty of the Catholic equivalent,[31] while An-

---

[25] Kramer and Sprenger, *Malleus* 2, q. 1, chap. 15, pp. 147ff.

[26] Castañega, *Tratado* 23, p. 145; Ciruelo, *Treatise* 3.7, p. 254.

[27] G. Henningsen, "El banco de datos del Santo Oficio: Las relaciones de causas de la Inquisicion española," *Boletín de la Real Academia de la Historia* 174 (1977): 547–570, at 549.

[28] Castañega, *Tratado* 2–3.

[29] Ciruelo, *Treatise* 1.1, pp. 67f., 77; contrast Aquinas, *Summa* 1, q. 90ff.

[30] Ciruelo, *Treatise* 1.1, p. 77; 1.2, pp. 83ff.; Castañega, *Tratado* 4–5.

[31] See Murúa, *Historia del Origen* (1590), 3.45, pp. 269f., on Andean confession: diciendo palabras fingidas dan sus penitencias y con palabras equivocadas les dan a entender que no dejen los rituos y dioses antiguos.

dean priests and ritual specialists were thought to threaten the authority and social status of Catholic priests and missionaries.[32]

Two different methods of explanation, one anchored in an appeal to reason and the other in an appeal to the authority of sacred doctrine, were in tension in Castañega's and Ciruelo's thinking. This tension had been latent in Aquinas but became explicit once practical applications of his teaching were contemplated. On the side of reason, Castañega and Ciruelo endeavored to show that the devil and demonic spirits had no real power, so that rituals addressed to them of necessity remained inefficacious. In addition, such rituals were inefficacious because they involved scientific misapprehensions. Diseases had natural causes and could be cured by "natural medicines" administered by a qualified physician, while prayer would procure spiritual sustenance for the sufferer. Nostrums and amulets, by contrast, achieved nothing because they contained no inherent virtue to combat a given disease, while the ritual formulas spoken in spells and enchantments were vain words without power.[33] Such vain words had to be distinguished from prayers invoking the omnipotence of God and especially from the words spoken by a priest when administering the sacraments. These latter were invested by God with "a supernatural divine power to bring about the effects."[34] In short, medicines worked because they had a natural power the effects of which could be studied by observation; and certain words when spoken by a priest had divine power, although words in general did not.

This distribution of natural and divine power in the universe was mirrored and made effective in society by different groups of experts. Priests administered words imbued with divine power, while physicians, as a result of prolonged study, administered the natural power inherent in certain plants and minerals. There was therefore no such thing as knowledge "infused by God without the need of a teacher's instruction or the study of books," while treatises of secret wisdom such as those allegedly written by King Solomon could be shown to be forgeries.[35] Ciruelo thus considered the practices he described as "idolatrous superstition" to threaten not only true religion and scientifically accurate knowledge but also the proper ordering of society. Where, in the realm of theory, truth confronted falsity, in society the ranks of true experts—priests, physicians, and theologians, administering words and things of power—confronted clandestine groups of false experts administering words and things that had no power.

Yet when arguing in the light not of reason but of doctrinal authority,

[32] See below, chap. IX.1.
[33] Ciruelo, *Treatise* 3.4, 7.
[34] Ciruelo, *Treatise* 1.2, p. 97.
[35] Ciruelo, *Treatise* 3.1, pp. 183ff.

Castañega and Ciruelo did not find matters to be so unambiguous, because the activity of demons, posited in sacred doctrine, overlapped with the workings of nature. The natural causation of storms was well understood, but Ciruelo would not altogether rule out the possibility of demons causing storms, even though he conceded that such storms were indistinguishable from natural ones. For this reason, he thought, storms should not be exorcised.[36] Similarly, diseases had natural causes, but on occasion people fell ill because a spell had been cast on them.[37] Unlike demonic interference in the weather, Ciruelo thought, spells and demonic possession in human beings could be diagnosed, so that here the remedy of exorcism was applicable, along with medical care. The exorcist was to be an ordained priest, who by virtue of his office wielded the same power over demons as Christ's apostles had done. As described by Castañega and Ciruelo,[38] and in Christian literature beginning with the New Testament, exorcism was a duel between the exorcist and a demonic force acting through the possessed person. The exorcist's charge that the demon should come out of his victim was confronted by the demon's countercharge; accusation met with denial, just as would happen in a court case pleaded by lawyers. In this way, a demon possessing a human being all too easily acquired an audience and riveted its attention, thereby gaining further power. This was why Castañega and Ciruelo warned against sensational exorcisms involving dialogue and confrontation with demons. Instead, exorcism was to follow the measured and precise ritual laid down by the Catholic church, so that demonic power was overcome not by any individual's wisdom or ability but by the institutional and impersonal collective power of the church.

In Mexico and Peru, exorcisms were customarily performed in accordance with these rules. Demons dwelling in human beings were adjured by the cross of Jesus Christ to declare their identity and purposes and to come out of their victims.[39] In difficult cases, the exorcist would explicitly set any worth he might himself possess to one side and call instead on the power of Jesus, the merits of the saints and the virtues of miraculous Christian images.[40]

Demonic power was thus real, not imaginary. Yet, its most profound impact on human affairs was not to be looked for in open displays of control over situations or individuals—as might become evident, for instance, in exorcism—but in its more subtle workings in the imagination.

[36] Ciruelo, *Treatise* 3.9; similarly Castañega, *Tratado* 19.

[37] Ciruelo, *Treatise* 3.5, pp. 237ff.; Castañega, *Tratado* 16, on true and false relics and holy medals.

[38] Castañega, *Tratado* 20–21; Ciruelo, *Treatise* 3.8.

[39] Las Casas, *Apologética Historia* 255, pp. 550f.

[40] Ramos Gavilán, *Historia . . . de Copacabana* 1.6, pp. 26f.; 1.15, pp. 51ff.; 2.19, pp. 132ff.

At issue here was the functioning of demonic power within the most intimate fabric of the human soul.

Dreams were a case in point. The divinatory dreams of prophets and patriarchs had been discussed by Aquinas[41] and in greater detail by Barrientos. According to Barrientos, the nature and content of a given dream, its truth value, depended on the role of the imagination in it. Excess in food and drink brought vaporous images before the imagination of the dreamer, while an abstemious and virtuous person saw lucid and clear dream images.[42] Only such persons "of subtle imagination," among whom Barrientos, as later Ciruelo, counted the patriarch Joseph and the prophet Daniel, were capable of experiencing and especially of interpreting prophetic dreams.[43] Furthermore, just as in waking life, recollection and abstemiousness, along with an ability to seclude oneself from the clutter of sense perceptions, led to lucid phantasms and hence to a truthful understanding of natural phenomena,[44] so also in sleep, the dreamer's ordered and disciplined moral and mental habits would result in lucid and true dream images.[45] But a dissolute person incapable of recollection, whose imagination registered vaporous dream images, would mistake these for divine visitations and would, moreover, be captivated by demonic illusions or even worse, would be deceived by them, thanks to "mistaking the image for the thing itself."[46] Dissolute living was thus liable to result in disordered, misleading fantasies and dream images and in erroneous interpretations such as Satan exploited for his own purposes. Given that many missionaries in Peru did not consider Andean laws and customs to have inculcated an appropriate moral and ethical discipline, these missionaries also judged Andeans to be especially vulnerable to Satan's machinations.[47]

Two issues are at stake in these judgments. First, Castañega and Ciruelo, like the missionaries later, described a universe in which divine power, articulated through the beliefs and rituals of the Catholic church, was paralleled and rivaled at every stage by its counterpart, the power of demons. Neither God nor the demons controlled human free will; yet the order of nature was disposed in such a way as to provide a series of step-

[41] Aquinas, *Summa* 2.2, q. 95, a.6.

[42] Barrientos, *Tratado del dormir*, in his *Vida y obras*, pp. 29, 40, 41f. See also Aquinas, *Summa* 2.2, q. 172, a.4, on prophecy and *bonitas morum*; *Summa* 2.2, q. 173, a.2, on prophetic judgment as distinct from simple visionary experiences such as those of Pharaoh, Nebuchadnezzar, and Belshazzar.

[43] Barrientos, *Tratado del dormir*, pp. 53f.; Ciruelo, *Treatise* 2.6. For Spinoza's different opinion about the prophet Daniel, coupled with his different evaluation of imagination, see below, Epilogue at n. 62.

[44] Barrientos, *Tratado del dormir*, pp. 41f., 55.

[45] Barrientos, *Tratado del dormir*, p. 54; Aquinas, *Summa* 2.2, q. 172, a.1 ad 2.

[46] Barrientos, *Tratado del dormir*, pp. 56, 58.

[47] See below, chaps. VI, IX.1.

ping stones whereby demons, through conditioning a person's body, were capable of influencing the imagination, and hence other faculties of the soul as well. The resulting cosmic battle between good and evil, which was acted out with particular intensity in human beings, was ultimately directed by divine providence. Thus it was possible to say that God permitted the sufferings of Job and the temptations of Anthony in the desert,[48] even though it was impossible to specify precisely how he did so. As Castañega expressed it, God permits the perdition of certain individuals "after they are confirmed in error; as the prophet says, 'He abandons them, according to the desire of their hearts.' " But we are not told what being confirmed in error amounted to.[49]

The second issue concerns the manner of demonic appearances. In the footsteps of Aquinas and the early Christian apologists, Castañega and Ciruelo, like later missionaries in Peru, thought that the demons imitated divine actions, as, for instance, when they appeared before the imagination in dreams or created false phantasms before the eyes of a waking person.[50] Alternatively, demons could be induced to display themselves to human fantasy by illicit rituals counterfeiting the true rituals of the church.[51] Either way, the demons laid claim to a power of causation that rivaled the divine power of causation, and with it they usurped the right to adoration belonging only to God. As the painter Joachim Patinir saw it, demons tempted the hermit Anthony by hiding their demonic substance under the accidents of beautiful young ladies, thereby not merely arousing carnal sensibilities but also seeking to shift the saint's attention away from God (fig. 5).

The reasoning that explained eucharistic visions and transubstantiation was thus the exact counterpart to the reasoning that explained the nature and functioning of demonic power in human affairs. For the separability of substance and accidents served to elucidate the inner workings of divine miracle and demonic manipulation alike. This is, of course, logical and to be expected, because the same psychology and natural philosophy underlay theories of divine and demonic action. Demons and the devil did not act in a different human or natural universe merely because they were evil. Rather, the universe was one and the same throughout. From late antiquity on, Christian theologians had rejected the Manichaean polarity of two clearly separable cosmic principles of good and evil. As a

[48] Ciruelo, Treatise 1.2, p. 90; 3, p. 237.

[49] On the inscrutable will of God, see below, chap. III.1.

[50] See Ciruelo, Treatise 2.6, p. 162 and Castañega, Tratado 7. For a late antique antecedent, see Chrysostom, In epistolam I ad Corinthos homilia XXIX, in Migne, Patrologia Graeca 61, cols. 239–243. For the same theory regarding demonic activity in the Andes, see below chap. V.2 at nn. 32ff., Las Casas; chap. VI at nn. 105ff., Acosta.

[51] Ciruelo, Treatise 1.3, p. 109.

2. RELIGION AND POLITICS

result, they were forced to contend with the grinding dilemma of the intermingling of good and evil in the terrestial city.[52]

Human society and an individual's free will thus sustained the heavy obligation of discriminating between divine and demonic power, the operations of which by their very nature appeared to be deceptively similar. Indeed, in their discussion of visions, Theresa of Avila and many other mystics were constantly caught in the dilemma of differentiating visions caused by God from those caused by demons. Divine visions brought inner peace and tranquillity, the mystics thought, whereas demonic ones were ultimately a source of disquiet and discontent. Yet even if someone experiencing a vision might in this way be able to distinguish its origin, the criterion was a fragile one, because disquiet and tranquillity were not measurable in any sense external to the individual experiencing them. Similarly, Castañega differentiated the good intention of sacraments from the evil intention of demonic "execraments," but without being able to resort to any more palpable distinctions.[53]

The task of differentiating divine and demonic causation was at once a theological and a scientific one. On the one hand, theologians and priests endeavored to explain which ritual actions and which words enshrined approved intention and efficacy and which did not, while also carrying out those approved ritual actions and speaking the accompanying words. Physicians, on the other hand, were trained to know which natural substances had curing properties in relation to which diseases and practiced their profession on this basis. These well-known arguments differentiating divine from demonic agency, which Ciruelo stated with great care,[54] were in the seventeenth century reiterated to Andeans. Reason and observation of natural phenomena, the Indians were told, would reveal to them the falsity of their own ancient religion.[55] If thus the burden of articulating theological and scientific information in terms of everyday life rested on specially designated groups of professionals and experts, set aside as they were from the rest of society by status, privilege, and attire (cf. fig. 25; see also figs. 27, 41), the burden of acting on the basis of such information weighed on every member of society at large. The reason was that the most insidious, and at the same time the most efficacious, way in which demonic power could manifest itself was thought to involve the individual imagination.

The social fabric was therefore ordered by multiple landmarks—rituals both secular and sacred, groups of publicly designated experts, learned

[52] R. A. Markus, *Saeculum: History and Society in the Theology of St. Augustine* (Cambridge, 1970).
[53] Castañega, *Tratado* 3, p. 30.
[54] Ciruelo, *Treatise* 3.12.
[55] See below, chap. IX.1.

and religious traditions—capable of guiding the individual imagination toward an acceptance of divine power as expressed in the teachings and ceremonies of the Catholic church. Trials conducted in secret by the Inquisition culminated in meticulously orchestrated public ceremonies that exalted the authority of church and state and humiliated and disgraced those who had offended against it (fig. 7).[56] Theological and ceremonial precedents, once established in the peninsula, were adapted to the specific circumstances of early colonial Peru.[57] Individuals who placed themselves outside the landmarks of ritual and authority could therefore be readily identified as victims of demonic deception, and even as devotees of demonic power. This is one reason why, in early sixteenth-century Spain, the *alumbrados* provoked such ferocious reaction and repression,[58] and why later Theresa of Avila was so careful to subordinate her visions and religious experiences to priestly authority.[59]

In their different ways, Barrientos, Castañega, and Ciruelo perceived their society as being polarized between demonic and divine power. Demonic power was recognizable in rituals not practiced by the Catholic church, in authority not defined by canonical texts, and in the activities of experts whose skills were not officially approved. But the mode of describing and analyzing things divine as opposed to things demonic was identical to that used, later, to contrast Christian ritual and belief with Andean counterparts. There existed no distinct vocabulary of otherness or difference to portray religious phenomena and religious experience outside, or to one side of, the Catholic church. Indeed, in Spain all parties to the conflict of Judaism, Christianity, and Islam found themselves riveted in the spell of the same concepts. For Jews, therefore, the "idolatrous superstition" was Christianity.[60] Other critics of Christianity referred to the Mass as "a work of witchcraft"[61] and to Christian religious images as idols.[62] Martín de Castañega was painfully aware of this very difficulty when explaining how easily "execraments" imitated sacraments: "What

---

[56] Berruguete, Auto da Fé (Museo del Prado, *Catálogo de las pinturas*, inventory 618, p. 58). Note also, in the same series by Berruguete, St. Dominic supervising the burning of heretical books (Prado, *Catálogo*, inventory 1305, p. 58). This is a frequent theme in the sixteenth century; see, e.g., Cristobal Llorens, St. Dominic superintends the burning of Islamic and Jewish books (Valencia, Museo de Bellas Artes, inventory 448).

[57] See below, chap. IX.1.

[58] M. Bataillon, *Erasmo y España* (1950); C. F. Fraker, "The 'Dejados' and the *Cancionero de Baena*," *Hispanic Review* 33 (1965): 97–117.

[59] Francisco de Ribera, *Vida de Santa Teresa de Jesús*, ed. J. Pons (Barcelona, 1908), chap. 10, pp. 129ff.; see also, Santa Teresa de Jesús, *Camino de Perfeccion*, ed. J.-M. Aguado (Madrid, 1929), chap. 23.

[60] Yosef ha-Kohen, *Emeq Ha- Bakha (El Valle del Llanto)*, transl. P. Leon Tello (Madrid, 1964), pp. 127f.

[61] *FIRC* 2: 320, obra de hechicería.

[62] *FIRC* 2, no. 391; cf. no. 84; where Lope de Malvenda says, "El alguazil de los padres; digole el alguazil de los idolos."

7. Auto da fé: Dominican friars urge the condemned (at the bottom of the stairs, left, and next to the stake, right) to die repentant, thereby accepting the sentence as justified. The cooperation of the secular state in these proceedings, which are directed by the chief inquisitor on the tribunal, is spelled out by the presence of mounted guards and soldiers.
Pedro Berruguete; Prado, Madrid.

could a non-Catholic say, a person who has no faith in the sacraments of baptism, confirmation, holy orders and extreme unction, other than that these sacraments are mere superstitions, with all their rituals and anointings? The sacrament of extreme unction appears exactly like some piece of witchcraft, when they anoint the sick person's eyes, ears, nose, mouth, hands, his loins and his feet."[63]

The absence of conceptual alternatives to this carefully nuanced, yet deeply subjective, system of differentiating religious truth from religious error, the works of god from the works of demons, became explicit in Peru. Spaniards in the Andes continued defining religious difference and otherness in the familiar fashion. But the locus of difference and otherness, and hence of demonic agency, shifted. In Peru otherness and demonic agency were no longer to be encountered merely in a small number of individuals who might step beyond the boundaries of shared knowledge, belief, and ritual, or in a different but somehow familiar religious tradition, such as Judaism. Rather, in Peru, otherness defined the vast majority of people. Moreover, otherness pertained not merely to religion, but extended to language, social organization, and every conceivable aspect of everyday life.

When Spaniards confronted Andean people, therefore, the familiar scale of nuances that had served in the peninsula to distinguish truth from error, and god from demons, collapsed into a consolidated sense of a difference that was total. The early accounts of Peru abound with comments about the exteme difficulty of describing and explaining the new land and its people to the reader who had not seen them. Occasionally, comparisons between the customs of Spanish Muslims and Andean Indians were deployed to explain the unknown in the light of the known,[64] but in the last resort such comparisons were of limited use.

To the countless political and religious differences between Andeans and Spaniards with which the early writers on Peru contended, warfare added the difference between conquered and conquerors. In the eyes of Spaniards, this difference too was anchored in religion. The men of Pizarro rallied under the battle cry of the Virgin and Santiago and accordingly described themselves as Christians. Back at home, the Christianity of some of the invaders might well have been questioned,[65] but in Peru such doubts did not arise until much later. The empire of the Incas was conquered in the name of the Christian god, who endowed the conquerors with a personal and political identity defined by the vast difference and inequality between themselves and the people of the Andes. The

[63] Castañega, *Tratado* 3, p. 29.
[64] MacCormack, "The Fall of the Incas," *History of European Ideas* 6 (1985): 421–445.
[65] J. A. del Busto Duthuburu, "Tres conversos," *Revista de Indias* 27, nos. 109/110 (1967): 427–442.

Spanish invaders of the Andes thus constructed a conceptual framework, a set of poles of likeness and difference, within which Andean religion could be observed and remembered in the light of Christian doctrine allied with military success.

Yet if this had been all, the story of Spanish perceptions of Inca and Andean religion, and the concurrent story of the evolution of Andean religion in colonial times, would be a simple one. There is, however, no sense in which either story is simple. For the criteria that had been evolved in Christian Spain to evaluate and judge religious truth and religious error were ambiguous, seeing that no set of absolute and unshakable distinctions could be drawn between the one and the other. Applied to the religion of the Incas and to the religion of Andean people in colonial times, these criteria, buttressed though they were by military superiority at the outset and by political hegemony subsequently, did not over time and in the eyes of different Spanish observers deliver a uniform verdict. Moreover, Andeans soon understood the equivocal, two-edged character of the invaders' vocabulary of religious truth and error. Spaniards might well describe Andean sacred images as idols. But Andeans in turn came to be convinced that Catholic religious images were "the idols of Spaniards," while the demon-conquering cross of Jesus was simply a "stick."[66]

[66] MacCormack, "Pachacuti," *American Historical Review* 93 (1988): 960–1006.

INVASION OF PERU
AND FIRST CONTACTS,
1532–1535

THE INVASION of the Andes that resulted in the capture and subsequent death of the Inca ruler Atahualpa in the city of Cajamarca in northern Peru had been planned and prepared over a considerable period. For more than a decade, Francisco Pizarro and his future companions in arms had searched out whatever information could shed light on the lands and peoples that might one day be found to the south of the Spanish settlement and seaport of Panama. In 1524 Francisco Pizarro and Diego de Almagro set sail in two ships and a small brigantine to explore the coastline that extended out toward the south, but they found it rugged and forbidding. The pilot Bartolomé Ruiz was therefore sent ahead in one of the ships, and it was he who stumbled across clear proof that perseverance was likely to be richly rewarded. Near the equator Ruiz encountered a sailing craft carrying a precious and exotic cargo to be exchanged in Mexico for the spondylus shells that Andeans valued for both ritual use and personal adornment. This cargo fired the imagination of the Spanish adventurers. It consisted of

> many pieces of gold and silver for the adornment of their persons to exchange with their trading partners. Among these pieces were crowns and diadems and belts and daggers and protective leggings, breastplates, and pincers, and small bells and strings and bunches of beads, ruby silver, and mirrors adorned with the said silver; and cups and other vessels for drinking. They carried shawls of wool and cotton and shirts and coats . . . and many other garments, most of them beautifully worked with elaborate craftsmanship. The colors were red and crimson and blue and yellow and all the other colors diversely worked into figures of birds, animals, fish, and plants. They carried some small scales similar to the Roman kind for weighing gold, and many other things. Among the strings of beads were some containing small stones of emerald and chalcedony and other precious stones and pieces of crystal.[1]

[1] Joan de Samano, *Relación*, ed. R. Porras Barrenechea, p. 66. I thank Rolena Adorno for her help with translating this passage.

Bartolomé Ruiz was able to capture three men from among the crew of the Indian craft, who learned to be interpreters and accompanied the Spanish adventurers on subsequent expeditions. By 1532 several more interpreters had been recruited, but the level of communication they facilitated was rarely more than elementary.[2] Indeed, years elapsed before the invaders gained any clear understanding of Andean thought and social order.

The earliest written accounts of the Incas and their land are thus full of meticulously remembered concrete observations that were formulated in whatever basic terms lay readily to hand in the invaders's existing vocabulary. Llamas figured as "sheep of the land"[3] and sacred buildings were often called "mosques."[4] Similarly, several of the earliest chroniclers did not preoccupy themselves with the intricacies of Inca nomenclature and simply referred to the Inca ruler by the name of his capital, as "the Cuzco."[5] For further clarity, a distinction was sometimes drawn between "the old Cuzco" and "the young Cuzco" to refer to the Inca Guayna Capac, who had died before the invaders arrived, and his son Guascar, the older brother of Atahualpa.[6]

With lapse of time, Spaniards in the Andes learned to dispense with such crude vocabulary because they acquired a more intimate knowledge of Andean thought and culture. At the same time, increasing familiarity with the Andes sharpened a set of contradictions in Spanish perceptions of the Andes that were present from the beginning. The commercial cargo that Bartolomé Ruiz had captured was only the first of innumerable indicators of the high level of Andean material and political culture to claim the invaders' attention. The Inca road system, Inca construction and architectural design, and above all, Inca administration were repeatedly described as unrivaled in Europe. Pizarro's secretary, Francisco de Xerez, thus remembered how on 15 November 1532, the eve of Atahualpa's capture, the Spaniards had seen for the first time the fine dwellings of Cajamarca, its temple of the Sun, it's defenses, water supply, and road

[2] See, for instance, on the confusion that arose among the invaders regarding a gift sent to them by Atahualpa, [Estete], *Noticia* (1924), p. 23; Mena, *La conquista*, in *Las relaciones primitivas*, ed. R. Porras Barrenechea (1937), p. 81 with n. 9.

[3] *Relación francesa*, in *Las relaciones primitivas*, ed. R. Porras Barrenechea, p. 75; Sancho, *An account* 14, p. 129.

[4] [Estete], *Noticia* (1924), p. 25.

[5] E.g., *Relación francesa*, ed. R. Porras Barrenechea, pp. 74, 77; Mena, *La conquista*, ed. Pogo, p. 250.

[6] Xerez, *Verdadera relación*, p. 96; Mena, *La conquista*, ed. Pogo, pp. 266, 272, 274. A precedent of sorts for this procedure appears in Hernando del Pulgar's *Crónica de los Reyes Catolicos*, Biblioteca de autores españoles, vol. 70 (Madrid, 1953), pt. 3, chaps. 36, 58, etc., where, as a shortcut for using Arabic names, the rival kings of Granada are described as "el Rey viejo" and "el Rey mozo."

system.[7] Another of Pizarro's men recalled feeling afraid as he surveyed this Inca provincial capital from the mountain road on which the Spanish host was descending into the valley where the city was situated. Looking down at the Inca Atahualpa's encampment at a small distance from the city, he wrote: "we were astounded. For we had not thought that Indians could possess so proud an abode, or so many tents, and so well appointed. Nothing similar has been seen in the Indies so far, and it caused to all of us Spaniards great confusion and fear."[8]

Inca religion, by contrast, was criticized and attacked from the outset. Initially, Spaniards had difficulty with the idea that Andeans knew nothing about Christianity, that the message which was to be proclaimed "to the ends of the earth" and which constituted one of the criteria of the unity of mankind, had somehow not been heard in the Andes. It thus seemed natural that Andean religious rituals and beliefs should enshrine some residue of that message. Yet these pious hopes were prone to being disappointed. Objects which at first glance seemed to be crucifixes[9] and crosses, garments which resembled chasubles and bishop's mitres,[10] myths which apparently recalled Noah's flood[11] and the preaching of the apostles, on closer inspection turned out to be so many illusions. What had at first been perceived as likenesses or resemblances, however distant, between Andean religion and Christianity therefore collapsed into difference. And in due course, the differences Spanish observers noted between Andean religion and Christianity became, quite simply, so many indicators of Andean error. For, so the reasoning went, if Andeans had indeed in the past known of the true religion, it was obvious that they had forgotten or misrepresented it because the devil had imprinted their minds with illusory images such as had also proved to be a powerful means of demonic deception back in Europe (figs. 8 and 9).[12]

Observations of the Incas and their subjects that might have been capable of feeding reflection on what was in some way comparable between Andean religion and Christianity were thus formulated in terms of contrasts. In due course, accordingly, there remained few mediating nuances, few shades of chiaroscuro, that an observer might employ to paint a tableau capable of revealing the interrelated layers of meaning that gave weight to Andean religious belief and practice. The resulting polarity be-

[7] Xerez, *Verdadera relación*, pp. 103f.

[8] [Estete], *Noticia*, p. 25.

[9] [Estete], *Noticia*, p. 16.

[10] Zárate, in M. Bataillon, "Zárate ou Lozano?" *Caravelle* 1 (1963): 25.

[11] Zárate, ibid., p. 24.

[12] See Gonzalo Fernández de Oviedo y Valdés, *Historia general y natural de las Indias*, Biblioteca de autores españoles, vol. 117 (Madrid, 1959), pt. 1, bk. 5, Proemio, p. 111b: tienen el entendimiento bestial y mal inclinado; Betanzos, *Suma* (1987), 1.3, p. 18a, author retells the myth of Ayarcache as Andeans tell it, i.e., "segun que ellos lo fantasean."

ala prouincia que de su nombre se llamò Pachamaca,donde el residia,que es quatro leguas
dela ciudad delos Reyes, y q̃ duro Pachamaca
muchas edades,hasta que los Christianos llega
ron al Peru,que entonces nunca mas pareciò,
por donde se cree que deuia de ser algun demo
nio que les hazia entẽder todas estas vanidades,

creen que antes de todo esto vuo diluuio,y q̃
quando vino se escaparon las gentes en grãdes
cueuas que para ello auian hecho enlas muy
altas sierras llenas de todos bastimentos,y tapa
das las pequeñas puertas que tenian,por mane
ra que la lluuia no les pudiesse entrar,y q̃ quan
do creyeronque ya las aguas abaxauan, echa-
uan

8. Andeans converse with the demon Pachacamac. "Pachacamac endured
for many ages," states the accompanying text, "until the Christians came
to Peru. But then he never appeared again, so that it is thought he must
have been some demon who made them believe all these vanities." Agustín
de Zárate, *Historia* (Antwerp, 1555), fol. 19v. Biblioteca
Nacional, Madrid.

la paz q̃ prometé sustétá. La guerra q̃ tuuierõ
con los Españoles se dira adeláte en su tiépo
y lugar. Muy gráde es el dominio y señorio q̃
el demonio enemigo de natura humana, por
los pecados de aquesta géte sobre ellos tuuo,
permitiédolo Dios: porq̃ muchasvezes era vi
sto visiblemente por ellos . En aq̃llos tabla-
dos teniá muy grandes manojos de cuerdas
de cabuya a manera de crizneja: la qual nos a
prouecho para hazer alpargatas, tã largas q̃te
niã a mas de quaréta braças cada vna de aq̃-
stas sogas. De lo alto del tablado atauã los In
dios q̃ tomauan en la guerra por los hóbros,
y dexauã los colgados, y a algunos dellos les
sacauan los coraçones, y los ofreciã a sus dioses

9. Human sacrifice in the Andes sponsored by the devil appearing as an
illusory monster, attended by other such monsters. The illustrator has dramatized the accompanying text of Cieza's *Crónica* (Antwerp, 1554), which
merely states: "The dominion and lordship that by God's permission the
devil . . . exercised over those people because of their sins, was very great"
(chap. 19). Benson Collection, University of Texas at Austin.

tween truth and falsity, the works of god and the works of the devil, pervades accounts of Andean religion from the moment of first contact to the end of the seventeenth century and beyond.

These difficulties in the way of conceptualizing whatever nuanced likeness and difference might after all be perceived in Andean religion were aggravated by the momentum of conquest; the momentum, that is, of desecrating Andean temples, shrines, and holy places. As almost every contemporary observer noted, the reason that first brought Spaniards to Andean religious centers such as the pyramid of Pachacamac, the city of Cuzco, and the holy island of Titicaca, was the lust for treasure. But if the theft of temple treasures was to be somehow legitimated, their sacred quality had to be gainsaid, and this could only be done by denying that the deity to whom the treasures had been dedicated was indeed a deity.

1. THE DEVIL AND DIVINATION

A beginning was made in the undertaking of devaluing and desecrating Andean holy objects when, on the day after their arrival in Cajamarca, Francisco Pizarro's host encountered the Inca Atahualpa in the city's central square. The capture of Montezuma in Mexico had revealed the demoralizing and disorganizing effect the ruler's captivity could have on his subjects, and plans were therefore laid as to how to capture the Inca at that first formal meeting. When Atahualpa and his majestic retinue had ceremoniously entered the square, the Spaniards sent forward the Dominican friar Valverde to explain to him the sovereign claims of the Christian religion and the falsity of his own. The significance of Valverde's explanation was merely formal, for as several historians noted later, it was inconceivable that the Inca could have understood even a fraction of whatever was said on that occasion. However, the friar claimed that Atahualpa had rejected his exhortation to become a Christian and called on the Spaniards to avenge this offence against their god. When thus the Inca was captured and imprisoned, a preliminary proof—if such was needed—had been obtained of the falsity of his religion.[1] An agreement was then made whereby the Inca should purchase his freedom with a room full of gold treasure, most of which was to be collected from temples. The Inca himself ordered his subjects to transport the gold to Cajamarca, but in addition, parties of Spaniards were sent out to hasten the collection and to acquaint themselves with the land and its people.

Three Spanish eyewitnesses described Hernando Pizarro's violent entry into the holy of holies of the temple pyramid of Pachacamac, which rises above the coastal dunes of the Pacific Ocean just south of Lima. Pa-

[1] MacCormack, "Atahualpa y el libro," *Revista de Indias* 48 (1988): 693–714.

chacamac was consulted for oracles, and people came to his shrine in pilgrimage from far and wide, bringing offerings of gold, silver, and textiles.[2] The site was surrounded by shelters for pilgrims and by the tombs of noblemen who had desired to be buried in proximity to their god.[3] Some half century before the invasion, the Incas incorporated this sanctuary into their network of imperial holy places by erecting next to Pachacamac's pyramid another taller one to the divine Sun.[4]

The treasure-seeking Spaniards who arrived there in January 1533 were received by the local nobility and by the attendants of the deity. Some of the temple's precious objects were reluctantly handed over, but the priests were unwilling to admit the intruders into the sanctuary, because "no one was permitted to see the god."[5] Indeed, pilgrims felt honored to be allowed merely to touch the walls of the great pyramid,[6] and the privileged few who were admitted into the proximity of the god fasted twenty days before ascending the pyramid's first step and for an entire year before reaching its peak.[7] The priests who met the Spanish newcomers thus offered to convey a message to Pachacamac but would not admit them to the temple. However, Hernando Pizarro and his men overrode all objections and insisted on being accompanied into the divine presence. Passing many doors during the winding ascent of the pyramid, they finally reached its peak, where a small open space gave access to an artificial cavern made of branches, its posterns decorated with leaves of gold and silver. A door bejeweled with corals, turquoises, and crystals and flanked by two guardians closed off this holy spot. Upon the Spaniards demanding that the door be opened, a tiny, dark room was finally revealed, its walls painted with animals of land and sea.[8] In the center of the room stood a wooden pole, the top of which was carved into the figure of a man. All around, the ground was covered with small offerings of gold and silver, which had accumulated there over many years. This was the seat of Pachacamac, a two-faced deity who on the one hand created and sustained human beings, made the crops grow, and cured disease, but on the other hand brought disease[9] and caused earthquakes and the overflowing of the sea. So it was that, as one of Pachacamac's worshipers told

---

[2] Estete, in Xerez, *Verdadera relación*, p. 137.
[3] Gasca, *Descripción del Perú*, pp. 53f.; Cieza, *Crónica* 72, p. 213.
[4] Cieza, *Crónica* 72; see below chap. III.1 at nn. 14–17.
[5] [Estete], *Noticia*, p. 38.
[6] Estete, in Xerez, *Verdadera relación*, p. 137.
[7] Hernando Pizarro, *Relación*, pp. 176–177.
[8] Gasca, *Descripción del Perú*, p. 53.
[9] P. Duviols, *Cultura andina y represión* (1986), p. 8. For an important discussion of Pachacamac's qualities, see T. Gisbert, "Pachacamac y los dioses del Collao," *Historia y cultura* (La Paz) 17 (1990): 105–121.

Miguel de Estete, a member of Hernando Pizarro's force, "All things in the world lie in his hands."[10]

But the Spaniards, exalted by their spectacular success in the service of the apparently invincible cause of their god, had no ears for such reasoning. The jeweled door of Pachacamac's dwelling had led them to expect on the other side some elaborately worked treasure chamber. Finding instead an unadorned holy place of ancient simplicity, they expressed a profound contempt. "Seeing how vile and despicable the idol was," related a member of the expeditionary force,

> we went outside to ask why they paid such reverence to something so worthless. And they were astounded at our boldness and, defending the honor of their god, said that he was Pachacamac, who healed their infirmities. As we understood it, in the cavern the devil appeared to those priests and spoke with them, and they entered with the petitions and offerings of those who came in pilgrimage; and indeed, the entire kingdom of Atahualpa went there. Seeing the vileness that was there and the blindness in which all those people lived, we brought together the leaders of the town and opening their eyes in the presence of all, that cavern, into which very few people had ever entered, was opened and broken down. And when they saw our resolve and grasped what we said of how they had been deceived, they themselves gave a show of being glad. Thus, with great solemnity, we erected a tall cross on that dwelling place that the devil had held so much as his own.[11]

Other Spaniards also thought that "a demon had been in that idol and spoke with those who came to ask him something."[12] In the opinion of one of the invaders, the oracle fell silent after its desecration, thereby demonstrating its demonic nature: "Pachacamac endured for long ages, until the Christians came to Peru. Thereafter he was never seen again, whence it is thought that he must have been some demon, who made them believe all these vanities"[13] (see fig. 8).

But Hernando Pizarro, the leader of the expedition, was more skeptical; he doubted that the devil, in the guise of Pachacamac, really talked

---

[10] Estete, in Xerez, *Verdadera relación*, p. 137; M. Rostworowski, *Estructuras andinas de poder* (1983), pp. 42ff. For earthquakes, see [Estete], *Noticia*, p. 39; *Runa yndio*, ed. Urioste, 20.243; cf. 23.292.

[11] Quotation from [Estete], *Noticia*, pp. 38–39, abridged. See also E. Guillén, *Versión Inca*, pp. 20f. Estete's story follows a well-established typology of confrontation between Christian god and pagan idol; for a Norse example, see T. Andersson, "Lore and Literature in a Scandinavian Conversion Episode," in *Festschrift Klaus von See*, pp. 261–284.

[12] Sancho, *An Account*, transl. Means, chap. 10, p. 97.

[13] Zárate, in M. Bataillon, "Zárate ou Lozano?" *Caravelle* 1 (1963): 23; but see further below, chap. III.1 at nn. 14–17.

with the priests. Rather, he thought that the oracle was a priestly fabrication designed to exploit the local nobility. To confirm his hypothesis,
he arranged for one of the god's most intimate attendants to be questioned under torture, but was unable to extract the desired explanation.
As Hernando Pizarro himself wrote to the Audiencia of Santo Domingo,
his victim "remained convinced of his erroneous opinion, so that it was
impossible to find out any more from him as to whether they really hold
Pachacamac to be their god."[14] Hernando Pizarro's hypothesis about the
exact functioning of Pachacamac's oracle had precedents in early Christian apologetic against Greek and Roman deities but was as much out of
step with Andean reality as was the theory that a demon spoke in the
guise of the god.[15]

For the Andean gods regularly availed themselves of human speech to
declare their intentions. It was not only the image of Pachacamac, but
also the divine Sun of the Incas in Cuzco that spoke through human in-
termediaries. When the young nobles of Cuzco were initiated into adulthood, they swore to serve the Inca and the Sun loyally; this act of homage
was formally received by an Inca lord standing in the holy spot, or *huaca*,
known as Yavira. This lord responded to each young man's oath "in the
name and place of the Sun and the huaca . . . and said that the Sun wished
him to be *auqui*, lord."[16] Similarly, during the part of the ceremony of an
Inca's inauguration that took place in Coricancha,[17] someone speaking on
behalf of this temple's image of the Sun named the Inca, although Spaniards speculated that the Sun's statements were either made by the devil
or by "some Indian whom they hid away so that he could respond [to the
questions that had been addressed to the Sun]."[18] Another deity whose
voice was mediated through a human voice was Apurimac, "the Lord
who Speaks." In 1536 Atahualpa's brother Manco Inca passed Apurimac's
shrine near Cuzco in the company of the Spaniard Francisco Martín. As
Martín later told the story, Manco Inca "caused the devil to speak to him
in front of his very eyes, and he [Martín] said that he heard the voice of
the devil, which responded to Manco Inca's question, and Manco said to
him, 'Listen to how my god speaks to me.' "[19]

[14] H. Pizarro, *Relación* (1920), p. 177.

[15] But the problem persisted: twenty years later, Augustinian missionaries at Huamachuco were in doubt as to whether the devil or a priest with a falsetto voice spoke in a local
oracle, Religiosos Agustinos, *Relación*, p. 21.

[16] Betanzos, *Suma* (1987), 1.14, p. 68a. I here translate the Spanish *idolo* with "huaca."

[17] Quechua, "enclosure of gold": the temple of the Sun in Cuzco.

[18] Sarmiento, *Historia Indica* 29, p. 235a; see further below, chap. III.3 at nn. 32–33; chap.
IX.2 at nn. 116–118.

[19] Pedro Pizarro, *Relación* 14, p. 81; see further below chap. II.2 at nn. 53–55. The juxtaposition of different cultural and social orders is still an important feature in Andean myth;
see Dillon and Abercrombie, "The Destroying Christ," in *Rethinking History and Myth*, ed.
J. D. Hill (1988).

That the Spanish newcomers should interpret such phenomena in the light of apparent biblical antecedents and parallels from classical antiquity and even from Christian Europe was to be expected.[20] But this European and Christian perspective closed the door on any detailed understanding of the network of reciprocal favor and obligation that in the Andes linked the gods with men, and to which human beings speaking on behalf of the gods gave a voice. For throughout the Andes oracular statements were uttered not by anyone who happened to feel so inclined but by specific individuals "who were appointed for this task" and spoke on behalf of a deity.[21] Most of the invaders, however, were not interested in tracing these networks of reciprocal obligation between Andean people and their gods. Rather, they juxtaposed Andean religion with Christianity in order to pinpoint error in the one and truth in the other.

Nonetheless, in challenging Pachacamac, the invaders unwittingly stumbled upon a point of tension in Andean and Inca religion of which Andeans also were aware, although in terms that differed from those of their Spanish critics. Oracular shrines both great and small abounded in the Andes; their principal role was to legitimate political power by establishing and then articulating consensus. In the course of doing this, the oracular deities also predicted the future. Because such predictions were capable of generating either support or dissent at times of political uncertainty, they were taken most seriously and were carefully remembered. The Inca intervention on the cult site of Pachacamac had resulted in a negotiated settlement that was still remembered two generations later. Pachacamac himself, speaking through his priests, had conceded that the presence of the divine Sun of the Incas on his cult site "could not be avoided"[22] and therefore granted permission for the construction of the Sun's pyramid next to his own. Thereafter, Pachacamac and the Sun coexisted on the site,[23] thus giving cultic and religious expression to the political role of the Incas in the region. However, the coexistence of the two deities was complicated and not altogether harmonious, as is spelled out in the adjustments that myths about Pachacamac, whose name means "maker of the world," underwent after the advent of the Sun and the Incas.

One of these myths, perhaps formulated before the Incas' arrival, and in any case independently of their presence, told how Pachacamac

---

[20] See, for example, Augustine, *City of God* 8.23–24; MacCormack, "Calderón's *La aurora*," *Journal of Theological Studies* 33 (1982): 448–480.

[21] Cieza, *Crónica del Perú. Primera Parte* (hereafter *Crónica*), 43, p. 142, Cañari; 48, p. 157, Puerto Viejo; 80, Guanuco; 100, Collas; Cieza, *Segunda Parte* 28, p. 84, Vilcanota. See also Betanzos, *Suma* 1.32, p. 149b, Inca Pachacuti speaks to the Sun in Coricancha.

[22] Gasca, *Descripción del Perú*, p. 59.

[23] Cieza, *Crónica* 72, p. 214.

made the sky and the earth and everything in them, and he also made the ocean, which he contained in a certain vessel and entrusted to a man and his wife. But the couple negligently broke the vessel, and the water flowed out into the space it now occupies. Pachacamac said that the ocean was to remain thus spread out, although he punished the man and his wife for their misdeed by changing him into a monkey and her into a fox.[24]

Other accounts of Pachacamac's creation focused on human social order. One of these relates how Pachacamac sent to earth two pairs of stars, the first of which became the ancestors of kings and lords, while the other procreated the common people, servants, and the poor.[25]

Thanks to Inca intervention, such accounts of Pachacamac's creation were supplemented by myths of solar origin that the Incas had appropriated from Lake Titicaca.[26] In one of these myths we learn of rival creations, and the Sun of the Incas has become Pachacamac's father.[27] The creator of the first age after the flood, who was Con, son of the Sun and Moon, came from the North. He raised mountains, laid out valleys, and also made the human beings of those times. Because some of those human beings angered him, he converted their land into what is now the desert of coastal Peru. Henceforth Con's people gained sustenance from the plants and fruits that grew by the streams running from the Andean mountains across the desert plain to the ocean. Next there came, this time from the South, another son of the Sun and Moon, who was Pachacamac. Con disappeared, and Pachacamac turned Con's now leaderless people into the birds and animals of the Peruvian coast. Pachacamac then created the Indians of the present time and taught them agriculture. They therefore worshiped him as god, and their lords were buried near his shrine, in those funerary structures that the Spanish invaders were later to comment on.[28]

Another myth documenting the presence of the Inca Sun at Pachacamac's sanctuary described conflict between the two deities in yet more explicit terms. In the beginning, Pachacamac made a man and a woman, but there was no food. The woman prayed to the Sun, who did not send

[24] Gasca, *Descripción del Perú*, pp. 52f., with Barnadas ad loc.
[25] Calancha, *Corónica moralizada* 2.19, p. 935; cf. p. 934, myth of three eggs.
[26] Cf. below chap. III.2.
[27] Zárate, in M. Bataillon, "Zárate ou Lozano?" *Caravelle* I (1963); Calancha, *Corónica Moralizada* 2.19, pp. 930f.
[28] Zárate, in M.Bataillon, "Zárate ou Lozano?" *Caravelle* I (1963): 22f. Zárate appears to have taken the myth from Rodrigo Lozano, on whom see also R. Porras Barrenechea, "Crónicas perdidas" (1951), rpt. in his *Los cronistas* (1986), pp. 695f. Gómara used this same version, discussed by M. Rostworowski, "El sitio arqueologico." *Revista del Museo Nacional* 38 (1972): 315–326, focusing on Con. For the noblemen's tombs, see above n. 3. For Con and Pachacamac in Collao, see T. Gisbert (above, n. 9).

food but impregnated her with a boy-child. Pachacamac became jealous and dismembered the child, making maize out of the child's teeth, yucas out of the ribs and bones, and fruits and vegetables out of the flesh. But the mother grieved for her child and prayed to the Sun until he made another boy-child out of the dead one's umbilical cord. This second child was Vichama. Pachacamac, in revenge, killed the mother and created human beings, along with the lords who were to rule over them. Vichama now sought to destroy Pachacamac, but when Pachacamac "went out to the sea where now his temple stands," thus becoming invisible, Vichama turned his fury against the people Pachacamac had created and transformed them into stones. Later he and the Sun repented themselves of this deed and made the lords of those people whom they had converted to stone into holy presences and objects of worship, the huacas. And since the world was now devoid of men, and there was no one to worship the Sun and the huacas, Vichama begged his father the Sun to create new people. The Sun therefore gave Vichama three eggs, one of gold from which kings and lords were to come forth, another of silver to produce royal and noble women, and another of copper to produce common men and their wives and children.[29]

Yet other myths, while making some concessions to the Sun of the Incas, left Pachacamac with a dominant role in the formation of the natural and human world.[30] As one Spaniard expressed it, from the time when the Incas arrived on the coast, people there "worshiped both the Sun and Pachacamac as gods, but in such a way as to give precedence to Pachacamac."[31]

However, not all deities acquiesced in Inca overlordship. In Chacalla, some seventy kilometers northeast of Pachacamac, the people "prayed to and talked with" their local huaca so that Topa Inca Yupanqui, Guayna Capac's father, might die.[32] Topa Inca was informed of this undertaking and ordered all the men of the place to be killed. Nonetheless, when Guayna Capac came to rule, the people of the nearby village Acupayllata in turn consulted their own huaca, in the hope that Guayna Capac should die and that "there should be no more Incas to conquer them." Since this huaca had earlier claimed credit for the death of Tupa Inca Yupanqui, the enterprise seemed to be a plausible one.[33] But it did not survive the wrath of Guayna Capac, who, like his father, avenged himself by killing all the men of the village. Furthermore, he resettled the survivors elsewhere, away from their insubordinate huaca.

[29] Calancha, *Corónica moralizada* 2.19, pp. 931ff.
[30] See sources cited above, nn. 27–28.
[31] Gasca, *Descripción del Perú*, p. 60.
[32] *Justicia* 413, fol. 219v, p. 186; cf. Rostworowski's introduction, p. 62a.
[33] *Justicia* 413, fol. 226v, p. 188.

The influence of the huacas of Chacalla and Acupayllata did not reach far beyond their communities, and the Incas were therefore able to make short shrift of both of them. Other deities were more powerful, and their resistance or noncooperation required the Incas to devise carefully designed strategies extending over long periods. Before setting out to suppress a revolt in Quito, Tupa Inca Yupanqui consulted Catequil, a regionally respected oracular deity in Huamachuco, in order to learn whether he would return victorious. Catequil's priests responded in the negative, and the outcome proved them right. Much wealth and prestige therefore accrued to the oracular deity. But when, years later, the Inca Guayna Capac passed in the vicinity of the shrine, he ordered the site to be destroyed, by way of punishing the deity for venturing to predict an Inca's death. The priests were, however, able to snatch their god's statue from the flames and in due course another temple was erected for him.[34] Next, Atahualpa, who was then ruling in Quito, tried his luck with the oracle. He sent messengers to Catequil to inquire after his chances of success in the war he was planning against his brother Guascar, who controlled Cuzco. Possibly Atahualpa was hoping to win the region of Huamachuco peacefully by gaining the support of one of its principal deities. But Catequil did not give the desired response. When thus the victorious Atahualpa gained control of Huamachuco, he exacted spectacular vengeance on the deity and his priests. Atahualpa himself killed the aged priest who had delivered the offending oracle; Catequil's image was overthrown and its head thrown into a river; and finally, Catequil's treasures were confiscated and the entire cult site was devastated in a fire that burned for over a month.[35]

Pachacamac also was found on more than one occasion to have made unwelcome pronouncements, which furthermore had been proved wrong in the outcome. But the considerable power of the god and the immense respect in which he was held had on earlier occasions prevented Atahualpa from retaliating. However, a long-awaited opportunity presented itself when the Spaniards demanded a room full of gold as Inca Atahualpa's ransom. The Inca apparently believed that he could both escape from his captors by providing the ransom they demanded, and that he could at the same time settle his grievance against the over-mighty Pachacamac. He therefore ordered the representatives of Pachacamac who were in Cajamarca to surrender the god's treasures to the Spaniards,

[34] Arriaga, *Extirpación* 2, pp. 23f., with Calancha, *Corónica moralizada* 2.32, p. 1062.
[35] Religiosos Agustinos, *Relación*, pp. 25–26; Betanzos, *Suma* 2.16; Sarmiento, *Historia Indica* 64, p. 268ab; further below, chap. IV.1 at nn. 1ff. For Manco Inca's vengeance on Guaribilca, whose people had sided with the Spaniards, see Titu Cusi, *Relación de la conquista*, pp. 106f.; for Inca Pachacuti's vengeance on rebellious priests, *Relación anonima*, p. 167b.

because, as he somewhat aggressively expressed it, "This Pachacamac of yours is not god." Atahualpa's reasons for challenging Pachacamac's divinity were manifold. First, the cure he had recommended to the Inca's father, Guayna Capac, during the latter's last illness failed to work and Guayna Capac had died, even though he had been especially devoted to Pachacamac.[36] Next, during the war between Guascar and Atahualpa, Pachacamac predicted that Guascar would win, which he did not.[37] And finally, he had erroneously predicted that Atahualpa would defeat the Spaniards. Francisco Pizarro used the Inca's disenchantment to inform him that "Pachacamac was the devil, who was talking to them in that place and was deceiving them. [And he said] that God was in heaven, and other things of our holy faith."[38] Yet as seen by Atahualpa and the priests of Pachacamac, the problem was not so straightforward. Bearing in mind what had happened to Catequil, Pachacamac's priests may well have intended to support Atahualpa by predicting his victory over the invaders, although earlier the much more cogent policy had obviously been to ally the oracle to the Inca Guascar in Cuzco,[39] rather than to Atahualpa in distant Quito. Thus, where Andeans found themselves with the task of stage managing a delicately tuned, but not infallible, network of sacred power that had developed over centuries, Spaniards regarded all aspects of that network as either demonic delusion or priestly fabrication.

2. THE LAST INTI RAIMI AND THE END OF IMPERIAL RELIGION

Confrontations like the one that resulted in the overthrow of Pachacamac orchestrated Spanish appropriation of sacred property throughout the period of the conquest. In February 1533, Francisco Pizarro sent Martin Bueno, Pedro Martín, and a certain Zárate to investigate the imperial city of Cuzco and bring back what treasure they could lay hands on to contribute to the ransom of Atahualpa.[1] Atahulpa, still hoping to gain his freedom, arranged for the three to be accompanied by an Inca lord and to be assisted in all particulars of their journey.[2]

Upon arriving in Cuzco, the Spaniards made their way to the temple

[36] Cieza, *Segunda Parte* 66, p. 193.
[37] Cf. Santacruz Pachacuti, *Relación de antiguedades*, pp. 302, 314ff., with J. Szeminski, *Un kuraka* (1987), p. 61, and below, chap. VII.2 at nn. 22ff.
[38] Pedro Pizarro, *Relación* 11, pp. 57f.; cf. Xerez, *Verdadera relación*, pp. 124, 127.
[39] For the crystallization of regional loyalties in the war between the two brothers, cf. E. Guillén, *Versión Inca* (1974), p. 106, testimony of Curi Huaranga from Socoya in Yauyos province, "soldado de Guascar contra Atabalipa."
[1] J. Hemming, *Conquest of the Incas*, pp. 64f.
[2] Pedro Pizarro, *Relación* 11, p. 56; Cristóbal de Mena, *La conquista*, ed. Pogo, p. 254; Xerez, *Verdadera relación*, p. 129.

of the Sun, which was commonly known as Coricancha, the "enclosure of gold." This edifice, dedicated to the mythic ancestor of the Inca rulers, who described themselves as sons of the Sun,[3] was the center of the Inca state religion. Coricancha had been built on the outcrop between the rivers Tullumayu and Huatanay, so that the rising sun shone on its southeastern face.[4] This part of the building was adorned with a band of plaques of gold to catch the sun's rays. The plaques, which measured a finger's thickness and the width of a span, were arranged beneath the roof line in such a way that "the more the wall faced away from the sun, the lower was the quality of the gold."[5] Using copper crowbars, the three Spaniards pried loose seven hundred of these plaques and removed them, while the people of Cuzco stood by watching in silence.[6] The Spaniards also took from the patio of Coricancha what they thought was a "seat where [the Incas] made their sacrifices," which was large enough for two men to recline on it and was made entirely of gold.[7] This seat, worth twenty thousand *castellanos*, became the prize of the conqueror Francisco Pizarro.[8]

Although the treasure seekers encountered no active resistance, they found themselves in a tense situation, because the Inca general Quizquiz, who only gave a reluctant assent to Atahualpa's permission for these acts of despoilment, was encamped nearby with thirty thousand soldiers.[9] Nonetheless, the three Spaniards continued their search for treasure and collected from various dwellings in Cuzco a large number of gold vessels that were in due course transported to Cajamarca. In a structure they described enigmatically as "another very large house," which could have been either the palace of Guayna Capac or part of Coricancha, they discovered "many clay vessels covered with gold leaf." But they refrained from breaking these vessels and from stripping off the gold "so as not to

[3] [Estete], *Noticia*, p. 52

[4] See J. H. Rowe, *An Introduction to the Archaeology of Cuzco* (1944), pp. 37f. For an excellent description of Inca Cuzco, see J. Hyslop, *Inka Settlement Planning*, chap. 2.

[5] Mena, *La conquista*, ed. Pogo, p. 256; Pedro Pizarro, *Relación* 14, p. 92. A finger thick, Las Casas, *Apologética Historia* 58, p. 301; Cieza (*Segunda Parte* 27, p. 80) mentions plaques four fingers thick. Unlike Las Casas, Cieza does not appear to have personally seen any of this wall decoration of Coricancha. A span equals about nine inches. For similar plaques decorating buildings elsewhere, see Lothrop, *The Inca Treasure* (1938), pp. 58f. According to Betanzos, *Suma* (1987), 1.28, p. 136, the gold plaques were installed by Tupa Yupanqui, using gold he brought to Cuzco as war booty.

[6] Mena, *La conquista*, p. 256; Xerez, *Verdadera Relación*, p. 149.

[7] Mena, *La conquista*, p. 256.

[8] Pedro Pizarro, *Relación* 11, p. 59. Mena, *La conquista*, p. 256, mentions a gold seat worth nineteen thousand pesos, and Ruiz de Arce, *Relación*, p. 371, mentions one worth eighteen thousand castellanos. Possibly these are all the same seat, which would confirm that the "otra casa" mentioned by Mena (below, n. 10) was indeed Coricancha.

[9] Xerez, *Verdadera Relación*, p. 149.

anger the Indians."[10] In this same place, one of the Spanish looters reported,

> there were many women. And there were two embalmed bodies of
> Indians, and next to them stood a living lady wearing a gold mask
> on her face, fanning away dust and flies with a fan. The [embalmed
> bodies] held in their hands very fine gold staves. The lady would not
> let the [Spaniards] enter unless they took off their boots. Doing as
> asked, they went in to see those dried bodies and removed many fine
> pieces from them. But they did not take everything, seeing that the
> lord Atahualpa had asked them not to do so because [one of the em-
> balmed bodies] was his father.[11]

With this minimal expression of deference toward the great Inca Guayna
Capac, the three looters returned to Cajamarca.

But few restraints controlled the invaders' conduct when they returned
in full force later that year, after the Inca Atahualpa had been killed. The
process of looting combined with desecration that now followed was an
orderly and deliberate one, and all the more devastating for that. Yet at
this time the rituals of Coricancha and of the other shrines and holy places
of Cuzco were still being performed, and through chance observations
and descriptions by the invaders we gain a glimpse of Inca Cuzco as it was
before its destruction.

Juan Ruiz de Arce, whose father had taken part in the conquest of Granada, thus inspected Coricancha, where, he was informed, "all the rulers
of the land are buried." He thought that this edifice was a *monasterio* for
nobly born ladies who lived there, each in her cell, attended by her serving women.[12] Walking round, he noted that like the outside of the building, so all the rooms inside it were decorated with a gold band a span in
width running beneath the roofing. He also saw statues of llamas and
women sculpted in gold, as well as different kinds of golden vessels. In

---

[10] Mena, *La conquista*, p. 256; Hyslop, *Inka Settlement Planning*, pp. 44–45, describes this
structure and an adjacent "otra casa" containing a gold seat as being parts of Coricancha
without qualification. If one could show that the gold seat mentioned by Pizarro is identical
with that mentioned by Mena and that mentioned by Ruiz de Arce, it would confirm Hyslop's conclusion; cf. above, n. 8. Regarding the mummified body of Guayna Capac, mentioned below at n. 11, this does not inevitably have to be looked for in Coricancha. See
Betanzos, *Suma* (1987), 2.1, p. 208a, the mummified body of Guayna Capac is in his palace
of Casana; *Suma* (1987), 1.32, p. 149b, body of Pachacuti on his estate of Patallacta; but see
also 1.30, p. 142a, where the body of Pachacuti is to be placed with the bodies of earlier
Incas: presumably in Coricancha.

[11] Mena, *La conquista*, pp. 256f.

[12] *Monasterio*, "monastery" or "convent." Ruiz de Arce seems to have confused Coricancha with nearby Acllahuasi, the "house of the chosen women" of the Sun, which did function as a convent. Possibly Ruiz de Arce conflated Coricancha with Acllahuasi because the
model in his mind was some peninsular prototype such as Las Huelgas de los Reyes in
Burgos, a convent for nuns and a royal mausoleum at the same time.

the center of the courtyard, he noticed there stood, next to what he thought was a fountain, a golden seat of great value and to one side of it, a sacred image, also of gold. The image, in the shape of a young boy, represented the divine Sun of the Incas; it was clothed in a tunic of the finest cloth and wore on its head an Inca imperial headband.[13] The "fountain" was an *ushnu*, an opening giving access to the underground drains that channeled liquids poured as sacrifice into the earth, thereby sustaining its powers.[14] The golden seat had been mounted over a rock that likewise had the form of a seat. Here was the place where on certain days the Sun was thought to "seat himself."[15] Ruiz de Arce stopped in this courtyard to watch the ceremonial that was being performed. He observed how at noon the golden seat was uncovered and the women of the monasterio produced a dish of maize, another of meat, and a jar of *chicha*,[16] all of which they offered to the Sun. Two attendants then brought a silver brazier, in which the meat and maize dishes were burned, while the chicha was poured into the ushnu. Finally, those present "raised their hands to the Sun and gave him thanks."[17]

This ritual, with its distinct phases of offering food and chicha to the Sun, burning the food and then pouring the chicha into the ushnu, closely resembled the ritual that on certain days was performed for the Sun in the central square of Cuzco known as Haucaypata.[18] On such days, the image of the Sun went to the square accompanied by a pair of attendants bearing "the arms of the Sun," which consisted of two hatchets mounted on long, elaborately decorated staves. Enthroned in the center of the square on a

[13] Ruiz de Arce, *Relación*, pp. 371f. For the seat, above, n. 8; particulars on attire of Sun's image, Betanzos, *Suma* (1987), I.11, p. 52a.

[14] Sarmiento, *Historia Indica* 36, for the ushnu in Coricancha; Pedro Pizarro, *Relación* 15, p. 90 and Molina, *Fábulas* 74 and 79 for that in Haucaypata; Rowe, "An Account of the Shrines," *Nawpa Pacha* 17 (1979): 74f. shrine no. 24. Cristóbal de Albornoz, *Instrucción*, p. 176, "sentavanse los señores a bever a el sol en el dicho uzno"; cf. p. 179. J. Hyslop, *Inka Settlement Planning*, pp. 69–101, provides an illuminating discussion of the literary and archeological data on ushnus in Cuzco and elsewhere. See also Zuidema, "El ushnu," *Revista de la Universidad Complutense* 28 (1979): 330, suggesting that the monastery Ruiz de Arce saw was Hatun Cancha, adjacent to Acllahuasi; cf. [Estete], *Noticia*, p. 45. According to Garcilaso de la Vega (*Comentarios reales* 4.1, p. 121b), no women, not even the acllas, entered Coricancha; but this assertion, perhaps made by Garcilaso to approximate the acllas to Christian nuns, is contradicted by Molina, *Fábulas*, p. 100, referring to the cult of the moon in Coricancha, and by Sarmiento, *Historia Indica* 36.

[15] Pedro Pizarro, *Relación* 15, p. 92; for the Sun "sitting on" solar pillars, see below chap. VIII.1 at n. 40.

[16] *Chicha* is maize beer. The term was imported from Central America, and in Spanish has superseded the Quechua term *aka* (Gonzalez Holguin, *Vocabulario de la lengua general*, p. 18).

[17] For the entire ceremony, see Ruiz de Arce, *Relación*, pp. 371–372.

[18] Sarmiento, *Historia Indica* 36. The chicha that was poured into the ushnu was mixed with the ashes of sacrificial food; a little of the chicha was first offered to the Sun in a libation. Cf. Guaman Poma, *Nueva Crónica*, p. 246 [248], where the Inca "drinks with the Sun," here figure 17.

seat adorned with multicolored featherwork, the Sun received offerings of food and chicha. The burning of the food was marked by a solemn silence, after which the ashes and the chicha were discarded into the ushnu in the usual fashion.[19] This ushnu in Haucaypata had a gold cover, and one of its underground canals went to Coricancha.[20]

At night, the image of the Sun dwelt in a small room constructed of the finest Inca masonry. This room also was adorned with a band of gold plaques, probably resembling the ones that Ruiz de Arce mentioned seeing elsewhere in Coricancha.[21] Here, the golden cult image of the Sun representing him as a young boy was attended by virgins, daughters of Inca nobles, who had been chosen to serve the deity. At dusk, the image "was put to bed" and "slept" until the next morning.[22] The room was appropriately furnished with another seat or "couch" for the Sun to repose upon, this one decorated with irridescent feathers.[23]

It was around the time when Ruiz de Arce inspected the monasterio, that Diego de Trujillo, who had been at Cajamarca when Atahualpa was captured and killed, forced his way into Coricancha. Thirty-eight years later, he still remembered the episode vividly:

> We entered the House of the Sun, and Vilaoma, who was the priest according to their law, exclaimed, "How can you come into this place where no one enters without first fasting for a year, and even then he enters bearing a burden and walks unshod?" Without taking any notice of what he said, we went inside.[24]

The systematic pillaging of Coricancha, and its conversion into the monastery of the Dominicans followed soon after this act of desecration. One of the very few objects that were saved was the cult statue of the Sun as a young boy. The Spaniards looked hard for this image but did not find it until 1571.[25] It must have been at the time when Coricancha became a Christian building that the maize garden of the Sun next door to it was destroyed. The maize that grew here was specially watered by hand. Three times annually, at seedtime, during the harvest, and when the young Inca noblemen were initiated into adulthood, the Sun's garden was

[19] Pedro Pizarro, *Relación* 15, p. 91.

[20] Pedro Pizarro, *Relación* 15, p. 90 and Molina, *Fábulas*, pp. 74, 79: during Citua, four hundred young men set out from here toward the four directions of Tahuantinsuyo to drive out evils. See further below, p. 195ff.

[21] Pedro Pizarro, *Relación* 11, p. 59; 14, pp. 91f.

[22] Gasca, *Descripción del Perú* p. 57.

[23] Pedro Pizarro, *Relación* 15, pp. 92f.; Gasca, *Descripción*, p. 57; Betanzos, *Suma* (1987) I.11, p. 52a, also mentions the irridescent feathers, "de pajaros tornasoles."

[24] Diego de Trujillo, *Relación inédita*, pp. 63f.

[25] See below, chap. III.2 at nn. 103–107 and chap. VI at nn. 1 and 47, with fig. 29.

adorned with maize plants made of gold, "with their cobs and leaves made just as maize is in nature, all of very fine gold."[26]

Next to the divine Sun, the mythic ancestor of the Incas, it was the mummified bodies, usually described by Spaniards as *bultos*, of deceased Inca rulers that stood at the center of the religious and ritual life of Cuzco. One of the invaders saw what he believed to be the mummified bodies of all the dead Incas "embalmed and dressed in many garments, one over the other . . . with diadems on their heads" (see figs. 10 and 51) in a burial place a league distant from Cuzco.[27] The mummies had probably been removed to this place for their protection, because normally they participated in public life in the city. As Ruiz de Arce noted, they were housed, at least some of the time, in Coricancha. Nearly forty years after the invasion, Pedro Pizarro, the conqueror's brother, still remembered his profound astonishment at the scene which greeted him on arriving in the central square of Haucaypata. Here stood the palaces of the Inca rulers, including that of Atahualpa, the entrance of which was adorned with plaques of silver and other metals,[28] and it was here that the living and the dead interacted on a regular basis. "It was a remarkable thing to see," wrote Pedro Pizarro, "the people who lived in this City of Cuzco":

Most of these people served the dead . . . whom every day they carried to the main square, setting them down in a ring, each one according to his age, and there the male and female attendants [of the mummies] ate and drank. The attendants made fires in front of each of the dead . . . in which they burned everything they had put before them, so that the dead should eat of everything that the living ate, which is what was burned there in the fires. The attendants also placed before these dead bodies certain large pitchers which they call *birques* . . . and there they poured the chicha that they gave to the dead person to drink, showing it to him; and the dead toasted each other and the living, and the living toasted the dead.[29]

The rituals of offering sustenance and sacrifice to the dead (see fig. 10) closely resembled the corresponding rituals addressed to the Sun. After being poured into the birque, the chicha to be consumed by the mummies was, like the Sun's chicha, discarded into the ushnu of Haucaypata along with the ashes of the mummies' solid food.[30] The world above ground,

[26] Pedro Pizarro, *Relación* 15, p. 92; cf. Guillén, *Versión Inca de la Conquista* (Lima, 1974), p. 125, testimony of Don Diego Cayo Inca, describing how Manco Inca removed from Coricancha what perhaps were its last ornaments.
[27] [Estete], *Noticia*, p. 47; one league is five to six kilometers.
[28] [Estete], *Noticia*, p. 45.
[29] Pedro Pizarro, *Relación* 15, pp. 89f. free translation; Guaman Poma, *Nueva Crónica*, p. 287 [289].
[30] Pedro Pizarro, *Relación* 14, pp. 89-92.

CAPITVLOPRIMERO ENTIERO DEL IGA
VICAILLAPA·AIA·DEFVTO

pucullo

yllapa·
defunto

en tierro   como

10. The Inca ruler pours a libation of chicha into a sacrificial receptacle for
his deceased ancestor and his consort, whose embalmed bodies are watching the transaction. The burial tower in the background contain bones of a
dead person of long ago. Drawing by Guaman Poma, *Nueva Crónica*, p. 287.
Royal Library, Copenhagen. Photo from facsimile, Paris 1936.

where the Sun, the living, and the mummies interacted, was thus every day brought into contact with the hidden, but equally vital, forces of the earth.

The presence of the deceased Incas in Cuzco was the upshot of protracted arrangements, some of which the first Spaniards to settle in Cuzco were able to glimpse in passing. One of these Spaniards thus noticed that each of the mummies in Haucaypata had at its side a small box, which he compared to a Christian reliquary, containing "the nail parings, hair clippings, teeth, and other items they had cut from their limbs" while alive.[31] At about the same time, Francisco Pizarro's secretary Pedro Sancho learned that some of a deceased lord's nail parings and hair-clippings were usually incorporated into a clay image representing him and that these images likewise received veneration.[32] No one was permitted to lift his eyes to look at the living Inca, to touch his sacred person, or even to touch one of the vessels from which he had eaten.[33] It was by way of safeguarding the sacred person of an Inca ruler in its entirety and forever that throughout the ruler's life his hair clippings and other bodily remains were set aside for safekeeping in order to be redeployed in his cult after death.

Daily contacts between the living and the dead in Haucaypata took the form not only of ceremonious feasting but also of political interaction. For, as the Spaniards were surprised to find out, the mummies of Inca rulers and their consorts retained in perpetuity the services of their kinsmen and attendants and also their palaces and other belongings, such as herds of llamas, lands, textiles, and ornaments.[34] As a result, the dead possessed considerable political power, which they exercised through their kinsmen. Pedro Pizarro learned this from a poignantly remembered personal experience. He had come to Cuzco before the bulk of the invading army had occupied the city, in order to gain permission for the marriage of a royal lady to an Inca general allied to the Spaniards. The lady, so Pedro Pizarro understood, was in the service of some great lord in Cuzco, and he was the one whose assent had to be obtained. Reaching Cuzco, Pedro Pizarro sought out the lady and was astounded to discover that the lord in question was a deceased Inca. He found the lady in Hau-

---

[31] [Estete], *Noticia*, p. 55. For a later account and explanation of the observance, told with Garcilaso de la Vega's customary charm, see *Comentarios reales* 2.7, p. 52b.

[32] See Pedro Sancho, *An Account of the Conquest* 19, p. 170, about the preserved body of Guayna Capac: "[it was] lacking only the tip of the nose. There are other images of plaster or clay which have only the hair and nails which were cut off in life and the clothes that were worn, and these images are as much venerated by those people as if they were their gods" (transl. Means).

[33] S. MacCormack, *Children of the Sun and Reason of State: Myths, Ceremonies and Conflicts in Inca Peru*, 1992 Lecture Series, Working Papers no. 6, Department of Spanish and Portuguese, University of Maryland, College Park (1990).

[34] Sancho, *An Account* 17, p. 159; Pedro Pizarro, *Relación* 10, p. 52.

caypata, along with a male companion, the two of them seated on either side of the Inca's mummified body, which was enthroned in the square along with the other mummies, each with its attendants. Through an interpreter, Pedro Pizarro presented his question. The lady glanced at her companion and he at her, and together they informed Pizarro that their lord favored the match.[35]

The daily rituals of Haucaypata and of the city of Cuzco at large were punctuated from time to time by exceptional celebrations to mark specific current events. Such celebrations highlighted the ritual and political continuity of the Inca empire through time by activating mythic and historical memory in the context of the present. The Spaniards in Cuzco watched one such celebration early in the year 1534. In December 1533, Manco, a son of Guayna Capac, had been chosen Inca under Spanish overlordship.[36] It would soon become evident that his authority was only acceptable to the invaders insofar as they could exploit it for their own ends. But meanwhile the two sides acted in harmony and for what appeared to be their mutual advantage. Manco Inca had thus assisted the Spaniards in driving his own mortal enemy Quizquiz and the army of Quito back to the north.

To celebrate this joint victory and the new ruler's inauguration, the deceased Incas, each accompanied by his own retainers, were carried into the square in a procession that was headed by Manco Inca in his litter with the litter containing Guayna Capac's mummy at his side.[37] Having arrived in Haucaypata, the mummies were placed on their seats. The feasting, interspersed with sung recitations extolling the "conquests made by each one of these lords and his valor and accomplishments," began at sunrise and continued until dusk, when the mummies were escorted back to their abodes. The entire celebration lasted for over a month.[38]

The Inca rulers going back to the mythic founder Manco Capac were thus present to witness and enhance the glory of their youngest representative. This interaction of past and present was made explicit both in the recitations about the deeds of past Inca rulers and in prayers of thanks addressed in the course of the festival to the divine Sun, originator and protector of the Incas, for his continuing favor. Finally, as the priest of the Sun, speaking as the head of the Inca lineage,[39] reminded Manco, the great Inca ancestors were to inspire him to imitate their achievements.[40]

Yet, the Spanish presence compromised and threatened to destroy the

---

[35] Pedro Pizarro, *Relación* 10, pp. 53f.

[36] Sancho, *An Account* 11, p. 105; 12, p. 111.

[37] Cf. Guaman Poma, *Nueva Crónica*, p. 256 [258], depicting how a mummy is transported during "the festival of the dead."

[38] [Estete], *Noticia*, pp. 54–56.

[39] Pedro Pizarro, *Relación* 15, p. 91.

[40] [Estete], *Noticia*, pp. 54–56.

coherence of this political philosophy that the Incas enacted in the ceremonies of their capital, just as earlier it had destroyed the authority of Pachacamac. Christian ceremonies in Cuzco had so far taken place alongside the Inca ones. For instance, at Christmas 1533, the Spaniards celebrated a Mass and then read out the *requerimiento* with as much solemnity as could be mustered, fancying that its demands had been understood and accepted.[41] Even had this been the case, it was, in the opinion of one sharp-sighted Spaniard, improbable that the Inca leaders intended to abide by such involuntary agreements for longer than absolutely necessary.[42] But because Spaniards were now arriving in Cuzco in increasing numbers, their hold on the city tightened, and the disintegration of the fabric of Inca ceremonies, along with the religious and political meaning that sustained them, became irreversible.

On 23 March 1534, Francisco Pizarro performed a ritual in Haucaypata to mark the Spanish refoundation of the Inca city. Indeed, it was as though that city had never existed, for the new Cuzco's recognized inhabitants and property owners—*vecinos*—were all to be Spaniards. Haucaypata was proclaimed to be the new city's main square, and on its upper, northeastern end a site was appropriated for the cathedral. Next, a gibbet atop a set of preexisting steps was erected in the center of the square to make palpable the judicial authority claimed by the conquerors.[43] With the dagger he carried in his belt, Francisco Pizarro made some marks on this gibbet by way of carrying out a formal act of taking possession and of founding the city.[44] Possibly the steps on which this gibbet was erected formerly supported the ushnu of Haucaypata, in which case a fundamental aspect of Inca imperial ceremonial would have come to an end at this time. A fountain was subsequently constructed in the center of the square, but the ritual link that the ushnu had established between the world of daylight above ground and the waters and earth beneath it was ruptured for good.[45]

Having laid claim to the city of Cuzco, the invaders distributed its sacred buildings and palaces among themselves under the pretence that they

[41] Sancho, *An Account* 12, pp. 112f.; on the requerimiento, a formulaic demand that the people of the Americas submit to the sovereignty of Spain or be conquered by force, see L. Hanke, "The 'Requerimiento' and Its Interpreters," *Revista de Historia de America* 1 (1938): 25–34.

[42] [Estete], *Noticia*, p. 54.

[43] Betanzos, *Suma* (1987), 1.11, p. 52b, royo; Betanzos, *Suma* (1967), 1.11, p. 33b, rollo.

[44] G. Lohmann Villena, *Francisco Pizarro Testimonio. Documentos oficiales, cartas y escritos varios* (Madrid, 1986), pp. 163ff.; Sancho, *An Account* 14, p. 130.

[45] Hyslop, *Inka Settlement Planning*, pp. 38–40; J. Sherbondy, "El regadío, los lagos," *Allpanchis* 20 (1882): 3–32. For the appearance of the ushnu, cf. Betanzos, *Suma* (1987), 1.11, p. 52b: "a stone in the shape of a sugarloaf . . . with a belt of gold," understood to be a popular representation of the Sun. Cf. below, chap. III.2 at n. 111.

were uninhabited.[46] Casana, the palace of the Inca Guayna Capac and property of his mummy, was thus assigned to Francisco Pizarro, while his former companion in arms Diego de Almagro took the palace of Inca Guascar.[47] Similarly, all over Cuzco, Spaniards ousted the Inca inhabitants from their dwellings.

Elsewhere in Peru also the invaders were taking possession of the land by first desecrating holy places and then occupying dwellings and fields, thereby displacing the Inca and Andean owners. Among the sites to be thus appropriated was the temple of the Sun on the Island of the Sun in Lake Titicaca, which according to some Inca myths was the parent shrine of Coricancha in Cuzco. The Titicaca temple of the Sun in turn was associated with that of the Moon on the neighboring island of Coati. It was over Titicaca, according to one myth, that the Sun had first risen, and from here that the mythic ancestor of the Inca rulers had set out to settle in Cuzco. The pre-Inca temples of the Sun and of the Moon were expanded and beautified by Tupa Inca Yupanqui. Also, state settlers drawn from forty-five different nations of the Inca empire were brought to nearby Copacabana for the service of the holy places and to attend to the needs of the pilgrims who came here from far away. The entire settlement was ruled by an Inca lord from Cuzco.[48] In 1534 two Spaniards were sent from Cuzco to investigate this site and the region at large. According to Pedro Sancho, they came back with glowing reports of the area's gold mines. They had also learned about the two island sanctuaries:

> In the middle of the lake there are two islets, and on one of them is a mosque and house of the Sun which is held in great veneration, and to it they come and make their offerings and sacrifices on a great stone . . . which either because the devil hides himself there and speaks to them or because of an ancient custom or on account of some other cause that has never been made clear, all the people of that province hold in great esteem, and they offer there gold, silver and other things. There are more than six hundred Indians serving in this place, and more than a thousand women who make chicha in order to throw it upon that stone.[49]

[46] R. Rivera Serna, "Libro primero de cabildos de la ciudad del Cuzco," *Documenta* 4 (1965): 459.

[47] Rivera Serna, "Libro primero," p. 469.

[48] In general, see A. F. Banderlier, *The Islands of Titicaca and Koati* (New York, 1910); also, W. Espinoza Soriano, "Copacabana del Collao," *Bulletin de l'Institut Français des Études Andines* 1, no. 1 (1972): 1–15; S. MacCormack, "From the Sun of the Incas," *Representations* 8 (1984): 30–60; T. Bouysse-Cassagne with P. Bouysse, *Lluvias y Cenizas. Dos Pachacuti en la Historia* (La Paz, 1988).

[49] Sancho, *An Account* 18, p. 163 (transl. Means).

In about 1543 Copacabana, where pilgrims used to embark for the two holy islands, became the *encomienda*[50] of a Spaniard.[51] By this time the sanctuaries of the Sun and Moon would have been destroyed. But local gossip had it that before the Spanish treasure seekers arrived there in 1534, the people of Copacabana had thrown the sacred treasures into the lake.[52]

The shrine of Apurimac, "the Lord who Speaks," where the Spanish believed the devil to be conversing with humans[53] came to a more dramatic end. The building, an elaborately adorned hall, stood near the Inca suspension bridge spanning the deep chasm of the river Apurimac, with the rock face rising almost vertically on either side of the riverbed. The hall was the home of a heavy wooden shaft, its girth that of a stoutly built man, which was regularly anointed with sacrificial blood. Apurimac is a male name, but the sacred shaft which represented the deity was endowed with exclusively female characteristics. Girded by a band of gold adorned with two large golden breasts, the shaft was dressed in very fine women's clothes. These were held together by means of a large number of long golden pins, *topos*, such as women used.[54] From the shaft's head, which was flat on top, little round bells of gold and silver were suspended. On either side, arranged in a row, stood smaller shafts similarly attired which were also anointed with sacrificial blood, but it was in the central shaft that, as the Spaniards understood it, "the devil talked" to worshipers. Asarpay, a lady of the Inca imperial family, possibly a daughter of the Inca Guayna Capac, served as priestess of this deity. When the Spaniards despoiled and took away the sacred shaft, this lady veiled her head and calling on Apurimac threw herself into the chasm of the river.[55]

Amidst all this upheaval, not long before Asarpay killed herself, a Spanish clergyman, perhaps a certain Bartolomé de Segovia, observed how the maize harvest was being garnered in the valley of Cuzco. It was April 1535, and the times were daily getting grimmer. Yet after the work of harvesting was completed, the Inca lords of Cuzco, headed by Manco Inca as ruler of Tahuantinsuyo, "the four parts of the Andean world,"[56]

---

[50] Spanish, "estate."

[51] Espinoza Soriano, "Copacabana del Collao" (1972), p. 8.

[52] Garcilaso, *Comentarios reales* 3.15.

[53] See above chap. II.1 at n. 19.

[54] E.g., Guaman Poma, *Nueva Crónica*, p. 138, Coya Mama Ocllo.

[55] Pedro Pizarro, *Relación* 14, pp. 82–83; copied by Cobo, *Historia* 13.20. Cristóbal de Albornoz, *Instrucción*, p. 181, was told that Apurimac "era una piedra a manera de Indio de gran supersticion." Could this be compatible with the shaft Pedro Pizarro saw, or had the real Apurimac already been forgotten? For a suicide resembling that of Asarpay in Cajatambo, see below, chap. IX.2 at nn. 66–69; see also Duviols, *Cultura andina y represión* (1986), p. 474. For sacred suicide during the Taqui Onqoy, Molina, *Fábulas*, p. 132; similarly, still in the early seventeenth century, Duviols, *Cultura andina y represión* (1986), p. 496 and C. Romero, "Idolatrias," *Revista Historica* 6 (1918): 182, 194.

[56] Cf. Gonzalez Holguin, *Vocabulario de la lengua general*, p. 336.

gathered once more to celebrate the imperial festival known as Inti Raimi, "Festival of the Sun," which marked this time of year. The festival's purpose was to honor "the Sun and all the huacas and shrines of Cuzco, to give thanks for the past harvest, and to make supplication for harvests to come."[57] It was the last occasion that they were able to do this, for during the following harvest season, Manco Inca was preparing to expel the Spaniards from Cuzco. The attempt failed, and Manco, with his followers, retired to the forests of Vilcabamba, leaving Cuzco in ruins for the Christians to take over undisturbed. But in 1535 our clergyman watched the celebration of Inti Raimi and described some of what he saw. Although he felt that the splendor and solemnity of the festival ought to inspire Christians to perform their religious obligations with greater devotion, he could not entirely suppress the vocabulary of contempt and indignation at the "abominable and detestable" ritual that was being addressed to the divine Sun. This vocabulary of difference, of the contrast between Christian truth and Andean error, was becoming well established as a language of perceived descriptive and analytical validity. Nonetheless, our clergyman was moved by the beauty and majesty of the celebrations he had observed, and seventeen years later still remembered the days of the festival in some detail.[58]

After the maize and other crops had been garnered, he wrote, the people of Cuzco "brought out into a plain that faces toward the point where the sun rises as one leaves the city, all the figures[59] from the shrines of Cuzco. The ones of greater authority were placed beneath elaborately worked feather awnings that were a splendid spectacle to behold. These awnings were aligned with each other [in two parallel rows] so as to form an avenue . . . over thirty paces wide." In this avenue lined by awnings, each sheltering a "figure" attended by servants and chosen women,[60] stood the Inca lords of Cuzco. Spaniards recognized these noble Incas by their large golden ear ornaments, which expanded and elongated the wearer's earlobes, thereby earning Inca lords the Spanish epithet *orejones*, "long-ears." Describing the appearance of the lords of Cuzco, the cleric thus wrote:

> They were all orejones, very richly dressed in cloaks and tunics woven with silver. They wore bracelets, and the disks on their heads were of fine gold and very resplendent. They stood in two rows, each of which was made up of over three hundred lords. It was like a procession, some on one side and the others on the other, and they

[57] [Bartolomé de Segovia], *Relación*, p. 81b.
[58] [Bartolomé de Segovia], *Relación*, p. 82a; on date and authorship, see Porras Barrenechea, *Cronistas* (1986), pp. 315ff.
[59] These seem to have been mallquis; cf. below at nn. 65–70.
[60] [Segovia], *Relación* p. 82a.

stood very silent, waiting for sunrise. When the sun had not yet fully risen, they began slowly and in great order and harmony to intone a chant; and as they sang, they each moved forward . . . and as the sun went on rising, so their song intensified. The Inca had his awning in an enclosure with a very fine seat, at a little distance from the line of the others. And when the singing began, he rose to his feet with great authority and stood at the head of all, and he was the first to begin the chant; and when he began, so did all the others. And when he had stood a while, he returned to his seat and stood there to talk with those who approached him. And at certain times, at regular intervals, he went to his own group of singers,[61] where he stood for a while; and then he turned round. And so they sang from the time when the sun rose until it had completely set. And since until noon the sun was rising, they heightened their voices, and after noon they slowly softened them, always in step with the movement of the sun. During all this time they offered sacrifices, for to one side, on a mound with a tree, were Indians who did nothing other than cast meat onto a great fire and burn it to be consumed in the flames.

In another spot, llamas were set loose for random distribution among the populace of Cuzco: the solemnity of the imperial celebration was temporarily suspended when everyone rushed forward to grab an animal, while the aristocratic onlookers burst into laughter.[62] In the course of the morning, two hundred young women, walking in files of five, brought jars of chicha and baskets of coca leaf for the Sun, and many other ceremonies and sacrifices were performed, which, so the cleric thought, "would take too long a time to describe."

When the sun was getting ready to set, they showed great sadness in their bearing and in their song because of the sun's coming departure, and they deliberately dulled their voices. And when the sun had set completely, so that it disappeared from their sight, they expressed great shock, and with hands joined, they adored the sun with the most profound humility. Next, they removed all the equipment of the celebration, took down the awnings, and went home.[63]

In this way, the Sun was honored for eight or nine days in succession, and at the end of each day, the "figures" were returned to their abodes, to be brought forth again on the following day. Once the celebration of this festival of the Sun, which concluded the maize harvest, had been completed, Manco Inca initiated the plowing of the land for the next crop.

[61] The Spanish term is *coro*.
[62] This episode in the celebration was also noted by Cobo, *Historia* 13.27, p. 214b.
[63] [Segovia], *Relación*, p. 82b.

At the end of all the festivals, for the last one, they brought a large number of digging sticks, which formerly used to be of gold, and after certain preparations, the Inca took a digging stick and began to break the earth with it, and the other lords followed. This was the signal for everyone in the empire to do the same. Without the Inca inaugurating [the plowing season], there was no one who would have ventured to break the earth, nor would they have thought that the earth would produce [a harvest] unless the Inca were the first to break it.[64]

This description of harvesting and plowing in Cuzco is unique for being the only extant detailed account by an eyewitness of a major Inca festival, the only account which conveys, however simply and haltingly, something of the immense splendor, dignity, and beauty of these celebrations (see fig. 18). Even so, the description is incomplete, because the writer could say nothing about the theological and political significance of the festival, or rather, set of festivals, that he witnessed. This fragmentary quality is not particular to this account. Rather, it pervades to a greater or lesser degree all extant descriptions of Andean religion. Christian Spain and Europe offered no precedents that might have enabled the invaders either to comprehend Inti Raimi and similar festivals in their mythic, political, and religious context, or to describe them in a nuanced and differentiated terminology. A case in point is the mummies, which participated so prominently in the festivals and the daily life of Inca Cuzco. On occasion, the mummies were described quite cogently as "[dead] Indians [looking] like embalmed bodies"[65] or as "embalmed bodies dressed in many garments, one over the other . . . with diadems on their heads."[66] But usually they were referred to more cryptically as "those dried figures,"[67] or "those dead people."[68] Similarly, the clergyman who watched the Inti Raimi of 1535 referred to "all the figures from the shrines of Cuzco."[69] A little later, he expanded this ambiguous expression in a way that suggests that it was indeed the mummies, not religious images in general, that attended the celebration. After sunset on each of the days of Inti Raimi, the cleric wrote, the participants in the festival

returned these figures and evil relics to their houses and shrines . . .
And it should be noted that these figures of idols that they displayed

---

[64] [Segovia], *Relación*, pp. 82bf.

[65] Mena, *La conquista*, ed. Pogo, p. 256: Indias en manera de enbalsamados.

[66] [Estete], *Noticia*, p. 47; cf. p. 55. See figs. 10 and 51.

[67] Mena, *La conquista*, p. 258, referring to Guayna Capac and another mummy as "aquellos bultos secos."

[68] Pedro Pizarro, *Relación* 10, pp. 52f.; 15, p. 89, estos muertos.

[69] [Segovia], *Relación*, p. 82a, todos los bultos de los adoratorios del Cuzco.

under these awnings were of the past Incas who ruled over Cuzco. Each one present was served by a crowd of attendants who all day long waved away the flies with fans of feathers . . . and by his *mamacona*, who are like women living in seclusion, and under each awning there were twelve or fifteen of them.[70]

The term "evil relics" suggests that Christian relics, many of which were dead bodies of saints, in some way resembled these Inca "figures," and that the latter were therefore indeed mummies. Yet there remains room for ambiguity as to the identity of the "figures" at the Inti Raimi of 1535, because the same Spaniard who noticed that each mummy possessed a small box containing hair clippings and the like also encountered in Cuzco itself and in neighboring shrines over twenty statues of gold and silver "which must have been the portraits of some deceased ladies. For each one of them had its team of pages and serving women as though they were alive. These served and cleaned with such deference and respect as though [the deceased ladies] were present in their own bodies, and cooked food for them to eat, carefully prepared and delicious, as though the deceased were really going to consume it."[71] These statues, which Pedro Sancho described as goddesses whom the Incas fed and talked with "as if they were women of flesh," were "dressed in beautiful and very fine clothing."[72] They thus resembled the mummies quite closely. The dead were accordingly present and active among the living not only as mummies but also as portraits, and it is therefore not inconceivable that the "figures" which the cleric saw at the Inti Raimi of 1535 were portraits, not mummies. Spaniards never fully understood the religious and political significance of representations of deceased Inca nobles and rulers and their consorts, although during subsequent decades, they did on occasion return to the issue.[73]

The early Spanish accounts of the Incas, packed with all kinds of information though they are, at the same time raise numerous queries as to what the writer really saw or meant. This is so not only for the modern reader: readers in sixteenth-century Spain also encountered the problem of explaining and reformulating what could be learned about the Incas from those early accounts.

A small but telling example of this process of interpretation occurred in the reception of our cleric's description of harvest and plowing in Cuzco. A few years after being completed, this description was quoted

[70] [Segovia], *Relación*, p. 82b, bultos y reliquias pessimas; aquellos bultos de idolos. I have translated the term *beatas* as "women living in seclusion." The *mamacona*, "mothers," were the senior women dedicated to the service of the Sun and the dead.
[71] [Estete], *Noticia*, p. 46.
[72] Sancho, *An Account* 14, p. 129.
[73] See below, chap. III.3 passim.

and slightly altered by Bartolomé de Las Casas in his *Apologética Historia*, and in 1575 Jerónimo Román, in his *Repúblicas del Mundo*, published a further adaptation of Las Casas' version. Las Casas and Román both wrote to defend and explain the civilizations of America, and their revised wording of our passage reflects this purpose. Las Casas thus omitted the Christian terms of contempt that the clergyman had thought necessary to insert into his description. He also elaborated one phrase. Where the clergyman had written that the Inca "talked with those who approached him" but had not been able to say what the subject was, Las Casas wrote that the Inca stood "talking with and despatching those who brought business . . . he talked and made provision for what was needful."[74] Jerónimo Román elaborated this phrase a little more by saying that the Inca "talked and dispatched matters of importance for the kingdom."[75] Like Las Casas, Román had no direct knowledge of Peru, and this is perhaps why in his mind's eye he pictured Manco Inca, like the king of Castile, transacting public business with the grandees of his realm.[76] The change in wording is small, but it is indicative both of the impossibility of recounting the hitherto unknown except in terms of the known, and of the vast process of fragmentation and transformation that Andean reality underwent in the course of being described by Europeans.

[74] Las Casas, *Apologética Historia* 189.

[75] Jerónimo Román, *Republica de las Indias Occidentales* (1575), 1.21.

[76] For comparable imagery in Castile, see a text popular in the sixteenth century, *The Poem of the Cid*, ed. and transl. R. Hamilton and J. Perry (London, 1984), laisse 135, cf. laisse 99; *Crónica del Señor Don Juan segundo* (in Biblioteca de autores españoles, vol. 68), year 1419, chaps. 1–4.

 III

THE INCAS AND
THEIR SPANISH HISTORIANS,
1535–1552

THE GOLDEN treasure of Atahualpa reached Seville in 1534 and provoked a sensation. Some special items from the vast collection of heavy gold pitchers, gold llamas, sacred images, and temple furnishings that were stored in the Casa de Contratación were sent to Toledo so that the emperor Charles V, who was holding court there, could see them before they were melted down. Among the many seekers of advancement who set out for Peru upon seeing the Inca treasures in Seville was Pedro Cieza de León.[1] Cieza began his American career as a soldier of fortune, but his attention soon shifted to what could be learned about the peoples of the Andes and their past. Although he was only one among a number of Spaniards to record what they had learned about the Andean past during the years immediately following the invasion, his was the first account to combine observation with sustained reflection and analysis.

Cieza spent fifteen years in the New World, from 1535 until 1550, years that witnessed the first stages of the transformation of the Inca empire into a colonial state.[2] By 1547, when he reached the lands formerly controlled by the Incas,[3] several other Spaniards were also developing an interest in the Andean past, whether for administrative purposes[4] or to satisfy their personal curiosity. Cieza thus supplemented his own researches with information given him by the Dominican Fray Domingo de Santo Tomás, author of the first Quechua grammar and dictionary, and by Don Pedro de la Gasca, president of the Audiencia of Lima between 1547 and 1550, who extended official patronage to Cieza's studies.[5] Passing

---

[1] Cieza, *Crónica, Primera Parte* (hereafter *Crónica*), 104; *Tercera Parte* 79; cf. Xerez, *Verdadera relación*, p. 152 and a list of items sent from Peru that appears in *Relación francesa 1937*, ed. R. Porras Barrenechea, pp. 76f.

[2] See Pease's excellent introduction to Cieza as a historian in *Crónica*, pp. xxff.

[3] Pease, ed., Cieza, *Crónica*, p. xxiii.

[4] E.g., Espinoza Soriano, "El primer informe," *Revista Peruana de Cultura*, nos. 11–12 (1967). The first volume of Iñigo Ortiz de Zúñiga's *Visita de la provincia de León de Huanuco en 1562*, ed. J. V. Murra, also contains the visita of 1549 of the Chupachus; see pp. 289ff. This was first published by M. Helmer, as "*La visitación de los Yndios Chupachos.* Inka et encomendero," *Travaux de l'Institut Français des Études Andines* (Lima) 5 (1955–1956): 3–50, q.v. for the historical context.

[5] Cieza, *Crónica* 61; 62; 64. On Domingo de Santo Tomás, see also *Crónica* 90; 95. On La Gasca, see Cieza, *La Guerra de Quito*, 234, in Pedro Cieza de Leon, *Obras Completas*, ed.

through Potosí in 1549 (see fig. 11), Cieza met there the lawyer Juan Polo de Ondegardo, who was to become one of the greatest authorities on matters pertaining to the Incas. Like Polo and several more of his Spanish contemporaries in the Andes, Cieza kept notebooks, and he also studied and copied for his own future use notes made by others.[6] Above all, he was a meticulous observer and asked questions tirelessly.[7] In Cuzco he interviewed Don Garcia Cayo Topa, one of the few surviving descendants of Guayna Capac.[8] As such, Cayo Topa was also known to the *quipucamayos*, keepers of Inca historical traditions, who some years earlier had been questioned about the Inca past by Vaca de Castro.[9]

Two vecinos of Cuzco translated what the quipucamayos had to say, Francisco Villacastin and Juan de Betanzos.[10] Cieza mentioned a conversation about Andean antiquities between Villacastin and one of his own acquaintances, but he apparently did not know of Juan de Betanzos, who was working on his own history of the Incas at the very time that Cieza was staying in Cuzco.[11] Betanzos, who perhaps had begun studying Quechua while still in the Caribbean,[12] was married to Dona Angelina Cusirimay; this lady was Atahualpa's niece and consort and later had two children by Francisco Pizarro.[13] It was from Dona Angelina and her kinsmen that Betanzos learned the historical traditions of the Incas that he endeavored to translate for Spanish readers.[14] Twenty years later, Pedro Sarmiento de Gamboa consulted over one hundred quipucamayos in Cuzco before writing his *Historica Indica*, which was then verified by representatives of the twelve royal Inca lineages.[15]

Betanzos, Cieza, Sarmiento, and their contemporaries were much more methodical and reflective in their approach to the Andes than the first invaders who recorded their impressions in writing had been. Moreover, these later historians brought to light entirely new fields of Andean

C. Saenz de Santa Maria (Madrid, 1985), vol. 2; cf. Cantù in her edition of Cieza, *Segunda Parte*, pp. xxixff. On Pedro de la Gasca, see also T. Hampe Martínez, "Don Pedro de la Gasca y la proyección del mundo universitario salmantino en el siglo XVI," *Mélanges de la Casa Velazquez* 22 (1986): 171–195 and T. Hampe Martínez, *Don Pedro de La Gasca* (1989).

[6] See Pease, ed., Cieza, *Crónica*, pp. xxiii-xxv; Cieza, *Crónica* 64; Polo de Ondegardo, *Informe al licenciado Muñatones*, p. 130, todos los borradores que entonces hize.

[7] E.g., Cieza, *Crónica* 21, p. 77; Cieza, *Segunda Parte* 4, p. 6; 30, p. 93; 38, p. 112; 46, p. 136.

[8] Cieza, *Segunda Parte* 6, p. 13; 38, p. 112.

[9] Quipucamayos, p. 72.

[10] Quipucamayos, p. 21.

[11] Cieza, *Segunda Parte* 30, p. 93, for Cieza in Cuzco in August 1550. Betanzos finished a first draft in 1551; see *Suma* (1987), 1.14, p. 70b.

[12] See Martin Rubio's introduction to Betanzos, *Suma* (1987), p. xiii.

[13] Betanzos, *Suma* (1987), 1.47, pp. 197f. For some further particulars on Doña Angelina, see Maria Rostworowski de Diez Canseco, *Doña Francisca Pizarro. Una ilustre mestiza, 1534–1598* (Lima, 1989), pp. 18ff.

[14] Betanzos, *Suma*, Preface.

[15] For Sarmiento's informants, see G. Urton, "Historia de un mito," *Revista Andina* 7, no. 1 (1989): 155–160 and his *History of a Myth*, pp. 63–70.

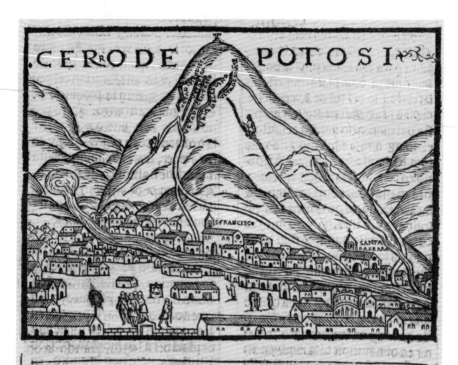

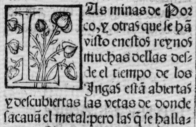

As minas de Po=
co, y otras que se há
visto enestos reynos
muchas dellas def=
de el tiempo de los
Ingas está abiertas
y descubiertas las vetas de donde
sacauá el metal: pero las q̃ se halla=

y bien assentado q̃ ay en toda aq̃=
lla comarca. Y porque los Indios
llaman Potossí a los cerros y co=
sas altas, quedosele por nóbre Po
tossí, como le llamá. Y aunque en
este tiépo Gonçalo Piçarro anda
ua dando guerra al visorey, y el
reyno lleno de alteraciones causa=

11. "The mountain of Potosí," showing, near its top, the silver mines discovered in 1547. Below, the newly founded city with the conventual church of San Francisco for Spaniards, and the Indian parish church of Santa Barbara. In the foreground, the *casa de la moneda* and main square. Pedro Cieza de León, *Parte Primera de la Chrónica del Perú* (Seville, 1553), fol. CXXIIv. Biblioteca Nacional, Madrid.

thought and experience. They thus recorded, for the first time, a number of Inca and Andean myths. The first invaders had made no mention of myths and little mention of Inca history. As Betanzos realized, the reason for their silence was that neither they nor their interpreters ever learned the relevant languages in sufficient depth. But when Betanzos, Domingo de Santo Tomás, and others began studying Andean languages systematically,[16] and after Andeans and Spaniards had lived side by side for some years, a more sophisticated interchange became possible.

However, this was not a simple matter of Spaniards understanding more about the Andes than they had done formerly. For in the very process of translating and writing down what they were told, Spaniards inevitably introduced notions of their own that had, strictly speaking, no Andean counterparts. One such notion concerned the historicity of the long-distant past. Sixteenth-century Europeans interpreted the book of Genesis and Greco-Roman myths of origins as historical narratives, not as mythic or allegorical accounts of creation and human beginnings. It was thus natural for Spaniards to view Andean myths of primeval floods and conflagrations and of the origins of society as historical narratives of a similar kind.[17] This led Cieza, Betanzos, and the other sixteenth-century historians of the Incas to extrapolate from legendary accounts they heard about Inca origins and social organization the history of a dynasty of twelve rulers, going back some five hundred years or even longer.[18] Although historicizing Andean myths in this fashion amounted to misunderstanding them profoundly, the dynasty had its uses, because it provided the invaders with a conceptual framework within which they could understand Inca imperial expansion.[19] As for Andeans, they were not interested in their past in the same way, or for the same reasons as Spaniards. In the course of the sixteenth century, Andeans did however learn to explain their history in terms that Spaniards found intelligible and at times to exploit Spanish preconceptions to their own advantage.[20] This process of translating and adapting Inca mythic and historical narratives

[16] Betanzos, *Suma* (1987), Preface, p. 7; Cieza, *Crónica* 43, p. 143. Precedents for language study by missionaries existed in the peninsula; for Granada, see R. Ricard, *Études et documents pour l'histoire missionaire de l'Espagne et du Portugal* (1930), pp. 209–228.

[17] Cieza, *Segunda Parte* 3, p. 4, thus compared Andean flood stories to the Greek myth of the flood of Thessaly; he clearly viewed all these accounts as historical, as most of his contemporaries would have done. Similarly, Sarmiento regarded Plato's account of flood and cataclysm in the *Timaeus* as historical; see his *Historia Indica* 3–5, pp. 201ff.

[18] Sarmiento's date for the death of the first Inca Manco Capac is 665 A.D., *Historia Indica* 14, p. 220a.

[19] See J. H. Rowe, "Absolute Chronology," *American Antiquity* 10 (1944–1945): 265–284 and further below, chap. III.3, n. 1.

[20] A particularly clear example is examined by G. Urton, *History of a Myth*. For a commercial counterpart to this political and cultural phenomenon, see J. Murra, "Aymara Lords and Their European Agents," *Nova Americana* 1 (1970): 231–243.

led to various distortions in how Spaniards understood the Andean past. What concerns us here, however, is not primarily this reformulation of Inca history during the sixteenth and seventeenth centuries[21] but the changing perceptions of Inca and Andean religion that accompanied it.

The missionary Fray Domingo de Santo Tomás supplied information not only to Cieza but also to fellow Dominican Bartolomé de las Casas, with whom he campaigned against the perpetuity of encomiendas in Peru.[22] Cieza's work in turn was one of the sources Las Casas used.[23] A shared purpose inspired Cieza and the two Dominicans: to learn the religious customs of the Indians "so as to make them understand the path of truth, so that they will be saved."[24]

Although more could be learned about the Inca past when Betanzos, La Gasca, Cieza, and their contemporaries interested themselves in this subject, the land they saw was no longer the flourishing empire that had greeted the Spaniards in 1532. Cuzco was beginning to be described in relation to its Spanish, not its Inca, landmarks,[25] and parts of it had acquired a dirty and neglected air.[26] Travelers crossed the river Apurimac by means of a rope, because the Inca suspension bridge had been destroyed. As for the oracle, it was a memory only.[27] The great Inca palace and temple of Tumebamba, where Guayna Capac had held court, were deserted, and the local *curaca*[28] had become a Christian.[29] The temple of Vilcas, built by the Incas to mark the geographical center of their empire, was likewise in ruins—"It was what it is no longer," as Cieza put it.[30] The curaca of Xauxa had been baptized and called himself Don Cristóbal; he showed Cieza round the local Inca temple of the Sun and the temple of the regional prophetic deity, Guaribilca, who also was the divine ancestor of the people of Xauxa. The sacred images had been destroyed by the

[21] I plan to return to this topic in the companion volume to this book, which will deal with sixteenth- and seventeenth-century concepts of myth and history in the Andes. Aside from the issue of Inca chronology, see, on the difficulties encountered by missionaries in understanding and interpreting Andean myth, T. Bouysse-Cassagne, O. Harris, T. Platt, and V. Cereceda, *Tres reflexiones sobre el pensamiento andino* (La Paz, 1987), pp. 11f., 16ff.

[22] Las Casas and Domingo de Santo Tomás, *Memorial*, in Las Casas, *Obras* 5: 465. *Encomienda* describes a grant of Indians to a Spaniard to whom they owe tribute payments and labor services.

[23] Pease, ed., Cieza, *Crónica*, pp. xviif. To the passages there cited, which Las Casas quoted from Cieza, add Cieza, *Crónica* 89, p. 252 = Las Casas, *Apologética Historia* 57, p. 299, on Vilcas.

[24] Cieza, *Crónica* 64, cf. 23. Missionary work was also a crucial stimulus for Spaniards to learn Quechua; for an important discussion of the effect this had on the language, see B. Mannheim, *The Language of the Inca since the European Invasion* (1991), chap. 3, sec. 1.

[25] Betanzos, *Suma* (1987), I. 3, p. 17a.

[26] Cieza, *Segunda Parte* 35, p. 106.

[27] Cieza, *Crónica* 91.

[28] Quechua, "lord."

[29] Cieza, *Crónica* 44.

[30] Cieza, *Crónica* 89.

friar Valverde in 1533, so that the oracle fell silent; the buildings were in ruins and overgrown with shrubs.[31]

Cieza experienced, as he expressed it, "no small sorrow" when contemplating the passing away of the Inca order of things[32] and the possibility that the very language of the Incas might disappear.[33] Betanzos likewise was deeply aware of the changes he was witnessing. Change, so much of it a perceived change for the worse, inspired the historians of the mid-sixteenth century not only to record, but also to explain, what they knew future generations would not be privileged to see. Officials and missionaries, by contrast, were led to write about the Andes by the more practical needs of colonial government and were therefore less committed to produce a reasoned and readable text. It was historians who in the sixteenth and early seventeenth centuries created the conceptual forms that still guide much of our research into the Andean past. Yet without the inquiries of the missionaries and officials of early colonial Peru, those conceptual forms would be less richly endowed with life and diversity than in effect they are. Beginning therefore with the researches of Cieza and Betanzos, we will continue later with the more detailed, but frequently less focused, information recorded by officials and missionaries.[34]

1. DIVINATION AND THE DEAD

The impact of Christianity in South America was predominantly violent and destructive; nonetheless, from time to time the Indians glimpsed another dimension in the religion that the invaders sought to impose on them. Cieza recorded one such occurrence. He repeatedly expressed repugnance at the widespread custom of burying alive wives and servants of distinguished individuals, so that they might follow their deceased masters into the next world, and was surprised that some women would even commit suicide voluntarily to be with their dead husbands. An incident that occurred during Cieza's earliest years in America, while he was serving under Juan de Vadillo between 1537 and 1539, thus remained fixed in his mind: "I still remember, when I was in the province of Cartagena some twelve or thirteen years ago, while the licentiate Juan de Vadillo was its governor and judge, how a boy escaped from a village called Pirina and fled to where Vadillo was staying, because they wanted

---

[31] Cieza, *Crónica* 84; cf. Titu Cusi, *Relación de la Conquista*, pp. 106f., on the destruction of Guaribilca by Manco Inca because Guaribilca, along with the Guanca Indians, had sided with the Spaniards.

[32] Cieza, *Segunda Parte* 22, p. 66.

[33] Cieza, *Segunda parte* 24, pp. 72f.

[34] Cieza, Betanzos, and some aspects of Sarmiento will be discussed in the present chapter; for the reports of officials and missionaries, see chap. IV.

to bury him alive with the lord of the village, who had died at that time."[1]
To bury the living seemed to Cieza an "accursed custom," which was
explicable only if one bore in mind the extraordinary power of demonic
illusion in the lives of "these gentiles."[2] There were thus concrete reasons
why one should wish to convince the Indians of the Christian "path of
truth."

However, the victory of the Christian god was not as speedy or as complete as might be suggested by the incident of Pirina, or by the conversion
of Don Cristóbal of Xauxa. Cieza thus went on to tell how, only two
years before he passed through Xauxa, Don Cristóbal's father, Alaya, had
been buried with all pomp and circumstance according to the ancient rituals, which included the burial of "a great number of live women and
servants."[3] Indeed, when some years later Don Cristóbal himself died, he
in turn was followed into death by some of his people.[4] In 1549 Manco
Inca's brother Paullu Inca died in Cuzco as a Christian, but his people
solemnly commemorated the anniversary of the death with as many of
the old observances as they were able to perform in the officially Christian city.[5] Indeed, as Cieza learned from Domingo de Santo Tomás,
shortly before Paullu died, one of his servants heard the voices of the old
gods recalling him to those same ritual banquets that Christian missionaries were urging their charges to renounce:

> One of his servants informed Paullu Inca that near the fortress of
> Cuzco he had heard loud voices, which shouted amid a great noise,
> "Why, Inca, do you fail to preserve [the customs] it behoves you to
> preserve? Eat and drink and rejoice, for soon you will no longer eat
> and drink and rejoice." He who reported these voices to Don Paullu
> heard them for five or six nights. And within a few days, Don Paullu
> died and he who heard the voices as well. Such are the tricks of the
> devil and the snares that he uses to capture the souls of them who
> put their trust in auguries.[6]

Throughout the Andes divine powers were locked in a combat that the
missionaries sought to direct by means of publicly enacted ceremonies of
conversion and by exorcisms such as Castañega and Ciruelo had envi-

---

[1] Cieza, *Crónica* 62, p. 194; see Aranibar, "Necropompa," *Revista del Museo Nacional* 36
(1969–1970), for a critical reading of this and related passages, distinguishing Inca from
Andean burial practices. For Vadillo, see Fernández de Oviedo, *General y natural historia de
las Indias*, ed. J. Pérez de Tudela y Bueso, Biblioteca de autores españoles, vol. 120 (Madrid,
1959), bk. 39, Proemio, p. 337.
[2] Cieza, *Segunda Parte* 24, pp. 72f.; cf. *Crónica* 33, 51, 100–101.
[3] Cieza, *Crónica* 62.
[4] Polo de Ondegardo, *Notables daños*, p. 106.
[5] Cieza, *Segunda Parte* 32, 61.
[6] Cieza, *Crónica* 62, p. 195.

sioned for the very different circumstances obtaining in Spain.[7] But in one sense the two situations were similar, for in both Spain and Peru access to supernatural power was a means of exercising social and political control and therefore required legitimation. Andeans thus found themselves caught between rivaling ritual orders, one accessible to themselves and the other manipulated by the invaders.

Cieza related two conversion stories that illustrate this conflict. In 1547 the people of Lampaz near Lake Titicaca asked their parish priest for permission to celebrate the time-honored festival that marked the potato harvest and would prognosticate the next year's crop. Permission was granted and the elaborate ritual was set in motion, only to be interrupted at its culminating point by a recent convert, who loudly reproved the villagers for indulging in this "diabolic rite." Subsequently, another villager approached the priest begging for baptism because a beautiful figure wearing shining white robes had appeared to him at night in a nearby Andean holy place. Once baptized, this villager set fire to his house, distributed his women and property among his kin, and urged conversion on his fellows.[8] Another conversion story related how an ethnic lord in Popayan was beleaguered night and day by demons, who threw stones, lifted him in the air, dangled evil visions before him, and yelled Indian war cries. In despair, the lord journeyed to the nearest church, was baptized, and saw no more of demons.[9] In both these stories, the visionary experience conforms to Christian norms, to what Andeans had been told of the supernatural world by missionaries. For the figure in shining robes matches the appearance of angels in European visions, while uproarious and threatening demons are a staple of Christian hagiography from the desert fathers onward.[10]

But not everyone was equally suggestible. On his long travels through the former Inca empire and adjacent regions, Cieza was confronted again and again with the disquieting reality that God continued to permit the demons to hold dominion over Andean souls. Ciruelo had distinguished between the public idolatry and superstition of the gentiles of antiquity and the clandestine superstition of his own day; Cieza did the same.[11] Public idolatry had come to an end with the fall of the Inca empire, but clandestine idolatry persisted, especially in rituals of divination. Ciruelo's

[7] Above, chap. I.2, p. 42; description of an exorcism in Cumana, Las Casas, *Apologética Historia* 99, pp. 520f. and 245, p. 520.

[8] Cieza, *Crónica* 117. For a discussion of the ritual in Andean terms, see T. Bouysse-Cassagne, *La identidad aymara* (1987), pp. 262–272.

[9] Cieza, *Crónica* 118.

[10] For some of the earliest examples of such demons, see Athanasius, *Life of Anthony* 6, 8–9, 11–12 and Jerome, *Life of Paul the Hermit* 7–8, both translated in R. J. Deferrari, *Early Christian Biographies*, The Fathers of the Church, vol. 15 (Washington, D.C., 1952).

[11] Ciruelo, *Treatise* I.2, pp. 92ff.; Cieza, *Crónica* 43, 62; *Segunda Parte* 29.

devil, who thanks to his great age and fine memory was an "excellent historian" and easily deceived the simple with probable but incomplete prophecies,[12] was thus the exact counterpart of Cieza's devil, who "because of his subtlety and astuteness and because of his great age and the experience he has in everything, speaks to the simple and they listen to him."[13] The prophetic god Pachacamac was a case in point. It was Don Pedro de la Gasca and Cieza who had been the first to learn that when the Incas conquered the valley of Pachacamac, they considered it politically wise to establish the state cult of the divine Sun alongside the existing cult of Pachacamac, rather than attempting to eradicate this ancient worship.[14] As Cieza understood it, "The demon Pachacamac was happy with this agreement and displayed great contentment in his responses. For in one way or the other, he received his honors, and the souls of those wretched simple folk remained in his power." The strategy of survival that had worked so well for Pachacamac in Inca times worked once again after the Spaniards arrived. Cieza was thus told that

> in secret retreats this wicked demon talks with the old people: for seeing that he has lost his influence and authority and that many of those who formerly served him now hold the contrary opinion and have recognized their error, he says to them that the god whom the Christians preach and he are one and the same thing. . . . And with deceits and false appearances he manages to prevent them from receiving the water of baptism.[15]

Contrary to what the Spaniards who in 1533 desecrated Pachacamac's shrine had so confidently expected, this violent intrusion and the subsequent preaching of Christianity thus did not entirely destroy the god's power. What changed was that the public rituals of the ancient sanctuary were replaced by clandestine ones, and where formerly priests had spoken on behalf of Pachacamac, he himself now spoke in the memories of his

---

[12] Ciruelo, *Treatise* 2.8, p. 173.

[13] Cieza, *Crónica* 48.

[14] Cf. above, chap. II.1 at nn. 22ff.

[15] Cieza, *Crónica* 72, quoted by Las Casas, *Apologética Historia* 131. Pachacamac was not the only place that Cieza believed to have been inhabited by a demon: see, e.g., *Segunda Parte* 7, p. 17, Guanacaure was "algun demonio." Cf. Betanzos, *Suma* (1987), 1.11, p. 49b: "El demonio los traiga ofuscados y en cada parte que se lo demonstraba ofuscados les decía mil mentiras y engaños . . . y en los tales lugares do ansi le vían ponían piedras en su lugar a quien ellos reverenciaban y adoraban y como les dijese unas veces que era el sol y otras en otras partes decía que era la luna y a otros que era su dios y hacedor e a otros que era su lumbre que los calentaba e alumbraba e que ansi lo verían en los volcanes de Arequipa en otras partes decía que era el señor que habia dado ser al mundo e que se llamaba Pachacama." Perhaps the vision of the sun in the volcano of Arequipa should be juxtaposed with Inca Pachacuti's vision of the sun in the well Susurpuquio; see below, chap. VII.1 at nn. 11ff.

worshipers.[16] Spaniards thus felt called upon to continue investigating demonic activity among human beings. Like Castañega and Ciruelo in Spain, so Cieza in Peru was concerned to learn what exactly the demons did and to fathom the extent of the divine forbearance allowed their activities to persist. "God knows," Cieza wrote, "why he permits the devil to speaks to these people and to hold such great power over them, so that they are so greatly deceived by his sayings."[17] But Cieza saw in addition a crushing human responsibility, for he thought that had it not been for the internecine wars among the Spaniards in Peru and for their terrible abuses of power, the Indians could have been saved from the demons quickly and easily.[18]

As it was, Andean rituals and the beliefs that sustained them persisted. Cieza thus recorded a variety of Andean opinions about the afterlife and the nature and existence of the soul. These opinions were expressed, Cieza thought, in the widespread custom of burying with deceased lords their wives, retainers, possessions, and food, so that they might enjoy in the hereafter the same status and pleasures as in terrestial life.[19] On the surface, such information reveals little that is specific to the Andes, for topics such as these constituted a well-established rubric of ethnographic inquiry by Greek and Roman historians, some of whom Cieza had read.[20] Also, rituals of burial were a subject of missionary exhortation to converts from Islam in Granada,[21] for it was considered unbecoming for these converts to bury their dead according to non-Christian rites. As regards the delights of eating, drinking, and feasting in the next life, Christian apologists against Islam regularly reproached Muslims for adhering to a worldly and materialistic image of the future beyond the grave.[22] There were thus reasons for Cieza's interest in these matters that were independent of what he saw in the Andes, and he accordingly described Andean beliefs and practices relating to the dead with reference to ideas he brought with him from Spain.

These ideas were especially dominant in Cieza's perception of the stateless societies beyond the northern frontier regions of the Inca empire. Just as historians of the Greco-Roman Mediterranean had felt that the semi-

---

[16] Similarly, the gods in Puerto Viejo did not dare to speak in public, but did speak in secret, Cieza, *Crónica* 49, p. 160.

[17] Cieza, *Crónica* 33. Cf. Kramer and Sprenger, *Malleus Maleficarum* 1.12–13, 18, p. 85.

[18] Cieza, *Crónica* 101, cf. 23.

[19] E.g., Cieza, *Crónica* 33, 62, 63, 90.

[20] Cieza quoted the preface of Diodorus Siculus; see his *Crónica*, Proemio, p. 14. For possible European antecedents of Andean burial customs, see Diodorus Siculus, *Library of History*, ed. and transl. C. H. Oldfather (Cambridge, 1960), 1.91–95, on embalming the dead in Egypt.

[21] A. Domínguez Ortiz and B. Vincent, *Historia de los moriscos* (1978), p. 270.

[22] See Ricoldo de Montecrucio, *Reprobación del alcoran* (Seville, 1501), chap. 9; cf. chap. 1.

sedentary and nomadic peoples beyond its confines lacked a recognizable cultural and religious profile, so Cieza thought that to the north of the Inca empire people had "no religion at all, as we understand it, nor is there any house of worship to be found."[23] Given that in those regions there existed no architectural expression of worship, it followed that people "adhere to no beliefs of any kind."[24] Or, if there was some religious belief to be found, "they adhere to it in error."[25]

One such erroneous belief, fostered by the devil, was the expectation that the next life would be filled with the same material delights that life on earth bestowed on the fortunate.[26] Yet this belief in an afterlife was not entirely erroneous, since it expressed some apprehension of the resurrection of the body that Christians believed in. About Quimbaya, Cieza thus reported that notwithstanding the absence of any explicitly formulated religious belief, "These people do have the understanding to think that there is in man more than a mortal body. They do not believe that there is a soul, but some transformation that they conceive of. And they believe that all bodies will resurrect, but the devil makes them understand that it will be in a place where they will enjoy great pleasure and repose."[27] It was under the civilizing influence of the Incas, as Cieza perceived it, that Andeans learned to believe not only in the immortality of the body but also in that of the soul. Traveling on the Inca royal road from Quito to Tumebamba, Cieza stopped in Tacunga, a village of *mitimaes*, Inca state settlers. Like the Stoics of classical antiquity,[28] these people derived their religious beliefs from beholding the splendor of the universe: "So far as we understand them, they believe in the immortality of the soul and know that there exists a maker of everything in the world, because when they contemplate the greatness of the sky and the movement of the sun and of the moon and the other marvels [of creation], they believe that there exists a maker of these things."[29] Likewise, the Chancas of the central Andean sierra, which at the time of the Spanish invasion was controlled by the Incas, who had imposed their religion on the area, "believed

[23] Cieza, *Crónica* 28, p. 97; cf. 33, p. 111, about Indians of Quillacingas and Pastos.
[24] Cieza, *Crónica* 24, p. 84, on Quimbaya: no tienen creencia ninguna. Cf. 33, p. 111, Pasto. On the ancient Mediterranean, see J. Vogt, *Kulturwelt und Barbaren. Zum Menschheitsbild der spätantiken Gesellschaft*, Akademie der Wissenschaften und der Literatur in Mainz, Abhandlungen, geistes- und sozialwissenschaftliche Klasse (1967), no. 1. Cieza's distinction between the Incas and their subjects on the one hand and other less civilized polities on the other perhaps rested on Andean precedent; see T. Bouysse-Cassagne, *La identidad aymara*, pp. 154ff.; F. M. Renard-Casevitz, T. Saignes and A. C. Taylor-Descola, *L'inca, l'espagnol et les sauvages* (Paris, 1986).
[25] Cieza, *Crónica* 23, p. 82, Indians of province of Carrapa believe in a creator but "creenlo mal."
[26] Cieza, *Crónica* 24, p. 85; 33, p. 111.
[27] Cieza, *Crónica* 24, p. 85.
[28] Cicero, *De natura deorum* 2.2,4; 6.16ff.
[29] Cieza, *Crónica* 41, p. 136; cf. *Segunda Parte* 3, p. 4.

in the immortality of the soul, which they call *xongon*, which is also the term for heart."[30] Among the Yungas of the coast near Lima, treasures, equipment, and food deposited in burials also indicated that the Andeans believed in "the immortality of the soul and that man has more than a mortal body," and that there existed another world where the dead "would eat and drink as they did before they died."[31]

How did the Indians come by these notions? Cieza thought that despite considerable diversity, Andean burial customs and beliefs regarding the afterlife displayed a certain coherence and consistency and might therefore ultimately provide some clue as to where the Indians had originally come from.[32] However, he did not pursue this theme that was to preoccupy subsequent historians of the Indies so deeply.[33] Instead, Cieza had recourse to an explanation that lay much closer to hand. This was the capacity of demons to interfere in human affairs by assuming material bodies.[34]

Many of the first invaders had speculated that demons communicated with their Andean worshipers by lodging themselves in images of gods, as for instance in the image of Pachacamac. The dead, by contrast, spoke through their human representatives. This was the case not only in Cuzco, where the mummies of deceased Inca rulers were represented by their kinsfolk, but also elsewhere.[35] Throughout the Andes, Spaniards despoiled graves richly furnished with gifts for the departed,[36] and on occasion observed that even after the invasion and Christian missionizing had taken their toll, the dead were still being honored with elaborate funerary rituals and continued being revered long after these rituals were completed. Cieza was in Cuzco when the anniversary of Paullu Inca's death was being commemorated,[37] and in Collao he watched people observe the anniversary of a kinsman's death with llama sacrifice and libation of chicha at the tomb.[38]

Nonetheless, times were changing. By the time Cieza reached Peru, the ritual framework within which the mummies of Inca rulers and lords had communicated with the living through representatives specifically appointed for this purpose had been destroyed. Gonzalo Pizarro had burnt the mummy of Inca Viracocha, and the other mummies had been

---

[30] Cieza, *Crónica* 90.

[31] Cieza, *Crónica* 62.

[32] Cieza, *Crónica* 63, referring to the lost first chapter of *Segunda Parte*.

[33] E.g., Sarmiento, *Historia Indica* 2–5; Acosta, *Historia natural y moral* 1.16–25; and especially Gregorio Garcia, *Predicación del santo Evangelio en el nuevo mundo* (1625).

[34] Cf. above, chap. II.2 at n. 53.

[35] Duviols, *Cultura andina y represión* (1986), p. 474, priest of Tanta Carhua who had been sacrificed as capacocha.

[36] Cieza, *Crónica* 62, p. 193; 63, p. 197.

[37] Cieza, *Segunda Parte* 61, p. 178, August 1550.

[38] Cieza, *Crónica* 101, p. 277.

hidden away by their custodians, to be revered in secret.[39] Similarly, on the coast, Don Jerónimo Loayza, archbishop of Lima, had ordered the dead who were being revered to be buried in the ground, where the bodies would decompose.[40] What was left for Cieza to observe, therefore, was only some fragments of the elaborate ceremonial order whereby the dead and the living had interacted before the invasion. The presence of the dead could on occasion still be felt in society, but they no longer acted through their publicly designated human representatives. This is why Cieza repeatedly expressed the opinion that the dead did somehow communicate with the living, or rather, as he understood it, demons, in the guise of the dead, were communicating with human beings.[41] Changes in Andean religious observance brought on by the invasion and by missionary activity thus led to interpretative changes. Where Pedro Pizarro had learned by personal experience how the dead communicated with the living,[42] Cieza was left to speculate that this communication was demonic, but was for some reason tolerated by God. "Such great secrets exist in these nations of the Indies," he wrote, "that only God is able to comprehend them."[43]

In Cieza's opinion, the phenomenon of the devil communicating with human beings in the guise of deceased kinsmen pervaded the Andes. He observed it among the Cañari on the Inca frontier[44] and in Puerto Viejo. Here, people saw the devil in illusions,

> walking through the fields, appearing to people in the form of persons already dead whom they had known, or who perhaps were their fathers and kinsfolk. It looked as if they were passing by in their state and dignity as when they had lived in the world. Thanks to such vain apparitions, these abandoned people followed the will of the devil, and buried in sepulchers living beings and other things so that the deceased should depart with greater honor. This was their manner of obeying their religion and of fulfilling the commandment of their gods; and they thought that the dead would go to a delightful and blessed place, where they would live eating and drinking, as they were accustomed to do in this world when they were alive.[45]

"Illusions of the devil" could also be seen in Riobamba near Quito, where lords long dead were found "walking through their fields, adorned with

[39] Cobo, *Historia* 12.11, p. 77b; Hemming, *Conquest of the Incas*, p. 298.

[40] Cieza, *Crónica* 63, p. 197.

[41] Cieza, *Crónica* 28, p. 96, demons acting through the dried corpses of slain enemies in Cali. This was not a cult of the dead such as was practiced to the south in Inca lands, but Cieza considered the two phenomena to be equivalent; see Cieza, *Cronica* 63, p. 195.

[42] See above, chap. II.2 at n. 29.

[43] Cieza, *Crónica* 33, p. 111.

[44] Cieza, *Crónica* 44, p. 147.

[45] Cieza, *Crónica* 48, p. 159; cf. G. Taylor, "Supay," *Amerindia* 5 (1980): 47–63.

the attire they took with them and accompanied by the women who had entered the tomb with them alive."[46] Further south, in the valley of Ica, a similar situation obtained. For here,

> when the will of God was pleased to give the devil power, it allowed him to adopt the appearance of lords already dead, and to show himself in their very own guise and stature, exactly as they were in the world, with some semblance of servants and adornment. Thus [the devil] led them to suppose that [their lord] lived happily and peaceably in another realm, just as they had seen him here. Therefore the Indians, considering those false appearances to be true, give more care to preparing their tombs and burials than to any other matter.[47]

Likewise, in Huanuco, in the highlands of northern Peru, Cieza heard that as a result of demonic persuasion, women stayed by the side of their deceased husbands; the very thought of their fate appalled him.

> When the lords of these villages died, [the people] did not place them into their graves alone, but had them be escorted by the most beautiful living women. . . . Thus, when [the lords] are dead and their souls outside the body, these women whom they bury [alive] await the dread hour of death, which it is so fearful to endure, in order to join the deceased, having been placed into those great caverns that are their graves. And [the women] consider it to be a great felicity and blessing to go with their husband or lord and believe that soon they will attend to serving him as they have been accustomed to do in this world.

"This custom," Cieza continued, "arises from what I have said on earlier occasions, which is that they see, according to what they say, on their farms and in the sown fields, appearances of the devil, who looks like the lords who have already died, and they are accompanied by their wives and have the objects that were placed in the tomb with them."[48] In the highlands around Lake Titicaca also, the devil walked about in the fields looking just as the dead had done in their lifetime. Accordingly, the Collas "were deceived by the devil . . . with false appearances he made, for by means of his illusions he created an impression of people who had already died, walking through the fields, and it seemed to the Collas that they saw the dead adorned and clothed just as they had been placed in the

---

[46] Cieza, *Crónica* 43, p. 141.

[47] Cieza, *Crónica* 62, p. 194. For a possible American precedent for these notions, see Peter Martyr, *De orbo novo . . . decades* (Alcala, 1530; Graz, 1966), 1.9, fol. xxr: a detailed account of the dead appearing as phantasms and offering to have sexual intercourse with women. "Ast quum ad opus pervenitur, evanescunt," writes the sensible Peter Martyr; but contrast Kramer and Sprenger, *Malleus Maleficarum*, pt. 1, q. 3, pp. 21ff.

[48] Cieza, *Crónica* 80.

tomb."[49] The Collas therefore built for their dead burial towers of masonry infinitely finer than that employed for the houses of the living. When a lord died, the corpse was escorted to the tomb amidst much solemnity, drinking of chicha, and sacrifice of llamas. Some of the women, children, and servants who were to accompany the lord were killed, while others were placed living into the tomb.[50]

The capacity of the devil to create illusions, pictures in the imagination that had no true substance, affected even Christians. At the oracular shrine of Coropona, for instance, Spaniards had seen devils walking about in the guise of an Indian,[51] and Cieza himself had heard the devil respond to Indians in an oracle in the village Bahayre in Cartagena.[52] As for Andeans, Cieza thought, they were doubly vulnerable because they lacked the guidance of revealed religion. Nonetheless, the relationship between the dead and the living that Cieza described as being so regularly spelled out in Andean burial customs can assist us in grasping a crux of Andean thought and conduct. For Cieza was too meticulous an observer to overlook, on his long travels, the specifically Andean perception of the dead as continuing participants in human affairs.

In Cuzco, the mummies of deceased Incas participated in the affairs of the living and invited and toasted each other in the main square. Elsewhere, the dead were remembered as being present in the tomb. In the coastal valleys of Chincha, the dead were placed into burial vaults grouped by lineage, and their clothes were periodically renewed.[53] In Puerto Viejo, Cieza saw shaft graves in which lords were buried with their wives and belongings, and which were constructed in such a way as to allow chicha to be poured through a hollow reed to flow to the deceased for his continued sustenance.[54] In 1621 the priest Hernandez Principe described an Inca tomb of this type in Ocros in the Peruvian central sierra.[55] Here a young woman had been buried alive as capacocha[56] before the advent of the Spaniards and still responded to her people's needs through her priests.[57] Cieza himself noted, as we have seen, that the dead communicated with the living, although he explained the phenomenon as demonic communications.[58]

[49] Cieza, Crónica 101, p. 277.
[50] Cieza, Crónica 100, p. 275; burial towers in Collao with doors facing east, Cieza, Crónica 63, p. 196.
[51] Cieza, Segunda Parte 28.
[52] Cieza, Segunda Parte 41, p. 122.
[53] Cieza, Crónica 63, p. 197.
[54] Cieza, Crónica 51.
[55] Hernández Príncipe, in Duviols, Cultura andina y represión (1986), pp. 471–474.
[56] On capacocha, see below, chap. IV.3 at nn. 116–133; chap. IX.2 at nn. 46–69.
[57] See R. T. Zuidema, "Shaft Tombs," Journal of the Steward Anthropological Society 9 (1977): 133–178.
[58] Cieza, Crónica 62, about the dead of the Yungas; 28, about the dead in Cali.

Tombs were often located in the very fields where the dead were observed walking about, and sometimes the spot was chosen by the deceased while still alive.[59] Just as the living Incas shared their capital city with dead ancestors, so throughout the Andes, the countryside was inhabited by the living and the dead jointly. When Cieza described these countryside burials, he was thinking of the individual tombs of lords whose funerary possessions attracted the attention of treasure-hunting Spaniards, although he also observed that a burial place was at the same time a holy place, huaca,[60] situated "in the mountains, where they go to worship."[61] The full pattern of coexistence and interpenetration between the mundane everyday world of the living and the numinous world of the dead was revealed during ecclesiastical inquiries of the seventeenth century, which showed that all the members of entire lineages, not merely isolated individuals, were buried, generation after generation, in the open country, in the fields and wastelands belonging to each individual's kin group.[62]

Andeans perceived the land differently from Spaniards. It was not merely that the majestic heights of the Andes and the far-flung plains of the lowlands sustained the presence of the living as much as that of the dead. It was also that these heights and plains, and the springs and lakes that demarcated them, were so many pointers to humanity's remote origin from, and identity with, that august environment. Cieza glimpsed something of this Andean perception of the land. In Ayavire he heard that Inca Pachacuti had waged war against the inhabitants, leaving very few of them alive. These survivors "went through the sown fields calling upon their dead ancestors for a long time, and lamented their ruin with groans of profound emotion, and the destruction that had come upon them and their people."[63] A time of terrible change and upheaval was thus also a time to remember ancestors and origins, and thereby to recreate a collective identity.

In many places, collective identity was spelled out in myth and sacred architecture. In Xauxa, the capital of the Guanca people, Cieza was thus shown a spring called Guaribilca. A temple of the same name had been constructed near it; there also were three or four sacred *molle* trees and a place for sacrifice. The spring itself was approached by a stone stairway and enclosed by an ancient tripartite wall. It was oracular and had given

[59] Deceased chooses the spot, Cieza, *Crónica* 43, p. 141, Riobamba; see also Murúa, *Historia* (1590), 1.8, p. 65. For the dead walking about in *sementeras* and *heredades*, cf. above at nn. 44ff. Tombs are in *sementeras* and *heredades*, Cieza, *Crónica* 62, p. 194, Yungas; 98, p. 270, Canas and Canches.

[60] Cieza, *Crónica* 63, p. 197.

[61] Murúa, *Historia* (1590), 1.8, p. 65.

[62] See below, chap. IX.2 at nn. 87ff.

[63] Cieza, *Crónica* 98, pp. 270f.

origin to the man and woman from whom the three lineages or *parciali-dades* of the Guanca people were descended. When the Incas conquered the region, they built a splendid temple of the Sun near this spot. Apparently, their intervention met with resistance, since according to a myth from Cuzco, the creator Tecsi Viracocha converted Guaribilca into stone for rebellion.[64] Another myth, which Cieza was told in Xauxa itself, perhaps refers to the same upheaval of the Inca takeover. Five suns had appeared in the sky, people recounted, which produced such a radiance that all the local deities—whom Cieza described as demons—fled amidst cries of pain and grief, and Guaribilca was never seen again. Nonetheless, the ancient cult to the ancestral spring Guaribilca continued alongside the Inca state cult of the Sun.[65]

When Cieza was traveling to La Paz on the Inca royal road of Colla-suyo, he passed through Urcos in the valley of Cuzco. Nearby was the holy mountain Ausangate, where, as Juan de Betanzos had heard, the creator Contiti Viracocha had stopped at the beginning of time to call forth from within the earth the people who were to live in the place. Later, those people erected a splendid temple, huaca, on top of the mountain where the Creator had sat down.[66] Urcos was one of many other places where the Creator or one of his companions had called forth people from the earth, or from a spring or mountain.[67] Cieza, when in Urcos, was told a different, more regionally specific myth about the origin of the people there, a myth that explains particularly clearly the bonding Andeans felt with the land that had raised them. "In times past," he wrote, the people of Urcos

> greatly venerated a temple that they called Auzancata. Near it, they say, their ancestors saw an idol or demon whose appearance and dress was like their own, and with whom they held converse, offering sacrifices according to their custom. And these Indians tell that in times past they were convinced that souls that left the body went to a great lake . . . which was their place of origin, and from there the souls entered the bodies of those who were being born. Later, when the Incas ruled over them, they became more polished and intelligent and adored the Sun, although they did not forget to revere their ancient temple.[68]

[64] Cristóbal de Molina, *Fábulas*, p. 53.
[65] Cieza, *Crónica* 84.
[66] Betanzos, *Suma* (1987), 1.2, p. 14b.
[67] Betanzos, *Suma* 1.2.
[68] Cieza, *Crónica* 97; on Apu Ausangate now, see B. Condori and R. Gow, *Kay Pacha*, pp. 43ff. Sallnow, *Pilgrims of the Andes*, p. 35, citing Santacruz Pachacuti on comets emerging from Asoncata. On Ausangate and the pilgrimage of Qoyllur Rit'i, Sallnow, *Pilgrims*, pp. 79, 91f., 129f., 183, 211ff. See also below, sec. 2 at n. 77 for Viracocha's golden seat.

1. DIVINATION AND THE DEAD

What distinguishes this myth from many others of its kind is the theme of the lake as the place whence the people of Urcos first came and also the place to which their souls returned at death and whence again they set forth for a new life. For the idea that the same place constitutes both beginning and end, origin and destiny, was merely hinted at in other Andean myths.[69]

Throughout the Andes, people thought their ancestors had sprung from the land itself, from mountain or rock, lake or spring. A place of origin, often described as *pacarina*, from *pacari*, "dawn,"[70] and *paccarini*, "to be born,"[71] was a point fixed in the environment, where geographical space and human time intersected. This was made clear in the early seventeenth century by the Andean nobleman Joan Santacruz Pachacuti Yamqui, who recorded one of several myths about the origin of the Incas. The deity Tunupa gave his staff of sovereignty to Apo Tampo, the "Lord Place of Sojourn," or "Lord Inn,"[72] who was to become the father of the first Inca. An explanatory note written into the margin of the manuscript by a seventeenth-century Quechua scholar states, "This Apo Tampo is Paccarectampo," a term that translates as "Inn of the Dawn."[73] Paccarectampo in turn was the place not far from Cuzco whence the Incas came forth. To be buried in the open country in the way that Cieza described thus meant in some general sense to return to one's origin. However, since tombs were located on land belonging to one's kin group, this return could also be conceptualized as specific and concrete. Places of origin, like the dead, were recipients of offerings for the increase of crops, animals, and humans. Ritual action spelled out the connection between a kin group, beginning with its first ancestors and proceeding down to its living members on the one hand, and that kin group's means of sustenance in the land on the other. To make sacrifice to the dead thus amounted to making sacrifice to the land, to a pacarina, and the success of the harvest depended on such sacrifices.[74]

The relationships Andeans perceived between life and death, and between humanity and the natural environment were profoundly different from their Spanish and Christian equivalents. The land surrounding the

[69] See Montesinos, *Memorias antiguas historiales* (1882), pp. 82–83, who describes how a pre-Inca king was buried and his boy successor inaugurated at Tambotocco, for "if fortune were to persecute the child king, they could seclude and hide him in that cave [of Tambotocco] as in a shrine."

[70] Domingo de Santo Tomás, *Lexicon*, p. 158.

[71] Gonzalez Holguin, *Vocabulario de la lengua general*, p. 267; see also Szeminski, *Un kuraka* (1987), pp. 99f.

[72] Gonzalez Holguin, *Vocabulario de la lengua general*, p. 337.

[73] Pachacuti Yamqui, *Relación de antiguedades*, ed. Jiménez de la Espada, p. 266, note by Avila; see also Cristóbal de Albornoz, *Instrucción*, p. 169. On Paccarectampo as a place, see G. Urton, *History of a Myth* (1990).

[74] Cf. below, chap. IX.2 at n. 113.

people of the Andes told the story of their first ancestors as much as it told their own story and the story of those yet to come. It was right that the familiar dead were seen walking through the fields they had once cultivated, thus sharing them with both the living and with the original ancestors who had raised the first crops in the very same fields.[75]

The cleric who described the last solemn celebration of the maize harvest in Cuzco in 1535 also understood something of these Andean relationships between mankind and nature. The Sun, he explained, had given a mother to all things; even the earth had a mother. So did the maize and other crops and animals. Vinegar was the mother of chicha and water the mother of vinegar, and the sea had a mother who was called Mamacocha. Nuggets of gold were tears that the Sun wept, and as such—that is, as somehow sacred—were offered to the Sun. Similarly, deceased lords were buried with attendants and possessions and were worshiped as "fathers from whom the lineage had come forth."[76] Death was therefore the great leveler not because, as in Christian thought, it reduced all human beings to equality in relation to each other and before god. Rather, death was a leveler because by means of it humans were reintegrated into a network of parents and offsprings that embraced the entire natural order.

Cieza looked at this order of things with a certain puzzlement, because he thought Andean religious ideas, diverse, contradictory, and demonically inspired as they appeared to him, were out of step with Andean political and economic achievements, which he greatly admired. However, the Incas had imposed a certain regularity, dignity, and predictability on this vast diversity of belief and practice. A parallel change had taken place in the development of Andean political forms. Cieza produced a penetrating analysis of the functioning of stateless societies beyond the frontiers of the Inca empire,[77] where, as he understood it, religious observance centered around the dead of a given social group and accordingly varied from one region to the next. But in Inca lands, as Cieza saw it, religion had become unitary and more rational, in that regional cults of the dead had in part been superseded by the Inca state cult of the divine Sun.

2. Cuzco, the Ruling City

The importance of the Sun in Inca religion was evident even to the first invaders, preoccupied though they were with warfare and looting. "In each settlement," Pizarro's secretary, Francisco de Xerez, had observed,

[75] Cf. *Runa yndio*, ed. Urioste, secs. 356, 389, 394, 403, 446, for Yawri Llancha as a place of origin and return.
[76] Bartolomé de Segovia, *Relación de muchas cosas*, p. 76a.
[77] See Salomon, *Lords of Quito* (1986), pp. 21ff.

"they make their mosques to the Sun."[1] Another of the invaders noted that the cult of the Sun was particularly prevalent in the central Andean highlands, and that the ruling Inca was known as "Son of the Sun."[2] In Cuzco, the sheer splendor of Coricancha and the ceremonious dignity of those of the city's daily rituals and seasonal festivals that were still being observed when the invaders began to settle there impressed them with the central role of the Sun in the Inca state cult. But it was only toward midcentury that Cieza, Betanzos, and others began to reflect on the cult of the Sun in any detail.

Cieza described this cult in terms of the religious organization of the empire, where Coricancha stood at the center of a far-flung network of solar shrines in Inca provincial capitals. At the same time, the cult of the Sun in Cieza's eyes constituted evidence of a more advanced religious rationality than he had observed among Andean peoples other than the Incas.

Throughout his extensive travels, Cieza collected information on the temples that the Incas had erected to the divine Sun, their vast apparatus of sacred buildings and storehouses along with their staff of chosen women, artisans, and religious specialists. The solar temple of Vilcas, he thought, had been serviced by forty thousand individuals, forty of whom were gatekeepers,[3] while the less important temple of Xauxa still had a staff of eight thousand.[4] These and many other Inca foundations[5] served to establish the Inca solar cult alongside preexisting regional cults, which local people continued to observe.[6] The model for all these temples was Coricancha, which, so Cieza learned, had originally been the dwelling place of Manco Capac, the mythic founder of the Inca dynasty, and was converted into the "House of the Sun" by the ninth Inca.[7]

Like all Spaniards, Cieza was an admirer of Inca architecture, but when it came to describing Coricancha, words somehow failed him. After hesitantly comparing Coricancha to the Torre de Calahorra of Cordoba and to the Tavera Hospital, which he had seen while passing through Toledo in 1552, he mentioned the temple's treasures and adornments, including its garden containing maize and llamas, with their herders carrying slings

---

[1] Xerez, *Verdadera relación*, p. 104.

[2] [Estete], *Noticia*, p. 52.

[3] Cieza, *Crónica* 89, p. 253; cf. Pedro de Carbajal, *Descripción fecha de la provincia de Vilcas Guaman . . . 1586*, in *Relaciones geograficas de Indias*, vol. 1, ed. Jiménez de la Espada, Biblioteca de autores españoles, vol. 183, p. 218.

[4] Cieza, *Crónica* 84.

[5] Cieza, *Crónica* 72, 80, 103, etc. Cf. C. Morris, "Establecimientos estatales en el Tawantinsuyu: una estrategia de urbanismo obligado," *Revista del Museo Nacional* 39 (1973): 127–141; C. Morris and D. Thompson, *Huanuco Pampa* (1985).

[6] Cf. Cieza, *Segunda Parte* 41, pp. 122f., Incas consult oracle regarding Cari and Capana.

[7] Cieza, *Segunda Parte* 8, 27.

and shepherd's crooks all made of gold[8]—but these things were a memory only by the time Cieza reached Cuzco in 1549.

Nonetheless, Cieza was able to interview some of the old Incas who were still living in Cuzco,[9] and from their statements he correlated some aspects of Inca religious observance with Inca myth. Cieza and Betanzos were the first to record continuous renderings of myths of creation and origin as told in Cuzco. In Andean eyes, the two themes—the creation of the world and the origin of the Incas, or the origin of human beings in a given place—went hand in hand. The myths we have of Inca origins are thus all prefaced by a myth of creation.

Before launching on his account of Andean beginnings, Cieza defined the chronological boundaries of his statements according to the norms of European sacred and secular history. Sacred history applied in particular to accounts of creation and the origin of mankind. Here, Catholic chronology required that Andean origins be dated to some time after the flood in which, according to the book of Genesis, all mankind except Noah and his kin were destroyed.[10] Andean accounts of inundations and cataclysms, Cieza thought, must therefore refer not to Noah's flood but to "some lesser flood in these lands, like that of Thessaly."[11] As for the rise of the Incas as told in myth, Cieza recounted it within an evolutionary sequence, although in the absence of writing in the Andes,[12] he could supply no exact dates. As Cieza understood it, before the Incas the people of the Andes lived as a rulerless crowd, without fixed government and social order, in what Spaniards called *behetrías*.[13] The rise of the Incas therefore marked the Andean transition from chaos to culture.

Long before the Incas ruled, Cieza was told by his informants in Cuzco, the world was dark, so that people prayed for light until the sun rose over Lake Titicaca. A tall, white man came from the South, making plains into mountains and mountains into plains and causing springs to flow from rocks. He went toward the North, teaching people to live in harmony, and was called Ticsiviracocha, "Beginning of all things, Father of the Sun." Another such man then came, who healed the sick and made the blind see by his word alone. But in Cacha, in the Vilcanota valley south of Cuzco, people despised him and were about to stone him to death when fire fell from heaven, causing them to repent. The man then went away as far as the sea in the West and spreading out his cloak, disappeared

---

[8] Cieza, *Segunda Parte* 27, p. 81.

[9] Cieza, *Segunda Parte* 6.

[10] Cf. Don Cameron Allen, *The Legend of Noah* (1949).

[11] Cieza, *Segunda Parte* 3, p. 4. Regarding the flood of Thessaly, Cieza perhaps informed himself from Diodorus Siculus, whom he mentions; see Diodorus, *Library of History*, ed. and transl. C. H. Oldfather (Cambridge, 1954), 1.10; 3.62, 10. A more popular author in Cieza's day, Ovid, *Metamorphoses* 1, 261ff., tells the story in a mythological vein.

[12] Cf. Cieza, *Segunda Parte* 9, p. 23.

[13] See Covarrubias Horozco, *Tesoro*, s.v. behetria; Cieza, *Segunda Parte* 4, p. 6.

amid the waves. Hence, he was called Viracocha, which Cieza translated as "foam of the sea," and a splendid temple was built for him at Cacha.[14]

In Cuzco, Cieza learned that the first Incas were three brothers and their three sisters who had emerged from a cave in nearby Pacaritambo, the "House of Coming Forth,"[15] whence they set out to find a place in which to settle. One of the brothers, Ayar Cache, aroused his siblings' envy by his daring. They sent him back to the cave under pretence of needing certain gold implements that had been left behind there, and then barred the mouth of the cave, thus burying him inside. Journeying on, they encountered Ayar Cache flying in the air on wings of many-colored feathers, urging them to descend lower into the valley and to settle in Cuzco. He instructed them to worship him under the name of the nearby sacred rock of Guanacaure and promised that he in return would guide their future destiny. Ayar Cache then made known the rituals of initiating young men into adulthood and of inaugurating the Inca sovereign. Having finished speaking, he and Ayar Uchu, one of the other brothers,[16] turned into stone, while the third brother, Ayar Manco, henceforth to be known as Manco Capac, "king and wealthy lord," journeyed on to Cuzco with the women. On arrival, he prayed to the Sun and to his brother at Guanacaure and then settled peaceably among the people who were already living in the valley. His first abode was "a small house of stone roofed with thatch that they called Coricancha, which means 'enclosure of gold.' "[17] When Manco Capac died and his death had been mourned, his son Sinchi Roca was inaugurated "with the customary ceremonies"[18] of marrying his sister,[19] fasting in seclusion, and then receiving the imperial headband in Coricancha (cf. fig. 12).[20]

Cieza felt discontented with these accounts of creation and Inca origins that he had so laboriously patched together from what his informants in Cuzco told him. Just before concluding the story, he thus observed: "I have laughed at what I have written about these Indians. I tell in my writing what they told me in theirs"—they were reading from quipus[21]—"and rather than adding a single thing, I have omitted much."[22]

[14] Cieza, *Segunda Parte* 5. The name of the deity Viracocha occasioned much perplexity during the sixteenth and seventeenth centuries. See further below n. 72 and chap. VIII.2, with n. 9.

[15] The translation is Cieza's. For a synoptic account of different versions of the Inca myth of origins, see Urton, *History of a Myth*, pp. 13–14, 18–22.

[16] For Ayar Uchu, see below, chap. IV.I, n. 18.

[17] Cieza, *Segunda Parte* 8, p. 21; 27, p. 79.

[18] Cieza, *Segunda Parte* 31, p. 94.

[19] Cieza, *Segunda Parte* 7, p. 19, with 31, p. 95.

[20] Cieza, *Segunda Parte* 7, pp. 19–20. The ceremonies of an Inca's inauguration are discussed in more detail below, chap. III.2.

[21] The term is Quechua, and describes the knotted cords used by the Incas for recording information.

[22] Cieza, *Segunda Parte* 8, p. 21.

By way of making some sense of the myth, Cieza placed it, as best he could, into a historical context. It was not only in Cuzco but elsewhere in the Andes that Cieza heard how, in some remote past, a warlord had gathered the people of the place under his sway, thereby creating an ordered society where before only behetrías had existed. At Hatuncolla on Lake Titicaca, "a most valiant lord called Çapana" established his sovereignty,[23] while another lord, Cari, ruled in nearby Chucuito.[24] The rise of Manco Capac in Cuzco followed the same pattern, for until he brought social and political order to the region, "the people were living in confusion, were killing each other, and were enveloped in their vices."[25]

Having once established themselves, it was natural, Cieza thought, that the Incas should "magnify their origin"[26] and lay claim not only to exalted deeds but also to a certain superhuman status. It was for this reason that Manco Capac, like all his successors, claimed to be a son of the Sun,[27] and that he prayed to the Sun and founded the new city of Cuzco in the name of the creator "Ticsiviracocha and of the Sun and of his other gods."[28] As Cieza understood it, the Inca solar cult extended back to the very beginning of Inca history. But the imperial elaboration of that cult was the work of the ninth Inca, Yupanqui. For it was under his patronage that Coricancha, the edifice with all its adornments that Cieza so much admired, was erected and that Inca dominion expanded far beyond the region of Cuzco.[29]

Thanks to his extended travels and unceasing inquiry, Cieza could describe certain aspects of the network of religious, economic, and political relationships that extended throughout the Andes and of which Coricancha was a focal point. These relationships found expression both in the festival cycle of the Inca empire and in Andean sacred topography as reformulated by the Incas.

Cieza placed Inti Raimi, the celebration of harvest and plowing, into a wider context of Inca myth, ritual, and belief than the cleric who watched this festival in 1535 had been able to do.[30] Much had changed in Cuzco

---

[23] Cieza, *Segunda Parte* 4, pp. 6f.; 6, p. 15. On this Çapana's descendant, see Cieza, *Segunda Parte* 41, p. 121.

[24] Cieza, *Segunda Parte* 4, p. 7; cf. chaps. 41–43.

[25] Cieza, *Segunda Parte* 6, p. 13.

[26] Cieza, *Segunda Parte* 6, p. 13.

[27] Cieza, *Segunda Parte* 6, p. 15.

[28] Cieza, *Segunda Parte* 8, p. 21.

[29] Cieza, *Segunda Parte* 27, pp. 79ff.

[30] There is little agreement in the sources about the names of Inca festivals and about the names of the months in which they were celebrated. Cieza, *Segunda Parte* 30, p. 90, described Hatun Raimi, "Solemn Celebration," as a thanksgiving for the harvest, when "se avían de rendir graçias y loores al gran Dios Hazedor . . por les aver dado buen año de cosechas." On the other hand, he thought the festival marked the time of plowing, p. 93. Bartolomé de Segovia described the harvest thanksgiving he witnessed in May as "gracias al Sol por la cosecha," *Relación de muchas cosas*, p. 81b. Molina, *Fábulas*, pp. 67, 68, described the festival celebrated in May as Intip Raimi, "Festival of the Sun," its purpose being to keep

during the intervening fifteen years, as is evident from Cieza's description of the celebration: "I remember how, when I was in Cuzco in August 1550, the Indians and their wives, having gathered the harvest, entered the city and created a great uproar. They were carrying digging sticks and maize straw and made merry, singing and saying how in the past they used to celebrate their harvests."[31] Although the festival's ancient splendor had fallen prey to the invaders' greed and their missionary zeal, Cieza pieced together some elements of the ritual as observed before the invasion. The month of August, when Cieza saw Indians entering the city carrying their digging sticks, was the time of plowing.[32] In Inca times, this phase of the festival had begun with a fast of ten or twelve days, followed by sacrifice and feasting. Next, all gathered in Haucaypata after midday to sing the "ballads and carols that had been composed for such occasions by their ancestors in thanksgiving to their gods." In the center of the square the image of the creator Ticsiviracocha was displayed on cloth of feathers, adorned with gold and precious stones. Before this image, the Inca and the nobles of Cuzco, followed by the common people, would take off their sandals and perform the customary gestures of worship. Next to the Creator were arrayed the images of the Sun and Moon and of other gods, along with the mummies of the deceased Incas.[33] These sacred personages were the principal protagonists in Inca cosmology and history as outlined in the myths of creation and Inca origins that Cieza recorded. Their presence in the celebration of harvest and plowing validated the Inca past and projected it onto the present, thereby helping to perpetuate the imperial order of things.

The political dimension of the religion of the Incas stood out particularly clearly when, every year, the most renowned oracular huacas of the empire visited the city of Cuzco.[34] Among them were Guanacaure, Vilcanota from twenty-six leagues east of Cuzco, where "the Sun was born,"[35] Ancocagua, Coropona, Apurimac, and Pachacamac.[36] As subsequent inquiries revealed, the visit of these eminent huacas to Cuzco

---

the Sun young. But his name for the month of May suggests the activity of breaking the earth; see note 32 by Urbano and Duviols in Molina, *Fábulas*, p. 66. Molina, *Fábulas*, p. 118, placed the harvest itself in April, which month he called Ayriguay. Polo de Ondegardo placed it in May and called the month Hatuncuzqui Aymoray. According to Polo, the "fiesta del Sol," or Inti Raymi, took place in the month of June, Aucay Cuzqui; see Polo, *Errores* 8, fol. 10v. See further, M. S. Ziolkowski, "El calendario metropolitano Inca," in *Time and Calendars in the Inca Empire*, ed. M. S. Ziolkowski and R. M. Sadowski (Oxford, 1989).

[31] Cieza, *Segunda Parte* 30.

[32] See Guaman Poma de Ayala, *Nueva Crónica*, p. 250 [252], but note divergences in Molina, *Fábulas*, p. 73, and Polo, *Errores*, fol. 10v.

[33] Cieza, *Segunda Parte* 30.

[34] Cieza, *Segunda Parte* 29; see further below, chap. IV.3 at nn. 96ff.

[35] Molina, *Fábulas*, p. 69; see further below, chap. IV.2 at n. 46.

[36] Cieza, *Segunda Parte* 28; note especially p. 84, on a capacocha sacrifice being offered to Vilcanota every year, showing that this huaca was included among those which undertook the pilgrimage to Cuzco every year; see *Segunda Parte* 29, p. 89.

took place between August and September as part of the purificatory festival of Citua.[37] Cieza was told how the huacas, accompanied by their priests, were solemnly received by the Inca and his court and were displayed in Haucaypata. They were then questioned individually about events of the coming year: war and peace, the harvest, and the Inca's well-being. Once the questions had been weighed and considered, and sacrifices had been made, the priests who spoke on behalf of each huaca responded. The following year, the huacas who had prophesied truthfully were rewarded by the Inca with offerings of gold and silver objects, textiles, and llamas, which were sent to the relevant shrines in a solemn procession known as *capacocha*, "imperial obligation."[38] The huacas who had been mistaken, on the other hand, "received no offering, but rather lost reputation."[39]

A carefully balanced system of patronage and censure of provincial shrines thus placed the Inca rulers in their capital city at the hub of Andean sacred space.[40] At the same time, the mobilization of Andean oracles for Inca purposes spelled out that sacred space was tantamount to economic and political space. It was the Inca who commanded the huacas to come to Cuzco from distant parts, and it was the Inca who rewarded or censured the huacas' prophetic statements. Yet periodic conflicts between Inca rulers and regional oracular huacas made clear that the Inca's power over the empire's huacas depended on the successful manipulation both of opinion[41] and of the redistributive functions of the Inca state.[42]

Cieza was the first Spaniard to list a set of major Inca shrines, mostly in the region of Cuzco, in all of which, as in Coricancha, human sacrifice was offered and "the devil was seen and gave answers."[43] In Cieza's mind, these two issues, the human sacrifices made by the Incas and the oracular responses they received at their principal shrines, were connected, just as oracular responses and demonic appearances were connected with the custom observed throughout the Andes of burying women and servants along with their deceased lords. But in the second volume of his history of Peru, which deals with the Incas, there is a subtle shift in attitude as Cieza comes to discuss Inca human sacrifice. In his first volume, Cieza had described many Andean funerary customs, including the burial of

[37] Molina, *Fábulas*, p. 73; the ceremony Cieza described, *Fábulas*, pp. 94f.; cf. below, chap. IV.3 at nn. 91ff.

[38] For translation of the term, see Gonzalez Holguin, *Vocabulario de la lengua general*, pp. 199–200, s.v. Qquelcca huchayachac; huchachani . . . ; huchachapayani, etc., with G. Taylor, *Runa yndio* (1987), pp. 29–30. See further below, chap. IV.3, n. 115.

[39] Cieza, *Segunda Parte* 29.

[40] Cf. below, chap. VII.1 at nn. 37ff. for a memory of this ceremonial in the early seventeenth century.

[41] Cf. above, chap. II.2 at nn. 56ff.

[42] See J. V. Murra, *The Economic Organization of the Inca State* (Greenwich, Conn., 1980), chap. 6.

[43] Cieza, *Segunda Parte* 27, 28.

living human beings, as being still current, or current within very recent memory. The human sacrifices of the Incas, by contrast, were a matter of past history, and to describe them did not inevitably entail the obligation of making an ethical judgment regarding the rights and wrongs of such sacrifice.[44] Where thus Cieza abhorred the custom of burying the living with the dead, when it came to Inca human sacrifice, he was ready to reproduce the ideas of those of his Inca informants who described their lost world as coherent and intelligible, without applying a Christian perspective to what he learned.

Among the huacas to receive human sacrifice, which the Incas described by the same term, *capacocha*, which they used for the processions of imperial gifts to veridical prophetic huacas,[45] Guanacaure was one of the foremost. For it was here that Ayar Cache dwelt in the form of a stone, so as to be a beneficent presence and oracle for the lords of Cuzco.[46] Cieza therefore selected Guanacaure as representative of the huacas that were honored by the sacrifice of human lives and described the ritual as it was performed there, apparently during the annual visit of prophetic huacas to Cuzco. This was one of several imperial occasions when human sacrifice was offered to important huacas.[47] The males who had been chosen to die wore their finest attire, and having listened to a discourse by the officiating priests, drank chicha from golden cups. They then

> solemnized their sacrifice with songs declaring that to serve their gods they offered their lives in this manner, and considered it happiness to exchange life for death. And having grieved in this way, they were killed by the priests . . . [who] buried them in their graves all around the oracle. And these they regarded as canonized saints, believing firmly that they were in heaven serving their Guanacaure.[48]

An analogous ritual was observed for sacrificing women, both at Guanacaure and at the other great shrines of the Inca empire that gave oracles.[49]

By describing the capacocha offered to Guanacaure in its mythic and ritual context, and by outlining themes of the official indoctrination of

[44] Francisco de Vitoria considered human sacrifice a ground for war against Indians; see his *Relectio de indis*, pt. 3, pp. 101–116.

[45] Cieza, *Segunda Parte* 29, p. 89; cf. Hernández Principe in *Cultura andina y represión*, ed. Duviols (1976), pp. 471–474 about a girl sacrificed as capacocha in Ocros; cf. below, chap. IX.2 at nn. 48ff.

[46] Cieza, *Segunda Parte* 7, p. 16. Cf. Betanzos, *Suma* (1987), 1.4, p. 19; Sarmiento, *Historia Indica* 12, p. 216.

[47] See Sarmiento, *Historia Indica* 13, p. 217b, human sacrifice for initiation of young men; 40, p. 245b, for victory; 31, p. 237a, in general. See further below, chap. IV.3 at nn. 116ff.

[48] Cieza, *Segunda Parte* 28, pp. 83f. Cf. Betanzos, *Suma* (1987), 1.31, p. 145a, celebration of an Inca's funeral, who, like Cieza's victims for human sacrifice, "es casi canonizable como a santo."

[49] Cieza, *Segunda Parte* 28, p. 84.

victims, Cieza conveyed something of what the sacrifice may have meant in Inca eyes. Elsewhere he used his reading of Greek and Roman authors to render the Incas intelligible by comparing their achievements to those of classical antiquity. About the celebration of harvest and plowing in Cuzco he thus wrote: "Let the reader believe that I am convinced that neither in Jerusalem, Rome, or Persia, nor in any other part of the world, did republic or king ever join in one place such wealth of gold, silver, and precious stones as was brought together in this square of Cuzco when this festival and other similar ones were celebrated."[50] Other comparisons involved Christian themes, as when Cieza observed that only noble and good Inca rulers, "compassionate toward Indians and generous in granting favors," were honored as mummies: "These their blindness canonized as saints, and they honored their bones without understanding that their souls burn in hell, but instead believed that they were in heaven."[51] Just as Castañega had compared the sacraments of the church to the "execraments" of magicians and false priests,[52] so Cieza here compared saints and mummies. While in theological terms, mummies were to be abhorred, in conceptual terms, the comparison between mummies and saints allowed Cieza to move a little closer to Andean reality.

Throughout his long work, Cieza struggled to evaluate the religious achievement of the Incas. Catholic theology as formulated both in Spain and, for the most part, in the Americas, dictated that Indian souls did indeed burn in hell. But that was not the whole story. For, like some of his contemporaries, Cieza found that the terminology of the pagan religions of European classical antiquity was somehow applicable to the Incas. Like those gentiles of the ancient Mediterranean, therefore, the Incas during Hatun Raimi and at other times used rites of divination.[53] For instance, when founding Cuzco, the mythic first Inca Manco Capac, had looked for favorable omens:

> Turning his eyes toward the hill Guanacaure, he prayed for favor to his brother, whom he already revered as divine, and looked to the flight of birds and the signs of the stars and other auspicious prodigies.[54]

Guanacaure was indeed oracular, but the observation of "the flight of birds" was a Greek and Roman, not an Inca, means of divination, which Cieza probably read about in an ancient historian such as Diodorus Sicu-

[50] Cieza, Segunda Parte 30, p. 92. For the prevalence of examples from ancient history in writings about the Americas, see J. González, La idea de Roma (1981).
[51] Cieza, Segunda Parte 30, p. 92; see also Segunda Parte 11.
[52] See above, chap. 1.2 at n. 63.
[53] Cieza, Segunda Parte 30.
[54] Cieza, Segunda Parte 9.

lus whom he mentioned in his general preface, and transferred to the In-cas. Elsewhere also, classical antiquity guided Cieza's perception of the Incas, who, he believed, had imposed more elevated forms of worship on their subjects. Thus, the Cañari

> regarded the Sun as sovereign deity. They believed the same as oth-ers, to wit, that there is a maker of all created things, whom in the language of Cuzco they call Ticibiracoche. And although they had this understanding, formerly they adored trees and rocks, the moon and other things.[55]

As for the Incas themselves:

> They set great store by the immortality of the soul . . . They be-lieved in a Creator of things, and the Sun they regarded as sovereign deity, building great temples to him. And deceived by the devil, they adored trees and rocks, like the gentiles. In their principal temples they had many beautiful virgins, like those in the temple of Vesta in Rome, and the laws they observed were almost identical.[56]

In short, although the Incas never achieved complete clarity in their con-cept of deity, their progress in this matter resembled the religious evolu-tion of the ancient Mediterranean. Cieza thus recalled having read "in many histories, if I am not mistaken," that people used to adore bulls, cocks, and lions. Even the Greeks, although "excellent men, among whom letters flourished for a long time," fell into this error, along with the Egyptians, Bactrians, and Babylonians, and even the Romans. How-ever, the ancient gentiles also took to adoring as divine their benefactors, "such as Saturn or Jupiter or another individual of this kind, so that now it was men who became divine, not animals."[57] Similarly the Incas adored the sun and moon, which stood far above plants and animals in the hier-archy of being, but nonetheless did not give up the lower cults "which the imagination suggested to them."[58]

With respect to politics, Cieza described his journey southward from Panama as an itinerary leading from diverse behetrías to the ordered mon-archy of the Incas, while in religious terms he witnessed a shift from the

---

[55] Cieza, *Crónica* 43, p. 142.

[56] Cieza, *Crónica* 38, p. 124.

[57] For the worship of benefactors according to the Hellenistic philosopher-historian Eu-hemerus, see the fragments from his works assembled in Diodorus Siculus, *Library of His-tory*, ed. and trans. C. H. Oldfather (Cambridge, Mass., 1939), bk. 6, especially 1.8–10. Cieza could have encountered these fragments in the *Praeparatio Evangelica* of Eusebius; see F. Jacoby, *Die Fragmente der griechischen Historiker*, vol. 1, pt. A (Leiden, 1957), no. 63, pp. 302f. Another author popular in the sixteenth century who dealt with this issue was the early Christian apologist Lactantius; see his *Institutes* 1.

[58] Cieza, *Crónica* 50.

worship of the lowliest aspects of creation to the worship of the sun, the most exalted of all God's creatures. Cieza's long journey thus took him, as he viewed it, through ascending cultural stages that had first been mapped in the history of the ancient Mediterranean, until he reached Cuzco. He perceived in the Andes what was intelligible within the framework of this trajectory and ordered his data in harmony with it.

Cieza's contemporary Juan de Betanzos, by contrast, perceived in his own peninsular culture few guidelines whereby to understand the Inca past.[59] He had been a resident of Cuzco for some years by the time he began composing his *Suma y narración de los Incas*,[60] for which the principal informants were the kinsfolk of his wife, Doña Angelina Cusirimay. His work's Cuzco-centered perspective, favorable to Atahualpa and hostile to Guascar, reflects their memories, interests, and preoccupations. Possibly it even reflects their actual words, in that Betanzos regarded himself as a translator only, whose task it was to "preserve the manner and order of the Indians' speech."[61]

Like Cieza, Betanzos began his account of the Incas with the paired myths of Andean creation and Inca origins. But where Cieza endeavored to contextualize the myths by locating them within Biblical chronology and within a Spanish model of the evolution of society, Betanzos recounted them without such a framework,[62] and true to his promise, retained a good many Quechua turns of phrase in his Spanish version. For example, Betanzos interspersed his text with the refrain "they say," not because, like Cieza, he sought to distance himself from his narrative, but because Quechua speaking storytellers used this refrain to highlight that the narrative in question was not a private invention.[63] Another Quechua expression used in mythic narratives which Betanzos retained was "in the ancient times," *ñaupa pacha*.[64] Betanzos' faithfulness to his informants was a matter not only of idiom but also of substance. He thus told how, in the ancient times, the creator Conticiviracocha made "the sun and the day," and this is exactly what his informants are likely to have said, because in the later seventeenth century, Andean people still spoke of Sun and Day, Inti and Punchao, as a complementary unit.[65]

---

[59] Betanzos' reference to Merlin, a figure of knightly romance, at *Suma* (1987), 1.5, p. 21b is merely incidental.

[60] The title can be translated as "Complete Account of the Incas."

[61] Betanzos, *Suma*, Preface.

[62] On the historicity—or lack thereof—of accounts of Inca origins recorded by sixteenth-century Spaniards, cf. below, chap. III.3, n. 1.

[63] "Dicen" is the phrase Betanzos used; cf. *Runa yndio*, ed. Taylor, 1.1, ñiscas and 6.46, ñispa.

[64] Betanzos, *Suma* (1987), 1.1, p. 11a; *Runa yndio*, ed. Taylor, 1.1, 7.6, etc.

[65] Betanzos, *Suma* (1987), 1.1, p. 11a and b; Duviols, *Cultura andina y represión* (1986), pp. 89, 91, Sol llamado Punchao; cf. p. 66. Elsewhere, similar parallelisms are applied to other figures in the divine universe. See Santacruz Pachacuti Yamqui, *Relación*, fol. 9v = p. 248 in

But even though Betanzos reproduced the phrasing and some of the ideas of his informants much more closely than did other Spaniards at this time, he found Inca and Andean concepts of god and creation confusing.[66] In the myths of origin he heard, the Creator figured both as one individual deity, called either Contiti Viracocha[67] or simply Viracocha,[68] and as a group of originating deities, who were described in the plural as "Viracochas,"[69] or else as Contiti Viracocha's "people."[70] Apparently, Betanzos did not perceive any connection between this plurality of originating deities and the different ethnic groups of the Andes, each of which had its own place of origin.[71] Such a connection would have rendered the plurality of Viracochas of whom Betanzos was told more intelligible. Nonetheless, he listened to the myths carefully and wrote them down without imposing on them the fixed and defined characteristics of the Judeo-Christian god.[72]

People who lived in the ancient times, Betanzos recounted, when there was no light, served some other lord. Next, at Tiahuanaco, the Maker Contiti Viracocha made the sun and the day, the moon and stars, and turned those earlier people to stone for having offended him. Out of stone he made different kinds of people, with lords to rule over them, with pregnant women, and babies in cradles.[73] His attendants, the Viracochas who were with him, distributed these people to caves and rivers, springs and mountains in the different parts of Peru, and then called them to come forth to inhabit the land.[74] Finally, Contiti Viracocha sent two further Viracochas, one to Condesuyo and the other to Antisuyo, while he himself went on the royal road toward Cuzco calling the people out of the earth.[75]

Jiménez de la Espada's ed.: the aged Manco Capac calls on Viracocha on behalf of his son, mentioning "intica quillaca ppunchaoca tutaca" (sun, moon, day, night); Molina, *Fábulas*, p. 67, statue of "Punchao ynca, que era el Sol"; cf. p. 91, prayer to "Punchao ynca inti yayay." See Rowe, "Eleven Inca Prayers" *Kroeber Anthropological Society Papers* 8–9 (1953), no. 10, p. 93, with comments on these words.

[66] See Betanzos, *Suma* (1987), I.11, p. 49, wondering whether the creator is the Sun or Viracocha. Cf. Rowe, "The Origins of Creator Worship," in *Essays in Honor of Paul Radin* (1960), pp. 408–429; F. Pease, *El dios creador andino* (1973).

[67] Betanzos, *Suma* (1987), I, p. 11a, etc.

[68] Betanzos, *Suma* (1987), I, p. 11b; 2, p. 13a, el Viracocha en Tiaguanaco; p. 14a, Viracocha. See Szeminski, *Un Kuraca*, pp. 12ff.

[69] Betanzos, *Suma* (1987), I.2, p. 13, estos viracochas.

[70] Betanzos, *Suma* (1987), I.1, p. 11a, cierto numero de gente; los suyos.

[71] Cf. above, chap. III.1 at nn. 70ff.

[72] Cf. P. Duviols, "Los nombres Quechua de Viracocha, supuesto 'Dios Creador' de los evangelizadores," *Allpanchis* (Cuzco) 10 (1977): 53–74; Betanzos, *Suma* (1968), I.11, p. 31b, mentions the Sun in the volcano of Arequipa, a notion that could not be assimilated to Spanish concepts of deity.

[73] Betanzos, *Suma* (1987), I.1, p. 11b.

[74] Betanzos, *Suma* (1987), I.1–2, pp. 12a–13a.

[75] Betanzos, *Suma* (1987), I.2, p. 13ab.

The myth now shifts its focus to the region of Cuzco and its Viracocha, who was identical with Contiti Viracocha from Tiahuanaco. At Cacha in the valley of Cuzco, the Cana people, who emerged from the earth armed, attacked Contiti Viracocha until fire fell from heaven. But later they built a temple for their Maker.[76] Continuing thence to Urcos, Contiti Viracocha called people forth from a high mountain, where later a golden seat was placed, with his statue on it.[77] In Cuzco, Viracocha made a lord, Alcabicca, and left word that later there should be *orejones*, Incas. Finally, he went North to Puerto Viejo where he rejoined his own people and vanished away over the sea.[78]

In the ancient times before there were Incas, Betanzos was told, Cuzco was a village with thirty little houses, the inhabitants of which were ruled by Alcabicca. At that time, a cave in Pacaritambo opened and let forth four brothers and their four sisters.[79] They were all dressed in the finest cloth, woven with gold; the men carried halberds[80] of gold, and the women had golden vessels and pitchers with which to prepare food. Near Guanacaure, the eight siblings tilled some fields. Standing on the top of Guanacaure, Ayar Cache with his sling threw rocks at three mountains, making them all into plains, whereupon his siblings sent him back to fetch more gold implements from the cave of Pacaritambo, and then treacherously imprisoned him there.[81] Next, the remaining brothers and sisters moved to Matagua and from there saw the valley of Cuzco. It seemed proper that one of the brothers should stay at Guanacaure to be an object of worship[82] and talk to their Father the Sun. Ayaroche rose to perform this task; displaying large wings, he flew heavenward and descending again, announced that the Sun ordered his brother Ayar Manco, henceforth to be known as Manco Capac, to lead his sisters and remaining brother, Ayarauca, to settle in Cuzco. Ayaroche then turned to stone. Shortly thereafter, one of his wings was broken away when some neighboring Indians threw a rock at him, so that he could never fly again.[83]

---

[76] Betanzos, *Suma* (1987), pp. 13b, 14a.

[77] Betanzos, *Suma* (1987), p. 15a. On this site, see above, chap. III.1 at n. 68.

[78] Betanzos, *Suma* (1987), 1.2, pp. 14b–15b.

[79] On Pacaritambo as both an actual and a mythic place see G. Urton, "La historia de un mito," *Revista Andina* 7, no. 1 (1989): 129–216, noting in particular the comments of P. Duviols, pp. 200–201. Similarly now, G. Urton, *History of a Myth* (1990). See also R. T. Zuidema's interpretation of Betanzos' account of the myth in *La civilisation inca au Cuzco*, pp. 22f. Zuidema's central question is the meaning of this and other myths in Inca times. Urton, and, in a different sense this present discussion focus on the meaning of myths after 1532.

[80] The Spanish term is *alabardes*.

[81] Betanzos, *Suma* (1987), 1.3, p. 18ab.

[82] I translate as "object of worship" Betanzos' term *idolo*. For Guanacaure as marking a crucial phase in the journey to Cuzco, see G. Urton, "La historia de un mito," *Revista Andina* 7, no. 1 (1989), at pp. 169ff.

[83] Betanzos, *Suma* (1987), 1.4, p. 19ab.

Near Cuzco, Mama Huaco, the consort and sister of Ayar Cache attacked an Indian in a village where coca leaf and aji were grown, and killed him with such ferocity that the other Indians of that village fled to the valley of Gualla, where their descendants were still growing coca in Betanzos' day.[84] In Cuzco, with Alcabicca's leave, Manco Capac chose as his place of settlement the future site of Coricancha.[85] Soon, his last brother died, and Manco Capac himself was in due course succeeded by his son Sinchi Roca, who took as his consort Mamacoca, daughter of the lord of the nearby village Zano.[86]

Although Betanzos' account of Andean creation and Inca origins resembles Cieza's in many particulars, there is one overall difference between the two stories that highlights Cieza's editing and ordering of the material he collected from the Inca nobles of Cuzco.[87] Cieza associated the major institutions and formative ceremonies of the Inca empire with the time of the mythic founder, Manco Capac. He thus wrote that Coricancha was "as ancient as the city of Cuzco itself," but that, not unlike many European cathedrals, which also grew over the generations, it was expanded and beautified over time. Successive Incas, in particular the ninth Inca Yupanqui thus added both to the structure and to the adornment of Coricancha.[88] Similarly, he connected the inauguration ritual of Inca rulers with the initiation ritual for young men, which latter, he wrote, was laid down by Ayar Cache, who was converted into stone at Guanacaure.[89] He also thought that the brother-sister marriages of Inca rulers dated back to the beginning of Inca history.[90] This view of Inca beginnings harmonizes with the European and Spanish principle that the legitimacy and worth of political and religious institutions arises from their antiquity.[91]

Betanzos, by contrast, recorded what he learned from his wife's kinsmen without this European idealization of Inca origins. Even Cieza recognized that the Inca empire as the Spaniards found it was essentially the creation of the ninth Inca Yupanqui, who successfully defended Cuzco from conquest by the neighboring Chancas and devised the institutional and administrative fabric of the Inca state. He was therefore often referred

---

[84] Betanzos, *Suma* (1987), 1.4, p. 20a. Sarmiento also tells the story of Mama Huaco's ferocity toward the Guallas; see Sarmiento, *Historia Indica* 13, p. 218a.

[85] Betanzos, *Suma* (1987), 1.4, p. 20ab.

[86] Betanzos, *Suma* (1987), 1.5, p. 21a.

[87] Cieza, *Segunda Parte* 6, p. 13; 9, pp. 23f.; 31, p. 94, etc.

[88] Cieza, *Segunda Parte* 8, p. 22; 27, p. 79; cf. 31, p. 94, Coricancha enlarged by Sinchi Roca.

[89] Cieza, *Segunda Parte* 7, p. 17.

[90] Cieza, *Segunda Parte* 10, p. 25; 31, p. 95.

[91] Cf. Rico, *Alfonso el Sabio* (1984), pp. 113ff.

to by his epithet as Inca Pachacuti, the "Turning of the Time."[92] According to Betanzos, it was under Inca Pachacuti, not under the founder Manco Capac, that Coricancha had been built and that the ritual of initiating young people received its definitive form.

The Incas whom Betanzos interviewed thought of the construction of Coricancha not merely as an architectural but also as a ceremonial event. Before choosing the site, Inca Pachacuti surveyed the city for three days, and then, in accord with Inca custom, measured out the ground plan of the edifice with a cord.[93] Once the walls had been raised under the Inca's close supervision, five hundred women were chosen to serve the Sun in his house, along with a chief priest and two hundred male attendants.[94] A great sacrifice was then prepared for the Sun, consisting of maize, llamas, and cloth, which were all solemnly burned. The sacrifice included a number of boys and girls, dressed in precious cloth, who were buried alive in Coricancha as capacocha.

By way of consecrating the newly constructed walls of the temple, the Inca marked them with lines of sacrificial blood. Similarly, he marked the faces of the priest of the Sun, of the Inca nobles, and of the mamacona, women consecrated to the service of the Sun. The priest of the Sun in turn marked the faces of the common people when they brought their offerings of coca and maize.[95] This sacred action of making marks with sacrificial blood, which was known as pirani or arpay[96] was also performed on other occasions when the sacrifice of capacocha was called for. At an Inca's inauguration, children were sacrificed to the Maker, the face of whose statue was lined with their blood.[97] The faces of Inca rulers' mummies were similarly lined with the blood of child capacochas,[98] and other mummies were still marked with animal blood in the later seventeenth century.[99] Finally, in the course of being initiated into adulthood,

---

[92] Betanzos, Suma (1987), 1.17, p. 83b; Cieza, Segunda Parte 45–54. On the meaning of Pachacuti, cf. MacCormack, "Pachacuti," American Historical Review 93 (1988): 960–1006.

[93] Betanzos, Suma (1987), 1.11, pp. 49, 50; 2.5, p. 215b.

[94] Betanzos describes the priest of the sun as "mayordomo" and the attendants as "yanaconas," Betanzos, Suma (1987), 1.11, p. 50b. On yanaconas and on the acllas or chosen women who were, in some respects, their female counterparts, see Murra, Economic Organization (1980), p. 154.

[95] Betanzos, Suma (1987), 1.11, p. 51ab.

[96] Cf. Gonzalez Holguin, Vocabulario de la lengua general, p. 287: Pirani: era una ceremonia que del carnero, o cordero que avian de sacrificar con la sangre neva y fresca se embijavan con rayas en la cara, o cuerpo para tener parte en aquel sacrificio. Gonzalez Holguin, p.34, Arpay, sacrificio obra de sacrificar.

[97] Molina, Fábulas, p. 123, pirac; see also Pachacuti Yamqui, Relación, p. 259. For a similar and perhaps related observance during Corpus Christi in contemporary Macha, Bolivia, see T. Platt, "Andean Soldiers of Christ," Journal de la Société des Américanistes 73 (1987), p. 159.

[98] Polo, Errores 2.3, fol. 8r: sacrificabanles . . . niños, y de su sangre hazían una raya de oreja a oreja en el rostro del defunto.

[99] Pachacuti Yamqui, Relación, p. 259, Avila's note on arpamientos. See also Duviols, Cultura andina y represión (1986), p. 63, llegaba al dicho difunto y le asperxaba con chicha y

young men swore to serve the Inca and the divine Sun; before they did so, llamas were sacrificed and a line drawn from ear to ear across the young men's faces.[100] The application of this same ritual to a building, to human beings, to mummies and sacred images, reveals that Andeans, unlike Christian Spaniards, who made a radical distinction between animate and inanimate being, perceived a shared quality in these different entities, all of which could be described as *huaca*.[101] Betanzos thus wrote of Coricancha that it "was revered and held in great awe; . . . its stones and servants and yanaconas were all regarded as blessed and consecrated."[102]

The "House of the Sun" was now ready for its divine occupant. For a month, the goldsmiths of Cuzco worked on the cult image, while everyone fasted and a perpetual fire to consume the Sun's sacrifices was established in Coricancha. The image, known as Punchao, Punchao Inca, or simply Inti,[103] represented the Sun as a small boy, just as Inca Pachacuti had seen him in a vision,[104] and was dressed in the woven tunic, sandals, and head ornament worn by Inca sovereigns. As the Spaniards learned later, inside this image were preserved the hearts of deceased Inca sovereigns.[105] Inca Pachacuti approached the image reverently and barefoot, and placed it on the seat covered with cloth of irridescent feathers that later the Spaniards saw in Coricancha.[106] Before the image stood gold and silver braziers where its daily food and drink was burned, as though it "were a person who eats and drinks."[107]

Coricancha was an imperial and aristocratic place of worship. While the Inca ruler made sacrifice before the Sun, the Inca lords performed their devotions in an anteroom.[108] The common people were not permitted to enter at all but could only approach the building from the square Intipampa, outside its main entrance.[109] For them, Inca Yupanqui raised over the ushnu in Haucaypata, where in Betanzos' time stood the gibbet

---

sangre. But note the reason given for the ritual: that the soul can thereby reach the next world. Cf. Betanzos, *Suma* (1987), 1.11, p. 53a, who uses the term *arpa* simply for "sacrifice."

[100] Betanzos, *Suma* (1987), 1.14, p. 67b; similarly Polo, *Errores*, fol. 10r, copied by Murúa, *Historia del origen* (1590), 3.71, p. 346.

[101] See also Garcilaso, *Comentarios reales* 2.4, with the discussion below, chap. VIII.1 at nn. 9ff.

[102] Betanzos, *Suma* (1987), 1.11, p. 52b. On yanaconas cf. above, n. 94.

[103] "Day," "Lord Day," or "Sun," see Duviols, "Punchao," *Antropologia Andina* 1–2 (1976): 170; Molina, *Fábulas*, p. 67.

[104] See below, chap. VII.1 at n. 13.

[105] Salazar, *Relación*, p. 280; cf. below, chap. VI at n. 1.

[106] Pedro Pizarro, *Relación* 15, p. 93; Betanzos, *Suma* (1987), 1.11, p. 52a.

[107] Betanzos, *Suma* (1987), 1.11, p. 52b.

[108] "Patio," Betanzos, *Suma* (1987), 1.11, p. 52b; cf. Rowe, *Introduction to the Archaeology of Cuzco* (1944), p. 36.

[109] Intipampa means "square of the Sun." For its location, see Garcilaso, *Comentarios reales* 7.9 and J. Hyslop, *Inka Settlement Planning*, pp. 43, 61, 225; 326, n. 15.

that Pizarro had erected,[110] a stone shaped like a sugarloaf, its sharp end pointing upward, which was enclosed in a "belt" of gold.[111] This stone was carved at the same time as the cult image in Coricancha and likewise represented the Sun, but in a popular context.[112]

The sacred topography of Cuzco thus demarcated the imperial cult centered on Coricancha, where the ruling Inca, titled Intip Churin,[113] stood face to face with his divine parent, from the cult of the people at large, which centered on the public square. On certain occasions, the two cultic realms overlapped. After Coricancha had been inaugurated, the gold image of the Sun was carried around Cuzco on a small litter covered in cloth of gold, in order to bless the city,[114] and during the various festivals of the Inca calendar, it was displayed in Haucaypata amidst the Inca mummies, with whom it shared a common ritual. For like the mummies, the image of the Sun received sacrifice of food and drink which was known as *arpa*.[115] The same term described the nourishment of Inca lords,[116] who in other respects also enjoyed an almost divine status.[117]

Imperial Inca religion as remembered by the nobles whom Betanzos consulted was thus made up of clearly demarcated aristocratic and popular spheres. Cieza had understood Andean and Inca religion in terms of a hierarchy of ideas: gradually, the divine Sun of the Incas would prevail over those lesser concepts of divinity that Inca subjects tended to adhere to. The nobles of Cuzco whom Betanzos knew, by contrast, understood their religion in terms of a hierarchy of social relationships in which they and their Inca had stood at the apex. Imperial religion believed and participated in thus differed profoundly from imperial religion observed.

The same difference is apparent in Betanzos' account of Inca festivals. Where Cieza had selected the consultation of imperial oracles and the harvest celebrations as being representative of the Inca festival cycle, Betanzos' Incas started much closer to home, with the initiation of their own sons and daughters into adulthood. As understood by Cieza, the rituals of initiation went back to the very beginning of Inca history.[118] The in-

---

[110] Donde agora es el rollo, Betanzos, *Suma* (1968), 1.11, p. 33b. The 1987 edition of the newly found manuscript of Betanzos' *Suma* has "royo"; see p. 52b. For the translation, see Covarrubias, *Tesoro* (1611), s.v. rollo; also above, chap. 11.2, p. 72.

[111] Spanish, *faja*.

[112] On the "stone shaped like a sugar loaf" which was carved at the same time as Sun's golden image, Betanzos, *Suma* (1987), 1.11, p. 52b. See also p. 53b (1987), en medio de la pila [i.e., the ushnu] pusieron la piedra que significaba el sol. On ushnus, see above chap. 11.2, n. 14, with text; further, Dearborn and Schreiber, "Houses of the Rising Sun," in *Time and Calendars*, ed. Ziolkowski and Sadowski, pp. 61ff.

[113] "Son of the Sun," Betanzos, *Suma* (1987), 1.1, 17, p. 83b, and throughout.

[114] Betanzos, *Suma* (1987), 1.11, p. 53a.

[115] See above, chap. 11.2 at n. 30.

[116] Gonzalez Holguin, *Vocabulario de la lengua general*, p. 34; Betanzos, *Suma* 1.11, p. 53a.

[117] Cobo, *Historia* 13.35, pp. 136bf.

[118] See above, at n. 20. Molina also linked initiation with Inca beginnings; see *Fábulas*, p.

formants of Betanzos, by contrast, attributed the public formulation of
these rituals to Inca Pachacuti. It was Pachacuti who laid down that initiation should inaugurate the annual Inca festival cycle and should take
place in November and December, during a period that was reckoned as
the first month of the year.[119] Both Cieza and Betanzos described the rituals of initiation in some detail, but with differing emphasis. Where
Cieza[120] concentrated on the public aspect of initiation and said nothing
about the initiation of young women, Betanzos included women, mentioned many homely details, and revealed how a family ritual meshed
with the ritual of the Inca state.

The long round of initiation procedures began in a domestic context,
when the kinswomen of each young man to be initiated spun the yarn
for, and then wove, the four sets of ceremonial tunics and cloaks he would
need. In November the young men gathered together as a group to chew
the maize with which to prepare chicha for the festival, in order to start
fermentation. The women, meanwhile, fetched water for the chicha from
the sacred spring of Calizpuquio.[121] Although Betanzos learned much less
about women's initiation than he did about men's, he does show that the
successive phases of the initiation of young men unfolded side by side
with that of young women. Similarly, in Coricancha, the cult of the Sun
went hand in hand with that of his consort the Moon, Pacsamama. This
latter cult was in the care of women,[122] which is why Spanish historians,
all of them men, learned so little about it.[123]

Like the young men, so the young women began initiation with a fast.
They also received sets of ceremonial clothes, described as *acso* and *lli-*

101; also by Cobo, *Historia* 13.25, p. 208b, young men to be initiated were dressed like
"their ancestors when they came from the cave." Molina, *Fábuloas*, p. 107, dance *huari* is
derived from Manco Capac. Cf. Sarmiento, *Historia Indica* 12–13; Cabello, *Miscelanea antar-
tica* 3.9, p. 263, stating that initiation was instituted by Ayar Cache. Gutierrez de Santa
Clara, who professed to have received his information on initiation from Paullu Inca, also
derived the ritual from Inca beginnings. See Gutierrez de Santa Clara, *Historia de las guerras
civiles del Peru* 3.54, Biblioteca de autores españoles, vol. 166 (Madrid, 1963), pp. 253ff. This
account is disappointingly general and perhaps not as authentic as the author claims. See
M. Bataillon, "Gutierrez de Santa Clara, escritor Mexicano," *Nueva Revista de Filología Hispanica* 15 (1961): 405–440.

[119] Betanzos, *Suma* (1987), 1.14, p. 71b. In the text edited by Duviols, "Une petite chronique," *Journal de la Société des Américanistes* 63 (1974–1976): 280, non-Inca initiation is described as a domestic event.

[120] Cieza, *Segunda Parte* 7; cf. below, chap. 3.3 at nn. 58–61.

[121] Betanzos, *Suma* (1987), 1.14, p. 66ab; 15, p. 73b; cf. Cieza, *Segunda Parte* 7, p. 18. On
spinning and making chicha and *ojotas* see Molina, *Fábulas*, pp. 97ff. Cobo, *Historia* 13.25,
describing initiation used the same source as Molina or copied from Molina; preparation of
the chicha, Cobo, *Historia* 13.30, p. 220a.

[122] Molina, *Fábulas*, p. 100; cf. Santillan, *Relación del origen* 27, on Pachamama; Silverblatt,
Moon, Sun and Witches, pp. 47ff.

[123] On Pacsamama (Moon) in Haucaypata, along with the Maker, the Sun, and the Lightning, see Molina, *Fábulas*, pp. 103, 105, 106, 110.

quilla,[124] which they wore during the successive phases of initiation.[125] Next followed a short pilgrimage to Guanacaure, where young men and young women seem to have been paired as partners, and where the young men danced the dance *huari* that the Maker had taught Manco Capac when he came forth from Pacaritambo.[126] While at Guanacaure, the young men had their hair cut and attired themselves in their first set of ceremonial clothes, which were black tunics and white cloaks. At the same time, lines were drawn across their faces with the blood of llamas about to be sacrificed.[127] Next the young men changed into colored tunics[128] and visited the holy place Anaguarque, where the young women awaited them with cups of chicha.[129] The young men then ran to Cuzco,[130] and the following day went to Yavira. Here, their faces having once more been marked from ear to ear with sacrificial blood, they swore loyalty to the Sun and the Inca and put on tunics and cloaks elaborately woven with patterns,[131] as well as adult loin cloths known as *huara*.[132] Returning to Cuzco, the young men paraded in Haucaypata wearing puma skins to denote their courage[133] and then fasted for thirty days, while their elders chanted in honor of the Sun.[134] At the end of this period, the young men washed in the spring of Calizpuquio.[135]

For the last phase of their initiation, they were attired in the finest tunics so far and returned to their homes.[136] Here, their ears were pierced while they were inebriated with the chicha that had been brewed earlier. From now on they wore the ear spools that distinguished Inca nobles from other people (see figs. 16 and 21). A young woman's initiation also comprised a domestic aspect. This was linked to her first menstruation,

---

[124] *Acso* is a long rectangle of cloth used as a wraparound skirt; *liquilla* is a square shoulder cloth.

[125] Betanzos, *Suma* (1987), 1.14, p. 66b; Molina, *Fábulas*, p. 100.

[126] Betanzos, *Suma* (1987), 1.14, p. 66b; Molina, *Fábulas*, p. 102, 107; cf. Cobo, *Historia* 13.30, p. 219b. Echoes of Inca origins were common in imperial festivals; on such an echo during the festival of the December solstice, see Dearborn and Schreiber (see above, n. 109), pp. 57–58.

[127] Cobo, *Historia* 13.30, p. 219b.

[128] Betanzos, *Suma* (1987), 1.14, p. 67a.

[129] Betanzos, *Suma* (1987), 1. 14, p. 67a; Molina, *Fábulas*, pp. 105f.; Cobo, *Historia* 13.25, p. 211a.

[130] Cf. Ramos Gavilán, *Historia . . . de Copacabana* 1.23, p. 146, for a footrace at the young men's initiation as celebrated at Copacabana in the early seventeenth century. The custom probably dated back to Inca times.

[131] Betanzos, *Suma* 1.14, p. 67bf.

[132] Molina, *Fábulas*, p. 106.

[133] Cf. Guaman Poma, *Nueva Crónica*, p. 155, sesto capitan otorongo, with p. 83, segunda arma; see also *Runa yndio* 5.87–90, ed. Taylor, myth from Huarochiri about dancing in a red puma skin.

[134] Betanzos, *Suma* (1987), 1.14, p. 68bf.

[135] Ch-3:8. Titu Cusi, *Relación*, p. 69, using Christian terminology, calls this "rrebautizar."

[136] Cf. Cieza, *Segunda Parte* 7, p. 18.

when in the course of a family ritual she received her adult name[137] and began wearing adult dress.[138]

The day after the young men had their ears pierced, they fought a mock battle in Haucaypata in which they pelted each other with prickly pears launched from slings.[139] This battle, followed by a public feast,[140] completed their initiation, except for one final change of clothes: during the harvest celebrations of May and June, which the anonymous cleric and Cieza had described, the recently initiated men appeared in tunics woven with thread of gold and silver and adorned with irridescent feathers.[141]

This last detail reveals an aspect of Inca festivals that Spaniards other than Betanzos tended to overlook. The festivals were not isolated occasions celebrated one by one in the course of a calendar year. Instead, they formed an interconnected fabric of sacred time. The initiation of young men was followed by the summer solstice, the longest day of the year, which the Incas celebrated in its own right. And the celebration of harvest and plowing was followed by the winter solstice, the shortest day of the year, itself the occasion of a set of rituals. The festivals of December and June were accordingly brought into relation with each other not merely by ceremonies focusing on the course of the divine Sun but also by ceremonies focusing on growth and change in human society.

Calendrical time, marked by the movement of the sun, and human time, marked by the maturation of young people, were celebrated in conjunction. The initiation of young men epitomized human time and was interwoven with the celebration of the winter and summer solstices, which marked the recurring annual cycle of the seasons. In Cuzco as throughout the Andes, human time was thus integrated into the fixed and predictable rhythms of calendrical time. But not all human lives could be textured within such fixed and predictable rhythms. For the life and death of the Inca, on whom was focused a vast network of power, imposed their own distinct rhythms on his subjects. It was therefore said that with the inauguration of every succeeding Inca sovereign, time began afresh.[142] In the person of the ruler, human time, characterized by the sequence of birth, maturity, and death, was mediated to the Andean world without the modifications afforded by calendrical time. This mediation was ex-

[137] For men's adult names, see Titu Cusi, *Relación*, p. 69.

[138] Molina, *Fábulas*, p. 119; but see Ramos Gavilan's *Historia . . . de Copacabana* for the initiation of girls in February (1.23, p. 143; cf. 1.24, p. 151) and of boys in December (1.24, p. 150). Perhaps one of the two feast days of the Virgin of Copacabana, the Purification on February 2, was chosen to coincide with the pre-Christian initiation of girls.

[139] Betanzos, *Suma* (1987), 1.14, p. 69b; according to Molina, *Fábulas*, p. 61, this happened "en el primer dia de la luna."

[140] Molina, *Fábulas*, p. 111.

[141] Betanzos, *Suma* (1987), 1.15, p. 71b; on cloth in the Andes, see Murra, *Economic Organization* (1980), p. 79.

[142] Quipucamayos de Vaca de Castro, in *Relación de la descendencia*, p. 20.

pressed by means of the ceremonies and festivals that linked an Inca's death with the inauguration of his successor.

3. Incas, Mummies, and the Order of Time

The differences in outlook that distinguish Cieza's account of calendrical festivals from that of Betanzos also pervade the perception these two historians had of what was at stake in the succession of one Inca ruler by another.[1] In Cieza's eyes, legitimation of a particular Inca's dominion arose from compliance with certain rules which, he thought, governed the selection of an Inca and the public celebration of his inauguration. These rules, as Cieza understood them, originated in the very beginning of Inca history, during the initiation and inauguration of Manco Capac's son Sinchi Roca (see fig. 12), whom Cieza viewed as a historical, rather than a mythic, personage. Betanzos, by contrast, looked to precedents that were less distant in time and described in terms of ritual what Cieza described as history. As a result, Betanzos thought that an Inca's legitimation arose from a quite fluid spectrum of considerations, in which religion and politics were intimately intertwined. Above all, in the eyes of Betanzos' informants, legitimation did not result from a single issue or the ceremonious formulation of any definitive point in time, but from a long-drawn-out process of forming political and social relationships.[2]

---

[1] This present section (like, indirectly, the preceding one) touches upon the thorny question of Inca chronology. Several scholars have investigated, with widely different results, to what extent the accounts of Inca origins and of the Inca past that Spaniards collected in the Andes during the sixteenth and seventeenth centuries reflect historical reality. Since I plan to discuss this issue in a companion volume to this book, I mention here only the core of the debate. In his *Ceque System of Cuzco* and more recently in his *Inca Civilisation in Cuzco* and elsewhere, R. T. Zuidema has argued that the Spaniards interpreted Inca accounts of royal kinship and of social and political hierarchy within the Inca state in historical and dynastic terms. In other words, the Spaniards reformulated what Andeans told them in categories that were meaningful in Europe but that did not correspond to Inca and Andean realities. Explanations and modifications of Zuidema's argument include N. Wachtel's "Structuralisme et histoire: à propos de l'organisation sociale du Cuzco," *Annales ESC* 21 (1966): 71–94 and P. Duviols' "La dinastía de los Incas. Monarquía o diarquía? Argumentos heuristicos a favor de una tesis estructuralista," *Journal de la Société des Américanistes* 66 (1979): 67–83. J. H. Rowe, on the other hand, reads the sixteenth- and seventeenth-century accounts of Inca rulers, particularly from Inca Viracocha onward, as essentially historical; see his "Inca Culture at the Time of the Spanish Conquest," in *Handbook of South American Indians*, ed. J. H. Steward (Washington, D.C., 1946), pp. 183–330, at pp. 201ff., and his "Absolute Chronology in the Andean Area," *American Antiquity* 10 (1944–1945): 265–284. More recently, see J. H. Rowe, "La constitución Inca del Cuzco," *Historica* 9 (1985): 35–73, and note response by Zuidema, *Inca Civilization in Cuzco*, pp. 45–50 with n. 25. On the historicity of at least the more recent Inca past as perceived by Inca nobles in early colonial Cuzco, see J. H. Rowe, "Probanza de los Incas," *Historica* 9 (1985): 193–245, and on the colonial transformation of concepts of that past, see the important contribution by G. Urton, "La historia de un mito," *Revista Andina* 7, no. 1 (1989): 129–216. This article is a short version, accompanied by comments from other scholars, of Gary Urton, *The History of a Myth: Pacariqtambo and the Origin of the Incas* (Austin, 1990); see especially pp. 5ff.

[2] I would like to thank Tom Zuidema for discussing this picture with me.

12. The rituals of initiation into adulthood and of inauguration to sovereignty converge as Inca Manco Capac designates his young son, Sinchi Roca, by handing him the gold scepter, *tupayauri*. Manco Capac wears both the golden ear spools of adult men and the imperial headband of Inca rulers. Sinchi Roca, still a boy, by contrast, has no ear spools. The figure on the right holds Sinchi Roca's imperial headband (*mazcca paycha*) and shield. The shape of the shield has been adapted to follow European heraldic designs. Martín de Murúa, *Historia general del Perú* (c. 1611), fol. 21 r, pen and ink with colored washes. The J. Paul Getty Museum.

These relationships involved not so much individuals as entire lineages. During festivals the inhabitants of Cuzco and of all other cities and villages of the empire grouped themselves according to the moieties of upper and lower Cuzco, *anan* and *urin*.[3] Within each moiety they were ordered by lineages, every lineage being represented by its own mummies, much as Pedro Pizarro had observed.[4] In Cieza's opinion, Inca inauguration ceremonies, like corresponding ceremonies in Europe, proved a ruler's legitimacy, this being a value focused on the future. As Betanzos understood them, however, these ceremonies explained political and religious continuity, the interlocking of the present with the past, of the living with their mummies.

Betanzos learned from his informants in Cuzco the names of eight Incas, from the founder Manco Capac to Viracocha, of whose inauguration no particulars appear to have been known, and almost nothing was known about their deeds.[5] The story then reached Viracocha's younger son, Inca Yupanqui, who was renamed Pachacuti at his inauguration. Inca Yupanqui distinguished himself by his heroic defence of Cuzco against the Chanca invaders at a time when Viracocha himself, with his older son, Inca Urco, had ignobly withdrawn to safety at Xaquixaguana, near Calca.[6] At this time, Viracocha had already designated Inca Urco as his successor, and, in the words of Betanzos, expected that

> the lords of Cuzco would bestow [on Inca Urco] . . . the tokens of royalty, which were that no one, however mighty a lord, not even one of his brothers, should appear before him with shoes on his feet but only barefoot, and they would stand before him with lowered head for as long as they spoke with him or approached him with some message. He would eat alone without anyone daring to touch the food that he ate. He would be carried in a litter on the shoulders of lords. When he went out to the square, he would sit on a seat of gold; he would have a parasol made of dyed ostrich feathers. He would drink from goblets of gold, and the other vessels used in his dwelling would also be of gold.[7]

---

[3] Cf. Cieza, *Segunda Parte* 32, p. 97.

[4] See above, chap. II.2 at n. 29.

[5] Betanzos, *Suma* (1987), 1.5, pp. 21–22.

[6] Betanzos, *Suma* (1987), 1.6, p. 25a. On the Chanca war, see P. Duviols, "La guerra entre el Cuzco y los Chanca, historia o mito?" *Revista de la Universidad Complutense* 28 (117), (1979), volume entitled *Economía y sociedad en los Andes y Mesoamerica*, pp. 363–371.

[7] Betanzos, *Suma* 1.8, p. 31b; further on the veneration of the Inca's person, Cieza, *Segunda Parte* 13; 20, pp. 58f.; 28, p. 90. I anchor the present discussion in the sources to which I refer, in all of which the Inca rulers are listed as succeeding one another in a dynasty. For the problems of a possible Inca dyarchy and for the possible contemporaneity of certain rulers, see most recently, J. Szeminski, *Un kuraka* (1987), pp. 102ff., 105, 149. Note also the evidence given in 1582 by Cristóbal de Molina, author of *Fábulas y ritos de los Incas*: el ynga tenía señalado . . . una persona grave de su linaxe con quien se tratasen . . . los negocios

However, Inca Yupanqui's victory over the Chanca endowed him not only with popular support but also with an aura of divine protection, because before confronting the enemy in battle, the Creator Viracocha Pachayachachic had appeared to him in the figure of a man, promising assistance and success.[8]

The battle won, Inca Yupanqui brought the spoils and prisoners to Xaquixaguana for his father to tread underfoot in the traditional Inca gesture of triumph.[9] But because Viracocha wished Inca Urco to perform this ritual, Inca Yupanqui withdrew his spoils and prisoners and returned to Cuzco as de facto ruler, concluding the Chanca war, reconstructing the city, and regulating its religious observances.[10] Yet when the nobles of Cuzco suggested that he should assume the "headband of state," *mazcca paycha*,[11] that Inca rulers wore over their foreheads, and should perform the fast and the celebrations that traditionally accompanied this action, Inca Yupanqui refused. He could either accept the headband from Viracocha his father, he explained, or else he could take it from the head of Inca Urco, "along with the head itself," in return for the affront he had endured when Viracocha refused to triumph over his spoils and prisoners, in order that Inca Urco might do so.[12] To add force to his words, Inca Yupanqui emptied a cup of chicha on the ground and vowed that his blood should be spilled like the chicha if he did not receive satisfaction from his father.[13] The Inca nobles took their cue from this statement and persuaded Viracocha to return to Cuzco so as to endow his son with the headband of state. Seeing the splendor of the newly built city, Viracocha said to Inca Yupanqui, "Truly you are the Son of the Sun and I name you king and lord."

And taking the headband into his hands, removing it from his own head, he placed it on the head of Inca Yupanqui. It was a custom among these lords that when this was done, he who placed the headband on the head of the other at the same time had to give him the name that he was to bear henceforth. Thus Viracocha Inca, placing

---

... y esta segunda persona del dicho ynga se elexía el dia que a el alçavan por señor porque la eleción deste tocava a los sacerdotes del sol, *Informacion hecha en el Cuzco*, p. 280.

[8] Betanzos, *Suma* (1987), 1.8, p. 32ab. Further on the Inca's vision, below, chap. VII.1 at nn. 11ff.

[9] Cf. Betanzos, *Suma* (1987), 1.19, p. 95a.

[10] Betanzos, *Suma* (1987), 1.9–16.

[11] Gonzalez Holguin, *Vocabulario de la lengua general*, p. 232.

[12] Betanzos, *Suma* (1987), 1.17, p. 82b.

[13] See on this episode, T. B. Foster Cummins, *Abstraction to Narration: Kero Imagery of Peru and the Colonial Aftermath of Native Identity*, Ph.D. dissertation, University of California at Los Angeles, 1988, pp. 437–450. See also pp. 208ff. for the custom of drinking chicha out of an enemy's skull, which makes Pachacuti's threat all the more graphic. For head-shaped Inca drinking cups, called *Keros*, see Cummins, fig. 116; although they all date from the colonial period, such cups appear to recall this custom.

the band on Inca Yupanqui's head, said to him: "I name you, so that from today your people and whatever other nations you may conquer shall call you Pachacuti Inca Yupanqui Capac and Indichuri," which is to say, Turning About of the Time, King Yupanqui, Son of the Sun.[14]

However, this was not the end of the ceremonial duel between father and son. For Inca Yupanqui, now to be known as Pachacuti, completed his own investiture and made good on his vow by forcing his father to drink chicha from a common, soiled goblet before the eyes of the assembled Inca nobility:

> Viracocha, understanding what he had been ordered to do by the new lord, took the goblet and without replying one word, drank the chicha, and when he had drunk it, he abased himself and bowed before Pachacuti.[15]

By agreeing to drink chicha from anything other than one of the gold vessels set aside for the use of the Inca, and moreover from a soiled vessel, Viracocha renounced his own consecrated status and confirmed that of his son, whose command he had obeyed.

Pachacuti's accession to power could now be completed by performing a set of rituals that appear to have been established at an earlier phase of Inca history. The Inca and his consort, Mama Anahuarque,[16] along with her mother, retired to fast for ten days in seclusion, while the nobles of Cuzco sacrificed "to all the huacas around the city and especially in the temple of the Sun." These sacrifices included pairs of nobly born boys and girls, who were buried alive as capacocha with utensils of gold and silver such as were given to married couples.[17] Her fast completed, Mama Anahuarque, now clothed in royal attire, was greeted by the lords of Cuzco. Viracocha having exchanged a kiss with her, gave her certain villages as her "patrimony," while Pachacuti, having greeted her as his wife, gave her one hundred ladies, mamacona, to whom the priest of the Sun added another fifty. Finally, three months were spent in rejoicing and gift exchange, whereupon Viracocha returned to his estate of Xaquixaguana.[18]

---

[14] Betanzos, *Suma* (1987), 1.17, p. 83b.

[15] Betanzos, *Suma* (1987), 1.17, p. 83b.

[16] Sarmiento, *Historia Indica* 47, p. 253a; Guaman Poma, *Nueva Crónica*, p. 136; according to Cieza, *Segunda Parte* 46, p. 135, Pachacuti's coya had initially been married to Inca Urcon.

[17] Betanzos, *Suma* (1987), 1.17, p. 84; cf. the capacocha sacrifice for Pachacuti's funeral, Betanzos 1.30, p. 142b; Sarmiento de Gamboa, *Historia Indica* 42, capacocha for Tupa Inca Yupanqui's accession, and Betanzos, *Suma* (1987), 1.39, p. 177a, for his funeral. For a description of the sacrifice, Molina, *Fábulas*, pp. 120ff., discussed below, chap. IV.3 at nn. 118ff.

[18] Betanzos, *Suma* (1987), 1.17, p. 84bf.

The information Betanzos collected about Inca accessions is characterized by domestic intimacy and by details such as could only come from
personal acquaintance with the protagonists or their descendants and fa-
miliars. Twenty years later, another Spanish historian, Pedro Sarmiento
de Gamboa, once more questioned Inca informants still living in Cuzco.
His accounts of Inca accessions focus not on events within the inner circle
of the Inca royal clan but on public ceremonies performed in Coricancha.
Whereas the ceremonial events that culminated in Viracocha's drinking
from a soiled cup defined the relationship between Pachacuti and his father and brother, the ceremonies described by Sarmiento defined Pachacuti's position in relation to his other Inca kinsmen and the people of
Cuzco at large. These latter ceremonies spelled out that Pachacuti enjoyed
the support of the divine Sun, the royal deity who presided not only over
Cuzco but over the entire Inca empire. Here also, Pachacuti's claim to
rule arose from his victory over the Chancas. For thanks to this victory,

> Pachacuti found himself to be in a position of great power and the
> leader of many people. He thus ordered . . . a great sacrifice to be
> offered to the Sun in Indicancha, the House of the Sun, and then they
> went to ask the statue of the Sun who should be Inca. The oracle
> which they had there . . . answered that [the Sun] had designated
> Pachacuti Inca Yupanqui. At this response all those who had gone to
> make the sacrifice prostrated themselves before Pachacuti Inca Yu-
> panqui and called him . . . Son of the Sun.[19]

By way of implementing the oracle's statement, the Inca nobles returned
with Pachacuti to the temple of the Sun:

> And when they came before the statue of the Sun, which was of
> gold, the stature of a man, they found it holding the [imperial] head-
> band in its hand, as though freely offering it. Pachacuti, having made
> the customary sacrifices, came before the statue of the Sun, and the
> Sun's chief priest . . . took the headband from the hand of the statue
> and with much ceremony placed it on the forehead of Pachacuti Inca
> Yupanqui. Thereafter, all acclaimed him as . . . Son of the Sun,
> Lord, the Turning About of the World.[20]

This ceremony, which unfolded in the public and official space of Coricancha, complemented the more personal and intimate transactions that
had been described by Betanzos. The two accounts focus on different aspects of Pachacuti's accession procedures: one involved the inner circle of
Inca nobles, while the other was addressed to a wider public comprising

[19] Sarmiento, *Historia Indica* 29, p. 235a; for the oracle, cf. below chap. VI at nn. 1ff.
[20] Sarmiento, *Historia Indica* 29, p. 235ab. See also the Supplementary Note to this chapter.

the people of Cuzco and representatives of subject and allied peoples from all parts of the empire.

Ten years later, Viracocha died. Betanzos described how Pachacuti presided over the obsequies. The embalmed body of the deceased Inca was transported to Cuzco on a litter and was honored there "as though alive." Sacrifices of llamas, cloth, maize, coca, and chicha were offered to the embalmed body as sustenance, because it "ate and was a son of the Sun and dwelt with the Sun in the sky." After Pachacuti instituted the cult of his father's embalmed body, which Betanzos described as an "effigy" or *bulto*,[21] the Inca "provided that several other effigies should be made, as many as the number of lords who had succeeded after Manco Capac down to his father, Viracocha Inca."[22] The "effigies"[23] of these rulers were displayed on elaborately painted wooden seats decorated with many-hued feathers[24] and were given nourishment every morning and evening. Expenses thus incurred were defrayed by endowments of retainers, lands, and herds that, according to Betanzos, the Inca Pachacuti assigned to each of these rulers. He also laid down that individuals who came before the living Inca would first pay their respects to his ancestors and to the divine Sun. Finally, he decreed that poetic recitations relating their glorious deeds be performed regularly before the effigies of these Incas, so that "a memory remained of their ancient past."[25] Indeed, in Betanzos' day, the Inca rulers of the past were still revered and fed in secret.[26]

The ceremonies of Inca accession and funeral as developed during the long reign of Pachacuti Inca, drawn out though they were over many years, nonetheless articulated a coherent set of themes. These ceremonies

[21] Betanzos, *Suma* (1987), 1.17, p. 85b. For the term *bulto*, meaning, in early modern Spanish usage, "image," "effigy," or "figure," see Real Academia Española, *Diccionario de Autoridades* (Madrid, 1726, 1984), s.v. bulto.

[22] Betanzos, *Suma* (1987), 1.17, p. 85b. It is clear from Betanzos and other sources that these "figures" were not embalmed bodies but representations that stood in for such bodies; see in particular Titu Cusi, *Relación*, p. 100. He mentions remains of Manco Capac, which he describes as Vanacuri; see on this designation of an Inca ruler MacCormack, "Pachacuti," *American Historical Review* 93 (1988): 967f., on the dead Tupa Amaru as Inca Vana Cauri. Apart from Manco Capac's remains, Titu Cusi mentions the mummies of Viracocha, Pachacuti, Tupa Inca Yupanqui, and Guayna Capac and of women. The rulers whose "effigies" Pachacuti created and endowed with property and servants were legendary ancestors one of whose functions was to represent the genealogical distance of various Inca lineages from the ruling Inca (Zuidema, *Inca Civilization*, pp. 34–35 and his "Dynastic Structures in Andean Culture," in *The Northern Dynasties: Kingship and Statecraft in Chimor*, ed. M. E. Mosley and A. Cordy-Collins [Washington, D.C., 1990], pp. 489–505). Betanzos, like other Spaniards in the period here studied, considered these ancestors as historical personages, cf. above n. 1. It is not clear to what extent Betanzos was aware of differences between the embalmed bodies of recent Inca rulers and the representations of rulers of the mythic past that Pachacuti ordered to be made, since he described both as "bulto"; see above, n. 20.

[23] Spanish, *bultos*, Betanzos, *Suma* (1987), 1.17, p. 85b; (1968), p. 54a.

[24] Betanzos, *Suma* (1987), 1.17, p. 85b.

[25] Betanzos, *Suma* (1987), 1.17, p. 86a.

[26] Betanzos, *Suma* (1987), 1.17, p. 86b.

underpinned the different stages of Pachacuti's rise to power; they spelled out a continuing relationship, albeit a tense one, between Pachacuti and his father, thus establishing a channel for the transfer of power; and they adumbrated the divine status of both the living and the deceased Inca. Finally, the ceremonies represented the stages of the young Inca's emergence and the corresponding stages of the old Inca's advance toward death as an interlocking mechanism whereby a gradual and smooth transition from one ruler to the next could be achieved. In short, these ceremonies were designed to minimize the disruption and discontinuity resulting from an Inca's death. These same themes emerge in Betanzos' description of the retirement and death of Pachacuti and the inauguration of his son, Tupa Inca Yupanqui.

According to Betanzos, Tupa Inca Yupanqui emerged into public life under the protection of his older brother Yamque Yupanqui, who arranged his marriage to his sister Mama Ocllo. When Pachacuti felt the onset of old age, he recalled the two brothers from their northern military campaign and proposed to give the headband of state to Yamque Yupanqui's young son. Yamque Yupanqui countered that the band should be bestowed on Tupa Inca Yupanqui, to whom Mama Ocllo had recently borne a son.[27] Pachacuti ordered Mama Ocllo to return to the house of her sisters, where she had grown up and where presumably she was to fast in seclusion, took her baby son into his personal charge and placed the royal headband on his own son Tupa Inca Yupanqui, ordering him to be seated at his side (see fig. 13). Next, Mama Ocllo, now Coya,[28] thanks to her fast in seclusion, was married anew to her now royal husband, and the "customary sacrifices" were made to the Sun and the Inca mummies.[29] Another mazcca paycha was placed on the head of the young couple's six-month-old son, Inti Cusi Vallpa,[30] who received the epithet Guayna Capac, "Young Lord," and was from then on raised by the aged Pachacuti.[31]

Here also, Sarmiento told a different story, which, however, harmo-

---

[27] The story Betanzos records is clearly a version favored by the lineage of Tupa Inca Yupanqui, although it was not the only version in existence. Sarmiento, *Historia Indica* 42, p. 247a, also mentions an older brother when narrating Tupa Inca Yupanqui's inauguration, but calls him Amaro Topa Inca. In accord with his critique of the Incas, Sarmiento, *Historia Indica* 43, p. 248a, recounts the inauguration of Tupa Inca Yupanqui as having been conflict-ridden, since Amaro Tupa Inca did not yield to his younger brother's elevation without resistance.

[28] Quechua, "queen."

[29] Betanzos, *Suma* (1987), 1.27, p. 132a.

[30] Quipucamayos, *Relación de la descendencia*, p. 40; Sarmiento, *Historia Indica* 54, p. 258b, names him Tito Cusi Gualpa.

[31] Betanzos, *Suma* (1987), 1.27, pp. 131–132; Sarmiento, *Historia Indica* 47, p. 252b. Santacruz Pachacuti Yamqui also knew of these arrangements; see his *Relación de antiguedades* (1879), pp. 285–286.

13. The aged, white-haired Inca Pachacuti designates his adult son, Tupa Yupanqui, to become the next Inca by taking hold of his arm. Investment with the imperial headband, *mazcca paycha*, will follow this initial gesture of investiture. Martín de Murúa, *Historia general del Perú*, c. 1611, fol. 44v, pen and ink with colored washes. The J. Paul Getty Museum.

nizes with his earlier account of the inauguration of Pachacuti. For according to Sarmiento, Pachacuti arranged that Tupa Inca Yupanqui be educated in Coricancha, unseen except by the select few, and that he receive the imperial headband from the hand of the statue of the Sun, just as Pachacuti himself had done earlier.[32] As told by Sarmiento, this ceremonial served to overcome the resistance of Tupa Inca Yupanqui's older brother, whom Pachacuti had initially designated as his successor.[33] Stage-managed correctly, an Inca's public investiture with the imperial headband from the hand of the Sun could accordingly serve to weaken, and indeed to silence, dissent.

Betanzos and Sarmiento agreed that when Pachacuti came to die, diverse steps had already been taken to achieve a harmonious succession. Both historians recount how, feeling his end draw near, the venerable old Inca

> lifted up his voice and sang a poem which those of his generation still sing in his memory and which runs: "Ever since I flourished like the flower of the garden until this day have I laid down order and reason in this life and in this world, until my powers were exhausted; and now I am becoming earth." And saying these words of his poem, Inca Yupanqui Pachacuti died.[34]

Pachacuti had arranged that his death be kept secret for three days while the elevation of Tupa Inca Yupanqui was published abroad, so as to forestall the possibility of rebellion.[35] Then, in accordance with Pachacuti's

---

[32] Sarmiento, *Historia Indica* 42, p. 247ab; compare Murúa, *Historia general* (c. 1611), 1.22, p. 54: Tupa Inca Yupanqui is brought before the image of the Sun and receives the ruler's insignia. In Sarmiento's account, Tupa Inca Yupanqui's inauguration proper followed this episode, contrary to the sequence of events as given by Cieza, *Segunda Parte* 7, p. 19. Sarmiento's account of the Inca receiving the headband of state from the Sun highlights that the priests of Coricancha took a part in the ceremonial. They clearly took a part, albeit a controversial one, in the inauguration of Guascar; see Sarmiento, *Historia Indica* 66, p. 271b. The historical records set down on the quipus that Guaman Poma de Ayala consulted (see M. Mroz, "Paracronologia dinastica," in *Time and Calendars*, ed. M. S. Ziolkowski and R. M. Sadowski 1989, pp. 17–34) recounted Guayna Capac's investiture by the Sun in Coricancha. Guaman Poma's wording reveals that the occasion was complicated; see Guaman Poma, *Nueva Crónica*, p. 113: Como entraron al tenplo del sol para que lo elexieran el sol su padre por rrey, Capac Apo Ynga. En tres veses que entraron al sacreficio no les llamo; en los quatro le llamo su padre el sol y dixo Guayna Capac. Entonses tomo la bolla y masca paycha y se levanto luego. Y luego le mando matar a dos ermanos suyos y luego le obedecieron.

[33] Sarmiento, *Historia Indica* 43, pp. 247bf. Gaining the allegiance of the Inca nobility was a further, separate issue. See the Supplementary Note to this chapter for a ceremony, observed by the first Spaniards to reach Peru, whereby the Inca nobility acknowledged the new ruler.

[34] Betanzos, *Suma* (1987), 1.32, p. 149a; similarly, Sarmiento, *Historia Indica* 47, p. 252b.

[35] Betanzos, *Suma* (1987), 1.30, p. 141; see also Gutierrez de Santa Clara, *Historia de las guerras civiles del Peru*, Biblioteca de autores españoles, vol. 166 (Madrid, 1963), 3.49, p. 212ab.

behest, and in accordance with a ritual of mourning that was still observed in the Andes in the later seventeenth century,[36] the mourners went out into the fields which in his lifetime Pachacuti had loved and where he had inaugurated the imperial festivals of harvest and sowing. They displayed his clothes, ornaments, and armor, and called for him to come back, reminding him of his former pursuits, joys, and achievements. After fifteen days of calling for the deceased from morning to night, the most eminent of the mourners declared that the Inca was now in the sky with his father, the Sun. Whereupon the other mourners begged the deceased Inca to remember them, to send them favorable seasons, and to deliver them from their necessities.

Within the city, the festival of *purucaya*[37] was now celebrated in Pachacuti's honor, and his glorious deeds were reenacted in ritual combat and recited in songs. Sacrifices should be offered, the Inca had laid down, "in my palaces where I have slept and in other places and abodes where I have been."[38] The city of Cuzco was surrounded by a network of holy places, huacas, enshrining religious, mythic, and historical memories. Generation after generation, the number of such places as had been sanctified by contact with an Inca increased, and the veneration addressed to them in turn endowed that Inca's doings with a durability that extended beyond his own life span.[39] Such durability spoke as well through the cult of the mummies of deceased Incas that Pachacuti instituted.[40] He also provided for the cult of his own mummy of his gold effigy, and of a "figure"[41] of his hair clippings and nail parings such as the Spaniards had noticed in 1533.[42]

Betanzos' description of the inauguration of Guayna Capac and the subsequent death of Tupa Inca Yupanqui closely resembles his account of what had been done earlier, when Tupa Inca Yupanqui became Inca.[43] A generation after Pachacuti had first laid down a ceremonial order of Inca succession, this order was apparently working in a stable and predictable fashion. The same conclusion can be reached from Sarmiento's account,[44] even though this historian deliberately highlighted conflict and dissension in the functioning of the Inca state.

Yet, however refined and authoritative Inca ceremonial had come to be

---

[36] Duviols, *Cultura andina y represión* (1986), p. 13; cf. L. Huertas Vallejos, *La religión en una sociedad rural* (1981), pp. 60ff. and below, chap. IX.2 at n. 105.

[37] But note Gonzalez Holguin, *Vocabulario de la lengua general*, p. 297, who associates this term with calling for the deceased.

[38] Betanzos, *Suma* (1987), 1.31, pp. 145, 147b.

[39] Cf. below, chap. IV.3 at nn. 69–83.

[40] Betanzos, *Suma* 1.17, p. 85b.

[41] In Spanish, *bulto*.

[42] Sancho, *An account of the conquest of Peru* 19, p. 170; see above, chap. II.2 at n. 32.

[43] Betanzos, *Suma* 1.39–40.

[44] Sarmiento, *Historia Indica* 41.

during the decades after Pachacuti's death, it was capable of sustaining no more than a limited degree of discord and dissent. This became evident when Guayna Capac approached the day of his death. All Inca rulers had sons by more than one consort, so that to choose a successor entailed choosing the candidate's maternal kinsfolk.[45] Hence, the Inca nobles warned the ailing Guayna Capac, then residing in Quito, that if he did not name a successor himself, then the nobles, in making the nomination, "would become entangled in passions, because the kinsmen of one son of the Inca would wish him to rule so that he had ties of obligation toward them, and the others would desire the same [for their kinsman], so that some discord would arise between them."[46] Guayna Capac thus named his son Ninan Cuyoche to succeed him. When divinatory rituals carried out on his behalf gave a negative verdict, Guayna Capac named Atahualpa, who would not accept the charge, whereupon Guayna Capac named Guascar, but again the oracles were opposed. At this point, Guayna Capac died.[47] Guascar therefore went into the customary seclusion and fasted, after which the nobles of Cuzco bestowed the headband of state upon him and pledged their obedience. In Quito, meanwhile, the Inca lords ordered the body of Guayna Capac to be made into a mummy by having its internal organs removed,[48] drying it in the air, and attiring it in precious cloth and in gold and feather ornaments. The mummy was then solemnly escorted to Cuzco,[49] where Guascar celebrated a spectacular posthumous triumph for his father, and by way of legitimating his own succession, joined Guayna Capac's generals in trampling underfoot the deceased Inca's spoils and prisoners.[50] But neither the triumph nor the performance of that gesture of unbounded might, which had earlier occasioned so much dissension between Viracocha and his son Pachacuti, sufficed to win for Guascar the allegiances of the royal Inca lineages. Guascar thus threatened to disempower these lineages by confiscating the lands of their mummies for his own use.[51] There were conflicts even in Guascar's own lineage, for his mother refused to give her consent to his

---

[45] See Rostworowski, *Historia del Tahuantinsuyu* (1988), pp. 137–153.

[46] Betanzos, *Suma* (1987), 1.46, p. 194a.

[47] Betanzos, *Suma* (1987), 1.48, p. 200; Sarmiento, *Historia Indica* 62, p. 264bf. Contra: Cabello Valboa, *Miscelánea* 3.21, p. 363, Guascar was nominated much earlier.

[48] The internal organs of deceased Incas were kept inside the cult image Punchao; see below, chap. VI, n. 1 and text.

[49] Betanzos, *Suma* (1987), 1.48, p. 201b, with the mummy went Guascar's mother; but Sarmiento, *Historia Indica* 63, p. 265a, Guascar's mother had gone to Cuzco earlier.

[50] Murúa, *Historia general* (c. 1611), 1.42, pp. 119f.; more briefly, Sarmiento, *Historia Indica* 63, p. 265. See also Santacruz Pachacuti Yamqui, *Relación de antiguedades* (1979), p. 308, Guascar's mother married the mummy of Guayna Capac to establish Guascar's legitimacy. This episode suggests that the rules of Inca succession were infinitely more fluid than Spanish historians could envisage.

[51] Betanzos, *Suma* (1987), 2.1, p. 207a.

projected marriage to his sister Chuqui Huipa. As a result, the mummy of Guascar's grandfather, Tupa Inca Yupanqui, had to be called upon to help arrange the match.[52]

Meanwhile, the kinsfolk of Atahualpa's mother, who was a descendant of Pachacuti, backed Atahualpa to become Inca. Atahualpa, who was still in Quito, accordingly also celebrated Guayna Capac's obsequies by way of claiming entitlement to succeed his father as Inca.[53] He arranged for the making of two effigies of Guayna Capac's hair clippings and nail parings, one to accompany him on his expeditions and another to stay permanently in the city of Quito.[54] Perhaps it was one of these effigies that later Guascar's emissaries to Atahualpa encountered in Tumebamba. They offered it sacrifice and removed the Inca insignia which appear to have been kept at Tumebamba to help assert Atahualpa's claim to rule.[55]

Throughout their account of these events, Betanzos' informants, who were of the kin of Atahualpa, implied that thanks to performing the rituals of Guayna Capac's obsequies, Atahualpa had as good a claim to be his successor as did Guascar. However, irrespective of such reasoning, the civil war between Guascar and Atahualpa demonstrated that the ceremonial order that, according to Betanzos and Sarmiento, governed the passing on of power from one Inca to the next had not functioned successfully because an essential ingredient, Guayna Capac's unambiguous designation of a successor, was lacking. For unlike his ancestor Pachacuti, Guayna Capac did not live long enough to supervise the first stages of his successor's inauguration or to prepare the Inca lineages to accept his chosen candidate. The invading Spaniards, arriving at just the juncture when, after bitter warfare, Atahualpa had defeated Guascar, were the beneficiaries of precisely the kind of conflict that Guayna Capac's nobles had foreseen.

When it functioned successfully, however, the ceremonial order of Inca inaugurations and funerals was characterized by carefully orchestrated repetition and was executed, phase by phase, over extended periods of time. It was this long-drawn-out quality, this majestic slowness, that rendered the ceremonial efficacious. An Inca would nominate his successor; years later, when this Inca had died, the nomination would be reiterated by the nobles of Cuzco. This process could be repeated twice over when

---

[52] Murúa, *Historia general* (c. 1611), 43, p. 121f.; Cabello Valboa, *Miscelánea* 3.25, p. 399f. For hostility between Guascar and his mother, see Sarmiento, *Historia Indica* 65, p. 271a.

[53] Cf. Cieza, *Segunda Parte* 7, p. 20, an Inca must receive the headband in Cuzco; contra, Betanzos, *Suma* 2.5, p. 215ab.

[54] Betanzos, *Suma* (1987), 2.2, p. 209. For such effigies of Guayna Capac in Cuzco, see Betanzos, *Suma* (1987), 2.1, p. 208b.

[55] Sarmiento, *Historia Indica* 63, p. 266b. Possession of one's deceased predecessor's mummy was part and parcel of establishing a claim to rule. For the succession of Atahualpa, see Betanzos, *Suma* 2.26, p. 286a.

an Inca nominated not only his son, but also his grandson, to succeed him, as Pachacuti had done. Pachacuti's nomination of his grandson Guayna Capac was thus reiterated later by Tupa Inca Yupanqui.[56] The measured, quasi-eternal rhythms of Inca ceremonial spoke not only through the interlocking phases of obsequies and inauguration that followed one upon another in the course of many years but also through the rituals surrounding the mummies of deceased Incas. For as a mummy, endowed with inalienable palaces, lands, herds, and retainers, an Inca was in effect immortal, and, as Pedro Pizarro and other Spaniards learned when they first visited Cuzco, continued playing a role in the affairs of men.

An Inca's career was shaped by a twofold set of forces. On the one hand, while alive, he was set apart from humankind. He was carried in a litter by nobles and sheltered in the shade of a parasol such as no other person could use; his utensils and garments were made of uniquely precious materials, and his subjects approached him with gestures such as they addressed to the divine Sun and the huacas. On the other hand, after death, when the Inca had become a mummy and was in addition represented by a gold statue that had its own servants, courtly ceremonial endeavored to emphasize his human characteristics. Food and drink were served to the mummies and the statues morning and evening. The mummies, moreover, spent the day in public activities and at night returned to their palaces. At the same time, the deceased Inca lived "in the sky with his father the Sun."[57] In short, the living Inca's human life was extended into divine, supernatural life, while the deceased Inca's divine and supernatural life was extended into human life. In either case, the royal ceremonial spelled out how the Inca's existence transcended both the limits of human time and the rhythms of calendrical time. His dominion over his subjects was exemplified by his dominion over time.

Such perceptions were deeply alien to the finely tuned European reason and even to the searching power of observation with which Cieza addressed the Andean world. For him, the nature of a thing was characterized by its cause and origin. Following one of the Inca myths of origins, Cieza therefore began his discussion of Inca inauguration and death ceremonies with the initiation of young men. Where Betanzos described a ceremonial order governing Inca obsequies and inaugurations that reached its definitive form in the time of Pachacuti, Cieza traced this ceremonial order back to Inca beginnings. The initiation rituals that preceded an Inca's inauguration,[58] he thought, had not been laid down by

---

[56] Betanzos, *Suma* (1987), 1.39, p. 175.
[57] Betanzos, *Suma* (1987), 1.31, p. 145b.
[58] Cieza, *Segunda Parte* 7, pp. 19; contrast Sarmiento, *Historia Indica* 42–43, pp. 247af, where Topa Inca Yupanqui's designation by investiture with the headband preceded initiation.

Inca Pachacuti, as Betanzos had been told, but went back to the mythic past.[59] Indeed, as Cieza understood it, the fast and seclusion of the Inca designate took place while the young men were being initiated.[60] His fast concluded, the Inca was invested with the mazcca paycha, and this ceremony had to take place in Cuzco.[61] In Cieza's view, therefore, Atahualpa, who began his reign in Quito, was not a legitimate ruler.

In addition, according to Cieza, the ruling Inca must marry his sister, and his successor must be the eldest son of that marriage. The precedent for this observance, Cieza thought, had been set when the mythic founder, Manco Capac, married his son and successor, Sinchi Roca, to the latter's sister.[62] In this way "the succession to the kingdom was confirmed in the royal lineage."[63] Atahualpa was older than Guascar, but Guascar was born from the marriage between Guayna Capac and his sister Chimbo Ocllo, and thus, by the rules Cieza outlined, had a better claim to rule than Atahualpa.[64] Betanzos also mentioned the brother-sister marriages of Inca rulers but only at a later stage, when Pachacuti married his sister Mama Ocllo.[65] Here also, therefore, Cieza ascribed to the beginnings of Inca history a usage that in historical terms only arose later, although Inca myth did suggest an earlier precedent.[66]

Having thus established the rules of Inca succession, Cieza related how, with every Inca's death and his successor's inauguration, these rules came into play. They did so as antecedents and conditions to the unfolding of the rituals of mourning, of the establishment of worship for the old Inca's mummy, of the successor's seclusion and fast, of his investment with the headband of state, and of his marriage to his sister.[67] An Inca's death and the inauguration of his successor thus occasioned—or, in the case of Guayna Capac's death and the accession of Atahualpa, failed to occasion—a moment of legitimation that was crystallized in ceremonial action. According to Cieza, therefore, once the appropriate ceremonial had been performed, a new reign could unfold and its events could be narrated as occurring in a sequence of reigns that were linked to one another by male primogeniture from a brother-sister marriage.[68]

Regular sequences of reigns were a norm aspired to in fifteenth- and

[59] See above, chap. III.2 at nn. 18–20.
[60] Cieza, *Segunda Parte* 7, pp. 18–19.
[61] Cieza, *Segunda Parte* 7, pp. 19–20.
[62] Cieza, *Segunda Parte* 8, p. 22; 31, p. 95. Contra: Sarmiento, *Historia Indica* 15, p. 220b, he married a lady from Sano.
[63] Cieza, *Segunda Parte* 10, p. 25.
[64] Cieza, *Segunda Parte* 69.
[65] Betanzos, *Suma* (1987), I.26, p. 127b.
[66] Cf. Rostworowski, "Succession, Cooption," *Southwestern Journal of Anthropology* 16, no. 4 (1960): 417–427.
[67] See Cieza, *Segunda Parte* 31–38 passim; 45–46; 54–55; 61–63; 69–71.
[68] Cf. below, chap. IV.3 at n. 117, for the capacocha sacrifice at an Inca's accession.

sixteenth-century Spain, where, at the very time when Cieza was working on his *Crónica del Perú*, the historian Florián de Ocampo put the fin-
ishing touches on a history of Spain that traced the line of kings who had
ruled in the peninsula back to a grandson of Noah. Ocampo also published a version of the *Primera Crónica General* by Alfonso the Wise, a
work that likewise displays a deep preoccupation with the lineages of rulers. The legitimation of any one ruler was most convincingly established
by his place at the end of a long line of kings.[69] This perspective on the
past led Cieza to emphasize those aspects of Inca myth and ceremony that
could lead to the perception of Andean analogies to his peninsular model.
He therefore began his account of Inca inaugurations with that of Sinchi
Roca, son of the founder Manco Capac. By contrast, Betanzos and Sarmiento showed little interest in such distant precedent. Betanzos in particular adhered meticulously to the narrative of his Inca informants.
These informants provided a detailed account of Inca deaths and of properly legitimated inaugurations as understood by themselves, not as understood by sixteenth-century Spaniards. The succession of rulers they
considered relevant to themselves began with Viracocha and Pachacuti.
Betanzos thus thought that insofar as Inca rulers before Viracocha had an
identity, it was an identity activated for the most part by kinship and by
ceremonial. On the one hand, earlier Inca rulers were remembered as
progenitors of royal lineages; and on the other hand, their effigies, *bultos*,
were benficiaries of the cults and laudatory recitations that Pachacuti had
ordered those lineages to perform.[70]

Twenty years later, Sarmiento was given a very similar account of these
matters, but he appears to have found the story of the bultos incredible.[71]
He accordingly wrote that when Pachacuti instituted the rituals of Coricancha,

> he disinterred the bodies of the seven Incas of the past, from Manco
> Capac to Yaguar Guaca Inca, which were all in the House of the Sun,
> and adorned them with gold, placing masks on them, and head-

[69] On Alfonso the Wise, see Rico, *Alfonso el Sabio* (1984), pp. 113ff. Juan de Mariana
displayed similar genealogical preoccupations in his *Historia general de España*, Biblioteca de
autores españoles, vol. 30 (Madrid, 1950); see in particular 1.1 and 7–11. In the fifteenth
century, Alfonso de Santa Maria compiled a history of Spain that highlighted the succession
of rulers: "Reduxi ad modum arboris omnes qui in hac Hispania nostra regis diademate sunt
potiti," he wrote at the outset of his *Anacephaleosis* published by A. Schottus, *Hispania Illus-
trata*, vol. 1, Frankfurt (1608). See on this work and its intentions, R. Tate, "La 'Anacephaleosis' de Alfonso Garcia de Santa Maria," in his *Ensayos sobre la historiografía peninsular del
siglo XV* (Madrid, 1970), pp. 55–73.

[70] Betanzos, *Suma* (1968), 1.17, p. 54b: Pachacuti ordered "que luego hiziesen cantares
. . . en los loores de los hechos que cada uno destos Señores en sus dias ansi hizo." On
bultos, cf. above nn. 21–22.

[71] I would like to thank John Hyslop for drawing my attention to these parallel passages
in Betanzos and Sarmiento.

dresses which they call *chucos*, and disks, bracelets, scepters called *yauri* or *chambi*, and other gold ornaments. And then he arranged them in order of their antiquity on a platform richly worked in gold, and then he ordered splendid festivals with representations of the life of each Inca to be celebrated.[72]

The supposition that Pachacuti exhumed the bodies of his forebears reflects Spanish incomprehension of Andean attitudes toward the dead and of different Andean methods of representing the dead in society. In Christian thought, each human being is made up of a unique soul inhabiting a unique body. Indeed, selfhood and identity are predicated upon this fusion of each soul with its body, both in this life and after death, in the life to come.[73] In Inca and even in colonial Peru, by contrast, a person's identity had a social and consensual aspect for which there is little room in Christian thought. An episode from the reign of the Inca Guayna Capac will clarify this difference between Inca and Christian thought. During his wars on the northern frontier of the empire, Guayna Capac was accompanied by the gold statue of his mother, Mama Ocllo, which was normally housed in a splendid temple in Tumebamba and contained Mama Ocllo's womb. This statue provided the Inca with the means of extricating himself from a dangerous and embarrassing situation. Guayna Capac had been defeated by the Carangui and blamed the disaster on the nobles from Cuzco who let him fall from his litter during a battle.[74] He therefore humiliated those nobles by excluding them from regular distributions of supplies and ceremonial gifts. The nobles accordingly resolved to return home to Cuzco. When they were already on their way, however, Guayna Capac sent after them "the statue of his mother Mama Ocllo dressed in mourning, with her priests and with a Cañari lady who began speaking in the voice of the image." This lady, impersonating Mama Ocllo, succeeded in persuading the nobles to return to the service of the Inca.[75]

---

[72] Sarmiento, *Historia Indica* 31, p. 236b. Cf. Betanzos, *Suma* (1968), 1.17, p. 54a; also *Suma* (1987), 1.17, p. 85b.

[73] For a definitive statement of this doctrine, see Augustine, *City of God*, books 13 and 21–22. This is the teaching which, in simplified form, the missionaries inculcated in the Andes. See the two treatises in *Doctrina Cristiana y Catecismo* (1584) entitled "Exhortación para ayudar a bien morir" (foliated separately: fols. 1–10). However, one should also note that in Christian Europe, there inevitably existed loopholes and contradictions in theological teaching regarding burial and the nature of the dead as well as the resurrected body, and that precept was readily set aside by the exigencies of practice: see E.A.R. Brown, "Authority, the Family, and the Dead in Late Medieval France," *French Historical Studies* 16, no. 4 (1990): 803–832.

[74] For Mama Ocllo's statue in Tumebamba, see Murúa, *Historia general* (1613), 1.31, p. 81; Cabello Valboa, *Miscelánea* 3.21, pp. 364f. For Guayna Capac's accident in battle, Cabello, *Miscelánea* 3.21, p. 370.

[75] Cabello Valboa, *Miscelánea* 3.22, pp. 374–378.

The coya Mama Ocllo's identity and authority thus resided as much in her statue as it did in the person of the lady who spoke in her voice. But that is only part of the story. For her identity, in order to be functional, also required the recognition of society.

Whether, therefore, in the ceremonial formulated by Pachacuti, past Incas were represented as effigies of some kind or as mummies, the purpose was to make concrete their presence in the human and political world. At the same time, the parallel functions fulfilled by mummies and effigies are instructive, for they highlight a rift in sixteenth-century perceptions of the long distant, as distinct from the more recent, Andean past. Many Andeans whom Betanzos, Cieza, Sarmiento, and their contemporaries interviewed, personally remembered the reigns of Guayna Capac and Tupa Inca Yupanqui.[76] Viracocha and Pachacuti on the other hand stood just beyond the boundary of living memory; their reigns marked the point beyond which accounts of the past became sketchy and schematic. This was why Betanzos said so little about Incas before Viracocha. Moreover, as Betanzos and Sarmiento both made clear, the cults of these rulers were established by Inca Pachacuti as an expression of the new imperial order. Whatever historical importance these rulers may have had in their own right was thus absorbed within the framework of the Inca state. As all the early Spanish historians of the Andes were aware, there was little to be learned about the early Incas, and most of it was highly contradictory. In addition, the personal memories of Andean informants reached back to precisely the period when Inca society found the shape that the Spanish invaders were to encounter.[77] Historical circumstances as well as Inca methods of accounting for the past thus converged to make that past hard of access to the invaders.

In addition, it was in the nature of the narrative which Betanzos recorded, a narrative which drew on the memories of different individuals, that it should contain repetitions and contradictions. Critically acute historians, such as Cieza and Sarmiento, found this aspect of the Inca historical record infuriating. For in accord with the precepts of European historical writing, they regarded it as part of their task to explain or harmonize differences in their sources, thereby finding in the Andes a pattern of narrative and explanatory coherence such as was familiar from European written history. But the manner in which Andeans recounted their past made this very difficult to do. Betanzos, on the other hand, recorded stories as he heard them and left the critical evaluation that was

[76] Cf. Cieza, *Segunda Parte* 31, p. 94.

[77] I am not as convinced as is R. T. Zuidema that no historicity at all can be attributed to figures preceding Pachacuti (cf. above, n. 1), although I realize that the shift in the nature of our information about the last three or four Incas of the traditional dynasty needs more explanation than it has received if one does not subscribe to Zuidema's thesis in its entirety.

demanded by European historiography to one side. For instance, his Inca informants appear to have recounted Pachacuti's obsequies twice: they gave the first version in the form of Pachacuti's own instructions regarding what was to be done at his death;[78] the second version, beginning with the dying Pachacuti's song,[79] records how the instructions were carried out. These two versions do not agree in all particulars.[80]

However, despite such difficulties, a coherent picture of the observances marking an Inca's death and his successor's inauguration emerges from Betanzos. Firstly, these observances were flexible: they could be accommodated to widely differing circumstances, such as the tension-ridden inauguration of Pachacuti on the one hand, and the inauguration of Tupa Inca Yupanqui, which the sources describe as having been comparatively well prepared and peaceful, on the other. Secondly, the celebrations and ceremonies accompanying an Inca's death and his successor's inauguration extended far beyond the exact time at which these events occurred. As Betanzos' informants made clear, activities leading up to a well-prepared death and inauguration took up many years. If all went well during those years, the desires of most contending parties would be accommodated as a preliminary to the new Inca's inauguration. In addition, the meticulously slow and deliberate pacing of the ceremonial of an Inca's death and his successor's inauguration had been evolved, as Betanzos' informants stated repeatedly, to forestall rebellion among the empire's subjects.[81]

In practical and political terms, the ceremonial was designed to eliminate the possibility of sudden change by bringing the Inca's successor into the public limelight as early as possible. The religious dimension of the ceremonial, which exalted the Inca as Indichuri, "Son of the Sun," and spelled out his dominion over time both in life and after death, orchestrated this practical purpose. To fall victim to time was the lot of everyone except—so the ceremonial of Inca death and inauguration suggested—the Inca. In cosmic terms, at death the Inca returned to his origin, so as "to rest with his father the Sun."[82] In human terms, the dead Inca "as though alive"[83] participated in the doings of his successor by virtue of the services of his retainers and kinsmen, thereby empowering his lineage to partici-

[78] Betanzos, *Suma* 1.30–31.

[79] Betanzos, *Suma* (1987), 1.32, p. 149a.

[80] Betanzos, *Suma* (1987), 1.30, p. 142a, Pachacuti's mummy was to stay in Cuzco. Contra, 1.32, p. 150a, Pachacuti's mummy was in Patallacta; cf. 2.1, p. 208b, Guayna Capac's mummy on his estate in Yucay.

[81] Betanzos, *Suma* (1987), 1.126, p. 128a; 28, pp. 133bf.; 29, p. 137b; 30, p. 141a (cf. 33, p. 150a); 39, p. 171a.

[82] Betanzos, *Suma* (1987), 1.26, p. 128a. See above, n. 22, the dead Inca is called by the name of Guanacaure, a huaca strongly associated with Inca origins.

[83] Betanzos, *Suma* (1987), 1.39, p. 177b.

pate in the life of the Inca polity. Given these patterns and themes of Inca religious observance and political order, the Christian preoccupation that illusion and demonic activity were somehow at work fell by the way. Betanzos or his informants might mention in passing the demons who deceived Andean people and who spoke in the huacas of Cuzco, in the volcano of Arequipa, or in the image of Pachacamac.[84] But demons were not needed to explain the workings of Inca religion and politics to men who had an intimate understanding of both. Nonetheless, demonic activity and illusion remained potent concepts throughout the sixteenth century and beyond, because for most of the invaders these concepts integrated the new and unfamiliar with what was familiar and known. And in more practical terms, Spanish officials and missionaries appealed to the power of demons in the Andes by way of legitimating the different political order that they were in the course of implanting in the lands formerly ruled by the Incas.

Supplementary Note: Tocto

Francisco Pizarro's two secretaries, Pedro Sancho and Francisco Xerez, recorded particulars of the inaugurations of Atahualpa's successors, Tupa Huallpa and Manco Inca, that accord with and supplement the more informed and more detailed accounts by Betanzos, Cieza, and Sarmiento. Before an Inca was inaugurated, Xerez and Sancho learned, he had to fast for a certain period in seclusion,[85] in a building specially set aside for this purpose.[86] Then the lords of the empire, by way of promising obedience to the Inca, kissed his hand and cheek,[87] these being gestures that had counterparts in Castilian courtly ritual. But another ceremony that Pedro Sancho observed did not. When Tupa Huallpa had fasted, his lords assembled before him, and "each one came to offer him a white feather as a sign of vassalage and tribute." Similarly, Tupa Huallpa offered such a feather to express—so far as Sancho understood it—his homage to the emperor Charles V, and later the Inca lords offered white feathers to Manco Inca at his inauguration.[88] After the ceremony, the feathers, known as *tocto*, were burned.[89] Even in the later seventeenth century, such

[84] Betanzos, *Suma* (1987), 1.11, pp. 49bf.
[85] Xerez, *Verdadera Relación*, p. 156.
[86] Sancho, *An account of the conquest*, pp. 23, 111.
[87] Xerez, *Verdadera Relación*, p. 157.
[88] Sancho, *An account*, pp. 23, 25, 111.
[89] Cobo, *Historia* 12.36, p. 138b; cf. Gonzalez Holguin, *Vocabulario de la lengua general*, p. 344, s.v. ttokto. White feathers of a bird called *tocto* also adorned the heads of recently initiated young men after they fought their mock battle, Molina, *Fábulas* p. 111; and the same kind of feathers decorated tunics worn during the lesser Inti Raimi in December, Molina, *Fábulas*, p. 113; see also Murúa, *Historia general* (1611), 2.27 (vol. 2, p. 104, line 20 of 1962 ed.), the bird *tocto* is found in desert places and is used for sacrifice.

feathers were still burned as an ingredient in sacrifices to huacas and mummies.[90] When thus the Inca nobles approached their new ruler with white feathers in their hands—feathers that were later burned, just as in the seventeenth century feathers were still burned in the Andes to honor deities—these nobles were giving expression to the Inca's divinity as Son of the Sun.

[90] Duviols, *Cultura andina* (1986), pp. 29, 57, 71, 88, 94, 192, 279, etc., feathers of the bird Hasto Tucto offered in sacrifices; cf. p. 89, Hasto Tucto the sister of the *huaca* Llacssa Guari.

ANDEAN SACRED SPACE
AND TIME,
1552–1583

CIEZA WAS the first European to grapple seriously with Andean religious belief and observance, and the issues he raised in both his published and his unpublished writings were still recognized as fundamental a century later. Although much changed regarding things Andean during the later sixteenth century, works of history published by midcentury contributed significantly toward creating an initial understanding of the Andean world in Europe. The number of books about Mexico always far exceeded those about Peru, yet news from the Andes did circulate, so that by century's end Peru figured in some detail in Giovanni Botero's *Relationi universali* and in similar descriptions of the "theatre of the world." Among the more important publications about Peru that such authors could draw on were the first volume of Cieza's *Crónica*, published in Seville in 1553,[1] and the earliest Quechua grammar and lexicon, both of 1560, by Domingo de Santo Tomás, whom Cieza had known and consulted during his travels in the Andes. Francisco López de Gómara's best-selling *History of the Indies*, dealing principally with Mexico, was first published in 1552. Gómara derived some of his Peruvian information from the same source as did Agustín de Zárate, author of the *History of the Discovery and Conquest of Peru* of 1555. The two authors' account of myths of Pachacamac is thus almost identical.[2] Other works of history, personal memoirs, and administrative and ecclesiastical documents circulated in manuscript. In this way the Inca empire, which initially had been viewed as a remote and exotic polity, came to be included, in some fashion, within a European network of theories and ideas about the nature of political existence.

Cieza had collected his information not only from Andeans, but also from Spanish officials and missionaries. These men looked for the details of religious observance, including sometimes the rationale of that observance, so as to be able to supplant it with Christianity. Christianiza-

---

[1] Cf. M. Maticorena Estrada, "Cieza de León en Sevilla," *Anuario de Estudios Americanos* 12 (1955): 615–672.

[2] Above, chap. II.1; M. Bataillon, "Zárate ou Lozano?" *Caravelle* 1 (1963): 1–28.

tion had interested Cieza also, but in a historical and theological, more than an official or administrative, sense. Similarly, Betanzos took it for granted that Andeans would become Christians but did not concern himself with how this purpose was to be achieved. The Andes as viewed by historians thus differed from the Andes as viewed by those missionaries and secular officials who in the course of the latter half of the sixteenth century transformed the empire of the Incas into a colonial state by replacing Inca institutions with European ones.

To achieve this transformation, secular officials and missionaries collected detailed practical information not only about many aspects of Andean myth and cult, of religious observance and political power—topics that had earlier interested Cieza and Betanzos—but also about more technical issues regarding Andean and Inca sacred topography, the religious calendar, and particulars of daily and domestic religious practice. In 1583 the dignitaries of the Peruvian church met in the Third Council of Lima and laid down future missionary goals and strategies in what turned out to be a well-nigh definitive form. They were able to do this because they had at their disposal a very sizable body of information about the workings of Inca government and about Andean religion and social and economic organization. This information had been accumulated both by missionaries and by secular officials conducting formal inspections, *visitas*, of towns and villages.

The first visita to cover Peru in its entirety was that of Don Pedro de la Gasca in 1549.[3] Some visitas had as their aim not merely the collection of information, and hence, in due course, of revenue, but also the reorganization of Andean settlement patterns. The vast majority of Andeans were country dwellers living in small villages that often comprised only a few households. To gain control over this rural population, missionaries and secular officials favored resettlement in larger villages or small towns. Programs of resettlement, *reducción*, were implemented within twenty years of the invasion. As early as 1557, Damián de la Bandera, having inspected the province of Huamanga, was able to report to the Crown that its 672 villages had been reduced to 252, thereby facilitating the access of both missionary and tax collector.[4] But the most intensive and complete program of resettlement was organized somewhat later by the viceroy Toledo, who governed Peru between 1569 and 1581.[5] A network of

[3] See T. Hampe Martínez, *Don Pedro de la Gasca*, pp. 131–138. For an edition of part of the visita, see Gasca, *Visitación*, ed. Helmer (1955–1956); also printed in Iñigo Ortíz de Zúñiga, *Visita de León de Huanuco 1562* 1: 289ff. See also W. Espinoza Soriano, "El primer informe etnologico sobre Cajamarca," *Revista Peruana de Cultura* 11–12 (1967): 5–41.

[4] Damián de la Bandera, *Relación general de la . . . provincia de Guamanga* (1965), p. 176.

[5] Cf. R. Levillier, *Don Francisco de Toledo* (1935), pp. 246ff.; S. J. Stern, *Peru's Indian Peoples* (1982), pp. 76ff., 148ff. On the extent of the upheaval of the Toledan reducciones see T. Bouysse-Cassagne, *La identidad aymara*, pp. 40ff., with p. 373.

missionary village parishes, or *doctrinas*, thus came into existence. Many of them were laid out, just as Juan de Matienzo, *oidor*[6] of the royal *audiencia*[7] of Chuquisaca, had suggested in 1567, around a central square dominated by a church and by Spanish administrative buildings, behind which were huddled the humble houses of Indians (fig. 14; see also fig. 11).[8]

Yet, the hispanized appearance that many Andean villages and towns had acquired by the later sixteenth century was not often accompanied by hispanized and Christian conduct or belief on the part of Andeans. For although, outside Cuzco, Inca religion and ceremonial gradually fell into oblivion, the Incas themselves did not, and the old, established regional beliefs and practices had a much more powerful grip on Andeans than most missionaries anticipated. While thus the religion of the Andean present began to diverge from that of the Inca past, the task of historians who recorded this past likewise began to diverge from the task of the missionaries and secular officials who administered the viceroyalty of Peru. For secular officials and missionaries required a knowledge of the present. Besides, some official and missionary documents focus on Inca and Andean religion beyond the confines of Cuzco, whereas historians tended to concentrate on the capital. Finally, these documents show how Inca and Andean conceptions of sacred space and time changed and came to interact with their Christian counterparts.

These interrelations between Inca Cuzco and the imperial provinces, and between Inca past and colonial present, determine the order of our present discussion. We begin by considering Andean and Inca religion as practiced away from Cuzco. Then we turn to some memories of the religion of the Inca capital that were, for the most part, recorded in the later sixteenth century. And finally, we discuss the Andean protest movement of the 1560s known as *Taqui Onqoy*, or "Dance of Disease," along with the investigations into Inca religious practice by missionaries and colonial officials that accompanied and followed this movement.

1. REGIONAL CULTS AND THE INCAS

In 1552 the Augustinian order founded a convent in one of the Inca palaces of Huamachuco. Some years earlier, Cieza had passed through Huamachuco and had learned something of the recent history of the region. It had been absorbed into the Inca empire by Tupa Inca Yupanqui and Guayna Capac, who built roads, raised some fine buildings, and set aside part of the land as a royal hunting reserve. These were costly enterprises,

---

[6] Spanish, "judge."
[7] Spanish, "judicial council."
[8] Matienzo, *Gobierno del Peru* 1.14; fig. 14.

14. Juan de Matienzo, *Gobierno del Perú*: plan of the center of a resettlement village (*reducción*) displaying the new political order of colonial Peru. The main square is overlooked by church, prison, hospital, and hospice for Spanish travelers, and by the quarters of Spanish figures of authority. Only one Andean dignitary, the *tucurico* (royal official) is mentioned: his house, behind that of the *corregidor*, has no view of the square. New York Public Library, MS Rich 74, fol. 38r.

and Huamachuco was very far away from the center of Inca power in Cuzco. When thus the Spaniards arrived, they received a friendly welcome.[1] Indeed, the priests of the region's prophetic deity, Catequil, had already distanced themselves from the Incas on earlier occasions by uttering unwelcome predictions regarding Inca matters of state. Whether these priests had the oracle predict, correctly as it turned out, that Tupa Inca Yupanqui would die in the course of his wars in the North, or whether the oracle erroneously announced that Guascar would defeat Atahualpa, such statements, which publicized many of the tensions existing within the Inca state, damaged Inca prestige. Atahualpa therefore smashed Catequil's image and devastated his cult site.[2] Catequil, however, lived to see another day, because the priests and temple servants who resided at the foot of his holy mountain survived the Inca's onslaught and restored their god's worship. The head and three fragments of the body of Catequil's statue were recovered from a nearby river and were reverently erected in a newly constructed sanctuary, where the god received the traditional Andean offering of finely woven ceremonial cloth. But when the priests learned of the Spanish invaders' hostility to Andean deities, they transported the salvaged pieces of Catequil's statue to a remote mountain refuge, where the god continued to give oracles. This was the situation that the Augustinian friars encountered when they arrived in Huamachuco; in 1560, after eight years of missionary labor, they wrote an account of what they had achieved and learned.[3]

Eight years was long enough for the friars to gain a certain understanding of the relation between daily religious practice in the Andes and religious belief as formulated in myth. Other Spaniards, who lacked such long-term familiarity with a particular region, only glimpsed the existence of such a relationship, as Cieza did when he realized that the role of Guanacaure in the Inca foundation myth bore on this huaca's role in the festival cycle of Cuzco.[4] In the missionary endeavor of extirpating Andean religion, however, a clear and specific grasp of the interdependence of myth and cult was fundamental and was to form a staple of missionary discourse until, over a century later, the Catholic church lost interest in the issue.

Cieza had commented in passing both on the Inca state cult and on the regional cults of Huamachuco.[5] It was these latter that continued to be practiced after the Inca empire had come to an end and that there-

[1] Cieza, *Crónica* 81.

[2] See above, chap. II.1 at n. 29.

[3] Religiosos Agustinos, *Relación de la religion y ritos del Perú* . . . (1865; hereafter Religiosos Agustinos), pp. 25–26.

[4] Cieza, *Segunda Parte* 28, p. 83; cf. above, chap. III.2, p. 101.

[5] Cieza, *Crónica* 81, p. 237.

fore preoccupied the Augustinian friars most deeply. Local myths re-corded that the oracular Catequil was the offspring of the creator Atagu-ju's son, Guamansuri, and of a woman belonging to an earlier generation of beings. The missionaries understood these beings to have been "Chris-tians, who in the language of Huamachuco are called Guachemines."[6] These Guachemines killed Guamansuri for having corrupted one of their women, to wit, Catequil's mother. Catequil, however, grew up to be a valiant youth, who in turn

> killed the Guachemines, and the ones who survived he expelled from the land, and then he went up into the sky and said to Ataguju: "Now the earth is free, and the Guachemines are dead or exiled, and I beg you to create Indians to inhabit and work the earth."

The creator Ataguju therefore ordered Catequil to bring those Indians forth from the mountain Ipuna like a crop, by using digging sticks of silver and gold; and he promised that thenceforth these Indians would prosper and multiply.[7] Catequil obeyed the Creator's behest but was much feared because he was prone to killing people by hurling lightning, thunder, and lightning flashes[8] at them with a sling he had received as a gift from his mother. Since Catequil could wield a sling like a man, the cult statue that Atahualpa destroyed represented him anthropomorphi-cally.[9] At the same time, however, he was a mountain lord. Porcon, the cult site where he gave oracles, was a mountain with three peaks that represented him as Apo Catequil, "the Lord Catequil," flanked by his mother, Mama Catequil, and his brother, Piguerao. At the foot of this mountain was the settlement where in Inca times the priests and atten-dants of the sanctuary had resided.[10]

This myth of Huamachucan origins makes clear how quickly Andeans began to adapt inherited conceptions of the past to their experience of the invading Spaniards. All Andean myths of origins open with an earlier age that in some fundamental way differed from the current age. In Cuzco, for instance, Cieza heard that during that earlier age, people did not see the sun, while according to a myth from Pachacamac, there was no food in the first age.[11] The Andeans who told the Augustinian missionaries in

---

[6] Religiosos Agustinos, p. 22.

[7] Religiosos Agustinos, pp. 22–23: Catequil gave the order that his people should use digging sticks of silver and gold; perhaps he ordered that men have gold, and women silver, digging sticks, just as the Inca was specifically protected by the golden sun and his consort by the silver moon, cf. below, chap. VIII.1 at nn. 26–27.

[8] Spanish, *rayo, trueno, relampago.*

[9] Religiosos Agustinos, p. 25.

[10] Religiosos Agustinos, p. 25.

[11] Above, chap. III.1 at n. 29; Cieza, *Segunda Parte* 5, p. 8; Calancha, *Corónica Moralizada* 2.19, p. 931.

Huamachuco that their first age was an epoch of Christians were applying a familiar mythic motif to a new situation. They perceived the invading Christians as fundamentally different from themselves, as belonging to a separate epoch. Indeed, since the myths usually described preceding epochs as deficient, to call such an earlier epoch Christian amounted to saying that in comparison to Andeans, Christians were deficient. Perceptions of Christian deficiency were not restricted to Huamachuco. In his account of the invasion of Peru, Manco Inca's son, Titu Cusi Yupanqui, repeatedly stressed the conspicuous moral failings of Spaniards, sons of the devil who were consumed by envy and rapacity.[12] The Augustinian missionaries, however, interpreted the myth from Huamachuco differently. They believed that the Christians of that earlier Andean epoch were proof that, long ago, the gospel had been preached in the Andes by one of Christ's apostles.[13] Andeans in turn saw in the fact that their originator, Catequil, had killed the Guachemines, or Christians, an explanation for their sufferings from Spanish greed and oppression: for by oppressing Andeans, the Christian invaders were avenging their own Christian kinsmen, the Guachemines. This Andean interpretation of the myth led the missionaries, on their side, to suppose that the Indians

> are our enemies, along with the devil; because the Guachemines killed Guamansuri, the latter hates and fears the Christians and did not want the Indians to receive the law of the Christians. Indeed, there is no doubt that the hatred of the Indians for us is great.[14]

However much Christianity was at variance with Andean mythic discourse, the missionaries' engagement in this discourse reveals its power when under attack. For, in the last resort, the missionaries were forced to concede that Andean myth retained its explanatory validity even when it projected a negative interpretation of the Christian presence in the Andes.

As soon as the Augustinian friars had settled in Huamachuco in 1552, they searched out the fragments of Catequil's statue, which had by then been removed to its place of refuge. Having found these fragments, the missionaries ground them to a powder, which they secretly threw into a river, so that not even the tiniest piece of the statue could be retrieved for future worship. Catequil's llama herds were distributed among the poor, and some of his sacred cloth was made into Christian altar frontals.[15]

But it happened with the deity as it had with his myth. For Catequil

[12] Titu Cusi, *Relación*, pp. 36, 39, 52, 55.

[13] Different versions of this theory were current elsewhere in Peru (cf. Cieza, *Segunda Parte* 5) and were to gain further support later on; see below, chap. VII.3.

[14] Religiosos Agustinos, p. 24. As so often, the Spanish writer gives a very abridged rendering of the myth. Thus he does not explain how Guamansuri can both be killed and still hate the Christians.

[15] Religiosos Agustinos, p. 26.

resurrected manyfold, in that the Indians thinking of him as they walked and worked in their fields saw his many sons being revealed to them in diverse rocks and stones, which they therefore set aside as focal points of cult.[16] In Huamachuco, as everywhere in the Andes, the plains and the mountains, the sky and the waters were both the theatre and the dramatis personae of divine action. The vocation to be a priest, *alco*, could thus come to a person while performing daily tasks, such as collecting fire-wood or tilling a field in a distant *estancia*.[17] In the course of a contemplation occasioned, perhaps, by some object dancing on a surface of water, one would be led to a remote holy place and remain for some days, learning to converse with the divine presence residing there. A five days' fast, taking the form of abstinence from salt, aji,[18] chicha, and sexual intercourse, bestowed public validation on such a priestly vocation.[19] Alternatively, one could be called in a dream vision or during the performance of a religious ritual.[20] Whatever the particular form of the calling, the individual thus designated conversed with the holy presences of the land on behalf of his people. The voice of these holy presences was perceived by the priest either as an interior voice or as some external sound that his calling enabled him to interpret.[21] This intimate contact that religious specialists were accustomed to establish between themselves and the natural environment was not restricted to Huamachuco. For in Cuzco likewise the priest of the Sun would retire to the country so as "to contemplate and meditate more freely on the stars . . . and on the things of their religion."[22] The priests of Huamachuco also offered solemn sacrifices to the deities,[23] heard confessions, and imposed penances, such as undertaking a pilgrimage to a mountain holy place above the snow line.[24]

The missionary friars viewed such observances, which reminded them of Catholic confession and penance, as so many demonic imitations of true religion.[25] Furthermore, the devil appeared to Andeans in dreams as an eagle[26] or in waking visions as a serpent—as that serpent who figured

---

[16] Religiosos Agustinos, pp. 26f.

[17] Spanish, "farmstead in the high mountains."

[18] Term of Caribbean origin: a spicy condiment. The Quechua term, which Spaniards rarely used, is *uchu*; cf. Garcilaso, *Comentarios reales* 5.5, p. 154a. On fasting by abstaining from uchu, see Garcilaso, *CR* 6.24, pp. 224bf.; 7.6, p. 253a; 8.12, p. 309a. The term *uchu* appears in the name of one of the mythic Inca founding brothers, Ayar Uchu; see Garcilaso *CR* 1.18, p. 30b with Sarmiento, *Historia Indica* 12, p. 216b, Ayar Uchu Guanacauri. See also Max Hernandez et al., *Entre el mito y la historia*, pp. 21, 24.

[19] Religiosos Agustinos, pp. 17–18.

[20] Religiosos Agustinos, pp. 18–20.

[21] Religiosos Agustinos, pp. 20–21.

[22] *Relación Anónima*, p. 161b.

[23] Religiosos Agustinos, p. 21.

[24] Religiosos Agustinos, pp. 44–45.

[25] Religiosos Agustinos, p. 44; cf. p. 43 on Andean "baptism."

[26] Religiosos Agustinos, p. 18.

so prominently in Inca thought, as a figure for lightning or a sign of prosperity and first origins.[27] And when the friars had destroyed the statue of Catequil, it was the devil who spoke from the stones that the people of Huamachuco came to regard as Catequil's sons.[28] Finally, the devil could lead those he desired for his service to mountain retreats, so as to deceive them the more easily in that remote solitude;[29] and if such gentle and gradual deception failed, the devil entered a person violently, depriving him of his senses.[30] In short, the friars brought with them a variegated vocabulary for interpreting the religious experiences of Andeans. Yet their interpretation could hardly have been more distant from Andean self-perception.

For in Andean eyes, the holy places, or huacas,[31] of Huamachuco, imbued as they were with divine presences, represented the history and the concerns of the community. The deity who figured most prominently in cult was Catequil, who had brought the first inhabitants of Huamachuco forth from the mountain Ipuna, where people therefore sacrificed cloth and chicha.[32] The creator Ataguju on the other hand was, like other Andean creator gods, a more distant presence, who was worshiped with sacrifices but "lived in the sky and did not move from there."[33] Such creator gods gave expression to a first beginning that was logically satisfying and necessary, but was remote both historically and in terms of daily cult and daily concerns. Closer at hand was not only Catequil himself but a group of deities who protected individual villages. According to the missionaries, such a deity was "the common guardian of the entire village . . . the eye of the village,"[34] the divine presence being manifest in a great stone standing in or next to each village of the region. Some of these stones were endowed with protective power because they were deities or human beings transformed into stone, while others were associated with some event of transcendent importance.[35] But these Andean characteristics of sacred stones remained unknown to the Augustinian friars, who instead found the stones standing outside the villages of Huamachuco to be reminiscent of the guardian angels of the nations, about whom they had read in the church fathers: "As the theologians write, there is an angel who guards every republic and nation, but . . . the devil imitates what he sees and contrives to transform himself into an angel of light. Although here

[27] See Religiosos Agustinos, p. 39.
[28] Religiosos Agustinos, pp. 26f.
[29] Religiosos Agustinos, pp. 17f.
[30] Religiosos Agustinos, p. 19.
[31] Cf. Religiosos Agustinos, p. 23.
[32] Religiosos Agustinos, p. 23.
[33] Religiosos Agustinos, p. 14.
[34] Religiosos Agustinos, pp. 33–34.
[35] See for Cuzco, below, pp. 191ff.

he transformed himself into rock."[36] Other divine presences of the Andes supervised not so much places and individuals but recurring activities: dyeing and spinning wool,[37] and maintaining irrigation canals. Besides, the deities protected the crops and procreation, and they assisted in warfare.[38] Calendrical time was punctuated by rituals focusing on sun and moon, the morning star, and the Pleiades;[39] a further set of rituals subdivided the time of an individual's life span, from birth to name-giving and on to adulthood, marriage, and death.[40]

The Incas left these long-standing observances intact and joined in worshiping the ancient regional deities.[41] At the same time, their presence brought about a subtle restructuring of the divine world, just as it did of the social and political world. For the Inca state settlers arrived with their own holy presence, a small black figure called Topallimillay, who owned a rich store of weavings;[42] in addition, they revered the mummies of two Inca captains, one of which, the missionaries believed, was inhabited by a demon.[43] Finally, in Huamachuco itself stood the temple of the divine Sun of the Incas[44] which Cieza had seen and which, like all other regional temples of the state cult, was endowed with land and herds of llamas and was maintained by a staff of religious specialists and chosen women.

Institutionally these Inca cults, especially that of the Sun, were distinct from the regional ones, for they were supported from separate revenues and maintained by a separate staff of experts. But conceptually the different cults, whether local or Inca in origin, were continuous with each other. It had thus been the Inca Guayna Capac who had responded to a local need by instituting a cult dealing with irrigation, and the same Inca had chosen a local huaca to accompany him on his campaigns.[45] The people of Huamachuco in their turn served the state temple of the Sun, but they also included the Sun along with their other holy presences when making sacrifice at time of sickness, and they offered coca to the Sun as a remedy for fatigue during journeys.[46] Hence, the cult of the divine Sun did not merely consist of celebrating the great imperial festivals that were organized from Cuzco; rather, it comprised much more humble daily observances that were adhered to long after the Inca empire had fallen. For

---

[36] Religiosos Agustinos, pp. 33–34; cf. MacCormack, "Roma, Constantinopolis, the Emperor and his Genius," *Classical Quarterly* 25 (1975): 131–150.

[37] Religiosos Agustinos, pp. 32, 29, respectively.

[38] Religiosos Agustinos, pp. 33, 40 35, 31, respectively.

[39] Religiosos Agustinos, pp. 41f.

[40] Religiosos Agustinos, pp. 42ff.

[41] Religiosos Agustinos, p. 27.

[42] Religiosos Agustinos, p. 31.

[43] Religiosos Agustinos, pp. 32, 38.

[44] Religiosos Agustinos, pp. 40f.

[45] Religiosos Agustinos, pp. 33, 30, respectively.

[46] Religiosos Agustinos, p. 41.

the persuasive power of Inca religion resided not so much in its imperial prestige as in the fact that it converged with long established Andean religious traditions.[47]

The Augustinian friars were interested in the religion of Huamachuco as they saw it being practiced, for it was current observance that had to be extirpated before Christianity could be implanted. The historical dimension of cult and belief concerned the friars only incidentally, so that they said little about the religious impact of the Incas on the region for it had already become a matter of past history. Spanish officials administering secular visitas and inquiries, by contrast, were greatly interested in the Incas, because Inca precedent could be deployed to legitimate colonial taxation and administration.

The fragment of la Gasca's 1549 visita of Huanuco, the 1562 visita of Huanuco by Inigo Ortíz de Zúñiga, and the Lupaqa visita of 1567 by Garci Diez de San Miguel thus all provide detailed and specific information about regional contributions to the running of the Inca state. The religious component of these contributions is sometimes mentioned separately, but often it is not.

The 1549 visita thus specified that the Chupacho Indians of Huanuco maintained members of their community in Cuzco to perform various services. Among these Chupachos were 150 retainers for the mummy of Tupa Inca Yupanqui and another twenty for that of Guayna Capac.[48] There were also forty Chupacho men in Cuzco guarding the "women of the Inca," another four hundred to build houses,[49] and a number of weavers, dyers, herdsmen, and other specialists. In addition, the Inca had sent state settlers to serve as *huacas-camayos*, presumably for Inca huacas residing among the Chupacho.[50] Some tasks enumerated here are specifically religious, but all the tasks mentioned could include a religious aspect; cloth, for instance, was needed everywhere in the Andes for both sacred and secular purposes.

The visita of Huanuco in 1562 likewise shows that a clear distinction was not always drawn between serving the state and serving the state's religion. One informant said that people used to till the fields "of the Inca and the Sun, which was all one and the same,"[51] while another explained that sacrifices for the Sun and the huaca Guanacaure, the local representative of its namesake in Cuzco, were taken from the Inca's property.[52] There were nonetheless some obligations that were specifically religious.

---

[47] See T. Bouysse-Cassagne, *La identidad aymara*, pp. 282ff.

[48] Iñigo Ortíz de Zúñiga, *Visita de la provincia de León de Huanuco en 1562* (hereafter *Huanuco*), fol. 167r.

[49] *Huanuco*, fols. 168r, 166v, respectively.

[50] *Huacas-camayos*, "keepers of huacas," *Huanuco*, fol. 159r.

[51] *Huanuco*, fol. 12r; cf. fol. 22r, women for the Sun or the Inca.

[52] *Huanuco*, fol. 12v.

These included making periodic sacrifices of llamas, llama fat, guinea pigs, feathers, sea shells, coca and chicha to the Sun, the Moon, and the huacas,[53] conveying the Inca's gifts to the huaca Chaopibilca, which he favored,[54] and celebrating the great annual festivals.[55] Although the worship of the Sun was described as obligatory, several witnesses stated that they gave offerings to the Sun of their own accord, because "he bestowed growth on their harvests, their herds and their children."[56] Here, therefore, was a point where the obligatory worship of the Inca state intersected with those immemorial regional cults that were still practiced in the later seventeenth century.[57]

The Lupaqa of Lake Titicaca owed their considerable wealth to raising camelids, and this pastoral dimension of their existence is amply reflected in the visita: they maintained herds belonging to particular communities[58] and on occasion used these herds to pay their Spanish taxes and to defer the cost of public festivals.[59] Lupaqa memories of the Incas differed somewhat from those of the people of Huanuco. For although, like the people of Huanuco, they tilled fields for the Inca and the Sun and maintained members of their community to serve the Inca in Cuzco,[60] several witnesses remembered that they had sent young people to Cuzco not only to serve the Inca and the Sun but also to be sacrificed.[61] Persons to be sacrificed as capacocha were sent to Cuzco from all parts of the empire.[62] The fact that the Lupaqa mentioned them, while the people of Huanuco did not, may point to divergent interpretations of the capacocha. Perhaps the people of Huanuco regarded capacocha as something other than the tribute that Spanish officials were constantly inquiring about; the Lupaqa, by contrast, simply enumerated individuals to be sacrificed among the other prestations they furnished to the Inca state.

At any rate, both visitas afford a partial view of Andean religion in Inca times. People answered the questions put to them concisely; also, they remembered most clearly what concerned them or their immediate community. Don Pedro Cutinbo, one of the Lupaqa curacas, thus recalled that delegations of one hundred persons were formerly sent to Cuzco

[53] *Huanuco*, fol. 18v; cf. 24r, 30v, etc.
[54] *Huanuco*, fol. 141v.
[55] *Huanuco*, fol. 21r.
[56] *Huanuco*, fol. 30v; cf. 24r.
[57] Below, chap. IX.2, especially at nn. 37ff.
[58] Garci Diez de San Miguel, *Visita hecha a la provincia de Chucuito* (hereafter *Chucuito*), fols. 37r, 39v, 42r.
[59] *Chucuito*, fol. 19r.
[60] *Chucuito*, fols. 18v, 41r, 45r, etc.
[61] *Chucuito*, fols. 18v, 41v, 45r, 52r, etc.
[62] Cf. Pedro de Carabajal, *Descripción fecha de la provincia de Vilcas Guaman*, pp. 206, 218f., Vilcashuaman; Murúa, *Historia general* (1611), 2.29, pp. 109ff. For memories of this ritual in the seventeenth century, see below, sec. 3 at nn. 118ff.

with the firstfruits of quinua, and that his people used to send llamas for the initiation of the Inca and of other great lords, and the same for such persons' first haircutting.[63] But nothing Don Pedro said overlaps with what Betanzos or other historians whose information originated in Cuzco wrote about the great Inca festivals.

The interests of these historians led them to Cuzco and to what members of the Inca nobility could tell them. Cieza repeatedly drew attention to his Inca informants, whose statements, he believed, were trustworthy. Other historians, while less specific about their methods of gathering information, also tended to highlight what they learned in Cuzco or from Inca nobles. This Inca bias extends even to visitas and other administrative documents. The questionnaires to which answers were sought regularly included religious matters. In particular, officials wanted to know whether a given community was still administering lands, herds, and supplies that had belonged to the Inca, the Sun, or the huacas.[64] The answer was invariably negative.[65] Yet in the seventeenth century, ecclesiastical visitas revealed that while the Spaniards had indeed expropriated everything belonging to the Inca and to the deities of the Inca state, regional deities retained control of their lands, herds, supplies, and personnel.[66] Evidently, Andeans were committed to protecting from expropriation the property of their own regional deities and cared much less about what belonged to the Inca and his gods.

Correspondingly, the Andeans who speak in administrative documents remembered the Incas and Inca institutions from the vantage point of their village. We learn from Cieza that every year the Inca rewarded veracious oracular huacas by sending to their shrines a gift-bearing procession known as *capacocha*.[67] Cieza also mentioned that repercussions arising from such processions were under discussion in lawsuits then pending before the Audiencia in Lima.[68] The transcript of one such litigation, which began in 1549[69] and involved capacocha processions in the Chillon valley, north of Lima, is extant. If this is one of the cases Cieza had in mind,[70] then it is clear that these processions viewed from Cuzco conveyed a very different message from the one that mattered in the provinces.

---

[63] *Chucuito*, fol. 18v.

[64] *Huanuco*, question 8, p. 13; *Chucuito*, fol. 4r.

[65] *Huanuco*, fols. 11r, 17r, 23r, 33r, etc.; *Chucuito*, fols. 45r, 10vff., 16rv, 53v.

[66] See below, chap. ix.2.

[67] Above, chap. iii.2 at n. 38. For the meaning of the term *capacocha*, see *Runa yndio*, ed. Taylor, p. 331, chap. 22,11 note; also pp. 29–30; Further, above, chap. iii.2, n. 37.

[68] Cieza, *Segunda Parte* 29, p. 89; *Audiencia*, "high court."

[69] See Rostworowski (1988), p. 62.

[70] This is suggested by Rostworowski, *Justicia 413. Conflicts over Coca Fields* (1988; hereafter *Justicia 413*), p. 65.

IV. ANDEAN SACRED SPACE AND TIME

In the lawsuit, the people of Chacalla sued those of Canta for ownership of a coca field at Quivi. In Inca times, the Chacalla, who laid claim to the field as Inca state settlers, endeavored to strengthen this claim against the field's earlier occupants, the Canta, by directing capacocha processions across it. Very little is said in the lawsuit about the "many vessels of gold and silver and other objects, precious stones, loads of fine cloth, and much livestock" that, according to Cieza,[71] such processions conveyed to favoured huacas on behalf of the Inca. Rather, the witnesses described capacocha processions as serving a regional as much as an imperial purpose. The imperial purpose was to pray for the health, long life, and prosperity of the Inca and his coya.[72] The regional purpose was to define claims to land. The focus and core of a capacocha procession was an individual who in a gourd conveyed a mixture of sacrificial blood and *mullo*[73] to a huaca. This individual was a member of whatever ethnic group the land being traversed belonged to, each group being responsible for supplying a bearer to convey the blood and mullo across their own land. On pain of death the bearer could not spill even one drop of the mixture before reaching the huaca for whom it was destined. Relays of bearers were thus organized, each member of the chain awaiting his turn where his people's land adjoined the land of the previous bearer's people.[74] On certain occasions, boundary stones were placed at the point where the transfer occurred or where the capacocha had reached its term. In the litigation about the coca field at Quivi, the Canta alleged that the Chacalla had deliberately misinformed them as to the arrival of their participant in the capacocha relay, so as to be able to cross the field themselves, thus becoming entitled to place their boundary stone on it.[75] On one occasion, a Canta Indian had tried to halt the Chacalla bearer; because, as a result, a little of the blood was spilled, this Canta was instantly killed and buried on the site.[76] The capacocha procession as viewed from Quivi thus harnessed empirewide prayers for the Inca's welfare, while at the same time, the Inca's quasi-divine authority underpinned titles to land very close to home.

In the long judicial battle about the Quivi coca field, only one witness gave an account of a capacocha procession that has any clear resemblance with what we learn about capacocha from sources originating in Cuzco.

[71] Cieza, *Segunda Parte* 29, p. 89.
[72] See Rostworowski, *Justicia 413*, fols. 64rv, 84r, 178r (question 4), 187v, 202r, 206vf., 212r, 223r, 226v, 230rv, 234r, 236v, 256v.
[73] Quechua, "crushed sea shells."
[74] See Rostworowski, *Justicia 413* (1988), fol. 186v.
[75] Rostworowski, *Justicia 413* (1988), fols. 64rv, 178v (question 5), 212rff. See especially fols. 236v, 241r, 250r, 268r: the person carrying the gourd shouts, "Fasta aqui llegó mi capacocha, fasta aqui es mi termino," and places a boundary stone.
[76] Rostworowski, *Justicia 413* (1988), fols. 82r, 230rv, 245v; the Canta were thus afraid to stop the procession, fol. 82r, question 6; fols. 193rv, 202r, 223r, 226v.

This account, at the same time, appears to describe two different kinds of capacocha procession, one organized by the Inca and the other possibly not. A Spaniard was told in Quivi that in the time of Tupa Inca Yupanqui,

> the coca field belonged to the Canta. Under Guayna Capac, the Chacalla brought a capacocha that the Incas had entrusted to them at Xauxa. The ritual of handing over the capacocha consisted of first giving a little mullo to each Chacalla who was present and of then sacrificing llamas that had been brought from Cuzco, burning the flesh and retaining the blood. Next, the Chacalla men of tribute-paying age[77] each received a little blood in a gourd, along with gold and silver for the huacas. Carrying their gourds, they traversed mountains and crags praying to the huacas, the Sun, and the Earth that the Inca and his consort, on whose behalf they offered their sacrifice, always be young and live a long time. To certain renowned huacas they sacrificed Indians by burying them alive. Having made a sacrifice of this kind, the Chacalla passed below the disputed field to wash their gourds in the river of Quivi. If someone sinfully spilled a drop of blood or someone caused him to spill it, they killed and buried him in that spot. The Chacalla also entered part of the land they claim with another sacrifice, and under Guascar they entered again; and because the Canta were afraid of spilling the blood, they did not dare to hinder them.[78]

The capacocha involving the llamas from Cuzco was clearly organized by the Incas; moreover, the sacrifice of human victims by burying them alive which is mentioned as the conclusion of this ritual is familiar from Inca Cuzco. Indeed, according to Betanzos, this is what defined the Inca capacocha.[79] The "other sacrifice" at the end of the account from Quivi, by contrast, seems to have been organized not by the Inca but by the Chacalla themselves. The third entry into the disputed coca field, during Guascar's reign, likewise apparently not organized by the Inca, is probably identical with one of the two capacochas performed for Guascar that are mentioned elsewhere in the document.[80]

If indeed the litigation about the Quivi coca field involved two kinds

---

[77] Described in the document as "mancebos y hombres y ni biejos muy biejos" fol. 57r.

[78] Rostworowski, *Justicia 413* (1988), fols. 57r–58r, précis.

[79] Above, p. 112; for further mentions of capacochas from Cuzco, some referring to the same occasion, see Rostworowski, *Justicia 413* (1988), fols. 206vf., 212rff., 236v, 265v. In the later sixteenth century, Cristóbal de Molina, who served the parish of Nuestra Señora de los Remedios in Cuzco, learned that capacocha processions walked from Cuzco to their destination in a straight line "crossing ravines and mountains" and shouting their prayers for the Inca's well-being. See Molina, *Fábulas*, p. 127, cf. Cobo, p. 223b and above, chap. III.2 at n. 94. Evidently, this is the same kind of procession as the Spaniards heard described in Quivi.

[80] Capacochas for Guascar, Rostworowski, *Justicia 413* (1988), fols. 84r, 187v, 202r, 223r, 226v, 230rv, 245v, 297vff.

of capacocha, then this ritual conforms to a larger pattern describing the links between Inca state religion and the religion of the empire's provinces. The Inca state religion was formulated in terms of specific myths and rituals. However, although anchored in the natural environment of Cuzco and in the historical development of the Inca polity, these myths and rituals also focus on themes that had counterparts elsewhere in the Andes.

The coca field litigation reveals that the Incas had not been in the Chillon valley for long; the earliest Inca ruler known there was Tupa Inca Yupanqui. In less than three generations, however, the Incas had made themselves a force to be reckoned with.[81] The same was true in Chincha,[82] where Tupa Inca Yupanqui, who conquered the region, was the first Inca ruler known to the people and hence was viewed as the founder of the Inca dynasty.[83]

Chincha was famous for its agricultural wealth; Cieza remembered with delight walking through the region's irrigated green fields and described the pleasure-loving, affluent life-style of the Yunga nobles, as well as the unparalleled splendor of their burials.[84] The Incas themselves deferred to so much plenty, for the lord of Chincha enjoyed the unique privilege of being carried in a litter even when in the Inca's presence.[85] Such deference on the part of the Inca ruler notwithstanding, the changes brought by Inca intervention in Chincha were profound. They are outlined in three interdependent Spanish documents of the mid-sixteenth century.

Fray Cristóbal de Castro, prior of the Dominican convent of Chincha, which had been founded around 1542 by Domingo de Santo Tomás, assisted in the compilation of a report[86] describing the political, religious, and economic administration of the region. In 1563 the lawyer Hernando de Santillán consulted this report when responding to a royal questionnaire about Inca taxation.[87] Finally, information that had probably been collected by Domingo de Santo Tomás was copied after his death in an *Aviso* discussing landholding and the distribution of labor in Chincha under the Incas.[88]

---

[81] Dillehay, "Tawantinsuyu. Integration of the Chillon Valley," *Journal of Field Archeology* 4 (1977): 397–405.

[82] See Pease, ed., Cieza, *Crónica*, p. xxxiv.

[83] Gasca, *Descripción del Perú* (1553), p. 55; Pease, ed., Cieza, *Crónica*, p. xxxivf.; Cieza, *Segunda Parte* 60.

[84] Cieza, *Crónica* 66, p. 203; 60, Yungas; 62; 75, Ica.

[85] Pedro Pizarro, *Relación del descubrimiento* 9, p. 37; cf. Cieza, *Crónica* 74, p. 220.

[86] Cristóbal de Castro and Diego de Ortega Morejón, *Relación . . . del modo que este valle de Chincha* (1558), ed. Trimborn (1936), p. 246.

[87] Wedin, *Lo Incaico*, pp. 55f.; on the date, see F. Esteve Barba, ed., *Crónicas peruanas de interés indígena* (Madrid, 1968), p. xxx.

[88] *Aviso de el modo que havia en el gobierno de los Indios*, ed. M. Rostworowski, *Revista Española de Antropología Americana* 5 (1970): 163–173.

Inca penetration of this region brought to an end a long period of endemic warfare between the valleys of Chincha, Ica, and Limaguana, for which the only remedy had been the exchange of women in marriage.[89] The Incas unified the religious and economic organization of the region according to a schema that had been devised for all conquered provinces by Inca Pachacuti. The schema, which Inca nobles in Cuzco described to the historian Sarmiento de Gamboa in 1571, provided for construction of roads, tambos,[90] palaces, agricultural terraces, and forts on the basis of information which was collected about each region by official Inca inspectors, and was recorded on cloth or in the form of clay models.[91] Cristóbal de Castro, Hernando de Santillán, and the author of the *Aviso* all confirm that the Incas implemented precisely these kinds of projects in Chincha.[92] Secular as they sound, they entailed substantial changes in the practice of religion.

The Yunga of Chincha and adjacent valleys considered themselves to have been newcomers in their land; during an earlier epoch, this land had been inhabited by a generation of dwarves, whom the Yunga conquered and whose tiny bones could still be found in ancient burials. An oracle by the divinatory deity Chinchaycama, "the Creator of Chincha," which had issued from a sacred rock was associated with the advent of the Yunga in their valley. This sacred rock, also known as the *pacarisca* of the people of Chincha, was marked by a temple honoring the prophetic deity.[93] Even so, before the Incas came, the Yunga treated matters of religion somewhat casually. As Fray Cristóbal de Castro and his colleague Diego de Ortega Morejón were told, formerly, "the Yunga did not adore the Sun but the huacas, and not all of them but only those who responded [to requests for oracles], and this not always but only when they had need of them."[94] Among those who responded was Chinchaycama, who continued being worshiped alongside the deities of the Inca state cult.[95] Another dominant divine presence in these valleys was Pachacamac, who, so the story went, had appeared to Tupa Inca Yupanqui in a dream or vision, thereby occasioning this Inca's first journey to the region.[96]

But once the Incas had established themselves in Yunga lands, even the powerful Pachacamac had to accommodate himself to the state cult of the

---

[89] Castro and Ortega Morejón, *Relación*, p. 236; Cieza, *Crónica* 61, p. 192. Limaguana is the Cañete valley.

[90] Quechua, "way station."

[91] Sarmiento, *Historia Indica* 39, p. 244b; 45, p. 250a; for Quivi, see Rostworowski, *Justicia 413* (1988), p. 63.

[92] Castro and Ortega Morejón, *Relación*, p. 237; *Aviso*, p. 167; Santillán, *Relación del origen, descendencia, politica y gobierno de los Incas* 37–38, p. 114b.

[93] Albornoz, *Instrucción para descubrir todas las guacas*, p. 190; Cieza, *Crónica* 74, p. 220.

[94] *Aviso*, p. 246.

[95] Cieza, *Crónica* 74, p. 220.

[96] Santillán, *Relación* 28, p. 111; Castro and Ortega Morejón, *Relación*, p. 246; cf. Rostworowski, *Justicia 413* (1988), p. 54a; see further below, chap. VIII.2 at nn. 11–13.

Sun, although this did not prevent his devotees from esteeming him more highly than the Sun.[97] Apart from the cult of the Sun, the Incas imposed the cults of the living Inca and of the mummies of his predecessors. The consequences as perceived in Chincha were principally economic and increased with lapse of time.[98] For since property of the living Inca was employed, once he died, in the cult of his mummy, each succeeding Inca ruler laid claim to further resources for his own use. The informants of Fray Cristóbal de Castro and Diego de Ortega Morejón thus explained, with regard to the accession of Guayna Capac, the second Inca to rule in Chincha, that the people

> made a house for him in every administrative district[99] and gave him women from the entire kingdom and chacaras,[100] because the Incas considered it a point of honor not to take or use any woman or chacara or servant or anything else that belonged to their fathers, but rather, in all the valleys [new property] had to be given to them; and if the Christians had delayed in coming, all the chacaras and women and Indians would have belonged to the Sun and the Incas and their sisters and the huacas, because all these had servants and houses and chacaras every one individually.[101]

Spanish observers tended to differentiate lands, herds, and services used by the Incas for governmental purposes from those used for religious purposes. This distinction, being anchored in European concepts of relations between church and state, does not apply to the Inca empire, where politics and religion were coextensive. In his responses to questions about Inca taxation, Santillán accordingly stressed that this topic could not be understood without examining Inca religion.[102] For all obligations to the Inca arose, as he concisely expressed it, "por religión y señorío."[103] The same point was made by an Andean witness in the visita of Huanuco.[104]

The interdependence of Inca politics and religion is also apparent with regard to the administration of justice in the empire, which amounted to enforcing the correct performance of religious and political obligations to the ruling Inca. The entire weight of authority and administrative expertise that Inca officials were capable of mustering was brought to bear on

---

[97] Gasca, *Descripción del Perú* (1553), pp. 59f.; above, chap. II.1 at nn. 26ff.

[98] Castro and Ortega Morejón, *Relación*, p. 244; Santillán, *Relación* 54, cf. 34.

[99] Translating the Spanish term *repartimiento*.

[100] Quechua, "fields."

[101] Castro and Ortega Morejón, *Relación*, p. 239.

[102] Santillán, *Relación* 26; on the annual distribution of fields for the Sun, the huacas, the Inca, and the people, see also, Polo de Ondegardo, *Carta . . . para el doctor Francisco Hernández de Liébana*, p. 154.

[103] Santillán, *Relación* 56, "for religion and sovereignty."

[104] *Huanuco*, fol. 12r; above, at n. 51.

the task of creating and maintaining a social and economic order capable of meeting these obligations. Punishments exacted for infractions from local lords and their subjects by Inca ministers of justice could be ferocious. There was thus an Inca official bearing the title *ochacamayo*, "he who chastises sins and delicts."[105] Castro and Ortega Morejón were informed of a visit to Chincha of one such official, shortly before the Spaniards arrived:

> A woman from this valley of Chincha who had been set aside for the Inca had intercourse with a lord. An ochacamayo came to a certain place that was the prison of the Inca, eight leagues from this valley, and ordered all the curacas and their sons over the age of ten to be imprisoned, and without omitting a single one he had them all cast from a rock. . . . And often the Inca ordered a man to be killed if he had escaped with an *agra*, a "woman chosen for the service of the Sun."[106]

Although some Spaniards viewed such implacable administration of punishment for breach of the Inca's commands as lawless tyranny,[107] others admired the orderly workings of the Inca state and the interpenetration in it of politics and religion. The functioning of the imperial religion as a means of articulating authority, of creating consensus, and of thus maintaining order in society had already been apparent to Cieza; throughout the Andes, early colonial documents reiterate the same point. Santillán, perspicacious lawyer that he was, explained the issue very clearly:

> The religion that existed among these people was most carefully observed and comprised many ceremonies and sacrifices, because people were devoted to such things. Lords and Incas in particular held frequent converse with huacas and houses of religion and communicated to everyone else that they approximated more closely to the gods they adored than did other people, and that they knew the future. The principal means whereby they held all other people in subjection was this profession of observing their religion and worship.[108]

[105] Castro and Ortega Morejón, *Relación*, p. 242.

[106] Castro and Ortega Morejón, *Relación*, p. 242; I added the definition of *agra* from Gonzalez Holguin, *Vocabulario de la lengua general*, p. 15b, s.v. acllacuna.

[107] Cf. *Información hecha en el Cuzco* (1582), pp. 272; 280; 284, where the Spaniard García de Melo, followed by Cristóbal de Molina, the author of *Fábulas*, asserted that the Incas administered justice arbitrarily, while Inca informants stated that the Incas had laws and observed them.

[108] Santillán, *Relación* 33. Santillán's legal colleague and acquaintance Juan Polo de Ondegardo (see Santillán, 28, p. 112a) was in complete agreement; see Polo, *Muñatones*, pp. 132f.; below, sec. 3 at nn. 146–151.

For instance, when the Inca went to war, his decision was approved by gods (cf. fig. 40) and men. As informants in Chincha told Castro and Ortega Morejón: "Before the Inca Guayna Capac left Cuzco for the second time, he called an assembly and meeting of all the grandees and huacas of all the land and informed them in a parliament how it befitted his honor and that of his ancestors that he should go to conquer new lands."[109] Such displays of imperial purpose were effective because they were rooted in good administration. Santillán listed the twelve age groups, ranging from birth to death, which appeared on Inca census quipus and served as the basis for assessment of all forms of service to the state. The age group who served in the Inca's armies and tilled the fields was men between twenty-five and fifty: "They do all the work, for from among them [the Incas] took warriors, and they paid the tribute and carried it to Cuzco and worked the fields of the Inca and the curacas."[110] Men between fifty and sixty did lighter agricultural work, which included tilling vegetable fields, while younger men, Santillan thought, assisted in carrying burdens, in which they were joined by those between sixteen and twenty, who also picked coca. Women's work was similarly distributed by age.[111]

The coordination of the service of the Inca with age and with the tasks of survival endowed the imperial order with an all pervasive validity and authority that was also expressed in the annual cycle of festivals and ceremonies. Work was inseparable from celebration. Castro and Ortega Morejón, followed by the author of Aviso, described the annual plowing of fields, the inauguration of which in Cuzco the anonymous cleric had watched in 1535. This ceremony of the capital was reiterated annually in Chincha and throughout the empire. Just as in Cuzco the Inca inaugurated the plowing season by digging the sacred field Sausero,[112] so elsewhere it was the Inca's delegate or a local curaca who initiated the season. As in Cuzco, the work proceeded amid singing and dancing. The first fields to be dug were those of the community; crops from these fields were reserved for times of scarcity and for the cult of the Inca, the Sun, and the local huacas. Next followed the fields of the curaca, and then those of the people. Once the curaca had dug his share, lesser dignitaries

---

[109] Castro and Ortega Morejón, Relación, p. 239; see also p. 237.

[110] Santillán, Relación 11, pp. 106f.; Castro and Ortega Morejón, Relación, p. 238. Other listings of the Inca age groups: Ortíz de Zúñiga, Huanuco 1, p. 35; Señores que sirvieron al Inga Yupangui y a Topainga Yupangui . . . , Relación del origen e gobierno que los Ingas tuvieron, pp. 61–62, pp. 66–67. The latter source shows that the writer was familiar with Chincha; perhaps this accounts for the similarity between this document and the Relación by Castro and Ortega Morejón, which possibly the writer of "Señores" consulted. For a less rigid list of occupations, see Aviso, pp. 167ff. or Guaman Poma, Nueva Crónica, pp. 195ff. [197ff.].

[111] See Guaman Poma, Nueva Crónica, pp. 214ff. [216ff.].

[112] See below, sec. 2 at n. 12.

dug some distance, and finally, the work was completed by the common people.[113] The diggers, moving from the fields of the Sun, the Inca, and the huacas on to the fields of their lords, and finally to their own, gave expression to their community's sacred and political geography, while at the same time replicating the sacred and political geography of Cuzco, where the identical ceremony was being enacted under the direction of the Inca.[114] (See fig. 18.)

2. MEMORIES OF INTI RAIMI

The anonymous cleric who in 1535 watched the Incas in Cuzco sing to the Sun took much for granted. The buildings of the Inca capital that Spaniards so admired (cf. fig. 15) still spoke of the purposes for which they had been constructed, and much of the Inca topography of the city remained intact. When thus the cleric wrote that the ceremony he watched took place "in a plain that faces toward the point where the sun rises, as one leaves the city,"[1] a reader familiar with Cuzco could have identified the site. But the longer Cuzco was inhabited by Spaniards, the more opaque such casual references to its Inca topography became. Similarly, when the Inca festivals were no longer being celebrated, the timing of the maize harvest in relation to other festivals was obscured, along with the significance of that timing. Increasingly, therefore, understanding the Incas had to be rooted in a systematic grasp of Inca antiquities. Cieza and Betanzos had laid some foundations for antiquarian erudition. But after midcentury, treatises of antiquarian, rather than historical, content, usually written in response to an official inquiry, became something of a literary genre in their own right. Two of these treatises supply the context within which something of the significance of Inti Raimi in Inca times may be understood.

The first lists the huacas in Cuzco and its vicinity and appears to have been compiled in the later sixteenth century. In the mid-seventeenth century, the Jesuit historian Bernabé Cobo incorporated an abridged version of it into his *History of the New World*.[2] This treatise shows that the huacas of Cuzco were not randomly scattered in space but were aligned on sight lines, or *ceques*, that, like strings from the center of a quipu, ran from Coricancha[3] to points on and beyond the horizon in the four parts of the

[113] Castro and Ortega Morejón, *Relación*, p. 245; *Aviso*, p. 166.
[114] Correlation of the parallel ceremonies as celebrated in Cuzco and in the Inca empire at large, *Aviso*, pp. 165–166.
[1] Bartolomé de Segovia, *Relación de muchas cosas*, p. 82a; see above, chap. II.2 at n. 59.
[2] The treatise has been edited and translated by J. H. Rowe, "Account of the shrines," *Ñawpa Pacha* 17 (1979; hereafter "Account"), pp. 6–8.
[3] Cobo, *Historia* 13.13. The work of R. T. Zuidema, beginning with his *Ceque System* (1964) is fundamental to an understanding of the role of the ceque lines as expressions of

15. Doorway in Coricancha, Cuzco. The trapezoidal shapes of the opening and the niches in the background are characteristic of Inca architecture. Photograph by John Hyslop.

empire. The ceques were thus named and numbered after these four parts of Peru, "which are Antesuyu, Collasuyu, Contisuyu and Chinchay-suyu" (see fig. 24).[4] The second treatise, on Inca myth and the Inca calendar, was addressed in around 1574 to Bishop Lartaún of Cuzco by Cristóbal de Molina, cura[5] of Cuzco's Indian parish of Nuestra Señora de los Remedios. The antiquarian character of these authors' subject matter allowed little scope for either Cieza's eloquence and analytical acumen or for the intimate familiarity with Inca history that Betanzos picked up from Doña Angelina's kinsmen. But their methodical persistence yielded many details of topography, chronology, and nomenclature that had escaped the two historians, or had simply not seemed worth mentioning.

Betanzos located the celebration of the maize harvest in Limapampa, or, as he spelled it, Rimacpampa, which was "where the hospital now is . . . as you leave the city."[6] The list of ceque shrines that Cobo extracted from an earlier source confirms that Limapampa was the site where the maize harvest was celebrated, and provides more information about it. The first holy place on the second ceque of Collasuyu, which headed from Coricancha to San Sebastian, that is, "toward the point where the sun rises," as the anonymous cleric had specified,[7] was "Limapampa, where the chacara[8] of Diego Gil was made; there they held the festival when they harvested the maize, so that it would last and not rot."[9] Adjacent to Limapampa, according to Cobo's list of shrines, was the next huaca on Collasuyo's second ceque, which was called Raquiancalla: "It is a small hill that is in that chacara, in which there were many idols of all four suyus. Here a celebrated festival was held that lasted ten days."[10] Seeing that the Incas gathered in the field Limapampa, the elevation where they

social, political, and religious order among the Incas. My own discussion is focused to one side of his work because the questions asked in this book are defined as much by what was intelligible to Spaniards during the period here studied as they are by what was intelligible to Andeans.

[4] Gonzalez Holguin, *Vocabulario de la lengua general*, p. 336.

[5] Spanish, "parish priest."

[6] Betanzos, *Suma* (1987), I, chap. 14, end; chap. 15, p. 72a. According to Esquivel y Navia, *Noticias cronologicas de la gran ciudad del Cuzco* I: 139–140, the hospital was founded in 1546 and was moved to another site between July 1553 and 1557, that is, after Betanzos completed the *Suma y narración*. Betanzos is thus thinking of the first site, which, however, Esquivel y Navia does not name.

[7] Above, chap. II.2 at n. 59, with Cobo, *Historia* 13.27, p. 215a and Rowe, "Account," p. 42: Sausero, the third huaca on this ceque is "on the road to San Sebastian"; cf. below, sec. 3 at n. 78.

[8] Quechua, "field."

[9] Molina, *Fábulas*, p. 72 describing the rituals of the month of July, refers to the place as "Aucaypata adonde ahora llaman los españoles Limapampa que es abajo de Santo Domingo." Aucaypata is the main square, and is not "below" Santo Domingo. But if Limapampa is in part identical with Hurin (Lower) Haucaypata (see Hyslop, *Inka Settlement Planning*, p. 99), the difficulty can be resolved. Zuidema, "The Lion in the City," *Journal of Latin American Lore* 9 (1983): 252, locates the celebration of 1535 in Ayllipampa, the first huaca of Antisuyo's seventh ceque.

[10] Transl. Rowe, "Account" (1979), p. 41, Collasuyo 2,2.

made the sacrifices the anonymous cleric mentions should be this small hill Raquiancalla.[11]

From both Molina and Cobo's list of shrines we also learn that the harvesting and plowing with golden digging sticks that the anonymous cleric observed in 1535 began in a field called Sausero. This was another holy place near Limapampa, where the Incas sang to the Sun.[12] Sausero was the property of the mummy of Mama Huaco,[13] consort of the legendary first Inca, Manco Capac. A myth recounted that Mama Huaco was instrumental in initiating Inca agriculture in the Cuzco valley. On their migration from Pacaritambo to Cuzco, the first Incas dwelt for two years at Matagua, looking for fertile land. While there, Mama Huaco "took two golden rods and threw them toward the North. One of them reached within two arrowshots of an arable field called Colcabamba but did not sink into the ground, because the earth was loose and unterraced; thus they knew that it was not fertile land. The other rod reached further toward Cuzco and sank deep into the terrain called Guanaypata, so that they knew that this was fertile land."[14] The Incas laid claim to Guanaypata and cultivated it. It was therefore fitting that Mama Huaco's maize field should be the first to be harvested and plowed,[15] followed by other sacred fields belonging to the Creator, the Sun and Moon, the Thunder, the living Inca and Guanacaure; last came the fields of deceased Inca rulers.[16] The maize from Mama Huaco's field was used to make the chicha that was consumed in her honor,[17] just as the crops from other sacred fields served to provide for the cultic and personal needs of their owners.

The anonymous cleric described the singing to the Sun in Limapampa as an isolated, splendid occasion. But in fact this occasion figured in a continuous round of interrelated religious observances involving the sun. Betanzos thus pointed out that the initiation of young men was celebrated to honor the Sun,[18] while the maize celebrations beginning in May and ending in June were "another very solemn festival to the Sun."[19] Molina

---

[11] I thank John Rowe for pointing out that the celebration could not have taken place in modern Limapampa, when Abrazos meets Tullumayo, because there is no elevation nearby that could correspond to Raquiancalla.

[12] Rowe, "Account" (1979), pp. 42–43, Collasuyo 2,3. See also Cobo, *Historia* 13.27, p. 215a.

[13] Molina, *Fábulas*, p. 118, el cuerpo de la dicha Mamaguaca.

[14] Sarmiento, *Historia Indica* 13; cf. Sherbondy, "El regadio," *Allpanchis* 20 (1982): 12f.

[15] See Silverblatt, *Moon, Sun and Witches* (1987), p. 50; but note, according to Cobo, the field belonged to the Sun, Rowe, "Account" (1979), pp. 7–8.

[16] Molina, *Fábulas*, p. 118.

[17] Molina, *Fábulas*, p. 118.

[18] Betanzos, *Suma* (1986), I.14, p. 40b, phrase omitted in the 1987 edition. I thank Tom Zuidema for discussing with me the Inca calendar on which he is writing a book.

[19] Betanzos, *Suma* (1968), I.15, p. 45a = p. 71b (1987): otra fiesta al Sol muy solemne, celebrated in May, "que entonces comenzasen a coger sus maices comenzase la fiesta y durase hasta en fin de junio. (sic)

similarly referred to the celebrations accompanying the initiation of young Inca men in November and December as Capac Raimi, "Great Festival,"[20] and juxtaposed this occasion with the celebration of the maize harvest in May, which he callled Intip Raimi, "Festival of the Sun."[21] At both times, he noted, the Inca "drank with the Sun and the other huacas," the chicha that was to be consumed by these deities being poured away into the ushnu.[22] Polo de Ondegardo in turn saw common elements in December's Capac Raimi and the rituals of the planting season, which he noted were observed near the time of the winter solstice in June, when Christians celebrated Corpus Christi.[23] In the early seventeenth century, the Andean historian Guaman Poma de Ayala drew up a calendar of agricultural tasks as performed in his own day where May is the month of the maize harvest while in June, the potatoes were brought home. In Guaman Poma's Inca calendar, however, June was the time of the "lesser Inti Raymi," *moderada fiesta del Inti Raymi.*[24] At this time, the Inca "drank with the Sun for the Festival of the Sun," because, as Guaman Poma shows in his drawing for this occasion, the Sun was small and weak in June, during the winter solstice, and needed strengthening with sacrificial chicha (fig. 17).[25] The December solstice by contrast was celebrated as Capac Ynti Raymi, "Great Solemn Festival of the Sun,"[26] when the sun was mature and the moon full (fig. 16).

The celebrations of the two solstices were thus juxtaposed not only by reference to the Sun but also by reference to harvest and planting, and to the initiation of young men. The latter observance, which ended with the mock battle they fought with prickly pears in Haucaypata, Capac Inti Raimi, the summer solstice. After the mock battle, there remained only one more task for the young men to perform. This was a long series of fasts and sacrifices that began with the completion of their initiation and ended during the harvest celebration.[27] At this time, the young men were clothed in

> tunics woven of gold, silver, and irridescent feathers, and with feather ornaments, gold [head] disks and armbands. At this festival they made an end of their fasts and sacrifices that they had performed until then, beginning at the time when they were made orejones.

[20] Molina, *Fábulas*, p. 98.

[21] Molina, *Fábulas*, p. 67. For more on this aspect of the Inca calendar, see M. Ziolkowski, "El calendario metropolitano Inca," in *Time and Calendars*, ed. M. Ziolkowski and R. M. Sadowski (1989), pp. 129–166.

[22] Molina, *Fábulas*, p. 113.

[23] Polo de Ondegardo, *Errores* 8.1 and 7, fols. 9v–10v.

[24] Guaman Poma, *Nueva Crónica*, pp. 246f. [248f.] with 1143 [1153f.]–1147 [1157f.].

[25] For the toasting, see also Garcilaso, *Comentarios reales* 6.21.

[26] Guaman Poma, *Nueva Crónica*, p. 258 [260].

[27] Betanzos, *Suma* (1987), 1.15, pp. 71bf.

DEZIEMBRE
CAPAC·INTIRAIMI

lagran pascua
solene del sol

capac

16. The mature, fully grown Sun and the full Moon face each other from opposite quarters of the sky as the Incas celebrate the "Great Solemn Festival of the Sun" at midsummer. "In this month of December," explains Guaman Poma, "they observed the festival and solemn celebration of the Sun, because . . . the Sun is king and therefore lord of all the sky and the planets and the stars and all that exists." *Nueva Crónica*, p. 258, Royal Library, Copenhagen. Photo from facsimile, Paris 1936.

17. At midwinter, when the Sun is small, the Inca "drinks with the Sun during the Festival of the Sun," so that it may gain renewed splendor. The Sun's chicha was poured by the Inca into the *ushnu* in Haucaypata, whence it flowed to Coricancha. But Guaman Poma conceptualized the transaction in Christianized terms by envisioning that a demon transported the chicha to the Sun. *Nueva Crónica*, p. 246, Royal Library, Copenhagen. Photo from facsimile, Paris 1936.

And they now started living at ease and celebrating the festival . . .
addressed to the Sun for the crops.[28]

A group of such recently initiated orejones must have been among the
splendidly attired host of Incas whom the anonymous cleric watched in
1535, even though for him they were lost in the crowd because he could
not have known enough about the ordering of Inca society to tell them
apart. Similarly, he could not have watched all the rituals that preceded,
accompanied, and followed the singing for the Sun in other parts of
Cuzco.

But the subsequent inquiries by Cristóbal de Molina and by the anonymous author from whom Bernabé Cobo derived his account of Inca
festivals[29] elucidated some of these particulars—not, however, without
raising further difficulties and contradictions. Molina began his account
of the Inca year in May with Inti Raimi, while Cobo began in December
with Capac Raimi and the initiation of young men, just as Betanzos had
done. To complicate matters, the Inca months were lunar and did not
correspond to European ones. Molina observed in passing that the first
month of the Inca year began in mid-May, "give or take a day, on the first
day of the moon." But neither he nor any of the other early historians of
the Incas explained how exactly the Incas reckoned time.[30]

According to Molina, the festival season of the maize harvest opened
with llama sacrifices to the Sun, the Maker, and the Thunder. Prayers
addressed to the Maker of the world begged that he, the Sun, and the
Thunder "might always remain young . . . that all things might be at
peace, that people multiply, and that there might be food." A separate
prayer to the Sun asked "that he should always be young and should rise
shining and splendid," while Thunder and Lightning were asked to send
rain so the crops could grow.[31] The sacrifice with its accompanying
prayers states a recurring theme of the harvest festival, one that also
speaks through the Inca's toast to the Sun recorded by Guaman Poma. It
was that the deities, in particular the Sun, then at the lowest point of its
course, should remain young and strong. Similarly, in the course of the
capacocha sacrifice, people prayed that the Inca should always "be young
and strong and live a long time and that his consort should be young."[32]
The youth of the Inca and his consort, like the youth of the Maker, the
Sun, and the atmospheric deities, between them safeguarded the continuance of human life and of the established order.

[28] Betanzos, *Suma* (1987), 1.15 pp. 71b–72a = p. 45a (1968).
[29] Cobo, *Historia* 13.25–32; Cobo shares a number of details with Molina, but his source,
or one of his sources, seems to have been other than Molina.
[30] Molina, *Fábulas*, p. 66; see Ziolkowski, "El calendario" (above, n. 19).
[31] Molina, *Fábulas*, pp. 66f.
[32] Maria Rostworowski, *Conflicts over Coca Fields* (an edition of AGI Justicia 413), fol. 57v.

Cobo also mentioned these sacrifices that preceded the harvest.[33] But here and in his account of the other monthly sacrifices of the Incas he refers to a detail not found elsewhere. This is that, unlike Molina, Cobo thought that the sacrificial llamas were taken from the herds of the Sun and were "offered on the Sun's behalf" to the Maker Viracocha.[34] The Sun accordingly offered these sacrifices, rather than receiving them. The missionaries and historians who argued that the Incas differentiated between the Sun and the Maker of the world, between the creature and the creator,[35] thus had a significant piece of evidence on their side—which, however, most of them overlooked.

Molina and Cobo did not mention the singing to the Sun that the anonymous cleric in 1535 had found so moving but did describe rituals that were perhaps performed during those same days. The anonymous cleric had noted three phases in the singing to the divine Sun: sunrise, when the chant was barely audible; midday, when it was at its height; and sunset, when the voices finally faded away. Cristóbal de Molina details sacrifices that marked the same three phases in the course of the sun. At its rise, a llama was burned for Guanacaure, situated southeast of Cuzco, with the prayer: "Maker, Sun, and Thunder, may you always be young, may the peoples multiply, and may they live in peace." At midday, a llama was sacrificed in the patio of Coricancha; the ceremony perhaps coincided with a time when the gold image of the Sun sat on its throne in the patio of the temple and received its daily offerings.[36] Lastly, at dusk, another llama was sacrificed to the Sun on the hill Aepiran, over which it was at that same moment setting.[37] Like the singing, the sacrifices followed the sun's course from East to West. Cobo mentioned a further event that apparently occurred during the days when the Incas sang to the Sun. He noted that during the harvest season llamas were distributed to the people

[33] Cobo, *Historia* 13.27, p. 214b.
[34] Cobo, *Historia* 13.26, p. 212b; 13.25, p. 209a; similarly 13.27, p. 214b, for the fifth month "el mismo sacrificio"; also, p. 215a.
[35] See Molina, *Fábulas*, p. 67, [el sol] no conociendolo por Hacedor sino por hechura del Hacedor; further, below, chap. v.1 at nn. 15–26; chap. vii.3 passim; chap. viii.2 at nn. 2ff.; cf. Rowe, "Creator worship," in *Essays in Honor of Paul Radin* (1960); F. Pease, *Dios creador* (1973).
[36] Pedro Pizarro, *Relación* 15, p. 92; Sarmiento, *Historia Indica* 36. Perhaps these were the days when the image of the Sun stayed in Coricancha in order to receive this sacrifice, rather than going out to Haucaypata; cf. above, chap. ii.2 at nn. 17ff.
[37] Molina, *Fábulas*, p. 68. But note the context of this ritual during May, which Molina considered to be the first month of the Inca year. The ritual is preceded by the sacrifice of one hundred llamas for Inti Raimi, p. 67, and is followed by the pilgrimage to Vilcanota and other huacas, pp. 68f. The difficulty in correlating information from Cobo and Molina is that the two authors' divergence as to the beginning of the Inca year seems to influence their reporting of the sequence of events during April, May, and June. Regarding Aepiran, Urbano and Duviols, ad loc., suggest that it is the same place as Apian in Cobo's list of shrines; see Rowe, ed., "Account," p. 54, Cuntisuyo 6.1: Apian . . . una piedra . . . que estava en el sitio que oy tiene Santo Domingo.

of Cuzco, so that no one "great or small, should lack for a meal." This appears to be a reference to the same distribution of llamas that the cleric had observed in 1535.[38]

Subsequent days witnessed renewed sacrifices,[39] which preceded and accompanied the harvesting and plowing of Sausero, of other sacred fields, and of fields belonging to the Inca and the curacas; the reaping of fields belonging to the common people brought the harvest to an end. Both when harvesting and when plowing, the ruling Inca who began the work was assisted by the young men who had been admitted to the ranks of adult Inca nobles during the preceding November and December.[40] While harvesting, they sang *aravis*, "songs about the deeds of others, or about the memory of absent loved ones, or about love."[41] Having gathered the maize cobs, the harvesters carried them home in sacks slung over their shoulders.[42] Finally, when they plowed (fig. 18), wielding their golden digging sticks, which evoked the golden rods that had been thrown by Mama Huaco,[43] they again sang aravis but this time interspersed them with *hayllis*, "songs of rejoicing in war or [about] fields that have been well finished and conquered."[44] Befitting the triumphal theme of haylli, the plowmen, once their work was completed, returned to the main square, Haucaypata, resplendent in the tunics that they had won in warfare.[45]

During this same period or a little later, a pilgrimage was made to various huacas in and outside Cuzco, including the oracular shrine of Vilcanota, twenty-six leagues east of the capital, where "the Sun is born"[46]— an appropriate place to visit at the time of the winter solstice, when the days once more begin to lengthen. The pilgrimage thus meshes with the earlier prayers that the Sun, Creator, and Thunder should "always remain young" and with Guaman Poma's account of the Inca's toasting the winter Sun in order to give it new strength (fig. 17).

Once the maize had been brought home, had dried, and was ready to be shelled, the Inca set forth for a period of feasting and rejoicing at the

---

[38] Cobo, *Historia* 13.27, p. 214b; Bartolomé de Segovia, *Relación de muchas cosas*, p. 82b. But this latter author describes live llamas, whereas Cobo appears to refer to llamas that have been killed as sacrifices to the Sun.

[39] Cobo, *Historia* 13.27, p. 215a.

[40] Molina, *Fábulas*, p. 118; Cobo, *Historia* 13.27, p. 215a.

[41] Gonzalez Holguin, *Vocabulario de la lengua general*, p. 152, s.v. haravi; Molina, *Fábulas*, p. 118; Guaman Poma, *Nueva Crónica*, p. 245 [247]; Cobo, *Historia* 13.27, p. 215a.

[42] Cobo, *Historia* 13.27, p. 215a; Molina, *Fábulas*, p. 118; cf. Guaman Poma, *Nueva Crónica*, p. 244 [246].

[43] See also above, sec. 1 at n. 7, concerning Ataguju's golden digging sticks.

[44] Gonzalez Holguin, *Vocabulario de la lengua general*, p. 157b, s.v. haylli; Guaman Poma, *Nueva Crónica*, p. 250 [252].

[45] Cobo, *Historia* 13.27, p. 215a; cf. Molina, *Fábulas*, p. 118.

[46] Molina, *Fábulas*, p. 69; Cieza, *Segunda Parte* 28, p. 84.

18. Four lords, each representing one part of Tahuantinsuyo wield their digging sticks in unison. The women help by breaking the sod, while a crippled girl brings two cups of chicha, one to be offered to the earth, Pachamama, and the other for the diggers. Guaman Poma, *Nueva Crónica*, p.250, Royal Library, Copenhagen. Photo from facsimile, Paris 1936.

hill Mantocalla, the sixth holy place on the third ceque of Antisuyu.[47] The procession included two sacred images of women attired in exquisite textiles as well as two llamas of gold and two of silver, a reminder of the llamas that came forth with the first Incas from the window at Pacaritambo.[48] With the Inca came the men of royal lineage, but no women, for aside from the mamacona who prepared the chicha, women were barred from attending.[49] Possibly this was the first ceremonial occasion for the young men who had been initiated during the preceding December to be formally admitted to the exclusive company of adult men, with whom they would in due course fight the Inca's wars and administer his far-flung realm.[50] While the Inca and his company dwelt at Mantocalla, human effigies made of quisshuar wood—the material of the digging sticks that were used throughout the pre-Hispanic Andes[51]—were dressed in fine clothes and then burned.[52] After this the Inca returned to Cuzco in a solemn procession for which coca leaf, flowers, and many-colored feathers were spread in his way.[53]

Maize and Sun were linked throughout this protracted celebration of the winter solstice, harvest, and plowing. Among the fields of the Sun that were ceremoniously reaped and tilled at this season was one within the sacred enclosure of Coricancha, the crop of which was distributed throughout the empire as a token of fellowship and communion. Another such maize field was laboriously cultivated next to the temple of the Sun in the harsh mountain climate of distant Titicaca, while in Cuzco, Collcampata, the "garden of the Sun," was also planted with maize.[54] This garden was among the fields which were solemnly harvested and plowed by the Inca rulers in person during the festival season of May and June.[55] The interdependence of the Sun, the empire's principal deity, and maize, its prestige crop, is also explicit in the interlocking sequence of ceremonious events during this period. The season opened with the harvesting

[47] Mantocalla is where Dearborn and Schreiber "Houses of the Rising Sun," in *Time and Calendars*, ed. Ziolkowski and Sadowski, p. 59, suggest the singing to the Sun that the cleric observed in 1535 might have taken place.

[48] Molina, *Fábulas*, p. 70; Cobo, *Historia* 13.28, pp. 215bf., has a longer and more complicated description of the procession to Mantocalla and of the events that took place there.

[49] Cobo, *Historia* 13.28, p. 215b; Molina, *Fábulas*, p. 70.

[50] Note the oath of loyalty the young men at their initiation swore to the Inca: Betanzos, *Suma* (1987), 1.14, p. 68a; cf. Cobo, *Historia* 13.28, p. 215b; Molina, *Fábulas*, p. 69.

[51] Cobo, *Historia* 6.49, p. 255.

[52] Molina, *Fábulas*, p. 69, dance *huallina*; Cobo, *Historia* 13.28, p. 216a, dance *cayo* was danced at Mantocalla following the burning of the effigies; Polo, *Errores* 7, f. 10v.

[53] Polo de Ondegardo, *Errores* 8, fol. 10v; Molina, *Fábulas*, p. 71; Cobo, *Historia* 13.28, p. 216a.

[54] MacCormack, "From the Sun of the Incas," *Representations* 8 (1984): 45; Garcilaso, *Comentarios reales* 2.22.

[55] Garcilaso, *Comentarios reales* 5.2; Molina, *Fábulas*, p. 118; John Murra, "Rite and Crop," in *Essays in Honor of Paul Radin* (1960), pp. 393–407.

of Sausero and other sacred fields. Next came a festival of the Sun (part of which the anonymous cleric watched in 1535) that extended over a month or so and included the ceremonious opening of the plowing season. Finally, the time of celebration came to an end when the Inca made his excursion to Mantocalla. For after plowing, according to the informants of Juan de Betanzos, the lawgiver Pachacuti had laid down that there should be a pause in the round of celebration, so that people could "irrigate their lands, and begin to sow maize, potatoes, and quinoa." Similarly, Molina and Cobo placed the time for irrigation immediately after the Inca's visit to Mantocalla.[56]

The different events of the lesser Inti Raimi were thus attuned to each other so as to form a continuous whole, and the festival in its entirety formed a continuous whole with the other celebrations of the Inca calendar. A similar coherence and continuity speak through those parts of the ceremonies we have reviewed that relate to herding. For although like the harvest Inti Raimi and Capac Inti Raimi were predominantly agricultural, they did comprise a pastoralist strand, as indeed might be expected, considering the importance of wool and cloth in the Inca economy.[57]

The principal agents here were not humans but llamas. More precisely, llamas were represented as interacting with humans on an equal footing, and indeed as adopting human roles—this being what they still do in the puna[58] around Cuzco.[59] The interchangeability of llamas for human beings can be traced in Guaman Poma's survey of deities and rituals of the four parts of the Inca empire.[60] Guaman Poma conceived of the principal deity of Chinchaysuyo as a fusion between the oracular Pachacamac from the coast and Pariacaca, the lord of a glacier in Huarochiri; he depicted this deity, who dwelt in a rocky cliff, looking down on an approaching couple from Chinchaysuyo (see fig. 19) The man holds up a young child for sacrifice to the deity in the rock, while his wife offers the accompanying plate of *vaccri zanco*, maize bread mixed with sacrificial blood.[61] In Inca Cuzco, such a mixture of blood and bread, known as *sanco*, was eaten as a token of communion during the purificatory festival of Citua.[62] In the Inca hierarchy of the provinces of the empire, Chinchaysuyo was paired as anan with Collasuyo as urin. Similarly, in Guaman Poma's survey of rituals, his account of Chinchaysuyo should be matched with that

[56] Betanzos, *Suma* (1987), 1.15, p. 72a; Molina, *Fábulas*, p. 71; Polo de Ondegardo, *Errores* 8, fol. 10v; Cobo, *Historia* 13.28, p. 216b.
[57] See J. V. Murra, *Economic Organization* (1980), chap. 4; J. V. Murra, *Formaciones economicas* (1975), pp. 145–170.
[58] Quechua, "high altitude plateau."
[59] M. J. Sallnow, *Pilgrims of the Andes* (1987), pp. 133ff.
[60] Guaman Poma, *Nueva Crónica*, pp. 264–273 [266–275].
[61] Guaman Poma, *Nueva Crónica*, pp. 268f. [270f.].
[62] Molina, *Fábulas*, p. 79; further, below, sec. 3 at nn. 103–109.

19. Pariacaca-Pachacamac, deity of Chinchaysuyo, watches as parents offer him their child in sacrifice. Sacrificial smoke ascends to the deity like
prayers (cf. figs. 38–39). Pariacaca and Pachacamac were two separate deities
(cf. fig. 23), but Guaman Poma, viewing the coastal region from his distant
home in the Andean highlands, has merged them into one. *Nueva Crónica*,
p. 266, Royal Library, Copenhagen. Photo from facsimile, Paris 1936.

of Collasuyo. For Collasuyo, comprising the high Andes around Lake Titicaca, Guaman Poma represented Vilcanota as the principal deity. He also is depicted dwelling in a rock face. Collasuyo was famous for its huge herds of camelids. Accordingly, the sacrifice being offered to Vilcanota by a married couple of Collasuyo is a "black llama" (fig. 20).[63] Guaman Poma's iconography for this llama sacrifice of Collasuyo is identical to his iconography for the human sacrifice of Chinchaysuyo. While in Chinchaysuyo the man offers up the child, in Collasuyo he presents the black llama that the deity is to receive. And while in Chinchaysuyo the wife offers a plate of *zanco*, in Collasuyo she holds up three packs of coca leaf, eaten not only by humans but also—in certain exceptional circumstances—by llamas.[64]

The interchangeability of humans and llamas that Guaman Poma's pair of drawings reveals is also discernible in the Inca celebration of the winter and summer solstices. In addition, by examining a pair of ceremonial episodes involving llamas, we will see how in Inca thinking, the solstices were correlated to each other and were also integrated with other calendrical observances.

During Capac Inti Raimi in December, a sacrificial procession including a white llama made its way to the holy place of Guanacaure. For some time, this llama had been nourished on nothing but coca leaf and chicha, both normally consumed only by humans.[65] Moreover, the white llama was adorned with a many-colored tunic and with gold ear ornaments, matching the tunics and ear ornaments worn by humans. This animal, known as *napa*,[66] represented the first llama that had emerged from the Incas' pacarina[67] after the flood, when the current epoch began.[68] At the beginning of the lesser Inti Raimi, the napa llama was displayed once more, this time in Haucaypata. It stayed there for a month, was looked after by two yanaconas,[69] and was given chicha to drink. The llama was expected to kick over the vessel containing the chicha, thus making of it a sacrifice to help the maize form grains.[70] After the ritual of the napa llama in the square, a procession of dancers danced as far as a building that in Spanish times became the house of Diego de los Rios. It was situ-

---

[63] Guaman Poma, *Nueva Crónica*, p. 270 [272].

[64] E.g., Cobo, *Historia* 13.25, p. 209b.

[65] Cf. Sallnow, *Pilgrims*, pp. 133f.

[66] Quechua, "white."

[67] Quechua, "place of origin."

[68] Cobo, *Historia* 13.25, p. 209b.

[69] Personal retainers of the Inca; see Murra, *Economic Organization* (1980), pp. 153ff.

[70] Cobo, *Historia* 13.27, p. 214b; cf. Zuidema, "El ushnu," *Revista de la Universidad Complutense* 28, no. 117 (1979): 336, where this and the passages from Guaman Poma cited below are discussed. Zuidema suggests that the chicha the llama kicked over flowed into the ushnu.

20. The deity Vilcanota, who like his counterpart Pariacaca–Pachacamac is contained within a rock face, receives a black llama and coca from a man and woman of Collasuyo. Guaman Poma, *Nueva Crónica*, p. 270, Royal Library, Copenhagen. Photo from facsimile, Paris 1936.

ated on the street running north to south from the palace of Manco Capac to Limapampa.[71]

Guaman Poma described a ceremony at the very beginning of the Inca harvest season in April that likewise involved a llama in Haucaypata. But because now the llama was dressed in a many-colored woven tunic and wore gold earrings, Guaman Poma described it as colored or red, *puca llama*.[72] At the beginning of the maize harvest, the Inca "sang the song of the llamas, [which was entitled] *Colored Llama*, and the song of the rivers, that sound which they make. These are the songs proper to the Inca; like the llama, he sings and says 'yn' for a long time" (fig. 21).[73] The coyas, Guaman Poma continued, and the ñustas responded, singing gently "aravi, aravi," which, as we have seen, was a song for harvesting and plowing; and the llama sang as well.[74] A song of triumph, haylli, followed, and the conclusion was a mournful aravi, a love lyric, sung by the princesses and the young men. Fearing that his beloved would forget him, the young man in the lyric at the same time feared the approach of the consummation of the world in flood and darkness.[75]

Guaman Poma's drawing of this essentially festive episode in April is matched by another drawing of a mournful episode in October. Like Inti Raimi and Capac Inti Raimi, these two episodes are thus separated by exactly half a year. In October, Guaman Poma writes, the Incas prayed for rain amid tears and lamentation, "and they tied up black llamas in the public square and gave them nothing to eat, so they could help with the weeping."[76] The drawing corresponding to this text is the exact iconographic counterpart to the drawing of the colored llama, except here the theme is not joy but sorrow (fig. 22).[77] Either way, the llama is man's partner and equal.

The first llama to live after the flood figures repeatedly in Andean myths. One myth in particular illumines Guaman Poma's story of the Inca singing with the colored llama in Haucaypata. The myth relates how, in the ancient days, a llama saw in the stars that the sea would overflow and consume the earth in a flood. Thus it wept; "yn, yn," it kept repeating and refused to eat. The master became angry and threw the maize cob he had just finished eating at his llama. "How stupid you are,"

[71] Garcilaso, *Comentarios reales* 7.9; Cobo, *Historia* 13.27, p. 214b, the procession of dancers included a napa llama.
[72] Cf. puca in Gonzalez Holguin, *Vocabulario de la lengua general*, p. 292; Zuidema, op. cit. (above n. 70), p. 336; see Sarmiento, *Historia* 12, p. 215a, for a full description of the animal's adornments; also Murra, *Economic Organization* (1980), p. 58.
[73] Guaman Poma, *Nueva Crónica*, p. 243 [245] with 318 [320].
[74] *Coya*, Quechua, "queen"; *ñusta*, Quechua, "princess." For an analysis of the song's content and poetry, see B. Mannheim, "Poetic form," *Amerindia* 11 (1986): 41–64.
[75] Guaman Poma, *Nueva Crónica*, p. 318 [320].
[76] Guaman Poma, *Nueva Crónica*, p. 255 [257].
[77] Guaman Poma, *Nueva Crónica*, p. 254 [256].

21. The Inca, wearing strings of bells round his knees and ankles, is attended by princesses and courtiers while he sings with his colored llama in Cuzco's main square to celebrate the beginning of the harvest. Guaman Poma, *Nueva Crónica*, p. 318, Royal Library, Copenhagen.

22. Averting drought in October, under a meager, waning moon. Guaman Poma's caption reads: "Procession praying for water from god, the maker of man." On the llama that had been tied up without food he wrote: "The black llama helps with weeping and asking for water because it is hungry." *Nueva Crónica*, p. 254, Royal Library, Copenhagen.

the llama said and explained its premonition about the flood. The master therefore gathered up his belongings and with the llama ascended to a cave high up in the side of a mountain. There they both found refuge until the waters subsided. The people of today are said to be descended from this man, and their llamas from his llama.[78]

The white llama called napa that figured in the celebration of both Capac Inti Raimi and the lesser Inti Raimi thus brought to mind the beginning of the current order. For this napa llama stood for the llamas that had accompanied human beings on their very first journey: the journey from their pacarina to the abodes they were to occupy in space and time. Sarmiento recorded a variant of the Inca myth of origin in which Ayar Cache is sent back to the window at Pacaritambo to fetch not only the familiar gold vessels but also seeds and a napa llama.[79] A version of this myth was enacted when, by way of concluding the celebration of the lesser Inti Raimi, the Inca was accompanied to Matucalla by a procession including four life-size images of llamas, two in gold, called *corinapa*, and two in silver, called *colquinapa*. All four were dressed in finely woven tunics and were carried on the shoulders of Inca nobles. They were there "in memory of the llamas who they say came forth from the *tambo* with them"—another reference to first origins, specifically the Incas' emergence from Pacaritambo, the "House of the Dawn."[80]

The current order of things, into which those first llamas had accompanied their human fellow travelers, came into existence as the consequence of a cataclysm[81] and was expected to end in another cataclysm. The times, having turned once to bring the known world into existence, would in the future turn again to terminate it. This is what the song of the princesses and the young men darkly pointed to during the celebration of the lesser Inti Raimi. Beginning matched end, just as light matched dark, and the celebration of the December solstice pointed to the celebration of the solstice in June. There was thus no contradiction when men working the fields sang the mournful aravi alongside the triumphal haylli. These continuities reach beyond the political, the imperial, and even the religious content of Inca festivals to concepts of time and history that were shared by Andeans irrespective of Inca governance.[82]

While the anonymous cleric was walking through the streets and fields of Cuzco in 1535, therefore, he saw, even if he did not fully understand, a complex and many-layered representation of Inca and Andean religion

---

[78] *Runa yndio*, chap. 3; for a Cañari parallel, see Molina, *Fábulas*, p. 56.

[79] Sarmiento, *Historia Indica* 13, p. 215a.

[80] Molina, *Fábulas*, p. 70; cf. Sancho, *An account of the conquest of Peru*, transl. Means, chap. 14, p. 129: he saw in Cuzco four lifesize gold llamas that perhaps had a similar purpose.

[81] Cieza, *Segunda Parte* 3; cf. Betanzos, *Suma* (1987), 1.1, p. 11a; Zárate, in Bataillon, "Zárate ou Lozano?" *Caravelle* 1 (1963): 22f.

[82] MacCormack, "Pachacuti," *American Historical Review* 93 (1988): 960–1006.

and politics, a representation of the mythic past of the Incas, of the social and economic order of their empire, and also of the anticipated future, which would bring, sooner or later, the destruction of all that was loved and known. The invading Spaniards brought about this destruction much more quickly than the Incas and their subjects could possibly have imagined. Within less than a decade of the Spanish arrival, the ceremonies that the anonymous cleric had watched lived only in people's memories. For with the end of the Inca empire, imperial ceremonial lost its raison d'être.

However, this was far from being the case with regard to the ceremonies of harvesting and plowing that were practiced by Andeans beyond the confines of Cuzco, and even within Cuzco, but independently of the rituals of the Inca empire. The imperial rituals had been introduced in the wake of Inca armies and administrators by the great conqueror and legislator Pachacuti in the mid-fifteenth century. They were thus of recent origin; indeed, when the Spaniards came, aged Andeans, among them some of the people who were interviewed in Chincha, remembered how their region had been administered before the advent of the Inca. In Chincha and elsewhere, local people explained that it was the Incas who arranged that fields assigned to the state be ritually plowed and cultivated by the community. These ceremonial events were modeled on the Inca ceremonial of Cuzco.[83] Inca ceremonies left some traces in Spanish Peru but were much more fragile than the age-old rituals and beliefs that predated the empire. Many of these rituals were quite unconnected with the imperial rituals of Cuzco, for while the Incas were interested in celebrating their "father the Sun," their mythic origins and the political and social ordering of their empire, country people were more urgently concerned with averting crop failure and starvation.[84]

The harvest songs, aravi, of Andean villagers revolved around the theme that the maize should last for the year, and the same preoccupation was expressed in rural maize rituals. These songs and rituals that endured throughout the colonial period interested the ever-pragmatic Polo de Ondegardo much more than the bygone ceremonial of the Incas.[85] Polo thus described how at harvest time country people selected a well-grown cob of maize and ceremoniously placed it in a small container, pirua, which in turn was wrapped in a woman's shawl, llijlla. This was Zaramama, the mother of the maize. After a three nights' vigil in her presence, she was asked whether she had sufficient strength for the coming year. If the answer was no, the Zaramama was solemnly burned in her chacra of origin and another cob of maize was selected for the coming year, "lest the seed

---

[83] Aviso, pp. 165f.; cf. above, sec. 1 at nn. 113–114.

[84] Murra, "Rite and Crop," in Essays in Honor of Paul Radin, pp. 393–407.

[85] On the rituals of initiation, see Polo de Ondegardo, Errores 8, fol. 10r; cf. fol. 10vf., on Citua.

of the maize should perish."[86] Another kind of Zaramama was made of cornstalks and was dressed in a skirt like a woman, her llijlla being held in place by a silver *topo*.[87] Zaramama could also be a cornstalk that had borne many cobs, or a double cob, or a cob that had grown in an unusual shape or in unusual colors. Indeed, in harmony with the Andean tendency to find a genealogical principle in everything,[88] all cultivated plants had mothers, representations of their successful growth,[89] and the very earth received offerings as "mother," Pachamama. Throughout early colonial Peru, Zaramamas, along with the mothers of all the other plants, were ubiquitous.[90]

Andean rural cults and sacrifices endured because they gave voice to the ecology of the Andes and to Andean concepts of humanity. Every year the crops were planted and harvested, and every year they were exposed to the same natural hazards.[91] Yet, after 1532, Andeans, familiar with their own world, coexisted with people whose sacred time unfolded according to quite different rhythms. Superficially, however, some Andean and Christian festivals resembled each other. For example, the Catholic festival of Corpus Christi, with its elaborate procession of the eucharistic host, resonated in Andean perceptions with the Inca Inti Raimi, which had been celebrated around the same time of year. Commenting on this fact, Polo de Ondegardo observed that "the Indians nowadays, while appearing to celebrate our festival of Corpus Christi, in effect indulge in much superstition by celebrating their old festival of Inti Raymi."[92] Some of the resulting continuities were quite specific. Where thus, in former days, the people of Cuzco had scattered coca leaf, flowers, and many-colored feathers on the path of the Inca when he returned to the capital from the hill of Mantucalla, the same observance could in Christian times be performed for processions accompanying the eucharistic host at Corpus Christi. Extending this logic a little further, Andeans placed their own holy objects next to Christian images of saints.[93] In this way, while seeming to revere a Christian image, Andeans could secretly pay homage to their huacas. Indeed, the very appearance of Spanish religious images invited such an approach. For their sheer naturalism, their lifelike glass

---

[86] Polo de Ondegardo, *Errores* 6, fol. 10v; similarly, Cobo, *Historia* 13.27, p. 215.

[87] Quechua, "pin."

[88] Cf. Berthelot, "L'exploitation des métaux," *Annales ESC* 33 (1978): 960ff.

[89] Arriaga, *Extirpación* 2, p. 20, Mamacocha, Mamapacha; p. 28, Zaramama.

[90] Pérez Bocanegra, *Ritual*, p. 133; Duviols, *Cultura andina y represión* (1986), Index, p. 570, s.v. zaras mamas; cf. for Cocamama, pp. 398, 434.

[91] Cf. Murúa, *Historia del origen* (1590), 3.49, pp. 278–81; Calancha, *Corónica Moralizada* 2.32, p. 1065.

[92] Polo de Ondegardo, *Errores* 8, fol. 10v; cf. fol. 10r.

[93] Lima, *Segundo Concilio Provincial*, ed. R. Vargas Ugarte, Constitution for Indians 95. For similar continuities in Quito, see F. Salomon, *Native Lords of Quito* (1986), pp. 77ff.

eyes,[94] their blushing complexions, and their wardrobes filled with jeweled clothing,[95] invited Andeans to perceive in them the huacas and mallquis of Christians, whose very existence authorized the worship of their Andean counterparts.[96]

3. Taqui Onqoy and Inca Antiquities

In 1564 Luis de Olivera, priest of the repartimiento of Parinacocha in the bishopric of Cuzco discovered a movement of religious and political revolt that extended from La Paz to Chuquisaca, Cuzco, Huamanga, and even to Lima and Arequipa.[1] The movement was known among Andeans as *Taqui Onqoy*, "dance of disease."[2] In the words of a Spanish observer, its adherents, for the most part Indians who had become Christians, would "dance and tremble while moving in a circle, and in the dance they called on the devil and on their huacas and idols, at the same time abjuring . . . the true faith of Jesus Christ and all the teachings they had received from Christian priests."[3] The disease from which this ecstatic dancing, or, in the words of a Spanish resident of Huamanga, this "walking about like madmen,"[4] was to liberate its practitioners was the worship of the Christian god who favored only the Spaniards and had assisted them in conquering the Inca Atahualpa, but whose turn to be defeated was now at hand.[5]

The geographical extent of the Taqui Onqoy and its intensity astounded and frightened Spaniards. After all, the religion of the Inca state, highly visible as most of its manifestations had been when the invaders arrived, had all but come to an end by 1564. Most Inca holy places were derelict, and Inca temples had been destroyed or converted to Span-

[94] See T. Gisbert, *Iconografía y mitos indígenas* (1980), p. 103.

[95] See B. Gilman Proske, *Juan Martínez Montañes Sevillian Sculptor* (New York, 1967), pp. 52ff., 132ff., for his commissions from Peru and work by his followers there. A lively art market linked peninsular Spain with the Americas; see D. Kinkead, "Juan de Luzon and the Sevillian Painting Trade with the New World in the Second Half of the Seventeenth Century," *Art Bulletin* 66, no. 2 (1984): 303–310. For an example of a lifelike cult image in Spain, see E.M.A. Olmos, *Santa Maria de los Inocentes y Desamparados* (Valencia, 1968), figs. 19ff.

[96] Cf. MacCormack, "The Heart Has its Reasons," *Hispanic American Historical Review* 65 (1985): 460; "Pachacuti," *American Historical Review*, 93 (1988): 982ff.

[1] Molina, *Fábulas*, p. 78; Stern, *Peru's Indian Peoples* (1982), pp. 51–71; Spalding, *Huarochiri* (1984), pp. 147ff., and now the excellent study by R. Varón Gabai, "Taki Onqoy," in L. Millones, ed., *El retorno de las huacas*, pp. 331–405.

[2] Molina, *Fábulas*, p. 129; C. de Albornoz, *Informaciones*, ed. L. Millones, in *El retorno de las huacas* (hereafter Albornoz, *Informaciones*), p. 191.

[3] Albornoz, *Informaciones*, p. 205, with p. 213; cf. Albornoz, *Instrucción*, p. 194.

[4] Yaranga Valderrama, "Taki Onqo ou la vision des vaincus," in *Les mentalités dans la Péninsule Ibérique* (1978), p. 160; Albornoz, *Informaciones*, p. 99; for use of hallucinogenics, see Duviols, *Lutte*, pp. 113f.

[5] Molina, *Fábulas*, p. 130; cf. MacCormack, "Pachacuti," *American Historical Review* 93 (1988): 982ff.

ish uses. Moreover, the offerings of gold and silver, the herds, lands, and stores of *cumbi* cloth, maize, and other foodstuffs belonging to the Inca deities had been dispersed or confiscated. However, as the Augustinian friars in Huamachuco and other missionaries elsewhere had already learned, the regional deities who predated the Inca empire were not so easily disposed of, and it was those deities, more than the deities of the Inca state, that figured in the Taqui Onqoy. The movement's adherents thus believed that the Andean huacas, led by Pachacamac and Titicaca, were about to arise to drive the invaders from the land. A Christian observer reported:

> All the huacas of the kingdom that the Christians had burned and destroyed had risen to life again and were drawn up on two sides, the one side with the huaca Pachacamac and the other with the huaca Titicaca, which were the two greatest of the kingdom; these two had joined forces to give battle against God Our Lord, who, [the Indians] thought, had already been conquered. Furthermore, [the Indians thought] that the Spaniards of this land would soon die because the huacas would send all of them diseases and kill them all.[6]

Cristóbal de Molina, who was for many years cura of Nuestra Señora de los Remedios in Cuzco, learned very specifically what was at issue and how adherents of the Taqui Onqoy expected the future to unfold:

> When the Marquess [Francisco Pizarro] entered the land, God had defeated the huacas, and the Spaniards had defeated the Indians. But now the world was turning around, and God and the Spaniards would be overcome . . . and the sea would rise and would drown them, so that no memory would be left of them. . . . The huacas were walking about in the air, dried out and starving, because the Indians were not feeding them or pouring chicha. The huacas had therefore sown many fields of worms for planting in the hearts of Spaniards and of Spanish livestock and horses, and also in the hearts of Indians who remained Christians.[7]

The adherents of the Taqui Onqoy maintained careful contact with the Incas in exile at Vilcabamba and anticipated a return of the "time of the Inca."[8] Their theatre of action was bounded by the frontiers of the former Inca empire, and they addressed their sacrifices to "all the huacas and vilcas of the four parts of this land,"[9] in short, of Tahuantinsuyo.

But much had changed in the religious thinking of Tahuantinsuyo's

---

[6] Albornoz, *Informaciones*, p. 178; cf. p. 116. On Pachacamac and Titicaca, see further T. Gisbert, "Pachacamac," *Historia y Cultura* 17 (1990).

[7] Molina, *Fábulas*, p. 130; cf. Albornoz, *Informaciones*, p. 178.

[8] Molina, *Fábulas*, pp. 129, 130; Albornoz, *Instrucción*, p. 193.

[9] Molina, *Fábulas*, p. 133.

inhabitants during the preceding generation. The adherents of Taqui
Onqoy still honored the Maker Viracocha, the Sun, Moon, and stars by
addressing to them ancient Andean gestures of worship, such as blowing
coca leaves, just as they might have done in Inca times. Altogether, they
sought to renew the "rites and ceremonies of the time of the Incas."[10] But
the leading huacas of the Taqui Onqoy were not the deities of the Inca
state but Titicaca and Pachacamac, followed by the many regional deities
of the Andes.[11]

Moreover, the nature of these deities had changed in almost impercep-
tible but significant ways as a result of Christian missionizing and the
experience of colonial rule. In one sense, neither idol-smashing by missionaries nor the theft of sacred property by other Spaniards were particularly new in the Andes, for the Incas had not infrequently vented their
displeasure at Andean deities in precisely these ways. The worshipers of
Catequil in Huamachuco had rescued the fragments of their god's statue,
which in a fit of fury Atahualpa had ordered to be destroyed, and in the
1560s Andeans reconstituted in just the same fashion sacred objects and
images that had fallen prey to Christian missionaries.[12] Furthermore,
missionaries felt that the Andean deities, or "devils," were growing in
strength because instead of entering embalmed bodies, rocks, and other
material objects, as they had tended to do formerly, they now possessed
living human beings and spoke through them: "Now the huacas did not
enter rocks or clouds or springs in order to speak, but instead embodied
themselves in the Indians and made them speak. And [they ordered the
Indians] to keep their houses swept and in readiness in case one of the
huacas desired to seek shelter there."[13] Since the huacas spoke directly and
explicitly in the words of the person into whom they had entered, that
person represented the huaca and was revered as such.[14] These phenomena appeared to the missionaries as new and unfamiliar. But Andean deities had long been accustomed to communicate or deliver oracles
through the voices of human beings. The Sun of the Incas, Pachacamac,
Catequil, and many other deities both great and small all spoke in this
way with their worshipers. The Spaniards, on their side, had from the
outset interpreted this phenomenon by recourse to the long-established
Christian vocabulary of demonic possession,[15] exactly as they did once
again when confronted with the Taqui Onqoy.

Even so, the indwelling of gods in human beings as described by ad-

off[10] Blowing coca leaves, Molina, *Fábulas*, p. 133; rites and ceremonies, Yaranga Valderrama (above n. 4), pp. 149, 154.

[11] Cf. Albornoz, *Informaciones*, p. 93.

[12] Molina, *Fábulas*, p. 131.

[13] Molina, *Fábulas*, pp. 130–131; Albornoz, *Informaciones*, p. 178; see p. 191, the huacas
"se metían en los cuerpos de los indios e los hazían hablar."

[14] Albornoz, *Informaciones*, pp. 93, 140.

[15] Above, chap. II.1 passim.

herents of the Taqui Onqoy was not the same as it had been before the invasion, because it was in part conditioned by Christian notions of god dwelling in man that the missionaries had sought to inculcate for some thirty years. The missionaries claimed to be the messengers of an invisible, all-powerful deity whose authority could not be challenged and whose word was written in their book, the Bible. In response to these claims, the leaders of the Taqui Onqoy described themselves as the messengers of "Titicaca and the other huacas,"[16] who cared for Indians, while the Christian god and the saints were interested only in Spaniards.[17] Where the missionaries endeavored to explain to their Andean listeners the indwelling of the Holy Spirit in the Christian soul, Don Juan Chocne, one of the leaders of the Taqui Onqoy in Huamanga, denounced Christian teaching because "he bore within himself one whom they did not see, who told him these things, and it was he who gave them their food and their sustenance."[18] The missionaries claimed that the huacas were made of lifeless matter and thus could not see or hear, let alone respond to prayer. Many Andeans found this to be untrue, and an experiment confirmed their opinion. According to a Spanish priest living in Huamanga, some adherents of the Taqui Onqoy

> raised a cross in their meeting house and placed it into a corner. And their sorcerer preachers spoke in that house with their huacas and these same huacas gave answers to these preachers [who then said], "Look how this stick has not spoken for the cross, and he who speaks to us is our God and Maker, and him we ought to adore and what the Christians preach to us is a mockery."[19]

This was an apt response to the preaching of missionaries, who were prone to describing the Andean deities as a "mockery," *cosa de burla*. It was, moreover, from the invading Christians, who claimed to have conquered Peru under the protection of Santiago and the Virgin Mary,[20] that the proponents of revolt had learned to present the huacas as warlike and jealous. The huacas, when properly worshiped and fed with sacrificial food and drink, would drive out the invaders and would moreover cause the crops to grow and arrest the catastrophic demographic collapse that had been brought on by the invasion.[21] But these beneficial results could not be achieved unless Andeans separated themselves from the invaders

[16] Albornoz, *Informaciones*, pp. 93, 130; Albornoz, *Instrucción*, p. 194.
[17] Molina, *Fábulas*, p. 130.
[18] Albornoz, *Informaciones*, p. 225.
[19] Albornoz, *Informaciones*, p. 147.
[20] See Titu Cusi, *Relación de la conquista del Perú*, pp. 81, 86, 88.
[21] Albornoz, *Informaciones*, pp. 130, 147, 225.

by avoiding Spanish food and clothing, by not attending church and cat-echism class, and by not so much as entering Spanish dwellings.[22]

The teachers of the Taqui Onqoy also challenged the Christian moral code. They questioned the efficacy of sacraments administered by corrupt priests, asserting instead the sacred power of Andean priests and sha-mans,[23] and they affirmed the validity of trial marriage as practiced in the Andes. Above all, they insisted on the worth, indeed the necessity, of Andean religious observances. To fast thus meant to abstain from sexual contact, to drink no alcoholic beverages, and to eat no food seasoned with salt and aji.[24] Confession was valid only when made before Andean priests.[25] Similarly, food offered in sacrifice to the gods and the dead, like human food, had to consist of Andean products.[26] To choose Andean religion thus amounted to choosing Andean culture and returning to a life uncontaminated by the invaders.

Yet the very concepts of divinity that the teachers of the Taqui Onqoy relied on demonstrated that this could not be done. From a practical point of view also separation was impossible, as witness the uncovering of the Taqui Onqoy by Luis de Olivera and its subsequent extirpation, in the course of which the priest Cristóbal de Albornoz made his reputation. He destroyed many hundreds of huacas and confiscated their possessions, wrote a short treatise on methods of extirpation,[27] and in the opinion of his young Andean assistant, the future historian Guaman Poma de Ayala, was a severe but incorruptible judge, who "punished everything."[28]

The suppression of the Taqui Onqoy, which took several years, was followed in 1571 by the invasion and destruction of the Inca state in exile at Vilcabamba, which formed one of the highlights of Viceroy Francisco de Toledo's career in Peru. The two events marked the end of the first major phase in the colonization of the former Inca empire. Missionaries came to take for granted some smattering, however superficial, of Chris-tian knowledge among Andeans. Simultaneously it became clear that even if conversion itself was voluntary, continuance in Christian ways was unlikely to be. This realization underscored the usefulness of extir-pation as a reinforcement of Christianity as taught by word and—hope-fully—by example. But effective extirpation required expertise in Inca antiquities and in Andean religious lore. Missionaries thus had to learn to

[22] Molina, *Fábulas*, pp. 129, 130; Albornoz, *Informaciones*, pp. 80, 85.

[23] Albornoz, *Informaciones*, pp. 92f., 225.

[24] Albornoz, *Informaciones*, pp. 75, 93, 116, 126.

[25] Albornoz, *Informaciones*, pp. 75, 126; Polo de Ondegardo, *Errores* 5, fol. 8vf.

[26] Albornoz, *Informaciones*, p. 93; also [Polo de Ondegardo], *Instrucción* 3, fol. 2v; but see also Wachtel, *Vision des vaincus* (1971), pp. 212ff.

[27] This is the *Instrucción para descubrir todas las guacas del Perú*, ed. Urbano and Duviols (1988).

[28] Guaman Poma, *Nueva Crónica*, p. 676 [690].

differentiate survivals of Inca or Andean religion within Christian practice from mere local custom; in addition, they had to be able to recognize
signs of the clandestine performance of Andean rituals. Albornoz' treatise
on extirpation addressed both these desiderata. Other treatises on Inca
and Andean religion that date to the second half of the sixteenth century
were not specifically composed in response to the Taqui Onqoy but do
focus on the needs of missionaries and the not unrelated needs of secular
government. The most influential of these treatises was written by Juan
Polo de Ondegardo while *corregidor* of Cuzco in 1559. It helped the bishops assembled in the Second Council of Lima in 1567 to formulate the
decrees dealing with Indian parishes,[29] was published among the documents of the Third Council of Lima under the title *Errors and superstitions
of the Indians*,[30] and was frequently copied and plagiarized.[31] In addition,
the viceroy Toledo conducted antiquarian inquiries, some of which
touched on religion, by way of bolstering Spanish claims to sovereignty
in Peru, and his protégé Pedro Sarmiento de Gamboa wrote, in 1571, a
history of the Incas that had the same ideological intention.

The needs of extirpation and of secular government brought into existence a new, more systematic approach to Inca and Andean religion, of
which Polo de Ondegardo was the most eminent exponent, because he
learned to understand not merely the particulars of religious observance
and belief but the overall structures within which observance and belief
had meaning. A confrontation that took place in Chuquisaca, possibly in
the year 1566, between Polo and Domingo de Santo Tomás, who was at
that time bishop of the city, reveals what this could amount to in practical
terms.[32]

A number of baptized Indians had gathered to listen to Polo speak to
them on the subject of idolatrous worship. Fray Domingo was present,
and so, apparently, was Juan de Matienzo, one of the judges in the Audiencia of Chuquisaca, who recorded the incident in his treatise *The governance of Peru*. Matienzo felt that the clergy, and in particular Fray Domingo, had not done enough to destroy idolatry. "It is truly scandalous,"
he wrote,

[29] E.g., Lima, *Segundo Concilio Provincial*, Constitution for Indians 95, with Polo de Ondegardo, *Errores* 8, fol. 10v on Corpus Christi; see Wedin, *El concepto de lo Incaico* (1966),
pp. 78f.

[30] *Doctrina Christiana y Catecismo* (Lima, 1584; Madrid, 1985); for Polo's *Errores*, see pp.
265–283 of the Madrid edition, cited here according to the original foliation (fols. 7–16).

[31] By Murúa, among others; see Duviols, "Les sources religieuses [de] . . . Murúa," *Annales de la Faculté des Lettres d'Aix* 36 (1962): 267–277; also Duviols, *Lutte*, pp. 99ff. *Errores*
appears in an expanded version in Ramos Gavilán, 1.24. Perhaps he had access to the original, not the abridgement made for the Council.

[32] Matinezo, *Gobierno* 1.36, p. 120, writes "este año pasado," suggesting 1566, but this
overlaps with the Second Council of Lima, which met 1565–1567, and which Domingo de
Santo Tomás attended.

that this past year the licenciate Polo spoke to the Indians in the presence of their bishop and made them confess that they possessed the huacas he named to them, and that they were celebrating festivals for their idols, and he specified the huacas and the festivals and the days on which they were celebrating them. He told them how bad this was and that they ought not to do it any more. And they answered that no one had ever informed them that it was bad, and that now that they were being told, they would not henceforth do it.[33]

Fray Domingo, whom Polo was indirectly taking to task by upbraiding the Indians under his charge, did indeed lack zeal in the persecution of idolatry. It was during this same period that Fray Domingo, passing through the province of Chucuito, had set free a number of Indians whom the Dominican friars missionizing the area had imprisoned for sorcery.[34] The bishop's action did not stem from negligence or ignorance, but from the conviction, which he shared with his fellow Dominican Bartolomé de las Casas, that conversion to Christianity was an organic, and possibly a slow, process that must be voluntary.[35]

Matienzo and Polo, on the other hand, were convinced that Andeans would only become and remain Christians if forced to it, and then only if their objects of worship were destroyed. The two Spaniards had reached this conclusion long before the Taqui Onqoy, which, however, is likely to have strengthened it. Polo's feat of outlining the huacas of Chuquisaca was rooted in years of careful inquiry into Inca and Andean religious topography that had already led to major discoveries. While corregidor of Cuzco, Polo had thus found the hiding places of the Inca mummies which he consfiscated.[36] More relevant to his doings in Chuquisaca, it was at this same time, or at any rate by 1561,[37] that Polo discovered that the huacas of Cuzco were grouped along four clusters of ceques, or sight lines, that headed from Coricancha to the four parts of the empire.[38] This discovery had implications far beyond Cuzco, because the city's major huacas were replicated throughout the Inca empire, and every provincial capital of the Incas was built to be "another Cuzco." Huanuco thus had a huaca by the name of Guanacaure, with its endowment of lands and ser-

[33] Matienzo, *Gobierno* 1.36, p. 120.

[34] Diez de San Miguel, *Visita*, fol. 118v.

[35] See below, chap. v.1 at nn. 15ff., for voluntary conversion. But Garci Diez de San Miguel, who had conducted a careful visita of the region, wrote to Philip II in 1568 accusing the Dominicans around Lake Titicaca of grave negligence. "The Indians assert that they are well instructed," the visitor wrote, "but in effect they are not." See *Monumenta Peruana* 1, pp. 232f.

[36] See Duviols, *Lutte*, pp. 104–105.

[37] Polo de Ondegardo, *Informe . . . al Licenciado Briviesca de Muñatones*, p. 183 mentions his now lost letter on the ceques.

[38] Cobo, *Historia* 13.13; cf. above, sec. 2 at n. 2.

vants and treasures of gold and silver.[39] Guayna Capac's northern capital
of Tumebamba was deliberately constructed to resemble Cuzco and had
a temple of the Sun modeled on Coricancha, a huaca Guanacaure, and
other sacred places and institutions imitating those of Cuzco.[40] Indeed,
the very stones for its buildings had been brought from Cuzco.[41] Another
imitation of Cuzco was at Guarco on the coast, the city having been built
for the Inca to reside in: "and they say that the Inca ordered its neighbor-
hoods and elevations to be named after those of Cuzco."[42] The last copy
of Cuzco was Vilcabamba, where Manco Inca and his followers withdrew after they had failed to recapture the original Cuzco from the Spaniards.[43] Inca Cuzco thus was the conceptual model for other capital cities
of the empire, and its ceque lines were not unique. For such lines, radiating from a sacred center, could be superimposed on any landscape as a
system of ordering space. Wherever they were applied, the lines were
grouped in predictable patterns. This is why, in 1566, Polo was able to
use the knowledge he had gained of the ceques in Cuzco so as to reveal
their order in distant Chuquisaca.

Andeans formed different mental pictures of space than did Europeans.
What Polo had understood was how this Andean mental picture of space
functioned when applied to the holy places and objects of worship of Inca
Cuzco. The majority of these holy places must have been destroyed after
Polo made his discovery, so that the sequence of huacas on each ceque and
the sequence of the ceques themselves would have fallen into oblivion.
But the overall principles of ordering Andean space that the ceques epitomized remained operative. What was at issue in visual terms becomes
clear when we compare two maps, one drawn in 1586 by Diego Davila
Briceño to illustrate his account of reducciones he had organized in
Huarochiri (fig. 23) and the other drawn in the early seventeenth century
by the Andean noble Guaman Poma to illustrate his history of Peru (fig.
24). Davila Briceño's map, which was drawn in compliance with the
principles of sixteenth-century cartography, shows north at the left edge;
east is therefore on top. The map is bounded at the top by the eastern
mountain range of the Andes and at the bottom by the Pacific Ocean, on
which there are some ships. In the center, clearly identified, is Santa Maria de Jesús de Huarochiri, and four lines drawn from Santa Maria to
mark the four cardinal directions divide the map into four quarters. Gua-

[39] Ortíz de Zúñiga, Huanuco, ed. Murra, 1:30, 39. On the importance of Cuzco as a model
for other Inca capitals, see J. Hyslop, Inka Settlement Planning, chaps. 2 and 8.
[40] Garcilaso, Comentarios reales 3.24, p. 118a; Cabello Valboa, Miscelánea 3.21, pp. 364–
365; Murúa, Historia general (1611), 1.31, p. 81, lines 1ff.; cf. Borregán, Crónica, p. 84,
another Cuzco among the Cañari in the time of Guayna Capac.
[41] Garcilaso, Comentarios reales 8.5; cf. Cieza, Crónica 44, p. 145.
[42] Cieza, Crónica 73, p. 217.
[43] Guaman Poma, Nueva Crónica, p. 407 [409].

man Poma appears to have seen this or some similar map and modeled on it his own "World map of the kingdom of the Indies."[44] Here also, north is at the right edge, so that east, with the mountains of the Andes, is at the top. The Pacific, called Sea of the South ("Mar del sur") has fish and two ships. In the sea east of the Andes swims a *sirena* such as was soon to appear in church decoration in Cuzco and the Andean *altiplano*, and the entire representation is framed by a mature Sun and a waxing Moon.[45]

Guaman Poma's map thus displays at its center the city of Cuzco. Four lines radiating from the city divide the map into four parts. These lines do not, however, mark the cardinal directions, but, as Guaman Poma explains, the four suyos of Tahuantinsuyo, the Inca empire. Chinchaysuyo, to the north of Cuzco, is thus at the right. In accord with Guaman Poma's idea as to how the Inca empire functioned, each suyo is depicted as a kingdom in its own right, with a coat of arms and a pair of rulers.[46] Cuzco, displaying an Inca and his coya, is labeled as "the great city of Cuzco, head of this kingdom of Peru. Topa Inca Yupanqui, Mama Ocllo." If on this world map one superimposes a map of the city of Cuzco with its four clusters of ceques, once more placing north, or Chinchaysuyo, on the left side, it becomes clear that Guaman Poma's visualization of geographical space follows the Inca, not the European model, even though he deployed European geographical iconography to depict this Inca and Andean reality.

Polo de Ondegardo's account of Cuzco's ceque shrines is lost. Of the several other accounts of these shrines that came to be written during the later sixteenth century,[47] we have the abridged version which Bernabé Cobo included in his *History of the New World*. There is also the partial account of shrines in and near Cuzco, followed by a survey of shrines throughout Peru that the extirpator of the Taqui Onqoy Cristóbal de Albornoz included in his guidelines on extirpation.[48] These two lists reveal the meticulous sense of accountability with which the inhabitants of Inca Cuzco addressed their religious obligations.[49] Each holy place, however small, remote, or hard of access was entitled to its proper offerings: "If therefore they could not reach certain shrines to make the sacrifice because of rugged territory or because the place was covered in snow, the

---

[44] Guaman Poma, *Nueva Crónica*, pp. 983–984 [1001–1002], mapa mundi del reino de las Indias.

[45] The peripheries of the Andean world as here depicted correspond exactly to the worldview attributed to the Incas in c. 1608 by a mythographer in Huarochiri, who believed the limits of the world to be set beyond Titicaca at one end and Pachacamac at the other. "Beyond, there was not one settlement. There was nothing else." *Runa yndio* 22.8 (Taylor); 22. 278 (Urioste).

[46] Cf. Guaman Poma, *Nueva Crónica*, p. 982f. [1000f.].

[47] See J. Rowe, "Account of the shrines," *Nawpa Pacha* 17 (1979): 6–8.

[48] Albornoz, *Instrucción*, pp. 179ff.

[49] Cf. the analysis of shrines by Rowe, op. cit. (above n. 47), pp. 8–12.

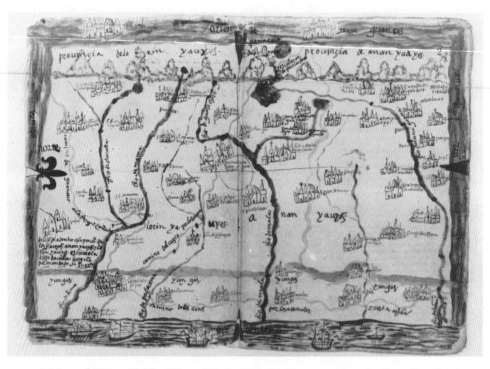

23. Map of Huarochiri by Diego Dávila Brizeño: lines marking the four directions, with west and the Pacific Ocean at the bottom, converge on the central *reducción* of the region, Santa Maria de Jesús de Guarocheri. In the lower left corner is Lima, described as Ciudad de los Reyes, and south of it is Pachacamac, marked as a village, not as the great Andean holy place it once was. But the deity Pariacaca, incarnate in a mountain, is clearly depicted (cf. figs. 19–20), along with the stepped path on which he was to be approached, top center. Real Academia de la Historia, Madrid.

ministers would walk up as far as they were able and from there they would hurl the sacrifice with slings, up to the peak."[50] The lore of these holy places—the prayers and rituals to be addressed to them and the sacrifices to which they were entitled—was kept alive in Inca Cuzco by over one thousand specialists, who were trained in this science from early youth.[51] The two lists of holy places preserved by Albornoz and Cobo, abridged and edited though they are, do give a certain insight into the

[50] Cobo, *Historia* 13.32, p. 223a; similarly Molina, *Fábulas*, p. 122; see also *Runa yndio* 22.19–20 (Taylor); 22.283 (Urioste); Cobo, *Historia* 13.1, pp. 148bf., mentions over one thousand specialists living in Cuzco who memorized matters of religious obligation.

[51] Molina, *Fábulas*, p. 127.

24. Guaman Poma's "map of the world of the kingdom of the Indies," with the Pacific Ocean at the bottom. Four lines marking the four parts of Tahuantinsuyo converge on Cuzco, depicted as Peru's spiritual and secular center: one coat of arms displays the pope's crossed keys and tiara, and the other the Spanish king's crown, with the towers of Castile and the lions rampant of Leon. These European blazons of power flank Tupa Inca Yupanqui with his consort, Mama Ocllo. *Nueva Crónica*, pp. 983–984, Royal Library, Copenhagen.

many-layered significance, and the sheer diversity, of Inca sacred knowledge.

In Cuzco there were, to begin with, the holy places associated with the mythic events of the pre-Inca epoch. The rock Guanacaure, which was sacred to Viracocha[52] and was deeply revered by the Incas, originated in that earlier time, emerging from the earth along with the huaca Apu Yauira.[53] After living a long time, Apu Yauira had ascended the hill Piccho, where he was metamorphosed into stone.[54] Guanacaure had brought

[52] Cobo, *Historia* 13.2, p. 150a.
[53] *Apu*, Quechua, "Lord."
[54] Ch-9:6 (I follow the abbreviations for the ceque shrines that have been devised by J. H. Rowe in his edition and translation of Cobo's list, cited above n. 47).

forth sons. But misfortune fell upon them, so that they also became stones; these stones were revered in the ravine Atpitan, near Guana-caure.[55] A huaca recalling the times before Viracocha went away across the sea was the house Mamararoy, "in which were venerated certain stones which they said were women of Viracocha, and that, walking at night, they had turned to stone."[56] Pachamama was Mother Earth, wor-shiped throughout the Andes. Yet near Cuzco she also had a more specific and more local face, for the field Ayllipampa, where miniature women's clothes were offered to her, was conceptualized as being Pachamama her-self.[57]

Other holy places recalled not the remote mythic past of the valley of Cuzco, but its pre-Inca history. Before the Incas came, the site of Cuzco was known as Aca Mama.[58] Among the original settlers whom the Incas had displaced after protracted warfare were the Guallas,[59] but the cave Atviturco, from which the first ancestors of the Guallas had sprung, was still revered in Inca times and was sprinkled with the blood of sacrificial llamas.[60] Similarly, the tomb of the lords of ayllu Ayauilla, who were kinsmen of a wife of Inca Viracocha, was remembered and revered, as was the tomb of Quilca, another non-Inca lord of the distant past.[61] An-other ancient holy place was Intirpucancha, a hall that had belonged to the first lord of Choco, the home of Pachacuti Inca's coya Mama Ana-guarque.[62] More closely connected with Inca origins and Inca history was Vicaribi in Piccho, the tomb of a lord of the ayllu of Maras, for according to one version of the Inca myth of origins, this ayllu had sprung from one of the windows of Pacaritambo along with the Incas.[63] Another holy place associated with Maras was the mountain Yauira, but by the time Molina recorded this information, the reason for its sanctity had perhaps been forgotten.[64] Members of Maras ayllu were, however, still living in Cuzco in the later sixteenth century.[65] Finally, on the hill Cinca next to the road leading from Cuzco to the Yucay valley, was a stone that the Ayamarca revered as their place of origin; to it, the solemn capacocha sacrifice was offered.[66] The Ayamarca were a group of pre-Inca ayllus from Cuzco that still numbered many members during the colonial and

[55] Co-1:6.
[56] Ch-8:8, transl. Rowe.
[57] An-7:1.
[58] Guaman Poma, *Nueva Crónica*, pp. 31, 84, 86.
[59] Sarmiento, *Historia Indica* 9, 13, 15.
[60] An-1:4.
[61] Sarmiento, *Historia Indica* 24, p. 229; Co-4:5; Cu-12:2.
[62] Cu-6:5; Sarmiento, *Historia Indica* 34, p. 239.
[63] Ch-9:5; Sarmiento, *Historia Indica* 11.
[64] Molina, *Fábulas*, p. 106.
[65] Sarmiento, *Historia Indica* 11.
[66] Ch-5:9; Sarmiento, *Historia Indica* 31, p. 237, Cinga.

republican periods.[67] Even in Inca times, they had maintained a certain independence, for they celebrated the initiation of their young men in October, independently of the date set for this ritual by their Inca overlords.[68]

The majority of holy places and objects of cult surrounding Cuzco evoked the origins and history of the Incas themselves. Several of these had already been holy in pre-Inca times but were adopted by the Incas. Yauira, revered by Maras ayllo, was the huaca where Pachacuti had decreed that the young Inca nobles who were being initiated were to swear loyalty to the Inca; it was here that they were given their adult loincloths and danced the dance huari, which dated back to the time when Manco Capac had come forth from Pacaritambo. Later Inca Guascar adorned the venerable huaca with two stone falcons.[69] Another huaca whose sanctity predated the Incas was Guanacaure. According to one version of the Inca myth of origins,[70] Guanacaure was the priest of a huaca whom Ayar Cache attacked and who was transformed into stone along with Ayar Cache himself. The Inca at his accession and the young Inca nobles during their initiation into adulthood visited Guanacaure and offered sacrifice there.[71] The huaca Guanacaure, which was an aniconic stone with tapering sides,[72] represented not merely Ayar Cache, but also his brother, the first Inca, Manco Capac. As such this stone was revered both by the lineage of Manco Capac himself and by all the royal lineages and accompanied the ruling Inca on campaigns.[73] After the advent of the Spaniards in Cuzco, Paullu Inca attempted to convert Guanacaure into a personal holy object by constructing a house for it next to his own house. But before long the Spaniards seized the venerable stone.[74] Other holy places that brought to mind the very beginning of Inca history included Caritampucancha, a small open space inside the Temple of the Sun, where Manco Capac had first settled;[75] Inticancha, the house of Manco Capac's sisters;[76]

[67] Rostworowski, "Los Ayarmaca," *Revista del Museo Nacional* 36 (1969–1970); see esp. p. 61, with Ch-6:7, Capi, the "root" of Cuzco.

[68] Molina, *Fábulas*, p. 97.

[69] Ch-9:6; Betanzos, *Suma* (1987), 1.14, p. 67b; Molina, *Fábulas*, p. 106.

[70] Cabello Valboa, *Miscelánea* 3.9, pp. 262f.

[71] Sarmiento, *Historia Indica* 56; Cieza, *Segunda Parte* 7; see chap. III.2 at nn. 126ff., cf. chap. III.3 at nn. 58ff. A related story is told by Pachacuti Yamqui, *Relación*, fols. 6vf. (pp. 241f.); see also Szeminski, *Un kuraka* (1987), p. 83.

[72] The "peña grande, figura de hombre" of Molina, *Fábulas*, p. 77, refers to the rock, not the portable huaca.

[73] Co-6:7, with Sarmiento, *Historia Indica* 14, p. 220; Titu Cusi, *Relación*, p. 100, lists Guanacaure as the first Inca.

[74] Co-6:7. On the opportunist Paullu, see Sarmiento, *Historia Indica* 67, p. 272ab, he seduces one of Inca Guascar's women and is spared by Chalcochima; cooperates with Spaniards (70, p. 276a).

[75] Cu-5:1.

[76] Cu-7:1.

the field Anaypampa, dedicated to the cult of Mama Ocllo;[77] and Sausero, dedicated to the cult of Mama Huaco.[78] When requesting favors from Mama Ocllo, it was customary to make offerings to her fountain Ticicocha, which was inside a house in Cuzco.[79]

Certain holy places were associated with the lives and deeds of particular Incas. Inca funerary ritual decreed that the kinsfolk of a recently deceased ruler should search for, and call upon, their lord in all the places that he loved to frequent when alive. Once it had been established that the Inca did not respond, that he had truly died, sacrifices were offered at these spots he had loved in his lifetime.[80] Some of these places were in due course integrated into the permanent network of shrines surrounding Cuzco and received offerings on a regular basis. Guayllaurcaja, for example, was a pass where the Inca Viracocha had been accustomed to rest, and Cusicancha was the palace where his successor, Pachacuti, was born. Both these sites became shrines.[81] The open space Cugitalis was venerated because the Inca Guayna Capac had a dream there that came true, and sacrifices were also made at a small house in Piccho where this Inca's mother used to sleep.[82] A very considerable number of huacas and holy places were associated with the Inca Pachacuti's victories in the Chanca war. Some of these marked sites where battles in the war had been won, while others were the *pururaucas*, divinely appointed warriors who, in accord with a dream the Inca had dreamt, fought for him and were then turned into stone.[83]

The shrines lining the ceques of Cuzco were thus a geographical representation of Inca myth and history. At the same time, the acts of worship addressed to these shrines endowed them with social and political significance—a significance made all the more explicit because the care of the different ceque lines was entrusted to the royal and non-royal Inca lineages of Cuzco.[84]

Apart from exemplifying the political and spatial ordering of Cuzco, and by implication of the empire, the ceque shrines guided worshipers through mythic and historical time. Finally, some of these shrines were

---

[77] Co-3:5.

[78] Co-2:3, with Molina, *Fábulas*, p. 118. Betanzos, *Suma* (1987), I.4, p. 20a, reports that Mama Huaco was the wife of Ayar Cache and that both were known for their ferocity; cf. Sarmiento, *Historia Indica* 13, p. 218a, where, however, Mama Huaco is the consort of Manco Capac. See M. Hernandez et al., *Entre el mito y la historia*, pp. 15ff.; 23ff.

[79] Ch-3:3.

[80] Betanzos, *Suma* (1987), I.31, pp. 145b, 147b.

[81] Ch-2:8, Ch-5:1.

[82] Ch-8:4, Ch-9:2.

[83] Rowe, "Account of the Shrines" (above, n. 47), pp. 9–10; below, chap. VII.1 at nn. 16–36.

[84] Rowe, "La constitucion Inca," *Historica* 9 (1985):35–73; R. T. Zuidema, *The Ceque System of Cuzco* (1964).

also markers of calendrical time. In Huamachuco, the Augustinians had noticed two huacas "in the East, where the sun is born."[85] These were probably pillars marking points on the horizon where the sun rose at a given time. Such pillars, described as *pacha unanchac*, "time marker" had been erected in Cuzco by Inca Pachacuti.[86] Two of these time markers were on the hill Sucana, "where the water channel from Chinchero runs. On it were two markers as an indication that when the sun arrived there, they had to begin to plant the maize. The sacrifice which was made there was directed to the Sun, asking him to arrive there at the time which would be appropriate for planting, and they sacrificed to him sheep, clothing, and small miniature lambs of gold and silver."[87] Appropriately, the hill Sucana was among the holy places visited during Inti Raimi.[88] The time markers surrounding Cuzco and other cities of the empire formed the network of such shrines[89] that served to implement the religious and agricultural calendar of the Incas. Betanzos had already outlined some of the religious festivals that were observed month by month, beginning with the initiation of young men in November and December. But after midcentury, and especially after the Taqui Onqoy, the Inca religious calendar attracted renewed interest, because it became clear to missionaries and secular officials that several Andean festivals, which the Incas had incorporated into their imperial calendar, continued to be celebrated. As Polo had observed, this was especially true of Inti Raimi, certain rituals of which were adapted to the rituals of Corpus Christi.[90]

Another Andean festival which the Incas had expanded into an imperial occasion and which Polo thought was still being celebrated in secret, was Citua, the expulsion of evils in August and September, during the Inca month Coya Raimi.[91] This was a time of rain, sickness, and potential food shortages in the Andes.[92] Betanzos described only the domestic and private aspects of Citua, without its imperial dimensions. People washed at night and then walked about with firebrands, saying that "they cast from themselves all pain and evil." Next, cloth, llamas, coca, and flowers

[85] Religiosos Agustinos, p. 41.

[86] Betanzos, *Suma* (1987), 1.15, pp. 73b–74, pacha unanchac at 74a, cf. p. 46a (1968). Gonzalez Holguin, *Vocabulario de la lengua general*, p. 269, "*pachacta unanchani*, to mark time to do something." See J. Hyslop, *Inka Settlement Planning*, pp. 226ff. for extant Inca astronomical markers.

[87] The Spanish writer writes "sheep" for llamas. Ch-8:7, transl. Rowe; cf. Ch-6:9, two markers for the beginning of summer; cf. Polo de Ondegardo, *Errores* 7, fol. 9v.

[88] Molina, *Fábulas*, p. 68, writes "Succanca."

[89] See R. T. Zuidema, "The Inca Calendar," in *Native American Astronomy*, ed. A. F. Aveni (Austin, 1977), pp. 219–259, at pp. 253ff.

[90] Polo de Ondegardo, *Errores* 8, fol. 10v.

[91] Coya Raimi, "Festival of the Queen," Polo, *Errores* 8, fol. 10v; 9, fol. 11r, on Ytu.

[92] Molina, *Fábulas*, p. 73; Cobo, *Historia* 13.29, p. 217a; Guaman Poma, *Nueva Crónica*, pp. 252 [254], 1155 [1165].

were offered to the waters at the confluence of the rivers Huatanay and Tullumayu.[93] Polo outlined the ritual of Citua in its imperial form, and Cristóbal de Molina described it in detail in the manual of Inca myth and ritual that he wrote in about 1574 for Bishop Lartaun of Cuzco.[94] In the mid-seventeenth century, Bernabé Cobo produced a very similar description; he may have used the same source as did Molina.[95]

Citua consisted of two interrelated sets of ceremonies: the expulsion of evils and the annual visit to Cuzco of the major huacas from all four parts of the empire, with their attendants and the curacas of their region. These latter ceremonies had already been described by Cieza.[96]

The festival began, according to Molina, with the arrival in Cuzco of the huacas. Citua did not have an entirely fixed ritual; rather, its exact course was planned every year by the Inca and his advisers on the day of the moon's conjunction with the sun.[97] The first phase of Citua was the expulsion of evils from Cuzco, which began when foreigners, along with persons suffering from physical defects, left the city,[98] while the Inca, with the nobles and people of Cuzco, awaited the appearance of the new moon in Coricancha. Once they saw it, they shouted, "Diseases, disasters, misfortunes, leave this land!" The message was taken up by warriors waiting outside Coricancha, who passed it on to another four hundred warriors gathered in Haucaypata. These warriors had been selected from the twenty royal and nonroyal lineages of Cuzco, and they now set out in four separate squadrons to the four suyos of the empire, each squadron running in the direction of the suyo to which their lineages belonged.[99] These were at the same time the directions in which the ceques that these lineages cared for were pointed. Here was one of the many occasions where the Inca ordering of space and time went hand in hand with the ordering of society. As they ran, the warriors, brandishing firebrands,

[93] Betanzos, *Suma* (1968), 1.15, pp. 45bf.; p. 72ab (1987).

[94] Polo de Ondegardo, *Errores* 8, fols. 10vf. Molina was regularly consulted regarding Inca and Andean antiquities; see his testimony in Albornoz, *Informaciones*, pp. 180ff., 223ff. See also, *Información hecha en el Cuzco* (1582); R. Porras Barrenechea, *Los Cronistas del Perú* (1986), pp. 349ff.

[95] This seems to account better for the similarity between Molina and Cobo than the hypothesis that Cobo copied Molina and some other source. For details in Cobo that are not in Molina, see Cobo, *Historia*, p. 218a, lavatorio general: all wash in water located on their own ceque; p. 219a, sacrificial meat eaten raw; also, Cobo's timing for the return of the *forasteros* is different, p. 218b, and Molina says nothing about burning thirty dressed logs of quishuar wood, Cobo, ibid. Most significant, Cobo says nothing about the visit of the huacas to Cuzco; cf. below.

[96] See above, chap. III.2 at nn. 34ff.

[97] Decisions about the festival are announced to waiting people, and statues of Viracocha and Thunder Chuquilla are taken to Coricancha, Molina, *Fábulas*, p. 73.

[98] Molina, *Fábulas*, pp. 73f.; Cobo, *Historia*, p. 217a, they leave before the consultation in Coricancha.

[99] Molina, *Fábulas*, pp. 74f.; Cobo, *Historia*, p. 217b; Rowe, "La constitucion" (above n. 84), pp. 37–38.

shouted "Evils go forth!"[100] Having run a certain distance, they were relieved by squadrons representing the state settlers who lived along the route, until the last squadron reached a fast-running river, where they washed themselves and their armor so that the river could carry the evils and sicknesses away to the sea.[101] In Cuzco, meanwhile, people shook out their clothes, and when they saw the dawn twilight coming, they went out to the springs and rivers to wash, each lineage to their own ceques.[102]

On the second day of Citua, people smeared their faces with a coarse maize porridge known as *sanco*, which was also spread on door lintels and storage places. The Inca mummies, having first been washed, were smeared with it too, and similarly the statues of the Sun, Viracocha, and the Thunder, as well as the huaca Guanacaure.[103] Springs too received sanco and were told "not to be sick."[104] Next came general rejoicing in Haucaypata, where the statues of the Sun, Viracocha, and the Thunder, various huacas, the Inca mummies, and the people of Cuzco, divided by their lineages of Anan and Urin Cuzco, were all assembled. The day passed with feasting and dancing to the music of panpipes.[105]

The following day witnessed the entry into Cuzco of a vast herd of llamas from all four suyos, four llamas being sacrificed to Viracocha, the Thunder, the Sun, and Guanacaure. The blood was sprinkled on gold platters filled with sanco, which was then given in communion to all present, after they had vowed to serve the deities and the Inca with a pure heart. The lungs of the sacrificed llamas were searched for signs of the future before being burned, and then each celebrant ate a little of the raw meat.[106] Next, all the remaining llamas were distributed among the people, while the priests prayed to Viracocha, the Earth, the Sun, and all the huacas for peace and plenty.[107] Prayer and sacrifice were followed by feasting and dancing.[108]

All was now in readiness to receive back the foreigners who had been required to leave earlier. For this purpose, the people of Cuzco, who on

[100] Guaman Poma, *Nueva Crónica*, p. 252 [254].
[101] Molina, *Fábulas*, pp. 74f.; Cobo, *Historia*, pp. 217bf.; Guaman Poma, *Nueva Crónica*, pp. 252f. [254f.].
[102] Molina, *Fábulas*, p. 75, with Cobo, *Historia*, p. 218a.
[103] Molina, *Fábulas*, pp. 76f., separates washing and smearing persons with sanco from doing the same to the Sun, Viracocha, the Thunder, the Inca mummies, and Guanacaure; he describes these actions as though they were performed in distinct phases. But it seems that all these rituals took place concurrently; more concisely, Cobo, *Historia*, p. 218ab.
[104] Cobo, *Historia*, p. 218a; cf. Betanzos, *Suma* (1987), 1.15, p. 72b, for a more detailed description.
[105] Molina, Fábulas, p. 78; Cobo, *Historia*, p. 218b.
[106] Molina, Fábulas, p. 80; Cobo, *Historia*, pp. 218–219a: according to Cobo, the forasteros come back before this communion, to share in it.
[107] Molina, pp. 81–95; J. H. Rowe, "Eleven Inca Prayers," *Kroeber Anthropological Society Papers* 8–9 (1953): 82–99. These prayers are not in Cobo.
[108] Molina, p. 96; Cobo, p. 219a.

preceding days had occupied Haucaypata, grouped according to their lineages, now clustered together on one side of the square, leaving the rest of it to the people of the imperial provinces. A ritual articulating social and political hierarchy within the city of Cuzco was thus supplanted by a ritual articulating such a hierarchy between capital and empire, rulers and ruled. The foreigners solemnly entered Haucaypata with their huacas, all being dressed in the finest attire of their regions. Having bowed before Viracocha, the Sun, the Thunder, Guanacaure, and the Inca himself, they found their places in the square and in their turn vowed to serve the deities and the Inca, whereupon they consumed their sanco sprinkled with sacrificial blood and a piece of meat from the llamas that had been sacrificed. Those who suffered from physical defects also returned to the city on this day, which was spent in feasting and dancing. On the last day of Citua, a llama was sacrificed, along with much fine cloth, and the Inca subjects who had come from the four suyos requested permission to return home, which they were granted. But they left behind in Cuzco the huacas they had brought with them, taking away those huacas who had come to attend Citua in the preceding year. Both the huacas and their people departed from the Inca's presence with gifts of gold and silver, cloth, women, and retainers.[109]

Cieza had described the Inca's gifts to the huacas visiting Cuzco as capacocha, specifying that these gifts rewarded huacas who had responded to the Inca's inquiry regarding the future with accurate prophecies.[110] Molina mentioned neither the inquiry nor the response of the huacas, but his observation that at the beginning of Citua the Inca lords deliberated how to celebrate the festival[111] may hint at the existence of this transaction. For conceivably, the subject of deliberation was the questions that, as Cieza wrote, were to be posed to the visiting divinatory huacas.[112] In that case, the foreigners, who were dismissed from Cuzco while the Incas were performing their rituals of purification and communion, now had time to consider their answers. Cieza wrote: "The priests . . . requested some time to respond . . . saying they desired to make their sacrifices, so that . . . their exalted gods would be pleased to respond what would come to be."[113] On rejoining the celebration of Citua inside Cuzco, the visitors could declare the responses of their huacas.

Cieza and Molina, like most other sixteenth-century authorities, wrote from an Inca perspective; rituals as performed and experienced by the subjects of Tahuantinsuyo interested them much less than Inca rituals.

[109] Molina, p. 96.
[110] Cieza, *Segunda Parte* 29, p. 89.
[111] Molina, p. 73.
[112] Cieza, *Segunda Parte* 29, pp. 87f.
[113] Cieza, *Segunda Parte* 29, p. 88.

They thus said nothing about Citua as perceived by any of the foreign visitors to Cuzco who witnessed it every year. Even so, Cieza grasped clearly the importance of Inca religion as a religion of empire. He thus described the political and social impact of Andean divination as controlled by Inca rewards and punishments.[114] Devotional and ritual particulars, on the other hand, meant little to Cieza. For Molina, the parish priest and missionary, by contrast, these particulars were of paramount importance.

Where thus Cieza had no more than mentioned the capacocha, the offering with which the Inca rewarded visiting prophetic huacas whose predictions came true, Molina provided an extensive description of the ritual and quoted the accompanying prayers.[115]

According to Sarmiento, it was Manco Capac who had instituted the capacocha, the sacrifice of a boy and a girl to Guanacaure during the initiation of young men.[116] This sacrifice appears to have been made from within the Inca clan. So was the capacocha which according to Betanzos Pachacuti decreed for the dedication of Coricancha, and also the capacocha for Pachacuti's own inauguration as Inca.[117] Molina, by contrast, learned of capacocha as an aspect of the religious reform of Inca Pachacuti, and as a method of correlating Cuzco with the four parts of the empire, the Incas with their subjects. In the capacocha Molina described, which marked an Inca's inauguration,[118] the human victims were not Incas but were sent to Cuzco from the four suyos of the empire. This information is confirmed by the visita of the Lupaqa, who in 1567 remembered that they had regularly sent to Cuzco "children for sacrifice."[119]

Upon arriving in Cuzco's Haucaypata, the capacochas were welcomed by the chief Inca deities and by the Inca himself, who decreed which offerings were to be assigned to the huacas of Cuzco and which to those of the empire at large. The latter returned home in those solemn processions that were described by witnesses in the litigation about the coca field in

---

[114] See above, chap. III.2 at nn. 38–39.

[115] For Cieza, see above, chap. III.2 at n. 38; for Betanzos, above, chap. III.2 at nn. 94ff. For the meaning of the term capacocha, cf. above, chap. III.2, n. 37. The same term was also used to describe offences committed against the sovereign; see Castro and Ortega Morejón, *Relación . . . de Chincha*, p. 240. Gonzalez Holguin, *Vocabulario de la lengua general*, p. 200, translated *hucha* not only as "pecado, daño, penitencia," but also as "justicia, pleyto, negocio." See further, Taylor, *Runa yndio*, pp. 29–30. In *Runa yndio*, chap. 22,11 with note, at p. 331, capacocha is a "ritual obligation." For a fine account of the ritual and its significance, see Sallnow, *Pilgrims* (1987), pp. 39ff. Cobo's account of capacocha, in *Historia* 13.32, p. 223, closely resembles that by Molina. See further Murúa, *Historia general* (1611), 2.29, vol. 2, pp. 109–111.

[116] Sarmiento, *Historia Indica* 13, p. 217b.

[117] Betanzos, *Suma* (1987), I.11, p. 51a; I.17, p. 87b.

[118] Molina, *Fábulas*, pp. 120f.; cf. Cobo, *Historia* 13.32.

[119] Garci Diez de San Miguel, *Chucuito*, fols. 18v, 41v, 45r, 52r.

Quivi.[120] In Cuzco the deities to whom capacochas were offered included Viracocha, the Sun and Moon, the Thunder, and Guanacaure. The accompanying prayers, as recorded by Cristóbal de Molina, implored Viracocha to preserve the health and safety of the Inca and of all human beings. One of these prayers ran as follows:

> Oh Viracocha, who says, Let there be day, let there be night; who says, Let dawn break, let it grow light; who makes the Sun, your son, to move in peace and safety to give light and illumination to the people you have created—oh Viracocha! Peacefully, safely shine on and illumine the Incas, the people, the servants whom you pastured, guarding them from sickness and suffering in peace and safety.[121]

Once the prayers had been said,

> —they suffocated the children, first giving those who were old enough something to eat and drink, and the little ones were fed by their mothers; for they said that the children should not arrive where the Creator was hungry and discontented. And with others they took the heart out of the living body and offered the hearts, still beating, to the huacas to whom the sacrifice was being made. And with the blood they anointed, almost from ear to ear, the face of the huaca, which they called *pirac*; and for other huacas they anointed the body with this blood. And so they buried the bodies jointly with the other sacrifices.[122]

Cieza had endeavored to explain to his readers that to those who practiced it human sacrifice was intelligible and tolerable, because in their eyes it was a noble and holy way of serving the gods.[123] Molina approached the issue in less intellectualized terms, by prompting the reader to regard the act of sacrificing a child as not incompatible either with parental nourishing and tenderness or with true devotion to the deity. At the same time, his simple prose highlights the tension between tenderness and violence, sharpened as they both were by the dignity of an elaborate ceremonial.

The litigation about the coca field in Quivi reveals that not all capacochas involved human sacrifice. This is confirmed by Molina who wrote: "It should be noted that they did not sacrifice children to all huacas but

---

[120] Above, sec. 1 at nn. 67ff.; Molina, *Fábulas*, p. 122, with 123, 126f.; 127; Cobo, *Historia*, pp. 222b, 223ab.

[121] Molina, *Fábulas*, pp. 123–125. The translation is by J. H. Rowe ("Eleven Inca Prayers," *The Kroeber Anthropological Society Papers* 8–9 [1953]; no. 6, pp. 90f.), with slight changes. As Rowe notes, the same prayer was, according to Molina, also spoken during Citua; see Molina, *Fábulas*, p. 87.

[122] Molina, *Fábulas*, pp. 123f.; for *pirac*, see above, p. 112f. See also *Runa yndio* 22, 11–12 (Taylor), 280 (Urioste), for capacocha sacrifice of a man and a woman to Pachacamac.

[123] Cieza, *Segunda Parte* 28, pp. 83f.; cf. above, chap. III.2 at nn. 44–49.

only . . . to the ones who were heads of provinces or lineages. In this manner they went walking throughout the land the Inca had conquered . . . making the said sacrifices until . . . the road reached the furthest . . . boundary marker the Inca had placed."[124] Guaman Poma depicted the placing of such a boundary marker on the *capac ñan*, the royal highway.[125] The Inca's capacocha processions thus defined the extent of his empire, just as regional capacocha processions defined the extent of a community's lands, while at the same time imploring the deities to protect the well-being of the Inca. The territorial and invocatory aspects of capacocha were remembered by a witness in the coca field litigation. He had heard from his father that

> the Incas used to go from Cuzco with certain ceremonies, which they said were the procession of the Inca, just as now the Christians say when they walk in procession praying; and that the Indians called it capacocha and that they went with it through all the lands of Peru, praying for the Inca. And he does not know if they were walking looking for lands or for some other reason.[126]

The well-being of the Inca was a primary concern of Inca religion. Both in Cuzco and throughout the empire, quipucamayos kept the most detailed records of offerings the Inca owed to each and every huaca in all the four suyos, lest some neglected huaca vent its anger on him.[127] This sacred record keeping was a fundamental factor in relationships between the Incas and their subjects.

While thus Cieza was right in regarding capacochas as gifts from the Inca to the huacas, this is only part of the story. For Molina shows that capacocha was also an exchange between the Inca and his subjects, center and periphery, an exchange which at the same time described and defined the boundaries of the empire.[128]

The logistics of the capacocha, the sending of victims to Cuzco, the return of some of them to be sacrificed in their homeland while others died in the capital, is analogous to the logistics of sending huacas to Cuzco during Citua.[129] Both these rituals articulated in religious terms the same interchange between capital and provinces that was also the

[124] Molina, *Fábulas*, p. 127; cf. p. 122.

[125] Guaman Poma, *Nueva Crónica*, p. 354 [356].

[126] *Justicia 413*, fols. 206vf.; cf. on "rogativos o plegarias" for the Inca, fol. 178r; cf. 63r.

[127] Molina, *Fábulas*, pp. 122, 127.

[128] Molina, *Fábulas*, p. 76.

[129] Perhaps the route for capacocha processions leaving Cuzco was the same as the route followed by the squadrons of warriors who expelled evils during Citua. Molina, *Fábulas*, p. 75, the first change of relay runners in Chinchaysuyo is Satpina; p. 71, for capacochas the first change of teams is Sacalpina. Could these be the same place?

driving force in Inca politics and economics.[130] But this was not an interchange between equals; rather, the interchange occurred within a pyramid of status and authority in which the Inca stood at the apex. Thus it was that observers from Chincha described the Inca as taking local resources for his own use.[131] At the same time, however, the Inca also redistributed resources, giving to Chinchaysuyo goods from Collasuyo, and vice versa, thereby supplying to each what was lacking in their immediate environment.[132] Furthermore, the Inca distributed to subjects and allies fine textiles and other high-prestige goods from Cuzco, just as, in a religious context, the capacocha delegations who returned home with their victims did so bearing gifts and privileges from the Inca.[133]

Molina's manual on Inca myth and ritual focused on the past but ends with a description of the Taqui Onqoy, which the author witnessed himself. This movement sought to expel the invaders and their god, but also articulated perennial Andean concerns with purification and liberation from evils such as had formerly been addressed during the Inca celebration of Citua.[134] In the early seventeenth century, Guaman Poma still perceived these continuities. Among the evils that Citua was to cure, Guaman Poma listed sara oncuy and pucyo oncuy, disease of maize and disease of springs, as well as taqui oncoc, "he who is sick from dance."[135] When later in his work Guaman Poma described the Christian calendar, he omitted all reference to these problems of the pre-Christian past; nonetheless, September remained the month when "diseases and pestilences and death walk about freely . . . and there is little food in all the kingdom."[136] Missionaries sought to impress on Andeans that health of soul mattered more than health of body and should be sought in Christian confession. But adherents of the Taqui Onqoy were convinced that confession and purification according to Andean rituals was more effective for physical and spiritual health.[137] Even in the late sixteenth century, Andean people were still accustomed "to wash themselves in rivers and springs while performing certain ceremonies, believing that with this they wash clean their souls from the sins they have committed, and that the current of the river takes them away. And they eat hichu, which is a kind of grass, and spit it out, declaring their sins to sorcerers, and in this

[130] See J. V. Murra, *Economic Organization of the Inca State*, chap. 6.
[131] See above, sec. I at n. 101.
[132] Castro and Ortega Morejón, *Relación . . . de Chincha*, pp. 245–246; Santillán, *Relación* 45.
[133] Textiles from Cuzco: Castro and Ortega Morejón, *Relación . . . de Chincha*, p. 237; further, below, chap. IX.2 at nn. 48ff.
[134] Cf. MacCormack, "Pachacuti," *American Historical Review* 93 (1988): 983ff.
[135] Guaman Poma, *Nueva Crónica*, p. 253 [255].
[136] Guaman Poma, *Nueva Crónica*, p. 1155 [1165].
[137] Albornoz, *Informaciones*, pp. 116; 120; 126; 130, adorando las dichas guaras . . . les yría bien . . . y ternían salud.

way they think they remain clean and purified of the diseases they suffered from."[138] Even where Christianity was rigorously enforced, the Andean thought patterns, the conception of evil as something concrete and tangible that could be physically driven out, prevailed. "Even today," the missionary friar Martin de Murúa reported in the early seventeenth century, "they maintain a strange error, which is, that after flagellating themselves during processions and [while walking the] stations of the cross on Maundy Thursday . . . they hang up their whips on crosses in cemeteries or at street corners and at the entrance of villages, saying that anyone who takes the whips down from there will take their sins with him."[139]

Spaniards tended to deride such attempts at eluding sin and evil as primitive and inefficacious.[140] At the same time, however, they recognized and even feared the power that crystallized in Andean expressions of purification and worship and sought to understand these phenomena by applying to them the cognitive vocabulary of imagination and illusion. Imagination was a channel through which God's communication with human beings could flow, but by the same token imagination could fall prey to demonic fraud, thus bringing forth erroneous illusion in place of true perception.[141] Cieza had reflected repeatedly on the nature and efficacy of such illusion.[142] Andeans buried living human beings with their dead lords because the devil convinced them with false visions[143] that this should be done. Similarly, it was by demonic illusion that the ancestors were seen walking through the fields they had formerly owned,[144] thus urging upon their descendants the necessity of funerary sacrifice.

Polo de Ondegardo likewise was convinced of the erroneous, illusory quality of Andean religious concepts and the practices that arose from

[138] Murúa, *Historia general* (1611), 2.34, vol. 2, p. 123.

[139] Ibid.

[140] Religious value judgments of this kind went hand in hand with the conceptual reorganization of Andean religious practice in accord with European norms. An early example came from the Augustinian friars in Huamachuco; see their list of over thirty deities to be extirpated, classified not according to any discernible Andean order but as they came to the mind of the writer (Religiosos Agustinos, pp. 27–43). Similarly, *Lima, Segundo Concilio Provincial*, Indian constitutions 99–110. Polo's treatises, abridged and edited for the Third Council of Lima, show the same characteristics: sacrifice, deities to whom sacrifice was offered and times when it was offered all appear in separate categories, Polo, *Instrucción*, sec. 1 with sec. 2; *Errores*, sec. 1 with 6; 14; see also secs. 7–9. Divination is separated from omens, *Instrucción* 4,5; *Errores* 4,11, and the cult of the dead is described in Christian terms, *Instrucción* 3, *Errores* 2. (*Instrucción* is only presumed to be by Polo de Ondegardo.) Note particularly that in the Andes, as in Europe, witches fly through the air and gain information by demonic means, Polo, *Errores* 10, p. 220; cf. Ciruelo, *Treatise* 2.10; G. Henningson, *The Witches' Advocate: Basque Witchcraft and the Spanish Inquisition* (Reno, 1980), p. 11; Levack, *Witch-Hunt* (1987), pp. 40–45 and now consult C. Ginzburg, *Ecstasies* (1991).

[141] See above, chap. I.1.

[142] Above, chap. III.1.

[143] "Engaña": e.g., Cieza, *Crónica* 62.

[144] Cieza, *Crónica* 100, 101.

them. Andeans, he thought, believed in the immortality of the soul, as Christians did, and it was for this reason that they buried the living with the dead. Thus it was that "from the great good of believing in the immortality of souls, the devil brought upon them a very great evil by causing the death of so many people."[145] Religious error came about, in the first instance, thanks to demonic illusion. However, once launched, it persisted and ramified quite independently of further demonic intervention. Polo could thus write of all Andean burial customs, vain as he thought them to be, as having been devised "in accordance with their imagination."[146] The same applied to other aspects of religion. The true account of man's origin after Noah's flood had been forgotten in the Andes, Polo thought. He thus viewed the foundation myth of the Incas, which enshrined many of their religious institutions and their claim to empire, as yet another product of the untutored Andegination.[147] Like the Incas in Cuzco, so people everywhere in the Andes told stories about their respective origins, "each one according to his imagination."[148] It was the same with all other aspects of religious thought and observance. Referring to his account of the ceque shrines of Cuzco, Polo thus wrote, "There were in this city, and within a radius of a league and a half of it, some four hundred sites where sacrifices were offered, and much property was expended on them for different purposes, from which the Indians imagine they derive benefit."[149] The very greatness and holiness of Cuzco was the outcome of "imaginations and opinions" that the Incas fostered about this city among their subjects.[150] It was thanks to these imaginations and opinions that year by year the Inca subjects brought their sacrifices and tribute to the center of empire and enhanced the glory of the city by their labor.[151]

By wrestling with theories of the imagination and, more broadly, with theories of cognition, of the origin of religious ideas, and of the nature of demonic intervention in human affairs, some Spaniards during the later sixteenth century endavored to explain the phenomenon of non-Christian religion. To their efforts we now turn.

---

[145] Polo de Ondegardo, Notables daños, p. 104.

[146] Polo de Ondegardo, Informe . . . al licenciado Briviesca de Muñatones, p. 140. See also [Polo], Instrucción 3, fol. 3r: las cabecas de los defuntos o sus phantasmas andan visitando los parientes.

[147] Polo de Ondegardo, Linage de los Incas, pp. 45, 48.

[148] Polo de Ondegardo, Linage de los Incas, p. 49.

[149] Polo de Ondegardo, Informe . . . al licenciado Briviesca de Muñatones, pp. 183–184.

[150] Polo de Ondegardo, Notables daños, p. 97. Polo goes on to report that the central square of Cuzco was covered with a thick layer of sand from the Pacific coast and that soil that was originally in the square was distributed elsewhere as being sacred; see further, Hyslop, Inka Settlement Planning, pp. 37–38.

[151] Polo, Notables daños, pp. 97–100.

THE IMPACT OF THEORY:
BARTOLOMÉ DE LAS CASAS
ON CULTURE, IMAGINATION,
AND IDOLATRY,
CIRCA 1560

IN 1559, AFTER years of research and writing, Bartolomé de Las Casas completed his great defence of Amerindian culture and religion, the *Apologética Historia.*[1] Materials reviewed in this work came from all parts of the Americas then known, and especially from the Caribbean, Central America, and the Andes. The book was a tract for the times. During the early, heady years after the invasion of Mexico, the conversion of the Indians to Christianity had promised to be a speedy task of a mere few years, and Las Casas' own early missionary enterprises had been conducted in this spirit. For during the early years after contact, some missionaries viewed the religious errors of the Indians as part and parcel of human nature untutored by revelation, and they thought that these errors could easily be remedied by substituting true and pure Christian teachings and rituals for false and impure pagan ones. Cortés himself thus experienced no qualms in appointing pagan priests in Mexico to perform Christian rites.[2] Religious observances in the Caribbean and the Central American mainland occasioned an utterly unshockable curiosity among the first Spaniards but little surprise, and the same attitudes prevailed in Peru during the early years after the invasion.

But by the mid-sixteenth century, missionaries and administrators had acquired some rudimentary grasp of Indian religion. Attitudes toward American paganism had become harsher and more censorious, because throughout the continent conversion to Christianity turned out to be a much more complex and protracted process than had originally been an-

---

[1] For the date, see E. O'Gorman, ed., Las Casas, *Apologética Historia* (hereafter *AH*), pp. xxi–xxxvi; on Las Casas' intellectual world, see A. Pagden, *The Fall of Natural Man* (Cambridge, 1982); M. Bataillon, *Estudios sobre Bartolomé de Las Casas* (Madrid, 1976); *Bartolomé de Las Casas in History: Toward an Understanding of the Man and His Work*, ed. J. Friede and B. Keen, (DeKalb, 1971); I. Pérez Fernández, *Bartolomé de Las Casas en el Perú. El espíritu lascasiano en la primera evangelización del imperio incaico (1531–1573)* (Cuzco, 1988).

[2] R. Trexler, "Aztec Priests for Christian Altars: The Theory and Practice of Reverence in New Spain," in his *Church and Community 1200–1600: Studies in the History of Florence and New Spain* (Rome, 1987).

ticipated,[3] while administering the conquered lands and peoples generated its own conflicts and controversies.

Las Casas never saw the Andes, but matters Peruvian first came to his attention when in Española he admired the treasure of Cajamarca on its way to Seville;[4] he also saw some of the gold plaques that had adorned the outer walls of Coricancha.[5] Among the Peruvian Dominicans whom he knew personally were Domingo de Santo Tomás, the founder of the Dominican convent of Chincha, Tomás de San Martín, the first provincial of his order in Peru, and Jerónimo de Loayza, first archbishop of Lima.[6] Las Casas knew Cieza and quoted his *Crónica*,[7] and he also read Cristóbal de Mena's anonymously published *Conquest of Peru* of 1534, as well as the *Conquest of Peru* by Xerez, which included Estete's description of the desecration of Pachacamac's temple.[8] Hernando Pizarro's letter on the same subject was perhaps familiar to Las Casas through Oviedo's *Historia*,[9] and, among other Andean materials, he quoted the anonymous cleric's account of the celebration of the maize harvest in Cuzco in 1535.[10]

In the *Apologética Historia* Las Casas defends Amerindian civilizations against their European detractors by demonstrating that these civilizations were comparable to those of the pre-Christian Mediterranean. Comparisons of Andean religion, and New World paganism at large, to the pagan religions and philosophies of classical antiquity were not new in mid–sixteenth-century Spain. But Las Casas wrote on the basis of an unusually far-ranging and detailed familiarity with the writers of both pagan and Christian antiquity.[11] He could deploy his arguments and utilize the ancient evidence in an incomparably more systematic and deliberate fashion than earlier authors had done.

New World religions are accordingly described in a comparative framework and in the light of theological and philosophical criteria. A

---

[3] For the Andes, see P. Duviols, *La lutte contre les religions autochtones dans le Pérou colonial* (Lima, 1971); cf. N. Farriss, *Maya Society under Colonial Rule: The Collective Enterprise of Survival* (Princeton, 1984), pp. 286ff.

[4] *AH* 133.

[5] *AH* 58.

[6] Marianne Mahn-Lot, *Bartolomé de las Casas et le droit des Indiens* (Paris, 1982), pp. 197, 215ff.

[7] Aside from his more general use of Cieza, Las Casas quoted the *Crónica* directly in *AH* 57 (compare Cieza, *Crónica* 89) concerning Vilcas.

[8] *AH* 56, 57, 133.

[9] Hernando Pizarro's letter, which was addressed to the Audiencia of Santo Domingo, is mentioned in *AH* 57, p. 295; The full text is quoted by Gonzalo Fernández de Oviedo y Valdés, *Historia general y natural de las Indias, Islas y tierra-firme del mar oceano*, first published by J. Amador de los Rios (Madrid, 1851–1855), pt. 3, 46.15. Las Casas would have had to consult this work in manuscript, because only its first part was printed in the sixteenth century (for this edition, see Select Bibliography). Possibly, therefore, he knew of Pizarro's letter directly from the Audiencia.

[10] *AH* 182.

[11] Cf. on Annius of Viterbo, *AH* 108.

far-flung series of parallels in the cultural evolution of America and pre-Christian and Christian Europe drove home this point. Citations from contemporary authors writing both about Europe and the Americas, from medieval philosophers and theologians, and from compendia of religious and secular history run side by side with citations from classical Greek and Roman authors, the Bible, and the fathers of the church. Las Casas conceded that polytheistic religions and even their more monotheistic descendants, such as the solar religion of the Incas, were indeed erroneous, but comparison demonstrated that the error was not specific to the Americas.

Las Casas' advocacy of Amerindian religions endowed his reading of the ancient and venerable texts that had guided and inspired European scholars for centuries with novelty and dramatic tension. Once the pagan gods of Europe had receded into the past and the cults that had been derided by the apologists of the early church had been supplanted by Christian worship, it was possible for the learned to look back to the old gods with nostalgia as having adorned that distant and revered antiquity with a patina of grace and charm.[12] Erudite interest in the denizens of a pagan Mount Olympus could thus go hand in hand with an unquestioning commitment to Christianity, as it did, for example, in the writings of the formidably learned theologian and scriptural exegete Alfonso de Madrigal (fig. 25) whose writings Las Casas often quoted. For at best the old gods continued to live a clandestine existence in the stories and rituals of superstitious country folk.[13] However, in the opinion of Las Casas, the gods of the ancient Mediterranean were neither the bearers of grace and charm, nor were they the relatively harmless focal points of rustic superstition. Rather, his comparisons between the pagan gods and cults of pre-Christian Europe and those of the Americas reinvigorated the ancient Christian apologetic against the persuasive power and moral corruption of Mediterranean paganism. The apologetic acquired a new dimension, however, because Las Casas sought to demonstrate that, unlike Greco-Roman religious ceremonies, those of pre-Columbian America had been performed with exemplary and sober dignity and that they had, in effect, enshrined a certain theological truth.

---

[12] J. Seznec, *The Survival of the Pagan Gods* (1953); M. Camille, *Gothic Idol* (1989).

[13] Above, chap. 1.2 at nn. 2ff.; Castanega, *Tratado*, chap. 6, p. 44; *AH* 97. In his commentary on Eusebius' *Chronicle*, entitled *Sobre el Eusebio* (Salamanca, 1506–1507), Alfonso de Madrigal followed established ancient precedent and treated the pagan gods as historical figures; a short treatise discussing several of the pagan gods in greater detail, entitled *Libro de las diez questiones vulgares*, was appended to the *Eusebio*. On the ancient and medieval background to Alfonso de Madrigal's approach to the history of religion, see J. D. Cooke, "Euhemerism: a Medieval Interpretation of Classical Paganism," *Speculum* 2 (1927): 396–410; also K. Traede in *Reallexikon für Antike und Christentum*, vol. 6 (Stuttgart, 1966), cols. 396–410. Further, below chap.v.1, n. 9.

25. The pagan gods made respectable: Alfonso de Madrigal's commentary on Eusebius' *Chronicle* and his *Fourteen Questions*, describing the ancestry, activities, and characters of the gods of classical antiquity, were published in Salamanca (1506–1507). The publication's sponsor was the impeccably orthodox Fray Francisco Ximenez de Cisneros, cardinal archbishop of Toledo, whose coat of arms serves as frontispiece. It depicts, inter alia, cardinal's hats and the Virgin Mary placing the priestly chasuble on Cisneros' predecessor, S. Ildefonsus. Department of Special Collections, Stanford University Libraries.

Among the ancient texts that acquired a new significance in this per-spective were Aristotle's *Nicomachean Ethics* and his *Politics*, to both of which Las Casas referred constantly. Aristotle had been concerned with the practice of virtue and the nature of knowledge in a humanistic and nontheological sense. Las Casas refocused Aristotelian virtue and cogni-tion toward explicitly theological goals. He wrote for readers who took for granted that the knowledge of god was the highest form of knowl-edge. The possibility of man's knowledge of god formed a cornerstone in Las Casas' arguments, because to prove that the Indians knew god in some form amounted to proving that the pagans of the New World were the cultural equals of those of pre-Christian Europe. According to Las Casas, Aristotle had believed in the innate capacity of all human beings for both virtue and knowledge:

> the disposition for virtue exists in all human beings even before it attains the consummation and perfection of actual virtues [practiced in living]. . . . [All human beings] have certain natural inclinations that are . . . seeds and beginnings of virtues, and later, when we per-form actions, . . . thus tilling the soil of our souls, these seeds reach the point of being virtues. Similarly . . . other kinds of seeds, which are of the sciences, have been naturally impressed on the understand-ing that we were given when we came into existence and that cannot be lost or corrupted.[14]

On this premise Las Casas constructed one of his principal arguments. It was that all human beings have the capacity to understand that there is a supreme god, and to seek him by acts of worship and sacrifice.

Similarly, Las Casas, having perused Cicero's dialogue *On the Nature of the Gods*, appropriated as his own the proofs for the existence of god that Cicero had put in the mouth of Balbus the Stoic.[15] But whereas Cicero had inquired how one might prove the existence of the gods, or of god, Las Casas accepted divine existence as self-evident and redeployed the venerable Stoic arguments to investigate how god could be discovered and known. Here also the issue is that all human beings know god in

---

[14] Las Casas, *AH* 186, p. 258. Here, as so often, Las Casa interprets Aristotle rather freely. He cites for his theory of seeds of virtues inborn in all human beings Aristotle, *Nichomachean Ethics*, book 6, which discusses the intellectual virtues. A passage Las Casas perhaps had in mind is *Nichomachean Ethics* 6.8.5–7, where *phronesis* (prudence) is first distinguished from theoretical knowledge such as is accessible to the young, and is then described as consisting of a knowledge of particular facts that can only be gained over time, by experience. A young person cannot therefore possess prudence. See also *Nicomachean Ethics* 2.1.1ff. and 2.2.8–9. For the seeds of the sciences in a person's understanding, Las Casas cites the *Posterior Ana-lytics*, see book 1.1, distinguishing actual and potential knowledge. On Las Casas' interpre-tations of Aristotle, see also the classic study, L. Hanke, *Aristotle and the American Indians: A Study in Race Prejudice in the Modern World* (Chicago, 1959).

[15] Las Casas, *AH* 71ff.

some form. For as the apostle Paul had written to the Romans,[16] God spoke to all men through his works. To discover him, therefore, one need only observe the natural environment. With this the ancient proof of god's existence became a proof of the possibility, indeed the inevitability, of knowing him:

> If you were to see a large and beautiful house, but did not see its lord or master, would you not judge him to be some notable and distinguished person? In the same way, beholding the great beauty of the world, so great a variety of things celestial and terrestrial, so great a compass of the earth, so great a breadth of the sea, and and everything so very beautiful, would it not be proof of ignorance and error if you failed to consider this universe to be the dwelling place and home of God?[17]

However, all this remained passive erudition, "old papers," as one Spaniard had written,[18] until confronted with the living religions of the New World. Las Casas himself described the transformation of his book learning into an active and engaged understanding of religious practice.

> Before New Spain, . . . Honduras, and Peru were discovered, I observed the care with which the Indians of these islands, especially those of Española and Cuba, offered a part of the harvest they had gathered as firstfruits, and I began to realize that the obligation of making sacrifice to God is an aspect of the natural law. Earlier, I had read, but had not myself witnessed, that, as St. Thomas demonstrates in the *Secunda secundae*, question 85, article 1, "the offering of sacrifices belongs to the natural law"; also, I have mentioned the opinion of Porphyry that all the ancients offered firstfruits. Now when all men do something by their own inclination and without being taught, there is a clear argument that the action is of the natural law. . . . When thus I sometimes asked, "Who is this Cemi [to whom you sacrifice firstfruits]?" they answered, "He brings rain and sun and gives us children and the other benefits we desire." And I rejoined, "This Cemi who does these things for you also cares for me," thus employing the opportunity of telling them something about God.[19]

The Americas were like an open book in which succeeding phases of mankind's religious history could be read in clear characters. The story began with the simple and natural worship of the peoples of the Carib-

[16] Romans 1:20, quoted in *AH* 74, p. 382.

[17] Las Casas, *AH* 72; for the simile of the house and its master, see Cicero, *De natura deorum* 2.6.17.

[18] Castañega, *Tratado*, p. 4.

[19] Las Casas, *AH* 166; cf. 186, end.

bean, Florida, and Brazil, and culminated with the elaborate and splendid cults of the Aztecs and Incas. The observations of ancient historians and geographers and the theories of philosophers and Christian apologists regarding humanity's religious evolution were borne out and made concrete in the New World.[20]

The *Apologética Historia* opens with an account of the influence of New World climate and geography on human life,[21] followed by an analysis of the faculties of the soul, its powers to reason, to know, and to inspire action.[22] This synchronic philosophical and anthropological discussion is the prelude to a diachronic historical and political account of New World cultures. Here the social organization and statecraft of the American nations are shown to conform to the principles outlined by Aristotle in his *Politics* and by the medieval commentators on that work, in particular Aquinas. As Las Casas understood him, Aristotle[23] had posited six groups of persons as necessary components of a fully evolved society: farmers, artisans, warriors, merchants or propertied persons, priests, and persons occupied with government.[24] In the passage Las Casas had in mind, Aristotle had differentiated the common people—farmers, artisans, traders—from notables, men distinguished by wealth, birth, virtue, or education. Aristotle did not mention priests. But Las Casas, in accord with his interpretation of Aristotelian cognition as applicable to the knowledge of god, recognized among these notables a class of priests. The most convincing American examples of complex societies, in which the six classes of persons could be clearly identified, were to be found in Mexico and Peru. The main body of the *Apologética Historia* is divided into six rubrics, one for each of the Aristotelian classes of persons. The discussion of religion in Mexico, Peru, and the Americas generally figures under the fifth rubric, that of the priests.[25]

The organizing principles that pervade both the philosophical and the historical parts of the *Apologética Historia* schematized and idealized the New World, for information gathered in the Americas was reproduced under, and tailored to harmonize with, the organizing principles that Las Casas derived from Aristotle. Amerindian civilizations were thus shown to have been what the civilizations of the Old World had often failed to be: ordered creations of natural reason. As a result, Amerindian civilizations speak in the *Apologética Historia* with a very European voice; they

[20] For antecedents of this reasoning in medieval Spain, see the illuminating article by C. F. Fraker, "Abraham in the 'General Estoria,' " in *Alfonso X of Castile: The Learned King*, ed. F. Marquez-Villanueva and C. A. Vega, pp. 17–29.

[21] *AH* 1–22, 24.

[22] *AH* 23–41; cf. Isidore of Seville, *Etymologiarum sive originum libri XX*, ed. W. M. Lindsay (Oxford, 1966), 9.2; 97; 105.

[23] Aristotle, *Politics* 4.4.1.

[24] Las Casas, *AH* 46.

[25] Las Casas, *AH* 71–194.

have lost their particularity. But this loss was countered by a gain. For by structuring argument and subject matter in this fashion, Las Casas was able to step to one side of the simple conclusion that Amerindian religions were erroneous merely because they differed from Christianity. In the historical, administrative, and ecclesiastical inquiries that Las Casas had consulted, this conclusion had arisen with a certain inevitability, because these inquiries posited knowledge of the Christian god as a self-evident norm, departures from which were considered worthy of note simply because the norm was taken for granted. But Las Casas did not take this norm for granted. Firstly, he anchored his discussion of the knowledge of god in a model of knowledge and cognition in general. Secondly, he viewed religion as a conglomerate of theological tenets and their expression in cult, sacred history, and myth. He discussed this conglomerate in historical terms and within the framework of an inquiry into what constitutes human society, and not simply in a framework of what constitutes true religion, in isolation from its social, cultural, and political ramifications. We will turn first to this historical aspect of the *Apologética Historia*.

1. THE WORSHIP OF ONE GOD

The salient theme of the historical parts of the *Apologética Historia* is religious change. Las Casas thus argued that just as societies evolved from primitive simplicity into a fully articulated body politic such as Aristotle had described, so also did the concept of divinity. From primitive and simple conceptualizations of divinity and primitive, simple cultic actions to match them, human beings throughout the world progressed to more exalted theological ideas and more elaborate and dignified forms of worship and religious art and architecture. Refinement of theological and philosophical culture went hand in hand with the refinement of material culture. One documented the other.

This approach to the study of religious expression had been pioneered by humanist historians and editors of classical texts, who were accustomed to impress on their readers the beauty and splendor of sacred architecture in the ancient Mediterranean.[1] Las Casas[2] insisted that the temples of pre-Columbian America were of a piece with these fabled

---

[1] This theme is especially prominent in accounts of ancient Rome: see, e.g., Lucio Fauno, *Delle antichità della città di Roma, raccolte e scritte da M. Lucio Fauno . . . Libri V. Revisti hora e corretti dal medesimo Autore* (Venice, 1552). On Du Perac's maps of ancient and sixteenth-century Rome and their antecedents, see F. Ehrle, *Roma Prima di Sisto V. La pianta di Roma Du Perac-Lafrery esistente nel Museo Britannico* (Rome, 1908), pp. 8ff. Cf. *AH* 132f. For the wider intellectual context, see M. Ryan, "Assimilating New Worlds in the Sixteenth and Seventeenth Centuries," *Comparative Studies in Society and History* 23 (1981): 519–538.

[2] Las Casas, *AH* 128–129.

monuments. Regarding Peru, he described Coricancha with its sacred maize field and the pyramid of Pachacamac in some detail,[3] also mentioning, perhaps from Cieza, the temples of Quito, Riombamba, Tomebamba and Vilcas,[4] while from Estete's *Relación* in Xerez' *Conquest of Peru* he extracted references to the temples of Junin, Cajamarca, and Xauxa.[5] The architectural beauty of these temples was matched by the richness of the sacrifices that were offered there and by the refinement of their rituals. Las Casas accordingly ended his discussion of Amerindian religion by quoting in its entirety the anonymous cleric's description of the celebration of the maize harvest of 1535 in Cuzco.[6]

This elaborate festival demonstrated the truth of a proposition that was central to Las Casas' interpretation of Amerindian religion: dignified religious rituals, such as those of the Incas, that were worthy of the divine majesty and performed in an appropriate architectural setting by trained experts were unthinkable without a highly diversified social and political structure, with its concomitant professional specialization of public servants, priests, musicians, dancers, architects, painters, sculptors, and artisans. Such a society, truly worthy of admiration, was the product of long-term evolution and change that extended from the dawn of history to the present.

In the Andes, as Las Casas understood it, a notable phase in this process of change was marked by the advent of the Incas, some five or six hundred years before the Spanish invasion. He derived this division of Andean history into the pre-Inca and Inca periods from Cieza.[7] It was a meaningful division in both political and religious terms, because the Incas had introduced more elevated and more highly organized forms of worship in the Andes when they supplemented the diverse regional cults with their own imperial cult of the divine Sun.

Religion was accordingly defined not by an immutable body of doctrine but by cultural and political change and advance. God was known not thanks to a unique and lapidary revelation; he was discovered, rather, in a series of steps, resulting in a gradually growing acquaintance. God, on his side, worked through history, making of it a *praeparatio evangelica*[8] such as the early Christian apologist Eusebius, whom Las Casas cited frequently, had traced in the cultures of the ancient Mediterranean. Las Casas described this process, in which the Americas were of course in-

---

[3] *AH* 58, 126, 131. In accord with this book's central theme, I highlight the Andean evidence that Las Casas cited in the *Apologética Historia*, although the argument I present could equally well be conducted in the light of his account of other parts of the Americas.

[4] *AH* 56, 57.

[5] *AH* 57.

[6] *AH* 182; cf. R. Marcus, "Las Casas Pérouaniste," *Caravelle* 7 (1966): 25–41.

[7] Cieza, *Crónica* 38; cf. 105, p. 284, with *AH* 250.

[8] Latin, "preparation for the gospel."

cluded, in two different ways that sometimes intermingle. One was anchored in the writings of Greek and Roman philosophers and historians, and the other in the Bible and Christian history and theology.

These two groups of authorities confront each other in the *Apologética Historia* in a dramatic tension. In the Greek and Roman sources, Las Casas found reasons for viewing humanity's religious history in a positive light. One could suppose, first, that crude and inadequate notions of deity and morality had over time been elevated and refined, and second, that even those early notions had contained a core of truth. The Bible by contrast suggested that the reverse was the case, that human history began with the expulsion from Paradise and continued, more often than not, in reiterated falls from righteousness. Yet, in the Christian extension of biblical history, these same lapses and occasional recoveries could be viewed, in the manner of Eusebius, as a preparation for the gospel, as a process that culminated in the coming of Jesus and in the worldwide mission of Christianity.

In Europe, most parts of which had been Christian for over a milennium, these contradictory interpretations of pre-Christian history had ceased to be of much practical interest. But in the Americas the day to day observations of missionaries, officials, historians, and administrators added weight to one side or the other.

By means of frequent recourse to the ancient philosophers and historians, Las Casas demonstrated that, like the pagans of the ancient Mediterranean, those of the New World recognized a divine presence in natural phenomena.[9] This perception of divinity led to worship, for living and surviving in the natural environment entailed experiencing need and dereliction. These in turn induced human beings to implore higher powers for rescue and salvation. In pre-Inca Peru, accordingly,

> two groups of people were more religious than others and more devoted to the gods, that is to say, those who lived in the mountains and those who lived on the coast. Those in the mountains were concerned for their crops, which were often lost because it did not rain, or were blighted by snow or frost. The people of the seashore were anxious for their fisheries. For such needs they had gods who presided over their activities, and they resorted to these gods with devotion and sacrifice when they saw fit.[10]

Unusual features to be found in the landscape, whether cave or crag, or even, as in Manta, a fine emerald which Cieza also had mentioned as an object of worship, were considered to be endowed "with some partici-

[9] Las Casas, *AH* 74, 121.
[10] *AH* 126; cf. 124 and 182.

pation in divinity."[11] Hence resulted the vast plethora of divine beings and presences who figured so prominently in the descriptions of Andean religion that Las Casas had consulted. But Las Casas interpreted this evidence in a new way. As in ancient Rome,[12] so in the Andes, the diversity of human needs for which supernatural aid was sought resulted in a diversity of divine beings or functions. However, while both the Christian apologists from whom Las Casas derived much of his information about the ancient Mediterranean and Spaniards in the Andes found a great deal to criticize in this phenomenon and condemned pagans for worshiping the creature in the place of the Creator, Las Casas, while accepting this criticism as valid, also set forth a different rationale for divinizing aspects of nature. It was a natural and good impulse for man to humble himself in the face of visible sublimity; it was natural and good to revere and honor it. For "whatever nobility, whatever excellence and virtue is to be found in created things . . . is nothing other than a trace, a light and gentle footprint, of divine perfection."[13] The very search for this divine perfection gave expression and form to the innate and God-given human potential for perfection, because it gave expression to the orientation of human beings toward their final goal, which was to see and enjoy God. But whereas in Europe the earlier phases of this search lay buried in the remote pre-Christian past, in the Americas there were still nations who adhered to innocently primeval concepts of divinity.

These were the peoples of Brazil, Paraguay, and Florida, as well as those of Cuba and Española, whom Las Casas had watched offering first-fruits to their god Cemi. Because among these peoples there existed as yet no diversification of trades and no centralized political authority, they built no temples, offered no elaborate sacrifices, and made no idolatrous images; indeed, many of them made no images of any kind.[14] These nations, although in space and time they had traveled as far as all the others from human origins in the terrestrial Paradise, remained spiritually close to those origins and to Paradise because their material culture had changed little over the milennia. Most often their worship was addressed to the sun, to whom they gave simple offerings of food, drink, and objects of personal adornment. Although these nations had no understanding of the divine qualities and thus lacked a particular and specific knowledge of God, their general concept of him was so close to the truth that "one needs only to help them to substitute the Creator, the Sun of Justice, for the sun, the material creature; to the Creator they will then offer, with

[11] *AH* 126; Cieza, *Crónica* 50.
[12] *AH* 103–105.
[13] *AH* 74.
[14] *AH* 124, p. 651, Cibola and Rio Grande; p. 655, La Plata; *AH* 168, p. 181, Florida; cf. *AH* 191, p. 283.

less labor than is required for sacrifices of flour and feathers, the sacrifice that he asks for, which is their souls."[15]

This was a very different portrait of primitive religion from the one Cieza had drawn on his travels beyond the northern borderlands of the Inca empire. Throughout these regions, Cieza noted, the Indians adhered to "no religion of any sort"; there were no temples, and such rituals as were observed were of the most primitive kind.[16] All that could be said for these people was that they were "without malice."[17] Yet this absence of malice constituted something of a moral vacuum, for the people thus endowed at the same time ate the flesh of their defeated enemies and kept the skin and bones as trophies, in which the devil was accustomed to make his appearances.[18] Cieza had thus found himself confronting a certain failure, an absence of clearly formulated creed and its ceremonial and architectural expression. Las Casas, by contrast, discovered that the innocent and pure beliefs and customs of earliest humankind about which he read in his ancient sources[19] had in the New World been perpetuated down to his own day.

Elsewhere in the Americas, however, the formation of states and empires had brought with it more complex concepts of god and more refined and elaborate rituals. The advent of the Incas which initiated the second epoch of Andean history, marked a clear-cut phase in the Andean branch of this universal religions evolution. For the Incas united the many small Andean chiefdoms and lordships into an ordered empire and superimposed a unified imperial worship on the multifarious cults of Andean peoples. The definitive formulation of Inca religion was the work of the great general and legislator Pachacuti, whose name, as Las Casas had read in his sources, meant the "turning about of the world."[20] Las Casas felt he understood why Andeans had bestowed this epithet on their ruler. It was because "He brought them to a higher and more civilized state than the one they had enjoyed earlier, and because of this advance and improvement it seemed to them that the world had turned from one side to another."[21] In the Andes as in Europe, humanity's original knowledge of the invisible creator God had been dispersed by lesser cultic preoccupations. But in the time of Pachacuti, knowledge of this god, whom, according to Las Casas, Andeans had called Viracocha, reemerged:

[15] *AH* 187, p. 265.
[16] Cieza, *Crónica* 19, 24, 28, 33.
[17] Cieza, *Crónica* 28, 33.
[18] Cieza, *Crónica* 28, Cali.
[19] *AH* 42, 46, 47; note p. 254 on the golden age.
[20] *AH* 126, p. 659. The source cannot be Cieza, who does not mention this epithet of Inca Yupanqui.
[21] *AH* 121, p. 639.

This king and his successors had a more correct and accurate knowledge of the true God, because they thought that God existed and that he had made heaven and earth, the sun, moon, and stars, and all the world. Him they called Condici Viracocha, which in the language of Cuzco means "maker of the world." They said that this god dwelt in the far end of the world and that from there he looked upon it, governed it and provided for all its needs. Him they held to be god and lord, and to him they offered their principal sacrifices.[22]

Concurrently, as Las Casas understood it, Pachacuti reformulated the ancient American and Andean conception of the sun as god and provider.[23] The sun was accordingly regarded as "the principal creation of god," who "speaks and makes clear what God commands. And in this they did not wander far from the truth, because, as we read in St. Dionysius, in the fourth book of the *Divine Names*, apart from men and angels no creature shows forth the attributes and excellencies of God as clearly as does the sun. . . . Therefore they served and honored him and offered him sacrifice."[24] For this deity Pachacuti erected the temple of Coricancha on the site of his own and his ancestors' palace in Cuzco and installed in it, so Las Casas thought, an image "all of gold, with the face of a man and rays of gold, just as [the sun] is painted among ourselves."[25] The sun of Dionysius the Areopagite and its Inca representation in the form of a golden solar face are a long way both from the Sun, divine ancestor of the Inca dynasty, and from the solar cult image that was displayed in Coricancha. For the actual image was a gold statue representing the Sun as a young boy, inside of which were preserved the hearts of deceased Inca rulers.[26] Here, as elsewhere, Las Casas recast the information he found in his Andean sources to fit to the framework of his comparisons between Old World and New World pagan religion.

Pachacuti thus reminded Las Casas of Numa Pompilius, the second king of Rome and its religious founder. Numa had derived his legislative authority from his divine consort, the prophetic nymph Egeria. Similarly, Pachacuti called himself Indichuri, "Son of the Sun," by way of claiming that "whatever he did and commanded was done, commanded,

[22] *AH* 126, p. 659.
[23] *AH* 124, 187.
[24] *AH* 126, p. 659.
[25] *AH* 126, p. 660; quoted by Jerónimo Román, *Repúblicas del Mundo. República de las Indias Occidentales* (1575), I.5, fol. 361r, col.a; also Cobo, *Historia* 13.5, p. 157a; *Relación anonima*, p. 158a, idolo de oro . . . como Sol con sus rayos. See below, chap. VII.3 at n. 90, on Pachacuti Yamqui; P. Duviols, *La lutte contre les religions autochtones*, pp. 131f.; P. Duviols, "Punchao, Idolo Mayor del Coricancha," *Antropología Andina* 1–2 (1976): 156–183.
[26] Antonio Salazar, *Relación sobre . . . Don Francisco de Toledo*, p. 280, cf. above, chap. III.2 at n. 104.

and ordained by the Sun,"[27] that is, by divine authority. Pachacuti thus rivaled one of the great religious lawgivers of classical antiquity.[28] Furthermore, the priority he bestowed on religious matters, Las Casas thought, demonstrated that he was a "most excellent, prudent, and devout prince, a prince truly happy and blessed," whose achievements might well serve "as a singular example, most worthy of imitation," for the Catholic princes of Europe.[29]

The late antique Christian apologist Eusebius had interpreted the transition from republic to monarchy in the Roman empire as a theological, not merely a political, evolution, for in his opinion monarchy, the rule of one man, mirrored the sway of the one god over the universe and human society. It was thus thanks to the working of divine providence that Jesus was born into a Roman empire recently transformed into a monarchy.[30] Las Casas, who had read Eusebius carefully, discerned a parallel evolution in the Andes. For here also the rule of a great monarch, the Inca Pachacuti, had led to more refined theological understanding and to more dignified forms of worship, which were destined to be fully articulated later in a Christian framework.

But this, the organic progression toward a true concept of God by natural reason and gradual political change, was only part of the story. For in the Andes, as throughout the world, progress in the conceptualization of God had been paired with regress; enlightenment in one area produced error in another. This regress in man's religious evolution was documented not only in the Bible, but also by Josephus in his *Jewish Antiquities* and by many Christian historians as well.

The problem they had all endeavored to resolve was the origin of false religion and idolatry. The Bible set it down as an unquestionable fact that Adam knew his creator and spoke to him face to face. Las Casas found evidence that some trace of this knowledge had survived in the Americas, in that the Indians knew of a creator god: "In many parts of Tierra Firme, people had specific knowledge of the true God, believing that he had created the world and was its lord and governed it. To him they resorted with sacrifices, cult, and worship and with their needs. In Peru they called him Viracocha, which is to say, creator and maker, lord and god of everything."[31]

How then was it that idolatry had become all but universal? Writing

[27] *AH* 251, p. 581.
[28] Cf. Cabello Valboa, *Miscelánea antártica* 3.18, p. 339, for Pachacuti as Numa. But Cabello mistakenly attributed the title Pachacuti to Tupa Inca Yupanqui, not to Inca Yupanqui.
[29] *AH* 251, p. 580.
[30] See on Eusebius' political theology, Erik Peterson, *Der Monotheismus als politisches Problem* (1935), with A. Momigliano, "The Disadvantages of Monotheism for a Universal State," in his *On Pagans, Jews and Christians* (Middletown, 1987), pp. 142–158.
[31] *AH* 121, p. 638.

during the late first century of the Christian era in the Roman Empire, Josephus had associated the origin of false religion with the expansion of political power, in particular the power of Nimrod, the "mighty hunter before the Lord." In a departure from the text of Genesis, Josephus converted Nimrod into the builder of the Tower of Babel, the engineer of an enterprise that epitomized blasphemous pride.[32] Where thus Aristotle had viewed the exercise of political power as the natural and positive outcome of man's social instincts, Josephus proposed a negative interpretation of such power. Quoting Josephus, Las Casas explained that Nimrod "was the first to venture to draw human beings away from the fear and hope of God and to substitute for this fear and hope his own power."[33]

Here was a biblical and Christian schema of humanity's early religious history that ran quite contrary to the model Las Casas had found in Greek and Roman writers. According to this schema, divine worship was gradually transformed into the worship of kings. Thinking of this process, Las Casas was reminded of a passage in the invective against idolatry in the Book of Wisdom.[34] Here the writer denounced reverence for kings as a "hidden trap for mankind," because, so he thought, it was one of the root causes of idolatry. In the Andes, as Las Casas learned from Cieza and from Dominican missionaries,[35] the transition from simple reverence and respect to idolatry could be tangibly documented in rituals of royal burial.

And yet this was not an entirely negative transformation, because the advance in material and intellectual culture that accompanied and underpinned religious change could not be altogether discounted. Nimrod notwithstanding, Las Casas thought, royal government remained "the most noble and natural" form of government, and even before the Incas kings had governed in the Andes.[36] During this early epoch, they controlled no more than village-sized communities and ruled benevolently and justly as

---

[32] Genesis 10:8–12, 11:1–9; Josephus, *Jewish Antiquities* 1.113ff.

[33] *AH* 75, p. 390.

[34] Book of Wisdom 14:16ff. (I translate the title from the Latin Vulgate Bible that Las Casas used. In English the work is better known as Wisdom of Solomon); *AH* 249, p. 569. On reverence for kings as an incentive to idolatry, see in general P. Burke, *The Renaissance Sense of the Past* (New York, 1969), pp. 39f. The underlying point of reference usually is Wisdom 14; see J. D. Cooke, "Euhemerism: a Medieval Interpretation of Classical Paganism," *Speculum* 2 (1927): 396–410. For a Spanish exegete, see Alfonso de Madrigal, *Sobre el Eusebio. Primera Parte* (Salamanca, 1506), p. LXVI; a collection of further citations on our passage is in Cornelius a Lapide, *Commentarius in Librum Sapientiae* (Venice, 1717), ad loc., and argumentum. Jerónimo Román (*República Gentilica* 1.2, pp. 4f.) probably derived his information from Las Casas; cf. below, chap. VII.3 at n. 90. See also Antonio de la Calancha, *Corónica moralizada* 2.10, p. 822, and Alonso de la Peña Montenegro, *Itinerario para parrocos de Indios* (Antwerp, 1698), 2.4.5. For José Acosta's highly original interpretation of Wisdom 14, see below, chap. VI at n. 81.

[35] *AH* 249, p. 572, nuestros religiosos.

[36] *AH* 248.

"elder kinsmen and fathers." When these kings died, their subjects buried them with honor and remembered them with gratitude. Like Cieza, Las Casas dwelt on the solemnity of Andean funerary rituals and on the splendid offerings that were deposited in the tombs of the mighty.[37] These noble ceremonies imperceptibly transformed mourning into worship, so that, with passage of time, the royal dead attained an all but divine status in the hearts of their former subjects: "Lords who had governed well and justly, and with love and gentleness, and who had furthered their people, were regarded as more than human, and little by little people esteemed them as gods, offered them sacrifice, and resorted to them with invocations at their times of need."[38] The religious, even idolatrous, awe that characterized Andean attitudes toward dead rulers intensified under the Incas. The Incas held sway over far more extensive lands than earlier kings had done, and the splendor of their courtly rituals matched their power. In their day, therefore, a much more elaborate funerary ceremonial articulated not only religious but also political concerns. It was a token of Inca political wisdom that, to forestall rebellion, this ceremonial insured that a ruler's death would not be disclosed before his successor had gained control of the government.[39] Only then did the new ruler and his subjects express their profound veneration for the royal deceased in solemn celebration and sacrifice.[40] This Andean ruler cult was ennobled by the luster of ancient precedent by being juxtaposed, in the narrative framework of the *Apologética Historia*, with the divinization of great human beings in the pre-Christian Mediterranean.[41]

One of the authors whom Las Casas cited repeatedly on the question of divinization was the Greek universal historian Diodorus Siculus. Diodorus, like the early Christian apologists after him, adopted as his own the theory of Euhemerus, according to whom the gods of the different nations had once been human beings: kings, inventors, culture heroes.[42] This theory explained both why there were so many gods and why they were endowed with human characteristics, passions, predilections, and hatreds. Polytheism, whether in Europe or the Americas, could thus be understood in historical terms as the product of cultural and political advance, of change for the better.[43]

But this did not alter the fact that in strictly religious and theological

[37] *AH* 249.

[38] *AH* 126, cf. 259.

[39] See above, chap. III.3, at n. 35, the evidence of Betanzos. But Las Casas does not seem to have known this text. Rather, he used an unknown source about the Incas.

[40] *AH* 260; cf. 126, p. 660, on the political wisdom of not enforcing the solar cult too rigorously.

[41] *AH* 76–77.

[42] Cieza also had read Diodorus; cf. above, chap. III.2 at n. 55.

[43] Cf. *AH* 122.

terms, polytheism was a change for the worse. The momentum of this negative change was accelerated by the confusion of languages and the scattering of the nations over the earth that terminated the building of the Tower of Babel. For as long as only one language was spoken and all human beings dwelt together, idolatry and "ignorance [of God] could not spread among the nations," because they could teach each other and the old could teach the young.

> But when the languages were divided and the nations, each with its separate language, went forth to different lands, the young men who succeeded the old ones . . . thought that the shadows, traces, and signs of God [that inhere in created things] were the divine truth itself and therefore accepted them as divine. . . . And because they did not lift their considerations beyond what they saw and felt with their bodily senses, they resembled people walking in the night. Such people usually regard the shadow or likeness, the sign or trace, of things they perceive with their bodily eyes . . . to be those actual things. For instance, a person looking for a man or object he much desires fancies the shape of a tree he sees at a distance to be that man or object he is looking for. The proof of this argument is the diversity of gods . . . whereby some people regard one cause as divine, and others another. This could not have occurred except by the diversity of languages, for if all the nations had been one, in unity of language, they would have agreed in their ignorance; . . . they would have agreed to set up one single god.[44]

This argument, that human beings in the course of traveling from their origins in time and space set in motion a twofold theological error, recurs throughout the *Apologética Historia*. On the one hand, along with the diversity of languages, the diversity of physical environments, which resulted in different occupations, produced a diversity of divine beings. Fishermen invented different gods from farmers, and fishermen speaking different languages called their gods by different names. On the other hand, visible and tangible reality—celestial bodies, natural forces and features in the environment, and powerful human beings, whether dead or alive—did duty for the invisible and intangible reality that is the true God.[45] Monotheism was supplanted by polytheism, and, at the same time, visible and finite parts of creation supplanted the invisible, infinitely powerful Creator. In short, true knowledge of god was supplanted by erroneous imagination.[46] In this perspective, human history is the history

[44] *AH* 74, p. 383.
[45] *AH* 75–76; cf. 105.
[46] *AH* 75, p. 388.

of a false vision of god, of a long-continued falling away from original innocence.

This falling away was least pronounced among those nations in the Americas who preserved a primevally simple manner of life. But among most of these nations, just as in pre-Christian Europe, passage of time, diversity of language, migration over the far-flung American continent, and technological advance had dispersed the specific knowledge of god.[47] This was the regress that dogged all human progress, the cost of civilization.

So, at any rate, many of the Christian writers on whom Las Casas drew had believed. Las Casas, however, found a contradiction, even a conflict, in the story. For it was the very nobility of aspiration of the simple searcher after God that led him to adhere with all possible perseverance to the mistaken object of his desires; yet this same nobility of aspiration, the more noble because it was persevering, precluded that the searcher could ever recognize his error.

Nonetheless, the regress implicit in this error in turn brought forth a progress. This is one of the points where the biblical method of interpreting religious history that Las Casas employed converged with what he had read in Greek and Roman philosophers and historians regarding the gradual refinement of concepts of deity. In the Andes this process was exemplified by Pachacuti's religious reforms, anchored as these were in the workings of natural reason. On the one hand, Pachacuti had revitalized the original Andean knowledge of the creator god Viracocha. And on the other hand, he reformulated the ancient American and Andean conception of the sun as god and provider into the divine Sun of the Incas.[48]

Progress and regress were in tension, even in conflict, in Inca religion as interpreted by Las Casas. The issue is revealed in its sharpest form in his discussion of human sacrifice. How could the cruelty and pain involved in human sacrifice be compatible with the rationality and order Las Casas perceived in Inca religion?[49] He responded to this dilemma in a twofold argument that elucidates more precisely the functioning of progress and regress in the history of the human search after god.

Las Casas read in Porphyry and other ancient authors that the earliest sacrifices human beings in Europe had offered to honor and thank the gods and to implore their favor were fruits, herbs, and incense,[50] and the same had been the case in the Andes.[51] These humble offerings were in

---

[47] *AH* 121, pp. 639f.
[48] *AH* 124, 187.
[49] Cf. *AH* 183, p. 245, on abolition of human sacrifice by the emperor Hadrian.
[50] *AH* 144.
[51] *AH* 182.

accord with the innocent, if primitive, idea of deity held by the people of the age after Noah's flood. Continued reflection heightened the awareness of divine majesty, so that more costly sacrifices were prepared, that is, sacrifices of animals. The next step was to lay before the deity the most precious sacrifice of all, a human life:

> The nations who offered human beings in sacrifice to their gods had attained a more noble and worthy estimation of the gods and therefore possessed superior understanding and a clearer rational judgement than all other nations. And those who gave their own children in sacrifice for the well-being of the people outstripped other nations in religious devotion. [52]

Among them were the Carthaginians and certain individuals such as Agamemnon, who sacrificed his daughter Iphigenia so that the Greek fleet could set sail for Troy. In the Andes, human sacrifice was, according to Las Casas, introduced by the Incas, as was to be expected, given the exalted notions of deity that had inspired Pachacuti's religious reforms. Inca human sacrifice took two forms. On the one hand, children were offered to the gods on solemn occasions, and on the other, certain individuals were buried alive with deceased Incas. According to Las Casas, Pachacuti Inca was accompanied into the grave by those of his wives and servants who chose to be buried with him of their own free will so as to continue in his service in the next world. [53]

Here was a very different rationale for this form of human sacrifice from that posited by Cieza when he pondered the fearsome death of the ladies and servants whom Andeans buried alive with deceased lords. Cieza saw no explanation for this custom other than demonic illusion. Las Casas, by contrast, regarded elaborate and costly religious rituals— even those that were costly in human lives—as tokens of a politically advanced society and as expressions of deep reflection on theological and moral questions. The dictate of natural reason which underlay human sacrifice, namely, that the gods were owed the greatest offering human beings could lay before them, was confirmed by the gods themselves in their oracles, as for instance the oracle of Apollo at Delphi. [54] But these divine pronouncements entailed a difficulty. For who spoke in the Delphic oracle and in the other divinatory shrines of both the Old World and the New? The response to this question marks the precise juncture at which the progress that Las Casas traced in the formation of man's concept of deity veers into regress.

---

[52] *AH* 183, pp. 244f., compressed translation.
[53] *AH* 260; cf. Betanzos, *Suma* (1987), 1.30, pp. 141b–142b, with C. Araníbar, "Notas sobre la necropompa," *Revista del Museo Nacional* 36 (1969–1970): 108–142.
[54] *AH* 183, p. 246.

He who pronounced the oracles was not some human being called Apollo but a most astute and evil demon . . . who with God's leave and because of man's sins gave responses and deceived people in that temple of Delphi. . . . They called him Delphic Apollo not because he was a man. Rather, [a demon] took the name of that Apollo who was king of the people of Delphi and son of Latona. . . . This demon himself confessed his identity when he vaunted himself as being more astute and wiser than other demons. His words, recorded by the Sibyl as being his response to an inquiry as to how prayer should be addressed to him, are these: "Knowing all things, wise in all things, you who are conversant with all things, hear us, oh Demon."[55]

Thanks to the notorious ambiguity of his responses, it was never possible to pin any error or lie on the demon of Delphi. Such ambiguity had been a favorite method of demonic deceit from the very beginning, for it was by means of ambiguous statements that the serpent had deceived Adam and Eve in Paradise,[56] and the devil, as Cieza had observed, continued holding the Indians of Peru in subjection by exactly the same means.[57] The authority and fame of the Delphic oracle was nonetheless universal, and its teachings were accepted and obeyed without question.

Human sacrifice was only one of the many pagan aberrations that the demon of Delphi taught his devotees. He also instructed them to offer sacrifices to "sticks and rocks" and to "idols of stone, wood, gold, and silver." He offered assistance at times of need and inspired poets to tell fables about false gods.[58] Throughout the world, demons claiming the identity of dead kings[59] uttered oracular statements similar to those of Delphi so as to propagate their teachings. A further means of communication employed by demons was "illusions and phantasms that they paint in the imagination" of children, young virgins, and other impressionable individuals.[60] One of these was the Pythia, "a virgin girl and priestess," who acted as representative of the demon Apollo of Delphi and pronounced his sayings.[61]

It thus appears that the entire fabric of pagan belief and observance that Las Casas had described so meticulously as the outcome of reasoned reflection and of political and cultural change and progress must also be

[55] AH 81, p. 420.
[56] AH 81, p. 421; cf. Cieza, Segunda Parte 29, p. 88.
[57] Cieza, Crónica 48, p. 158, responde equívocamente, que es decir palabras con muchos entendimientos.
[58] AH 82, p. 426; 91, p. 473.
[59] AH 82, p. 424.
[60] AH 91, p. 473.
[61] AH 80, p. 416.

understood not simply as a simultaneous regress, a departure from primeval purity, but as anchored in illusion, in fictions of the imagination. This is the same conclusion that had been reached by Cieza de Leon when he thought about the rationale of burying people alive, by the cleric who had watched the maize harvest in Cuzco in 1535, and by Juan Polo de Ondegardo when reflecting on the religious foundations of Inca political power. But Las Casas went further in his analysis of this issue, by referring it to the functioning of the faculties of the soul, the functioning, that is, of human cognition.

2. DEMONS AND THE IMAGINATION

Las Casas understood cognition in Aristotelian and Thomist terms. "The soul never thinks without a phantasm, a mental image," Aristotle and Aquinas had said,[1] and Las Casas agreed. Mental images, formed by the imagination, arise from sense perceptions[2] and constitute the foundation for thought. The five senses, as Las Casas and other Aristotelians understood it, emit "crude" images[3] that are gathered together into common sense, are processed and refined by the imagination, located at the top of the head, and are then passed on to the intellect in order, finally, to be stored in memory (fig. 26).[4] The intellect is the locus of all human understanding, including that concerning the existence of God or the gods. Notwithstanding its exalted object, this understanding begins with sense perception. It is attainable by means of the faculties innate in man, that is, by natural reason, without the assistance of divine grace. Hence, all human beings, Las Casas maintained, have a concept of deity. The adequacy or inadequacy of that concept depended on how it was formed, because intemperance, emotional imbalance, distress, and the passions could disrupt the cognitive process by blurring both the sensory "crude" images that the imagination received and the images that imagination in turn sent forth to the intellect.

In his description of the workings of cognition, Las Casas used the Aristotelian and Thomist sources that were familiar to his Spanish contemporaries. But when it came to providing examples of a well-tempered soul in whom the different faculties functioned harmoniously, Las Casas turned to the Indies, for in his eyes it was among Indians more than among Europeans that "natural gentleness and modesty," arising from a

[1] Aristotle, *On the Soul* 3.7, 431a17.

[2] Aristotle, *On the Soul* 429a2, imagination is a movement arising from sensation.

[3] Imagenes gruesas, Las Casas, *AH* 25, pp. 127, 130.

[4] Joannes Romberch, *Congestorium artificiose memorie V.P.F. Joannis Romberch de Kyrspe Regularis observantie predicatorie: omnium de memoria perceptiones aggregatim complectens* (Venice, 1533), fol. 12r; Las Casas, *AH* 26, pp. 133–134, For applications of these and related ideas in the new world, see R. Taylor, *El arte de la memoria en el nuevo mundo*.

Et quoniã hec pars ſi humidioz ſit q̃ oportear
male retinet acceptas ſpeciesꞁhinc eſt q̃ pleri̷
q̃ huic defectui mederi intendentesꞏ diuerſis
modis vnctionũ hanc parté excⁱccare moliun̄ Jn mó
tur꞉de quo alibi locus opportunus꞉ diuerſi di̷ ſtudédi
uerſa ſentiunt꞉caure auté adhiberi remediũ Jn noꞏ
conſultius mihi perſuaſum habeo꞉ru vel nʳani̅ ma ocij
de hoc habero intentioné vel que ipſe apd̄ ex̷ lⁱrarij
pertiores legerⁱꞏ medicos rene . Quod ad hũc
locũ atrinet naturali memozie non medicinis
ſed locis z ĩiaginibus ſuffragandũ cenſuimus
                                          B iiij

26. How the brain works: the perceptions of sight, hearing, smell, and taste, the fifth sense of touch being omitted, are combined into common sense (sensus communis) and are passed to imagination (fantasia and imaginativa) and thence to reason, which is divided into its thinking and evaluating aspects. The result is stored at the back of the head in memory.
    J. Romberch, *Congestorium artificiose memorie* (Venice, 1533).
    Biblioteca Nacional, Madrid.

certain "nobility, restraint, and balance inherent in their dispositions," were especially to be found.[5]

Nonetheless, a cloud loomed over the knowledge of God attainable by all human beings, because the sin of the Fall, along with subsequent sins committed by each individual, impaired the workings of human reason and perception.[6] This is why, in the last resort, the true knowledge of God could only be revealed knowledge, and why, in the absence of revelation, idolatry was universal. The Fall changed the natural order of things because it transferred the true knowledge of God from the realm of human cognition to the realm of grace, however much traces of divine knowledge could be apprehended from creation. Secondly, it was as a result of the Fall that cognitive, political, and material progress was inevitably paired with regress and that the demons exercised so sweeping an influence both in nature and in human affairs.

From late antiquity onward, Christian theologians identified the demons as Lucifer and the angels who had fallen with him, and debated the nature and extent of their interference in human affairs. Given that in Christian eyes all the gods of pagan antiquity were demons, their number was considerable, and so was the diversity of their activities. In describing these activities, Las Casas ranged from Ovid's Circe, who transformed the companions of Ulysses into animals[7] to similar feats by witches in Christian Europe about whom he read in scholastic writers and in the late medieval manual for inquisitors that bore the picturesque title *Hammer of Witches*.[8]

Some of the authors whom Las Casas quoted were inclined to view the transformation of human beings into animals and other magical performances attributed to witches as poetic fancies, while other authors were more credulous. The authors of the *Hammer of Witches* insisted that the transformations wrought by Circe were "only an appearance," because "the animal shapes were drawn out of the repository or memory of images" stored in the mind of the onlookers and were then "impressed on their imaginative faculty."[9] Las Casas, by contrast, cited Augustine and believed that such a transformation could have happened.[10]

Such divergences notwithstanding, the texts Las Casas collected convey a coherent message. What is at issue is not primarily how each of the strange and extraordinary occurrences or prodigies that Las Casas recounted should be interpreted. Rather, these stories reveal how fluid was

[5] *AH* 36, p. 190.
[6] *AH* 73, p. 377.
[7] *AH* 92, p. 476.
[8] *AH* 95, p. 492; 98, p. 512.
[9] Kramer and Sprenger, *Malleus* 2, q. 1, chap. 8, p. 123.
[10] *AH* 92, p. 476, citing Augustine, *City of God* 18.16–18, who is equally uncertain.

the boundary between the demonic and the natural world, between the world subject to the laws of God and the world permeable to the wiles of demons. In theory, of course, the entire universe was governed by the laws of God, and the fact that apparently these laws were not always and everywhere obeyed was attributed, as Las Casas expressed it, to the "secret judgements of God, which are many, but never unjust."[11] But in practice, the demons were ubiquitous.[12] Indeed, in the sublunary sphere, they accounted for many of the phenomena that later Newton was to explain by reference to the force of gravity; but unlike the force of gravity, demons were individuals and were therefore endowed with will and a sense of purpose,[13] which was to supplant the worship of God by the worship of themselves in human hearts. This purpose of the demons was a force to be reckoned with, because by virtue of controlling the material world they were capable of controlling the human body and hence could influence the soul, anchored as it was in the perceptions of the bodily senses.[14] This Thomist blend of cosmology and psychology was taken for granted far beyond the frontiers of Catholic Spain and beyond the sixteenth century. In Shakespeare's *Tempest*, for instance, the demon, or as Shakespeare described him, the "airy spirit" Ariel, having first shipwrecked the King of Naples and his entourage, then struck their souls with a suicidal frenzy.[15]

The absence of clear-cut boundaries between the divine, the human, and the demonic worlds as perceived by Las Casas also speaks in his interpretation of the Bible. For at times he discerned demonic activity where the text, interpreted strictly, mentions none. In the book of Exodus, for example, we read that Aaron challenged the sorcerers of Pharaoh by transforming his rod into a serpent, whereupon the sorcerers did the same, but Aaron's rod, of course, swallowed up their rods. As Las Casas understood the story, however, the sorcerers had called demons to their aid with secret incantations and had made a pact with them. Similarly, he thought, sorcerers performed rain ceremonies and conjured hail and

---

[11] *AH* 92.

[12] Above, chap. 1 passim.

[13] See *AH* 87, cf. 24–25; but note Aquinas, *Summa* 1, q. 110, a.1; a.3 resp., angels move all matter. Wolfson, "Souls." *Dumbarton Oaks Papers* 16 (1962).

[14] See *AH* 87, p. 452, story of Job.

[15] Shakespeare, *The Tempest*, see act 1, sc. 2, lines 198–215; cf. act 3, sc. 3, lines 58–60, for Ariel's explanation. It is worth observing that the Aristotelian account of sense perceptions that underlies the texts here discussed did not inevitably entail belief in demons. Note, e.g., Don Diego Hurtado de Mendoza, *Guerra de Granada*, ed. B. Blanco-Gonzalez (Madrid, 1970), p. 391, on the site of the battle of Munda: hoy en dia . . . se ven impresas señales de despojos, de armas y caballos; y ven los moradores encontrarse por el aire escuadrones . . . estantigas llama el vulgo español a semejantes aparencias o fantasmas, que el vaho de la tierra cuando el sol sale ó se pone forma en el aire bajo, como se ven en el alto las nubes formadas en varias figuras y semejanzas.

storms, "all of which the demons bring about, provided that God has given his leave."[16]

Las Casas was not alone in his interpretation of Holy Writ but rather, drew on a long exegetical tradition. A test case in this tradition was the story of Saul and the witch of Endor.[17] On the eve of his last battle against the Philistines, Saul asked the witch to bring back from the dead the spirit of the prophet Samuel to counsel him on his course of action. Samuel appeared as an old man enveloped in a robe and predicted Saul's death and defeat. Augustine, Aquinas, Nicolas de Lyra, and Alfonso de Madrigal, all of whom Las Casas consulted,[18] had repeatedly pondered this story. For how was it possible that someone who had died could cross the divinely appointed barrier between the living and the dead? Exegetes thus speculated as to whether a demon had assumed the appearance of Samuel and spoken in his voice or whether God himself had intervened to permit Samuel to appear. Like everyone before him, Las Casas remained in a quandary:

> Augustine . . . holds that the apparition was by witchcraft, that it was not the soul of Samuel but some demon. But there are good reasons for the other view, that Samuel did not appear by the power of the witch or her magic art, as though the demons could force Samuel to come and speak; for they had no power over him who was in the limbo of the just. Rather, God wanted to send him to announce Saul's death.[19]

Here also demons were not explicitly mentioned in the original text, although the Old Latin translation used by Augustine described the witch of Endor as "pythonissa," while Jerome in the Vulgate text available to Las Casas translated the Hebrew as "mulier pythonem habens."[20] Jerome employed the identical term for the prophetic girl whom Paul exorcised in Philippi. This same story in turn was adduced by Las Casas in his discussion of the divinatory activities of demons.[21] *Pytho*, Las Casas thought, was precisely a familiar spirit or demon,[22] a personalized evil force capable of entering and possessing a human being.

The bodies of demons were ethereal, invisible to the human eye and

---

[16] Exodus 7:11ff., quoted *AH* 87, p. 450; 88, p. 453.

[17] 1 Samuel 28:3ff.

[18] *AH* 101.

[19] *AH* 101; cf. Augustine, *Quaestiones ex Veteri Testamento* 27, *Patrologia Latina* 35, col. 2230f.; *Quaestiones ad Simplicianum* 2.3, *Patrologia Latina* 40, col. 142; *Quaestiones ad Dulcitium* 6, *Patrologia Latina* 40, col. 162; cf. Kramer and Sprenger, *Malleus* 1, q. 16, p. 80; Castañega, *Tratado* 4, p. 38.

[20] 1 Kings 28:7.

[21] *AH* 80, p. 417; Acts 16:16.

[22] *AH* 79, p. 411.

inaudible to the human ear. To act visibly and audibly in this world, demons possessed themselves of material bodies. Such bodies could simply be vapors and clouds. But demons also inhabited statues of pagan deities, which according to Hermes Trismegistus, cited by Augustine in a passage of the *City of God* that in turn was cited by Las Casas, were made specifically to house them.[23] And finally, Las Casas knew of instances, beginning in New Testament times, of demons possessing themselves of human beings. Among these latter, some uttered prophecies.[24] In the footsteps of early Christian apologists and church fathers, Las Casas thus speculated that a demon in the guise of some dead king named Apollo had inspired the prophecies of the oracle at Delphi, which were spoken through the mouth of Apollo's priestess the Pythia. This view of Delphic prophecy entailed a major recasting of pagan thinking on the topic. In a passage of the *Phaedrus* that Las Casas quoted,[25] Plato reflected on the nature of prophetic and poetic ecstasy. Both were characterized by a suspension of rational awareness, even though after ecstasy receded, reason would interpret the sublime truth that had been captured in ecstatic vision. Subsequent ancient writers dramatized ecstatic perception as a subjection of a human being's body and soul to divine energy. The Roman poet Lucan thus described the prophetic utterances of the Pythia as resulting from a conflict between her will and the god's prophetic force, which invaded her being. Recoiling in terror from the intense impact of divine power and cognition, she battled against the suspension of her conscious identity with raging desperation. In the grip of the god's violent intrusion, the priestess uttered the prophetic words that he put into her mouth and of which her human faculties remained ignorant.[26]

Here, in the eyes of Las Casas as of late antique Christians, was a clear example of demonic possession. Like those Christians, Las Casas thought that the high esteem that Plato's Socrates had bestowed on the divine madness of prophets and lovers, so far from revealing a sublime truth, made clear just how "profoundly the devil has deceived both the wise and the foolish of this world."[27] In his own account of the functioning of the Delphic oracle, Las Casas therefore mentioned Plato and Lucan, but quoted verbatim John Chrysostom's Christian interpretation of pagan prophetic inspiration. When the Pythia, Chrysostom had said in a sermon,

> ascended the sacred seat, the devil entered into her from the secret lower parts, and she became filled and enraged with an infernal fury,

[23] Augustine, *City of God* 8.23; G. Fowden, *The Egyptian Hermes* (Cambridge, 1986), pp. 209f.; Las Casas, *AH* 29, p. 148; see also *AH* 100, p. 523.

[24] *AH* 79–83.

[25] *AH* 79, p. 414; Plato, *Phaedrus* 244b.

[26] Lucan, *Pharsalia* 5.123ff.

[27] *AH* 79, p. 414.

unloosened her hair, and foamed at the mouth, so that a hundred men could not hold or hinder her. In this state of rage, she threw herself on the ground, and thus recumbent the petition for an oracle was put before her. She responded with what the demon commanded her to say, without feeling anything or knowing what she said. . . . This was the divine and holy rage that the gentiles thought came from heaven.[28]

But in effect, the rage did not come from heaven. Rather, the demon who had seized the Pythia's body deranged her sense perceptions so that her imagination could not convey true images to her intellect, and she raved of the phantasms the demon put before her. The demons were able to do all this because, as Aquinas had so carefully explained regarding the Eucharist and eucharistic visions, the accidents of an object, its external appearance, were separable from its substance.[29] In the case of a demonic vision, therefore, the sense of sight, and hence imagination and intellect, were deluded by a false appearance. As Cieza had observed, demons could make themselves visible to Andeans in the guise of their forebears,[30] and in the same way they were accustomed to appear to Europeans in the guise of animals, humans, or even angels.[31]

The concept of demonic activity affected European thinking about the Andes, and about America in general, in two ways. First, as we have seen, the demons were thought to disguise themselves as deities and to hide in the bodies of the dead. It was by virtue of understanding the revealed truth of Christianity that Spaniards in the Andes considered themselves to be immune from such deceptions. But in addition, apart from being deceivers par excellence, the demons were thought to wield real power, because their control over matter was real. Perhaps it was from one of his fellow Dominicans that Las Casas received a rendering of an Andean myth of origins. At any rate, the myth led him to suppose that, like Christians, the Incas had some knowledge of the presence of demonic energies in the environment.

> They affirmed that before he created the world, the Creator Viracocha had a son called Taguapica Viracocha, who contradicted his father in everything. Whereas the father made men good, this son made them evil, both in body and soul. . . . The father made springs and the son dried them up . . . so that finally, the father became wroth and threw his son into the sea to die an evil death, but he never did die. This fiction or imagination appears to signify the fall of the

[28] *AH* 80, p. 417; Chrysostom, *In Epist. I ad Cor. Homilia XXIX, Patrologia Graeca* 61, col. 242.

[29] Above, chap. I.1 at nn. 34–37.

[30] Above, chap. III.1 at nn. 44ff.

[31] *AH* 95, citing Kramer and Sprenger, *Malleus* 2, q. 1, chaps. 8ff.

first evil angel, who was created a son of God, but his pride made
him evil and always contrary to God his creator. He was thrown into
the sea, according to the words of the Apocalypse, chapter 20, "The
devil was cast down into the abyss."[32]

Divine antagonisms figure regularly in Andean myths of origins.[33] In the
north of Peru, the concept of Viracocha the creator was readily transformed into that of Viracocha the destroyer,[34] and a primeval confrontation between the deities Con and Pachacamac[35] had given rise to the order
of things on the coast near Lima. The same Pachacamac, lord of the pilgrimage sanctuary that was desecrated by Hernando Pizarro and his men,
was worshiped for his beneficent, and feared for his destructive power.[36]
To Las Casas, however, the myth of Viracocha and his son and antagonist
made a different point. For although, like other mythic, non-Christian
perceptions of the supernatural, the story was, in his eyes, only a "fiction
or imagination,"[37] it did demonstrate that Andeans had somehow apprehended the pervading presence of a personified evil in the world, an evil
endowed with the faculties of deliberation and volition.

Exploration of the Americas thus led to discovering there an order of
things that was already familiar from Europe. At the same time, the encounter with demons in the Andes, as elsewhere in America, reempha-
sized the urgency of existing theological issues. On the one hand, everyone knew that human beings were endowed with free will, which by
virtue of being free cannot be subject to demonic influence without in
some sense willing it. But on the other hand, the demons were active in
man's terrestrial environment to such an extent as to make the reality of
free will questionable. As a result, each individual soul in its human body,
each member of society, was perceived to be a tiny focal point in the
cosmic battle between God, the giver of free will, and his antagonists, the
devil and the demons. In Europe, institutions and rituals both secular and
sacred had over the centuries been devised to map the social landscape in
which this battle was fought out and to assist the individual combatant in
arriving at a theologically and politically approved result.[38] In the New
World, corresponding institutional and ritual markers appeared at first
sight to have been nonexistent. The import of Las Casas' comparative
approach to the study of religion was that he showed this not to have been

[32] AH 126.

[33] Duviols, "Une petite chronique, Journal de la Société des Américanistes 63 (1974–1976):
276f.; cf. 281, n. 8; see also M. Rostworowski, Estructuras andinas del poder, pp. 21ff.

[34] Benzoni, Historia del nuevo Mundo, p. 64.

[35] Zárate, in M. Bataillon, "Zárate ou Lozano?" Caravelle 1 (1963): 22f.; cf. above, chap.
II.2 at nn. 27ff.

[36] Duviols, Cultura andina y represión (1986), p. 8.

[37] AH 126.

[38] Above, chap. I.2. at nn. 56–59.

the case; for in the New World, as in Europe, human relations with the supernatural were defined and regulated by institutions and rituals that were comparable to European ones. Domestic economy underpinned the proper functioning of each individual's powers of reason, and deliberation, and hence free will, while the political economy of society at large regulated relations between individuals.[39]

Throughout the ancient Mediterranean, demons spoke ambiguously from hollow statues and possessed themselves of human beings, while in Las Casas' own Spain and Europe they were still active in rituals of sorcerers and witches.[40] At this level, there was little to choose between Europe and America except that Europe was assisted in its battle with the demons by the teachings and ceremonies of revealed religion. The authors of the *Hammer of Witches*, Castañega, and Ciruelo all described the Catholic procedures for exorcising demons, be this to avert thunderstorms, locusts, or other natural disasters such as demons could mobilize, or be it to free a human being from demonic possession.[41] There was need for such exorcisms in the New World also.

Las Casas heard from an eyewitness how the Dominican missionary Pedro de Cordoba exorcised a demon who had entered a young Indian shaman in Paria, much as the demon of Delphi had entered the Pythia.[42] Attired in his priestly stole, holding a cross in his left hand and a bowl of holy water in his right, Pedro de Cordoba addressed the demon in the name of Jesus and demanded to know where the demon took his devotees' souls. To certain "pleasant and delightful places" was the answer. Whereupon the friar forced the demon to confess that the true destination of those souls was hell and then exorcised him from the shaman.[43]

But even though the power through whom Pedro de Cordoba and other missioneries exorcised demons was the power of Jesus, the task that Las Casas had appointed for himself was not to contrast the true Christian religion with the false religions of the Americas or even of classical antiquity. Rather, the task was to understand the nature and origin of human perceptions of God. This involved explaining how non-Christian concepts of deity, concepts, that is, that were formed without the assistance of revelation, came about in cognitive terms, even though demons interfered in the formation of such concepts. Because concepts of deity varied from one civilization to another, Las Casas also sought to understand the reasons for cultural and religious difference.

---

[39] *AH* 40–45.

[40] Above, chap. 1.2 at nn. 7ff., and note Las Casas' extended discussion of incidents selected from the *Hammer of Witches: AH* 95, pp. 492ff.; 98, pp. 512ff.

[41] Kramer and Sprenger, *Malleus* 2.2, chap. 6, pp. 179ff.; Castañega, *Tratado* 21–22, pp. 127ff.; Ciruelo, *Treatise* (1977), 3.8, pp. 265ff.

[42] *AH* 245, p. 550.

[43] *AH* 245, p. 551; see also *AH* 81.

In practical terms, the issue was whether Amerindian humanity was more vulnerable to demonic deceptions than Europeans, given that many Spaniards described Indians as credulous and simpleminded. Cognition and psychology, therefore, had to be examined in American, not only in European terms. As Aristotle had made clear, the soul learns and knows by means of processing the perceptions of the bodily senses.[44] Hence, Las Casas inquired into how the human body was conditioned in the New World by the natural environment, by personal habit, and by society. Cultural and religious difference thus became, at least in part, a question of geographical environment and historical conditioning. The theory stems from Ptolemy and his commentators, but its systematic application to the Americas was new.

Las Casas first demonstrated that thanks to its climate and the astral influences prevailing over it, the American continent was an environment "most blessed and favorable for the nature and condition of man."[45] Human souls, he explained, were equal and the same at the time when God infused them into bodies. What would in due course begin to distinguish one soul from another was the body in which it dwelt, and that body was conditioned by climate and the stars prevailing over the region where a person was born. There were variations even within Europe; Spaniards thus considered the peoples of northern Europe to be slower of understanding but more warlike than themselves, and attributed these differences to climate and the stars. Las Casas, who like other theologians was intent on avoiding the determinism implicit in acknowledging climactic and astral influences on human beings, differentiated such influence on the soul from that on the body. He explained that material bodies, air, clouds and stars could not work either good or ill in the soul, because it was an immaterial spirit. Yet insofar as these bodies conditioned the human body, they also brought an indirect influence to bear on the soul. Therefore, "when God wishes to infuse a perfect soul endowed with all the natural virtues, he begins with the body. . . . And thus, according to variations in the disposition of the body, there result different kinds of communication [between body and] soul. . . . For this reason, some have thought that the celestial bodies make the souls of men such as they are."[46]

While climate and the stars affected the human soul willy-nilly, the formation of an individual's habits depended on how that individual deployed free will. These habits, moreover, determined the quality of his sense perception and imagination at a much more intimate and enduring level than climate or stars. The "impetuous movement of sensible things and of sensual affections and of vapors and fumes that rise up from the

[44] *AH* 24, p. 118.
[45] *AH* 33, p. 168; see also chaps. 1–22 and 24.
[46] *AH* 23, p. 117; cf. 84, p. 437, the stars do not control free will.

stomach and the heart,"[47] as well as "worldly and temporal cares" and "anger, joy, fear, and sadness,"[48] disturbed the ordered working of both sensation and imagination, and hence also of cognition.

In describing the personal habits of Indians, just as in describing their political and religious institutions, Las Casas was guided as much by his apologetic purpose as by the sources he had collected.[49] He thus created an idealized, paradisal image of the New World and its people before the advent of Europeans, the exact opposite of what had come into existence with Spanish settlement in America and the establishment of colonial government.[50] But before these upheavals, the Indians had lived as abstemiously as "the holy fathers in the desert"; their sparing use of alcohol could not be rivaled by that of a "most observant monk"; and their sexual mores were exemplary.[51] For walking barefoot, as many Indians did, "especially if they go altogether naked, tempers and dissolves desire and mortifies inclination for sexual acts. . . . Washing oneself often in cold water, as the Indians do day and night, has the same effect . . . and likewise eating and drinking sparingly. Similarly, avoiding idleness, as these people do . . . For one will never find Indians, whether at home or in the fields, not working with their hands."[52] Furthermore, the Indians were indifferent to wealth and lived together peacefully, without accumulating possessions or coveting each other's property. They were thus altogether exempt from those passions and inner conflicts and disorders that cloud and confuse the images gathered by sense perception and forwarded to the imagination.[53]

The characteristics of society at large stem from the inclinations and habits of the individuals of whom it is constituted. Just as Plato and Augustine had seen individual virtues and vices reflected in the city, so Las Casas found the qualities he observed in individuals writ large in Amerindian societies.[54] The early Christian apologists supplied him with a rich and colorful documentation of the drunkenness and sexual excess accompanying festivals of the pagan gods in the ancient Mediterranean. The images of deity that arose from such celebrations matched the moral corruption of the celebrants.[55] When Indians honored their gods, by con-

---

[47] *AH* 26, p. 113.

[48] *AH* 27, p. 137.

[49] Cf. A. Gerbi, *Nature in the New World: From Christopher Columbus to Gonzalo Fernández de Oviedo* (Pittsburgh, 1985), pp. 353f.

[50] Cf. *AH* 28 with 37, on *tristeza*; further, Las Casas, *Del unico modo* 5.4, p. 90; 6, p. 99, on conversion.

[51] *AH* 35, pp. 182, 184, 185.

[52] *AH* 36, p. 187.

[53] *AH* 36–37.

[54] *AH* 40–42.

[55] *AH* 75, p. 391.

trast, order, dignity, and sobriety prevailed,[56] and this reflected not only on the perfection of their social and political order but also on their concepts of deity.[57] Their natural and social environment and their own inner dispositions had thus endowed the Indians with faculties capable of apprehending the images of himself which God had projected onto his creation.

Nonetheless, in America as in Europe, the knowledge that could be gained in this way was limited. For firstly, the Fall deranged the flow of human cognition. And secondly, the face-to-face familiarity with God that Adam had experienced in Paradise had been forgotten with passage of time. The true worship of one God could therefore only be arrived at as a gift of grace, by revelation. For what is accessible to natural reason is not the knowledge of God himself, but only the conclusion that a supreme divinity must exist.[58] From this conclusion, certain uncommonly reflective individuals had, with time, deduced some of God's qualities. One of these was Aristotle;[59] the Inca Pachacuti was another.[60] For the rest, the worship of many gods in the guise of some material object, practiced throughout the world and at all times, was proof that idolatry was the natural response to humanity's need for an object of worship. Indeed, the very functioning of the human mind, when reinforced by demonic deceptions, made idolatry almost inevitable. This conclusion, spelled out by Las Casas in the light of his experience of the New World, had already been arrived at in a theoretical sense by Thomas Aquinas.

In his comments on Aristotle's distinction between sense perception and imagination,[61] Aquinas had supplied an example designed to clarify the difference between the two that impressed itself on Las Casas. A given sense perception can only occur when the corresponding object is actually displayed before the senses. But acts of the imagination can be voluntary. A person may thus imagine compound images, corresponding to no specific objects, such as a mountain of gold.[62] This capacity of the imagination to create images not represented in physical reality was often exploited by demons, who thanks to their control over matter presented to the imagination configurations of matter resulting in fraudulent images "the efficacy of which they well know."[63] The seductive quality of the mountain of gold in European, if not in Indian, eyes spelled out to Las

---

[56] *AH* 35.

[57] *AH* 71, 127.

[58] *AH* 71–73.

[59] *AH* 71, p. 371.

[60] *AH* 126.

[61] Aristotle, *On the Soul* 427b17.

[62] Aquinas, *In Aristotelis librum de anima commentarium* 3, Lectio 4, 633. See further above, chap. I.1 at n. 28.

[63] *AH* 96, p. 499.

Casas' readers the demons' capacity of endowing idols, oracles, and prodigies with an ineluctable power to convince. Artists in their own right, the demons had the power to "paint and impress on the imagination . . . pictures and images, phantasms and specters" that dazzled and deceived their human victims.[64]

More often than not, such specters led people to make idols and indulge in idolatrous rituals. On the island Española, an Indian listened to the wind, or rather to a demon, rustling in the leaves of a tree. A sorcerer interpreted the demon's message, which instructed the Indian to carve the tree into a statue and to build a shrine for its cult.[65] The incident did not lack Mediterranean precedent. Reviewing the infamous gods of the Greeks, Las Casas quoted the mocking words that Horace had put into the mouth of a wooden statue of Priapus, the lascivious protector of gardens and orchards: "Formerly the trunk of a fig tree, I was a useless log, when a craftsman, intent on carving a stool or a Priapus, decided I should be a god. A god I therefore am, a terrible fright to thieves and the birds. For my arm, a red stake protruding from my lewd groin, keeps away the thieves, and the reed fixed on my head scares the importunate birds."[66]

Idolatry was natural, not only because the unaided human faculties rarely avoided the traps of demonic illusion and were in any case incapable of attaining the direct knowledge of the one true God, but also because it was a long established-habit. As Aristotle had written, "Habits that are rooted in custom dispose human inclination in the same manner as does nature"; they are therefore most difficult to change.[67] The very games of children revealed how, over centuries and milennia, idolatry had become deeply rooted in the human heart. For children, without instruction from anyone "perform divine worship in their manner and according to their ability, by making small altars and adorning them as they can. And from bits of cloth and clay suitable for the purpose they make small idols, which are what we call dolls. By all this they demonstrate clearly our natural love and inclination for divine worship, be it true or false."[68]

Ensnared by demons as the faculties of the soul must inevitably be in the absence of revealed knowledge, they yet speak of the innate human desire and yearning for a focus of veneration and worship. The games of children are a poignant illustration of precisely this yearning. In the absence of the true knowledge of God, human beings will persist in yearning for erroneous embodiments of God, because to do so is rooted in the

---

[64] *AH* 96, p. 499.

[65] *AH* 120, pp. 634f.; copied by Jerónimo Román, *República de las Indias Occidentales* (1575), 1.2, fol. 355v.

[66] Horace, *Satires* 1.8, quoted in *AH* 78, p. 407; cf. *AH* 153, p. 98.

[67] *AH* 74, p. 386.

[68] *AH* 74, p. 386.

makeup of the soul. To explain this yearning, Las Casas incorporated the affective vocabulary of Plato and Augustine into his Aristotelian psychology.

Plato had described the soul as a compound of reason, anger or courage, and desire.[69] Las Casas reformulated this model of the soul by describing courage and desire as ancillary to Aristotle's reason.[70]

> The object of reason is truth, in particular divine truth; . . . the object of the desiring faculty is sweetness and delectation; and the object of the irascible faculty is to combat whatever impedes the desiring faculty, thus serving and honoring that delight which the desiring faculty seeks. Hence our reason is always insatiably avid and hungry for truth, our desire constantly hungers for delights and sweetnesses, and our irascible faculty opposes obstacles in the path of desire. . . . It thus follows that our reason cannot exist without some true or false opinion and belief; nor can our desiring faculty exist without desires and delights and other passions, in which it mixes objects both worthy and unworthy; nor can the irascible faculty exist without serving and honoring what it ought or ought not to serve and honor.[71]

Sometimes Las Casas interpreted the irascible faculty, by means of which the objects of reason and desire are attained, in an Augustinian sense, that is, as the will.[72] When desire is "simple affection without passion or uproar in the soul," it is validated and attains its goal by an act of the will.[73] In a well-ordered soul, reason, desire, and will motivate ethical and social behavior[74] and guide a person's yearning for God. This was an ordered, affective, and emotive yearning, rather than a merely dispassionate intellectual pursuit of truth. The will, whereby it is in a person's power "to perform certain actions, or not to perform them, or to do the opposite,"[75] endowed human action with purpose and emotive force.

But what of the images that demons projected onto the imagination from the physical environment, analogous as these were to the outcomes of drunkenness, disease, and insanity?[76] Las Casas illustrated this issue by reference to that stereotype of Christian ascetic theology, the image of a

---

[69] Cf. W.K.C. Guthrie, *A History of Greek Philosophy*, vol. 4, *Plato: The Man and His Dialogues* (Cambridge, 1975), pp. 422ff., 476ff.

[70] *AH* 73, p. 376.

[71] *AH* 73, pp. 376f.

[72] Ibid.

[73] Acto de la voluntad, *AH* 73, p. 376.

[74] Cf. *AH* 40.

[75] *AH* 41, p. 216; cf. above, at n. 38 (this section).

[76] *AH* 88, p. 453.

seductive woman (see fig. 5).[77] Such an image could congeal in a man's senses thanks to seeing an actual woman; but it could also be derived from fumes emanating from his body when drunk, sick, or insane; equally, it could be composed by demons out of airy substances. Whatever its origin, the image passed from the external senses to the imagination, where it aroused the desiring faculty and hence clouded the intellect, seeing that "the soul never thinks without a phantasm."[78] The issue, however, was that the will could withhold assent from the act of fornication that would follow in the wake of untramelled desire.[79] In the Americas, it was thus the "well-inclined will" of the Indians that led them to celebrate the festivals of their gods in dignified sobriety and not in debaucheries such as Las Casas read about in the church fathers and pagan authors of classical antiquity. Indeed, the Indians resembled a hero of Christian hagiography, the hermit Anthony, who, as Las Casas had read in the saint's biography,[80] was tempted, but not seduced, by the figures of illusion whom the devil paraded before his eyes.[81]

Yet not all demonic illusions had such clear-cut moral contours; many were much harder, indeed impossible, to recognize. Idols are visible and touchable, and they engage desire by promising concrete, tangible, and in themselves blameless benefits. The delight and pleasure they offer is instantaneous: "For carnal men, devoted to sensible things and unable to raise aloft their spirit so as to enjoy the things of the spirit, the cult of idols is more delightful and captivating than the cult and adoration . . . of God."[82]

Las Casas' argument about the origin and nature of Amerindian religions is poised in a tightly drawn balance. On the one hand, he argued that Amerindian polities favored the positive development of a person's natural endowments and that Amerindian religions articulated a noble and enduring yearning for truth, that is, for God. On the other hand, he had to explain why Amerindian religious practice was for the most part focused erroneously on material objects and a plurality of gods.

The demons, ever watchful, inculcated error in human minds and imaginations; with passage of time this error gathered momentum. Idolatry in the New World had its counterparts in the religious practices of the Greeks and Romans and even of the Jewish people as described in the

---

[77] *AH* 88, pp. 455f.
[78] Quoted in *AH* 88, p. 455.
[79] *AH* 88, pp. 457f.
[80] Athanasius, *Life of Anthony*, in *Early Christian Biographies*, ed. J. Deferrari (Washington, D.C., 1952); see chaps. 6, 9, 11 and 12 for incidents mentioned by Las Casas in *AH* 95, p. 492.
[81] Cf. above, chap. 1.1 at nn. 50ff. and figs. 5–6.
[82] *AH* 163, p. 155.

Hebrew Bible.[83] Secondly, long-established custom gained the force, authority, and seeming authenticity of nature. As a result, the innate human yearning for God became focused on tangible and immediate purposes and visible objects of worship that had all been insinuated into the imagination by demons. Once lodged in the imagination, they were accepted as valid by reason and thus acquired the persuasive power of the truth itself.

Amerindian history, like that of Europe, told how cultural and theological progress in the outer world unfolded alongside simultaneous regress: one was inseparable from the other. Cognition, anchored in sense perception and imagination, and thus prey to demonic illusion, told the same story about the inner world of the human soul. The ubiquity of these processes in Europe, both ancient and modern, as well as in the New World, disqualified them as means of evaluating Indian intellect and imagination as somehow more prone to error than those of Europeans. In particular, vulnerability to demonic illusion and hence to the idolatrous worship that the demons fostered was the common human lot. By way of explaining this state of affairs, Las Casas appealed, in the footsteps of Augustine, to the "secret judgments of God, which are many, but never unjust."[84] Earlier, Cieza, having outlined beliefs in a pleasantly materialistic afterlife held by the Indians of Pasto, had written in a similar vein, "There exist such great secrets among these nations of the Indies that only God comprehends them."[85] To leave the definitive explanation of history to the judgments of god amounted to understanding history without imposing on it verdicts and value judgments derived from Christian theology. Revealed religion stood at the peak of religious truth, but other human endeavors, however much religion was intertwined with them, could be evaluated and understood according to human, and indeed secular, criteria.

3. GAINS AND LOSSES

Sixteenth-century Catholicism could accommodate, as Las Casas demonstrated, a comparative study of religions, provided that Christian doctrine was excluded from the comparisons. Christian revealed truth stood on a different level from truth reached by even the finest human minds. In strictly theological terms, it remained the touchstone of true doctrine. Like Cieza, Las Casas was therefore able to admire the religious achievements of the Incas, while at the same time condemning any theological

[83] *AH* 85.
[84] *AH* 92; cf. 96, p. 499; 120, p. 635, divine permission for demonic phantasms and idolatry.
[85] Cieza, *Crónica* 33, p. 111; cf. p. 112 on divine permission.

continuity Andean converts might discover between their old religion and Christianity. Las Casas had read about the desecration of the temple of Pachacamac[1] and learned from Cieza[2] and from Dominican missionaries that, although public worship at the site came to an end, the ancient deity lingered in people's memories and merged with the Christian god. Las Casas viewed this shift in religious perception as yet another example of demonic fraud. Pachacamac had informed his worshipers:

> I have been angry with you because you have abandoned me and accepted the god of the Christians. But I have set aside my anger, because the god of the Christians and I have agreed that you should serve us both, and both he and I are well pleased that you should act in this way.[3]

So, far from losing anything, the demon increased his influence and insulted the divine majesty by insinuating his own worship into the worship of God.

Such aspects of Andean religion as were acceptable in Christian terms were cultural and political. In 1564 Las Casas responded to a set of queries regarding the administration of Peru.[4] One query concerned treasures that had been deposited in Andean burials and sanctuaries: could they be lawfully confiscated by Spaniards? And if not, did treasures already removed have to be restored, and to whom?[5] Las Casas insisted that full restitution be made. His reasons mesh with the argumentation of the *Apologética Historia*.

Treasures deposited in temples, he argued, should be restored to the donor or his heirs, because such treasures had been given to an idol on the tacit condition that it was God. "The natural understanding and knowledge that the gentiles had, although confused, was to seek the true God." Since the condition was not fulfilled, and since the donor would not have made his gift had he understood the recipient to be a false god, the treasure reverted to the donor himself or his heirs. It could not be confiscated by Spaniards.[6]

Treasures robbed from burials should be restored to those burials, for the purpose of depositing them there had been to attain for the deceased "the greatest temporal good there is in the world, which is honor, fame, and glory, and to live forever in the memory of men." Furthermore, this honor extended to the heirs and kinsmen of the deceased, and so did in-

[1] Las Casas, *AH* 57.
[2] Cieza, *Crónica* 72.
[3] *AH* 131, p. 687; cf. above, chap. III.1 at nn. 14–17, on Cieza's report about Pachacamac.
[4] For the date, see Las Casas, *Doce Dudas*, principio 8, p. 498b.
[5] Las Casas, *Doce Dudas*, questions 7–8.
[6] *Doce Dudas*, octava duda, first conclusion, p. 528a.

famy and affront if the treasures were robbed: "This is confirmed because the Son of God did not despise the glory of his burial, of which Isaiah says, 'And his burial shall be glorious.' " Las Casas added with his characteristic acerbity:

> Let me inquire from those knights and excellent lords, who own chapels in churches, where they have deposited many objects of value, such as harnesses, shields, banners, armor of gold and silver, tombs covered in cloth of silk and brocade, whether the dead who arranged for these objects to be deposited there and the living, their descendants and heirs, regard all these objects as abandoned property? And whether he who robs or removes them by force does an injury to the dead, and to their living heirs and descendants?[7]

The obligation of restitution extended not only to the treasures of temples and tombs, Las Casas thought, but to the land of Peru itself, which rightfully belonged to the Inca government in exile at Vilcabamba.[8]

What was at issue was not only the much-debated question of the "just titles," the legitimacy of Spanish dominion in the Indies, but also the possibility of evangelization, which Las Casas regarded as the only defensible reason for any kind of Spanish presence overseas. But this had to be a peaceful presence that did not compromise the harmonious functioning of the various Indian polities, because only then could the Indians convince themselves of their own free will that Christianity was true. A person's capacity for learning and understanding was conditioned by external factors such as climate, health, war and peace, and by internal ones, such as states of mind, joy, fear, and sadness.[9] Yet, in Las Casas' eyes, the oppression that Spaniards had brought upon Indians created among them a permanent state of sadness, *tristeza*, and despair such as prevented them from contemplating, and hence understanding and accepting, the Christian religion.[10]

Although the wholesale restitution of Peru to the Incas was never seriously considered in official circles, Las Casas' reasoning and that of likeminded theologians in Spain did not go unheeded. The majority of Las Casas' adherents were friars;[11] the pressure they exerted through the

---

[7] *Doce Dudas*, septima duda, pp. 525bff. The argument that grave goods are in no sense abandoned property stands at the center of Las Casas' treatise *De Thesauris in Peru*.

[8] *Doce Dudas*, principio 3; 4, pp. 491f.; undecima duda, pp. 531–536.

[9] *AH* 27, p. 137, above, sec. 2 at nn. 45–48.

[10] Las Casas, *Del unico modo* 5.4, p. 90; 6, p. 99; *AH* 37, see especially p. 142 on tyranny. In the later sixteenth century, a Jesuit in Peru expressed similar opinions, *Relación Anonima*, pp. 181aff.

[11] M. Bataillon, "Las doce dudas peruanas resueltas por Las Casas," in his *Estudios sobre Bartolomé de Las Casas* (1976), pp. 301–314; C. S. Assadourian, "Las rentas reales," *Historica* 9 (1985): 75ff., see also the *Memorial* on encomiendas coauthored by Las Casas and Domingo de Santo Tomás, in Las Casas, *Obras* 5: 465–468.

confessional on veterans of the invasion to restore some part of their gains to the rightful owners was sometimes effective.[12] The debate on the just titles, by contrast, lost such practical applicability as it originally possessed once colonial government was established irreversibly.[13] This debate did, however, help to keep alive the memory of the Incas. For those who questioned the legitimacy of Spanish rule in Peru often did so by drawing comparisons between colonial misrule and the ordered and equitable government of the Incas.[14]

When thus, in 1569, the viceroy Toledo arrived in Peru with the charge of devising a lasting government for the former Inca empire, he accompanied all his measures with careful investigations of Inca precedents. In the outcome, however, he often ignored or overrode these precedents because he found them to be incompatible with Christian teaching, thereby contradicting the assertions of Las Casas and his Peruvian adherents.[15] Regarding treasures deposited in Inca burials, for instance, Toledo's inquiries revealed that "All the Incas and Indians understood that they would be resurrected in body and soul because a Viracocha would come who would turn about the earth, and for this reason they ordered treasures to be secretly buried with them, so that they would have them available when they were to be resurrected and would not live in poverty."[16] Two of Toledo's supporters explicitly took Las Casas to task for his idealized description of Andean religious practice. One was the writer of the *Parecer de Yucay*, addressed to the viceroy after 1572.[17] He considered the comparison between Andean and Christian burials inappropriate because the former were "an infamous memory of some lord condemned in hell." This theoretical concern was paired with a practical one, because long after Polo de Ondegardo had seized the mummies of Inca rulers from their custodians, nonroyal mummies everywhere continued to attract

[12] Lohmann Villena, "La restitución," *Anuario de Estudios Americanos* 23 (1966): 21–89; Lohmann Villena, "El licenciado Francisco Falcón," *Anuario de Estudios Americanos* 27 (1970): 131–194; cf. *Monumenta Peruana* 1: 228f., on a Jesuit in Spain consulting Domingo de Soto on restitution.

[13] See Noreña, *Studies in Spanish Renaissance Thought* (1975), pp. 94ff., especially pp. 101f.

[14] On the lawyer Francisco Falcón, see Lohmann Villena (above, n. 12); see also Falcón, *Representación*, especially pp. 139–155; Morales, in Assadourian (above, n. 11), pp. 114–117.

[15] Hemming, *Conquest of the Incas* (1970), pp. 411ff.

[16] Francisco de Toledo, *Informaciones acerca del Señorío y gobierno de los Incas*, pp. 192f. For the statement that "habia de venir un Viracocha que revolviese la tierra," see S. MacCormack, "Pachacuti," *American Historical Review* 93 (1988): 960–1006. Possibly Toledo's informants were reporting beliefs associated with the Taqui Onqoy; note the subsequent statements, p. 193: Algunos testigos dícen que les decían que la dicha resurrección había de ser para esta vida, y otros, que ahora entienden, por lo que les enseñan y predican en la doctrina, que esta resurrección no ha de ser para esta vida sino para la otra.

[17] *Parecer de Yucay*, p. 460. See also Mustapha, "Encore le Parecer de Yucay," *Ibero-Amerikanisches Archiv* 3, no. 2 (1977): 215–231, and M. Bataillon, "Comentarios a un famoso Parecer contra Las Casas," in his *Estudios sobre Bartolomé de Las Casas* (1976), pp. 317–333.

worshipers.[18] The other refutation of Las Casas' views on funerary treasures is by the distinguished lawyer Juan de Matinezo, who also pointed
out that Andeans still frequented the burial places of their ancestors,
which should therefore be destroyed.[19] Furthermore:

> Regarding what the bishop says, that they placed treasures in their
> tombs to preserve their honor, this is not to be believed, for neither
> did they have any honor, nor is it possible to show that they were
> even capable of honor. Nor did they deposit the treasures for any
> reason other than the inducement of the devil, thinking that they
> would rise again to live once more in this world, and to enjoy and
> use those things they deposited in the tombs.[20]

Despite all the contempt for the conquered peoples of the Andes that
speaks through this passage, Matienzo's assessment of the motives for
placing treasures in tombs was considerably closer to Andean realities
than were the elaborately constructed arguments of Las Casas. Las Casas
validated aspects of Andean and Amerindian religion at the cost of ideal-
izing and schematizing them in terms that were suggested by classical,
patristic, and medieval authorities. He therefore cannot bring us much
closer to understanding Andean people, either before or after the invasion, in their own terms.

Las Casas did, however, close the door on arguments for European
religious and cultural superiority by establishing categories of analysis capable of reaching beyond the boundaries of one specific culture and religion. He did this by developing a series of tensions between different,
even opposing, focal points of inquiry. Progress, an increasingly refined
conception of god, was accordingly paired with regress, the polytheistic
diffusion of divine qualities resulting from a more diversified social order.
On the one hand, he posited given and unchangeable factors, such as different geographical environments and hence human occupations, that
condition religious preoccupations and the perception of divinity.[21] On
the other hand, such preoccupations and their ritual expression were a
matter of human choice. However, human choice, being anchored in
cognition, was in turn conditioned and limited by the worldwide activity
of demons.

This method of analysis, counter posing the given with the variable,
the involuntary with the voluntary, the negative with the positive, and,
ultimately, a universe ordered in a fixed and predictable way with human
free will, pervades both the historical and the philosophical sections of
the *Apologética Historia*. In his description of Amerindian religions in dia-

---

[18] *Parecer de Yucay*, p. 468.
[19] Matienzo, *Gobierno del Perú* 1.39.
[20] Matienzo, *Gobierno del Perú* 1.39, p. 130.
[21] Cf. *AH* 74, arguing that idolatry is natural to human beings.

chronic and historical terms, Las Casas focused on Amerindian cultural and political achievements, thus setting to one side the problem that from the Christian standpoint, which he himself also subscribed to, these religions were erroneous. Nonetheless, the nature and cause of religious error were fundamental, and are dealt with as a question of how the human soul learns and knows. Here, discussion centers on the one hand on the cognitive capacities and successes of human beings and on the other on their cognitive failures, anchored as these were in the Fall and in the all-pervasive activity of demons in the natural environment. In this sense, Las Casas attained his purpose: it was to understand Andean and Amerindian religion not as a human failure but as a human achievement, erroneous indeed, but nonetheless a document to the endeavor of discovering why one lives, and how one can live.

The *Apologética Historia* was not published until 1909.[22] But the Augustinian friar Jerónimo Román had access to a manuscript copy of the work that he excerpted liberally in his *Repúblicas del mundo* of 1575.[23] A second edition, revised in accord with the instructions of the inquisitorial censor, appeared in 1595. Román introduced a degree of organization into the disparate materials that make up the *Apologética Historia* by discussing as separate entities the Hebrew kingdoms of the Old Testament, classical antiquity, Christian Europe, the Islamic states and some non-Christian states of Asia and America. However, the influence of Las Casas is visible on every page. Worship was natural to humanity, and it was laudable that "we human beings naturally bow before God to worship him, even when we do not know who he is."[24] Civilization, however, took its toll. Jerónimo Román thus documents both the theological progress and the regress that was entailed in cultural and political advance. In the far-distant, primitive ages of human history, which in some parts of the Americas were perpetuated into the present, human beings carried the concept of one god in their hearts and expressed it in simple rituals.[25] With increasing civilization, basic theological ideas became more elaborated and refined. At the same time, the cult of the diverse deities suggested by nature and the human imagination was expressed more elaborately and sumptuously in civilized societies than in simple ones,[26] while from the time of Nimrod, the cult of kings added a hitherto unknown register of false gods.[27]

Nonetheless, like Las Casas, so Jerónimo Román considered the rav-

[22] See E. O'Gorman, ed., *Apologética Historia*, p. ciii.
[23] See Román, *República Ind.* (1575), 1.1, fol. 355r.
[24] Román, *República Ind.* (1575), 1.2.
[25] Román, *República Gentilica* (1575), 1.1; *República Ind.* (1575), 1.2; *República Septentrional* (1595), 2.
[26] Román, *República Gentilica* (1575), 1.1; *República Ind.* (1575), 1.2; 5, 7, 21.
[27] Román, *República Gentilica* (1575), 1.2, especially p. 4, quoting Wisdom 14; cf. *República Ind.* (1575), 2.12.

ages of original sin to be capable of being circumscribed and delimited by political and cultural institutions. This conviction arose out of Román's positive and hopeful evaluation of human nature in general and of his own intellectual and spiritual evolution in particular. As he explained to his readers in the preface to the *República Gentilica* of classical antiquity, when he was young, he had been deeply engrossed in writings of the pagan Greeks and Romans and had neglected the sacred and more spiritual works of Christian authors. However, just as the uncultivated earth was fertile of its own accord but when tilled gave richer harvests, and just as craftsmen progressed from the basic accomplishments of the beginner to the perfection of maturity, so also, Román thought, age and continuing study had brought him greater wisdom and discretion. This humanistic evaluation of personal culture and of the evolution of civilizations was to find a certain resonance in the work of Garcilaso de la Vega the Inca who read Román's work and quoted it in his *Royal Commentaries of the Incas*.[28]

Another Peruvian author who read Jerónimo Román's *Repúblicas* and from it derived and adapted some of Las Casas' ideas was the Franciscan friar Luis Jerónimo Oré, author of a manual on missionary teaching that was published in Lima in 1598.[29] He was born into a prominent family in Huamanga,[30] and in 1612 paid a visit to Garcilaso de la Vega in Cordoba.[31] Like Las Casas, Oré thought that the Indians were culturally prepared to receive the Christian message. In the *Apologética Historia*, Las Casas recounted how at a time of pestilence the Athenians dedicated an altar to the "Unknown God," and how later St. Paul, when visiting Athens, explained that this God was the true god whose message he was preaching. Jerónimo Román reproduced the story,[32] and Jerónimo Oré thought that the apostle's message could as appropriately have been addressed to the Incas and their subjects. For in the course of his own preaching in Peru, in particular in the Franciscan *doctrinas* of Xauxa and the Colca valley,[33] Oré had learned to appreciate the spiritual yearning and refinement of Andean people. In his missionary manual he thus reproduced in translation an Inca prayer invoking the Creator, which he attributed to Pachacuti. "Where are you? Perchance in the height of

[28] Garcilaso de la Vega, *Comentarios reales* 1.4, end, on the name of Peru; 2.2, p. 43b, contradicting Román's view of Pachacamac, expressed in *República Ind.* 1.5, fol. 361v, and taken from Las Casas, *AH* 131, p. 687. Garcilaso, *Comentarios reales* 5.18, cites Román about the pururaucas; cf. below, chap. VIII.1 at n. 23.

[29] Oré refers to Román in his *Symbolo*, chap. 9.

[30] S. Stern, *Peru's Indian Peoples* (1982), pp. 100f., 118f., 170.

[31] Garcilaso, *Historia general del Perú* 7.30; cf. J. Heras, "Bio-Bibliografia de Fray Luis Jerónimo Oré O.F.M. (1554–1630)," *Revista Historica* 29 (1966): 173–192.

[32] Las Casas, *AH* 79, p. 408; Román, *República Gent.* 1.4, fol. 10v.

[33] For St. Paul in Athens, Oré, *Symbolo*, chap. 9; for Franciscan doctrinas, chap. 17; see also Tibesar, *Franciscan Beginnings* (1957). But note that Oré entirely overlooks his own order's campaigns of extirpation; see Duviols, *Lutte*, pp. 90ff.

heaven, or here below, or in the clouds and mists, or deep in the abyss?[34] Hear me and answer me, grant what I beg," the Inca had prayed. It was this same Inca, Oré thought, who had learned by natural reason that the Sun could not be god because it never rests and can be obscured by a cloud.[35] The Inca also sent two emissaries to the shrine of Pachacamac near Lima, who were informed there that the Maker of the Universe was invisible.[36] The book of nature had prepared Andeans to comprehend the revealed book of God. They had learned to see in this life the invisible God mirrored in his visible creation and were therefore ready to be taught that in the next life God would be for all human beings the mirror through whom to behold his creatures.[37]

It was by way of providing such teaching that Oré composed for Andean Christians a cycle of hymns in Quechua that expounded the central Christian doctrines.[38] Like Domingo de Santo Tomás, Oré considered the Quechua language to be as refined a vehicle for the elucidation of the Christian mysteries as Latin,[39] and since Andeans were ready to comprehend the faith, he expected that the distance between Andean religion and Christianity would soon be bridged. We know of one reader who very much agreed with Jerónimo Oré. This was Guaman Poma de Ayala.[40] The prayer to the Creator that Oré had attributed to Pachacuti provided Guaman Poma with one of the prototypes to the similar prayer that he in turn reiterated throughout his long history of Peru, calling on the Creator in the four corners of the world.[41] Guaman Poma also echoed Oré's confidence in the spiritual maturity of Andeans, their readiness to be Christian priests, artists, and teachers.[42] When Oré published his manual in 1598, he was hoping to receive official ecclesiastical permission to circu-

---

[34] See J. Szeminski, "Las generaciones del mundo," *Historica* 7 (1983): 71 on this formula.

[35] Cf. below, chap. VI at n. 45 for this reasoning.

[36] A similar story was recorded by Santillán, but about Tupa Inca Yupanqui (see below, chap. VIII.2 at n. 13); Oré refers to the Inca in question as Capac Yupanqui Inca. The prayer closely resembles one of the prayers that according to Cristóbal de Molina were recited for Citua, Molina, *Fabúlas*, pp. 81f., cf. p. 94. Oré's rendering of the prayer is in *Symbolo*, chap. 9, p. E7v. Also in chap. 9, Oré recounts the same myth about the Flood from Cañaribamba as appears in Molina, *Fábulas*, pp. 55f.

[37] Oré, *Symbolo*, chap. 2, p. A3.

[38] Oré, *Symbolo*, chap. 18.

[39] Oré, *Symbolo*, chaps. 17–18; Domingo de Santo Tomás, *Gramatica o Arte*, Preface.

[40] Guaman Poma, *Nueva Crónica*, pp. 912 [926], 1080 [1090]; Adorno, "Las otras fuentes de Guaman Poma," *Historica* 2 (1978): 137–158; Adorno, "El arte de la persuasion," *Escritura* 8 (1979): 167–189; Adorno, "The Rhetoric of Resistance: The 'Talking' Book of Felipe Guaman Poma," *History of European Ideas* 6 (1985): 447–464.

[41] Guaman Poma, *Nueva Crónica*, pp. 51, 54, 912 [926], etc. See J. Szeminski, "Las generaciones del mundo," *Historica* 7 (1983): 69–109; cf. MacCormack, "The Fall of the Incas," *History of European Ideas* 6 (1985): 466; Adorno, "The Rhetoric of Resistance," *History of European Ideas* 6 (1985), at p. 458.

[42] Cf. Guaman Poma, *Nueva Crónica*, p. 673 [687], Indian sculptor; pp. 17ff., Martin de Ayala, priest.

late for use in Christian worship translations of other prayers supposedly composed by the Inca Pachacuti.[43] But this permission appears never to have been granted. In Europe, the later sixteenth century brought with it a hardening of theological frontiers between Catholics and Protestants. In Catholic lands, the teachings of the Council of Trent, which concluded in 1563, were imposed systematically. The newly found doctrinal rigor and precision that emerged from the Council had repercussions in the New World also. In Peru, the ecclesiastical dignitaries attending the Third Council of Lima in 1583[44] promulgated a set of carefully formulated canons governing the organization of the church and published a catechism and model sermons for the instruction of Indians. Great emphasis was laid on extirpation and on the need to distance Andean converts from their old religion.[45] For men of the ecclesiastical mainstream, extirpation was to be the policy of the future.

[43] Oré, *Symbolo*, chap. 9.

[44] For the Council of Trent, see *Diccionario de historia ecclesiastica de España*, ed. Q. Aldea Vaquero and others, vol. 1 (Madrid, 1972), s.v. Concilio de Trento, pp. 483–496. The catechetical publications of the Third Council of Lima are collected in *Doctrina Christiana y Catecismo para Instrucción de los Indios*. Jerónimo Oré perhaps attended the Council of Lima; see his *Symbolo*, chap. 12.

[45] Cf. Duviols, *Lutte*, pp. 144ff., 196.

THE MIND OF THE MISSIONARY:
JOSÉ DE ACOSTA ON
ACCOMMODATION AND
EXTIRPATION,
CIRCA 1590

ON 21 SEPTEMBER 1572, thirty-six years after Manco Inca had secretly left Cuzco to found his government in exile at Vilcabamba, an Inca ruler once more entered the ancient capital. He was Tupa Amaru, Manco's son. It was an astounding spectacle, for the Inca came as a prisoner, having been captured some days earlier by the expeditionary force the viceroy Toledo had sent to annex Vilcabamba (cf. fig. 29). In the face of considerable opposition from the notables of Cuzco and members of religious orders, Toledo insisted that this last representative of the old order be executed. On the appointed day, over one hundred thousand Indians with their curacas, along with the Spanish inhabitants of Cuzco, were gathered in Haucaypata to witness the death. The Inca rode into Haucaypata on a donkey draped in black and from the scaffold turned to address the assembled multitude. Next, in the words of an eyewitness:

> Raising both hands, with his face turned to where most of the curacas were standing, the Inca Topa Amaru made the sign that Indians are accustomed to make toward their lords and in his mother tongue said with a loud voice . . . "Oiariguaichic!" At that very instant, the shouting, grieving, and crying out ceased . . . and there was a silence as though not a living soul were present in the square. So great was the authority and sovereignty the Incas held over their subjects. And what he said in his mother tongue . . . was the following: "My lords, here you have come, from all the four suyus; hear now that I am a Christian and they have baptized me, and I wish to die in the law of God, and I must die. Everything that so far I and the Incas my ancestors have told you, that you should adore the Sun, Punchao, and the huacas, idols, rocks, rivers, mountains, and vilcas, is false and a lie. And when we said that we were going to go in to speak to the Sun, and that he commanded that you should do as we ordered you to do, and that he spoke to us, it was a lie. For it was not the Sun but

we who spoke, for the Sun is a lump of gold and cannot speak. My brother Titu Cusi informed me that when I planned to say anything to the Indians, I should arrange to enter alone before the idol Punchao, and no one should come with me; and that the idol Punchao would not speak with me, because it is a lump of gold; and that afterwards I should come forth and tell the Indians that Punchao had spoken to me and had said what I wanted to tell them, because in this way the Indians would comply better with what I was ordering them to do. And that what should be revered was what was inside the Sun Punchao, which is the hearts of my ancestors the Incas."[1]

The death of the Inca brought with it the demise of such vestiges as still endured of imperial Inca religious observance. The bodies of deceased Inca rulers that the anonymous cleric had seen during the celebration of the maize harvest in 1535 had been confiscated by Polo de Ondegardo some years before the annexation of Vilcabamba. The clandestine worship that these relics of empire had continued to receive thus came to an end.[2] But in Vilcabamba, the traditional cult was perpetuated on a lesser scale around the mummies of Manco Inca and of other members of his family. The cult image of the Sun that Tupa Amaru referred to in his speech from the scaffold had been taken from Coricancha before the Spaniards were able to seize it and was then removed to Vilcabamba by Manco Inca.[3] The Spaniards who invaded Vilcabamba captured both the mummies and this image, which they had been searching for during nearly forty years. As Toledo proudly wrote to a correspondent in Spain, no Inca "either dead or alive" now remained in the last stronghold of the old religion, "no descendant of theirs, and no captain or idol."[4]

Tupa Amaru's conversion and speech from the scaffold were the outcome of intensive pressure exerted on him during the days of his imprisonment by missionary priests. Among them were the Augustinian friar Augustín de la Coruna, bishop of Popayan, the expert on Inca antiquities Cristóbal de Molina, and the Jesuit Alfonso de Barzana, who had arrived in Lima two years earlier as one of the founders of his order's mission in Peru.[5] Tupa Amaru's account of his interaction with the cult image of the

[1] Salazar, *Relación sobre . . . Don Francisco de Toledo*, pp. 279–280; see also Toledo's letters on the subject of Punchao in *Gobernantes del Peru. Cartas y Papeles*, ed. R. Levillier, vol. 4 (Madrid, 1924), pp. 344f.: Punchao "es de oro vaziado con un corazón de masa en una caxica de oro dentro del cuerpo del ydolo y la masa en polvos de los corazones de los yngas pasados . . . tenía una manera de patenas de oro a la redonda para que dandoles el sol relumbrasen de manera que nunca pudiesen ver el ydolo sino el resplandor"; cf. pp. 501f. On radiance as an Andean numinous quality, cf. below, chap. VII.1 at nn. 68–72.
[2] See M. Rostworowski, *Tahuantinsuyu*, pp. 56ff.; P. Duviols, *Lutte*, pp. 104f.
[3] Betanzos, *Suma* 1.32, p. 150a.
[4] R. Levillier, *Gobernantes del Perú. Cartas y Papeles*, vol. 4 (Madrid, 1924), p. 342.
[5] Murúa, *Historia general* (1611), 1.85, pp. 270f.; Hemming, *Conquest of the Incas* (1970), pp. 442f.; *Monumenta Peruana* 1: 235 (n. 7), 240, 290, 354.

Sun corresponds to one of the established Christian theories on the issue of pagan oracles: if a non-Christian religious image was said to speak, this was either because a demon inhabited the image and spoke through it or because a human interlocutor of the image falsely claimed that it had spoken. This latter theory had been proposed for the image of Pachacamac by the skeptic Hernando Pizarro.[6] The historian Sarmiento de Gamboa proposed a related hypothesis for the image of the Sun in Coricancha, namely, that "some Indian whom they had hidden behind the image" did the talking.[7] Betanzos also explained the working of oracles in terms of deception. He thus wrote about Inca Pachacuti that "whenever he wanted to raise up some idol, he entered the house of the Sun and pretended that the Sun spoke with him and that he likewise replied, so as to make his followers believe that the Sun commanded him to raise up these idols and huacas, and so that they should adore them."[8]

Such an interpretation of the Inca's converse with the Sun is not entirely incompatible with Andean religious experience. In the later seventeenth century, a religious leader from Cajatambo explained to a visitor of idolatries[9] that the voice of the deity—who was a mummy—with whom he spoke was not an external phenomenon but rather, that the spirit of the mummy "descended into his heart" so that he heard the voice "within himself."[10] The Inca rulers who said that they spoke with their "father the Sun" thus had in mind not a conversation between two partners but an abstracted state of consciousness or absorption in the deity. It was in such a state of absorption in his Wamani that the dancer Rasu Ñiti in José Maria Arguedas' short story danced his last, and his greatest, dance.[11] What Tupa Amaru spoke of in his speech from the scaffold was this absorption, but his conversion to Christianity had shriven it of its Inca religious and cultural context.

The public staging of Tupa Amaru's self-denunciation and death followed a format that had been developed by the extirpators of the Taqui Onqoy. Some years earlier, Don Juan Chocne, one of the leaders of that movement, had appeared before the assembled inhabitants of Cuzco with some of his companions and had retracted his teaching before being punished for it.[12] In Huamanga, similarly, adherents of the movement had

---

[6] See above, chap. II.1 at n. 14. See also Betanzos, *Suma* (1987), 1.32, pp. 149f., the Inca pretends to talk with image of the Sun.

[7] Sarmiento, *Historia Indica* 29, p. 235a; cf. above, chap. II.1 at n. 16–19.

[8] Betanzos, *Suma* 1.32, pp. 149bf.

[9] Member of an ecclesiastical commission charged with investigating and punishing adherence to Andean cults.

[10] Duviols, *Cultura andina y represión* (1986), p. 143; see further below, chap. IX.2 at n. 117.

[11] J. M. Arguedas, "La agonía de Rasu-Ñiti," in his *Relatos completos*, ed. M. Vargas Llosa (Madrid, 1983), pp. 210–220. I thank Sara Castro-Klarén for drawing my attention to this story. See her essay "Discurso y transformación de los dioses en los Andes: del Taki Onqoy, a 'Rasu Ñiti,' " in *El retorno de las huacas*, ed. L. Millones (Lima, 1990), pp. 407–423.

[12] Albornoz, *Informaciones* (1971), pp. 147 (name spelled Juan Chono), 225.

declared themselves to have been in error[13] and were paraded through the city's streets.[14]

Such violent and dramatic displays of Christian and Spanish superiority over Andean weakness and error could be observed regularly in colonial Peru (fig. 27).[15] Sometimes, however, the spectacle, while still inculcating the lesson of Andean inferiority, was not quite as intimidating. Around the time when Tupa Amaru was executed, the Jesuits were beginning to construct their church in Cuzco above the foundations of the palace of Guayna Capac.[16] In 1579 José de Acosta, then provincial of the Jesuit order in Peru, described to fellow Jesuits in Spain how the work was organized in the customary Andean fashion, as a cooperative venture and festival.

> For the foundations [the Indians] have brought ancient cut stone in such quantities that even if the church were to be twice as large, there would be a surplus. They take these stones from old buildings . . . of the time of the Incas. Organizing themselves by ayllus, or kin groups, to carry the stones to our church, and dressing as for a festival with their feather ornaments and adornments, they come through the city singing in their language such things as occasion devotion, for instance: "Come, brothers, let us bring stones to construct the house of the Lord . . . there they teach us the law of our God and Redeemer. . . ." The Incas, who were the lords of this land, labor with most fervor, and the Cañari, who . . . pride themselves on always having been loyal to the Spaniards, compete with them. . . . Even women transport stones and do their work while singing.[17]

Missionary indoctrination was thus accompanied by public construction and patronage of the arts. At a more basic level, the face of Peru was being transformed by a policy of resettling Indians in Spanish-style villages known as *reducciones*. Initiated sporadically in the 1550s,[18] the program was extended to the entire viceroyalty by Toledo (cf. fig. 14). The religious goal of the reducciones was to move the Indians away from their ancestral mummies and huacas, because these continued to attract wor-

---

[13] Albornoz, *Informaciones* (1971), pp. 80, 82f., 112f., etc.

[14] Guaman Poma, *Nueva Crónica*, p. 675 [689].

[15] Cf. MacCormack, "Atahualpa y el libro," *Revista de Indias* 48 (1988): 701; Guaman Poma, p. 525 [529]; cf. p. 557 [571].

[16] *Monumenta Peruana* 1: 472; cf. 4: 455.

[17] *Monumenta Peruana* 2: 618.

[18] See, e.g., Diego Dávila Brizeño's description of the reducciones he created in Huarochiri, in *Relaciones Geográficas de Indias—Perú*, ed. Jiménez de la Espada, Biblioteca de autores españoles, vol. 183 (Madrid, 1965), pp. 155–165; for Juan de Matienzo, who advocated reducciones, see G. Lohmann Villena, "Juan de Matienzo," *Anuario de Estudios Americanos* 22 (1965): 767–886; Matienzo, *Gobierno* 1.14

27. Injustices of colonial evangelism: a parish priest, empowered by the pastoral charge of watching over the consciences of the faithful, abuses a penitent. Guaman Poma, *Nueva Crónica*, p. 576, Royal Library, Copenhagen.

ship even from those who had been baptized.[19] In the course of extirpating the Taqui Onqoy, Cristóbal de Albornoz and others had destroyed an immense number of mummies and huacas. But missionaries of the later sixteenth century and of the seventeenth discovered that notwithstanding this and subsequent campaigns of extirpation, many objects of worship remained and many others were reconstituted out of charred fragments in conformity with ancient Andean precedent.[20]

Missionary teaching, reinforced by coercion and resettlement, led Andeans to reformulate their religious concepts but not to drop them entirely. Indeed, sometimes missionaries attempted to utilize existing belief, or what they regarded as existing belief to explain their message and thus unintentionally helped Andean concepts to live on in a Christian framework. One such concept was the devil and another the Creator or Supreme Being.

Cieza was convinced that the devil inspired Andean funerary observances and thought that Andeans had a name for him: "There is no doubt that Andeans see the devil transfigured [in the guise of their departed lords]. Throughout Peru, they call him Sopay." This Sopay, Cieza thought, also entered into the bodies of the dead in order to speak with the living.[21] Cieza's illustrators completed the picture by representing the devil talking with Andeans not in the guise of an Andean lord but equipped with horns, tail, and goat's feet (cf. fig. 8). Some twenty years later, the Inca Titu Cusi Yupanqui accepted a negative definition of the term *supay* as valid but reversed its application: if supay there was, it was not Andeans but Spaniards who thanks to their demonic greed and lust for power epitomized a principle of evil.[22] Yet there was room for doubt as to whether this was a complete interpretation of the Andean sopay, for in his Quechua *Lexicon* of 1560, Domingo de Santo Tomás translated *cupay* as "good or evil angel," "demon or domestic goblin," and finally, in a late antique pagan sense, as "good or evil demon." Conversely, the Christian devil was defined in the friar's lexicon as *mana alli cupay*, a *supay* who is "not good."[23] As Domingo de Santo Tomás understood it, the Andean cupay was not necessarily evil. The Quechua lexicon published by Antonio Ricardo in 1583 also translated the term as bearing diverse connotations: *zupay* is "demon, phantasm, a person's shadow."[24]

[19] *Monumenta Peruana* 1: 467ff., a Jesuit observer of Toledan reducciones.
[20] See above, chap. IV.1 at n. 15; below, chap. IX.2 at nn. 2ff.
[21] Cieza, *Crónica* 62, p. 192.
[22] Titu Cusi Yupanqui, *Relación*, pp. 37, 64. See further Szeminski, *Un kuraca* (1987), pp. 42f., for Inca Guascar's denunciation of huacas, whom he describes as *supay*. Further, G. Taylor, "Supay," *Amerindia* 5 (1980): 47–63.
[23] Domingo de Santo Tomás, *Lexicon*, p. 46v (110).
[24] Domingo de Santo Tomás, *Lexicon*, fol. 279; Antonio Ricardo, *Vocabulario y phrasis*, p. 32.

The Quechua *Vocabulario* of 1608 by Diego Gonzalez Holguin gave a wider range of meanings for the word. *Cupay* could be a vision, phantasm, or ghost. But other usages revealed the negative, evil component of the concept. These included seeing evil phantasms or spirits, being possessed by a demon or devil; speaking with the devil; and making oneself wicked, like a demon.[25] Indeed, in his treatise on missionary work among Indians, completed in 1577, the Jesuit José de Acosta regarded such a meaning as established: *zupay* was God's adversary.[26] This same meaning occurs in Acosta's sermons accompanying the catechism for Indians promulgated by the Third Council of Lima in 1583. Here, Indians were exhorted to stay away from evil angels, or *cupay*, who encouraged them to worship huacas, consult sorcerers, and commit sins provoking the divine wrath.[27] Acosta's fellow Jesuit, the author of the *Relación anonima*, on the other hand, thought that in Inca times, Andeans knew of the invisible Creator, Illa Tecce Viracocha, and his angelic ministers and also of his evil adversary Cupay, whom they abhorred.[28] Similarly, in the early seventeenth century, the Inca Garcilaso de la Vega explained that the Incas had distinguished good from evil, and God from *supay*, which latter term they never pronounced, he asserted, without first spitting.[29] Garcilaso's contemporary Guaman Poma by contrast thought poorly of Inca religion. He therefore identified Inca deities as *supay*,[30] and thought that in colonial times it was *supay curaca*, the demon lord, who prevented Andeans from fulfilling their Christian obligations.[31] His illustrations match his words: along with the Inca, a devil with tail and claws offers chicha to the divine Sun (fig. 17),[32] while elsewhere an Andean priest is shown praying and sacrificing before a horned and clawed devil with a tail (fig. 28).[33]

According to Domingo de Santo Tomás and Antonio Ricardo,[34] the devil's adherents would go "to the inner world, the house of the devil" (*ucupachaman cupaypa guasiman*). Ucupacha was the inner world of Andean cosmology, but *cupaypa guasi*, "house of the devil," was a Christian neologism in Quechua. Domingo de Santo Tomás appears to have been aware of this fact, but Garcilaso attributed the term *cupaypa huacin*, as

[25] Gonzalez Holguin, *Vocabulario de la lengua general*, p. 88.

[26] José de Acosta, *De procuranda Indorum salute* (in Spanish in his *Obras*; hereafter *De procuranda*), 1.15, p. 422b; 5.10, p. 563a.

[27] *Doctrina Christiana*, Sermon 6, fol. 34v.f.

[28] *Relación anónima*, p. 154b.

[29] Garcilaso, *Comentarios reales* 2.2, p. 44a.

[30] Guaman Poma, *Nueva Crónica*, p. 262 [264].

[31] Guaman Poma, *Nueva Crónica*, p. 861 [875].

[32] Guaman Poma, *Nueva Crónica*, p. 246 [248].

[33] Guaman Poma, *Nueva Crónica*, p. 277 [279].

[34] Domingo de Santo Tomás, *Gramatica o Arte*, fol. 89r; Antonio Ricardo, *Vocabulario y phrasis*, p. 153, s.v. infierno.

28. The demonization of Andean religion: two Andean priests supervise a sacrificial ritual, the beneficiary of which is a devil. Both priests are depicted as elderly, for, as missionaries regularly complained, it was the elderly who maintained the ancient religion of the Andes most devotedly. Guaman Poma, *Nueva Crónica*, p. 277, Royal Library, Copenhagen. Photo from facsimile, Paris 1936.

used for "hell," to pre-Christian times,[35] by way of drawing attention to the theological sophistication of the Incas. Indeed, all sixteenth- and seventeenth-century definitions of *cupay* and *cupaypa guasi* figured within the wider framework of attitudes to the theological value of Inca and Andean religion.

At the same time, the missionaries sought to transform the ambivalent Andean conception of cupay into a clear-cut Christian one, so that a Christian Spanish god could be contrasted with an Andean cupay and demonic Andean deities and ancestors.[36] This Christian dualism affected views of the Andean past, in that Garcilaso and Guaman Poma both interpreted the pre-Hispanic *cupay* as the equivalent of the European "devil." Yet the term did recover a certain ambiguity, born of the inequities of colonial society. It was "their *zupay*," Acosta noted, who urged Andeans not to serve Spaniards except in situations of extreme duress,[37] while over thirty years later, Garcilaso wrote that Andeans called those Spaniards *zupay* "who proved to be harsh and cruel and of an evil disposition."[38]

Just as the Andean supay was juxtaposed with the Christian devil, so also the Andean creator god with the Christian one. Almost from the beginning, Spaniards questioned Andeans about their concept of a creator. Indeed, Andean myths of origins describing how a founding deity, who was often called Viracocha or Tecsi Viracocha, brought forth the people of different Andean regions from lakes and mountains, caves and streams invited comparisons with the Christian god and with the story of creation in Genesis.[39] Possibly the Inca Pachacuti sought to subordinate the Sun to the Founder Viracocha in philosophical and theological terms.[40] But this subordination was never made fully explicit and consistent in cult.[41] For unlike Christian Spaniards, Andeans did not require that every theological idea be consistently translated into ritual. This is one reason why, throughout the Andes, regional and Inca cults could be performed side by side.[42] Christian logic, however, brought with it theological and ritual exclusiveness by tolerating the worship of one god

[35] Garcilaso, *Comentarios reales* 2.7; cf. Duviols, *Lutte*, pp. 37–39.

[36] Cf. Acosta, *De procuranda* 5.10, p. 563a.

[37] Acosta, *De procuranda* 3.17, p. 488b.

[38] Garcilaso, *Historia general* 1.40, p. 76a.

[39] J. H. Rowe, "Creator worship," in *Essays in Honor of Paul Radin* (1960), pp. 408–429; see especially Cieza, *Segunda Parte* 3,5.

[40] Rowe (1960), pp. 421–423; on the Andean aspects of the concept of "Hacedor," see Szeminski, *Un Kuraca* (1987), pp. 76–79.

[41] Molina, *Fábulas*, pp. 61, 67, 76, etc., statues of, and sacrifices to, Sol, Hacedor, Trueno; but note pp. 81ff.; 94, prayers to the Hacedor Ticsi Viracocha. The only prayer recorded by Molina that is addressed to the Sun was a prayer for the Incas, p. 91; cf. p. 51 for pre-Inca times.

[42] See above, chap. IV.1 at nn. 41–47.

only. Andeans took note of this change. From the Taqui Onqoy onward, Andean religious teachers reciprocated Christian exclusiveness by discouraging the worship of the Christian god and the use of Hispanic dress and food.[43] Nonetheless, Christian logic conditioned the manner in which Andean concepts of deity were explained both by Spaniards and by Andeans.

Around 1551, Juan de Betanzos described how Inca Pachacuti had met with his nobles to regulate the religious affairs of Cuzco.[44] Some twenty years later, Cristóbal de Molina also mentioned such a meeting, at the same time attributing to the Inca the argument that the Sun cannot be the supreme deity.

> This Inca had such power of understanding that he set himself to consider the respect and reverence his ancestors bestowed on the Sun, seeing they adored it as God, even though, circling the world every day, the Sun never had any rest or respite. He therefore discussed with the members of his council that it was impossible for the Sun to be God, the Creator of all things. For if it were, it would not be possible for a little cloud passing before it to deprive its light of radiance. And if the Sun were the creator of all things, it would sometimes rest and would shine on all the world from one place and would command whatever it wished. But seeing that this was not the case, there was another who ruled and directed the world, and he was Pachayachachic, which means "Maker."[45]

Pachacuti therefore constructed the temple of Quishuarcancha in Cuzco; this contained the Maker's gold statue in the guise of a ten-year-old boy.[46] Since Punchao was also represented as a boy, Guaman Poma thought some connection had existed between him and the Maker. In his drawing of the captivity of Inca Tupa Amaru, a Spanish soldier carries in his outstretched hand a small seated statue of a human figure. But as though Guaman Poma were not certain as to whether this was indeed the statue the Spaniards had found, he drew above it the statue of another seated figure, surrounded by a circle of solar rays (fig. 29).[47] Possibly Guaman Poma did not invent this overlap between Punchao and the Maker but rather recorded accurately a regional and provincial perception of the two Inca deities as a conglomerate.

After Molina, several other Spaniards reiterated Pachacuti's argument

---

[43] Albornoz, *Informaciones*, pp. 63f., 75, 80, 85, 178; cf. p. 147, Andean teachers point out a logical flaw in Christian exclusiveness: if Christianity were true and consistent, only the baptized, not the unbaptized as well, should be allowed to enter churches.

[44] Betanzos, *Suma* 1.14.

[45] Molina, *Fábulas*, p. 59.

[46] Molina, *Fábulas*, p. 59.

[47] Guaman Poma, *Nueva Crónica*, p. 449 [451].

29. The captive Inca and his god: having occupied the Inca retreat of Vilcabamba, the captain Martin Garcia de Loyola leads by a chain the last Inca,
Tupa Amaru, wearing his regalia, while a Spanish soldier carries the image
of the Inca empire's principal deity. Guaman Poma depicts the latter as having a double form, that of the Sun or Maker represented as a small boy,
surmounted by another small boy within a solar circle of rays.
Nueva Crónica, p. 449, Royal Library, Copenhagen.

about the Maker and the Sun. In 1586 Cabello Valboa copied it from Molina himself.[48] Luis Jerónimo Oré and the Mercedarian missionary Martín de Murúa may have learned about it independently,[49] as perhaps did José de Acosta.[50] Later authors, however, used one of the existing sources, without collecting independent information.[51]

Irrespective of this Spanish interest in the issue, the later Incas certainly did occupy themselves with the problem of deity. In 1558 Castro and Ortega Morejón recorded that Pachacuti's successor, Tupa Inca Yupanqui, was led to intervene in the valley of Pachacamac, also known as the valley of Yzma, because he dreamed that "the Creator of all was to be found in the valley of Yzma." Some years later, Santillán wrote that Tupa Inca Yupanqui had spoken of the Creator in Yzma (Irma) when he was still in his mother's womb.[52]

Tupa Inca Yupanqui's dream or oracular statement has no European parallel. By contrast, Pachacuti's argument about the Sun and the Creator resembles in general terms the oft-repeated European argument for the Prime Mover. There is also a more precise parallel; this is the explanation offered by the historian Josephus, who was frequently cited by sixteenth-century missionaries and historians, for why the patriarch Abraham left his home in Chaldea:

> He was the first boldly to declare that God, the creator of the universe, is one, and that, if any other being contributed anything to man's welfare, each did so by his command and not in virtue of its own inherent power. This he inferred . . . from the course of sun and moon . . . for, he argued, if these bodies were endowed with power, they would have provided for their own regularity, but since they [rise and set at varying times] it was manifest that [they render their] services not in virtue of their own authority but through the might of their commanding sovereign.[53]

Josephus appealed to the ancient philosophical principle that a perfect and divine movement must be a regular movement, and that the movements

[48] Cabello Valboa, *Miscelánea antártica* 3.15, pp. 309f.

[49] Oré, *Symbolo* 9; Murúa, *Historia del origen* (1590), 1.7, 1.11. Both Oré and Murúa call the Inca in question Capac Yupanqui, possibly pointing to a common source; cf. Murúa, *Historia del origen* (1590), 3.44, p. 267, Capac Yupanqui builds Quishuarcancha, the temple of the Maker.

[50] Acosta, *Historia natural y moral de las Indias* (hereafter *HNM*), 5.5.

[51] Blas Valera, in Garcilaso, *Comentarios reales* 8.8, p. 304b; cf. 9.10, p. 346b, same argument attributed to Guayna Capac; Cobo, *Historia* 12.12, p. 78b.

[52] Castro, *Relación . . . del modo que este valle de Chincha*, p. 246; Santillán, *Relación* 28; cf. above, chap. IV.1 at n. 96; below, chap. VIII.2 at n. 13.

[53] Josephus, *Jewish Antiquities* 1.156, transl. Thackeray. This passage had already attracted the interest of the compilers of Alfonso el Sabio's *General Estoria*; see C. Fraker, "Abraham in the 'General Estoria,'" in *Alfonso X of Castile: The Learned King*, ed. F. Marquez-Villanueva and C. A. Vega, pp. 17–29.

of sun and moon, which vary day by day, are therefore neither perfect nor divine. The Inca Pachacuti, on the other hand, argued that movement in itself betrays subordination. Aside from this issue, however, the two arguments do resemble each other. What is new about Pachacuti's argument, as compared to Abraham's in Josephus, is the idea that the sun cannot be divine because it is so easily obscured by a cloud. Pachacuti's argument is the only piece of philosophical reasoning the Spaniards ever attributed to the Incas. However Molina's informants in Cuzco may originally have formulated Pachacuti's argument, some aspect of it brought to his mind a pattern that was familiar to him from European religious traditions.

Inca philosophy notwithstanding, it had been the cults of the Sun and the huacas, much more than the cult of the Maker, that dominated in the religious life of the empire.[54] And in colonial Peru the divine Sun, rather than the Maker, the founder Viracocha, or even Pachacamac, lived on in worship.[55] Even colonial Christianity sometimes accommodated the Inca Sun as the Sun of Justice, somewhat as Las Casas had envisaged it.[56] The decorative program of the churches of Andahuailillas and Colquepata thus included prominent representations of the Sun painted as a face with rays,[57] rendered in the same iconography that Las Casas had attributed to the cult image of the Sun in Coricancha.[58] Contemporary Andeans are still familiar with this imagery. In Sonqo near Cuzco, the sun is addressed as Jesus Christ,[59] and on the small domestic altarpieces from Ayacucho depicting the birth of Jesus, a large sun is often seen rising behind the child in the crib (fig. 30).

But such accommodation of European Christianity to Andean religious thought had limitations in colonial Peru. This is evident in the works of Acosta, author of a systematic treatise, completed in 1577, on Christian missionary strategy in the Americas and of the highly influential *Natural and Moral History of the Indies*, first published in 1590. In a theological treatise also published in 1590, Acosta explained how, in theoretical terms, he viewed the role of accommodation in Christian teaching.[60] Accommodation, as understood by Acosta, was a method of ex-

---

[54] Molina, *Fábulas*, p. 51.

[55] Duviols, *Cultura andina y represión* (1986), pp. 72, 91; cf. 95, Guaris hijos del Sol; 122, the Moon, wife of the Sun; 151, Sun creator of men, Moon, creator of women; 161, Sol Punchao.

[56] Above, chap. v.1 at nn. 15–24.

[57] Gisbert, *Iconografía* (1980), pp. 29ff.

[58] Above, chap. v.1 at n. 25.

[59] See C. J. Allen, *The Hold Life Has* (1988), p. 52; also G. Urton, *At the Crossroads* (1981), pp. 67f. and T. Platt, "The Andean Soldiers of Christ," *Journal de la Société des Américanistes* 73 (1987): 149, 160f.

[60] On accommodation, see A. Funkenstein, *Theology and the Scientific Imagination* (1986), pp. 11f., 213ff., 222ff. The origins of accommodation go back to classical antiquity; see P. Hardie, *Virgil's Aeneid: Cosmos and Imperium* (Oxford, 1986), p. 27, citing Cicero, *De*

30. Andean sunrise and nativity of Jesus: the sun rises in a blaze behind the Christ child in the crib on this contemporary domestic altarpiece from Ayacucho, painted by Nicario Jiménez Quispe.

pounding scripture by extending its meaning to topics the scriptural author did not mention and could not have known about. Thus, the vision of devastation and the sun going down at noon that God showed to the prophet Amos[61] referred in a literal sense both to the death of Jesus and to the sack of Jerusalem by the Romans. But by accommodation, the same words could be extended to signify the devastation of Catholic churches during the wars of religion in Europe, even though the prophet

---

natura deorum 1.15.41: [Chrysippus] volt Orphei Musaei Hesiodi Homerique fabellas acomodare ad ea quae ipse . . . de deis immortalibus dixerat ut etiam veterrimi poetae . . . Stoici fuisse videantur.

[61] Amos 8:9.

did not have these events in mind.[62] This method of interpreting the sacred text, Acosta wrote, increased the understanding and joy of those who were sincerely committed to the faith. But there was no room for such a reading in debates with heretics or in teaching gentiles, who had to be brought to understand and accept the literal and historical sense before they could hope to attain "the privilege of accommodating the scriptures."[63] In terms less critical of Andean audiences, the Jesuit author of the *Relación anónima* made the same point when he stressed that the Indians should be preached to "historically . . . taking from the historical narration loving and tender exclamations conducive to penitence and reform, or exclamations of trembling and awe, conducive to the fear of God and to turning away from vice."[64] The idea that accommodation was inappropriate in missionary Christianity accords with Acosta's emphasis on the necessity of extirpating all residues of pagan thinking and observance, without allowing any overlap between Andean religion and Christianity. For in Acosta's opinion, as outlined in his manual for missionaries, Andean religion was an unstructured conglomerate of rural worship and superstition. In the forty years that had elapsed between the invasion and Acosta's arrival in Peru, Spanish perceptions of Andean religion had changed, and so had Andean religion in itself.

Cieza had been overwhelmed by the splendor of Inca religious architecture and the elaborate economic and political apparatus of Inca worship. He thus differentiated the Inca state cult from regional cults, which struck him as being less rational and ordered. Similarly, Domingo de Santo Tomás had been impressed by the grace and grammatical consistency of the Inca language, Quechua, and considered it to be a worthy vehicle in which to convey Christian doctrine adequately and even elegantly.[65] When thus Las Casas argued in the *Apologética Historia* and elsewhere that Andeans and other peoples of the New World should be taught the gospel on the basis of what they already knew, he built on and elaborated the perceptions of some earlier students of the Americas. But the tenacious adherence of Andeans to their old beliefs and rituals led subsequent adminstrators and missionaries to view the issue quite differently. One of them was Polo de Ondegardo, whom Acosta knew personally and from whose writings he learned almost everything he knew about Inca religion.[66]

---

[62] Acosta, *De Christo revelato* 3.5. For the exegetical tradition within which Acosta worked and the terminology which he used, see H. de Lubac, *Exégèse médiévale: les quatre sens de l'Écriture* (Paris, 1954–1964).

[63] Acosta, *De Christo revelato* 3.8; cf. 3.14.

[64] *Relación anónima*, p. 187b.

[65] MacCormack, "The Heart Has its Reasons," *Hispanic American Historical Review* 65 (1985): 448f.

[66] Acosta, *De procuranda* 3.22, 5.9–10; HNM 6.1; also 4.7; 5.4; 6–7; 23; 27; 6.18; 20–22; 7.27. On Acosta's ethnography see A. Pagden, *The Fall of Natural Man* (1882).

By 1572, when Acosta arrived in Peru,[67] the majority of the first con-querors had died, as had the majority of Andeans who had seen or served the last Incas. Depopulation had changed the face of the countryside and Spanish settlement had changed the social order. Most Andeans had ex-perienced some contact with Christian teaching and had been baptized. But this did not mean that they had given up their old religion. Acosta thus noted that childbirth, marriage, disease, and burial remained so many opportunities for articulating pagan beliefs,[68] and that Christian teaching had done little to eradicate the customs that expressed such be-liefs.[69] Ritual drinking, which accompanied not only festive occasions but also the performance of agricultural tasks, was an especial threat to Chris-tian doctrine and morality.[70] In 1583 the bishops assembled at the Third Council of Lima reiterated these and similar points. Inca religion, by con-trast, was a memory only. Spanish opinion of the cultural and intellectual value of Andean religion became correspondingly more gloomy and critical.

Human knowledge and institutions, Acosta thus thought, had reached their most perfect state in Europe, and compared to the Americas, Eu-rope was "the better and more noble part of the world."[71] Elsewhere, Acosta repeated from the *Parecer de Yucay*[72] the metaphor of Peru as an ugly daughter whose appearance was redeemed only by her dowry, that is, Peru's mineral wealth. In cultural terms, Acosta felt that Quechua lacked the basic vocabulary that was necessary to convey Christian teach-ing. For instance, to match the "sparse and attenuated knowledge" An-deans had of the true God, Quechua had no generic term whereby to refer to him. There were thus only the specific names Andeans gave to god, such as Viracocha, Pachacamac, and Pachayachachic, "creator of heaven and earth." Moreover, the worship of this deity was everywhere mingled with diverse idolatries.[73] Finding little previous knowledge to build on, missionaries thus had to be patient and persistent teachers.[74]

When describing different kinds of idolatry, Las Casas had employed categories that were developed by the writers of classical antiquity and the early church. Like his ancient sources, Las Casas thus regarded the gods of the Egyptians as a case apart.[75] The Greek and Roman gods, on the other hand, could be classified into distinct types. Quoting, among

[67] Mateos, ed., Acosta, *Obras*, p. xi.
[68] Acosta, *De procuranda* 5.10, p. 563.
[69] Acosta, *De procuranda* 4.4; cf. *Monumenta Peruana* 1: 421–425.
[70] Acosta, *De procuranda* 3.20–23.
[71] Acosta, *HNM* 5.1.
[72] Acosta, *HNM* 4.7, p. 143 = *Parecer de Yucay*, p. 462.
[73] Acosta, *HNM* 5.3.
[74] Acosta, *De procuranda* 5.15, 6.11.
[75] Cf. Las Casas, *Apologética Historia* 75, 76.

others, Diodorus, Vergil, Ovid, and especially Augustine, Las Casas enumerated the select gods who lived on Mount Olympus, the lesser gods
who were offsprings of unions between a deity and a mortal being, and
the gods presiding over aspects of nature.[76] Acosta was familiar with these
and similar sources and extracted from them the distinctions between different types of gods that he discussed in his manual for missionaries. But
the conclusions he reached differed from those of Las Casas. He differentiated the astral deities of ancient Babylonia from the gods created by
Greek poets, on the one hand, and from the animal gods of the ancient
Egyptians, on the other. The worship of images and dead kings described
in the Book of Wisdom was in Acosta's eyes a particularly powerful form
of idolatry; he thus appended it as a subcategory to the gods of Egypt.[77]
Regarding Andean and American religions, Acosta saw little of positive
value in them but merely noted that all three kinds of idolatry were amply
represented in the Americas.[78] Where thus Las Casas had interpreted the
offering of firstfruits on the island Española as an example of Indians
complying with the natural law,[79] Acosta, who observed such rituals in
the Andes, classified them as simply another manifestation of the idolatry
that missionaries had to find a way of suppressing.[80]

In his Natural and Moral History of 1590, Acosta presented a new and
more abstract definition of idolatry that arose in part from his reading of
the Book of Wisdom and in part from his own direct observation of Andean
religion and his reading of earlier writers on the Andes.[81] Following the
Book of Wisdom, Acosta distinguished two principal types of idolatry, one
derived from nature and the other from human invention. Idolatry derived from nature viewed as worthy of worship the visible power and
beauty of the celestial bodies, natural phenomena, and the elements, thus
disregarding the invisible power and beauty of the creator.[82] In the Andes,
Acosta had observed, this worship derived from nature was focused either on objects of general significance, the sun, moon and stars, the earth,
and the elements; or else on particular objects, that is, the Andean huacas,
rivers and springs, trees and mountains. Similarly, Acosta distinguished
two subordinate branches in the idolatry that the author of the Book of

---

[76] Las Casas, Apologética Historia 105; Augustine, City of God 7.1–28. Medieval and late
medieval scholars in Spain had already classified the ancient gods by tracing their genealo-
gies. See for example, Alfonso X el Sabio, Primera Crónica General de España, ed. R. Menén-
dez Pidal (Madrid, 1977), chap. 4 and in particular, Alfonso de Madrigal, Libro intitulado las
catorze questiones del Tostado and his Eusebio (cf. fig. 25).
[77] Acosta, De procuranda 5.9, pp. 559af.; 5.10. See also above, chap. v.1 at n. 34.
[78] Acosta, De procuranda 5.9, p. 560a.
[79] See above, chap. v, introduction, at n. 19.
[80] Acosta, De procuranda 5.10, p. 563b.
[81] Acosta, HNM 5.2; for earlier discussions of the origin of idolatry according to the Book
of Wisdom, see above, chap. v.2, n. 59.
[82] Wisdom 13, with Acosta, HNM 5.4.

Wisdom had derived from human invention. Some objects of worship
were pure invention, such as idols and statues of wood, stone, or precious
metal; objects that "neither are nor ever were anything." Alternatively,
what was worshiped "vainly or in flattery" was the dead or their possessions. Acosta then gave Andean and Mexican examples of the resulting
four types of idolatry. In this new classification, the Inca cults of the Sun,
the Moon, the stars and the earth Pachamama, of the huacas, of the Inca
mummies, and of man-made holy objects and images all found their respective places,[83] as they had done earlier in the comparativist schema of
Las Casas. But unlike Las Casas, Acosta regarded these four different
forms of worship that he encountered in the Andes and the Americas at
large not as positive documents of human aspiration toward the good and
true, however erroneously focused, but as error pure and simple.

Acosta did, however, agree with Las Casas, of whose work he knew,[84]
that as societies changed, so did their forms of idolatrous worship.
"Where the exercise of temporal power had advanced furthest, there idolatry also increased."[85] But he did not believe that a pure and simple form
of worship had existed anywhere in the world at the dawn of history; to
look for survivals of such worship in parts of the Americas was thus a
vain pursuit. Rather, just as Cieza had supposed that many of the nations
beyond the frontiers of the Inca empire practiced "no religion at all" and
had no temples, so Acosta held that these simple societies lived "without
king, without law, and without covenants."[86] Such societies, lacking
fixed places of residence, chose leaders only at times of extreme need and
stood at the lowest point of cultural, political, and religious development.[87] Next came societies, such as the those of the Incas and Aztecs,
with cities, established forms of government, magistrates and laws, armies and organized religion.[88] Finally, China and Japan were examples of
societies that had writing and that approximated most closely to the civilized Christian nations of Europe.[89] Just as Aristotle had described all
people other than the Greeks as barbarians, so for Acosta the world beyond Europe was peopled by one or another of his three kinds of barbarian nations. "Barbarian" was not only a cultural and political definition
but also a moral and religious one: it described all non-Christians. Las
Casas, who had also reviewed the term, differed from Acosta in one cru-

[83] Acosta, *HNM* 5.4–6; 9.
[84] Acosta, *HNM* 7.27.
[85] Acosta, *HNM* 5.27, p. 267; cf. *De procuranda* 5.9, p. 561; cf. Polo, *Errores* 13, fols. 14rf.
[86] Acosta, *De procuranda*, Proemio, p. 393.
[87] Cf. Acosta, *HNM* 1.25, p. 64; 4.2, pp. 142f.
[88] Acosta, *De procuranda*, pp. 392bf.; *HNM* 1.25, 6.11.
[89] Acosta, *De procuranda*, p. 392a; cf. *HNM* 6.19, where the natives of America are divided
into three classes of society: monarchies, behetrías, and "gobierno totalmente bárbaro . . .
andan como fieras y salvajes."

cial respect, for to him Europeans, depending on their conduct, could also be barbarians.[90]

Acosta's three types of barbarians called for three distinct missionary strategies. People who lacked kings, laws, and covenants, he thought, could only be converted by force, that is, by missionaries working in company with soldiers to protect their lives.[91] Nations such as the Incas and Aztecs, once the work of evangelization had begun, should be governed by a Christian ruler to enforce their continued adherence to Christianity. Only the highly civilized nations of Asia could be converted by the same method as had been used by the apostles for the Greeks and Romans, that is, by peaceful and reasoned teaching involving no change of government.[92]

Apart from justifying, at any rate by implication, both Spanish colonial government in the Americas[93] and religious coercion, these opinions of Acosta's had repercussions on his interpretation and evaluation of Inca and Andean religion. Although he compared Inca and Andean deities to those of the ancient Mediterranean,[94] he saw a fundamental difference between Peru and the Americas on the one hand and ancient Greece and Rome on the other. When comparing the missionary work of his own contemporaries to that of the apostles and early Christians, Acosta was "tormented in soul" to understand why in the early days of the church Christian teachers regularly performed miracles, whereas in his own day miracles were almost unheard of. The difference, he resolved after long reflection, lay not so much in the virtues of the teachers, however much the lives and doings of the apostles and early Christians were exemplary. Rather, the difference lay in the missionaries' audience. The Greeks and Romans had been distinguished by their intelligence and reasoning ability. God granted to the apostles, who were simple men, the divine authority to perform miracles because there was no other way in which they could have convinced their oversophisticated listeners. The situation in the Americas presented a complete contrast:

> What need is there of impressive miracles when what is lacking is a higher intelligence that might experience some curiosity regarding the sublimity of our doctrine? There is need for only one miracle among these people of the New World, a great and singular miracle, most efficacious in inculcating the faith. This is that [the missionary's] mode of life be in accord with what he preaches.[95]

[90] Las Casas, *Apologética Historia* 267, p. 653.
[91] Acosta, *De procuranda* 2.8.
[92] Acosta, *De procuranda*, Proemio, pp. 392ff.
[93] Cf. Acosta, *De procuranda* 2.11.
[94] E.g., Acosta, *HNM* 5.4; 5.
[95] Acosta, *De procuranda* 2.9.

That missionaries should live virtuously is a common theme of the colonial church. It went hand in hand with the even more frequently reiterated desideratum, that the Indians should acquire such civilized and morally acceptable customs as were a prerequisite for comprehending Christianity.[96]

Unlike Las Casas, Acosta was convinced that the Indians lacked such customs, that the very fabric of Amerindian societies militated against true religion. Las Casas had noted in passing that the author of the *Book of Wisdom* had denounced reverence for kings as one of several causes of idolatrous worship and that evidence of such reverence could be found in Peru.[97] Acosta had in mind this same passage in the *Book of Wisdom* when constructing his twofold classification of idolatrous objects of worship. He thus interpreted its relevance to the Americas in much broader terms than Las Casas had done. Missionaries, Acosta suggested, should use the very words of this and similar biblical passages to impress on their charges the vanity and perversity of worshiping natural phenomena,[98] or corruptible objects of wood, stone, or metal, of greeting the rising sun, feeding the dead, and consulting diviners. For such observances had been brought into existence by "covetous priests and the might of kings."[99] This was no mere empty rhetoric, for even after Tupa Amaru's death, the people of the Andes did not forget the Incas. Figures of the Inca were still to be found among domestic objects of worship in the late sixteenth century and long beyond,[100] and the Inca himself appeared in visions urging Andeans to obey the precepts of their old religion.[101]

In the *Natural and Moral History*, Acosta thus interpreted the cult of kings as described in the *Book of Wisdom* as the pivot of Andean idolatry. "This was the wretched delusion of human beings," the author of *Wisdom* had written, and Acosta reiterated his view:

"At one time they yielded to affection and sentiment, and at another they [indulged in] flattering kings, thus imprisoning the unspeakable name of God in rocks that they adored as divine." . . . Portraits and statues of the dead gave rise to . . . idolatrous worship of idols and images. . . . Looking to our Indians, they reached the fullness of their idolatries by the very same stages that Scripture describes. . . . The [bodies of] Inca rulers were [preserved] in Cuzco, each in his chapel and shrine. . . . And each left his treasures, possessions, and income to maintain the shrine where his body was placed along with

[96] Cf. MacCormack (above, n. 64), pp. 456ff.
[97] See above, chap. v.1 at nn. 34ff.
[98] Acosta, *HNM* 5.4.
[99] Acosta, *De procuranda* 5.10, pp. 562f.
[100] *Doctrina Christiana*, Sermon 18.
[101] *Monumenta Peruana* 5: 208 (1592 A.D.).

a crowd of ministers and family members who performed his cult.
. . . Not content with this idolatry of dead bodies, they also made
statues; each king while alive had his idol or statue made of stone,
which was called *guaoiqui*, i.e., brother . . . and received the same
reverence as the Inca himself. These statues were taken to war and
led in processions to obtain rain and good weather, and were honored with festivals and sacrifices.[102]

Acosta's guide in all matters of Andean religion was Polo de Ondegardo, whom he often quoted verbatim.[103] His theological interpretation
of Andean religion, however, was his own. Having classified different
aspects of Inca and Andean religion according to his distinction between
objects of worship derived from nature and others derived from human
invention or imagination,[104] Acosta described all American religious observance as a series of demonic imitations of true belief and ritual.[105] As
Ciruelo and others had understood it earlier,[106] the devil produces plausible imitations of truth, the better to deceive human beings. In Peru, this
theory found extensive corroboration. For, as Acosta and the missionaries of the seventeenth century saw it, just as God was served by Christian
priests and different kinds of religious specialists, such as monks and
nuns, so in Peru was the devil;[107] and just as churches were the dwelling
places of God, so Andean temples like the pyramid of Pachacamac and
Coricancha had been the devil's dwelling places.[108] Andean confession
and rituals of ablution and purification were so many demonic imitations
of their Catholic equivalents,[109] while the Inca Citua was a demonic
"shadow and image" of the Eucharist.[110] Even the Christian Trinity had
been imitated:

In his own fashion, the devil has introduced a trinity into idolatrous
worship, for the three statues of the Sun [in Cuzco] were called
Apointi, Churiinti, and Intiquaoqui, which is to say, the father and
lord Sun, the son Sun, and the brother Sun. In the same fashion they
named the three statues of Chuquiilla, who is the god presiding over
the region of the air where it thunders, rains, and snows. I remember

<hr />

[102] Acosta, *HNM* 5.6, abridged translation. On *guaoque* see Cobo, *Historia* 13.11 and below, chap. IX.1 at n. 32. On the Inca practice of split inheritance here referred to by Acosta,
cf. above, chap. IV.1 at n. 101.

[103] E.g. Acosta, *HNM* 5.28 = Polo, *Errores* 8, fol. 9vf.

[104] Cosas imaginadas, Acosta, *HNM* 5.6.

[105] Acosta, *HNM* 5.1.

[106] Above, chap. 1.2 at nn. 36ff.; cf. Kramer and Sprenger, *Malleus* 2.1.5.

[107] Acosta, *HNM* 5.14.

[108] Acosta, *HNM* 5.11.

[109] Acosta *HNM* 5.17, on Ytu, from Polo, *Errores* 9, fol. 11r; *HNM* 5.25, cf. 26 for
Mexico.

[110] Acosta, *De procuranda* 6.12, p. 569; cf. above, chap. IV.3 at nn. 108–109, for Citua.

when I was in Chuquisaca, a worthy priest showed me a document that I had in my keeping for some time, in which he had investigated a huaca, or shrine, where the Indians professed to adore Tangatanga, this being an idol of which they said that in the one there were three, and in three one. And since the priest marveled at this, I think I told him that the devil steals whatever he can of the truth for his lies and deceits, and does so with that infernal and stubborn pride with which he always desires to be like God.[111]

These demonic trinities emerge from Acosta's interpretation of Andean data in accordance with Christian preconceptions. Acosta's intellectual heir, the seventeenth-century Jesuit historian Bernabé Cobo,[112] copied from Pedro Pizarro the information that Coricancha contained, apart from the image Punchao, an anthropomorphic statue of the Sun known as Apu-Inti, with two attendant statues known as "the Sun's guards," Churi-Inti and Inti-Guauqui. They each carried a hatchet mounted on a long staff sheathed in a cover, these hatchets being "the Sun's weapons."[113] The three statues did not, however, form any kind of trinity. Of the three names Acosta gives for the Thunder, Illapa and Chuquyilla are synonyms,[114] and the Thunder's statue in Cuzco was known as Chuquiylla Illapa,[115] so that here also, there is no trinity. Indeed, perhaps Acosta derived his Inca thunder trinity from the Spanish distinction between relámpago, rayo and trueno, for in his Tesoro of 1611, the lexicographer Covarrubias defined relámpago as "the fire and radiance that apparently precedes thunder [trueno] and lightning [rayo]."[116]

Nonetheless, Andeans did conceptualize some deities in groups of three. Thus, in Inca Cuzco, prayers and sacrifices were addressed to Vir-

[111] Acosta, HNM 5.4 = Polo, Errores 1.3, fol. 7v, for three names of the Thunder, with Rostworowski, Estructuras, pp. 39ff. See also Murúa, Historia del origen (1590), 3.51, on Chuquilla, Catuilla, Intiillapa as "hombre en el cielo con una porra," and contrast the poetic rendering of the same concept in Garcilaso, below, chap. VIII.1 at n. 47. Murúa, Historia del origen (1590), 3.71, p. 346 mentions three statues of Sol, and three of Trueno—padre, hijo and hermano—in Capac Raimi. Garcilaso, Comentarios reales 2.1, p. 42b; see also 2.5, p. 49b, on the Tanga Tanga trinity, corrects Acosta on the three statues of Chuquilla.
[112] Cf. P. A. Means, Biblioteca Andina (New Haven, 1928; Detroit, 1973), pp. 349ff.
[113] Pedro Pizarro, Relación 15, pp. 90f.; Cobo, Historia 13.5, pp. 157bf.; for a similar hatchet, see the picture of Guayna Capac in Guaman Poma, Nueva Crónica, p. 112. Churi means "son" and guauqui means "brother," so that the image of the Sun was shown as being attended by its son and brother. Sarmiento, Historia Indica 29, the statue of gold "tamaño de hombre" represented the Sun. Further, Sarmiento, 31, p. 237a, Inca Pachacuti added at the Sun's right side a statue of Viracocha Pachayachachi and at his left side Chuquiylla (relámpago), who was Inca Pachacuti's guauqui.
[114] Domingo de Santo Tomás, Lexicon, s.v. relámpago; Rostworowski, Estructuras, p. 41.
[115] Molina, Fábulas, p. 67.
[116] Cf. Cabello, Miscelánea antártica 3.15, p. 311; Murúa, Historia general (1611), 1.20, vol. 1, pp. 47,32; Garcilaso, Comentarios reales 2.1 (end), denies the authenticity of the thunder trinity and the trinity of Sun and Thunder.

acocha, who was also described as the Maker or Pachayachachic, the Sun, and the Thunder;[117] moreover, the three deities were commonly housed together.[118] Similarly, at the holy place Chuquipalta near Cuzco, the Maker Pachayachachic, Intiillapa, the "Thunder of the Sun," who was also the "brother" of Pachacuti Inca,[119] and Punchao were represented together as three upright stones and received joint sacrifices.[120] In Huamachuco, the Augustinian friars had found that the regional deity Catequil was revered with a mother and brother,[121] and similar groups were worshiped elsewhere.[122]

Echoes of these divine groups survive in colonial religious painting from the later seventeenth century onward, when clerical supervision of ecclesiastical art became less stringent. From that time on, the Christian Trinity was frequently painted in the Andes as three men of the same age whose chests are at times adorned with solar disks (fig. 31). The canonical image of the Trinity, by contrast, shows God the Father as older than Jesus, while the Holy Spirit is represented as a dove (fig. 32). European precedents for the heterodox Trinity of three men of the same age exist, but they are very few (fig. 33).[123] In the Andes, by contrast, the heterodox Trinity became ubiquitous, precisely because it was capable of evoking a pre-Christian and widely held belief. Even those Andean groups of three that included a female deity were in some instances translated into a Christian Trinity: a late seventeenth- or early eighteenth-century portrait of Nicholas of Bari in Cuzco is surmounted by a Trinity composed of Jesus partnered by the Virgin Mary as divine mother with the Holy Spirit as a dove hovering between them (fig. 34).[124]

However, such paintings fell outside the boundaries of orthodoxy as defined both by Acosta and by most missionaries of the sixteenth and seventeenth centuries. The central doctrines of Christianity could not be

[117] Polo de Ondegardo, *Errores* 1.3, fol. 7v; Molina, *Fábulas*, p. 67.

[118] Molina, *Fábulas*, pp. 61f.; Sarmiento, *Historia Indica* 31; Cabello, *Miscelánea antártica* 3.21, p. 365, about Tumebamba.

[119] Rowe, "An Account of the Shrines," *Ñawpa Pacha* 17 (1979), Ch-2:3.

[120] Cf. Murúa, *Historia del origen* (1590), 3.51, p. 286, three chief deities, Ticsiviracocha, Sol, Trueno; cf. Rowe, "An Account of the Shrines" (1979), Ch-4:8.

[121] Above, chap. IV.1 at n. 10.

[122] Rostworowski, *Estructuras andinas de poder*, pp. 77ff.; Cabello, *Miscelánea antártica* 3.18, p. 333, statues in Cuzco of Sol, Ticciviracocha, and Mama Ocllo Ynga Illo, set up by Pachacuti Inca.

[123] The manuscript of the Spinola Hours (John Paul Getty Museum, Malibu, California, MS Ludwig IX 18, fol. 10v), illuminated in Ghent or Malines in c. 1515 by Gerard Horenbout, displays another close precedent to the Andean iconographies here mentioned. Three men wearing red copes and crowned with identical crowns are seated next to each other on a wide throne. Each of the three holds a scepter; the central figure raises his right hand in blessing, while the two at the sides jointly hold a cross-bearing globe.

[124] A painting of the same period in the Museo de Arte, Lima, displays a similar iconography. Saint Nicolas of Bari is surmounted by a Trinity consisting, from left to right, of God the Father, the Virgin Mary, and Jesus.

31. The Andean Trinity: three equal, identical men with hands interlocked crown the Virgin Mary, dressed in the starry cloak of heaven. On the altar in the foreground, which is being decorated by two angels, are a monstrance for the eucharistic host, flowers, and candleholders. Material reality—the altar—thus fuses into the visionary reality of angels and deities (cf. figs. 2–3). Museo Municipal, Cuzco, by kind permission of the director.

33. A Spanish antecedent of the late fifteenth century for the Andean Trinity of three identical men. Jesus as Man of Sorrows, with his pierced feet resting on the globe, is held by God the Father, right, and the Holy Spirit, left. Miguel Ximénez, Prado, Madrid

accommodated to Andean interpretations, and indeed, the vast majority of ecclesiastical works of art in the Andes depict Christian ideas and teachings according to the traditional iconographies. Notwithstanding some exceptions,[125] the polarity that Acosta, like the bishops of the Third Council of Lima, perceived between Christian truth and Andean demonic

[125] For Oré, see above, chap. v.3 at nn. 30–45; for Pérez Bocanegra, see R. T. Zuidema, "Catachillay: The Role of the Pleiades, the Southern Cross, and α and β Centauri in the Calendar of the Incas," in *Ethnoastronomy and Archaeoastronomy in the American Tropics*, ed. A. F. Aveni and G. Urton (New York, 1982), pp. 203–229 at pp. 216f.

32. The orthodox Trinity, three separate persons in one divine substance: God the Father holds the crucified Jesus, the two being joined by the uniting love of the Holy Spirit, who is depicted as a dove. Domenico El Greco, Prado, Madrid.

RETRATO D SAN NICOLAS D BARI
que esta en su Ioloesta Parrochial de la Villa de ....

34. Nicholas of Bari, patron saint of children, is watched over by an Andean Trinity of Jesus, the Holy Spirit in the guise of a dove, and the Virgin Mary, who holds in her hand a priestly stole for her protégé. Museo Santa Catalina, Cuzco.

imitations or perversions of it became increasingly important in mission- ary instruction. Although the idea of this polarity is anchored in matters of religion, its substance was for the most part cultural and ethnic. Over a generation after the collapse of the Inca political order, which some early Spanish observers had admired so profoundly, many administrators and missionaries became convinced that there was no valid Andean social or political stucture. A Jesuit supporter of Viceroy Toledo's resettlement program thus wrote that the Indians had not become Christians because, living in scattered hamlets, "they have not been able to learn the social and political skills that are a prerequisite to becoming capable of the law of God. . . . [Instead,] they live in wild terrain like savages; even when they do join together in villages, their custom is to dwell in narrow poor quarters, dark and dirty, where they associate together and sleep like pigs."[126]

These harsh words resolve the dilemma of cultural and religious differ- ence, over which some earlier observers of Andean societies had labored so painfully, into a simple matter of Andean inferiority to European and Christian norms. This was the very resolution that in their different ways Cieza and Las Casas, among others, had endeavored to avoid. Acosta in his turn also settled for Andean inferiority, although he arrived at his con- clusion via his own distinct route, by classifying non-European humanity into three types of barbarians. There was no further need here for appeal- ing to demonic manipulations of the environment, and hence of human sense perception and imagination, in order to explain religious difference; for once religious difference was understood principally as an aspect of cultural and political evolution, the dichotomies that Las Casas had con- structed between progress and regress, between the voluntary and the given, god and devil,[127] became superfluous. Different cultures were or- dered in relation to each other according to a single hierarchy of values that placed Europe at the top.

Acosta was therefore free to understand the role of imagination in thought and cognition without taking stock of the demons, one of whose uses had been to diversify this hierarchy. Not that Las Casas and others had deliberately deployed the demons in their arguments so as to achieve a multiple hierarchy of cultural and religious achievements. Rather, their acknowledgment of the presence of demons in the universe amounted to an acknowledgment of the possibility of religious error, even their own. The avoidance of religious error could be sought only in revelation, which was addressed to all human beings equally. Acosta, by contrast, seeing that revelation had been delivered to the peoples of the world in a definite historical sequence, stressed that it had been addressed to Europe

[126] *Monumenta Peruana* I: 467 (1572 A.D.).
[127] See above, chap. v.1 at nn. 47–48.

first for reasons which could not be challenged. One could, of course, ask "why God called one people before another, and left that other in its blindness for so long." But like Augustine, whom he cited, Acosta thought that to insist on investigating or explaining such issues was to query divine justice and mercy.[128]

The issue was not new in the Indies, for Cieza and Las Casas, among others, had asked themselves why for so long God had "given the devil power" to control Indian souls.[129] But where Las Casas and Cieza had framed a theological question, Acosta thought in more historical terms. Taking it for granted that the culture and social order of Europe set the tone for the entire race, God had, as Acosta saw it, displayed his power so as to bring the world into contact with European norms. The universe could be seen to function intelligibly, so that nature and human history converged organically with divine revelation. The demons were present in the universe, but they did not determine the workings of its physical or human structure. It was sufficient to understand that divine dispensation had made of Peru the ugly daughter;[130] whether or not the demons had compromised the knowledge of god in the Andes was of merely secondary interest.

Acosta could therefore construe imagination in a more strictly Aristotelian sense, setting to one side the question of the influence of demons. This shift in emphasis in the exegesis of Aristotle was the work of Acosta's Jesuit contemporaries. Francisco Suarez and the authors of the Coimbra commentary on Aristotle's *De anima* noted that the discussion about the role of imagination in intellection was at the same time a discussion about the immortality of the soul. For Christian Aristotelians the intellectual part of the soul was immortal but depended on the mortal human body for the input of sense perceptions mediated by imagination. Given therefore that "the soul does not think without a phantasm," it would follow that the soul is mortal after all, because it cannot function without the support of its mortal components; this conclusion would seem to be inescapable unless it could be shown either that the imagination which supplied the phantasms was not part of the body, or that there was some aspect of intellect not dependent on imagination fed by sense perceptions. Suarez and the Coimbra commentators addressed this dilemma by arguing that the aspect of the imagination that forms the phantasms was, in effect, an aspect of intellect and was therefore immortal.[131] This aspect of

---

[128] Acosta, *De procuranda* 1.5.

[129] See above, chap. III.1 at n. 17, chap. V.2 at nn. 11ff.

[130] For the phrase "ugly daughter," see *Parecer de Yucay*, p. 462, and for the general conception of the Americas as less favored than Europe, Acosta, *HNM* 4.2, pp. 142f.

[131] Aristotle, *Commentarii Collegii Conimbricensis . . . in libros De Anima* ad 3.3; Suarez, *Tractatus tertius De anima*, pp. 56aff. I omit discussing here the new questions regarding the relation of soul and body, and the soul's manner of using sense perceptions which result from this way of constructing the soul.

imagination was thus not affected by material or demonic disturbances in the environment. It was from such work by his fellow Jesuits that Acosta learned to evaluate the imagination without reference to demons.

To consult the imagination and temper it with reason and experience, he believed, was to think speculatively. A case in point was the problem of how one could comprehend the shape of the universe. If one adopted a mental image of the universe as constructed "in the manner of a house that has its foundation on earth and its roof in the sky," one would arrive at an absurd image of "antipodes" in the Americas who walked with feet in the air among plants growing upside down. Such antipodes were ruled out by sense perception, by the actual experience of those who lived in the Americas. In order to match their sense perceptions with reason, i.e., in order to understand these sense perceptions, the mental image of the house must be replaced by another mental image, because "we cannot understand that the sky is spherical and the earth stands in the centre without imagining it."[132]

But imagination was not simply retrospective; it could do more than construct mental images for what experience had already made plain.

Acosta thus speculated on how human beings could have reached the New World before the compass was invented and before ocean-going ships were built. It was not by some adventurous voyage from Europe, whether planned or accidental, he suggested.[133] Rather, there must exist some as yet unknown land bridge that gave access to the Americas from Asia. There was, Acosta wrote, "no reason or experience to refute my imagination or opinion that the continents are joined and continuous in some part."[134] Acosta's theory of the land bridge was thus founded in speculative imagination, a form of imagination that was not fed by sense perception. Rather, this form of imagination functioned precisely in the absence of sense perception and tangible experience and thus differentiated human beings from animals.[135] Indians were therefore also endowed with it, some of them to a high degree. Like other Spaniards, Acosta could not withhold his admiration from the empire builder Pachacuti. According to an Inca legend, Pachacuti, before engaging in the crucial battle in which he defeated the Chanca confederacy, saw a vision in which the Creator Viracocha promised to send him aid; so it was that heaven-sent soldiers fought in the battle alongside Pachacuti's men, and later turned to stone. In this form, Acosta found the legend unacceptable but suggested instead that Pachacuti had invented both the vision and the heavenly help to enhance his prestige: "And the imagination and inven-

---

[132] Acosta, *HNM* 1.7.
[133] Acosta, *HNM* 1.10ff.; cf. D. C. Allen, *The Legend of Noah* (1949).
[134] Acosta, *HNM* 1.20, p. 56.
[135] See Aristotle, *Commentarii Collegii Conimbricensis in libros De Anima*, commenting on Aristotle, *On the Soul* 3.3; also q. 1, art. 5; and p. 500, *Tractatus de anima separata.*

tive power of this Inca were so remarkable that thanks to them he won the most outstanding victories."[136] Acosta's reinterpretation pleased Antonio Herrera, official historian of the Spanish Crown, who repeated it verbatim in his *General History of the Indies*, published in 1615.[137] Some forty years later, the Jesuit Bernabé Cobo reproduced this same reinterpretation yet again.[138]

What was excellent about Inca statecraft, as Acosta, Herrera, and Cobo saw it, was therefore a product of imagination. Like Suarez and the Coimbra commentators, Acosta still construed imagination within the Aristotelian and Thomist framework that was compatible with Catholic orthodoxy. But his contemporary, Juan Huarte, author of the influential, often reprinted, and several times translated *Enquiry into human talents* of 1575 did not.[139] Huarte used the familiar Aristotelian terminology of intellect and sense perception, memory and imagination, but was not interested in proving either that in a virtuous human being these faculties functioned in harmony with each other or that the soul was immortal. Rather, to be exceptionally gifted for a particular skill or branch of knowledge amounted to distemper much more than to harmony or balance. Persons of excellent memory, Huarte thought, were often stupid; similarly, a highly mobilized imagination was unlikely to go hand in hand with good reasoning and memory.[140] But persons of imaginative power could not only be fine artists and authors; they would also make skilled physicians, and above all, they could successfully lead armies and govern commonwealths.[141]

Huarte's book, although a considerable success among its readers, fell foul of the inquisitorial censor. For in setting aside the hierarchy of intellect, imagination, and sense perception that constituted the Aristotelian soul in its Thomist guise, Juan Huarte made of intellect not the immortal part of the soul but merely one of several aspects of human talent. In a passage that was deleted by the censor, he described the immortality of the intellect as being incapable of proof and suggested that it was an organic, corporeal faculty, just like the imagination.[142] Altogether, the book abounds in sallies against the established academic order, culminating in Huarte's assertion that the truly talented need no teaching,[143] and that ratiocination results from "the nature of living beings, without a teacher."[144] Just over a generation earlier, Pedro Ciruelo had maintained

[136] Acosta, *HNM* 6.21, p. 308.
[137] Herrera, *Historia General* 5.3.9.
[138] Cobo, *Historia* 12.10, p. 75a.
[139] Cf. Noreña, *Studies in Spanish Renaissance Thought* (1975), pp. 220ff.
[140] Huarte, *Examen de ingenios*, chap. 5, censored.
[141] Huarte, *Examen*, chap. 8.
[142] Huarte, *Examen*, chap. 6.
[143] Huarte, *Examen*, chap. 4, p. 107.
[144] Huarte, *Examen*, chap. 5, p. 100.

the exact opposite in order to buttress Catholic teaching.[145] Not surprisingly, therefore, Huarte's contrary opinion also fell victim to the censor.

Nonetheless, the tide was turning on the Thomist understanding of Aristotle's *De anima* with which we opened. Men had begun to read, with care and deliberation, not merely in the books of the learned but also in the book of nature. In Acosta's treatise on the New World, therefore, an account of what he called "the works of nature" preceded his account of human achievements, which he called the "works of free will." In the next generation, Acosta's fellow Jesuit Bernabé Cobo similarly wrote side by side about the natural history of America and the history of American humanity. This change of mood reached far beyond the preoccupations of the learned. One Jesuit missionary thus wrote from Peru how during an expedition to the Chunchos he had looked out from a mountaintop over the vast Amazonian jungle, dreaming that his eyes might sweep as far as the Caribbean Sea. His heart had opened up with a yearning to journey among those gentiles in their unknown land, and to undertake such a journey "seemed to me to be the most blessed destiny that could befall me on earth."[146] Another traveler of the end of the century was moved to note how the new stars of the southern hemisphere rose out of the ocean as the sails of his ship billowed before the tropical winds on the route southward from Panama to Lima.[147] In Acosta's eyes likewise, works of human art and skill paled when compared to the works of God: the ebb and flow of the sea, the flowering of the fields, the wild torrent of a river.[148] Yet Acosta was not as intrepid a turner of the pages of nature's book as his extensive travels and naturalist's observations might suggest. For in the course of his discussion of the imaginative faculty of the soul, Acosta was most careful to echo Aquinas in saying that intellect, the highest, most noble part of the soul, "participates in that supreme and original light" that is God, and is therefore immortal.[149] For this reason, when contemplating the beauty of nature, his mind turned precisely to that light, to the "Divine Wisdom that silently and without ever tiring nourishes and delights our reflection."[150]

In his work as a missionary, however, Acosta resigned himself to the reality, as he saw it, that this very "sublimity of our doctrine"[151] would remain inaccessible to the "short intelligence" of his Andean charges. The soul could be free of the demons, but the cost was high.

---

[145] See above, chap. I.2 at n. 35.
[146] *Monumenta Peruana* 2: 250.
[147] Ocaña, *Un viage fascinante*, p. 36.
[148] Acosta, *HNM* I.3, p. 22.
[149] Acosta, *HNM* I.7, p. 28; cf. Aquinas, *Summa* I, q. 12, a.5; 7; 11.
[150] Acosta, *HNM* I.3, p. 22.
[151] Acosta, *De procuranda* 2.9, p. 446a.

THE INCA AND HIS GODS:
THE TURN OF THE CENTURY IN
THE ANDES

ACOSTA'S OFTEN reprinted and several times translated *Natural and Moral History* marks a watershed in European perceptions of Andean and Inca religion. The theological dilemma that in different ways had troubled both Cieza and Las Casas so deeply, that demons and the devil should have gained power over so many souls, did not preoccupy the historians who wrote about Andean religious practices in the later sixteenth century. Assessing whether, and to what extent, human responsibility entered into the practice of idolatrous religion—which is where an evaluation of the role of imagination in cognition had figured in the discussion—was therefore not as urgent an issue as it had been earlier. In Europe also, theological interests shifted away from the demons. Acosta who viewed imagination as an aspect of speculative thought, not as a potential vehicle of demonic illusion, was therefore in step with the thinking of his contemporaries in Europe. The Andean ramifications of the problem did not interest him as deeply, since he was content to attribute the perceived religious errors of Andeans primarily to their cultural and intellectual limitations.

But historians of the Incas who were not as well informed as Acosta about leading theological and philosophical currents of thought in Europe continued following more old-fashioned approaches. Acosta's contemporary Miguel Cabello Valboa, who in 1586 completed his *Miscelánea antártica*, a history of the Incas set in a framework of world history, thus attributed the first idolatries to the pride of the tyrant Nimrod.[1] Once set on its course, idolatrous religion spread, thanks to the efforts of demons and the vagaries of human imagination.[2] For Cabello, the growth of royal power and the impact of demons on the imagination thus remained valid explanations of the origin of Andean idolatry. Other historians of the later sixteenth century, like Sarmiento de Gamboa, polymath, adventurer, and loyal supporter of the viceroy Toledo, and the Mercedarian

---

[1] For Cabello's date of writing, see Cabello Valboa, *Miscelánea antártica* 3.33, p. 483. On Nimrod, Cabello 1.4, p. 28; 1.13, p. 78.

[2] Cabello Valboa, *Miscelánea antártica* 1.13, p. 79; 3.12, p. 288; cf. 2.1, p. 84.

missionary Martín de Murúa, took demonic activity in the Andes for granted and saw no need to explain it.[3]

More specifically Andean issues, whether factual or interpretative, had also been resolved in what appeared to be a satisfactory manner. Cabello and Murúa[4] thus derived their information about the Inca religious calendar directly from Polo de Ondegardo's *Errores* as edited for the Third Council of Lima,[5] without investigating the many particulars that remained obscure. Similarly, the organizing principles that the Incas applied to the geographical distribution of their holy places attracted no further attention from these historians. Murúa merely repeated from one of his sources that there were some 340 of these holy places in Cuzco and vicinity[6] but said nothing as to how they were arranged. These historians lacked both the inquisitive acumen of Cieza or Polo de Ondegardo and Acosta's analytical sharpness. But their more leisurely and episodic narratives preserve, albeit somewhat disjointedly, many episodes from Inca oral tradition that had been overlooked or ignored earlier.

What was new in the writings of the later sixteenth century that deal with Inca and Andean religion came, for the most part, from Andeans. Cieza had claimed authority for his narrative because, inter alia, he consulted Andean and Inca informants. One of the first Andeans to make a historical and literary statement in his own right was the Inca Titu Cusi Yupanqui, who ruled in Vilcabamba after his father, Manco Inca, was killed. In 1570 Titu Cusi dictated an account of historical events in the Andes from the Spanish invasion up to his own day to a missionary friar who translated what the Inca had said into Spanish.[7] In Cuzco during the preceding year, members of Capac Ayllu, which was the kin group of Tupa Inca Yupanqui, made a notarized declaration of their forefathers' conquests.[8] Soon Andeans themselves took up the pen. Among them were two Andean nobles. Don Phelipe Guaman Poma de Ayala from Huamanga completed his long history of Peru from creation to his own day in 1613.[9] Given that the Incas had curtailed his family's power, Gua-

[3] Murúa, *Historia del origen* (1590), 3.9, p. 189; 3.15, p. 201.

[4] Cabello, *Miscelánea antártica* 3.19, pp. 350ff.; Murúa, *Historia del origen* (1590), 3.71, p. 346; Murúa, *Historia general* (1611), 2.38–39; cf. Duviols, "Les sources," *Annales de la Faculté des Lettres d'Aix* 36 (1962): 267–277; further on Murúa's plagiarisms, J. H. Rowe, "La mentira literaria," *Libro de homenaje a Aurelio Miro Quesada Sosa* 2: 753–761.

[5] Polo de Ondegardo, *Errores* 8–9.

[6] Murúa, *Historia del origen* (1590), 1.9, p. 67; cf. *Historia general* (1611), 1.31, p. 81, on Tumebamba. For new information on Murúa, see John Rowe's research on the mss. (forthcoming).

[7] For the date, see Titu Cusi, *Relación de la conquista*, p. 133; arrangements for recording the Inca's account, pp. 125–131; see F. Salomon, "Chronicles of the Impossible: Notes on Three Peruvian Indigenous Historians," in R. Adorno, ed. (1982), pp. 9–41 at pp. 12ff.; R. Chang-Rodriguez, "Writing as Resistance: Peruvian history and the *Relación* of Titu Cusi Yupanqui," in R. Adorno, ed. (1982), pp. 41–64.

[8] Rowe, "Probanza de los Incas," *Historica* 9 (1985): 193–245.

[9] Adorno in Guaman Poma, *Nueva Crónica*, p. xlii.

man Poma was critical of many aspects of Inca religion and government. Don Joan de Santacruz Pachacuti Yamqui Salcamaygua, from Canas and Canchis, halfway between Cuzco and Lake Titicaca, by contrast, thought favorably of the Incas; his account of Peru from Inca origins up to the Spaniards' entry into Cuzco was written at about the same time as Guaman Poma's history.[10] Guaman Poma and Pachacuti Yamqui both wrote as Christians. Indeed, Guaman Poma claimed that his father had welcomed the Spaniards at Cajamarca as Inca Guascar's emissary and had become a Christian at that time.[11] Pachacuti Yamqui, by contrast, viewed the time span that had elapsed between the advent of the Spaniards and his own day as longer in terms of generations than did Guaman Poma. Like Guaman Poma, Pachacuti Yamqui thought that his family had converted to Christianity when Pizarro and his Spaniards confronted Atahualpa in Cajamarca. And like Guaman Poma and Titu Cusi Yupanqui, he perceived in this encounter a potential for peaceful coexistence. But unlike Guaman Poma, he located the encounter four generations back into the past. For he thought that it was not his father but his great-great-grandfathers who had become Christians at Cajamarca and had abjured the "demons and devils, hapiñuñu, achacalla."[12]

Guaman Poma accounted for the time span between his own day and the capture and death of the Inca Atahualpa in chronological terms by narrating intervening events: the first contact with the Spaniards, the civil war among the invaders, the capture of Vilcabamba, and the death of Tupa Amaru (fig. 29), along with the doings of the viceroys, enumerated one by one, all find room in his pages. Titu Cusi also offered an account in chronological order that extended from 1532 to his time of writing in 1570. Pachacuti Yamqui, on the other hand, was less acculturated to European chronological narrative and therefore viewed the time span between the invasion and his own day differently. He concluded his story with a description of Manco Inca, Friar Valverde, and Francisco Pizarro ceremoniously and peacefully entering Coricancha, which he regarded as a temple not of the Inca Sun but of the Maker Viracocha.[13] In terms of his own family history, this event took place four generations earlier. In religious and conceptual terms, it took place in a different epoch. As a

[10] The manuscript's cover sheet, on which is written

son. 4 quadernos + [sign of the cross] Relación de antiguedades deste Reyno del Pirú es notable

is not part of the author's original manuscript. Also, the writing is in a different hand from the two hands of the main body of the text. Cf. Salomon (above, n. 7), pp. 16ff.; G. Harrison, *Signs, Songs and Memory in the Andes*, pp. 55ff.

[11] Guaman Poma, *Nueva Crónica*, pp. 375 [377f.], with 14f.

[12] Pachacuti Yamqui, *Relación*, fol. 1r, pp. 231f.

[13] Cf. Pachacuti Yamqui, *Relación*, fol. 9v, pp. 248f.

result, Pachacuti Yamqui avoided having to account for the dilemma that the bearers of the religion he himself agreed was the true one were also the destroyers of the Andean social order—a dilemma that occasioned Guaman Poma much inner conflict. In addition, Pachacuti Yamqui's estimation of Andean religion in his own day differed from Guaman Poma's. Guaman Poma had learned from extirpators and missionaries to view the Andean beliefs adhered to in his own time as superstitions. Similarly, he described Andean rituals practiced by his contemporaries as sorcery performed at the instigation of demons, who in the guise of Andean deities still wielded power over souls. Pachacuti Yamqui, by contrast, was not concerned with any of these issues. For in his view, non-Christian supernatural powers belonged to a past epoch that had been brought to an end by the *pachacuti,* the "turning about of the times" produced by the advent of the Spaniards.[14] The occurrence of the pachacuti did not mean that these powers had ceased to exist. They had, however, come to exist in a different realm, in *ucupacha,* described sometimes as the world inside the earth and sometimes as hell.[15] According to the Christian doctrine that Guaman Poma subscribed to, the huacas and demons would always exist, although they could and would be dispossessed and disempowered. In Pachacuti Yamqui's less acculturated universe, by contrast, the power of the dwellers in ucupacha was at all times real and would remain so, even if at most times this power was remote from the dwellers in this world, *cay pacha.*

Around 1608, some half-century after Domingo de Santo Tomás and other missionaries had first alphabetized Quechua, a Christian Andean compiled and recorded in Quechua some of the myths and historical traditions of Huarochiri. The work was undertaken at the instance, and for the use, of the extirpator of idolatries, Francisco de Ávila.[16] Like Guaman Poma and Pachacuti Yamqui, the anonymous author from Huarochiri wrote as a Christian. Here also, therefore, the Andean deities were categorized as demons. But this categorization was not imposed as consistently by the compiler from Huarochiri as it was by Guaman Poma and Pachacuti Yamqui. Rather, the ideas and values of Francisco de Ávila and other missionaries only figure in the myths from Huarochiri as one of several thematic strands.[17]

Whatever was the degree of Christian impingement on the ancient deities, Andeans viewed the characters and histories of these deities in an

---

[14] See Jan Szeminski, *Un kuraca* (1987), on hapiñuñu, huacas, and demons, pp. 47, 56ff., 79ff., 95, 100f.; MacCormack, "Pachacuti," *American Historical Review* 93 (1988): 960–1006; T. Bouysse-Cassagne with P. Bouysse, *Lluvias y cenizas* (1988).

[15] Gonzalez Holguin, *Vocabulario de la lengua general,* p. 350, cf. 556, s.v. infierno; Ricardo, *Vocabulario y phrasis,* p. 86; Guaman Poma, *Nueva Crónica,* p. 70; cf. Allen, *The Hold Life Has* (1988), pp. 62ff.

[16] On the date and on authorship, see G. Taylor in *Runa yndio* (1987), pp. 15ff.

[17] *Runa yndio,* e.g., 9.133; 20.246; 24.319; 25.347 (ed. Urioste).

infinitely more nuanced manner than did their Spanish contemporaries. Whether, therefore, the tension between Andean and Christian signification was articulated or whether it was left latent, it affected the vanquished much more deeply than it could possibly affect the invaders and conquerors. Nonetheless, there exists a significant thematic coherence and continuity between the Andean and Spanish authors of the first century after the invasion. Paradoxically, this coherence and continuity documents not so much whatever supremacy Christian thinking might have gained in the Andes but rather the limits that had so far been encountered by representatives of the invading and dominant culture to imposing their own preoccupations and interests on the vanquished. For however much Spaniards might be convinced of the superiority of their own religion, at the turn of the sixteenth to the seventeenth century the history of Peru as perceived in all our sources was still primarily the history of Tahuantinsuyo. Directly or indirectly, the themes of historical discourse were therefore being determined by Andeans.

An example of such a theme is the vision Pachacuti Inca saw before he fought the Chanca confederacy. Betanzos heard about this vision from Inca nobles in Cuzco, and twenty years later so did Sarmiento and Cristóbal de Molina. Pachacuti Yamqui, although his home was not in Cuzco, also knew of this vision, and related issues were raised by Guaman Poma and by the poet-mythographers of Huarochiri. Spaniards discussed prophetic words and events regarding the end of the Inca empire as frequently as did Andeans. Even Andean claims that Christianity in the Andes went back to before the Spanish invasion were taken up and elaborated by Spanish authors.[18] Both where they differ and where they converge, Andean and Spanish writers on matters of religion reveal how the people of the Andes appropriated and reformulated missionary Christianity. These convergences and differences also show how missionary Christianity conditioned what Andeans thought of their old, but now outlawed, gods and cults. At the same time it is clear that the gods continued to live in Andean hearts, their worship still remembered and often still practiced.

1. The Vision of Inca Pachacuti

Visionary experiences were common in the pre-Hispanic Andes. They were also common in Catholic Christianity, and the Spanish took a lively interest in the subject. On his long travels, Cieza accordingly recorded a

[18] Vigneras, "Saint Thomas," *Hispanic American Historical Review* 57 (1977): 82–90, the theme was in origin European; cf. Gavilán, *Historia . . . de Copacabana* 1.7–11; Calancha, *Corónica moralizada* 2.2, pp. 714ff. But the theme's development was not exclusively European. For Mexico, cf. J. Lafaye, *Quetzalcoatl and Guadalupe: The Formation of Mexican National Consciousness, 1531–1813* (Chicago, 1976).

variety of visions of the dead. In Huamachuco the Augustinian friars learned that people sought out their deities in mountain solitudes, and several Inca rulers had visions that Spaniards commented on. The Inca Viracocha, for instance, was given this name because the Maker Viracocha appeared to him one night in Urcos, where he was especially worshiped,[1] and the Inca Lloqui Yupanqui, when grieving over his childlessness, saw a vision of the Sun in the form of a man, promising him distinguished descendants.[2] Cieza was told that the sixth Inca, Inca Roca, was in pain after his ears had been pierced for initiation and retired to a mountain near Cuzco called Chaca, where he spent the night. At that time, there was a shortage of water in the city, so that Inca Roca prayed to Ticsi Viracocha, Guanacaure, the Sun, and his ancestors to show him a place where an irrigation canal could be constructed. While praying, the sound of a great thunderclap caused the Inca to lay his left ear to the ground. Blood flowed from the ear, and suddenly the Inca heard the noise of water running underground. "Taking stock of the miracle," *misterio*, the Inca ordered an irrigation canal to be built, which brought a beautiful stream of water to Cuzco.[3] Inca Roca's association with water continued after his death, because his mummy was carried in procession through fields and *punas* when rain was needed. On these occasions, the mummy's face was covered.[4] The covered face reveals a link between the dead Inca Roca and the thunder that he heard when he came upon the underground stream, because the statue in Coricancha representing Chuquilla Yllapa, who was the "lightning, thunder, and lightning bolt" had "the form of a person, although his face was not visible."[5] This link is confirmed by Cristóbal de Albornoz, the extirpator of the Taqui Onqoy, and by Guaman Poma, who both described Inca mummies as *yllapa*. Such terminology was meaningful in the Andes because lightning and the dead epitomized a cosmic imbalance tending either to generation or to destruction.[6] Inca Roca's *misterio* identified him with precisely the cosmic forces that he experienced.

At the end of the sixteenth century, Martín de Murúa learned of another meteorological encounter, this one experienced by Inca Pachacuti before he became ruler.[7] After it had rained for a month without inter-

---

[1] Sarmiento, *Historia Indica* 24, p. 228b; Molina, *Fábulas*, p. 84; above, chap. III.1 at n. 68.

[2] Sarmiento, *Historia Indica* 16, p. 221a.

[3] Cieza, *Segunda Parte* 35, pp. 105f.; cf. Rowe, "An Account," *Ñawpa Pacha* 17 (1979): 74, nos. 21–22.

[4] Cobo, *Historia* 12.9, p. 73b; Niles, *Callachaca* (1987), pp. 121–124.

[5] Molina, *Fábulas*, p. 67.

[6] Albornoz, *Instrucción*, p. 167; Guaman Poma, *Nueva Crónica*, p. 287 [289]; cf. Gonzalez Holguin, *Vocabulario de la lengua general*, p. 652, rayo; Domingo de Santo Tomás, *Lexicon*, p. 300, yllapa; Gade, "Lightning," *Anthropos* 78 (1983): 770–788; Earls and Silverblatt, "La realidad física," *Proceedings of the 42nd Congress of Americanists* 4 (1976): 314–323.

[7] Murúa, *Historia del origen* (1590), 2.1, pp. 105–106.

ruption, so that people "were afraid that the earth would turn, which they call *pachacuti*," the prince Inca Yupanqui saw a figure carrying a trumpet in one hand and a staff in the other at a place called Chetacaca or Sapi, above Cuzco. The prince begged this figure not to blow his trumpet, because people feared that if he did, the "earth would turn," and suggested that the two should become brothers. The figure refrained from blowing the trumpet and after some days became stone. The prince acquired the epithet Pachacuti, meaning "turning of the earth, or else, deprived and disinherited of his own." The site of the encounter, Sapi, meaning "root," was a huaca that consisted of "a very large quinua root which the sorcerers said was the root from which Cuzco issued and by means of which it was preserved. They made sacrifices to it for the preservation of the said city."[8]

The location and nature of the encounter imply that what was at stake was both the destiny of Cuzco, which could have been destroyed in a pachacuti, and also the destiny of Prince Pachacuti, whose name could mean that he was later to be "deprived and disinherited"—presumably by his father and hostile brother.[9] At times of crisis such as this, the Andean deities were wont to manifest themselves, as they still do today.[10]

Several other historians attributed to Inca Pachacuti a different, less threatening vision that fortified his resolve to fight the Chanca war. The simplest and earliest version of the story was recorded in 1551 by Juan de Betanzos.

Betanzos was told by his wife's Inca kinsfolk how Pachacuti, when preparing to defend Cuzco against the Chancas, retired by night to a deserted place where he prayed for help to the creator Viracocha Pacha Yachachic. He then fell asleep and, dreaming, saw Viracocha in the form of a man promising to send "people" to lend support in the coming battle and assuring him of victory. The same happened on subsequent nights, until, the night before the battle, Viracocha alerted the waking Pachacuti of the enemy's approach.[11] Later, Pachacuti built Coricancha in honor of "him whom he had seen before the battle,"[12] but because of the blinding radiance of his dream vision, he was now uncertain as to whether the personage he had seen was Viracocha or the divine Sun. Resolving that "it must have been the Sun," he ordered a statue to be made of pure gold representing the Sun in the form of a one-year-old boy. It was dressed in an exquisitely woven tunic and sandals and wore on its head an Inca head-

---

[8] Transl. Rowe, "An Account," *Ñawpa Pacha* 17 (1979), Ch-6:7; see further, Rostworowski, "Los Ayarmaca," *Revista del Museo Nacional* 36 (1969–1970): 61.

[9] Above, chap. III.3 at nn. 6–18.

[10] See Sallnow, *Pilgrims of the Andes* (1987), p. 88.

[11] Betanzos, *Suma* (1987), 1.8, p. 32ab.

[12] Betanzos, *Suma* (1987), 1.11, p. 50a.

band surmounted by a gold disk.[13] The statue was given a beautifully worked wooden seat covered in cloth of many-colored feathers and received offerings of food and chicha in a golden brazier.[14] Betanzos thus identified the statue of the personage whom Pachacuti saw in his vision with the principal cult image of the divine Sun in Coricancha. This was the image that the Spaniards finally captured in 1572 during the Vilcabamba campaign (cf. fig. 29).

The variants of the story about Pachacuti's vision that later historians recorded focus around four issues. Betanzos notes merely that Pachacuti saw a personage in a blinding radiance; but other accounts of the vision add that it involved a crystal or a mirror, that is, a shining object the meaning of which we will seek to discover. Second, according to Betanzos, the Creator promised to send "people" to help the Inca in battle, but in his descriptions of the fighting this historian mentioned no such people. Later accounts, however, do. Third, the ambiguity regarding the divine personage whom the Inca saw is borne out in subsequent accounts, and therefore (the fourth and last issue), Andean opinions diverged as to who was represented in the statue that Pachacuti later set up.

In 1572 Sarmiento, whose *Historia Indica* was based on information he collected from Incas still living in Cuzco, wrote that before the Chanca assault, Pachacuti was fasting and praying to Viracocha and the Sun at the spring Susurpuquio outside Cuzco, pondering how to resist the enemy.

> There appeared to him in the air a person like the Sun, consoling and fortifying him for the battle. And he showed the Inca a mirror in which he pointed out the provinces that he was to conquer, and that he was to be the greatest of his lineage. . . . The Inca took heart and receiving the mirror, which subsequently he always had with him in both peace and war, he returned to the people.[15]

During the battle, the Chancas saw "coming down from the mountains a great quantity of people whom [the Incas] say Viracocha, their Creator, had sent for their assistance, and [the Chancas] began to flee."[16] These are the "people" whom, according to Betanzos, the personage of the vision had mentioned, although Sarmiento himself said nothing about that personage's initial promise to send these people. Las Casas,[17] followed by Jerónimo Román, mentions both the vision, which was of the Sun, and the supernatural help in battle:[18] "Even now, when this valiant battle

---

[13] Betanzos, *Suma* (1987), 1.11, pp. 50a, 51b.

[14] Betanzos, *Suma* (1987), p. 52b.

[15] Sarmiento, *Historia Indica* 27, p. 232b.

[16] Sarmiento, *Historia Indica* 27, p. 233a.

[17] Las Casas, *Apologética Historia* 250, pp. 576f.

[18] Las Casas, *Apologética Historia* 250, pp. 576f.; Jerónimo Román, *República de las Indias Occidentales* (1575), 2.11, fol. 385b; 385a.

[against the Chancas] is discussed, the Indians say that all the stones that stood in that field changed into men to fight for them, and that the Sun did all this to fulfil his promise to the brave Inca Pachacuti."[19] Acosta encountered a similar tradition.[20] Here it was Viracocha, not the Sun, who appeared in the vision and promised to send Pachacuti "people who would succor him without being seen." Subsequently, Pachacuti explained to his warriors that these heaven-sent helpers had been changed into rocks, *pururaucas*. They accompanied later Incas into battle as talismans, and Pachacuti ordered them to be worshiped as huacas.[21] Bernabé Cobo's excerpts from a list of Cuzco shrines accordingly named two of them as recipients of cult.[22]

In the early seventeenth century, Don Juan de Santa Cruz Pachacuti Yamqui returned to the subject of the pururaucas, but according to him, rocks became men, not vice versa. Before the Chanca attack on Cuzco, the Inca Pachacuti saw at the holy place Callachaca[23] near Mantocalla, where Inca rulers celebrated part of the maize harvest,[24] a very beautiful white boy who in the name of the Creator promised him victory. During the battle, an old priest of Coricancha, hoping to impress the Chanca with a numerical superiority that the Incas did not in fact possess, lined up a row of rocks on a hillside. He equipped these rocks with shields, helmets, and cudgels so that from a distance they would look like soldiers. At a crucial juncture in the battle, these pururauca rocks rose up and with their ferocious fighting gained victory for Pachacuti.[25]

Andean myths abound in stories about metamorphoses from the non-human to the human and vice versa. When Viracocha created this present world, he called forth human beings from their *pacarinas*, places of origin, which were springs, lakes, and mountains, or he made human beings out of stone or clay, thus transforming inanimate nature into animate human nature by the power of his word.[26] The emergence of Inca Pachacuti's supernatural helpers from rocks occurred by an analogous act of creation. Transformations of animate beings into inanimate rocks were even more common in this Andean environment where the European distinction between nature on the one hand and man and culture on the other was absent.[27] Such a transformation might convert a moment experienced fleet-

[19] Román, fol. 385a; further, below, chap. VIII.2 at nn. 25ff.
[20] Acosta, *HNM* 6.21, cf. above, p. 278, on Acosta's rationalization of the story, for which, see further Cobo, *Historia* 12.10, p. 75; 13.8.
[21] Garcilaso criticized this version, *Comentarios reales* 4.21 with 5.17–18.
[22] Co-1:1; Cu-4:1; for other human shaped rocks, see Niles, *Callachaca* (1988), pp. 186ff.
[23] An-4:3.
[24] An-3:6; above, chap. IV.2 at n. 47.
[25] Santacruz Pachacuti Yamqui, *Relación*, pp. 270–271.
[26] Making human beings out of clay, see Molina, *Fábulas*, p. 51.
[27] Cf. above, chap. III.1 at nn. 69–75; Molina, *Fábulas*, p. 53.

ingly into permanence. A myth from Huarochiri thus told how the deity Chaupi Ñamca, after a long series of unsatisfactory lovers, at last found her perfect companion, and being metamorphosed into rock, she said, "With him I will stay for ever."[28] Stone huacas resembling "two persons embracing each other" were thought to bring good fortune in love and were still sought after in the later seventeenth century.[29] But the petrified embrace could be ambivalent. According to Pachacuti Yamqui, the huaca Guanacaure transformed into stone two of the original Incas, a brother and his sister. Manco Capac tried to liberate them from Guanacaure's deathly grip by beating the huaca with his royal rod *topayauri*. Guanacaure claimed that the two had sinned with each other and would not let them go, but at the same time he announced great good fortune to Manco Capac.[30] This story is a variant of one episode in the myth of the first Incas' migration from Pacaritambo to Cuzco. According to the more common account of this episode, one rendering of which was recorded by Cieza, Ayar Cache, one of the Incas to emerge from Pacaritambo, abided in a petrified state at Guanacaure and was revered there by succeeding generations of Incas.[31] Cabello was told another variant of the myth; it was that a sorcerer whose anger Ayar Cache had incurred turned him into rock.[32] The significance of petrification in Andean thought was thus ambiguous. On the one hand, it entailed the loss of conscious existence, and therefore Ayar Cache's brothers mourned for him. But on the other hand, Ayar Cache remained at Guanacaure as a protecting, auspicious presence for his brothers.[33] Or, as Pachacuti Yamqui told the story, Guanacaure, having petrified two of the Inca siblings, promised Manco Capac good fortune.

The pururaucas, soldiers metamorphosed into rock, whom the Incas carried into battle and whom the people of Cuzco worshiped,[34] were lasting reminders of Inca Pachacuti's vision and of the supernatural aid bestowed on him when, as his name implied, he "turned about the time"[35] by saving Cuzco from the Chanca invaders and inaugurating a new order of society. At the same time, the pururaucas were more than this, for they epitomized a process of creation and metamorphosis that was ubiquitous in the Andes and that Pachacuti, in the footsteps of the first founder, Manco Capac, once more made specific to the Incas. Manco Capac, ac-

[28] *Runa yndio* 10.146 (ed. Urioste); 10.24 (ed. Taylor); on Chaupi Ñamca's shrine, see Spalding, *Huarochiri*, pp. 98f.

[29] Montesinos, *Memorias antiguas* (1882), pp. 116f.

[30] Pachacuti Yamqui, *Relación*, p. 242 = fols. 7rf.; cf. Szeminski, *Un kuraca* (1987), p. 83.

[31] Cieza, *Segunda Parte* 7, p. 16; cf. above, chap. III.2 at nn. 16–17.

[32] Cabello Valboa, *Miscelánea antártica* 3.9, pp. 262f.

[33] Cabello, p. 263; Cieza, *Segunda Parte* 7, p. 17.

[34] Cobo, *Historia* 13.8.

[35] Betanzos, *Suma* (1987), 1.17, p. 83b.

cording to the myth of Inca origins, had led the Incas forth from their pacarina of Pacaritambo. Pachacuti reiterated this creating act by coming forth from Pacaritambo himself, while also validating this act by victorious warfare.[36] The Inca empire described as Tahuantinsuyo, "all of Peru, its four parts,"[37] extending in all directions from Cuzco, consisted of all the geographical space that was culturally meaningful. Similarly, Inca time extended from a creative act central to the present, such as Pachacuti's Chanca victory, back to all the other culturally meaningful creative acts, including Viracocha's original creation of the present dispensation. One strand in Pachacuti's vision thus makes clear how the Incas focused divine creative energy on their empire.

The mythographers of Huarochiri thought that when the Incas were in the lowlands, which were classified as *urin*, "low," they worshiped the Maker Pachacamac, but that in the sierra of the Andes, in lands that were *anan*, or "high," they worshiped primarily their Maker the Sun.[38] Just as urin and anan were necessary to each other, so a distant deity, be he Sun or Pachacamac, stood in tension or correlation with a counterpart who was close at hand. Spaniards were more prone to finding this contradictory than Andeans, who perceived different aspects in a given deity without finding ambiguity or conflict. Pachacuti Yamqui could conceptualize Viracocha and the Sun as coverging with each other,[39] while the Spaniard Betanzos had found it confusing to be told at one time that the Maker was Viracocha and at another that he was the Sun.[40] At the same time, Inca concepts of deity were not static but changed with the expansion of the empire.[41] Possibly, therefore, it is such political and social changes as much as converging aspects of deity that speak in the accounts of Pachacuti's vision by Betanzos and other Spaniards.

As Betanzos understood it, Pachacuti saw Viracocha, but later, the dazzling luminosity of his vision led the Inca to suppose he had seen the divine Sun, whose statue he therefore placed in Coricancha. Sarmiento's Inca informants thought that Pachacuti had seen "a person like the Sun," but that the helpers in battle were sent by Viracocha. Here also, ambiguity prevails, for Pachacuti's vision did not harmonize with the cultic arrangements that, according to these same informants, he later enacted. The Inca caused two golden images to be made:

[36] Sarmiento, *Historia Indica* 30, p. 236a.
[37] Gonzalez Holguin, *Vocabulario de la lengua general*, p. 336.
[38] *Runa yndio* 22.2–6 (ed. Taylor); 276 (ed. Urioste).
[39] Pachacuti Yamqui, *Relación*, pp. 257f.; fol. 14r; Szeminski, *Un kuraca* (1987), pp. 27, 64–76.
[40] Betanzos, *Suma* 1.11, p. 49b (1987); p. 31a (1968).
[41] Rowe, "Creator worship," in *Essays in Honor of Paul Radin* (1960), pp. 408–429; MacCormack, "From the Sun of the Incas ," *Representations* 8 (1984): 30–60.

One of these he called Viracocha Pachayachachic. This was to represent the Creator the Indians speak of, and the Inca placed this image at the right hand of the Sun. The other idol he called Chuquiylla, which was to represent the lightning, and he placed it at the left hand of the image of the Sun. This idol was much revered by everyone. Pachacuti took it as his *guaoqui*[42] because he said that they had met and talked in a desert place, and that [Chuquiylla] had given him a serpent with two heads, saying that while it was in his possession, no ill would befall him.[43]

Every Inca had a *guaoqui*, a divine double, or, as Sarmiento explained it, an "idol or demon whom each Inca elected for his companion to give him oracles and responses."[44] Manco Capac's guaoqui was the bird called Inti,[45] "whom everyone venerated and feared as something sacred, or, as others say, enchanted, and they thought that this bird made Manco Capac lord, so that people obeyed him."[46] This bird was bequeathed from one ruling Inca to the next as an inalienable inheritance and token of sovereignty of fearsome sacrality. The first to venture to look upon the bird Inti face to face was the audacious Inca Mayta Capac, who spoke with it as with an oracle and hence both learned the future and became wise.[47]

Like the Inca, so his guaoqui owned herds, lands, and male and female retainers to serve its cult. When the Inca died, this cult continued to be addressed to the guaoqui, alongside the cult to the Inca's mummy.[48]

Pachacuti's guaoqui, the lightning under the name Chuquiylla, "radiance of gold,"[49] articulated this Inca's central position in the cosmic order, both as expressed in nature and as replicated in politics and ritual. This position was not dissimilar from that of Inca Roca's mummy, the illapa on the ground that called forth the illapa in the sky. Lightning and the accompanying atmospheric phenomena, rain, hail, storms, whirlwinds, and the rainbow, represented cosmic forces of meteorological imbalance and war.[50] It was sometimes pictured as the serpent *amaru*, so that Chu-

[42] Quechua, "brother."

[43] Sarmiento, *Historia Indica* 31, p. 237a; cf. 47, p. 253b, the guaoqui is called Indi Illapa and is a gold statue.

[44] Sarmiento, *Historia Indica* 14, p. 220a; cf. Cobo, *Historia* 13.9.

[45] Quechua, "Sun."

[46] Sarmiento, *Historia Indica* 12, 214b; for the other Inca guaoquis see Sarmiento, 15, pp. 220bf.; 16, 221b; 23, 228b; 25, 230b; 54, 258bf.; 62, 265a. Perhaps Murúa, *Historia del origen* (1590), 1.8, p. 64, same wording as Murúa, *Historia general* (1611), 1.13, p. 39, also refers to guaoquis: Mandó [Inca Roca] levantar ciertas piedras y estatuas en su nombre para que en vida y en muerte se les hiciesse la misma veneración y onra que a los yngas reyes. See also Cobo, *Historia* 12.11, p. 77b.

[47] Sarmiento, *Historia Indica* 12, 214b; 17, 222b.

[48] Cobo, *Historia* 13.10, p. 164a.

[49] Cobo, *Historia* 13.7, p. 160b.

[50] Earls and Silverblatt, "La realidad fisica ," *Proceedings of the 42nd Congress of Americanists*

quiylla's gift to Pachacuti of a two-headed serpent was the gift of his own representation, highly appropriate at a time of impending war. In choosing Chuquiylla as his guaoqui, Pachacuti represented his own role as warrior, and later as Inca and reformer, in terms of cosmic principle. According to the oral tradition recorded by Sarmiento, Pachacuti's Chuquiylla was worshiped along with the Sun and the Creator in Coricancha. But another tradition had it that Pachacuti erected a separate shrine for Chuquiyllapa in Cuzco's Totocache district; it was in this shrine that Polo de Ondegardo found Pachacuti's mummy.[51]

Those historians of the Incas who supposed that Pachacuti's Chuquiylla was worshiped in Coricancha along with the Creator and the Sun sought to harmonize the cult of this Inca's guaoqui with his interest in the Creator Viracocha. This theme is also reflected in those accounts of Pachacuti's vision that state that he saw, not Chuquiylla, nor yet the Sun, but the Maker. The earliest of these accounts is that of Betanzos, although Betanzos in the end settled for the view that Pachacuti had seen the Sun. A little later, Polo de Ondegardo reiterated that Pachacuti had seen Viracocha, who explained to the Inca "that he was the universal creator and that because he had created the sun and everything else, it was right that he should receive greater veneration" than other deities.[52] This didactic and theological dimension of the vision also appears in Acosta's version of it, where Viracocha promises to send invisible helpers in battle, having first complained to the Inca that although he had created the universe, Andeans worshiped the Sun, Thunder, and Earth much more devoutly than himself.[53] After his victory, therefore, Pachacuti raised the statue of the Creator Viracocha above those of the Sun and the Thunder that flanked it.[54]

Here, as in Las Casas' earlier account of Pachacuti's religious reforms,[55] theology and cult go hand in hand in complete coherence and harmony, as Christian example, which was never far from our historians' minds, suggested they should. However, because Inca religion changed contin-

---

4 (1976): 314–323 passim; Albornoz, *Instrucción*, p. 166, a "guaca que llaman acapana que era aplicada a las guerras . . . a quien piden favor. Esto es unos rayos que haze el cielo." Cf. Gonzalez Holguin, *Vocabulario de la lengua general*, p. 12, acapana, celajes o arboles de la mañana.

[51] Cobo, *Historia* 13.7, p. 160b; Rowe, "An Account," *Ñawpa Pacha* 17 (1979), Ch-2:3; Acosta *HNM* 6.21, p. 308, with Ch-1:2, the mallqui had been brought there from Pachacuti's palace at Patallacta, where he had died.

[52] Polo de Ondegardo, *Informe . . . al licenciado Briviesca de Muñatones*, p. 153.

[53] Acosta, *HNM* 6.21, p. 307; p. 308, Pachacuti assigned no sacrifices to the Creator, because, having made everything, he needs nothing. The reasoning bears a distant resemblance to the Christian idea that God does not require sacrifices and offerings but a willing heart (Hebrews 10:5–11:16).

[54] Acosta, *HNM* 6.21, p. 308.

[55] See above, chap. v.1 at nn. 20–26.

uously in the light of current political and cultural aspirations, theology was at times out of step with cult. This reality ran counter to Catholic Christian principles. The divergent accounts of Pachacuti's vision, filtered though they are through the perceptions of the second generation of Spanish historians writing in the Andes, afford a glimpse of one particular phase of Inca theology and cult in the making.

A most revealing account of Pachacuti's vision, by Cristóbal de Molina, adds yet another dimension to the spectrum of changes in Inca religion. Furthermore, this account allows us to perceive a link between Pachacuti's vision and the vision and dream of a Christian Andean lord in the late sixteenth century. As a result, we will understand the role of the mirror or crystal that according to some accounts figured in Pachacuti's vision.

Molina did not explicitly link the occasion of Pachacuti's vision to the Chanca war, but like Sarmiento, he located the vision at the spring Susurpuquio. Before he became Inca, Pachacuti passed this spring

> and saw falling into the spring a sheet of crystal, inside which he saw the figure of an Indian, as follows: On his head, from the back of the neck, came three radiant rays, all like sun rays, and from where the arms meet [the torso], some twirling serpents. On his head was an Inca headband; the ears were pierced, and in them were Inca earspools; and his attire was that of an Inca. From between his legs sprung the head of a lion, and on his shoulders was another lion, whose legs seemed to embrace the two shoulders. This shape and appearance caused Pachacuti to flee, but the shape of the statue called him by his name from inside the spring and said, "Do not be afraid. I am your father the Sun and know that you will conquer many nations. Take very great care to worship me and remember me in your sacrifices."[56]

When he became Inca, Pachacuti had a statue made "exactly like the one he had seen in the mirror"[57] and ordered that throughout the empire the Sun be worshiped with the Creator. This is the only extant account of such a statue in Inca Cuzco, but aspects of the statue's iconography appear in pre-Inca depictions of supernatural beings (figs. 35–36).[58] The figure

[56] Molina, *Fábulas*, p. 60.

[57] Molina, *Fábulas*, p. 61; I translate Spanish *espejo* as "mirror": Molina is not consistent in his account of the vision, since what Pachacuti saw in the first instance was a sheet of crystal.

[58] I am most grateful to John Hyslop and Vuca Roussakis at the American Museum of Natural History in New York for their most generous help in finding the items depicted in figs. 35 and 36. The iconography shown in fig. 35 is very widespread, an unusual example being the woven glove of the middle horizon period at the Brooklyn Museum, New York, accession number 58.204. See also, A. Cook, "The Middle Horizon Ceramic Offerings

of the vision who was portrayed in this statue was clearly not identical with the figure whom, according to Betanzos, Pachacuti had ordered to be portrayed as the Sun in the guise of a very young boy. Furthermore, the theological import of Pachacuti's vision as described by Molina was at loggerheads with this Inca's own arguments against the divinity of the Sun, which Molina also recorded.[59]

On the other hand, Pachacuti's vision shares some elements with visions experienced by other Andeans. The first missionaries to work at Huamachuco described a genre of vision that could lead someone to become a priest. The person would see in the water of a lake

> a small gourd very beautifully worked and [go] to catch it, but by the cunning of the devil the little gourd flees and sinks below the water; and at other times it swims playfully above the water, and the person is so entranced by this as to become dazzled, and then the devil takes him to the huaca and teaches him [the office of priest].[60]

Although the friar who wrote this account in 1560 apparently did not understand the nature of the object that danced on the water, he did capture its entrancing, dazzling quality. Some fifty years later, a literate Andean recorded in Quechua a cycle of myths and stories from Huarochiri. One of these stories describes a vision and a dream experienced by the writer's contemporary, the Christian curaca Don Cristóbal Chuqui Qasa from the village of Chiqa. One night Don Cristóbal went to the shrine of the huaca Llocllay Huancupa, a son of Pachacamac, to meet his lover.[61] In the dark, he saw how this devil, *supay*,

> made appear before his eyes a blinding light resembling the reflection in a silver plate which touched by sun rays, blinds human eyes. Seeing it, he almost fell to the ground. Reciting Our Father and Ave Maria he fled to the little house where the woman was living. Halfway there, [the devil] dazzled him three times, and when he reached the place another three times, and [then] . . . another three times.[62]

Although for a long time the devil Llocllay Huancupa would not go away, Don Cristóbal recited all the prayers and all of the catechism he knew and

from Conchopata," *Ñawpa Pacha* 22–23 (1984–1985): 49–90. For the lion on the visionary figure's shoulder, cf. *Runa Yndio* 5, 87–90 (ed. Taylor): the primeval hero Huatiacuri defeats his rival by dancing with a red puma. Regarding the vision of Pachacuti, see also Engl, "La aparición del Sol," *Revista Española de Antropología Americana* 5 (1970): 123–134.

[59] Molina, *Fábulas*, p. 59.

[60] Religiosos Agustinos, *Relación*, pp. 19–20. The term I translate as "dazzled" is *tonto*.

[61] Possibly what was at issue was not merely meeting his lover but also worship. See Tello, "Idolatrías de los Indios Wankas," *Inca* 1, no. 3 (1923): 654, for an example of cultic action combined with "ofensas de Dios sensuales." Further, Pachacuti Yamqui, *Relación*, p. 263.

[62] *Runa yndio* 20.250–252 (ed. Urioste); 20.45 (ed. Taylor, whose translation I follow).

35

35–36. Inca Pachacuti's vision of his father the Sun as a composite being with human and animal aspects recalls the appearance of earlier supernatural beings and their attributes.

35. Ceremonial vessel of the Tiahuanaco period depicting the Creator, his head circled by birds, felines, trophy heads, and maize stalks. The head of the Sun in Pachacuti's vision was circled by rays, while a lion held its paws round his shoulders. American Museum of Natural History, New York. Neg. no. 313605 (Photo Irving Datcher and H. S. Rice) courtesy Department of Library Services, American Museum of Natural History.

36. Tunic from Viru or Chicama Valley depicting beings with head and ear ornaments, and a human or feline creature in their bellies. Compare the headband and earspools, and the lion between the legs of the figure seen by Inca Pachacuti. American Museum of Natural History, New York. Neg. no. 329755 (Photo Rota) courtesy Department of Library Services, American Museum of Natural History.

36

was at last able to overcome him. But the next day, the huaca returned in
a dream vision.[63] He called Don Cristóbal most insistently and when he
came dazzled him "as he had done before, with the silver."[64] In Don Cristóbal's dream, the huaca was being fed by his priest, who addressed him
as Creator of man, but the huaca itself could not reply. All that emerged
from the huaca's throat was an unarticulated sound and the noise of him
munching the coca that he had been given in sacrifice. Meanwhile Don

[63] See Taylor, ed., *Runa yndio*, p. 315, n. 6.
[64] *Runa yndio* 20.15 (ed. Taylor) 20.263 (ed. Urioste).

Cristóbal noticed two bands of painted figures surrounding the room. On one band, there was "a very black little devil with eyes like silver coins who held in his hand a staff. . . . Above, there was the head of a llama. Above again the little devil and above the head of the llama."[65] When the huaca had finished eating, Don Cristóbal exploited his muteness by challenging him to declare whether he or Jesus Christ was god, and then something was thrown. Shortly, Don Cristóbal woke up.[66]

Elements that Don Cristóbal's vision has in common with the vision of Pachacuti in its several renderings make it possible to investigate what these visions communicated to their visionaries beyond what can be learned from each incident in isolation.

Don Cristóbal was overwhelmed by the blinding, dazzling radiance in the "silver reflecting the light of the sun" that appeared before his eyes. Similarly, when Pachacuti thought back to his vision, according to Betanzos, what impressed him most was its radiant, dazzling quality, thanks to which he could not discern the identity of the personage who had appeared to him. According to one of the two accounts of Pachacuti's vision recorded by Sarmiento, the Inca standing by the spring Susurpuquio saw lightning, while according to Molina, Pachacuti saw a sheet of crystal falling into the spring Susurpuquio—the crystal, one might say, struck the spring like lightning. The image of lightning in these visions explains their blinding quality.[67] For the Inca, lightning, evocative of upheaval, change, and war, pictured what he was to expect in the immediate future.

But there was a further, and quite different, component in the vision, which stood at the beginning of Pachacuti's career as ruler of Cuzco and the empire. According to Molina, he saw the Sun in a sheet of crystal which fell into the spring Susurpuquio,[68] while according to Sarmiento, the Sun at Susurpuquio showed him in a mirror the lands he was to conquer.[69] Pachacuti Yamqui recounted that when Inca Roca was born, he was anointed in water brought from Lake Titicaca. This water was called "water forming drops of crystal to make kings."[70] When according to Titu Cusi his father Manco became Inca, he was carried in a "litter of gold

---

[65] *Runa yndio* 21.23 (ed. and transl. Taylor); 21.266 (ed. Urioste).

[66] *Runa yndio* 21.270 (ed. Urioste); 21.31 (ed. Taylor); cf. Pachacuti Yamqui, *Relación*, pp. 259f., a huaca is reviled by the Inca Capac Yupanqui.

[67] The quality of radiance, being an important aspect of Andean perceptions of divinity, was also exemplified in the cult image of Punchao in Coricancha, described by the viceroy Toledo as having "una manera de patenas de oro a la redonda para que dandoles el sol relumbrasen de manera que nunca pudiesen ver el ydolo sino el resplandor," Letter dated 20 March 1572, in *Gobernantes del Peru. Cartas y Papeles*, ed. R. Levillier, vol. 4 (Madrid, 1924), p. 345, and similarly p. 502.

[68] Molina, *Fábulas*, p. 60.

[69] Sarmiento, *Historia Indica* 27, p. 232b.

[70] Pachacuti Yamqui, *Relación*, p. 262 = fol. 15r; cf. Szeminski, *Un kuraca* (1987), p. 56.

and crystal."[71] Guaman Poma also described the Inca's litter as adorned with crystal, *quispi*.[72] In short, *quispi* crystal, whatever exactly the term means, was an attribute of sovereignty. Pachacuti's vision of it marked the divinely sanctioned beginning of his reign.

Concurrently, Inca interpretation associated Pachacuti's vision with the Sun, the divine parent of Inca rulers. According to Molina, the apparition described himself as "your father the Sun," and according to Betanzos, Pachacuti concluded that his radiant vision had shown him the divine Sun. The solar imagery was still present in Don Cristóbal's vision of the "silver reflecting the light of the sun." However, Don Cristóbal, being a Christian, interpreted his vision as demonic. Unlike Pachacuti, Don Cristóbal was not expecting to receive any illumination or understanding from his vision. Rather, having once been alerted in his waking vision to the continued existence of the huaca Llocllay Huancupa, Don Cristóbal fought against the huaca when it reappeared in a dream vision and considered himself to have emerged victorious in this combat against a demon.

The imagery of Don Cristóbal's vision, however, was Andean, not Hispanic or Christian. Like the visionaries of Huamachuco who were being called to the priesthood by a local deity, and like the Inca Pachacuti, so Don Cristóbal perceived the divine presence in terms of a radiance. Even the imagery of the painted frieze in the room where the huaca Llocllay Huancupa was eating is Andean, albeit demonized by the superimposition of Christian imagery of the devil. The "very black little devil with eyes like silver coins" and holding a staff in his hand is thus matched on textiles by staff-bearing human and animal figures with brightly colored eyes, whose headdresses are suggestive of demonic headgear in Christian iconography (fig. 37),[73] and the painted frieze in two bands in

[71] Titu Cusi Yupanqui, *Relación*, p. 28, fol. 10v.

[72] Guaman Poma, *Nueva Crónica*, p. 334 [336]; Gonzalez Holguin, *Vocabulario de la lengua general*, p. 465, s.v. cristal; Ricardo, *Vocabulario y phrasis*, p. 129, s.v. cristal; Guaman Poma, *Nueva Crónica*, p. 332 [334] writes "quispi perlas." Sarmiento's *espejo*, "mirror," is an anachronism; see Garcilaso, *Royal Commentaries* 1.22, p. 35a, before the invasion, Andeans knew no mirrors. But a mirror's shining surface evokes the crystalline quality of whatever the Inca saw. Cf. above, n. 57.

[73] For the item shown in fig. 37, see Linda S. Ferber and others, *The Collector's Eye: The Ernest Erickson Collections at the Brooklyn Museum* (New York, 1987), p. 26; the Metropolitan Museum of Art has another piece of the same cloth, which is a skirt, acquisition number 33.149.43. For further textile images evocative of Don Cristóbal's vision, see A. Jiménez Borja, *Paracas. Colección arte y tesoros del Perú*, ed. J.-A. de Lavallé and W. Lang (Lima, 1983), e.g., pp. 42, 56, 84–85, 114–115; cf. late intermediate textiles and ceramics from Pachacamac: M. Uhle, *Pachacamac: Report of the William Pepper, M.D., Ll.D., Peruvian Expedition of 1896* (Philadelphia, 1903), pp. 26, 30, plates 5.2; 6.1. An impressively demonic figure carrying staff and trophy head appears on a coastal Tiahuanaco textile (Metropolitan Museum of Art, New York, inventory 28.64.15), published by P. A. Means, "A Group of Ancient Peruvian Fabrics," *Bulletin of the Needle and Bobbin Club* 2, no. 1 (1927), which I was not able

37. The image in the mind of Don Cristóbal "of a very black little devil with eyes like silver coins" and holding a staff originated not so much in the Christian iconography of his own day but in residual memories of earlier depictions such as this round-eyed creature embroidered on a skirt from Paracas, its face ringed by trophy heads. Brooklyn Museum, New York, Ernest Erickson Collections.

which this little devil appeared recalls not only bands of figures shown on textiles (see fig. 36) but also the painted animal friezes that adorned the external face of the pyramid of Pachacamac.[74] Pachacamac was Llocllay Huancupa's father; traits in the decoration of Llocllay Huancupa's shrine as seen or imagined by Don Cristóbal that are reminiscent of the pyramid of Pachacamac may thus serve as a pointer to qualities the two deities shared.

A salient characteristic of huacas was that they spoke. Llocllay Huancupa first made himself known to the people of Chiqa by speaking to them, explaining his identity and his purpose in coming.[75] The Incas commonly held converse with the Sun, and whoever the deity was that appeared to Pachacuti, he spoke. But once Llucllay Huancupa had revealed himself in Don Cristóbal's eyes as a demon, *supay*,[76] he could no longer speak. In this instance, the presence of Jesus Christ in Don Cristóbal's mind had ruptured the bond of verbal and ritual converse whereby he had engaged in relationships of reciprocity with the Andean deities. This relationship of reciprocity was ruptured in different terms when in 1572 Tupa Amaru declared from the scaffold that it was not the divine Sun who had spoken to him and his ancestors in the cult image, but that the speaker had all along been only the Inca himself.

2. PROPHECY AND THE END OF TAHUANTINSUYO

To begin converse with the deities entailed a process of search leading up to recognition. Like other Andean visions or intimate experiences of divinity, so the vision of Inca Pachacuti followed this course. Faced by the threat of his city's destruction by the Chanca enemy, the Inca retired to a solitude in search of enlightenment. The deity appeared, identified himself, and promised succor. In due course, the Virgin Mary and Christian saints revealed themselves to Andean devotees in accord with this pattern. The Virgin of Copacabana, who was known especially to favor Andeans,[1] was a case in point. From the later sixteenth century onward, devotees hoping for a miracle would seek out the Virgin in her shrine, would behold her revealed whether in a dream, or through a Mass, or by contemplating her image, and would then be cured.[2] But in colonial Chris-

---

to consult. Thanks to Susan Bergh at the Brooklyn Museum and to Christine Giuntini at the Metropolitan Museum of Art for their help with these textiles.

[74] See Duccio Bonavia, *Mural Painting in Ancient Peru*, transl. P. Lyon (Indiana, 1985), pp. 135–137.

[75] *Runa yndio* 20.238 (ed. Urioste); 20.10 (ed. Taylor).

[76] *Runa yndio* 21.270 (ed. Urioste); 21.20 (ed. Taylor).

[1] Oré, *Symbolo*, chap. 8.

[2] Ramos Gavilán, *Historia . . . de Copacabana* (Lima, 1988), 2.22, p. 316; similarly 2.16, pp. 280, 282; 18, p. 293; 25, pp. 337f.; 26, p. 343, etc.

tianity, the exercise of sacred and priestly authority by Spaniards obscured or hindered direct, sustained contact between Christian deity and Andean devotee. By contrast, such contact stood at the center of non-Christian religious experience in the Andes.

One of the most frequently repeated Andean prayer formulas consisted of a series of questions that worshipers addressed to the deity. "Where are you? Who are you?" worshipers asked, in order to discover in the exchange of question, answer, and free-floating statement a deity's identity and powers.[3] The huaca Lloqllay Huancupa, who was a stone, was discovered by a woman working in her field and was helped to declare himself through the assistance of Cataqillay, a huaca sent by the Inca. "Who are you? What is your name? What have you come for?" Cataquillay asked, thereby introducing Lloqllay Huancupa to his prospective worshipers.[4] Santacruz Yamqui recorded Manco Capac's prayer for his son and successor, Sinchi Roca; it invoked Viracocha, the Founder and Creator, and at the same time addressed to him the familiar inquiry after his whereabouts.[5] Similarly, the formula for summoning huacas in the name of the Maker that Santacruz Yamqui attributed to the Incas inquires, "Who are you? Which one [of the beings the Maker has created] are you? What do you say? Speak, say it!"[6]

Because conversing with deities was so important in Andean religion, a variety of experts specialized in such converse and in benefiting their society with the knowledge thus obtained. The first Spanish historians of the Incas who saw some of the divinatory shrines still in operation did not investigate how and by whom the divine responses, instructions, and prophecies were delivered because they accepted as sufficient explanation the theory that the devil spoke in these shrines or that the transaction was fraudulent. Although such explanations continued to be considered valid, the extirpation of divinatory practices was a high priority among missionaries,[7] with the result that these practices were examined more closely in the later sixteenth century. Molina, Cabello, Murúa and Guaman Poma,[8] among others, accordingly described divinatory rituals and recorded some of the different titles and activities of the priests involved in them.

[3] See prayers in Guaman Poma, Nueva Crónica, pp. 50, 54.
[4] Runa yndio 20.4ff. (ed. Taylor); 20.236ff. (ed. Urioste).
[5] Pachacuti Yamqui, Relación, p. 284 = fol. 9v; Szeminski, Un kuraca (1987), pp. 28ff.
[6] See Szeminski, Un kuraca (1987), p. 36; Pachacuti Yamqui, Relación, p. 260 = fol. 15r.
[7] Cf. Matienzo, Gobierno 1.23, p. 80.
[8] Molina, Fábulas, pp. 62f., with notes by Urbano and Duviols ad loc.; cf. p. 72; Cabello, Miscelánea antártica 3.12, p. 287; Murúa, Historia general (1611), 2: 32–34; Guaman Poma, Nueva Crónica, pp. 248f. [250f.], 261f. [263f.], 277 [279], 279ff. [281ff.]; see also Relación Anónima, pp. 164ff.

Molina and Cabello[9] mention among diviners the *calparicu*, "those who see the fortune and outcome of things they are asked about." *Callpa* means "faculty" or "power," and could refer to the three faculties of the Aristotelian soul, the sense perceptions, inner senses, and intellect.[10] But the term also had a specifically Andean meaning. A ritual hunt in Huarochiri during November to obtain rain was equivalent to walking in "the footsteps of the deity Tutay Quiri, walking his *callpa*."[11] Callpa was also the divinatory ritual carried out before an Inca began a war[12] and before an Inca's inauguration, to ascertain whether his would be an auspicious reign. When Guayna Capac lay dying, Cuxi Topa Yupanqui, chief priest of the Sun, performed the callpa by opening a llama to read from its lungs the destiny of the two possible candidates for the succession, Ninan Cuyoche and Guascar, whom Guayna Capac had named. But the verdict was negative for both of them[13] and was confirmed by the outcome.

Virapirco was a priest who divined by watching the smoke rising from the fat (*vira*) of animal sacrifice.[14] Guaman Poma depicted two similar rituals, both performed by a priest bearing the title *vallaviza*. In July, when fields were assigned to those who were to cultivate them for the coming year, vallaviza and the ruling Inca observed the smoke rising from a sacrificial fire kindled to sustain the Sun, now growing again after the winter solstice (figs. 38–39).[15] A more explicitly divinatory sacrifice performed by vallaviza involved boiling fat and sanco,[16] feathers, coca, silver, gold, and foodstuffs in a new cauldron (fig. 28).[17] Faithful to his Christian education, Guaman Poma thought that "inside the cauldron speak the demons," and that other oracles were delivered by "ghosts and evil spirits," "phantasms," and the dead. Cabello similarly mentioned a priest designated as *ayatapuc*, "who inquires from the dead . . . in whom the devil disguises himself."[18] A priest named *cauiacoc*, "one who hiccups," prophesied while intoxicated, that is, in a condition of submersion "in the state of his imagination," when sense perceptions, as Cabello saw

[9] Molina, *Fábulas*, p. 62; Cabello, *Miscelánea antártica* 3.12, p. 289; for a discussion of the varieties of Inca priests and diviners, see M. Rostworowski, *Historia del Tahuantinsuyu*, pp. 204–208.

[10] Gonzalez Holguin, *Vocabulario de la lengua general*, p. 45.

[11] *Runa yndio* 11.20 (ed. Taylor); 11.158, 159 (ed. Urioste). See also Taylor's introduction to his edition (1987), pp. 25f.

[12] Sarmiento, *Historia Indica* 40, p. 245b; 58, p. 260a.

[13] Sarmiento, *Historia Indica* 62, p. 264b.

[14] Cabello, *Miscelánea antártica*, p. 289; Molina, *Fábulas*, p. 63, writes "viropiricoc," described by Duviols and Urbano as "vocablo incorrecto o desconocido." Cf. Religiosos Agustinos, *Relación*, p. 15, smoke from coca rises to the Creator Ataguju.

[15] Guaman Poma, *Nueva Crónica*, p. 248 [250].

[16] See above, chap. IV.3 at nn. 103ff.

[17] Guaman Poma, *Nueva Crónica*, p. 277 [279].

[18] Cabello, *Miscelánea antártica*, p. 287.

38. Smoke rises from a sacrificial fire, watched over by the Inca with an aged priest, and sustains the Sun. Guaman Poma, *Nueva Crónica*, p. 248, Royal Library, Copenhagen. Photo from facsimile, Paris 1936.

39. The prayer of Andean Christians rises to the Christian god like sacrificial smoke. Guaman Poma, *Nueva Crónica*, p. 821, Royal Library, Copenhagen.

it, were disturbed and intellect dormant.[19] *Camasca* was a diviner or visionary empowered by the Thunder, or by other deities or forces of nature.[20] The brief description Molina gave of this empowerment is reminiscent of the vision of Don Cristóbal. *Camascacuna* claimed that "the grace and virtue that some of them possessed was given to them by the Thunder, saying that when lightning fell and someone was terror-stricken, after he returned to himself, the Thunder had shown him this art, either of healing with herbs or of giving answers to questions that were put to him."[21]

The capacity of transforming vision into action and of speaking words of authority was an essential aspect of the exercise of power and sovereignty as perceived in the Andes. At the beginning of time, a creating deity "worked great things with his word" and "gave sight to the blind with his word alone,"[22] while Inca Pachacuti was empowered to rule by his ability to achieve victory, which in turn arose from his vision and converse with deity. Such converse in itself amounted to exercising power.[23] The point is made by a historical myth from Huarochiri. On one occasion, when his armies had been defeated by the Cañari, Tupa Inca Yupanqui summoned the huacas of the empire to Cuzco for a special reunion to advise him.[24] The huaca Maca Visa, who had assisted the Inca in war on an earlier occasion, proved helpful once more. He suggested a strategy, went to war on the Inca's behalf, won a resounding victory, and was duly honored in return. Another consultation, recorded by Guaman Poma, took place at a time of drought when Tupa Inca Yupanqui interrogated the huacas as to who among them had brought on the emergency (fig. 40).[25] At issue was how the Inca and the huacas should interact. On the one hand, the huacas were able to cause drought and pestilence and actually did so if human beings failed to serve them; but on the other hand, without sacrifices, the huacas would roam the land afflicted and hungry, looking like desiccated corpses.[26] Because the Inca controlled and supervised the service of the huacas throughout his empire, distributing to each exactly what was his due and keeping careful records of every transaction,[27] he was also entitled to question them and learn from them.

---

[19] Cabello, p. 288.

[20] Taylor, "Camay," *Journal de la Société des Américanistes* 63 (1974–1976): 231–244; Taylor, ed., *Runa yndio* (1987), pp. 24–25.

[21] Molina, *Fábulas*, p. 64; cf. Albornoz, *Instrucción*, pp. 167f.

[22] Cieza, *Segunda Parte* 5, p. 9 (Lima).

[23] Cf. *Relación Anónima*, p. 167b, Inca Pachacuti punishes insubordinate priests.

[24] *Runa yndio*, chap. 23; cf. 19.228–229 (ed. Urioste) = 19.1–8 (ed. Taylor); Spalding, *Huarochiri*, pp. 103ff.

[25] Guaman Poma, *Nueva Crónica*, p. 261 [264].

[26] Molina, *Fábulas*, p. 130.

[27] See above, chap. III.2 at nn. 38–39; also *Runa yndio* 22.283 (ed. Urioste) = 22.19–21 (ed. Taylor).

40. Tupa Inca Yupanqui consults the *huacas* of his empire. Guanacaure, one of the most important huacas of Cuzco, sits on the rock at the left, watching as Tupa Inca Yupanqui speaks: "Huacas and villcas, who among you has said, 'Let it not rain, or freeze, or hail'? Speak up. That is all I have to say!" "Not us, Inca," the huacas reply. Guaman Poma, *Nueva Crónica*, p. 261, Royal Library, Copenhagen. Photo from facsimile, Paris 1936.

The Inca's prophetic insight, anchored as it was in what he learned from the huacas, was a direct expression of his political and economic power and in turn perpetuated this power.

The Inca thus made his power real and concrete by conversing with the huacas.[28] He was the channel through which their energy was mediated to his subjects. When thus Guaman Poma pondered how it could have been that the Inca empire fell, he thought it was the Inca's visionary capacity and the power of his speech that had failed, not merely his military strength:

> Topa Ynga Yupanqui spoke with the huacas and Guayna Capac Ynga wanted to do likewise. But they did not want to talk or respond in anything. And he ordered all the lesser huacas to be killed; the major ones survived. They say that Paria Caca replied that there was no more scope for speaking and ruling because without fail the men whom they call Vira Cocha[29] were to rule and bring a very great lord in [Guayna Capac's] time or subsequently. This is what the huacas and idols said to the Inca Guayna Capac. And he was very sorrowful because of it.[30]

Guaman Poma was not the first to believe that Guayna Capac had known of the advent of the Spaniards. Cieza noted in his *Crónica* that Guayna Capac had been informed of Pizarro's exploratory expeditions and had predicted the Spaniards' return. "This he will have said from an utterance of the devil," added Cieza.[31] In the second part of his work he repeated the story, although he now thought that perhaps it was "fable."[32] Similarly, in 1552 Francisco López de Gómara suggested that Guayna Capac had come by his knowledge regarding the arrival of the Spaniards in the natural course of events. Having been informed about their early explorations on the coast of South America, the Inca anticipated that they would return.[33]

However, the theory that an Inca had foretold the invasion proved more attractive. On the one hand, it harmonized with the Christian view that demons spoke in the oracles consulted by the Inca. And on the other hand, Andeans themselves, in their endeavor to comprehend the cataclysm that had overwhelmed them, searched for supernatural explanations. These in turn buttressed the Christian theory that the Inca derived

---

[28] Places where such converse had occurred figured in Inca sacred topography, see Rowe, "An account," *Ñawpa Pacha* 17 (1979), Ch-8:4, a huaca where Guayna Capac had a prophetic dream.

[29] I.e., the Spaniards.

[30] Guaman Poma, *Nueva Crónica*, p. 262 [264].

[31] Cieza, *Crónica* 44, p. 148 (Lima).

[32] Cieza, *Segunda Parte* 69, p. 200 (Lima).

[33] Gómara, *Historia*, chap. 115.

his prophecy from demons. Las Casas thought that the Sun had informed the Inca Pachacuti of the end of Tahuantinsuyo without explaining how Sun and Inca communicated.[34] Some fifty years later, Garcilaso de la Vega likewise thought that the advent of the Spaniards had been foretold by both Viracocha and Guayna Capac without the help of demons.[35] But Murúa and Guaman Poma[36] attributed a demonically inspired version of the prophecy to Tupa Inca Yupanqui, and other picturesquely elaborated accounts of such prophecies were repeated by later historians of the Incas.[37] In addition, Murúa, Garcilaso, and Guaman Poma[38] suggested that the Inca hosts who accompanied Atahualpa at Cajamarca did not attempt to repulse the Spanish assault because they were expecting to meet Viracocha's emissaries, in fulfilment of the much repeated prophecy. This argument appears to rest on a certain foundation in historical reality.

When passing through Cuzco in 1550, Cieza heard that at the very beginning of the Spanish invasion, some Andeans saw a positive and divinely ordained dimension in it. The Spaniards, he was told, arrived shortly after Atahualpa's generals had captured Guascar, thus ending the civil war between the two brothers. Atahualpa's victory was followed by a bloodthirsty campaign of vengeance against Guascar's supporters in Cuzco. At this very time, news of Atahualpa's capture reached the city, and when soon afterwards the three Spaniards whom Pizarro had sent to despoil Coricancha and other sanctuaries arrived there, they were initially greeted as emissaries and sons of Viracocha and were moreover called by the Creator's name.[39] Although it soon became evident to all Andeans that the impact of Viracocha's emissaries was far from what had been anticipated by Guascar's adherents in Cuzco,[40] the divine epithet that had been applied to them endured, and the story of how they had come by this epithet was also told to Polo de Ondegardo.[41]

If indeed a number of Andeans had viewed the Spaniards as somehow connected with Viracocha, and if their coming had been foretold by an Inca ruler, then the warfare and violence of the invasion must be perceived

---

[34] Las Casas, *Apologética Historia* 259, p. 617.

[35] Garcilaso, *Comentarios reales* 5.28; 9.14–15; *Historia General* 1.39, 2.6.

[36] Murúa, *Historia general* (1611), 1.89, pp. 10f.; 90, p. 15; Guaman Poma, *Nueva Crónica* p. 262 [264]; see also 378 [380].

[37] Anello Oliva, *Historia* 1.2.12–13; Salinas y Cordova, *Memorial* 1.6, p. 58; 7, p. 71; Calancha, *Corónica Moralizada* 1.16.7; León Pinelo, *Paraiso* 2.20, p. 303.

[38] Murúa, *Historia general* (1611), 1.59, p. 176; Garcilaso, *General History* 1.20, p. 44; Guaman Poma, *Nueva Crónica*, p. 386 [388].

[39] Cieza, *Segunda Parte* 5, p. 11.

[40] Cf. Benzoni, *Historia* (Lima, 1967), pp. 64–65.

[41] Polo de Ondegardo, *Informe . . . al licenciado Briviesca de Muñatones*, p. 154; Acosta, *HNM* 6.22; see also Cieza, *Segunda Parte* 38, pp. 112f., with Murúa, *Historia del origen* (1590), 1.10, p. 68 and Sarmiento, *Historia Indica* 24, pp. 228f.

as needless and tragic.[42] It was precisely to persuade his readers of this opinion that the Inca Garcilaso de la Vega[43] and the historians who followed him recounted these matters. But in the process, the Inca's prophecy itself, thanks to being detached from its Andean context, was converted into historical fiction.

But this context is clear in Guaman Poma, in whose eyes Guayna Capac's inability to converse with the huacas and the failure of his prophetic insight augured the failure of his political power. Guaman Poma expressed this failure in terms of prophetic speech, while other Andeans thought that the end of Guayna Capac's empire had been foreshadowed by prophetic events.

One of the myths of Huarochiri recounted how Cuni Raya Viracocha[44] summoned Guayna Capac to accompany him to Lake Titicaca. While there, Cuni Raya sent emissaries, camasca, to his father Pachacamac in the Lower World, to bring back one of his sisters. One camasca brought back a little chest, which Cuni Raya gave to the Inca, saying, "Inca, you and I must divide this land. I will go to one region and you to the other." And then he shouted, "You and I will never meet again." When Guayna Capac opened the chest, lightning fell in that region. He found in the chest a beautiful dwarf lady with curly, golden hair and said, "I will never leave here, but will stay with my princess, my queen." The Inca therefore ordered a man of his own ayllu to announce in Cuzco that he was Guayna Capac. Then the Inca himself, his lady, and Cuni Raya disappeared. When the substitute Guayna Capac died, disputes arose about who should hold power, and the Spaniards arrived.

In some myths, Titicaca was the Incas' place of origin; the Lower World to which Cuni Raya's emissaries went was the coast, urin in relation to Titicaca's anan. But Andeans also conceptualized their own world as the world above, or "in the day," in relation to Castile, which was the world below, where the sun did not shine.[45] This world below, which could signify both the Pacific coast and Castile, was also the home of the dwarf lady, whose golden hair perhaps defined her as one of the newcomers. A further message that the dwarf lady conveyed had nothing to do with the invasion. In the mid-sixteenth century, people in Chincha told Spaniards that dwarfs were beings of an earlier epoch, whose tiny bones could still be found in ancient burials.[46] In staying with the dwarf lady, Guayna Capac thus located himself in the world of the dead. The light-

---

[42] Cf. Adorno, "Bartolomé de las Casas y Domingo de Santo Tomás en la obra de Felipe Waman Puma," *Revista Iberoamericana* (Madrid) 120–121, (1982): 673–679 at 678–679.

[43] See below, chap. VIII.2 at note 67.

[44] *Runa yndio*, chap. 14; for Cuniraya Viracocha see *Runa yndio* I.7 (ed. Urioste) = I.14–17 (ed. Taylor).

[45] Guaman Poma, *Nueva Crónica*, pp. 42, 368 [370].

[46] Above, chap. IV.I at n. 93.

ning that fell when Guayna Capac opened the chest from which she emerged betokened war and upheaval,[47] and Cuni Raya's farewell—"You and I will never meet again"—implies that the Inca would never again be able to gain prophetic insight by converse with this deity. Dividing the world into two parts perhaps echoes Andean myths of creation in which two creating deities set out on different paths to bring the human world into existence.[48] Like these creating deities,[49] Guayna Capac, his lady, and Cuni Raya all vanished, but they did not leave behind a created, ordered world. Rather, the disappearance of both the Creator and the Inca were the prelude to the destruction of the world as Andeans knew it.

Santacruz Pachacuti Yamqui recorded a myth about Guayna Capac that recounted the destruction of the Andean world not in a narrative of suggestion and allusion but in apparently historical and factual terms. On one of his campaigns, lightning bolts fell at Inca Guayna Capac's feet. After this evil omen, the Inca at midnight saw himself surrounded by thousands upon thousands of men, who were the souls of those who were to die in the pestilence that swept through the Andes in the wake of the Spanish invasion. The Inca, understanding that these souls were his enemies, returned to Quito. There, a messenger wearing a black cloak gave to the Inca a little locked chest that only he was to open. When Guayna Capac did so, out fluttered a host of small papers and butterflies foreboding evil,[50] which scattered until they disappeared. This was the pestilence of which Guayna Capac himself and many of his people were shortly to die.[51]

The messages that were delivered by the supernatural powers in these myths were definitive and final. During the Taqui Onqoy, the huacas, although starving and neglected, had still exhorted Andeans to return to the ancient cults, thereby joining human with divine energies so as to expel the Spaniards. By contrast, when Guaman Poma, Santacruz Pachacuti, and the mythographers of Huarochiri looked back to the Incas some forty years later, such a return was no longer a conceivable option. Spaniards at this time made of Inca and Andean prophecy subjects for antiquarian inquiry harnessed to missionary enterprise. But for Andeans, Christians though many of them had become, spoken prophecies and the prophetic events that myth attributed to the Inca past carried a different significance. They could not be a subject for antiquarian inquiry, because, as Don Cristóbal experienced, the huacas were alive, and they still had

[47] See above, sec. 1 at n. 6.
[48] Betanzos, *Suma* (1987), 1.1, p. 12a; 2, p. 13ab.
[49] Betanzos, *Suma* (1987), 1.2, p. 15b.
[50] See Guaman Poma, *Nueva Crónica*, pp. 281f. [283f.].
[51] Pachacuti Yamqui, *Relación*, p. 305.

power, even though this power could no longer be made manifest through officially recognized channels.

3. THE TRUE RELIGION IN ANCIENT PERU

The first Spaniards to study the Americas found it difficult to believe that Christianity had never been preached in the newly discovered continent. Early Christian hagiography had it that the apostles Bartholomew and Thomas had reached India, and as early as 1493 a missionary accompanying Columbus was compared, precisely, to the apostle Bartholomew.[1] Once launched, the idea that some apostle had preached in the Americas gained ground steadily, for there were considerations other than early Christian tradition to support it.

Long-established scriptural exegesis applied to the preaching of the apostles the verse from Psalm 18, "Their sound has gone out into all the world," which had to include the New World, and thus buttressed the extension of the legends of Thomas and Bartholomew to America. But with lapse of time, so it was thought in the early sixteenth century, the apostolic teaching had been engulfed by the age-old idolatrous religions of the New World.[2] Nonetheless, in the eyes of some Spaniards, certain aspects of American religious practice resembled Christian practice. Crosses found in Yucatan were thought to have been left behind by an unknown man of noble bearing[3] or by Spaniards who had fled there at the time of the Muslim invasion of the peninsula.[4] Las Casas gave credence to such theories, for he wrote in the *Apologética Historia* that in Yucatan and elsewhere in the Americas the Christian Trinity was not unfamiliar.[5] In 1586 Cabello de Valboa, who appears to have read this passage, produced supporting evidence from Peru.[6]

Indeed, by this time, the theory that Andeans had learned of Christianity from an apostle who had preached to them was well established. Cieza was told of such a theory when he visited the temple of Viracocha at Cacha, which housed the Creator's stone statue. This statue's long tunic

[1] For this and the following, see Vigneras, "Saint Thomas," *Hispanic American Historical Review* 57 (1977): 82–90; also J. Lafaye, *Quetzalcoatl and Guadalupe: The Formation of Mexican National Consciousness, 1531–1813* (Chicago, 1976).

[2] Fernández de Oviedo y Valdés, *Historia general y natural de las Indias*, ed. J. Amador de los Rios (Madrid, 1851), 1.2.7.

[3] Peter Martyr, *De orbe novo Decades octo* (Alcalá, 1530; Graz, 1966), 4.1, fol. 57r, quoted by Román, *República de las Indias Occidentales* 1.2, fol. 356v.

[4] Gómara, *Historia*, chap. 53.

[5] Las Casas, *Apologética Historia* 153, 154.

[6] Cabello, *Miscelánea antártica* 3.6, pp. 237–238; 3.9, p. 258, he likens the Inca Sun to the sun of Dionysius the Areopagite; cf. above, chap. v.1 at n. 24 and Las Casas, *Apologética Historia* 126, p. 659. The occurrence of this unusual comparison in the two works suggests that Cabello had access to a copy of the *Apologética*.

and head ornament reminiscent, Cieza thought, of a crown or tiara, suggested to certain Spaniards that it represented an apostle who had preached in these parts. Cieza was unconvinced,[7] but Betanzos, who also saw the statue, was inclined to believe that the individual it represented had worn an ankle-length white tunic, had held an object resembling a priest's breviary in his hands, and had his hair cut in the priestly tonsure.[8] The story of the apostle's preaching thus proliferated. In 1625 the Dominican Gregorio García, who arrived in Peru in 1587 and was convinced that remnants of apostolic teaching were to be found in Andean religion, published an erudite treatise on the subject.[9]

From the Andean point of view also, the story of the apostle's preaching had its uses, for it suggested that god had not delayed sending the gospel to the Americas until the Spaniards arrived, and that therefore the Americas were not, as Acosta had so disparagingly suggested, the less noble part of the world.[10] Furthermore, some Andean myths seemed to echo the passage in the Gospels in which Jesus sends the disciples on their first mission without money or spare clothing, instructing them to announce the coming of the kingdom, to preach and heal the sick, without asking for remuneration. And then Jesus said to the disciples, "If anyone will not receive you . . . shake off the dust from your feet as you leave that house or town. Truly . . . it shall be more tolerable on the day of judgment for the land of Sodom and Gomorra than for that town."[11] The cities of Sodom and Gomorra were wiped out by fire and brimstone from heaven as a punishment for their people's wickedness. The culminating proof of this wickedness was their contemptuous reception of two heaven-sent strangers.[12]

The myth of Viracocha at Cacha, which was told both to Betanzos and to Cieza, shares some motifs with these biblical episodes. On his Andeswide mission of calling human beings forth from the rocks, caves and springs that were their pacarinas, the Creator passed through Cacha, where he was met with hostility and was nearly stoned to death. Fire fell from heaven, and Viracocha went away to the sea where he spread out his cloak and disappeared among the waves. The people of Cacha recognized their error and erected for Viracocha a temple to house the stone statue which Cieza and Betanzos were shown.[13] Myths recounting supernatural

---

[7] Cieza, *Crónica* 98, p. 270; *Segunda Parte* 5, p. 10.

[8] Betanzos, *Suma* (1987), 1.2, p. 14b.

[9] Gregorio García, *Predicación* 6.5; J. L. Klaiber, "The Posthumous Christianisation of the Inca Empire in Colonial Peru," *Journal of the History of Ideas* 37 (1976): 507–520, examines the issue from a European vantage point.

[10] Acosta, *HNM* 5.1.

[11] Matthew 10:8–15; cf. Mark 6:10–11; Luke 9:3–5.

[12] Genesis 18:16ff.

[13] Betanzos, *Suma* (1987), 1.2, pp. 13bf. Cieza, *Segunda Parte* 5, pp. 9f.; cf. Sarmiento,

punishments for contempt of innocent strangers proliferated in the Andes. In the village Yanqui Supa on the road of Omasuyo, a poor stranger arrived while a festival was in progress. So far from offering him sustenance, the people mocked the stranger and drove him away, whereupon "divine justice" submerged the village in water.[14] Similar stories were told in Huarochiri. Paria Caca arrived at Yaru Tini during a festival and sat down in a corner. Only one man offered him drink and coca; this man was the only one to survive the hurricane in which Paria Caca consumed those villagers five days later. Another inhospitable village was consumed by Paria Caca in a red and yellow rain.[15] The Creator Cuni Raya Viracocha went about with his tunic and cloak in tatters, so that people drove him away as a louse-infested stranger, but they suffered retribution later.[16]

A version of the myth about Viracocha at Cacha that was told to Murúa shows the story in the process of being acculturated to Christianity. For here Viracocha has become a poor Spaniard and "blessed saint." The poor Spaniard came to Cacha from Tiahuanaco and reproved the people for their vices and their drunken festivals. When they threatened to stone him, fire from heaven destroyed the entire settlement.[17] A little later, Guaman Poma retold the story. The Spaniard was now the apostle Bartholomew, and the story's main point had become conversion. Bartholomew was given a hostile reception at Cacha, so that fire from heaven consumed the village. Bartholomew went to rest in a cave where the sorcerer Anti kept an idol through which he conversed with a demon. The demon told Anti in a dream that he could no longer enter the cave because the apostle was now dwelling there. Anti thus sought out Bartholomew, who ordered him to return to the cave and to converse with the idol, which thus found itself constrained to confess that "this poor man was more powerful than he himself, despite all his knowledge" (fig. 41).[18] Thanks to this experience, which resembles the experience of Don Cristóbal with the huaca–demon Llocllay Huancupa, the sorcerer Anti became Bartholomew's disciple and was baptized.

Guaman Poma dated this story to the time of Sinchi Roca, the second Inca, during whose reign, he thought, Jesus was born.[19] Bartholomew was only one of many wandering saints who were sent by God to test the charity of Andeans and to act as catalysts of divine justice: "If [Andean

---

Historia Indica 7, pp. 209bf.; Cabello, *Miscelánea antártica* 3.6, p. 237; see also Szeminski, *Un kuraca* (1987), pp. 49ff.

[14] Murúa, *Historia general* (1611), 1.38, p. 106.

[15] *Runa yndio* 25.342, hurricane; 26.348ff., rain (ed. Urioste).

[16] *Runa yndio* 2.9ff. (ed. Urioste).

[17] Murúa, *Historia del origen* (1590), 2.7, p. 122 = *Historia general* (1611), 1.88, p. 7.

[18] Guaman Poma, *Nueva Crónica*, p. 93.

[19] Guaman Poma, *Nueva Crónica*, p. 91.

APOSTOL
S. BARTOLO ME 92

41. The beginning of Christianity in the Andes: an Indian of Collao, having deposited his regional headgear (for which cf. fig. 20) at the foot of the cross that Bartholomew erected at Carabuco on Lake Titicaca kneels to revere the holy apostle. Guaman Poma, *Nueva Crónica*, p. 92, Royal Library, Copenhagen. Photo from facsimile, Paris 1936.

villagers] gave no alms, God punished them. By the prayer [of these saints] he burned them with fire from heaven, and in some places the villages were covered by mountains or became lakes, or the earth swallowed them."[20] Guaman Poma thus converted Andean myths of deities walking about unrecognized as poor strangers into myths about poor strangers who were unrecognized Christian apostles and saints.[21] But this was only one small aspect of his rethinking of Andean religious history. For not only had the apostle preached in the Andes, leaving behind "the church already established in the kingdom" long before the Spaniards arrived[22] but the Andeans themselves had known the true God from the very beginning of their history, when their first ancestor, a son of Noah, settled in the land and "brought God to the Indies."[23]

The core of this idea perhaps came to Guaman Poma as a result of studying the Quechua lexicon and grammar compiled by Domingo de Santo Tomás and the *Symbolo Catolico Indiano*, published in Lima in 1590 by the Franciscan missionary Luis Jerónimo Oré, whom he knew personally.[24] Both these authors thought that by means of their innate human faculties, Andeans had derived a truthful apprehension of God from "the book of nature," so that they were culturally prepared to understand Christianity.[25] Fray Domingo offered specific proof of this reality in his Quechua lexicon, where he translated many Christian theological terms into Quechua without using Spanish neologisms.[26] Fray Domingo and Jerónimo Oré did not construct as refined and subtle an edifice of human religious history as did Las Casas when positing the tension between man's original apprehension of God, simple but truthful, and the dispersion of this apprehension in the course of cultural and political development. But the two authors were in agreement with the positive evaluation of human cognitive possibilities that speaks in the *Apologética Historia* and

[20] Guaman Poma, *Nueva Crónica*, p. 94.

[21] The idea of the poor stranger warning of impending disaster goes beyond the pages of Guaman Poma. In 1720 a "poor old pilgrim" from Collao forewarned the people of Cuzco, engrossed as they were in sin and vice, of a coming epidemic, but to no effect; see Sallnow, *Pilgrims of the Andes* (1987), citing Esquivel y Navia, *Noticias* 2: 224.

[22] Guaman Poma, *Nueva Crónica*, p. 401 [403].

[23] Guaman Poma, *Nueva Crónica*, p. 25 with 49. Andean and Christian ideas continue to be correlated and confronted in contemporary times; see Dillon and Abercrombie, "The Destroying Christ," in *Rethinking History and Myth*, ed. J. D. Hill (1988).

[24] See Guaman Poma, *Nueva Crónica*, pp. 912 [926], 1079f. [1089f.]. For Guaman Poma's familiarity with Spanish writings, see the material assembled by Adorno, "Las otras fuentes," *Historica* 2 (1978): 137–158; also her "Bartolomé de las Casas y Domingo de Santo Tomás en la obra de Felipe Waman Puma," *Revista Iberoamericana* (Madrid) 120–121 (1982): 673–679, with her, "El arte de la persuasión: el padre de Las Casas y Fray Luis de Granada en la obra de Waman Puma de Ayala," *Escritura* (Caraca) 8 (1979): 167–189.

[25] Oré, *Symbolo*, chap. 2; Domingo de Santo Tomás, *Gramatica*, pp. 9ff.

[26] See Domingo de Santo Tomás, *Lexicon*, p. 57, baptizar; p. 93, cielo; p. 226, virgen; p. 111, diluvio; even for God, p. 111, he avoids the isolated Spanish term by translating as "living and true God." Acosta disagreed with this attitude; see above, chap. VI at n. 73.

in the treatise *Doce Dudas*, which deals exclusively with Peru. This latter work was also known to Guaman Poma.[27]

Guaman Poma's *Crónica* opens with a double account of man's earliest history, one biblical, the other Andean. The biblical account, like similar narratives of humanity's early history by European authors, outlines the generations of human beings, the growth of human wickedness and the corresponding divine punishments[28] during the four epochs before the birth of Christ. The Andean account, by contrast, stresses that throughout these four epochs, until the advent of the Incas, Andeans followed a pure religion, free of idolatry. They prayed to the one true God and understood that he was a trinity.[29] So it was that long before the Spaniards came, Andean prayers rose to the deity like smoke from a sacrifice, just as they were to do in Christian times (figs. 38, 39).

Guaman Poma's Andean differs from his European time scheme, for in his view idolatry began earlier in Europe than it did in the Andes, that is, during the second age, when Ninus was king and Abraham left Ur of the Chaldees at God's behest.[30] According to Cabello, whose *Miscelánea* Guaman Poma knew of and had perhaps read,[31] Ninus was the first to make a statue, which was of his father and which he compelled his subjects to adore.[32] Here and elsewhere, Cabello followed the Christian exegetical tradition which associated the growth of idolatry with that of royal power.[33] Guaman Poma did the same, but he drove the point home not with regard to some king of European antiquity but with regard to the Incas. As a member of an Andean noble family whose power the Incas had undermined, Guaman Poma was profoundly critical of their right to rule. His critique went hand in hand with his conception of Andean religious history. The Incas did not spring from a lineage going back to Noah such as would entitle them to rule as natural lords. For the first Inca, Manco Capac, "had no people, no land, no sown field or fortress, no noble descent or ancient ancestors, no *pacarimoc*[34] . . . to ascertain whether he was one of the sons of the first Indians . . . but rather, he said that he was a son of the Sun. The first Inca, Manco Capac, had no known father."[35] In holding that the Inca title "Son of the Sun" served to conceal a faulty claim to sovereignty, Guaman Poma agreed with some earlier

[27] Adorno (1982; above, n. 24).
[28] Guaman Poma, *Nueva Crónica*, pp. 23, 25, 27, 29.
[29] Guaman Poma, *Nueva Crónica*, p. 55; compare Oré, *Symbolo* 9, prayer of Capac Yupanqui to the Unknown God with Guaman Poma, p. 54, cf. 911 [925]f., prayer of Vari Runa; both pray, "Where are you?" Cf. above, chap. v.3 at n. 35.
[30] Guaman Poma, *Nueva Crónica*, p. 25.
[31] Guaman Poma, *Nueva Crónica*, p. 1080 [1090].
[32] Cabello Valboa, *Miscelánea antártica* 1.5, p. 36.
[33] Cf. above, chap. v.1 at nn. 32ff.; chap. vi at n. 102.
[34] Quechua, "founder of a lineage."
[35] Guaman Poma, *Nueva Crónica*, pp. 80–81.

Spanish historians, although he gave different reasons for his opinion.[36] Where Spaniards judged Inca governance in the light of European secular theories of sovereignty, Guaman Poma, whose Hispanic education came from missionaries, saw sovereignty in religious terms. He thought that the Inca title to rule had been devised by Manco Capac's mother and later consort, Mama Huaco, on the advice of demons speaking in huacas.[37] The practice of false religion thus lay at the very roots of Inca dominion.

When discussing the fourth Andean epoch, Guaman Poma noted the ruling dynasties that he believed had at that time held sway in the four parts, or suyos, of Tahuantinsuyo. Unlike the Incas, all four of these dynasties were the direct descendants of the son of Noah who had first come to the Andes.[38] In his account of the Inca period, he returned to the four suyos, but this time it was to discuss their different idolatrous cults, festivals, and burial practices, all of which had evolved under Inca governance[39] and matched Inca religious observances (cf. figs. 19–20). For just as the Incas revered the huacas of the vicinity of Cuzco, so throughout the four suyos, Andeans under Inca supervision[40] offered worship and sacrifice to their regional deities. Similarly, regional festivals and burial customs came to be laced with idolatrous accretions and corresponded to those of the Incas.

Guaman Poma described the first generation of Andean humanity, whom he called Vari Viracocha Runa, as being descended from "Spaniards,"[41] by which he meant that they were descended from the original man created by God. In this perspective, he viewed the Spanish invasion of Peru as a restoration of true religion, as the last in a series of events that began with the original settlement of the Andes and continued with the birth of Christ and the preaching of the apostle Bartholomew during the reign of the Inca Sinchi Roca. The apostle Bartholomew, accordingly, was the first "discoverer" of the New World,[42] to be followed in due course by Columbus and by Pizarro with his Spaniards.[43] Guaman Poma thus welcomed the campaigns of extirpation that destroyed, as he saw it, precisely those idolatrous accretions that had crept into Andean religious observance in Inca times.[44] As a young man, he cooperated in these campaigns as an assistant of Cristóbal de Albornoz, and in writing the Cró-

[36] Sarmiento, *Historia Indica* 9; Murúa, *Historia del origen* (1590), 1.2–3.

[37] Guaman Poma, *Nueva Crónica*, pp. 81–82.

[38] Guaman Poma, *Nueva Crónica*, pp. 75–77.

[39] Guaman Poma, *Nueva Crónica*, pp. 266 [268], 272 [274], 289 [291], 297 [299], 320 [323], 327 [329].

[40] Guaman Poma, *Nueva Crónica*, pp. 271 [273], 273 [275].

[41] Guaman Poma, *Nueva Crónica*, p. 49; cf. 60.

[42] Guaman Poma, p. 378 [380].

[43] Guaman Poma, p. 379 [381].

[44] Guaman Poma, p. 676 [690].

nica, he expected the information it provided on religious matters to be utilizable by future extirpators.[45] The argument underlying this attitude of Guaman Poma's was that extirpation would finally bring to fruition Bartholomew's teaching and reinvigorate the church that the apostle had left "already established." Indeed, Guaman Poma's own religious teacher was not any Spaniard but his stepbrother, the Christian priest Martín de Ayala, a "very great holy man." Martín de Ayala's biography prefaces the *Crónica*, thus underscoring one of its central themes, which was that in the last resort Peru's true Christians were Andeans, not Spaniards.[46]

This perception, however, was profoundly at loggerheads with the tenets that articulated the policies of church and state in Guaman Poma's Peru. When thus as an old man he contemplated the renewed campaigns of extirpation conducted by Francisco de Ávila and his assistants, extirpation displayed a face very different from the one he had observed some forty years earlier.[47] For the campaigns seemed to have become a mere pretence for confiscating Indian property, enriching corrupt officials, and disinheriting the Andean aristocracy.[48] Innocence was almost impossible to prove, Guaman Poma thought, given that Francisco de Ávila would confiscate as evidence for idolatry articles of adornment Andeans customarily wore and ceremonial vessels they used when celebrating Christian festivals.[49] In their affliction, Andeans could only call on the one true God with the same yearning their distant ancestors had felt for him in the first epochs of Andean history. "Where are you, God of heaven?" they would pray despairingly.[50]

The extirpations of the early seventeenth century thus led Guaman Poma to ponder elements of continuity in the fabric of Andean religious experience and expression from those first epochs down to his own time. When describing the first epochs, Guaman Poma mentioned how festivals were celebrated then with ceremonial drinking, with dancing, and with the singing of those songs of triumph and love, *haylli* and *aravi*, that Andeans still sang in his own day for harvest and plowing.[51] He thought, too, that these rituals should continue to be observed, because they had nothing to do with idolatry but rather underpinned the performance of those necessary community tasks that created the village surplus to sus-

---

[45] E.g., Guaman Poma, p. 267 [269]; see Adorno (1978; above, n. 24), pp. 151ff.

[46] Guaman Poma, pp. 14–21.

[47] Adorno (1978; above, n. 24), p. 154.

[48] Guaman Poma, *Nueva Crónica*, pp. 679 [693], 1094 [1104], 1129 [1139], and especially 1110ff. [1120ff.]. See also Guaman Poma, pp. 1111f. [1121f.], and Silverblatt, *Moon, Sun and Witches* (1987), pp. 148ff.

[49] Guaman Poma, *Nueva Crónica*, p. 1121 [1131].

[50] Guaman Poma, p. 1111 [1121] with 50, 54.

[51] Guaman Poma, pp. 59, 67; above, chap. IV.2 at nn. 84ff.; cf. Guaman Poma, pp. 52; 69, on burial without idolatry; 62; 73, on cult.

tain the poor and needy.[52] Similarly, in the fourth Andean epoch, philosophers bearing the titles camasca[53] and amauta[54] had learned to understand the courses of the stars, sun, and moon and on the basis of this knowledge were able to predict the future.[55] In Guaman Poma's eyes, such traditional Andean knowledge was legitimate and should continue to be valued in Christian times.[56]

Guaman Poma was not the only Andean thinker to trace the perception of religious truth in the Andes from the remotest antiquity to his own time. His contemporary Joan Santacruz Pachacuti Yamqui also found evidence that the one true god had been apprehended in the Andes from the beginning of remembered history. But Pachacuti Yamqui thought of the Incas more favorably than did Guaman Poma and therefore attributed to Inca rulers several of those fundamental perceptions of religious truth that punctuated the road to God on which human beings in the Andes had traveled.

Pachacuti Yamqui began his Andean history with the epoch of fortress construction, purunpacha.[57] One night during this epoch, the hapiñuños, who were demons, malevolent ghosts, or phantasms, were heard lamenting their overthrow, because on that night Jesus was born.[58] Soon a tall, white-haired stranger in flowing garments arrived who healed the sick by his mere touch and taught the Indians true doctrine, addressing them as his "sons and daughters."[59] This homeless stranger, whom the Andeans called Tunupa, was contemptuously received by everyone except the lord Aputampo of Pacaritambo. To him, accordingly, Tunupa gave a rod, Tupayauri,[60] that had been cut from his pilgrim's staff. After the birth of Aputampo's son, the first Inca Manco Capac, the Tupayauri turned into gold and became the Inca's scepter and his guarantee of victory in battle.[61]

---

[52] Guaman Poma, pp. 315 [317], 328 [330], 890 [904]f.; see especially 876 [890].

[53] Cf. above, sec. 2 at n. 45.

[54] Quechua, "wise man" see Taylor, ed., Runa yndio (1987), pp. 23–24.

[55] Guaman Poma, p. 72.

[56] Guaman Poma, pp. 883ff. [897ff.].

[57] This is comparable to Guaman Poma's fourth epoch (Guaman Poma, pp. 63ff.). On Guaman Poma's periodization, see Duviols, "Las cinco edades," in Time and Calendars, ed. M. S. Ziolkowski and M. Sadowski, pp. 7–16.

[58] Pachacuti Yamqui, Relación, p. 235; cf. Gonzalez Holguin, Vocabulario de la lengua general, p. 150, s.v. hapuñuñu, "phantasms or ghosts that used to appear with two large breasts (ñuñu) so that they could snatch (hapiy) with them." Cf. Ricardo, Vocabulario y phrasis, p. 42, fantasma o trasgo; Szeminski, Un kuraca (1987), pp. 56ff., 79ff.; G. Taylor, "Supay," Amerindia 5 (1980): 60; T. Bouysse-Cassagne, La identidad aymara, pp. 184f.

[59] Pachacuti Yamqui, Relación, p. 236.

[60] Rod of copper, Bertonio, Vocabulario, 365, 395.

[61] Pachacuti Yamqui, Relación, pp. 236f., 240f., 271. For an interpretation of this myth alongside the versions of it that are given by Betanzos and Sarmiento, and for what it reveals about the social organization of Cuzco, see R. T. Zuidema, La civilisation inca au Cuzco, pp. 19–26.

This story represents another Christianized variant of the Andean myth of the poor stranger, whom Pachacuti Yamqui identified with the apostle Thomas.[62] Like the apostles after Pentecost, Tunupa knew all languages. He performed miracles, owned nothing, and asked for no reward. He was thus the perfect missionary and like the missionaries of Pachacuti Yamqui's own day addressed the Indians as "sons and daughters."[63] At the same time, the name Tunupa describes the stranger as a manifestation or servant of the Creator Viracocha, who was revered in the Titicaca region.[64]

The myth of Tunupa as understood by Pachacuti Yamqui was closely intertwined with myths of Inca origins and with Inca history. For just as Tunupa bestowed on the Incas one of their royal insignia, so also his teaching determined a salient theme in their governance. This was the ongoing friction and conflict between different Inca rulers and the demons or huacas of the Andes. Whether a particular Inca at a given time favored the huacas or whether he did not, the relationship generated tension.

Manco Capac differentiated his subjects according to their places of origin or *pacariscas*, the principal place of origin being his own Pacaritambo. Although "an enemy of the huacas,"[65] he nonetheless smoothed the way for the "demons and devils *hapiñuñus*" to enter into these places of origin so as to deceive simple folk "with false promises."[66] At Villcasguaman, the Inca Pachacuti made war on a confederacy of seven huacas who displayed themselves in the guise of Andean lords, but he allowed other huacas to continue functioning.[67] Tupa Inca Yupanqui also fought against the huacas, but they multiplied nonetheless,[68] and during the minority of Guayna Capac, the traitor Guallpaya fostered the cults of Sun, Moon, and Lightning.[69] When ruling in his own right, Guayna Capac granted favors to Pachacamac and Rimac but found later that Pachacamac had delivered a false oracle.[70]

Notwithstanding the concessions that some Inca rulers made to the huacas, the relationship between huacas and Incas, as depicted by Pachacuti Yamqui, was for the most part adversarial. The first Inca, Manco Capac, lost two of his siblings in this conflict: they were turned to stone by the

[62] Pachacuti Yamqui, *Relación*, p. 236, cf. 237.
[63] Pachacuti Yamqui, *Relación*, p. 236: cf. below, chap. IX.1 at n. 80, on Avendaño.
[64] Szeminski, *Un kuraca* (1987), pp. 43f., 47f.; Gisbert, *Iconografía* (1980), pp. 35ff.
[65] Pachacuti Yamqui, *Relación*, p. 244.
[66] Pachacuti Yamqui, p. 246; cf. 247, on apachitas.
[67] Pachacuti Yamqui, pp. 273f.
[68] Pachacuti Yamqui, pp. 283ff.
[69] Pachacuti Yamqui, p. 294.
[70] Pachacuti Yamqui, p. 304; see also Szeminski, *Un kuraca* (1987), p. 61 on this Inca's problems with Pachacamac.

huaca Guanacaure, which soon became a focus of idolatrous worship.[71] The Inca Mayta Capac invited all the huacas of the empire to Cuzco by promising them a solemn procession and festival.[72] When they arrived, Mayta Capac had them enclosed in the foundations of a house that was being constructed for the purpose: "And they say that many idols and huacas fled like fires and winds, and others in the shape of birds, like Ayssavillca and Chinchaycocha and the huaca of the Cañari. . . . And they say that the entire land trembled at this taunt of the Inca more than in the time of his predecessors."[73] The Inca Capac Yupanqui wanted to converse with the huacas "as with his friends" and arranged to meet a certain huaca in a darkened house. But when the huaca arrived "with a rush of wind," the Inca had the door and windows thrown open and reviled the shamefaced deity as a fraudulent impostor, so that he fled "like thunder and lightning."[74] Other Incas likewise made the huacas tremble, even though they also sacrificed to them. The Inca Guascar on the other hand abjured all service to the huacas.[75] Pachacuti Yamqui considered this to have been a praiseworthy act, although earlier Andean tradition had criticized Guascar severely for his high-handed and arbitrary management of relations between himself and the representatives of sacred power.[76]

Pachacuti Yamqui's memory of Inca religious history, formulated as it was during Christian times and in the light of Christian instruction, thus enshrines much of what the missionaries taught, albeit in a modified form. The Christian cosmos was polarized between good and evil, god and devil. In the Andean cosmos by contrast, upper and lower, left and right, were complementary, just as the four suyos of Tahuantinsuyo were complementary to each other. These two cosmic orders coexist at several levels in Pachacuti Yamqui's narrative.

The Inca histories by Cieza, Betanzos, and Sarmiento reveal that an elaborate set of rituals, myths, and negotiations had orchestrated relationships of political and religious power between the Incas and the huacas, oracles, and pacarinas of the different parts of Tahuantinsuyo. These relationships were in constant flux, but ritual, myth, and diplomacy imposed a certain stability and continuity on them. Furthermore, ritual, myth, and diplomacy mediated the multifarious enterprises of aggression and dominance, support and demand for support, that the rulers of Ta-

---

[71] Pachacuti Yamqui, *Relación*, p. 243, with his note; his spelling for Guanacaure is Vanacaori. Formerly, the huaca was called Sanuc; see Pachacuti Yamqui, p. 241; also Sarmiento, *Historia Indica* 11, p. 214a; 13, p. 217b; 15, p. 220b.

[72] See above, chap. III.2 at nn. 34ff.

[73] Pachacuti Yamqui, *Relación*, p. 255.

[74] Pachacuti Yamqui, pp. 259f.

[75] Pachacuti Yamqui, pp. 261, 316.

[76] Betanzos, *Suma* 2.1, p. 207a; Sarmiento, *Historia Indica* 63, p. 266a.

huantinsuyo projected onto their subjects. This ebb and flow of hostility and cooperation between Inca rulers and the regions of the empire with their huacas, articulated as it was in an elaborate code of sacred diplomacy, stood at the hub of Inca politics.

A somewhat different picture emerges from Pachacuti Yamqui. As he understood Inca myth, ritual, and sacred diplomacy, they expressed an uneasy set of relationships between the Incas and the huacas, in which again and again Inca support for the huacas veered into hostility. This was because the Incas were frequently able to recognize the claims of the huacas as false claims. So it was, he wrote, that "the old men of our own time, the time of my father, Don Diego Felipe, are accustomed to say, that almost almost[77] the commandment of God [was being fulfilled in Inca times], especially the seven precepts [of the church]. They only lacked the name of God our Lord and of his son Jesus Christ, and this is public and well known among the old people."[78] Indeed, at times even the "name of God our Lord" shimmered with a certain clarity in the multifaceted crystal ball of Andean theological truth. In a ritual that foreshadowed Christian baptism, the child Inca Roca was sprinkled with water from Titicaca in order to endow him with the blessing of the holy Tunupa.[79] Moreover, this Inca's father, Capac Yupanqui, ordered a shrine to be erected for Tunupa, the entrance of which was flanked by a female huaca and her human lover, both of whom Tunupa had turned into rock for committing the sin of fornication.[80] Here, the Andean mythic motif of transformation into rock, which articulated one of the fundamental linkages between the human and the natural world,[81] has been converted into the Christian motif of sin and its punishment. Similarly, Pachacuti Yamqui thought Coricancha was dedicated not to the ancestral Sun of the Incas but to the Creator,[82] and that like Christian churches, this sanctuary offered asylum to delinquents who sought refuge there.[83]

One wall of Coricancha, according to Pachacuti Yamqui, was taken up by a depiction of the universe in which the Creator, flanked by the moon and the ray-encircled sun, was represented by an oval disk of fine gold. This disk was first installed by Manco Capac and was renovated by Mayta Capac.[84] It was not a cult image before which food, drink, and other things were sacrificed for the deity's sustenance. Rather, the golden disk

---

[77] Sic.
[78] Pachacuti Yamqui, *Relación*, p. 237; for the seven precepts of the church, *Doctrina Christiana*, Sermon 27, fol. 174v.
[79] Pachacuti Yamqui, *Relación*, p. 261.
[80] Pachacuti Yamqui, p. 263.
[81] Cf. above, sec. 1 at nn. 26–33.
[82] Pachacuti Yamqui, pp. 244, 327.
[83] Pachacuti Yamqui, p. 267.
[84] Pachacuti Yamqui, pp. 244, 256f.

was made "to signify that there is a Creator of heaven and earth."[85] Guascar added to the original composition another oval disk "like an image of the Sun," for which room was apparently found between the existing smaller ray-encircled sun and the moon. Pachacuti Yamqui described this second disk as "a disk of fine gold, which they say was the image of the Maker of the true sun, the sun called Viracochan Pachayachachic" (figs. 42, 43).[86] Similarly, Gonzalez Holguin translated Viracocha as an "epithet of the Sun, a name of honor of the God whom the Indians adored."[87] Just as Inca Pachacuti in his vision saw the Sun and the Maker almost interchangeably, and just as Betanzos was sometimes told by his Inca informants that the Maker was Viracocha and at other times that the Maker was the Sun,[88] so in Pachacuti Yamqui's rendering of the decoration of Coricancha, the Maker and the Sun stand in juxtaposition (see also fig. 29)

To these Inca formulations of deity, Christianity added a further strand. Las Casas had outlined an easy transition from the worship of the material sun to Christ, the Sun of Justice, and praised the Inca solar cult as addressed to the noblest of God's creatures.[89] As regards the cult image in Coricancha, Las Casas thought it was a gold disk, with a face and rays. Since Jerónimo Román copied this passage in his *República de Indias*,[90] it is not inconceivable that Pachacuti Yamqui was told of it. But one crucial difference distinguishes his gold disks representing the Maker and the Sun from the disk envisioned by Las Casas. For the latter had a human face, while Pachacuti Yamqui had in mind a non-iconic, abstractly conceived deity. Such a concept of deity was at home in the Andes and owed nothing to Christian teaching. Indeed, it was the missionaries who again and again spoke of god in anthropomorphic terms such as were alien to Andeans.

Unlike Guaman Poma, Pachacuti Yamqui did not engage in polemic, whether explicit or implied, against the invaders. He was, however, as eager as Guaman Poma to convince his readers that Andeans did not derive their theological knowledge exclusively from Spaniards. He thus argued not only that the golden plaque in Coricancha stood for a clear and distinct understanding of the Creator's existence but also that the great festivals of the Inca calendar articulated such a knowledge. The festival of

---

[85] Pachacuti Yamqui, p. 244.

[86] Pachacuti Yamqui, *Relación*, p. 257 with fol. 14r; for the copy in Villcas see p. 301; Szeminski, *Un kuraca* (1987), pp. 64–79; for figures, Pachacuti Yamqui, fols. 13v and 14r.

[87] Pachacuti Yamqui, p. 353.

[88] Betanzos, *Suma* (1987), I.11, p. 49b.

[89] Las Casas, *Apologética Historia* 187, p. 265 and 126, p. 659, respectively. Cf. above, chap. v.1 at nn. 15ff.

[90] Las Casas, *Apologética Historia* 126, p. 660; Duviols, "Punchao," *Antropologia Andina* 1–2 (1976): 11–58.

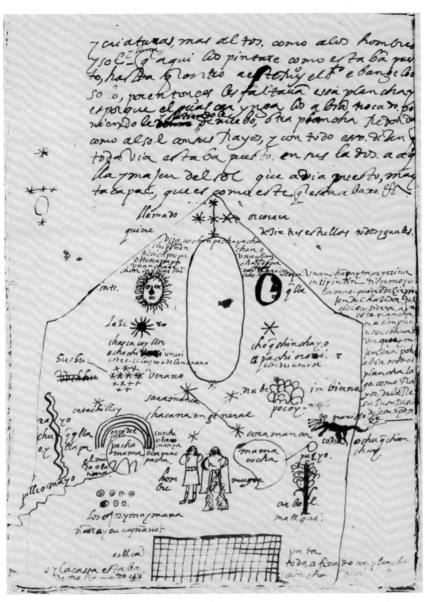

42. The universe according to Santacruz Pachacuti Yamqui: the world above contains the Maker, represented by an oval disk flanked by Sun, left, and Moon, right; the whole is surmounted by the Southern Cross. In the lower world, between "mother earth," surmounted by a rainbow, and "mother sea," stand man and woman. The male Sun watches over the man, while the female Moon watches over the woman. The Maker of all things is not defined by gender or anthropomorphic imagery. Biblioteca Nacional, Madrid, MS. 3169, fol. 145.

43. Santacruz Pachacuti Yamqui's drawing of the gold disk representing
the Maker that Manco Capac ordered to be displayed in Coricancha with,
below, Pacaritambo, the Incas' place of origin. The three "windows" in the
lower drawing represent the houses of Manco Capac's parents and of his
maternal and paternal ancestors. The trees stand for his father and mother.
Biblioteca Nacional, Madrid, MS. 3169, fol. 139.

Capac Raimi communicated to the participants that they should "know [God] with the intellect alone as powerful lord and ruler and creator" and should refrain from choosing as objects of worship even the most noble parts of the created order, such as human beings or the celestial bodies.[91] No missionary could disagree, for prescribed teaching insisted regularly that God is better known through intellect than through sense perception, which can only comprehend the created visible and tactile universe—the universe, that is, to which so much of observed Andean religious devotion was addressed. God, by contrast, was not to be understood as being contained in, and defined by, space and time.[92]

Santacruz Pachacuti, however, wanted to attribute such an understanding of God not to the missionaries but to his Andean forebears. Capac Raimi, he thought, was celebrated by the Incas as a foreshadowing of the eternal festival of the City of God in heaven. To celebrate Capac Raimi meant to be poignantly aware of the fragility and brevity of terrestrial life as compared with life in heaven. The Inca Mayta Capac would thus

> often say during those festal days when night fell: "Alas, how soon the festival is ended, and now only death is left us. For death must come, just as now night comes, sleep the image of death." And they would say many times: "Yet festivals also are the image of the true festival. Blessed are the rational creatures who in future times will attain, know, and understand the name of the Creator!"[93]

In anticipation of this knowledge, Mayta Capac would retire to Ttococachi, there to fast for an entire month.[94] The Inca Pachacuti also went to fast at Ttococachi, but under somewhat different circumstances. This Inca, according to Pachacuti Yamqui, witnessed a series of disquieting omens while conducting a military campaign in Condesuyo. The campaign completed, back in Cuzco a mysterious young stranger offered the Inca a book, which he ignored. Too late Pachacuti realized that the book might have explained the omens, which was why "the Inca fasted for six months in Ttococachi without knowing." [95]

In these stories, as so often elsewhere, Andean knowledge and understanding stood in tension with knowledge and understanding that came from elsewhere, whether this was through the teaching of Tunupa, the content of the mysterious book, or even the preaching that Pizarro's chaplain, Vincente de Valverde, had addressed to Atahualpa.[96] In the face

[91] Pachacuti Yamqui, *Relación*, p. 256.
[92] *Doctrina Christiana*, Sermon 5, fols. 27vff.; Oré, *Symbolo*, chaps. 3–6.
[93] Pachacuti Yamqui, *Relación*, p. 258.
[94] Pachacuti Yamqui, p. 258.
[95] Pachacuti Yamqui, p. 280; for Ttococachi see Rowe, "An Account," *Ñawpa Pacha* 17 (1979), Ch-1:1 and Ch-2:3.
[96] Pachacuti Yamqui, *Relación*, pp. 327f.

of so many alien imports, Pachacuti Yamqui, like Guaman Poma, endeavored to find indigenous Andean precedents for the knowledge of the true God. He thus posited as long rooted in the Andes a set of specifically Christian moral and metaphysical concepts.

These European ideas notwithstanding, Pachacuti Yamqui did capture certain aspects of Andean concepts of divinity with unique clarity. One is the aniconic and abstract dimension of these concepts. Tutored by missionaries, Andeans ended up seeing in their dreams and visions young men clad in shining raiment and black devils, just as European Christians did. But this imported iconography of the supernatural world did not entirely displace native Andean perceptions of divinity. Betanzos described how the Inca Pachacuti was overwhelmed by the imageless radiance of his vision, while Molina's Inca Pachacuti saw a sheet of crystal, a silvery gleam, dropping into the spring Susurpuquio, and it was only within the crystal that the Inca saw a figured representation of the divine Sun. Some dreams and visions dating from the colonial period retained this aniconic Andean core. Don Cristóbal saw the huaca Llocllay Huancupa as a dazzling spring of silver. Similarly, Santacruz Pachacuti's imagery of divinity was abstract. When the huacas fled from the Inca Mayta Capac, they had the appearance of fires and winds, while the huaca who conversed with the Inca Capac Yupanqui arrived with a rush of wind and left like thunder and lightning. The Creator himself was represented in Coricancha as a golden oval. Granted that Pachacuti Yamqui's visualization of this representation was perhaps derived not from any existing Inca image of the Creator but from his own conception of what such a representation ought to be, the golden disk corresponds felicitously to the radiant visions of Inca Pachacuti and Don Cristóbal.

Throughout the Andes, deity was often clothed in abstract, nonanthropomorphic guises. Andeans thus revered as their places of origin, or pacarinas, springs and mountains, lakes and rocks, none of which were ever endowed with a fully human identity. Santacruz Pachacuti's own visual rendering of the three "windows" in the rock of Pacaritambo from which the Incas had emerged accordingly consists of three rectangles, the central one being flanked by two trees representing the father and mother of the first Incas (fig. 43).[97] Similarly, the huacas who were revered in the vicinity of Cuzco were springs, rivers, irrigation canals, hills, mountains, caves, and plains.

Unlike Pachacuti Yamqui, Guaman Poma did at times apply anthropomorphic imagery to deities when depicting Andean rituals and concepts. He thus drew a tiny human-shaped figure on top of the rock of

[97] Pachacuti Yamqui, p. 249 = fol. 140; Sherbondy, *Mallqui: ancestros y cultivo de arboles* (1986).

3. THE TRUE RELIGION IN ANCIENT PERU

Pacaritambo with its three "windows" from which the Incas had come forth (fig. 44).[98] Elsewhere also his Andean holy presences are personalized by such figures (figs. 19, 20).[99] But these figures are dwarfed by the towering mass of sacred cliffs and crags, and in the drawing of the huacas whom Tupa Inca Yupanqui ordered to come to Cuzco, some are simply rocks unpermeated by human form (fig. 40).[100]

For ultimately, Andean deities defied description and definition in terms of a stable identity, whether human or nonhuman, that endured unchanged over time. Andean myths abound in tales of metamorphosis. But even without such explicit transformations, divine identity shifted and changed incessantly; it mocked human attempts at precise formulation.[101]

Like the God of the Hebrew Bible, who spoke to Moses from the burning bush, and to Job out of a whirlwind, Andean deities manifested themselves in visions of blinding radiance, and they came and departed like wind, fire, and lightning. However, witnessing these phenomena in their Andean guise, sixteenth- and seventeenth-century Spaniards could not recognize them as being endowed with theological momentum. Guaman Poma thus resorted to Christian historiography and Pachacuti Yamqui to Christian metaphysics to explain that the true God was at home in the Andes no less than in Spain and, moreover, that he had been at home in the Andes from remotest antiquity.

Many of Cuzco's holy places, as Pachacuti Yamqui saw it, were reminders of the age-old interaction between Andeans and their god, who was the true God. When the Spaniards came, the ancient meanings of these holy places were reaffirmed. Sapi was the root of Cuzco. Here, while still a prince, Inca Pachacuti had encountered a supernatural figure who threatened to cause the world to turn by blowing on his horn. Here also was an ancient root of a quinoa tree where sacrifice was made for the preservation of the city.[102] And it was here, on this venerable spot, Pachacuti Yamqui thought, that Cuzco's Christian epoch had been initiated.

[98] Guaman Poma, *Nueva Crónica*, p. 264 [266]; cf. 79.

[99] Guaman Poma, pp. 238ff. [240ff.]; 266 [268]–272 [274]. For the third quarter of the coat of arms, see A. Ricardo, *Vocabulario y phrasis en la lengua Quichua* (Lima, 1951), p. 38, choque ylla, rayo; p. 87, villca, ydolo. J. Szeminski, "Las generaciones," *Historica* 7 (1983): 99, translates Guaman Poma's "choqui ylla villca" as "Oro, tesoro, antepasado," while Urioste in his edition of Guaman Poma translates the phrase as "el noble del rayo o de oro." It would seem that Ricardo's dictionary definition is relevant to the depiction, because in the context posited by Guaman Poma's drawing, it recalls a ritual of Inca Cuzco; see Molina, *Fábulas*, p. 101, during the initiation ritual a prayer was spoken that began, "O Guanacauri, padre nuestro, siempre el Hacedor, Sol y Trueno y Luna no enbejezcan. . . ." See also Molina, *Fábulas*, p. 67, in May a sacrifice was made to the Sun, the Maker and "otro ydolo llamado Chuquiylla Yllapa que era la huaca del Relámpago y Trueno y Rayo."

[100] Guaman Poma, p. 261 [263].

[101] Cf. *Runa yndio* 1.7 (ed. Urioste).

[102] Above, sec. 1 at n. 8.

- 329 -

44. Armorial device of the Incas and of Cuzco. In the four quarters are
displayed: the Sun, deity of the Inca; the Moon, deity of his queen, the
Coya; the "Lightning" (*choqui ylla*) depicted as a star that has, like the Sun,
sixteen rays; and Pacaritambo surmounted by the human-shaped *huaca*
Guanacaure. The device is reminiscent of worship in Inca Cuzco, where
Sun, Moon, and Lightning were revered jointly. For Pacaritambo compare
fig. 43, and for Guanacaure see fig. 40. Guaman Poma, *Nueva Crónica*,
p. 79, Royal Library, Copenhagen. Photo from facsimile, Paris 1936.

After Manco Inca had become Inca, he and the Spaniards fought a battle against Atahualpa's general Quisquis.

> And so, they went to Capi, and the Marquess with the Inca, in the company of the holy Gospel of Jesus Christ, Our Lord, entered with great royal spendor and pomp of great majesty. . . . Fray Vicente went straight to Coricancha, the house constructed by the first Incas for the Maker. At last, the law of God and his long-awaited holy Gospel entered to take possession of the new vineyard . . . and there he preached like another Saint Thomas the apostle, patron of this kingdom.[103]

The preaching was both new and old: Peru was a "new vineyard,"[104] but Coricancha, the house of the Maker, was ancient. True religion was, as a result, far from being the exclusive possession of the Spaniards.

Writing in Andalucia, the Inca Garcilaso de la Vega, contemporary of Guaman Poma and Pachacuti Yamqui, arrived at a not dissimilar conclusion. But he travelled by a very different route. Guaman Poma and Pachacuti Yamqui spent their entire lives in the Andes, and their thinking was deeply embedded in the social and religious world that surrounded them. Garcilaso, by contrast, left Peru in 1560, at the age of twenty. He wrote surrounded by Spanish scholars, historians, and theologians, whose intellectual values he shared. But he did not entirely share their experience. For the experience which he chose to endow with significance and to write about was not so much his experience as the respected member of the Spanish intellectual aristocracy that he became in the course of long years of living in the peninsula. Rather, the experience that punctuated his life with images of haunting beauty and loss almost beyond the power of words to express was the vanished world of the Incas, the vanished world also of the Cuzco of his youth. To Garcilaso we now turn.

[103] Pachacuti Yamqui, *Relación*, pp. 327–328.
[104] For the image, see Matthew 20:1ff.

RELIGION AND PHILOSOPHY:
GARCILASO DE LA VEGA AND
SOME PERUVIAN READERS,
1609–1639

THE FIRST literary enterprise Garcilaso undertook after he settled in Montilla near Cordoba was the translation from Italian into Spanish of the *Dialogues on Love* by the Jewish Neoplatonist Leone Ebreo, which were first published in Venice in 1535.[1] Perhaps Garcilaso was drawn to Leone because Leone also had spent much of his life far from home, having been forced to leave his native Lisbon by Christian persecution. Certainly the *Dialogues* touched Garcilaso deeply. He wrote in the dedication of his translation to Maximilian of Austria how he had first read and translated short passages from the *Dialogues* for his own use "because I was enchanted with the gentle sweetness of their philosophy and with the beauty of which they treat." That was in 1586, when Garcilaso was beginning to make plans for writing the *Royal Commentaries of the Incas*, the first volume of which was published in 1609 and the second posthumously in 1617. Although Garcilaso did not explicitly refer to the *Dialogues* in this later work, Leone's philosophy was an Ariadne's thread running through his hand while he plotted his path in the labyrinth of facts and opinions that earlier historians had recorded about Andean and Inca religion. At times Garcilaso conveys an impression of learned timidity, for he appears to be hiding behind earlier writers, whose works he quoted with meticulous accuracy and exquisite courtesy. Among the more important of these earlier authorities are Cieza and Francisco López de Gómara, Agustín de Zárate, Jerónimo Román, through whom Garcilaso gained an indirect knowledge of Las Casas' *Apologética*, and José de Acosta. Garcilaso's deferential attitude toward these men of letters is explained by the reputation they enjoyed in Spain and Europe at large and by his own somewhat unconventional education "amidst arms and horses."[2] Yet behind this apparent timidity stands a self-willed thinker of

[1] This edition is reproduced in facsimile in Leone Ebreo, *Dialoghi d'Amore. Hebräische Gedichte. Herausgegeben mit einer Darstellung des Lebens und des Werkes Leones . . . von C. Gebhardt* (Amsterdam, 1929).

[2] Garcilaso, *Comentarios reales* (hereafter *CR*), 2.28, p. 84a; see Miro Quesada, *El Inca Garcilaso y otros estudios garcilasistas* (1971), pp. 477ff. Literature on Garcilaso is on the increase. A selection: Durand, "La biblioteca del Inca," *Nueva Revista de Filología Hispánica* 2

impressive erudition, whose subtle and all-pervasive originality stems not only from the Andean information he had drunk, as he wrote several times, "with my mother's milk" but also from his redeployment of Leone's philosophy in an Andean context.

Garcilaso's description of Leone's philosophy as being endowed with "gentle sweetness," *suavidad y dulzura*, must be understood carefully. For there is nothing soft, bland, or indeterminate to be found in the arguments that Filón and his beloved Sofía, who speak in the *Dialogues*, address to each other. The question to be resolved between them was whether Sofía would accept Filón's desire for her as compatible with, indeed as a necessary companion of, his love. At issue was the relation between physical and spiritual desire that arises from the will on the one hand, and spiritual love, a product of reason, on the other.[3] In expounding this relationship, Leone compared the knowledge that leads to love and desire among human beings to knowledge, love, and desire between God and man and then went on to expound knowledge and love as active within the person of God himself. Here Leone explained how divine love as perceived in the Hebrew Bible had also been fully comprehended by the Greek poets and philosophers, who frequently chose to express themselves in fable and allegory where the Bible used historical narrative. Leone thus applied reasoned explanation to a field of knowledge often torn apart by confrontations between sacred biblical and profane Greco-Roman erudition, and this is an aspect of his *suavidad y dulzura*. A very similar tone of "gentle sweetness" informed Garcilaso's description and discussion of Inca religion. In his estimation, the gulf between Christian truth and the religious ideas of the Incas had not been as absolute as some earlier authors had thought. But Garcilaso disliked confrontation and therefore passed lightly over areas of disagreement between himself and those authors, seeking instead to persuade his readers by placing before them his own alternative reading of Inca religion.

1. IDEAS OF THE HOLY

Given this agenda, Garcilaso interpreted Inca and Andean religion from the European and Christian point of view that he had been taught to adopt from infancy and that provided him with most of his historical and

---

(1948): 239–264 and *Nueva Revista de Filologia Hispanica* 3 (1949): 166–170; "Garcilaso," *Diogenes* 43 (1969): 14–21; Jakfali-Leiva, *Traducción, escritura y violencia colonizadora: un estudio de la obra del Inca Garcilaso* (1984); Brading, "The Incas and the Renaissance," *Journal of Latin American Studies* 18 (1986): 1–23; Zamora, *Language, Authority and Indigenous History in the Comentarios Reales de los Incas* (1988). The works of Miro Quesada and Durand, cited above, and R. Porras Barrenechea, *El Inca Garcilaso en Montilla* (1955), as well as J. Durand, *El Inca Garcilaso, clásico de América* (Mexico City, 1976), remain invaluable.

[3] Leone Ebreo, *Diálogo* 1.17a; 42b. Since what matters here is Garcilaso's reading of Leone Ebreo, I cite the latter's *Dialogues* from Garcilaso's translation.

philosophical terminology. To him, therefore, the Andean deities could not be the same living powers that they were for those of his contemporaries who were at home within the geographical and cultural sphere of those awesome presences. For unlike Don Cristóbal from Huarochiri, Pachacuti Yamqui, and even Guaman Poma, not to mention countless Andean villagers, the young Garcilaso spent as much time with Spaniards in the Peru that those same Spaniards were bringing into existence as he did with Incas and Andean people in the age-old Peru of huacas and the embalmed bodies of revered ancestors. It could not be otherwise, for "with the passage of time, the change of new events, and the modern histories of the new empire,"[1] the Cuzco where Garcilaso grew up was being transformed into a Spanish city, and the details of its Inca past were in the course of being forgotten. Yet Garcilaso wrote to arrest this process of forgetting. Leone Ebreo's "gentle sweetness" was not only the means whereby Garcilaso mediated to his readers the interests and opinions that Spanish historians had expressed about the Incas in the light of what he himself knew and thought. The "gentle sweetness" also articulated what Garcilaso had learnt in his youth from his mother's kinsfolk and the sense of loss he continued to experience as he reflected on the Andean past. But this sense of loss should not mislead Garcilaso's reader into overlooking the argumentative, polemical, and programmatic aspect of the *Royal Commentaries*. For Garcilaso's vision of Andean and Inca religion is a most meticulously crafted composite of history and theory, in which each piece of historical evidence is carefully set in its place in relation to each corresponding step of theoretical interpretation.

The overall framework of Andean religious history that Garcilaso adopted was pioneered by Cieza and elaborated by Las Casas in the *Apologética Historia*, followed by Jerónimo Román, whose *Repúblicas* of 1575, revised in 1595, Garcilaso knew well.[2] All three authors divided Andean religious history into a pre-Inca and an Inca epoch and argued that in the Andes, as elsewhere, the growth of religious refinement had gone hand in hand with cultural and political development. Taking this schema for granted, Garcilaso used it to interpret the Andean and Inca evidence he had collected himself.

In the first Andean age, before the advent of the Incas, the tenor of worship had been determined by basic human needs, hopes, and fears. During this epoch, religion had been everyone's private affair, so that there existed a plethora of gods particular to villages, lineages, and even

---

[1] Garcilaso, *CR* 3.23, p. 117a.

[2] Apart from sharing some of Jerónimo Román's ideas, Garcilaso cites him twice: *CR* 2.2, p. 43b and 5.18, p. 173b. Another work describing the "theatre of the world" that Garcilaso referred to was Giovannni Botero's *Relationi*; see *CR* 9.13, p. 351a; *Historia General del Perú* (hereafter *HG*), 1.7, p. 26a.

individual families.[3] For people "thought that someone else's god, occupied with someone else, could not help them, but helped only his own [devotees]. And thus they came to have so great a variety of gods, so many that they were without number."[4] These deities, which included plants, animals, rocks, and rivers, as well as the four elements, were worshiped for being endowed with qualities ranging from the fearful, admirable, or merely unusual down to the straightforwardly useful.[5] In regions that the refining influence of the Incas had not reached, such objects of worship survived, Garcilaso thought, until his own time. In Antisuyo, for example, the coca plant and the serpent *amaru* were revered, and in Manta people worshiped an emerald, this being a cult of which Garcilaso perhaps read in Cieza.[6]

Under the Incas, although those same unusual things—surprisingly beautiful or ugly, or noteworthy for some other reason—continued to attract reverent, curious, or admiring attention, this attention was no longer tantamount to worship. For the *amautas*, "who were their philosophers and the teachers of their republic"[7] had apprehended a certain hierarchy in the universe and decreed that people were to worship only "Pachacamac as the highest god and lord, and the Sun for the good he did to all, and that they should revere and honor the Moon as the Sun's wife and sister and the stars as ladies and attendants of his house and court."[8] Notwithstanding this new order of the worshipful that the Incas had introduced, the Spanish, according to Garcilaso, insisted on describing all objects of reverent attention indiscriminately as idols, because they misunderstood the different meanings of the Quechua term huaca. Not all huacas were idols, and they were not all worshiped.[9]

To clarify the issue, Garcilaso produced a philological analysis of the term. *Huaca* could be a temple or any sacred object or place. Some, but not all, of these were inhabited by demons posing as God and seeking to deceive Andeans into worshiping them. *Huaca* could also mean a burial place in the countryside or something that had been offered in sacrifice to

---

[3] Cf. Román, *República Gentilica* 1.13–14; see also *República de las Indias Occidentales* 1.2, fol. 355r.

[4] Garcilaso, *CR* 1.9, p. 19a.

[5] Garcilaso, *CR* 1.9–12.

[6] Garcilaso, *CR* 3.11, 4.17, 6.10, 9.8; cf. Cieza, *Crónica* 50.

[7] Cf. Taylor, ed., *Runa yndio* (1987), pp. 23f.

[8] Garcilaso, *CR* 2.4, p. 46b.

[9] Garcilaso may have had in mind the work of Acosta; for Acosta's classification of idolatry in *HNM* 5.2 see above, p. 265; *huaca*, see Acosta, *HNM* 5.2, p. 219; 4, pp. 221, 223; 5, p. 224; 9, pp. 230f. See also F. Pease, "Garcilaso andino," *Revista Historica* 34 (1983–1984): 41–52 at pp. 42f., on Quechua philology. For an excellent and new discussion of what *huaca* is, see Maarten J. D. Van de Guchte, *"Carving the World:" Inca Monumental Sculpture and Landscape* (Ph.D. dissertation, University of Illinois at Urbana-Champaign, 1990), pt. 4, chap. 9. Sadly, I had completed all but the very last details of this book by the time Van de Guchte's important dissertation became available for consultation.

the Sun. Another cluster of meanings was not primarily religious. For *huaca* could be applied to anything beautiful or excellent, as well as anything terrifying, monstrous, or remarkable, whether this was twins, individuals born with birth defects, or unusual rocks, stones, or mountains, including the entire Andean range of the Sierra Nevada.[10] Another kind of huaca was the heaps of pebbles and other objects, such as chewed coca and little sticks, that Spaniards noticed at the top of mountain passes, described as *apachita*, and considered to be a kind of idol. Garcilaso observed that, contrary to what Acosta had written,[11] these heaps were neither idols nor did Andeans call them *apachita*. *Apachecta* was the dative of the present participle *apachac* and meant "to him who causes to take away." Reaching the top of a mountain pass or of any arduous road, Andeans would set down their loads and understanding

> by natural reason that they ought to give thanks and make some offering to Pachacamac, the unknown god whom they adored in their minds, for having assisted them in that task . . . they would raise their eyes to the sky and lower them to the earth . . . and would repeat two or three times the dative *apachecta*. As an offering, they would pull out some eyelashes and blow them to the sky and discard the coca leaf they carried in their mouths, which they prized so much, saying, as it were, that they offered him the most valued thing they had to hand.[12]

Or else, Garcilaso went on, they might add some pebbles or sticks or a handful of earth to the piles of such things that were always to be found along regularly traveled paths. But none of this, Garcilaso argued, made apachecta into one of those objects of idolatrous worship that Spaniards were so prone to finding in the Andes.

Garcilaso thus dismembered the monolithic mass of idols, demons, and false gods that Spanish historians and apologists for Christianity were in the habit of discovering in Andean and Inca religion. Pachacuti Yamqui and Guaman Poma endeavored to do the same, but they chose a very different method of argumentation. For them, the operative argument in the demonstration that Andean or Inca religion had contained important elements of truth was that Andeans also had recognized the falsity of idols and had combatted demons and idolatrous practices. Garcilaso agreed that important, indeed fundamental, religious truths had been perceived in the Andes. At the same time, however, he showed that the notion of idolatry and demonic activity that historians and missionaries had adopted from the Christian apologists of late antiquity and had elaborated with reference to Andean and Inca religion were quite simply irrelevant

[10] Garcilaso, *CR* 2.4, pp. 47f.
[11] Acosta, *HNM* 5.5, p. 224.
[12] Garcilaso, *CR* 2.4, p. 48.

to the Andes. The demons were not nearly as active as had been supposed, and they were not active in the way that had been supposed; moreover, numerous objects traditionally described as idols on closer inspection turned out to be something else. Garcilaso was not the first or the only person to discern that the term *huaca* covered a wide variety of meanings and should not simply be translated as "idol."[13] He was, however, both the first, and for some centuries the only, person to grasp that Andean concepts of the holy differed radically from European and Christian ones. As a result, his account of Andean and Inca religious perceptions is infinitely more nuanced and differentiated than are those of any of his predecessors. With much tact and delicacy toward those historians who had differed from him, Garcilaso suggested to his readers that Andeans distinguished between different kinds and degrees of holiness and veneration.

Repeatedly, Garcilaso resorted to Quechua philology to make this point. But philology was not his only recourse. Among the deities with whom Spaniards populated the Inca pantheon was Illapa, the lightning flash, thunder, and lightning bolt.[14] Garcilaso thought they were wrong in believing that the Incas attributed divinity to Illapa. He therefore told one of his wry little stories about interactions between Indians and Spaniards in the Cuzco of his youth. Years earlier, when the Inca Guayna Capac was still living, lightning had struck a hall of his palace. The hall was immediately walled up so that no one could enter into it, because the Indians believed places where lightning fell to have been designated as "ill-starred, unlucky, and accursed" by the Sun.[15] When the Spaniards settled in Cuzco, that part of Guayna Capac's palace was assigned to Antonio Altamirano, and the "accursed" hall was opened and returned to regular use. The Indians found this action inexplicable, the more so when, some three years later, lightning struck that same spot again. "Now if the Indians had considered bolts of lightning to be gods," Garcilaso concluded, "surely they would have adored those spots as sacred and would have raised their most famous temples in them, saying that their gods, lightning, thunder, and lightning bolt, wanted to dwell in these places, having themselves designated and consecrated them."[16]

Christianity, in particular missionary Christianity, posited a universe polarized between pairs of opposites, the divine and the demonic, the sacred and the secular, good and evil. These divisions were spelled out in social differentiations between the clergy and the laity, as well as

[13] cf. Gonzalez Holguin, *Vocabulario de la lengua general*, p. 165, with Szeminski, *Un kuraca* (1987), pp. 93ff.

[14] Garcilaso, *CR* 2.23, p. 74b; see Acosta *HNM* 5.4, p. 221, copying Polo de Ondegardo, *Errores* 1.3, fol. 7v.

[15] Cf. Albornoz, *Instrucción*, p. 168: houses struck by lightning are walled up.

[16] Garcilaso, *CR* 2.1, p. 42b.

in spatial and temporal terms between consecrated and unconsecrated ground and between holy and ordinary days.[17] In the Andes, by contrast, perceptions of nature, society, and the holy were structured differently. As Garcilaso explained, a place or object could stand out from its environment for many different reasons. Where, for instance, in Christian Europe, priestly consecration was the only licit way of conferring inherent sacredness on a place, object, or person, in the Andes such a sacred quality could emerge in a variety of ways. According to Garcilaso, an object offered in sacrifice was sacred, was a huaca, but so was a snowy mountain. The sacred was thus capable of inhering in things independently of human action or ritual.[18] Furthermore, the Andean sacred was equally capable of generating attraction, as toward a lovely flower or plant, or aversion, "as when things depart from their natural course," for instance, when twins are born, or lightning strikes, or a volcano erupts.[19]

By anchoring this discussion of Inca religion in the meanings of the term *huaca* and not in any European or Christian conception of either "idols" or the sacred, Garcilaso was able to explain some basic principles of an Andean taxonomy of the holy. This taxonomy had no equivalents in sixteenth-century Christian thinking, because it classified as connected objects and concepts that in Europe were kept separate.

Moreover, this taxonomy made it clear that Andean and Inca definitions of reverence differed fundamentally from sixteenth-century Christian ones. The Spanish, whose reverence was focused on their one god, defined worship and adoration as the appropriate attitude with which to approach this god. Faced with a multitude of Andean huacas, Spaniards attributed to Andeans the same uniform attitude toward their huacas as they themselves cultivated toward their god. In making clear that Inca huacas were not worshiped and adored, that not even all of them were objects of cult, Garcilaso indicated just how profoundly different Andean concepts of the sacred were from their Christian counterparts. This difference applies both to Andean concepts of the sacred in themselves and to the manner in which they were organized. A case in point was the Inca solar cult.

On the one hand, this cult as described by Garcilaso was the upshot of the Andean interest in huacas: the Sun could be counted as one of these, although it far outstripped all terrestrial objects in splendor and beauty.[20]

---

[17] Cf. above, chap. 1.2 at nn. 35ff.

[18] Definitions regarding the nature of divine presence in the world played an important theological role in the late antique conflict between Christianity and paganism, and so again in the Andes. For late antiquity, see MacCormack, "*Loca sancta*: The Organization of Sacred Topography in Late Antiquity," in *The Blessings of Pilgrimage*, ed. R. Ousterhout (Champaign, 1990), pp. 7–40.

[19] Twins, Garcilaso, *CR* 2.4, p. 47ab; lightning, volcano, Albornoz, *Instrucción*, pp. 167, 170.

[20] Cf. Garcilaso, *CR* 2.1, p. 42.

But on the other hand, the Inca solar cult was political in nature, for as explained by Garcilaso, it arose directly out of the Inca myth of origins, which he described as "fables," or "historical fables," as distinct from "historical events."[21] This did not mean that the myth was false but that it must be understood in the same way that, according to Leone Ebreo,[22] we understand what Plato wrote, "in fables,"[23] of the origin of love in the *Symposium*, and what before him Moses wrote about the creation of the human race in the book of Genesis.

As a child, Garcilaso had been told a version of the Inca myth of origins by an aged Inca kinsman. The Sun had sent Manco Capac and his sister-consort Mama Ocllo, who were his children by the Moon, away from Lake Titicaca to found the imperial city of Cuzco. The site of the city was to be where the golden rod that the Sun had given to his children would easily sink into soft, fertile ground. The rod is evocative of the digging sticks that farmers used throughout the Andes, and the place where it sank into the ground at a single thrust was Guanacaure. Here, accordingly, Manco Capac and Mama Ocllo gathered people to build the city of Cuzco with Coricancha, the temple of the Sun, at its center.[24]

The structure of Coricancha, though stripped of its gold ornaments and converted into the convent of St. Dominic, was still standing when Garcilaso grew up in Cuzco. As he remembered the building some forty years later, its spatial layout articulated a theological message. At the sacred center of Coricancha was the Hall of the Sun, which the friars used for their church, and nearby, arranged around a cloister, were five other halls, one of which was dedicated to the Moon. In the Sun's hall was housed the gold image of the deity. Following Jerónimo Román, Garcilaso took this image to have been a gold disk in the form of a round solar face surrounded by rays and flames of fire, "just as painters paint it."[25] The mummies of deceased Inca rulers, Garcilaso had learned from an unknown source, were displayed on either side of the Sun's image, looking out at the people, while Guayna Capac, the last Inca to be stationed there before the Spaniards came, faced the Sun. Analogously, in the hall of the Moon, the image of the Moon, a woman's face, crafted on a silver disk, was flanked by the mummies of the Inca coyas,[26] while the mummy of Rahua Ocllo, Guayna Capac's mother, sat facing the divine ancestress.[27]

Another hall facing onto the cloister had been dedicated to the planet

---

[21] Garcilaso, *CR* 1.18, p. 29b; 21, p. 34b.

[22] Leone Ebreo, *Diálogo* 3, pp. 169b, 170b, 173a.

[23] In Spanish, *fabulando*.

[24] Garcilaso, *CR* 1.15–17.

[25] Garcilaso, *CR* 3.20, p. 113a, from Román, *República de las Indias Occidentales* (1575), 1.5, fol. 361r, col. a.

[26] Quechua, *coya*, "queen."

[27] Garcilaso, *CR* 3.21, p. 114a; cf. Cieza, *Segunda Parte* 27, p. 81 for Inca mallquis in Coricancha, and not on the deceased Inca's estate; cf. above, chap. III.3 at nn. 70ff.

Venus with the Pleiades and all the other stars, another to Illapa,[28] and another to the rainbow, *cuychu*: here a rainbow motif had been painted over the gold plaques lining the walls. The fifth hall was set apart for the use of the priests.[29] At one side of Coricancha was the Sun's maize garden, carefully irrigated by five watercourses, of which one was still flowing in Garcilaso's childhood.[30] This was one of the sacred fields to be solemnly harvested and plowed in the course of the Inti Raimi festival.

Convinced as he was that the Incas tended toward the worship of one god, Garcilaso explained the atmospheric and celestial forces that populated the Inca and Andean supernatural universe in terms of an ordered family of attendants on the Sun. This resembled the order of emanations, or reflections, of the one God that Leone Ebreo and other Neoplatonists had discerned in the Greco-Roman pantheon. It was indeed the case that the planet Venus, the Pleiades, and the stars at large were honored in the temple of Coricancha, but one needed to understand exactly how and why.

> Venus they called Chasca, which is to say "having long curly hair"; they honored this star because they said it was the page of the Sun, moving closest to him, sometimes in front and sometimes behind. The Pleiades they honored because of their strange position [in the sky] and the equality of their size. They considered the stars to be servants of the Moon, and therefore they gave them the hall next to that of their lady, so that they should be close at hand for her service.[31]

Similarly, Garcilaso asserted that contrary to what some Spaniards supposed, the three manifestations of Illapa were not adored as gods, let alone as some kind of trinity.[32] Rather, they were honored "as servants of the Sun. [The Incas] thought the same of them as the ancient gentiles thought of lightning, making it the instrument and weapon of their god Jupiter."[33] As for the rainbow, it was housed in Coricancha because the Incas had correctly understood that "it comes forth from the Sun, which is why the Inca kings took it for their arms and device, because they prided themselves on being descended from the Sun."[34]

[28] Comprising lightning, thunder, and lightning bolt.

[29] Garcilaso, *CR* 3.21–22; Rowe, *Introduction to the Archaeology of Cuzco* (1944), pp. 26–41, especially 29ff.

[30] Garcilaso, *CR* 3.23–24.

[31] Garcilaso, *CR* 3.21, p. 114a.

[32] See Garcilaso's polemic against Andean trinities invented by Spaniards, *CR* II.5, 6. *CR* 2.6, p. 49b is against "un autor" writing about the trinity Tangatanga; this unnamed author is Acosta, *HNM* 5.28; cf. above, chap. VI at n. 111; below, sec. 3 at n. 30.

[33] Garcilaso, *CR* 3.21, p. 114ab.

[34] Garcilaso, *CR* 3.21, p. 114b.

1. IDEAS OF THE HOLY

How the rainbow came forth from the sun, and what this meant, had been explained by Leone Ebreo. One strand of exposition in the *Dialogues on Love* demonstrates how movements of the soul that are activated in human love are paralleled in the cosmic order by the movements of the four elements, which also mingle with and love each other. The rainbow is the impression of the celestial fire of the sun on air—not on the light and serene air in the upper ranges of the sublunary sphere, however, but on the heavier and humid air that lies at a greater distance from the sun.[35] The rainbow thus exemplifies the order of the cosmos and the harmonious mingling of elements within that order; it is a case where one physical reality leads to an understanding of other such realities. At a more exalted and more abstract level of meaning, the rainbow, through which the one blindingly radiant light of the sun is impressed in multifarious colors on the watery clouds of the air, is an image for the blinding unity of God, which human understanding can only grasp through the gentle and diverse order of created nature.[36]

When thus Garcilaso stated that the Incas had "understood that the rainbow comes forth from the sun," he intended to imply that they had correctly apprehended how the cosmic order functioned and gave expression to this understanding in their sacred architecture, their concepts of divinity, and their festivals. However, unlike Leone Ebreo, the Inca amautas[37] did not articulate this understanding in abstract or theoretical terms but concretely, in the light of what was visible and tangible.[38] For example, Garcilaso explained, the Incas understood the solar year and were able to measure the course of the sun by means of columns erected for the purpose in and near Cuzco and other cities.[39] It was known, inter alia, that the shadow cast by these columns at midday became shorter the closer they were positioned to the equator.

Therefore they esteemed most of all the columns in [Quito] and vicinity as far as the seacoast, where, because the sun is in a plumbline, as bricklayers say, it casts no shadow at all at midday. For this reason they paid greater reverence to these columns, for they said that these were the sun's favorite seat, because here it sat straight and on the other columns it sat to one side. These and other similar simple things those people said in their astrology, because their imagination did not reach beyond what they saw materially with their eyes.[40]

---

[35] Leone Ebreo, *Diálogo* 2, p. 91a; cf. p. 53a.
[36] Leone Ebreo, *Diálogo* 3, p. 150a; cf. 199bf.
[37] Or "philosophers"; see Garcilaso CR 2.2, p. 43a.
[38] Garcilaso, *CR* 2.21–26.
[39] Garcilaso, *CR* 2.22–23.
[40] Garcilaso, *CR* 2.22, p. 73b.

Accordingly, the Incas dealt with the divine Sun, their ancestor, "as corporeally as if he had been a man like themselves," offering him dishes of food and toasting him with chicha.[41] And when Inca Viracocha won a victory, he sent a messenger to inform his divine father of the fact, "as though the Sun had not seen it."[42] It fitted with this Inca sense of the tangible and the concrete that in Coricancha the stars should be housed next to their lady mistress the Moon, and that there was likewise room in the temple for lightning, the servant of the Sun. What was expressed in the layout of the temple was what was visible in the sky. Accordingly, Garcilaso pointed out, unlike Europeans, the Incas did not imagine there to be more than one celestial sphere, nor did they imagine the signs of the zodiac to exist, and much less their influence on human affairs.[43]

The simple beauty and grace with which Garcilaso endowed Inca perceptions of divinity are derived, in the last resort, from Platonist sources, in particular Leone Ebreo. What Garcilaso remembered from the Cuzco of his childhood and youth was precisely what he could interpret in the light of these sources. His memories were therefore defined by some salient omissions. He said nothing of the gold statue of the Sun in the guise of a ten-year-old boy that figured so prominently in Inca cult, although this very statue was captured during the campaign against Vilcabamba in 1571 that he himself described.[44] Similarly, he said nothing of the cult of the Inca mummies in Haucaypata, even though he mentioned being shown some of these mummies by Polo de Ondegardo, who was very well informed on these matters.[45] And finally, despite considerable evidence to the contrary, he asserted that the Incas performed no human sacrifices.[46]

Nevertheless, Garcilaso did not invent his own version of Inca religion. He did, however, select and interpret evidence in the light of his Platonist convictions. This is clear, for instance, in his renderings and interpretations of Inca myth, especially when we compare them to those of other historians. Garcilaso's myth of the origin of rain and thunder is an example. Polo de Ondegardo, followed by Acosta and Murúa, had earlier explained that thunder (sic) in the Andes was called by the three names Chuquiilla, Catuilla and Intiillapa, and that the Indians pictured it as "a man who dwells in the sky carrying a sling and cudgel, and it is in his power to make rain, hail, and thunder, and everything else that belongs

[41] Cf. Guaman Poma, *Nueva Crónica*, p. 246 [248], fig. 17 in this book.
[42] Garcilaso, *CR* 5.19, p. 175.
[43] Garcilaso, *CR* 1.21, p. 72a.
[44] Garcilaso, *HG* 8.16.
[45] Polo de Ondegardo, *Errores* 2, fol., 7vf.; Garcilaso, *CR* 5.29, p. 189b.
[46] Garcilaso, *CR* 2.8, p. 54; similarly *Relación anónima*, p. 159a.

to the region of the air where clouds are formed."[47] In his childhood, Garcilaso had heard a different version of this myth. He was reminded of it by finding a similar one in the papers of the Jesuit mestizo Blas Valera. He thus reproduced the myth in the *Royal Commentaries*, along with an Inca poem on the same topic, which was also record by Valera.[48] The Maker of the world, Pachacamac, Garcilaso wrote, had brought into existence a *ñusta*,[49] the daughter of a king, whom he set into the sky to pour water from a pitcher when rain is needed on earth. At times, one of her brothers would break the pitcher, thereby causing thunder and lightning. Rain, hail, and snow thus resulted from the gentle action of the ñusta, while her more violent brothers caused the meteorological disruption of lightning and thunder.

Garcilaso's Incas portrayed every aspect of the visible world they perceived around them in a harmonious and beautiful mythic and cultic drama, the principal actors in which were the Sun and Moon and other celestial and atmospheric phenomena. Sacred buildings like Coricancha and the urban spaces of Cuzco and of the Inca provincial capitals that witnessed the annual round of festivals constituted the man-made stage upon which the drama unfolded. But there was a tension here, because behind the visible terrestrial and cosmic order, Garcilaso's Incas had perceived an invisible ordering Creator, so that much of their religious thinking concerned the appropriate formulation of the worship of the Sun in conjunction with the worship of this invisible Creator.

In the Inca poem about the rain ñusta, the divine Maker who had brought the ñusta into existence was described as "Pacharurac, Pachacamac," which Garcilaso translated as "the Maker of the world, the God who animates it." Explaining his translation, he wrote: "Pachacamac is to say, He who does in the universe what the soul does in the body. . . . *Cama* is to give soul, life, being, and substance."[50] Elsewhere, Garcilaso explained that

Pachacamac is a composite term made up of *pacha*, which is the entire world, and *camac*, the present participle of the verb *cama*, to animate. This verb comes from the noun *cama*, which is soul. Pachacamac is to say, He who gives soul to the entire world; and in its complete and entire significance it means He who does in the universe what the soul does in the body.[51]

[47] Polo de Ondegardo, *Errores* 1.3, fol. 7v; Acosta *HNM* 5.4; Murúa, *Historia del origen* (1590), 3.51.
[48] Garcilaso, *CR* 2.27, p. 80.
[49] Quechua, "princess."
[50] Garcilaso, *CR* 2.27, p. 80b.
[51] Garcilaso, *CR* 2.2, p. 43a.

Pachacamac was the deity whom according to Garcilaso the Inca amautas had identified as First Cause, Maker and Creator, higher even than the divine Sun.

In their worship, the Incas expressed both the nature of Pachacamac and the divine Sun and the relationship between them. For the Incas rendered to the Sun, as being the most noble part of the visible created universe, an exterior adoration that they expressed in ritual action and sacrifice. To Pachacamac, the supreme and invisible Maker and Creator, on the other hand, they offered the worship of their hearts, an interior adoration.[52] This worship involved no material transactions, no rituals or sacrifices; it was, rather, an utterly pure and simple spiritual adoration. Such a form of adoration was appropriate for Pachacamac not only because, as Creator, he stood in need of nothing but also because, being invisible, he was unknown.[53]

From the Incas, Garcilaso thought, the cult of Pachacamac had spread to other nations, although it there became contaminated with other forms of worship. Thus, on the coast, the great temple pyramid that Hernando Pizarro and his fellows later desecrated and despoiled was constructed for Pachacamac's worship. Here, according to Garcilaso, the Yunga people, still caught up in the primitive forms of worship of the pre-Inca epoch, set up their idols. These often took the form of fish, because fish was a staple food on the coast, while other idols in the image of a fox evoke one of the myths of nearby Huarochiri.[54] When the Incas gained political control of this entire region, an event that Garcilaso placed in the reign of Inca Pachacuti, they purified the temple of Pachacamac of its accretions and built next to it the pyramid of the Sun.[55] This double sanctuary was an eloquent monument to the paired cult of the divine Sun, the visible ancestor of the Incas, and the invisible and "unknown god"[56] and Maker Pachacamac.

In describing this invisible, unknown deity, perhaps Garcilaso had in mind the sermon Paul the Apostle preached to the Athenians about the altar they had dedicated to the Unknown God. The episode had earlier caught the attention of Las Casas followed by Jerónimo Román, whom Garcilaso had read. Acosta also mentioned the story.[57] Like the Athenians, the Incas did not, according to Garcilaso, have access to revealed truth, but, again like the Athenians, they perceived by natural reason that

---

[52] Garcilaso, CR 2.4, p. 46b.
[53] Garcilaso, CR 6.30, p. 232b.
[54] Garcilaso, CR 6.30, p. 232b; Runa yndio 5.42ff. (ed. Urioste); 5.21ff. (ed. Taylor).
[55] Garcilaso, CR 6. 31.
[56] Dios no conocido, Garcilaso, CR 2.4, p. 46b.
[57] Acts 17:23; Las Casas, AH 79, p. 408; Román, República Gentilica 1.5, fol. 10v; Acosta HNM 5.3.

a Supreme Being "who gives life to the universe and sustains it" must exist.[58] For the benefit of those Spaniards who could not believe that Indians were capable of conceiving of such a deity, Garcilaso quoted their own historian Agustín de Zárate, according to whose *History of Peru* first published in 1555, the Inca Atahualpa had explained to the missionary friar Valverde that Pachacamac "had created everything that was here."[59]

Yet the problem of Pachacamac's nature and identity was not so easily resolved, because from the beginning most Spaniards had been convinced that, whatever the Indians might say about Pachacamac, he was in actuality a demon who deceived credulous people with misleading prophecies. Garcilaso quoted two Spanish writers who took this view: one was Cieza[60] and the other was Jerónimo Román, who derived his information from Las Casas.[61] Both Cieza and Román wrote that in one of his prophecies Pachacamac had stated that he and the God of the Christians were one and the same and should therefore be worshiped together. To Cieza and Román, this prophecy was proof that Pachacamac was a demon endeavoring to retain his power within the Christian dispensation. Garcilaso, by contrast, thought that such an interpretation was yet another instance of the unwarranted demonization of Andean religious experience by the Spanish. The prophecy might indeed have been pronounced by a demon purporting to be Pachacamac, Garcilaso conceded; but from that it did not follow that Pachacamac himself was a demon.[62] If thus, he concluded, "they ask me who am Indian and a Catholic Christian . . . 'By what name do you call God in your language?' I would say, 'Pachacamac,' because in the general language of Peru there is no other name for God except this one."[63]

According to Garcilaso, the twofold exterior and interior worship of the Incas represented the culmination of Andean theology for several converging reasons. Wherever their power extended, the Incas had replaced the multifarious Andean cults addressed to objects satisfying the human need for food and shelter and to other objects arousing hope, fear, and wonder, with the one universal cult of the Sun. In practical and spiritual terms, the Sun superseded and replaced all those inferior objects of worship. For on the one hand, the Sun's light and warmth sustained all living beings, and therefore it stood higher in the life-giving chain of causation than any of the plants and animals that Andeans worshiped; and on the

[58] Garcilaso, *CR* 2.2, p. 43b.
[59] Garcilaso, *CR* 2.2, p. 43b; for Garcilaso's own account of this episode, see *HG* 1.22–27.
[60] Cieza, *Crónica* 72, cf. above, chap. II.1 passim; chap. III.1 at nn. 14ff.
[61] Las Casas, *AH* 131, p. 687; Román, *Rep. Ind.* 1.5, fol. 361v.
[62] Garcilaso, *CR* 2.2, p. 44.
[63] Garcilaso, ibid. The polemic is against Acosta, *HNM* 5.2, p. 220, who denies that there existed a generic term for "god" in Quechua.

VIII. RELIGION AND PHILOSOPHY: GARCILASO

other hand, the Sun's beauty and splendor raised it above all terrestrial counterparts, its excellence being most particularly discernible to the noblest of the senses, which was the sense of sight.[64] In training one's faculties on the Sun, therefore, one strove for the most exalted form of existence and the most exalted kind of understanding attainable on earth. This was why the worship of the visible Sun, paired as it was with the worship of the invisible Creator, Pachacamac, led the Incas to apprehend—albeit only in their customary concrete and unspeculative fashion[65]—a set of profound philosophical truths. It was from Leone Ebreo that Garcilaso learned how the truths that the Incas had apprehended in their religious observance could be articulated and explained.

Like other Neoplatonists, Leone Ebreo thought that traces of the intelligible universe, the realm of the divine intellect, were imprinted on the visible, material universe that is perceptible to the five senses. In addition, the intelligible and the material universe were related to each other by means of an interconnected hierarchy of existing things, ranging from the divine intellect and the ideas down to the world soul and down finally to animate and inanimate material bodies. In this hierarchy of existing things, soul had "a mixed nature of spiritual intelligence and corporeal mutation," much as Aristotle would have described it.[66] The relationship between the intelligible and the material universe, Leone thought, was pictured by the sun and moon, and could therefore be apprehended by human perception; for just as eyesight gives access to the physical universe, so the sight of the intellect gives access to the intelligible universe of the ideas. It is thus possible to understand that "the sun is the image of divine intellect, from which all other intellect is derived, and the moon is a semblance of the world soul, from which all other souls proceed."[67] More than that:

The light of the sun is not a body, nor is it a passion, quality, or accident of a body. . . . Rather, it is nothing other than the shadow of intellectual light or its resplendence communicated to the most noble of bodies. Hence the wise prophet Moses says about the beginning of the creation of the world that, when everything was a darkling confusion . . . the spirit of God, breathing on the waters of chaos, produced light. He intended to say that from the resplendent divine intellect visible light was brought forth on the first day of creation.[68]

[64] Garcilaso, CR 2.1; Leone Ebreo, Diálogo 3, p. 109b.
[65] Garcilaso, CR 2.2, p. 44b.
[66] Aristotle, On the Soul 3.3, 427a27, 427b28, and, in particular, 3.4, 429a21; Leone Ebreo, Dial. 3, p. 109a.
[67] Leone Ebreo, Diálogo 3, p. 109b.
[68] Leone Ebreo, Diálogo 3, pp. 110f.

Throughout the *Royal Commentaries* Garcilaso refused to explain to his readers whatever deeper or allegorical meanings could be derived from his text, thus inviting readers to apply such interpretation as they thought fit.[69] At the same time, Garcilaso posited a series of contradictions that pervade his entire work and in effect point to what he himself considered to be the most appropriate and most truthful interpretation. On the one hand, accordingly, the solar religion of the Incas was idolatrous, and Garcilaso himself repeatedly said so. On the other hand, Cieza, Las Casas, and others had already observed that in focusing their worship on the most noble and exalted of created beings, the Incas made an approach toward, or even glimpsed some aspect of, true religion. Garcilaso pressed this argument a little further. If it was truly the case that the light of the sun was the shadow of intellectual light communicated to the most noble of bodies, as Leone Ebreo had written, then one could not state so categorically that to worship the sun was idolatrous. This is indeed what Garcilaso suggested when he juxtaposed the exterior worship that the Incas expressed for the Sun with their interior worship of Pachacamac. But there were further issues at stake.

The question as to how exterior acts of worship such as fasting or offering alms should be balanced by interior ones, such as silent prayer and seeking God in one's heart, aroused much theological agitation in sixteenth-century Spain.[70] In fact, this was one of the most acrimoniously discussed questions of the Reformation and Counter-Reformation. Spaniards in Peru had thus been sensitized to the issue of exterior and interior worship, and discussed repeatedly whether Andeans had any conception of what was at stake. For the most part it was thought that they did not. Missionaries and officials who found that Andeans confessed their sins and afterwards performed acts of cleansing argued that the sins being confessed were only sins of action, not of thought; similarly, the cleansing was considered to be physical and exterior, not spiritual and interior.[71] Likewise, the Spanish supposed that when Andeans thought of the afterlife, they envisioned a physical, not a spiritual, state. Garcilaso did not take up any explicit position in this discussion. Rather, as so often, he made his opinion known by implying that the topic in hand had been misconstrued from the bottom up and was thus unfit for further comment.

He did this by revising what earlier historians had written about Inca veneration of huacas, pacarinas, mummies, and countless other objects to which, so Spaniards thought, worship was addressed. Garcilaso detected two assumptions that characterized Spanish attitudes to Inca religion, the

[69] See Garcilaso, *CR* 1.18.
[70] See Bataillon, *Erasmo y España*, pp. 196ff., 828ff.
[71] Polo de Ondegardo, *Errores* 5.2, fol. 9r; contra: *Relación anónima*, p. 165.

first being that Inca religion was <u>polytheistic,</u> and the second that it had been <u>demonically inspired.</u> According to Garcilaso, both of these assumptions were wrong. Undeniably, as Scripture explained, the devil deceived mankind. But this did not mean that all aspects of Andean religion were demonically inspired. Rather, before the Incas, and beyond their frontiers, religious observance was generally motivated by need, hope, and fear: in short, by ignorance. The devil could and did play a certain part in creating the resulting beliefs and rituals, but not to the extent that Spaniards imagined. When questioned, Garcilaso explained, the Indians

> do not dare to give an account of these things with the proper meaning and explanation of the terms, seeing that Christian Spaniards abominate everything they hear as things of the devil. Moreover, the Spaniards refuse to ask for information clearly and simply and assume that what they are told is of the devil, just as they imagine it to be. Also, errors arise because Spaniards lack a thorough knowledge of the General Language of the Incas, and do not understand the derivation, composition, and specific meaning of terms resembling each other.[72]

Indeed, there existed here an area of lamentable ignorance among the very Spaniards who claimed the greatest linguistic expertise, that is, the missionaries. In Cordoba, Garcilaso discussed with a Dominican friar who in Peru had taught Quechua to missionaries the meaning of the word *pacha*, as in Pachacamac, "meaning world, universe, and also . . . the sky and earth." The friar, seeking to display his expertise, said:

> "And it also means clothes, utensils, and house furnishings." I said, "Yes, but tell me, what difference is there in pronunciation in that case?" He said to me, "I do not know." I said, "You have been teaching the language and you do not know that?"[73]

After Garcilaso had explained the difference in pronunciation, "the teacher and the other friars who were present were greatly astonished."[74] Another egregious lexical error perpetrated by Spaniards concerned the term *huaca*. Garcilaso explained that *huaca* with the last syllable pronounced in the back of the throat is not a noun referring to idols but a verb meaning "to weep." But some Spanish historians whom Garcilaso courteously did not name, being ignorant of this crucial difference, wrote

---

[72] Garcilaso, *CR* 2.2, p. 44a, free translation.
[73] Transl. Livermore; see further on the point Garcilaso is making, B. Mannheim, *The Language of the Inca since the European Invasion* (1991), chap. 1, sec. 2.
[74] Garcilaso, *CR* 2.5, p. 49a.

that "the Indians enter their temples to make sacrifice with weeping and lamenting, which is what *huaca* means."[75]

What was at stake here was more than Spanish linguistic ignorance, for Quechua had been the vehicle of the very ideas and concepts that the historians whom Garcilaso discussed tended to claim were missing among the Incas.[76] Spaniards unable to distinguish the Quechua verb for weeping from the noun *huaca* and capable of confusing Pachacamac, the maker of the universe, with a maker of clothes and utensils were untrustworthy interpreters of Andean religion.

2. THE PHANTASM VIRACOCHA

Garcilaso's account of the Incas' exterior worship of the Sun and their interior adoration of Pachacamac, along with his analysis of Andean and Inca concepts of the holy, responded to a large variety of questions and criticisms that had been raised in Spain with regard to Andean and Inca religion. Among authors whom Garcilaso had read, the principal interpretative directions with regard to religion in the New World were represented by Cieza, Jerónimo Román, and Acosta. Cieza, deeply disturbed by what he saw as the theological and ethical implications of Andean and Inca religion, had attributed those Andean religious ideas that dismayed him most to demonic manipulation of the imagination. Acosta, on the other hand, was content to attribute those same ideas and observances to human responsibility. The deficiencies he perceived in Andean and Inca religion were thus, in the last resort, quite simply the outcome of what he viewed as Indian cultural inferiority. Garcilaso, while he considered Cieza's demons to be an unsatisfactory solution of the problem of religious difference, could not accept from Acosta that Andeans, and in particular the Incas, had been so significantly inferior to Europeans in their political and intellectual, and therefore in their religious, attainments. However, Acosta was only one of several among Garcilaso's earlier contemporaries struggling to interpret Amerindian religions. In particular, Las Casas' comparative *Apologética Historia* had given rise to Jerónimo Román's work on the *Republics of the World*, where pre-Columbian Mex-

[75] Garcilaso, *CR* 2.5 p. 48b; see Gómara, *Historia*, chap. 112; Zárate, in M. Bataillon, "Zárate ou Lozano?" *Caravelle* 1 (1963): 24: Guacas que es nombre de llorar, y assi lloran quando en aquellas templos entran. See further, on *guacanc* for "to weep" and also to refer to the sound made by animals, Domingo de Santo Tomás, *Arte*, chap. 23, fol. 71v. The friar whom Garcilaso had in mind appears to have been Gregorio García, who visited him, consulted the *Royal Commentaries* before they were published, and cited them in his *Origen* (1607), Preface, p. 8. In *Origen* 4.20, p. 463, García wrote that he learned from Garcilaso that Gómara had been mistaken in deriving *huaca* from *huacani*, "to weep," because the pronunciation of the two words was different. This merges with Garcilaso's story but places García in a less unflattering light.

[76] See Garcilaso, *CR* 7.4, p. 250b, on the civilizing impact of Quechua.

ico and Peru were discussed in admiring tones. Garcilaso studied this work carefully, and perhaps it was here, as well as in Leone Ebreo, that he found the inspiration for his juxtaposition of interior and exterior worship among the Incas.[1]

Yet, when considered in the context of the Andean evidence, this juxtaposition, with its monotheistic trajectory, created as many problems as it solved. Garcilaso demonstrated that there were no grounds for considering Andean and Inca religion as a mindless polytheism, a random conglomerate of myths, beliefs, and cults. However, in making this case, Garcilaso set aside much evidence that did not harmonize with his thesis. In particular, the authors Garcilaso read agreed that the creator god of the Incas was not Pachacamac, as Garcilaso insisted was the case, but Viracocha, or Ticci Viracocha.[2] Moreover, in Garcilaso's youth, traces of Viracocha's worship could still be found in the valley of Cuzco. A circle of five stones, a hill, a mountain, and a spring bore his name[3]—or possibly the name of Inca Viracocha, who was named after this deity.[4] And there was also Viracocha's temple, Quishuarcancha,[5] which was situated above the dwelling of Diego Ortiz de Guzman, whom Garcilaso knew.[6]

However, for someone raised in the Christian tradition, as Garcilaso had been, the figure of Viracocha raised a variety of problems and contradictions that made him hard to comprehend. Some myths of origins described Viracocha as more than one person.[7] Other myths depicted him as a single creator god, but yet others recounted how he wandered about Andean villages dressed in rags. Sometimes he acted beneficently, while at other times he manifested himself as a destroyer and trickster. In Jerónimo Román's *Repúblicas* Garcilaso will thus have read the myth of Viracocha the creator and his evil son, who ruined what the father had made, just as Lucifer corrupted the creation of the Christian god.[8] Finally, Viracocha's name, when translated, did not seem to produce a usable meaning. "Ocean of fat" is what Garcilaso, working within the limitations of sixteenth-century etymology, took the term to mean.[9] Hence, "Ticivir-

---

[1] Román, *República de las Indias Occidentales* 1.3, fol. 354va.

[2] E.g., Acosta *HNM* 5.3; 6.21, quoted by Garcilaso, *CR* 5.18; Rowe, "Creator worship," in *Essays in Honor of Paul Radin* (1960), pp. 408–429; Pease, *El Dios Creador Andino* (1973); Rostworowski, *Estructuras andinas de poder* (1983), pp. 30ff.

[3] Stone circle, Co-6:5; hill, Rowe, "An Account," *Ñawpa Pacha* 17 (1979): 73, no. 11; mountain, Cu-10:4; spring, An-6:5.

[4] Acosta, *HNM* 6.20.

[5] Molina, *Fábulas*, p. 59; Ch-6:2, ed. Rowe (1979), with p. 74, nos. 18–19.

[6] Garcilaso, *CR* 4.2, p. 123a; 7.9, p. 259a.

[7] E.g., Betanzos, above, p. 109.

[8] Above, chap. v.2 at n. 32; Román, *República de las Indias* 1.3, fol. 358r.

[9] Garcilaso, *CR* 5.21, p. 178b. But as so often, Gonzalez Holguin was on the right track, see his *Vocabulario*, p. 353: Viracocha. Era epicteto, del Sol honrroso nombre del Dios que adoravan los indios y de ay ygualandolos con su Dios llamavan a los españoles viracocha.

acocha" apparently was one of the divine names that Spaniards ignorant of Quechua had recorded in error. These Spaniards "give another name to God, which is Ticiviracocha. Of this name, I do not know what it signifies and neither do they."[10]

The name Pachacamac, "Maker of the World," on the other hand, did reveal what this deity was worshiped for. Furthermore, a tradition likely to have been preserved in the family of Garcilaso's great-grandfather, the Inca Tupa Inca Yupanqui,[11] suggested that the Creator whom the Incas worshiped was indeed Pachacamac. The earliest mention of this tradition occurs in the *Relación de Chincha* of 1558:

> Pachacamac, which is to say, "he who gives being to the earth," appeared in the form of a man to Tupa Inca Yupanqui where a palace now stands. He came in some dreams that the Inca had, [saying] that the creator of everything was to be found in the valley called Yzma.[12]

Hernando de Santillán heard a somewhat different and more detailed account of this same tradition:

> When the mother of Tupa Inca Yupanqui was pregnant with him, he spoke in her womb and said that the Maker of the Earth was among the Yungas, in the valley of Irma. A long time afterward, when the said Tupa Inca had grown up and ruled, his mother told him what had happened. He therefore resolved to look for the Maker of the Earth in the said valley of Irma, which is the valley now called Pachacama. There he prayed many days and undertook long fasts, and at the end of forty days, the Pachahc Camahc who they say was the Maker of the Earth spoke with him. He said that the Inca had been most blessed to find him, and that it was he who gave being to all things here below, and that the Sun was his brother and gave being to what was above. Therefore the Inca and those who were with him offered him great sacrifices and burned much cloth and gave him thanks for the favor he had bestowed on them. They asked him what sacrifices he wanted. The huaca told them through the rock in which he spoke to them that he had a wife and children and that they should build a house for him there in Irma. The Inca ordered it to be built in his presence, and it is a building that is standing today, of great height and splendor, which they call the great huaca of Pachacama.

This last fact was already noted by Domingo de Santo Tomás, *Lexicon*, fol. 177r, s.v. Viracocha. For a modern lexical study, see Szeminski, *Un kuraca* (1987), pp. 12ff.

[10] Garcilaso, *CR* 2.2, p. 24a. Elsewhere, Garcilaso wrote "Ticci Viracocha." Cieza, *Segunda Parte* 5, analogously translated Viracocha as "foam of the sea"; see above, chap. III.2 at n. 14.

[11] Gregorio García, *Origen* (1607), Preface, p. 8.

[12] C. de Castro and D. de Ortega Morejón, *Relación de Chincha*, ed. Trimborn (1938), p. 246.

. . . There the huaca said to the Inca that his name was Pachahc Ca-mahc, which is to say, He who gives being to the earth. And so the name of this valley of Irma changed to Pachacama.[13]

Some aspects of this account of Pachacamac are incompatible with Garcilaso's portrayal of the Creator but are substantiated in other sources. The myths of Huarochiri mention Pachacamac's children,[14] and sacrifices offered to Pachacamac are extensively documented. Garcilaso's Pachacamac, on the other hand, was invisible and received only the interior worship of the heart. Yet Garcilaso was not alone in holding such ideas. Cristóbal de Molina, for example, had explained that the Creator was "not born of woman, and immutable, and would have no end," and that he received only few sacrifices, while according to Acosta the Creator received nothing, because "being universal lord and creator, he did not need it."[15]

According to Santillán, Pachacamac revealed to Tupa Inca Yupanqui that he and the Sun worked in correlation with each other, one in the lowlands and the other in the sierra. Here also, the myths of Huarochiri agree.[16] If Garcilaso knew of such a tradition, he transformed the terrestrial juxtaposition of the Sun and Pachacamac, which had arisen from the cultural and physical geography of the Andes, into a cosmic and universal one such as was envisioned in Leone Ebreo's Platonist theology. Similarly, in ascribing the worship of Pachacamac to all Incas beginning with the earliest, he universalized a historical tradition that was of relatively late origin by extending it to the entire Inca period.

As a result, Garcilaso experienced great difficulties in making sense of those numerous Andean and Inca myths and cults where Viracocha rather than Pachacamac figured as Creator or chief deity. He did, however, find a way of doing so. When first broaching the topic of the Inca worship of Pachacamac, "the supreme God and Lord," he wrote, "Below, in its place we will treat of the god Viracocha, who was a phantasm that appeared to a prince, heir to the Incas, saying that he was a son of the Sun."[17] The prince here referred to was Viracocha, who was to become the eighth Inca of the traditional dynasty. His vision was described both by Garcilaso and by the historian Sarmiento de Gamboa, who collected his information in Cuzco not long after Garcilaso had left for Spain. According to Sar-

[13] Santillán, *Relación* 28, p. 111b.
[14] E.g., *Runa yndio*, chap. 14.
[15] Molina, *Fábulas*, pp. 55 (fol. 3v of MS for word "fin," omitted in transcription) and 51, respectively; Acosta, *HNM* 6.21, p. 308; but note, all these sources cite Viracocha as the Creator.
[16] *Runa yndio* 22.2–6 (ed. Taylor); 22.276 (ed. Urioste); above, p. 260.
[17] Garcilaso, *CR* 2.4, p. 47a.

miento, Viracocha Inca was initially given the name Hatun Topa Inca. When Hatun Topa was in Urcos,

> where there is the magnificent huaca of Ticci Viracocha, one night Viracocha appeared to him. In the morning, he called together his nobles, one of whom was Gualpa Rimache, his tutor, and told how that night Viracocha had appeared to him and promised him and his descendants great good fortune. Gualpa Rimache congratulated and saluted him with the name "O Viracocha Inca!" . . . and this name he kept for the rest of his life. Others say that he took this name because when he . . . had his ears pierced, he chose Ticci Viracocha as his sponsor.[18]

According to Sarmiento, Viracocha Inca brought about a turning point in the growth of the Inca empire, because he was the first to keep lands that Inca warriors invaded permanently occupied.[19]

Garcilaso gave Inca Viracocha's vision a different political context. As a member, through his mother, of the lineage of Tupa Inca Yupanqui, Garcilaso shared in his kindred's enmity against the lineage of Inca Pachacuti. This enmity had earlier fired the war between Guascar and Atahualpa and was still deeply felt in early colonial Cuzco.[20] Whenever possible, therefore, Garcilaso detracted from Inca Pachacuti's achievements. Where thus mainstream Inca tradition celebrated Pachacuti as recipient of a vision of the Sun or the Creator and as victor over the Chancas, Garcilaso attributed both these achievements to Inca Viracocha. The vision and victories of Inca Viracocha recorded by Sarmiento appear to have provided the foundation for this revision of Inca history. Apart from taking issue with established Inca historical traditions in his account of Inca Viracocha's life, Garcilaso also used this account to make a new and highly idiosyncratic contribution to discussions of Inca religion.

According to Garcilaso, Inca Viracocha's vision occurred while he was living in exile, herding the llamas of the Sun in the plain of Chita. Chita, situated on the route taken by the runners expelling evils during Citua, was the point at which travelers lost the city of Cuzco from sight.[21] In Garcilaso's narrative, the young Viracocha himself described what happened to him at Chita to his father, the Inca Yahuar Huacac:

> When I was resting at midday—although I cannot tell whether I was asleep or awake—I saw before me a strange man different from ourselves in dress and appearance. For he had a beard more than a palm

---

[18] Sarmiento, *Historia Indica* 24, p. 228b; see also the more concise account by Betanzos, *Suma* (1987), 1.5, p. 22b.
[19] Sarmiento, ibid.
[20] See Rostworowski, *Historia del Tahuantinsuyu* (1977), pp. 50–61, 85, 148ff.
[21] Molina, *Fábulas*, p. 75; An-3:6.

in length, and his garment was long and loose, covering him down to his feet. He had with him, tied by the neck, an unknown animal. He said to me: "Nephew, I am a son of the Sun and brother of the Inca Manco Capac and the coya Mama Ocllo Huaco, his consort and sister, your first ancestors. Thus I am brother to your father and all of you. My name is Viracocha Inca, and I come from our father the Sun to inform you . . . that most of the provinces of Chinchaysuyu are in revolt . . . therefore, tell my brother to prepare and forearm. . . . And to you I say that in whatever adversity may befall you, never fear that I shall fail you, for I will assist you in everything as my own flesh and blood."[22]

Although the old Inca was convinced that his son was "imagining nonsense [and pretending it was] revelations of his father the Sun,"[23] the Chancas did invade, and Viracocha defeated them. In battle, he was assisted by an army of twenty thousand allies, whose totally unexpected appearance he attributed "to the promise that his uncle, the phantasm Viracocha Inca, had made to him when he appeared to him in his dreams."[24] Even as the battle was being fought, it became the subject of Inca mythologizing:

> When the Incas saw succor reaching them, they did not pass over this opportunity of enhancing their deeds by telling fables and falsely attributing events to the Sun . . . They therefore shouted loudly, saying that the very rocks and shrubs of that plain were turning into men to fight in the service of their prince, because the Sun and the god Viracocha ordered it thus.[25]

By way of showing how Spanish historians tended to distort Inca evidence, Garcilaso then went on to quote from Jerónimo Román and Acosta the two somewhat different versions of this story of the pururaucas, stones that had been converted into men or men into stones.[26]

Later, Garcilaso went on, the Inca Viracocha constructed at Cacha a temple to the personage, "his uncle the phantasm" whom he had seen in his vision, with a statue resembling as closely as possible the appearance of this phantasm. At its feet was "a strange animal of unknown appearance with lion's claws, tied by the neck with a chain, one end of which was in the hand of the statue."[27] This edifice and the statue had earlier

---

[22] Garcilaso, CR 4.21, p. 143.

[23] Garcilaso, CR 4.22, p. 143b.

[24] Garcilaso, CR 5.17, p. 171b.

[25] Garcilaso, CR 5.18, p. 173, free translation.

[26] See above, chap. VI at n. 136 and chap. V.3 at n. 28.

[27] Garcilaso, CR 5.22, p. 180a; cf. Molina, Fábulas, p. 84, Viracocha at Urcos in a long white tunic, hair down to the belt, with "an eagle and a falcon carved in stone at the door of the huaca."

been inspected and described by Cieza and Betanzos, who both noted that some Spaniards considered the statue to represent one of the apostles who had supposedly preached in Peru.[28] In addition, Betanzos thought the statue held a book, but neither he nor Cieza mentioned the chained animal. Persons known to Garcilaso identified the apostle as Bartholomew, possibly because he was customarily represented with a chained devil at his feet (fig. 45).

Garcilaso's strange story of Prince Viracocha's vision is made up of diverse factual and speculative components. Like earlier historians recounting the vision of Pachacuti, Garcilaso sought to explain what exactly had happened regarding the pururaucas, the divinely appointed allies of the Incas during the Chanca war. In addition, he endeavored to explain who was seen in the vision and how precisely a vision such as Prince Viracocha experienced could occur.

No serious obstacles stood in the way of an interpretation of the story about the pururaucas because by the early seventeenth century, rationalization of Andean myth had become a well-established procedure, which Garcilaso himself adopted regularly. The task in hand was to find the historical core to any given myth, or, as Garcilaso termed it, "fable," whereupon fiction and historical fact could easily be separated. This is precisely what Garcilaso did in explaining the pururaucas as a fiction invented by the Incas themselves on the field of battle.

Regarding the personage seen in the vision, and how the vision occurred, Garcilaso applied to the problem insights he derived from Leone Ebreo and from the Aristotelian philosophical tradition of his day.

Whenever Garcilaso referred to the personage seen by Prince Viracocha in his dream or vision, he called him a phantasm, *fantasma*. As Garcilaso was aware, phantasms were the images that imagination abstracted from sense perception and passed on to intellect as the foundation for thought. These images could be lucid and true or vaporous and misleading.[29] Inca Yahuar Huacac was convinced that his son's phantasm was of the latter kind, that he was "imagining nonsense." The old Inca's judgment converged with Acosta's earlier description of one branch of idolatrous worship as being focused on imagined objects that "neither are nor ever were anything" beyond whatever statues or paintings might be created to represent them.[30]

While working on the *Royal Commentaries*, Garcilaso received a visit from the Dominican missionary Gregorio García, who had worked in Peru for some years. In his book on the origin of American Indians, which he published in 1607, shortly after this visit, García explained in

---

[28] Betanzos, *Suma* 1.2, p. 14; Cieza, *Crónica* 98; *Segunda Parte* 51.
[29] Above, chap. 1.1 passim.
[30] Acosta, *HNM* 5.2, p. 219; above, p. 266.

45. The apostle Bartholomew holding the devil under his feet by a chain. In his right hand, he carries a knife betokening his martyrdom by decapitation and a book inscribed with the words "I believe in the Holy Spirit." Wood relief by Felipe Vigarni, choir of Toledo Cathedral.

some detail and on the basis of an example often repeated in scholastic theology how the imagination produced images without foundation in reality. In waking life, he wrote, a person might see mountains and gold. In a dream the imagination could distill these into the phantasm of a golden mountain, such as could in turn be exploited by the devil for his own fraudulent purposes. This was exactly what in García's opinion had often occurred in the Americas.[31]

If Garcilaso was not reminded of this theory of the origin and content of Amerindian religion when conversing with Gregorio García, he still had ample opportunity to read about it in a more diffuse fashion in the many writers whom he quoted in his long work. He adopted from this popular theory the idea that an allegedly supernatural being could be derived from a phantasm, a mental image composed of distinct and disparate phenomena excerpted from waking life. The phantasm that Inca Viracocha saw was such a composite image, a strangely dressed individual presenting himself as an emissary and son of the Incas' visible deity, the Sun, and a brother of Manco Capac, who was long dead. In accord with established theological precedent, Garcilaso contemplated the possibility that Inca Viracocha's phantasm was of demonic origin:

It may well be believed that the devil, the master of all evil, produced the dream while the prince was sleeping, or that he appeared to him in that form while he was awake, for it is not known for sure whether he was asleep or awake. . . . The enemy of mankind may have done this to increase the credit and repute of the idolatrous religion of the Incas: seeing that the Inca kingdom was steadily growing and that the Incas were imposing their vain law and heathen superstition so as to be considered as gods and obeyed as such, he would appear to them in that form as well as in other guises the Indians mention.[32]

Garcilaso made no clear, unambiguous statement as to the nature of Inca Viracocha's phantasm but merely explored the different possibilities that could have brought it about, thereby indicating his own opinion of the strengths and weaknesses of Inca theology. While thus conceding that Inca Viracocha's phantasm and similar appearances could have been caused by the devil, Garcilaso was careful to limit the range and significance of demonic interference in Inca religion. Where, for instance, earlier authors had given the impression, even if they did not always explicitly state, that the Indians had worshiped the devil in the temple of Pachacamac,[33] Garcilaso pointed out that although the devil spoke there,

[31] Gregorio García, *Origen* 5.1; cf. above, pp. 26; 236.
[32] Garcilaso, *CR* 5.21, p. 179a, transl. Livermore.
[33] Cf. above, chap. II.1 passim.

this did not at all mean that Andeans worshiped him.[34] Similarly, he took
Acosta to task for asserting that the demonic trinity Tangatanga, "one in
three and three in one," had been worshipped in pre-Hispanic Chuquisaca.[35] The Trinity, Garcilaso explained, was a fact of Christian revelation,
which had not reached Peru before the Spaniards. To give credence to
pre-Christian trinities in the Andes would have amounted to attributing
to the Incas the very same demonic cults—imitations and perversions of
Catholic cult[36]—that Garcilaso stoutly maintained they did not practice.

Given that demonic agency was not particularly relevant to comprehending Inca concepts of deity, Garcilaso reflected instead on the scope of
imagination as a companion to thought, understanding, and action. A
childhood memory impressed on Garcilaso the impossibility of thinking
without resorting to phantasms.[37] One of his Inca kinsmen had shown
him the constellations, Garcilaso remembered. In the Milky Way,

> In those dark clouds that are spread over the length of it, they imag-
> ined there was the figure of a llama . . . suckling its baby. They tried
> to show this to me and said, "Do you see there the head of the llama?
> And there the head of the baby suckling? Do you see the body and
> the fore and hind legs of the two of them?" But I could only see the
> dark clouds and not the figures, which must have been because I
> could not imagine them.[38]

The act of the imagination is here conceived as interpreting sensory data
in the light of earlier cognitive experiences retained in memory. It was
these earlier experiences, as much as the sense perceptions of any given
moment, that tempered a person's understanding of ever new particulars,
even though, as Leone Ebreo had said, the number of these particulars far
exceeded the capacity of human understanding to encompass them.[39] At
issue was both the quality and the quantity or extent of human understanding.

On several occasions, Garcilaso compared European and Inca cultural
attainments. The Indians of Peru, he felt, "although not gifted at invention, are very talented in imitating and learning what they are taught."[40]
Using the terminology of Juan Huarte, a copy of whose *Inquiry into Human Talents* he had in his library,[41] Garcilaso contrasted the achievements

[34] Garcilaso, *CR* 2.2.
[35] Garcilaso, *CR* 2.5, p. 49b; Acosta, *HNM* 5.28.
[36] See above, chap. 1.2 at nn. 60–63.
[37] Cf. Aristotle, *On the Soul* 431a16; above, p. 24.
[38] Garcilaso, *CR* 2.22, pp. 74bf.; cf. Urton, *At the Crossroads* (1981), pp. 170f.
[39] Leone Ebreo, *Diálogo* 1, p. 34b.
[40] Garcilaso, *CR* 2.28, p. 83b; I use "talented" to translate *ingeniosos*.
[41] Durand, "La biblioteca del Inca," *Nueva Revista de Filología Hispanica* 3 (1948), no. 91,
and see above, p. 279.

of Indians in memory and imitation, at which they excelled, with their achievements in the realm of imagination and invention, where they were less distinguished.[42] Unlike Europeans, the Incas did not master the theoretical and speculative aspects of astronomy and natural science, because "they did not pass with their imagination beyond what they saw materially before their eyes."[43] For instance, they imagined that when the moon was in eclipse it was suffering from sickness, that the earth floated in water, and that at night the sun swam back to the eastern horizon underneath this floating earth.[44] Here, as in all other matters of natural philosophy, Inca reflections were concerned with observable secondary causes, not with speculation on the invisible primary cause or on first principles.[45] This state of affairs had repercussions in the field of religion. For unlike the nations of the ancient Mediterranean, in particular the Romans, Andeans and the Incas "did not know how to create imagined gods, such as Hope, Victory, Peace, and other similar deities, and because they did not raise their thoughts to invisible things, they adored what they saw."[46] By implication, therefore, Garcilaso dismissed the relevance to the Andes of one of Acosta's two "lineages" of idolatry, this being idolatry based on "things imagined or fabricated by human imagination."[47] The only imagined Inca deity—and therefore a highly anomalous one, as Garcilaso repeatedly mentioned—was the phantasm Viracocha.

In contemplating visible things, on the other hand, the Incas did arrive at the cult of the Sun, the noblest visible being, through which, as Leone Ebreo had explained, divine beauty was mediated to the human imagination as through a mirror or a crystal.[48] Moreover, by a further and truly great imaginative act, they discerned behind the visible Sun the invisible Creator, whom they called Pachacamac. He was the same Creator and Prime Mover who had earlier been discerned by the gentiles of classical antiquity.

Leone Ebreo's Platonism and his ideas on religious cognition pervade Garcilaso's entire work, however much, on occasion, he entertained theories of religious cognition at variance with Leone's thinking. Leone's world was ordered in a hierarchy of being at the peak of which stood the Creator, the God of the Hebrew Bible. Moses, the greatest of the prophets, was the only human being to have seen this God directly and simply, "with his intellect free and clear of the imagination." In this unique instance of prophetic insight, the laws of ordinary thought and cognition

[42] Garcilaso, *CR* 2.28.
[43] Garcilaso, *CR* 2.22, p. 73b.
[44] Garcilaso, *CR* 2.23.
[45] Garcilaso, *CR* 2.27, p. 79b.
[46] Garcilaso, *CR* 1.9, p. 19a.
[47] Acosta, *HNM* 5.2, p. 219.
[48] Leone Ebreo, *Diálogo* 1, p. 31a with 3, p. 167.

were suspended, so that imagination was not required to mediate understanding as it was at all other times, whether in waking, dreaming, or
ecstatic states. This was why "Scripture says of Moses that he spoke to
God face to face, as a man speaks with his friend."[49] Imagination could
not assist in this converse, because it could not comprehend divine infinity: for instance, infinite divine beauty could not be comprehended simply by multiplying in one's imagination the beauty of finite things. An
aggregate of finite things, however great their number, did not constitute
infinity.[50]

But in Leone's eyes, this did not mean that human beings other than
Moses had no perception of deity at all. Rather, sacred scripture gave the
reader an indirect or reflected image of divine beauty "as through a crystalline filter or a clear mirror."[51] Similarly, gentile myths reflected divine
truths, albeit more remotely. For example, the Greek myth of the birth
of Apollo and Diana, children of the sky god Jupiter and the terrestrial
deity Latona, was a poetic allegory of the first day of creation in Genesis.
In Greek mythic cosmology, Apollo and Diana represented the sun and
moon. The meaning of the myth, therefore, was that on the first day of
creation, God impregnated the earth with the radiant bodies of the sun
and moon which were to rise into the sky on the fourth day.[52] Similarly,
the beneficence of the divine Sun of Inca myth reflected the beneficence
of the invisible Pachacamac. Myths of this kind were mental images, creations of the imagination expressing some theological truth regarding the
nature or activity of the Creator, who in himself stood beyond the range
of imagination. As Leone Ebreo's Filón explained to his beloved Sofía:

> You well understand how a simple intellectual concept is represented
> in our imagination or is conserved in our memory, not in its unitary
> intellectual simplicity, but in a multifarious yet coherent image,
> which emanates from the one and simple concept and is represented
> in language by a separate multitude of words capable of being distin-
> guished individually. For the representation of the mind's concept
> stands in our imagination or memory, just as the sun impresses itself
> in limpid air and divine beauty exists in created mind. The concept
> is impressed on its extension, just as the light of the sun is repre-
> sented in opaque bodies and divine beauty and wisdom in the several
> parts of the created world.[53]

Leone Ebreo considered the role of the imagination in the apprehension
of religious truth to be held in balance and tension by its role in formulat-

[49] Leone Ebreo, *Diálogo* 3, p. 162.
[50] Leone Ebreo, *Diálogo* 3, p. 157a.
[51] Leone Ebreo, *Diálogo* 3, pp. 149, 150, 161b.
[52] Leone Ebreo, *Diálogo* 2, p. 82.
[53] Leone Ebreo, *Diálogo* 3, p. 200a.

ing political concepts and aspirations. Similarly, Garcilaso's phantasm Viracocha was a political as much as a religious construct. Whether, therefore, the phantasm Viracocha is construed as corresponding to Leone Ebreo's allegories of the personages of Greek myth, to the imagined Roman gods or even to an'impression of the light of the divine Sun on the "opaque body" of human imagination, it epitomized a certain political reality that was expressed in religious terms. For the Sun, deity of the empire, was at the same time the father both of the phantasm and of the Inca rulers and had bestowed on these rulers its own divine authority. The phantasm in its turn, like the imagined Roman gods in their day, was instrumental in Inca Viracocha's pursuit and attainment of victory and glory.

In his first *Dialogue*, Leone described the love of honor, glory, and power as being insatiable because it arose from the imagination, not from the senses. Loves arising from the senses, such as the love of food and drink, were satiable, because the senses to which they appealed were easily wearied by over-much exercise.[54] The imagination, on the other hand, was never wearied, and neither were the loves arising from it. Garcilaso expounded the repercussions of this fact in Inca politics.

On several occasions in the *Royal Commentaries*, he noted the Incas' ever-increasing lust for power—a concept that he perhaps derived from the Roman historian Sallust, whose works he owned.[55] For example, the fourth Inca, Mayta Capac, having visited all parts of his empire upon his accession, "turned his mind to the chief glory to which these Incas laid claim. This was to convert barbarian peoples to their false religion, for under the cloak of their idolatry they concealed their ambition and the lust of expanding their realm."[56] Throughout his reign, Inca Mayta Capac was thus consumed by the "lust and ambition of augmenting his kingdom."[57] Similarly, since the desire for "ruling is insatiable," Inca Viracocha was impelled to extend his people's conquests yet further.[58] This same passion for power had earlier led Viracocha to exile his father for having abandoned Cuzco to the Chanca invaders. The reason, Garcilaso suggested, was a mere subterfuge, but "since a prince's ambition and passion to rule are such that they will avail themselves of any apparent pretext, this ground was sufficient to deprive his father of the kingdom."[59] Although Garcilaso portrayed the lust for power as the negative aspect of imagination exercised in a political context, he also perceived that imagination could function positively in this realm, for he quoted Acosta's

[54] Leone Ebreo, *Diálogo* 1, pp. 24b, 29a, 40b; see also, on a lover's insatiable "abstract imagination" of his beloved, *Diálogo* 3, pp. 105f. and 134bf.; also 103.
[55] Durand (above, n. 41), no. 29.
[56] Garcilaso, *CR* 3.1, p. 85b.
[57] Garcilaso, *CR* 3.3, p. 90b.
[58] Garcilaso, *CR* 5.24, p. 182b.
[59] Garcilaso, *CR* 5.20, p. 177a.

admiring verdict of Inca Pachacuti, whose "imagination and inventive power were so remarkable that thanks to them he won the most outstanding victories."[60] Given that Acosta's Inca Pachacuti is Garcilaso's Inca Viracocha, this conclusion is confirmed by the enigmatic reason Garcilaso supplied as to why his Prince Viracocha had been banished to pasture the Sun's herds. From his youth up, Garcilaso declared, the prince had displayed an incorrigibly "evil disposition," leaving banishment and perhaps disinheritance as the only remedies.[61] Three years after being exiled, the prince saw the phantasm. A little later, having defeated the Chancas, he was chosen Inca, and his evil disposition was mentioned no more. The phantasm, by promising "to assist the prince in everything," inspired in him that same love of glory, honor, and power that Leone Ebreo had described as an insatiable passion residing in the human imagination. This passion, we are left to conclude, ousted the prince's evil disposition.[62]

Garcilaso endeavored to convince his readers that the Incas made the peoples of the Andes more humane and more noble. Their language, which they imposed wherever their power reached, fostered lucid thought and courteous expression. This argument led Garcilaso to reiterate an idea earlier expressed by Las Casas and Jerónimo Román, who were both following in the footsteps of the early Christian apologist Eusebius: Eusebius believed that monarchy, the rule of a single sovereign, was a necessary precondition for the full recognition of the one true God. The linguistic and political unification of the Andean world under the Incas accordingly occurred "not without divine providence," and this unification in turn greatly facilitated the preaching of Christianity. Indeed, the very worship of the divine Sun of the Incas led to the worship of the Christian Sun of Justice.[63] But from another point of view, Inca religion, like religion elsewhere, had been a most efficient instrument of political control. In the mid-sixteenth century, the lawyers Santillán and Polo de Ondegardo had already seen religion as a crucial factor in the effectiveness of Inca power. As a young man, Garcilaso talked with Polo,[64] but he is more likely to have derived his ideas about the role of religion in the body politic from the post-Machiavellian political theorists Jean Bodin and Giovanni Botero, whose writings he read in Spain.[65] According to both Bodin and Botero, the authority of religion, dexterously handled, was likely to ennoble and enhance princely authority; and according to Garcilaso, the Incas were not unaware of this fact. Ambition and greed (*ambición y codicia*)—stock phrases of seventeenth-century po-

[60] Acosta, *HNM* 6.21, in Garcilaso, *CR* 5.18, p. 174b; see also above, p. 278.

[61] Garcilaso, *CR* 4.20–21.

[62] See Garcilaso, *CR* 5.29, p. 191b, Inca Viracocha's views on education, parents, and children.

[63] Garcilaso, *CR* 7.4; 1.15, p. 25b.

[64] Garcilaso, *CR* 5.29.

[65] Garcilaso, *HG* 1.3, 7.

litical theorists—described excesses that a wise ruler would hold in check. It was, however, impossible to dispense with them altogether, because they were passions innate in the human soul, passions that, along with the love of glory, honor, and power, Leone Ebreo had counted among the insatiable affections of the imagination.

Garcilaso's discussion of Inca religion traverses a long and intricate course, passing from his explanation of Andean taxonomies of the holy to the conjoined cults of Pachacamac and the divine Sun and on to the ambiguous issue of the phantasm Viracocha. On the one hand, Garcilaso described the Incas as the precursors of the gospel, appointed by providence; but on the other hand, he also ascribed to them the shrewdness of pairing the awesome authority of religion with their own practical and political authority. Yet, paradoxically, it was thanks to this pairing that the Inca state and Inca religion came to an end at one and the same providentially designated moment, thereby paving the way for Christian revelation in the Andes.

Garcilaso was one of the several historians of the Incas who believed that the Incas themselves had prophesied the end of their empire and their religion.[66] To his mind, this prophecy on the one hand documented the excellence of the religious order established by the Incas and their range of vision, but on the other hand revealed that order as a finite and limited good. The first Inca ruler to foretell the advent of the Spanish invaders, Garcilaso thought, was Viracocha, the visionary of the phantasm, and Guayna Capac, the last Inca to rule before the invasion, repeated it.[67] In this context, Garcilaso raised another well-worn theme of Inca historiography. This concerned the question of why Andeans referred to the invaders as Viracochas. Garcilaso's first explanation was not new.[68] Because the Spaniards had appeared at the very time when Atahualpa had captured Inca Guascar, he wrote, Guascar's supporters were ready to greet them as Viracochas, heaven-sent emissaries and "sons of their god."[69] According to his second explanation, Andeans called the invaders Viracochas out of a somewhat unbecoming desire to flatter them,[70] and because their beards and attire bore a certain resemblance to the external appearance of the phantasm Viracocha that was believed to be a deity.[71]

It was surely by no unintended irony that the invaders of the Andes

---

[66] Cf. above, chap. VII.3 at nn. 28–38.

[67] Garcilaso, *CR* 5.28, p. 189a; 9.15; *HG* 1.25, p. 53b. According to Betanzos, *Suma* (1987), 1.29, p. 137, the coming of the Spanish was predicted in some detail as a reversal of the times (*pachacuti*) by the Inca Pachacuti. Betanzos' account highlights how soon after the invasion such stories began to circulate.

[68] See above, chap. VII.2, p. 308.

[69] Garcilaso, *CR* 5.21, p. 178a.

[70] Garcilaso, *CR* 5.21, p. 179a.

[71] Garcilaso, *CR* 5.21, p. 177b; divine Viracocha, see *CR* 2.27, p. 80b; 2.4, p. 47a, cf. 4.21, p. 143; also 5.18, p. 174b.

appear in Garcilaso's history of Inca and Spanish Peru as descendants or
semblances of an Inca ruler's phantasm, as "sons of the imagined god
Viracocha."[72]

3. CONVERSION AND *DESENGAÑO*

Garcilaso wrote his history of the Incas as an apologia, a work explicitly
designed to correct and supplement earlier writings on the Incas and the
Andean past. In spite of this openly declared purpose, however, the book
is pervaded by an immense, ever-present ambiguity and tension that
leaves no major statement unqualified. Ambiguity and tension were inherent in the story Garcilaso chose to tell, which culminated in the defeat
of his mother's people by the Spaniards, one of whom was his father (fig.
46). While thus on the one hand Garcilaso insisted on the validity of Inca
theology and religious practice, he maintained on the other that these
were no more than foreshadowings of Christian truth. And yet, so Garcilaso urged his readers, Christian truth could never have taken root in
the Andes had its way not been prepared by the Incas.

An example of the tension and ambiguity pervading the *Royal Commentaries* was the phantasm Viracocha which lived on in colonial Peru,
according to Garcilaso, not only in the capacity of ancestor or originator
of the invaders but also as a prototype of sorts of the Christian apostle who
had come to preach in the Andes. Like Cieza and Betanzos, Garcilaso
heard that this apostle had been represented in the statue that Inca Viracocha had dedicated at Cacha, and like his contemporary Guaman Poma,
he was told that the apostle in question was Bartholomew. But Garcilaso
considered both claims to be improbable; indeed, he demonstrated that
the statue could not possibly have represented the apostle.[1] However, in
spite of all this, Garcilaso did consider it worth recording that the phantasm Viracocha in the guise of the apostle Bartholomew was honored by
a Christian cult in colonial Peru. By implying that this cult was not entirely unwarranted he attributed to the phantasm in Christian times the
very existence and validity that he had denied to it in Inca times. Some
thirty years before he wrote his Inca history, Garcilaso recounted, the
mestizos of Cuzco wanted to adopt as their patron the "blessed apostle,"
who, so they thought, had been portrayed in the statue, and founded a
confraternity in his honor. In addition, the mestizos instituted an elaborate and costly annual festival celebrating the apostle, "although some
malicious Spaniards, seeing the trappings and finery they display on that

---

[72] Garcilaso, *CR* 5.28, p. 189a, hijos del dios fantástico Viracocha.
[1] Garcilaso, *CR* 5.22.

CON LA ESPADA

Y CON LA PLVMA

AVE MARIA

GRATIA PLENA

46. The Inca Garcilaso de la Vega's coat of arms. On the left, his Spanish
father's armorial devices, on the right those of his Inca mother, cf. fig. 44.
On the sides, Garcilaso's motto, adopted from his paternal kinsman the
poet Garcilaso de la Vega: "With the sword and with the pen." Frontispiece
of the *Comentarios reales* (Lisbon, 1609). Biblioteca Nacional, Madrid.

day, have said that they do it not for the Apostle but for their Inca Viracocha."[2]

These malicious comments were not the only ones of their kind, for all over Peru, Andeans and Spaniards disagreed with each other, and amongst themselves, as to whether Andean religious expression had any legitimate place within Christianity, and if so, how exactly it should be accommodated. Garcilaso thus remembered that when he was growing up in Cuzco, Spaniards were objecting to Andeans using the name of Pachacamac to refer to the Christian God. The issue evoked in his mind an incident he had witnessed when young. In 1557 the Inca Sairi Tupa, a nephew of Atahualpa, who ruled over the Inca empire in exile at Vilcabamba, resolved to leave his retreat, thereby resigning his sovereignty. It was a controversial decision, which Sairi Tupac claimed he had been commanded to make by the divine Sun and Pachacamac.[3] Sairi settled in Cuzco, where Garcilaso made his acquaintance. He was given to visiting ancient sites, the former house of the chosen women of the Sun, and the palaces of the Inca rulers, his ancestors, although most of them were now in ruins or occupied by Spaniards. He also visited the churches of the various monasteries that were being constructed, including the monastery of Santo Domingo, formerly Coricancha. There he would adore the eucharistic host, calling it "Pachacamac, Pachacamac." But "there was no lack of malicious persons who said when they saw him kneeling before the most holy sacrament in the church of Santo Domingo, that he did it to adore the Sun, his own father and the father of his ancestors, whose bodies had rested in that place."[4] Given that Pachacamac was the true God, whom the Incas had correctly apprehended by natural reason, Garcilaso at this juncture left the charge of these malicious persons pointedly unanswered.

For he had already explained that when the Incas became Christian, Pachacamac, the true God, continued to dwell in their hearts just as he had done formerly. At a different level, the divine Sun of the Incas also continued to figure in the spiritual universe of Andean converts to Christianity. European precedents for such a convergence between pagan and Christian religious concepts and ideas could be found in Leone Ebreo, whose Filón and Sofía drew their understanding of human, cosmic, and divine love as much from Greek philosophy and myth as they did from sacred Scripture. Indeed, sometimes it was a Greek myth that made obscure scriptural statements concrete and intelligible.[5] Throughout the Royal Commentaries, Garcilaso accordingly explained that the same had

---

[2] Garcilaso, CR 5.22, p. 180b.
[3] Garcilaso, HG 8.10, p. 144a.
[4] Garcilaso, HG 8.11, p. 146b.
[5] Leone Ebreo, Diálogo 3, pp. 170bff., Adam and Eve with Plato's androgyne.

been the case in the Andes. For the Incas had paired the interior worship of Pachacamac with the external cult of the divine Sun, the one expressed in silent devotion and the other in sacrifice and ceremony. This twofold worship anticipated and foreshadowed Christian observance, which likewise was composed of the adoration of the heart and external actions of reverence and cult. For in Christianity, the invisible Creator, whom Christian Incas using their own language should, according to Garcilaso, address as Pachacamac, had made himself manifest and visible in Jesus his son, the Sun of Justice.[6]

Another Christian tenet that Garcilaso, like earlier Cieza, found to have been foreshadowed in Andean and Inca religion was the resurrection of the body. As held in the Andes, the belief in the afterlife lacked refinement; what Andeans hoped for was not the vision of God and eternal glory but simply "tranquillity of soul, without cares, and rest for the body."[7] The ritual expression of this belief was correspondingly humble. As a child, Garcilaso had been puzzled to observe that people kept their hair clippings and nail parings in holes and cracks in the wall. Why was this being done? he asked and received this answer:

> You must know that all of us who have been born must return to live in the world—they did not have a verb to say "resurrect"—and the souls must rise from their burials with all there was of their bodies. And so that ours will not be held up looking for their hairs and nails, seeing how great an uproar and how much haste there will be on that last day, we place these things here in one spot, so that our souls will be able to rise more speedily.[8]

Rudimentary though both the ritual and the belief it epitomized appeared to be, they touched on a cornerstone of Christian teaching and therefore occasioned theological controversy. Two learned Jesuits of Garcilaso's acquaintance had urged him to include a mention of Indian beliefs in the afterlife in his earlier work, the *Florida*, but the censor removed the passage in question before publication. In the *Royal Commentaries*, Garcilaso stubbornly returned to his point, lest "so important a stone should be lacking from the edifice,"[9] that is, from his thesis that the Incas had laid a groundwork for even the most exalted of Christian doctrines.

Garcilaso therefore gave several examples of what he considered to be legitimate and even highly desirable continuities of thought and ceremo-

---

[6] Garcilaso, *CR* 1.15, p. 25b.

[7] Garcilaso, *CR* 2.7, p. 52b.

[8] Garcilaso, *CR* 2.7, pp. 52bf. The custom was still observed by Pérez Bocanegra in 1631; see his *Ritual, formulario e institución de curas*, p. 132, and above, p. 70, on Inca effigies of nails and hair.

[9] Garcilaso, *CR* 2.7, p. 53b.

nial between Inca and Christian festivals. Among the most significant of these continuities—as he saw it—were rituals of the festival of Inti Raimi and its attendant agricultural celebrations, which Andeans continued to celebrate in the guise of Corpus Christi. Polo de Ondegardo had already noted these same continuities and urged their extirpation.[10] But other Spaniards took a more tolerant view, as Garcilaso recounted in the context of one of his childhood experiences. The choir master of Cuzco cathedral had been pleased and impressed by the hayllis, songs of love and triumph, that Andeans were accustomed to sing for harvest and plowing. In 1551 or 1552 he therefore adapted this kind of composition for a chant to be sung at Corpus Christi.

> Eight mestizo boys from among my schoolfellows came out dressed as Indians, each carrying a digging stick. They enacted the song and haylli of the Indians in the procession, the whole choir joining in the chorus at the end of the stanzas. The Spaniards were pleased, and the Indians were most delighted to see the Spaniards solemnize the festival of the Lord our God, whom they call Pachacamac, with their own songs and dances.[11]

In 1555, after the defeat of Francisco Hernández Girón, when Garcilaso's father was corregidor of Cuzco, Corpus Christi was celebrated with especial solemnity, and the Spanish residents prepared elaborately decorated floats to be carried in the procession. Neighboring curacas came to Cuzco to take part in this procession, as they had done formerly for Inti Raimi. Some were decked in condor's wings, "just as angels are painted," and others appeared in lion skins, "in the same way as they paint Hercules." In drawing this comparison between Andean lords attired in skins of lions, or more precisely, of jaguars, and the Greek hero Hercules, Garcilaso quietly transposed to the Andes an argument that had been much used by Renaissance scholars, who perceived in the heroes and gods of classical antiquity counterparts to the heroes of the Hebrew Bible and even precursors of Christ.[12] In performing his labors, Hercules had freed men from evil, thus pointing to the ultimate liberation from evil that was wrought by Christ. The curacas dressed in jaguar skins adumbrated a similar lesson in the Andes. The Christianization of the Inca Inti Raimi in Cuzco accordingly constituted a further phase in the long and venerable history of humanity's journey to God, for one part of this history—the

---

[10] See above, IV.2 at nn. 85–92.

[11] Garcilaso, CR 5.2, p. 151b; similarly, Guaman Poma, Nueva Crónica, p. 783 [797], "hijos de principales" should dance before the Eucharist just as King David had danced before the Holy of Holies.

[12] M. Simon, Hercule et le Christianisme (Strasburg, 1950); J. Seznec, The Survival of the Pagan Gods (1953).

Christianization of Greek and Roman gods, heroes, and festivals in medieval and Renaissance Europe—was now being extended to the Andes. Others among the curacas celebrating Corpus Christi in Cuzco, Garcilaso continued, wore masks, or else carried emblems of the springs, lakes, mountains, and crags that had been their places of origin.[13]

> With many more solemnities, such as can be imagined, those Indians used to celebrate the festivals of their kings. And with the same solemnities—increasing them whenever possible—they in my day celebrated the festival of the most Holy Sacrament, our true God, redeemer, and lord. And they did it with the greatest contentment, as people who have already been disabused of the vanities of the gentile religion of their past.[14]

This state of having been disabused—*desengañado*—of earlier errors—*engaños*—was what according to Garcilaso made the perpetuation of Inca religious forms within Christianity possible. Indeed, with this particular phase of being disabused or undeceived, Andeans had attained spiritual maturity. For when Manco Capac first taught his solar religion to his subjects, he already "disabused people from the lowness and vileness of their many gods." "Let them look," he had said, "and their own eyes would undeceive them and show that the Sun raised the herbs, plants, and trees and the other things they adored for the service of men and the nourishment of beasts."[15] Because the Incas had bestowed on their subjects the blessings of true religious teaching and wise government, they were revered as gods. When later the Spaniards reproved Andeans for this devotion toward their former rulers "because they should know that the Incas were men like themselves, and not gods, they reply that they have already been undeceived of their idolatry, but that they adore the Incas for the many and great benefits they have received from them."[16]

To have lived through a state of engaño and gone on to attain desengaño was not merely a necessary precondition to comprehending Christian truth. Rather, the experience also brought with it a quality of soul deeply admired by Spaniards of the Golden Age,[17] and valued most particularly by Garcilaso himself. In attributing this quality to Andeans, he credited them not merely with religious virtue but also with cultural and, in particular, ethical stature. For desengaño was the attitude of a person unmoved by appearance and illusion, whether of wealth, influence, or

---

[13] Garcilaso, *CR* 6.20, p. 219, with *HG* 8.1, p. 128; see Sallnow, *Pilgrims of the Andes* (1987), pp. 56ff.
[14] Garcilaso, *HG* 8.1, p. 128a.
[15] Garcilaso, *CR* 2.1, p. 41b.
[16] Garcilaso, *CR* 2.1, p. 42a.
[17] Otis H. Green, "Desengaño," in his, *The Literary Mind* (1970), pp. 141–170.

power, the attitude of someone who will not substitute the "vain shadow of feigned good"[18] for the substance of true and lasting good. It is also desengaño that enabled one to discern the difference between the illusion, or engaño, of sense impressions sullied by demons and the physical reality conveyed by authentic and uncontaminated sense impressions. Andeans who, according to Cieza, thought they saw their ancestors walking about in the fields had been captivated by demonic engaño. Leaving other Andean peoples to one side, Garcilaso did not believe that such demonic illusion had affected the Incas significantly. But he did believe that like rulers of empires elsewhere, the Incas had been caught in another kind of illusion: the insatiable desire, which dwells in the imagination, for power. It was in the grip of this desire for power that Manco Capac had inaugurated the cult of the divine Sun among his subjects, and that his successors had perpetuated it. In renouncing both the cult and the spiritual illusion of false religion, the Incas also renounced the worldly illusion of power, thereby acquiring that quality of soul, desengaño, which characterized truly virtuous human beings.

When Garcilaso was a boy of five or six, he stood watching while the September ceremonies of Citua, the expulsion of ills, were being performed. But he was already in bed when torchbearers ran through the city at night expelling ills and then threw the contaminated torches into a stream so that the ills could be carried away to the sea. The next morning, however, he came upon one of those torches in a stream inside the city and watched how Indian children recoiled from it. The ritual was no longer being observed with the same care and solemnity as formerly, Garcilaso commented, for in the old days, the torches were not discarded within the city boundaries but far beyond them. Furthermore, the meaning of the festival was changing. It was not any longer "celebrated to expel ills, because the Indians were already in the course of being disillusioned, but rather in memory of the past times, because many of the aged people who had grown old in their gentile religion and had not been baptized were still alive."[19] *Ya se iban desengañando*: they were in the course of shedding their misapprehensions. Similarly, when Garcilaso was growing up in Cuzco, the Indians still venerated the crag where their prince, Viracocha, had seen the phantasm, but not for religious reasons: "They do not do it to commit idolatry, because by the mercy of God they are truly disillusioned with such idolatry as they had, but in memory of their king, who had been so good to them both in peace and in war."[20] *Bien desengañados están*: they are truly disabused of their idolatry. But this did

---

[18] Luis de León, *The Original Poems*, ed. E. Sarmiento, 2.20.
[19] Garcilaso, *CR* 7.7, p. 254b.
[20] Garcilaso, *CR* 5.25, p. 185b.

not mean that Incas and Andeans ought not to remember their pre-Hispanic and pre-Christian past.

Garcilaso's purpose in writing the *Royal Commentaries* was to record what was true, beautiful, and good about the Andean world that had been destroyed, and to pass lightly over its less estimable aspects. He remembered the Incas he wanted to remember, not the Incas who were capable of wiping out entire populations or the Incas who offered human sacrifice. This enabled him to confront in his own uniquely sharp and uncompromising way—undistracted by those arguments of moral outrage that exponents of one religion are prone to address to those of another—the dilemma of religious truth. Having little choice but to leave the truth of Catholic Christianity unchallenged, he focused his attention on the question of how the Incas might have learned what they knew about God and the holy. Much of his information came from his own childhood observations, when he, the unobserved observer, watched those ancient rituals, or when he asked eagerly naive and sometimes irreverent questions of his aged Inca kinsmen.[21]

Seeing that desengaño entailed both the discovery of religious truth and the process of growing older and wiser, it was first as an adult and then as an aging scholar that Garcilaso, himself growing in desengaño, looked at the historical process of desengaño that his mother's people had undergone. Like individuals, so also societies had the option of growing wise with age, growing in desengaño, or growing foolish. No other choice was possible. Garcilaso's story of Inca religion disclosed a twofold desengaño, the one of the Andean people and the other of Garcilaso himself. In describing Inca religion, Garcilaso described his childhood, just as Juan Santacruz Pachacuti Yamqui had done. "I declare," the latter had written at the beginning of his account of the Incas, "that when we were children, we heard ancient accounts and the histories and strange fables of the time of the gentiles,"[22] and then he proceeded to tell what he had learned from his elders. It was as impossible to forget those ancient tales as it was to forget one's childhood. And just as one could not attain desengaño without first passing through childhood and youth, so one could not attain a mature theological comprehension of God without first passing through fables and phantasms, and through corporeally concrete religious images such as the Incas had formed. Inca religion juxtaposed with Christianity thus did not correspond to any polarity of truth and falsity. Rather, according to Garcilaso, the two were complementary and continuous with

---

[21] E.g., Garcilaso, *CR* 1.15, p. 26a.

[22] Santacruz Pachacuti Yamqui, *Relación*, p. 234. In a less emotive fashion, the question of change and decline of cultures was treated by Garcilaso's friend Bernardo de Aldrete in his *Origen y principio de la lengua*; see 1.22, 2.6–7. Aldrete knew of Garcilaso's work and referred to it, *Origen* 3.13, p. 356.

each other, just as Upper and Lower Cuzco were complementary and continuous parts of the same whole, as the right arm needed the left, and as the older brother needed his younger fellow.[23] In this same way, Pachacamac in whose name "all of Inca theology had been enclosed,"[24] was now worshiped as the Christian God.

Inca religion was thus based in truth and capable of being absorbed into Christianity. Yet, despite his insistence on this issue, Garcilaso left several facets of the question as to how the absorption could take place to be elucidated by others. From Cieza onward, Spaniards had asked themselves whether some traces of Biblical history might be found in the Andes. Put differently, the issue was how the Indians had come to the New World. Given that the story told in Genesis, that all human beings were descendants of Adam and Noah, was interpreted as historically accurate by most scholars at this time, the question arose whether any aspects of this story were remembered in the Andes. For if any kind of historical memory existed among Andean people, it could in some way be incorporated into Christian history and the history of the world at large. The question continued being discussed in Garcilaso's day, but he refused to tackle it. "I do not interpose in matters so profound," he wrote regarding the possibility that the opening, or "window," in the rock of Pacaritambo, the Incas' point of origin, might in some way represent a window in Noah's ark. "I simply tell the historical fables I heard as a child from my people, and let everyone take them as he pleases and endow them with such allegory as he sees fit."[25] Similarly, he expressed no opinion regarding whatever overlap might have existed between Christian sacramental communion and the solemn eating of sacrificial meat and maize bread prepared by the women consecrated to the Sun during the festival of Inti Raimi.[26] The maize bread, *zancu*, Garcilaso wrote "may be the reason why some Spaniards have wished to affirm that these Incas and their subjects celebrated communion as Christians do. I have straightforwardly explained what the Incas did, and let everyone make what comparisons he wishes."[27] Comparisons were not long in coming. Indeed, they had already been made, and in his customary reticent and idiosyncratic fashion, Garcilaso took cognizance of this fact by undermining the very comparisons he avoided mentioning.

In the footsteps of European polemicists against witchcraft and their early Christian models, Acosta and others had argued that in Inca Peru

[23] Garcilaso, *CR* 1.16.

[24] Garcilaso, *CR* 2.25, p. 77a.

[25] Garcilaso, *CR* 1.18, p. 31a. For an exhaustive discussion of these issues by a contemporary of Garcilaso's, see G. Garcia, *Origen de los Indios* (1607).

[26] Garcilaso, *CR* 6.20, p. 219b; 22, p. 222b.

[27] Garcilaso, *CR* 6.22, end.

the devil imitated pure Christian rituals so as to deceive simple souls.[28] Acosta thus viewed the sacred maize bread that the Incas consumed at Inti Raimi as a demonic imitation of Christian eucharistic bread.[29] This was precisely one of the positions Garcilaso strove to discredit. Similarly, he considered demonized Andean versions of the Trinity such as Acosta had mentioned to be fictions of the Spanish imagination, because the Trinity was only knowable by revelation, to which Andeans only had access after the Spanish invasion. Moreover, to suppose that Andean people had fallen prey to such demonic trinities amounted to attributing too much power to the devil. The devil was present in Garcilaso's narrative, but usually only as a subsidiary or secondary cause of experiences and events. For true to the Platonic doctrines he had learned from Leone Ebreo, Garcilaso did not regard the devil as an agent in his own right. The devil might indeed whisper in obscure places[30] and further confound difficult situations,[31] but these activities had little explanatory significance.

Garcilaso's own desengaño consisted in recognizing that the Incas had lost their empire even though they were fully capable of practicing true religion and in taking stock of what he considered to be the continuities that linked Inca to Christian Peru. From these considerations it followed that ethical and intellectual stature did not necessarily go hand in hand with terrestrial success. Garcilaso therefore set aside the facile providentialism of historians like Francisco López de Gómara, who professed to believe that God had allotted the Americas to Spain in order to reward Spanish valor and orthodoxy and in order to propagate the gospel.[32] Desengaño, already introduced by the Incas, enabled Andeans to understand the gospel without much explanation, and certainly without the forcible extirpation of Andean religion that was gathering momentum in the early seventeenth century. Garcilaso thus shed a deeply problematic light on the vaunted labor of instructing and converting Indians. For many of these Indians, he suggested, became Christians of their own accord and needed little instruction.[33]

The *Royal Commentaries* were read widely and were translated into both French and English in the seventeenth century. In Spain and Peru, the work soon became canonical: no history of the Incas was complete without taking stock of Garcilaso. But his assessment of Inca religion, although never challenged outright, was only accepted selectively. Garci-

---

[28] Above, chap. IX.1 at nn. 5ff.; note the copy of Ciruelo in Garcilaso's library, Durand, "La biblioteca del Inca," *Nueva Revista de Filología Hispánica* 2 (1948), no. 97.

[29] Acosta, *HNM* 5.23.

[30] Garcilaso, *CR* 2.2, p. 44a.

[31] Garcilaso, *HG* 2.6, p. 89a; 13, p. 101a; 3.19, p. 210b; 6.8, p. 22b.

[32] MacCormack, "The Fall of the Incas," *History of European Ideas* 6 (1985): 423–424.

[33] Garcilaso, *HG* 2.8, pp. 91af., story of Alonzo Ruiz, quoted by Calancha, *Corónica moralizada* 2.19, p. 929.

laso wrote from a vantage point very different from that adopted by the clerical historians and polemicists of seventeenth-century Peru. Raised in a Cuzco still resonant with Inca memories and spending his adult life in Spain, he lacked the day-to-day familiarity with Andean village ritual and belief that had gradually convinced Peruvian churchmen that conversion to Christianity must entail a total transformation of native thought and conduct. At the same time, he lacked the cultural distance from Andean, and especially Inca, religious values that inspired these churchmen to insist on a form of Christian desengaño for Andeans that amounted to the elimination of most of their existing beliefs and practices.

Many missionaries—even Acosta, who criticized Andean religion severely—conceded that the Incas had attained certain fundamental theological insights, specifically that they knew about the existence of a Prime Mover and the immortality of the soul. But very few missionaries were prepared to countenance any of the ritual expressions Andeans gave to these and other beliefs, because Andean rituals articulated a social and political order incompatible with the colonial establishment. This reality conditioned the reception of Garcilaso's work in Peru and also in Spain.

Antonio de Herrera, official historian of the Spanish crown, thus followed Garcilaso in positing a twofold Inca worship of the "maker and creator of everything, through whom everything is governed," and of the divine Sun, "who came next in veneration."[34] In his account of festivals, sacrifices, and the religious calendar, however, Herrera followed Polo de Ondegardo and Acosta.[35] In Peru likewise, Garcilaso's readers were prepared to accept his interpretation of Pachacamac, despite much evidence to the contrary. But these same readers could not settle for the idea that conversion, the transition Andeans were to make from the engaño of their old religion to the desengaño of Christianity, amounted to no more than an organic growth toward wisdom and nobility of soul.[36] The Dominican friar Gregorio García, who visited Garcilaso in Cordoba, thus agreed with his host's interpretation of the relationship between Pachacamac and the Sun of the Incas.[37] But he also described the many cults that the Incas addressed to huacas. Similarly, in his history of Peru, which was completed in or before 1631, the Jesuit Anello Oliva agreed with Garcilaso that the Indians had known of Pachacamac, the sole "sustainer and creator of the world," and had worshiped him. But on the other hand, Oliva deployed the experiences and researches of missionaries in

[34] Antonio de Herrera, *Historia General . . . Década quinta* (1615), bk. 4, chap. 4, p. 116a, note: a este Viracocha hizieron un riquissimo templo que llamavan Pachiamac [*sic*].
[35] See, for instance, on Tangatanga and other trinities, Herrera, *Historia. Década quinta*, bk. 4, chap. 5, p. 116a = Acosta, *HNM* 5.28, p. 268.
[36] See below, chap. IX.1, p. 388.
[37] Gregorio García, *Predicación* 6.3, citing Garcilaso, *CR* 2.2; see also *Predicación* 6.6, citing *CR* 2.3 and *HG* 1.32; *Predicación* 6.8, citing *CR* 2.7, on the resurrection of the body.

his order to argue that the vast majority of Andean cults had nothing to do with monotheism.[38] Oliva's contemporary and fellow Jesuit, the historian Bernabé Cobo, also agreed with Garcilaso that the Incas had known of a single, universal Creator. But since the numerous sixteenth-century documents he consulted were full of cults to deities other than the Creator,[39] he considered this knowledge to have been confined to the elite.[40] Similarly, the extirpator of Andean religion Fernando de Avendaño drew attention to the Creator Pachacamac while at the same time upbraiding his Andean charges for persisting in the sin of idolatry.[41]

One of the most thoughtful of Garcilaso's Peruvian readers was the Augustinian friar Antonio de la Calancha, who published a history of his order in 1639. Like his contemporary, the Jesuit historian Bernabé Cobo,[42] Calancha made his own personal survey of the ruins of Pachacamac's sanctuary near Lima. This inspection led Calancha to conclude that human sacrifices had been offered there, a fact that Garcilaso had denied, at any rate for the period of Inca occupation. Regarding Pachacamac's personality, Calancha recounted a widely circulated coastal myth that he had read in the notebooks of a Jesuit extirpator of idolatries. The myth described successive phases of creation and destruction resulting from the conflicts between Pachacamac and his father, the Sun, and brother, Vichama.[43] Although Pachacamac figured in the myth as the maker of the original human couple, his dominant role was that of destroyer and avenger, a far cry from the loving deity described by Garcilaso in a passage that Calancha quoted in its entirety.[44]

Similar contradictions between Garcilaso's opinions and evidence pervade Calancha's work. In his historical survey of Andean and Inca religion, Calancha thus followed the treatise by Polo de Ondegardo that had been summarized for the Third Council of Lima, interspersing it with comparisons from the ancient Mediterranean.[45] Moreover, when studying the lives and labors of his fellow Augustinians, many of whom had been missionaries, Calancha encountered ample material from all parts of

[38] Anello Oliva, *Historia* 4.1–2, pp. 126–136.

[39] See on Cobo's sources, his own statement, *Historia* 12.2, pp. 58bff.

[40] Cobo, *Historia* 13.1, p. 148a; cf. 13.2, p. 150a, etymology of Pachacamac. The Sun as created, 13.5, pp. 156bf.; elite religion, 13.1, pp. 146a, 148a. On the other hand, Cobo agreed with Acosta that Quechua had no generic term for God; Cobo, *Historia* 13.4, p. 155ab = Acosta, *HNM* 5.3, p. 220. Also, according to Cobo, not Pachacamac but Viracocha was the Inca Creator (ibid). See also, Jose de Arriaga, *Extirpación* 6, p. 64, citing Garcilaso on apachetas.

[41] Fernando de Avendaño, *Sermones*, sermon 2, on Pachacamac; sermons 4–5, on idolatry.

[42] Cobo, *Historia* 13.17, pp. 186ff.

[43] Calancha, *Corónica moralizada* 2.19, pp. 930–935. See above, p. 60 for an outline of this myth.

[44] Calancha, *Corónica moralizada*, pp. 926ff.; cf. Garcilaso, *CR* 2.2.

[45] Calancha, *Corónica moralizada* 2.12, pp. 849ff.; cf. above, chap. IV.3 at nn. 29–31.

the Andes to impress on him the ubiquity of idolatrous practices unmodified by monotheistic inclinations of any kind.[46] He thus concurred with the missionaries of his order that conversion amounted to a fundamental transformation of a person's religious beliefs and observances, to desengaño from substantive error.[47] At times, however, Calancha found Garcilaso's evaluation of Inca religion irresistible and accepted it in the face of explicit evidence to the contrary that he cited himself, such as Polo's treatise. Similarly, he mentioned Fernández de Oviedo's *General History of the Indies*, which included the description of Pachacamac's sanctuary by Miguel de Estete, one of the Spaniards who had desecrated it and had helped to overthrow the god's image.[48] Nevertheless, Calancha asserted, following Garcilaso, that the worship of Pachacamac was imageless.[49] He also accepted Garcilaso's account of the Incas' twofold worship of the visible Sun and the invisible Creator Pachacamac,[50] although it differed fundamentally from all earlier accounts of Inca religion.

A complex rationale explains why Calancha adopted such contradictory views. He was able to agree with Garcilaso that the Incas had prepared the way for Christianity, that they had in some sense been God's instrument. At the same time, Calancha argued on behalf of his order that it also had been an instrument used by God to bring Christianity to the Andes. In the bitter rivalries that raged between the missionary orders of seventeenth-century Peru, Calancha was a fervent advocate of the Augustinians. As everyone knew, they had not been the first to arrive in Peru, although Calancha perversely argued that they had been the first to convert Indians.[51] The role played by his order's founder, Augustine of Hippo, in the conversion of ancient Rome was the same that the Augustinians of Peru played in the conversion of the Incas and Andean people in the Americas.[52] Calancha therefore agreed with Garcilaso and others who had explained Andean religion by comparing it to ancient Mediterranean paganism.[53] But unlike Garcilaso, he elaborated these compari-

---

[46] E.g., Calancha, *Corónica moralizada* 2.32, pp. 1060ff.; 2.34, pp. 1087f.; 3.2, pp. 1239ff.; 3.8–9, pp. 1298ff.; 3.18, pp. 1419, 1424; 3.33, p. 1585; 3.43–44.

[47] E.g., Calancha, *Corónica moralizada* 2.13, pp. 868–869.

[48] Above, chap. II.1 at n. 9; see Calancha, *Corónica moralizada* 1.10, p. 154, citing both Fernández de Oviedo's *Sumaria de la natural historia de las Indias* and his *Hystoria general de las Indias*. In *Corónica moralizada* 2.5, p. 770, Calancha again cites Oviedo, in a specifically Peruvian context. This suggests that the edition of Oviedo's *Hystoria general* that Calancha used was the one published in Salamanca in 1547, not the first edition of 1533, which did not deal with Peru. As is indicated on its title page, the 1547 edition was sold together with Xerez' *Verdadera relación de la conquista del Perú*, which in turn contained the *Relación* about the expedition to Pachacamac; see fol. XVIr of Xerez.

[49] Calancha, *Corónica moralizada* 2.19, p. 925; cf. 929; above, chap. II.1, p. 57.

[50] Calancha, *Corónica moralizada*, p. 926.

[51] Calancha, *Corónica moralizada* 1.20.

[52] See MacCormack, "Antonio de la Calancha," *Bulletin Hispanique* 104 (1982): 60–94.

[53] E.g., Calancha, *Corónica moralizada* 2.10, pp. 822ff., history of idolatry; p. 829, on natural, civic, and fabulous theology, derived from Augustine, *City of God* 6.6.

sons by means of historical and theological allegory.[54] Allegory served a twofold purpose. First, it enabled Calancha to make figurative claims for the importance of his order in the conversion of Andeans that could not be made in historical terms. Second, allegory provided Calancha with a dialectic of conversion.

This dialectic had been pioneered by another Augustinian, Alonso Ramos Gavilán, who published a history of the Virgin of Copacabana in 1621.[55] The book was graced by a set of prefatory verses in praise of the author by Calancha, who referred to it repeatedly in his own work. Ramos Gavilán told the story of how the Christian cult of the Virgin of Copacabana on the shore of Lake Titicaca supplanted the Andean cult of the Sun. This latter had been at home on the nearby island of the Sun and was integrated into Inca worship by Tupa Inca Yupanqui.[56] Ramos Gavilán regarded both the pre-Inca and Inca solar cults of Titicaca as creations of the devil.[57] The cult of the Virgin in Copacabana, by contrast, was the work of the Christian God, who had destined for his pure and perfect worship one of the centers of demonic activity in the Andes. In organizing his cult, according to Ramos Gavilán, the devil had seen to everything. He had inspired the Incas to construct a noble and dignified architectural setting and to arrange that the shrine of the Sun on the island be cared for by priests and consecrated virgins. Worshipers approached this majestic holy place only after careful purification and confession. All that the Christians had to do, therefore, was to reverse the orientation of the demonically inspired cult of the Sun of the Incas toward the cult of the one and only God. This is what was achieved with the induction into Copacabana of the image of Mary the mother of Jesus, who was himself the Sun of Justice.

Ramos Gavilán's schema of divine versus demonic worship, one being the mirror image of the other, reiterates the polarization of the cosmos and of human society between God and devil as described in fifteenth- and sixteenth-century treatises on witchcraft. When applied to the Andes, this polarization determined both what had to be given up in conversion and the quality of the accompanying desengaño. To achieve desengaño was to be undeceived, plain and simple. The nuances that gave Garcilaso's concept of desengaño its poignant, almost tragic dimension did not exist for men examining Andean religion in the light of the political interests of the Spanish imperial state and the Catholic church. Moreover, if Andean religion was indeed a demonic deceit or engaño, the mirror image

[54] E.g., Calancha, *Corónica moralizada* 1.14, p. 209, on Viracocha.

[55] On Ramos Gavilán, see Espinoza Soriano, "Alonzo Ramos Gavilán," *Historia y Cultura* 6 (1972): 121–194.

[56] MacCormack, "From the Sun of the Incas," *Representations* 8 (1984): 30–60.

[57] This was by now the established consensus of extirpators, cf. Romero, "Idolatrias," *Revista Historica* 6 (1918): 186, 192ff.; below, chap. IX.1.

VIII. RELIGION AND PHILOSOPHY: GARCILASO

of true religion, then desengaño was the highly desirable state of having been alerted to a fraud. Ramos Gavilán's examples of engaño and desengaño bear this out. The principal form of demonic engaño he described was the deeply rooted, and, as he saw it, unreasoning desire of Andean people to continue practicing their ancestral religion.[58] This desire resulted either from the devil "talking in retreats and obscure places, responding to questions in accord with the preconceptions of whoever was listening" or from outright demonic possession. That, at any rate, was what Ramos Gavilán learned when, in the course of exorcising a possessed woman, he forced the demons dwelling in her to confess in a loud voice "the deceits and superstitions" that they had introduced among the Indians.[59]

Calancha also believed in the reality of demonic possession, and he agreed that the devil imitated the true rites of the church. But he could not accept the Manichean simplicity of Ramos Gavilán's polarization of the cosmos and of human society between God and devil. For while desengaño was indeed the simple state of being undeceived from religious error, Calancha was too deeply steeped in his reading of Garcilaso, highlighted as this was by his reading of Augustine's *City of God*,[60] to settle for desengaño conceived in exclusively religious terms. Therefore, although conversion did entail the substitution of Christianity for Andean religion, this substitution was unthinkable without a political upheaval, that is, the end of the Inca empire. Calancha regarded Christian Peru as tantamount to Spanish Peru and did not consider the possibility, posited by Garcilaso, that the Incas might have become Christians without being conquered.[61] The conversion of Andeans to Christianity, therefore, had to entail their political desengaño, their renunciation of power.[62]

Calancha modified this message of Andean subjection—at least in theory—by clothing it in a language rich in imagery and historical allegory. The temple of Pachacamac had thus been the pagan "Athens of this monarchy," and even its ruins still lived for the Indians "as the temple of Solomon lives for the Jews, the Pantheon for the Romans and the house of Mecca for those who follow the sect of Mohammed." Yet, these noble titles notwithstanding, the sanctuary was, according to Calancha, deservedly destroyed by the Spanish invaders because the epoch of its glory had in effect been "an epoch of disgrace," the disgrace, that is, of religious

[58] Ramos Gavilán, *Historia . . . de Copacabana* 1.14–16, esp. p. 108; 1.21–23; 1.24, p. 159.
[59] Ramos Gavilán, *Historia* 1.6, p. 52; see also 15, p. 105; 16, p. 109.
[60] MacCormack (above, n. 52).
[61] Garcilaso, *HG* 1.24–25.
[62] MacCormack, "The Heart Has Its Reasons," *Hispanic American Historical Review* 65 (1985): 443–466.

error.[63] In Calancha's eyes, that disgrace had been remedied by the Augustinian order. Augustinian friars had gained the first converts in the Andes, he argued; they had also been the first to carry the gospel to the Inca empire in exile in Vilcabamba and had been instrumental in the conversion of the last Inca, Tupa Amaru.[64] In this perspective, the Inca empire had fallen not so much before Spanish military might as before the gospel, preached by humble friars. The triumph of the state resulting from the use of force was thus supplanted by the triumph of religion, which, so Calancha suggested with notable lack of realism, resulted from gentle persuasion.[65]

Despite this blinkered perception of Spanish missionizing, Calancha was able to refine Ramos Gavilán's somewhat crude idea of conversion and desengaño from religious error into a more subtle and searching conception of these two experiences. Like Garcilaso, he saw desengaño as both a political and a spiritual process, but unlike Garcilaso, he did not weave into this story about the collective desengaño of the Andean people the memory of his own maturation and his own disappointments. On the one hand, therefore, Calancha's perception of the desengaño of Andean converts to Christianity lost the human complexity and depth with which Garcilaso had endowed it. On the other hand, it acquired a certain public and political validity. For while Garcilaso wrote as an individual, Calancha wrote as the spokesman both of his order and of the Spanish and Christian Peru he called his homeland.[66] There is, however, a deeper difference that distinguishes Calancha's view of conversion and desengaño from that of Garcilaso. Garcilaso wrote with the conviction that, irrespective of cultural and religious difference, Andean people and Spaniards could confront each other somehow as equals. In actual fact, however, what defined relations between the two groups was inequality.[67] Calancha, who spent his entire life in Peru, took this inequality for granted. The desengaño he therefore considered appropriate for Peru's Spaniards and criollos was an awareness of the fragility of their own power and wealth,[68] while the desengaño appropriate for Andean converts to Christianity amounted, in the last resort, to a resigned acceptance of their nonparticipation in the exercise of power and the enjoyment of wealth.[69]

---

[63] Calancha, *Corónica moralizada* 2.19, pp. 924, 939; see also 4.8, p. 1876, Vilcabamba as Jerusalem.

[64] Calancha, *Corónica moralizada* 1.20; 4.2; 4.8, p. 1884.

[65] Calancha, *Corónica moralizada* 1.20; 1.29, pp. 433–438.

[66] Cf. B. Lavallé, *Recherches sur l'apparition de la conscience créole dans la Vice-Royauté du Pérou. L'antagonisme hispano-créole dans les ordres religieux. (XVIème–XVIIème siècles)*, Thèse . . . Bordeaux III, 28 Avril 1978 (Atelier national de reproduction des thèses: Université de Lille III, 1982).

[67] Stern, *Peru's Indian Peoples* (1982); Spalding, *Huarochirí* (1984).

[68] Calancha, *Corónica moralizada* 1.38, pp. 557ff.; 2.35–36.

[69] Calancha, *Corónica moralizada* 4.8, pp. 1879ff.; see also, MacCormack, "Calderón's *La*

47

47. Basilio Pacheco's rendering of the funerary procession of Saint Augustine of Hippo for the cloister of San Agustín in Cuzco. The procession is seen crossing the main square of Cuzco as it was in the painter's lifetime. In the background is the cathedral of Cuzco with the chapel of El Triunfo to the left. Cloister of San Agustín, Lima.

48. The engraving of Augustine of Hippo's funerary procession, by Schulte Adams Bolswert, after which Pacheco modeled his own composition. British Museum, London. Reproduced by courtesy of the Trustees of The British Museum.

49. Funerary procession of Augustine of Hippo, painted by Miguel de Santiago after Bolswert. Here, the engraver's design has not been adapted to fit the New World context of the cloister of San Agustín in Quito for which the painting was produced. San Agustín, Quito. Photograph by Alfonso Ortiz.

Anima beatissima in cælum transmissa, corpus non sine vberrimis suorum lacrymis, totiusq; vrbis et orbis luctu, incruento pro more sacrificio oblato, in basilica cathedrali D. Stephano sacra, terræ redditur. *Poss. c. 31.*

21.

48

49

This perception of colonial society was far from being peculiar to Calancha; rather, it was shared by a majority of lawmakers, clergymen and officials. In due course, therefore, Garcilaso's work was cited as evidence for the idea that the invasion of Peru and the consequent evangelization of the Indians were the work of divine providence, *tout court*.[70]

The issue was clearly understood by the Andean painter Basilio Pacheco, who in the mid–eighteenth century was commissioned to paint a cycle of pictures describing the life of Augustine of Hippo. These pictures were designed to adorn the cloister of the Augustinian convent in Cuzco. One of them represents the saint's funerary procession (fig. 47). The iconography follows a rendering of the same subject by the admired Netherlandish engraver Schulte Adams Bolswert (fig. 48) that had earlier inspired Miguel de Santiago, who painted a cycle of pictures on the life of Augustine for the Augustinian convent in Quito (fig. 49). The painting in Quito follows its prototype exactly, but Pacheco made two major alterations. First, he departed from Bolswert's original by depicting the funerary procession traversing, not a square in Hippo, where Augustine had in fact died, but the main square of Cuzco, where the Inca palaces have given way to the Cathedral and the Chapel of El Triunfo.[71] Second, Pacheco tranformed the figures of three kneeling onlookers, who in Bolswert's engraving observe the procession, into a portrait of himself. Bolswert's onlookers are fraught with emotion at the mournful spectacle passing before them. The Indian painter Pacheco, by contrast, ignores this spectacle and looks out at the beholder of his picture with solemn and distant composure. He witnesses Augustine's funerary procession without participating in it, while at the same time mediating the sacred action to the beholder of the painting. In short, Pacheco portrayed himself as the exponent of a twofold desengaño, as an outsider both to the gathering of people shown in his painting and to the community of friars who would day by day walk past this painting in their cloister.

---

aurora en Copacabana: The Conversion of the Incas in the Light of Seventeenth Century Spanish Theology, Culture and Political Theory," *Journal of Theological Studies* 32 (1982): 448–480. On Indians as "miserables," needing guidance, see Solorzano, *Politica Indiana* 2.28, Biblioteca de autores españoles, vol. 252, pp. 252ff.; Peña Montenegro, *Itinerario* 2, Tratado I.

[70] Diego de Cordova Salinas, *Crónica Franciscana de las Provincias del Perú*, ed. Lino G. Canedo (Washington, D.C., 1957), 1.2, p. 19–1.3, p. 25; 1.4, p. 32–1.6, p. 48; Antonio León Pinelo, *Paradiso* 3.19 pp. 303ff.

[71] Gisbert, *Historia de la pintura cuzqueña* (Lima, 1982), fig. 286 and p. 202; Courcelle, *Iconographie de St. Augustin*, vol. 3, plates 50 and 121 with p. 111. But Courcelle attributes the painting to a follower or student of Miguel de Santiago.

THE GREAT DIVIDE:
ANDEAN RELIGION IN THEORY
AND PRACTICE,
1621–1653

IN 1608 Fray Juan Ramírez, one of the four Augustinian missionary pio-
neers to work in Huamachuco,[1] died in the convent of his order in Trujillo.[2] He was nearly blind and had become an awesome old man. How
many years had he lived? one of the younger friars asked him not long
before his death. "Only few in the service of God and many in his disser-
vice," was the daunting reply.[3] Fray Juan had lived, at any rate, to see the
passing of an epoch. When he and the other founders of the Augustinian
Order arrived in Lima in 1551, they lodged in a simple private house that
had been given to them by a benefactor.[4] By the early seventeenth century, however, the Augustinians, like the other missionary orders in Peru,
owned a fine church, occupied elaborate and comfortable conventual
buildings, and had amassed a notable scholarly library (fig. 50). The writings of the time reflect these changes in the position of ecclesiastics in the
New World. Thus, Antonio de la Calancha, the friar who had ventured
to ask the aged Fray Juan about his life, admired the indomitable energy
with which the first Augustinians in Peru had traversed the length and
breadth of the Andes on foot, preaching the gospel. But Calancha himself, like many other religious of the early seventeenth century, lived the
sheltered existence of a man of learning. As such he devoted his time to
monastic administration, to research, and to weaving together the fragmentary accounts he was able to find of the Augustinian founding heroes
into an eloquent hagiography which was published in Barcelona in 1639
as the official history of his order. In his later years he lived in Lima,
where his learning and urbanity were appreciated by a circle of eruditi
reaching far beyond the Augustinian Order.[5]

---

[1] See above, chap. IV.1 at nn. 1ff.
[2] Calancha, *Corónica moralizada* 2.13, p. 897.
[3] Calancha, p. 896.
[4] Calancha, 1.21, p. 311.
[5] Cf. Bernardo de Torres, *Crónica Agustina*, ed. I. Prado Pastor (Lima, 1974), 4.24, pp.
826ff.; cf. for scholarly culture in Cuzco, W. Redmond, "Juan Espinoza Medrano: Prefacio
al Lector de la Logica," *Fenix. Revista de la Biblioteca Nacional* 20 (1970): 74–80.

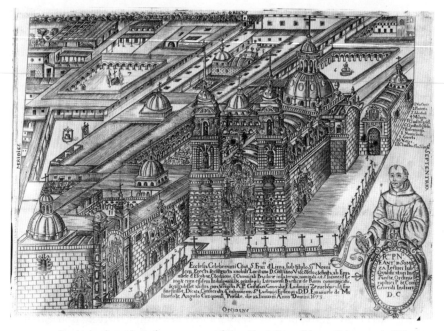

50. Spain in America: the convent of San Francisco, Lima. Friars and citizens of Lima met in the conventual church, accessible to the latter through the main portal, flanked by twin towers, and to the former through a side entrance from the principal cloister. The conventual buildings and grounds, used only by the friars, constitute a separate "city" within the city of Lima. Miguel Suarez de Figueroa, *Templo de N. Grande Patriarca San Francisco* (Lima, 1675). Biblioteca Nacional, Madrid.

A century after its foundation, Lima had become a sophisticated and elegant capital, graced by many cultivated persons who lived in, or passed through, the city and left their mark on its life. Among them were the jurist Juan de Solórzano, the Jesuit historian Bernabé Cobo, and the lawyer, antiquarian and bibliophile Antonio de León Pinelo, who in his *Paraiso*, completed in around 1650, wrote in admiring terms about the men of culture and learning whose company he had enjoyed in Lima.[6] Indeed, celebrations of the "merits and excellencies of the city of Lima" had become something of a literary genre, and its practitioners brought to it affectionate recollections of Limeño friends and acquaintances. One of those whose memory was cherished in this way was the Jesuit teacher and missionary José de Arriaga, author of a Latin treatise on rhetoric, whom

[6] See R. Porras Barrenechea, ed., Leon Pinelo, *Paraiso*, pp. viiif.

one of his students described as the "Cicero of eloquence and poetry's Vergil."[7] But there also was a sterner side to Arriaga's personality, for he wrote a book on extirpating idolatries that soon after its publication in Lima in 1621 became a classic, marking a new degree of professionalism and specialization in the rooting out of Andean religion. Indeed, the extirpation of Andean religion was at this time becoming so dominant a preoccupation amoung Peruvian ecclesiastics that it generated its own highly competitive and remunerative career structure.[8]

Although their interests and fields of expertise differed widely, the missionaries, scholars, and historians who conversed with each other about the Andean past in the convents and salons of Lima had one thing in common: their deep ambivalence concerning Inca and Andean religion. On the one hand, the publication of Garcilaso's *Commentaries* helped to crystallize a certain consensus that Inca religion represented a recognizable cultural achievement. On the other hand, persons familiar with the Andean past were convinced that whatever the merits of Inca religion might have been, they could not outweigh the huge conglomerate of Andean errors and "superstitions" that were still being practiced. The ambiguities that had endowed Garcilaso's vision of Andean religious history with tension and drama, and that captivated his readers even when they disagreed with him, were thus of little practical relevance in seventeenth-century Peru.

It was not only the era of heroic missionary endeavor that was coming to an end with the death of men such as Fray Juan Ramírez but also the first major epoch in Spanish perceptions of Andean life. In the experience of Fray Juan, who had been a late contemporary of Cieza de León, Betanzos, and Polo de Ondegardo, the Incas were a memory that was very much alive. This was still the case when, two decades later, Pedro Sarmiento de Gamboa and Cristóbal de Molina were making their inquiries. For all these researchers, investigation of the Andean and Inca past had gone hand in hand with personal observation. This continuity between practice and theory was beginning to come apart in the late sixteenth century.

Andeans interviewed in Cuzco by Molina and Sarmiento could still speak about the Inca state from their own experience, not merely from tradition. Garcilaso likewise availed himself of the personal memories of individuals who had lived under the Incas. But at the very time when Garcilaso was writing in Spain, a new generation of Andeans, who had been born in colonial Peru, began transforming the historical memory of the Incas into myth. Andean reality as observed and experienced ceased

---

[7] Salinas y Cordova, *Memorial* 2.7, p. 242.
[8] See Antonio Acosta in *Runa yndio* (1987), pp. 553–616.

to be continuous with the reality of the Incas. When, therefore, in the second decade of the seventeenth century, José de Arriaga and the other extirpators of idolatries scoured Peru for Andean objects of worship and for information about Andean myths, beliefs, and observances, the religious world they encountered differed significantly from the one that had been found by Cieza and Betanzos and their contemporaries. As a result, Spanish students of Inca religion and culture now derived their information not so much from face-to-face contact with Andeans but from earlier written documents produced by other Spaniards.

In 1653 Bernabé Cobo, then living in Lima, completed the most comprehensive extant history of the Incas. The work's importance stems from Cobo's intelligent use of documents that are now lost, and only to a lesser degree from what he added to these documents out of his personal experience. Calancha also was a skillful researcher in archives. Not that there was no personal experience to be gathered any more, no Andeans to consult. Indeed, the extirpators were dependent on their Andean interpreters and assistants. But since extirpation defined Andean religion as devoid of intrinsic value, its exponents lacked cultural authority. As a result, Inca and Andean beliefs, myths, and rituals provided raw materials to be molded by Europeans but could not modify the categories that these Europeans recognized as definitive. This is why Inca and Andean religion as perceived in seventeenth-century Lima gradually grew into a phenomenon somewhat to one side of the religion that was actually practiced in the Andean highlands and that the extirpators were endeavouring to uproot. It was next to inconceivable for seventeenth-century scholars to cross the divide that separated Andean reality from the Christian and Hispanic construct of that reality that they were in the process of erecting. Andeans thus enjoyed no recognition from exponents of the Christian learned tradition who evaluated and judged them. As a result, Peru became a land of two separate societies, or, as seventeenth-century jurists expressed it, "republics,"[9] between which little cultural exchange was possible.

1. THE VIEW FROM LIMA

In 1615, poor and getting old, Guaman Poma searched Lima for an ally and intermediary who might help to convey the manuscript of his *Crónica* to Spain, and perhaps arrange for its presentation to Philip III and subsequent publication. As a young man, Guaman Poma had worked with the extirpator Cristóbal de Albornoz, but this gave him, it seems, no usable contacts in Hispanic society. The manuscript of his *Crónica* did reach

[9] Spalding, *Huarochiri*, pp. 158, 296.

Spain, however. The intermediary, perhaps, was the young nobleman Buenaventura de Salinas y Cordoba, who at the time was serving as a page in the viceroy's household. In 1616 he became a Franciscan friar, and in 1630 he published a book entitled *Memorial of the Histories of the New World.* Fray Buenaventura began his work with an outline of the four Andean ages before the advent of the Incas, an outline that seems to be derived from Guaman Poma,[1] but without acknowledgment. Seventeenth-century authors tended to omit acknowledgment of unpublished sources except when bestowing praise or a compliment. However, since Fray Buenaventura was a passionate apologist for Andeans, it is striking that he said nothing about the origin of his Andean information—whether or not it was indeed from Guaman Poma—while on the other hand acknowledging European sources in detail and with care. A similar inability to recognize Andean intellectual and cultural achievements had earlier been noticed by Garcilaso, who therefore explained that the Inca amautas were professional philosophers, theologians, and historians.[2] Such a conception of the amautas, europeanized though it was,[3] did draw attention to the existence of Andean learned traditions. Yet, although one of the Peruvian eruditi to express agreement with Garcilaso on this issue was Antonio de la Calancha, Calancha's Lima offered Guaman Poma, a living exponent of Andean history and tradition, no public.[4]

This could happen because the European and Christian learned tradition, viewed in the light of its own standards, had served its Peruvian exponents well, and no reason appeared to exist for looking beyond it to other cognitive schemes. Andean and Inca religious belief and observance had been classified and understood in the light of criteria derived from the study of religion in the ancient Mediterranean and Christian Europe. The growing corpus of information on religion in the Andes that was being amassed by the extirpators continued to consolidate these old, established theories regarding the nature of non-Christian religion.

The same confidence in the resilience and versatility of European philosophy and theology that had inspired Las Casas to write the *Apologética Historia* still inspired scholars in seventeenth-century Peru, but their world was a grimmer and gloomier place. Las Casas had regarded many aspects of religious diversity and change as expressions of human prog-

[1] Salinas y Cordova, *Memorial* 1, pp. 13–14; Guaman Poma, *Nueva Crónica*, p. 48, with Murra/Adorno, ad loc.; Guaman Poma, p. 53; J. Imbelloni, "La tradición peruana de las cuatro edades," *Anales del Instituto de Etnografía* 5 (1944): 55–94.

[2] Garcilaso, *CR* 2.4, p. 46b; 21, p. 71b; 3.25, p. 119a; 4.19, p. 140b; 6.9, p. 205a; 7.10, p. 260b; cf. 9.15, p. 254a.

[3] See Taylor in *Runa yndio* (1987), pp. 23f.

[4] On the amautas, see Calancha, *Corónica moralizada* 1.14, p. 205; 2.18, p. 926. For a most illuminating discussion of the distance between Andeans and Spaniards in linguistic terms, see B. Mannheim, *The Language of the Inca since the European Invasion* (1990), chap. 6.

ress and discussed these phenomena within a broad comparative framework. Seventeenth-century scholars still used the comparative framework but tended to view religious diversity and change in more negative terms. When comparing the pre-Christian religions of Europe to those of the Americas, Las Casas had perceived in all these religions, but especially in those of the Americas, an evolution toward a profound and vital grasp of theological truth. A similar attitude motivated Garcilaso's interpretation of Inca religion in the *Royal Commentaries*, published in 1609. Twelve years later, José de Arriaga published his *Extirpation of Idolatry*, where he likewise compared Andean religion to Greco-Roman paganism. But he had nothing to say in favor of pagan religions, whether Greco-Roman or Andean. Despite arduous evangelizing labor, Arriaga lamented, idolatry in Peru was still flourishing. He conceded, however, that this was hardly surprising, for even in the "pure land" of Visigothic Spain "after six hundred years of preaching the gospel . . . idolatry continued to prosper and had by no means been uprooted."[5]

Imperceptibly, Peruvian missionaries had crossed the gulf separating the enterprise of preaching the gospel to all nations from that of extirpating non-Christian religion. The first missionaries in the Andes had looked for inspiration and example to the apostles and martyrs of the early church, men unburdened by institutional and political obligations. Extirpation, however, was impracticable without support from the secular state, so that the model of the post-Constantinian church, in which bishops and secular rulers had worked hand in hand, became more relevant in Peru. To explain the task that confronted missionaries in Peru, Arriaga accordingly quoted the decrees of the seventh-century Visigothic church councils of Toledo. The bishops assembled in these councils had repeatedly used language of a severity that was unparallelled in the annals of late-antique Christianity, in order to make provision for the "extermination of the sacrilege of idolatry" throughout the Iberian peninsula.[6] To apply these decrees to the Andes amounted to declaring that the heroic age of Peru's apostles, the first missionaries, had come to an end. Under the new dispensation, the apostolic labor of preaching and persuading was to be supplemented by the more authoritarian labor of implementing what had been preached by extirpation.

The policy of extirpation, along with a harsh intellectual rejection of religions other than Christianity, was, as Arriaga and several contemporaries noted approvingly, the order of the day throughout the Hispanic world. To such men, the expulsion of the Moriscos from Spain in 1607, after decades of debate and ever-intensifying legislative constraints, was a

[5] Pure land of Spain, Arriaga, *Extirpación* 1, p.3; idolatry, Arriaga, *Extirpación*, Preface, p. xxxi.
[6] Arriaga, *Extirpación*, Preface, pp. xxxif.

most laudable measure. The same attitude governed relations with Jews and Marranos.[7] In the Americas as in the peninsula, Jewish converts to Christianity and their descendants lived under the constant scrutiny of the Inquisition, a body of men that the learned Calancha considered to be an especial adornment, a "jewel" of viceregal government.[8] The statement is more than theoretical, for as a distinguished member of his order, Calancha would have been present at the several autos da fé that took place in Lima during the years of his residence there.[9]

The judicial rules under which the Inquisition prosecuted its victims, and the ceremonial order it observed when imposing its verdicts on society at large, provided extirpators of Andean religion with a procedural model.[10] During the procedure's opening phase, the extirpators cross-examined witnesses in exhaustive detail, in the expectation that whatever evidence might exist of non-Christian religious belief and observance would in due course come to light. Next, non-Christian objects of worship were ceremoniously burned in a public auto da fé and offenders were punished. Cristóbal de Albornoz and his fellow extirpators had already followed this order of events when prosecuting adherents of the Taqui Onqoy and suppressing their doctrines in the years after 1565. Campaigns of extirpation were renewed in 1607, when Francisco de Ávila began investigating cults, myths, and huacas in his parish of San Damián in Huarochiri.[11] In December 1609, he displayed his discoveries in Lima. Confiscated huacas and implements of cult, along with a large collection of ancestral mummies that Ávila had arranged to be removed from their places of burial, were piled up in the Plaza de Armas. In the presence of the populace, of the city's dignitaries, and of the Viceroy who surveyed the event from a balcony, Ávila preached in Quechua against idolatry, and then the accumulated mummies, huacas, and other sacred objects were put to the flame. The crowning event was the whipping of the Andean religious teacher Hernando Paucar. He, who according to Arriaga was "a great teacher of idolatry and spoke with the devil," had been tied to a stake in the square to witness the entire procedure, and after his terrible punishment was exiled to a Jesuit house in Chile.[12] In the course of the seventeenth century, similar rituals of destruction and punishment

[7] Duviols, "La represión del paganismo andino y la expulsión de los moriscos," *Anuario de Estudios Americanos* 28 (1971): 201–207; on the Marranos, Y. H. Yerushalmi, *From Spanish Court to Italian Ghetto. Isaac Cardoso. A Study in Seventeenth Century Marranism and Jewish Apologetics* (Seattle, 1971), chap. 1.

[8] Calancha, *Corónica moralizada* 3.16, p. 1389.

[9] Cf. Quiroz, "Expropriation," *Ibero-Amerikanisches Archiv*, n.s. 11, no.4 (1985): 407–465.

[10] For this model, see Beinart, "Jewish witnesses," *Essays in Honour of Ben Beinart* (1978), 1: 37–46.

[11] Cf. C. Romero, "Paliques bibliograficos," *Revista Historica* (Lima) 10 (1936): 192–228 at 201ff.

[12] A. Acosta in *Runa yndio* (1987), pp. 589ff.; Arriaga, *Extirpación* 1, pp. 6f.

were to be performed not only in Lima but in many Andean towns and villages.[13]

While the searching out and subsequent destruction of Andean objects of worship by missionaries was nothing unusual, the thoroughness of Ávila, Arriaga, and their numerous seventeenth-century followers was new. This investigative thoroughness—a certain controlled ferocity—had a bearing on research. The success of inquiries against idolatries depended very largely on the extirpator's ability to pursue them systematically. Polo de Ondegardo wrote the first major treatise designed to assist in formulating such an inquiry. The summary of this treatise published by the Third Council of Lima contains separate rubrics describing objects of worship, rituals of divination, confession and sacrifice, the calendar, different kinds of religious specialists, and finally objects for sacrifice. This order was determined less by any Andean significance of the subjects under discussion than by the convenience of the extirpator, who needed a clear-cut schema to follow.[14]

Arriaga composed his treatise on extirpation according to similar principles, discussing in turn objects of worship, religious specialists, sacrifices, and the religious calendar. He also provided prospective extirpators with a sample interrogation that appears to have been followed quite closely by the many readers of his work.[15] Apart from serving its purpose of helping extirpators, this interrogation reveals some relatively new preoccupations in the study of Andean religion, although some of these preoccupations had been adumbrated earlier by Polo de Ondegardo and his contemporaries in their investigation of Inca cults.

When searching for the Inca mummies that had been preserved in and around Cuzco, Polo noted that their cult was performed by specially designated members of each mummy's kin group. In due course, missionaries all over the Andes found that elsewhere also kin groups, or ayllus, provided for their ancestral mummies, especially those of their founders. Arriaga therefore instructed extirpators to find out the names and whereabouts of a community's mummies and above all to ascertain to which ayllu they belonged. He had himself worked in the central sierra, where the ubiquitous Andean moieties of anan and urin were described as

---

[13] For the chronology, see Duviols, *Lutte* (1971), chap. 2.

[14] Cf. above, chap. IV.3 at nn. 32ff.

[15] Arriaga, *Extirpación*, chap. 15; cf. Duviols, *Cultura andina y represión* (1986), p. 481; Arriaga's treatise was in part reprinted in 1647 in the *Carta pastoral de exhortación, e instrucción contra las idolatrías de los Indios del arzobispado de Lima* by the archbishop of Lima Pedro de Villagomes, Colección de libros y documentos referentes a la historia del Perú, vol. 12 (Lima, 1919); Villagomes also conducted campaigns of extirpation when bishop of Arequipa: *Constituciones sinodales del obispado de Arequipa hechas y ordenadas por el Illo y Rmo señor don Pedro de Villagomez . . . 1638*, Biblioteca Nacional, Madrid, MS. 723.

groups of newcomers called *llacuaz*, and of *huari* or *llactayoc*,[16] who were people indigenous to the region.[17] The religious life of llacuazes was dominated by their mummies, described in the Quechua of central Peru as mallquis. The oldest of these mallquis had been brought by the llacuazes when in the mythic past, they had come to settle, while the religious life of huaris centered on the immovable sacred landmarks or huacas that they associated with their origins and their history.[18] In addition, huaris had mallquis and llacuazes had huacas, but these were less central to their religious identity.[19]

Arriaga observed not only that different kin groups, or ayllus, revered different holy objects and thus followed independent ritual cycles, but also that these differences articulated community tensions and conflicts that could be exploited, seeing that hostile ayllus would probably "betray each other" to the extirpator.[20] He ought, therefore, to know the ayllu to which any individual he was questioning belonged and thence ought to learn additional details, such as the names and whereabouts of the curaca's personal huaca, of the huaca who was revered by the ayllu to prevent irrigation canals from breaking, and of huacas who brought rain and watched over cultivated fields. Furthermore, Arriaga specified, all households kept Zaramamas, Cocamamas, and other "mothers" who safeguarded the growth of crops and animals,[21] and all households celebrated the turning points of each member's life cycle, from birth to the baby's first hair cutting, to house-building when a couple married, and on to sickness and death.[22]

Beyond such cultic particulars, which affected the different ayllus and families in any given community as distinct and almost autonomous units, Andean villages lived a shared religious and ritual life that likewise, Arriaga noted, merited the attention of the extirpator. Religious rituals in which the entire community participated marked seedtime, harvest, and other events in the agricultural calendar.[23] In addition, each community as a whole was watched over by a communal huaca, a mountain or rock,

[16] From Quechua *llacta*, "village" or "settlement."

[17] See Duviols, "Huari y llacuaz," *Journal de la Société des Américanistes* 55 (1973): 153–191; Duviols, "Une petite chronique," *Journal de la Société des Américanistes* 63 (1974–1976): 288. This ordering of society was later replicated in cofradías, see E. R. Masferrer Kan, "Criterios de organización andina. Recuay siglo XVII," *Bulletin de l'Institut Français des Études Andines* 13 (1984): 47–61.

[18] Cf. Duviols, *Cultura andina y represión* (1986), pp. 226; 228; 229; 249; 250, cult of the mallquis of the first cultivators of certain fields.

[19] See below, sec. 2 at nn. 32ff.

[20] Arriaga, *Extirpación* 15, p. 138.

[21] Arriaga, *Extirpación* 2, pp. 28f.; 15, p. 139.

[22] Arriaga, *Extirpación* 6, pp. 56ff.

[23] Arriaga, *Extirpación* 2, pp. 19ff., differentiates private from public objects of worship; see also 4, pp. 52ff.; 15, p. 141.

who might have father, brother, wife, and children. Myths were told of these supernatural beings, who all had their special ministers, sacrifices, and community festivals.[24] These festivals, Arriaga observed, unfolded according to a common pattern that the extirpator should understand. Sacrifice to the huaca or mallqui being honored was attended by a night's vigil during which people sang, danced, and told myths and stories. Next came a five-day fast, consisting of abstinence from salt, aji, and sexual intercourse. While fasting, the Indians confessed their sins to officially designated confessors, who imposed penances and performed rituals of purification.[25]

To facilitate the extirpator's interrogation, Arriaga supplied the different titles of religious specialists: confessors, priests of diverse huacas, diviners, and guardians of the crops.[26] He also described the sacred attire woven of *cumbi* cloth and the silver adornments that Andeans wore when celebrating their festivals, so that extirpators would know which objects to confiscate and burn.[27] His sample interrogation furthermore alerted the extirpator to the neccesity of finding out what the different huacas looked like, how they were housed, and what clothes and ornaments they possessed.[28] For it was only when armed with such information that the extirpator had any hope of locating and identifying the huacas and of confiscating their property.

A comparison between Arriaga's treatise and the account of Andean religion that the Augustinian friars wrote in 1560, after working for eight years in Huamachuco, highlights the nuanced and differentiated quality of the former. In particular, Arriaga conceptualized Andean religious observances within their social and economic context, whereas the Augustinian friars for the most part could do little more than list deities and rituals. By Arriaga's time, the imperatives of extirpation, along with a significant body of erudition and expertise built up in the course of prolonged familiarity with the Andes, had sharpened the missionaries' powers of observation and classification.

A scholar and historian who greatly benefited by this accumulated erudition was Bernabé Cobo, who knew the published work of Arriaga,[29] regularly referred to Garcilaso, and also sought out manuscript copies of the writings of Polo de Ondegardo, Pedro Pizarro, Cristóbal de Molina

[24] Arriaga, *Extirpación* 15, pp. 138ff.
[25] Arriaga, *Extirpación* 5, pp. 49ff.
[26] Arriaga, *Extirpación* 3, pp. 32ff.; 15, p. 140; p. 142, pariana, for which cf. Guaman Poma, *Nueva Crónica*, p. 1138 [1148].
[27] Arriaga, *Extirpación* 5, p. 53; 8, p. 75.
[28] Arriaga, *Extirpación* 15, pp. 138, 140; 2, pp. 25f.
[29] Cobo, *Fundación de Lima* 3.22, Biblioteca de autores españoles, vol. 92 (Madrid, 1964), p. 238.

of Cuzco, Sarmiento, and others.[30] Cobo was the intellectual heir of José de Acosta. Like Acosta, he studied the human history of the American continent in conjunction with its natural history. And like Acosta, he found both the natural world and the people of the Americas deficient when compared to Europe. But this made them no less deserving of study.

By inclination, and also thanks to his experience as missionary and extirpator,[31] Cobo had eyes even for those details of Inca religion for which Europe and the ancient Mediterranean offered no parallels. Several earlier historians had referred to the participation of the mummies of deceased Incas in affairs of state, and the universal importance of mummies in Andean religion had been revealed by the campaigns of extirpation. Nonetheless, Cobo was the only historian of Inca religion to discuss the cult of Inca and Andean mummies in juxtaposition with the parallel cult of each Inca's *guauque*, his "brother" or divine double.[32] He also assembled information on the appearance and terminology of Inca royal insignia,[33] and interested himself in the logistics of Inca rituals.[34] Similarly, following a document of the later sixteenth century, he recorded that the shrines of Cuzco and its vicinity were arranged in a regular order along ceques, or sight lines, centering on Coricancha, and that, just as Arriaga had observed elsewhere in the Andes, these shrines were cared for by particular ayllus.[35] Cobo also explained, in general terms, the functioning of the Inca calendar and the astronomical measurements that the Incas took at the time of the spring and autumn equinoxes from the solar pillars erected for this purpose.[36] Finally, careful scholar that he was, Cobo took stock of the considerable confusion that had arisen among historians regarding the appearance of the Inca image of the divine Sun and attempted to resolve the difficulty by distinguishing, from the conflicting accounts, three different images.[37]

[30] Polo de Ondegardo, see Cobo, *Historia* 12.2, p. 59b; Pedro Pizarro, Cobo, *Historia* 6.13, quoting Pizarro 36, p. 249; Cobo, *Historia* 13.20, quoting Pizarro 14, pp. 81ff. Cobo also quoted Molina's *Fábulas*: e.g., Cobo 13.2, p. 151b = *Fábulas*, p. 55; Cobo, p. 152b = *Fábulas*, p. 57. Cobo 13.2 is a quotation from Sarmiento, *Historia Indica* 6, p. 207. Other earlier authors, see Cobo 12.2, pp. 59aff.; see further Rowe, "An Account," *Ñawpa Pacha* 17 (1979): 6f.
[31] Cobo, *Historia* 11.1, p. 10a; 13.10, p. 165b, saw mummies; 13.34, p. 226b, divination is hard to uproot, "cuanto ha mostrado la experiencia."
[32] Cobo, *Historia* 13.9–10; cf. above, chap. VII.1 at nn. 43–51.
[33] Cobo, *Historia* 12.36, cf. 13.32.
[34] E.g., on consecrated fire for sacrifices, maintained in a stone brazier next to Coricancha, Cobo, *Historia* 13.22, p. 204a; Inca accounting for sacrifices to be performed, Cobo 13.32, p. 223a; cf. Cobo 13.1, pp. 148bf., over one thousand specialists are employed in Cuzco in keeping alive the memory of matters of religion.
[35] See Rowe, "An Account," *Ñawpa Pacha* 17 (1979): 6ff.
[36] Cobo, *Historia* 12.37.
[37] Cobo, *Historia* 13.5, p. 157.

Cobo presented the diverse particulars of Andean and Inca religion he learned about in his sources in the tightly drawn cognitive framework that he had inherited from his intellectual ancestors, although he deployed it with much greater versatility and subtlety. Cobo's work thus exemplifies to perfection the heuristic power of the European and Christian learned tradition within which he thought and wrote, the tradition that the Jesuits were at this time deploying with such amazing success to chart non-European cultures in the Americas and in India, China, and Japan.[38]

Like Acosta,[39] Cobo regarded the Incas as "people of reason and less barbarous than other nations in this New World." They were capable of some speculative thinking and had therefore ascertained the existence of a Creator.[40] Nonetheless, thanks in part to their credulity and in part to the endeavors of the devil, they were plagued by a multitude of false gods.

Acosta had arranged these false gods into two categories or "lineages." One category consisted of objects of worship drawn from nature, such as the celestial bodies, earth and sea, mountains and lakes. The other consisted of products of human invention and imagination, including kings and the dead, who were worshiped for powers they were imagined to have but did not actually have, and idols representing animals, plants, and human beings. Acosta had derived this distinction between natural and imagined objects of worship (including idols fashioned by the human hand) from his knowledge of earlier writers on the Andes, from personal observation and above all from his readings in the Book of Wisdom.[41] When Garcilaso in turn reflected on Andean and Inca religion, on idolatry and Andean concepts of the holy, he argued that the interpretation of Inca religion as entirely idolatrous was too sweeping.

Cobo used the knowledge he acquired of Andean and Inca religion during over forty years of residing in Peru[42] to modify Acosta's view of Andean religion and reject Garcilaso's. Broadly speaking, he wrote, Andean objects of worship could be classified according to the two categories Acosta had used. In the first category were to be found "the works of nature, and in the second all the figures and idols that lacked all significance and being other than the matter of which they were formed and the shape with which they were endowed by their [human] maker."[43] However, where Acosta had included in the second category of idols both the

[38] See J. Spence, *The Memory Palace of Matteo Ricci* (New York, 1983).
[39] Above, chap. VI at nn. 92, 136.
[40] Cobo, *Historia* 13.1, p. 147b; cf. 11.7–8.
[41] See above, chap. VI at n. 102.
[42] See Cobo, *Historia*, Prologue, p. 4a; Mateos, ed., Cobo, *Obras*, pp. xiiff.
[43] Cobo, *Historia* 13.11, p. 166a.

Inca rulers and the dead, Cobo discussed these separately. Two issues were at stake.

First, by excluding living Incas and the dead from Acosta's category of imagined objects of worship, Cobo made this category more coherent. The dead and kings could be associated with idolatrous images and effigies as objects of worship because arguably, like these images, they were worshiped for imagined powers and qualities that they did not actually possess. On the other hand, it was inconsistent to juxtapose the cult of kings and of the dead with that of idolatrous images, because while idols are in themselves an invention, kings and the dead are not, even though, arguably, their powers are the result of human invention or imagination. By differentiating the cult of kings and the dead from the cult of imagined objects of worship, Cobo thus corrected an inconsistency in Acosta's analysis of idolatry.

Secondly, therefore, Cobo distanced the analysis of Inca and Andean religion from the analysis of idolatry that Acosta had derived, in the last analysis, from the Book of Wisdom. With this, biblical and Greco-Roman antecendents lost some of their former heuristic authority. Indeed, Cobo's own account of Inca religion, with its focus on phenomena such as the guauques of Inca rulers and the ceque shrines of Cuzco, for which there existed no clear European precedents, demonstrates that he thought this to be the case, even though he never argued it explicitly.

If therefore European antecedents and parallels were not as helpful in understanding Inca religion as had been assumed, then the entire comparative edifice erected by Las Casas and those who had followed him fell to the ground, and with it the apologetical purpose that had motivated them. This had been to demonstrate that American religions possessed not only cultural but also theological merit and that therefore they had prepared the way for Christianity. The historian who had made the most detailed and urgent case for the preparatory role of Inca religion was Garcilaso. Although Cobo accepted Garcilaso's views on Inca monotheism selectively, he did not agree with the main thrust of his interpretation of Inca religion. Cobo conceded that the Incas had attained "the knowledge that the true God and First Cause is one only,"[44] but throughout he emphasized the confused nature of this knowledge. For apart from adding "to the worship of the supreme Lord that of innumerable other things, which they venerated with equal respect and reverence," the Incas mingled "within this faint information they had about God a multitude of vanities and errors, attributing to him in their imaginations things very alien and unworthy of his most noble nature."[45] Moreover, the worship

[44] Cobo, *Historia* 13.1, p. 147a.
[45] Cobo, *Historia* 13.4, p. 155b.

of this supreme Lord emerged only late in Inca history.[46] The Incas referred to him by metaphorical titles like Ticciviracocha, which Cobo translated as "divine foundation." Such titles led him to agree with Acosta that the Quechua language lacked a generic term for "god," this being another indication that the concept of one supreme deity was not fully rooted in Andean thought.[47]

> They had no single proper term with which to name [the Creator]. For all the names they gave him were metaphorical . . . so that in the catechisms that have been written to instruct them in Christian doctrine, our word *God* is used, and we employ this same term whenever we speak with them, because their language has no term corresponding to *God*.[48]

In classifying Andean objects of worship or huacas according to Acosta's categories as either imagined or drawn from nature,[49] Cobo set aside Garcilaso's analysis of the concept *huaca*. But he appears to have reflected on it, because he used many of the same examples. Cobo thus made clear his opinion that Andeans and the Incas did in effect worship indiscriminately the wide array of natural objects and phenomena they described as *huaca*. Evidently, therefore, the concept *huaca* could not be deployed, as Garcilaso had done, to argue that Inca religion was essentially monotheistic. Neither could this concept be deployed to describe in any meaningful sense the order of nature. Cobo therefore enumerated the celestial bodies and atmospheric phenomena worshiped by the Incas not as classified in the Andes but according to the Ptolemaic order:

> After the Sun they worshiped the Moon and the stars, if we observe the order which these bodies maintain among each other rather than the order that the Indians followed in the veneration that they gave to them. For if we were to attend to this latter, we would now name Thunder, to whom they gave the second place after the Sun with regard to authority and honor.[50]

At issue was the validity of European and Christian, as opposed to Inca or Andean, modes of thought regarding the relationship between theo-

---

[46] I.e., under Inca Viracocha: Cobo, *Historia* 13.4, p. 156a. Cobo here adapted Garcilaso's date for Inca Viracocha's vision of his phantasm to the emergence of the deity Viracocha among the Incas.

[47] Cf. above, chap. VI at n. 73; chap. VIII.1 at nn. 7–8, 51. The term "Divine Foundation" to translate the name Viracocha is a tacit correction of Garcilaso; see further Szeminski, *Un kuraca* (1987), pp. 12ff. Molina, *Fábulas*, p. 53, translates Titiviracochan as "yncomprehensible dios."

[48] Cobo, *Historia* 13.4.

[49] Cobo, *Historia* 13.11.

[50] Cobo, *Historia* 13.6, p. 158.

logical and scientific knowledge. During the seventeenth century, the connection between natural science and Christian theology acquired a new and urgent relevance in Europe. For while Cobo as a young man was familiarizing himself with the Andes, his fellow Jesuits in Rome were battling against Galileo.[51] News of these duels as of other European intellectual events would have reached Lima, if only because the Jesuits circulated letters about each other's doings throughout the worldwide network of their order. In discussing Inca religion, Cobo thus reasserted the validity of the Ptolemaic view of the universe with more than usual care. However, whereas in Europe the central issue of debate was the configuration of the solar system, what was at stake in Peru was causation in the cosmos. Some sixteenth-century missionaries had already pointed out that Andean worship focused primarily on a variety of visible secondary causes, such as celestial bodies and atmospheric phenomena, and not on the invisible Creator and primary cause. If Andeans could amend their mistaken conception of the Sun and other idols as agents in their own right, these missionaries urged, then they would understand the necessity of worshiping the Christian God as the one and universal Cause.[52] The theme was thus an old one, but the scientific interests of seventeenth-century scholars gave it a new profile.

When Las Casas reflected on the nature of religion throughout the world, he concluded that all human beings had a conception of god, whether it was true or false, and that this conception was articulated in worship as a relationship of dependence and even of love. Cobo also pondered the nature of religion, but formulated it, with lapidary and scientific precision, in terms of causation and purpose: "The entire foundation of all religion and divine worship consists of the knowledge of the first cause, whether this is the true cause or a fictitious one, from which men believe they originated and on which [they think] they depend for the preservation of their being. [Beyond that, the foundation of religion is] the understanding of the end and the estate men hope to enjoy after this life."[53] The confused concern of Andeans with visible, secondary causes, such as the sun, the moon, the elements, and with their effects, did indeed point to the desire of Andeans to find God, that is, to find the first and invisible cause.[54] Again and again, however, they were deceived, *engañados*,[55] into thinking that some secondary cause was a primary one, for instance, that different constellations were the origin or cause of different

[51] See Funkenstein, *Theology* (1986); P. Redondi, *Galileo Heretic* (Princeton, 1987).
[52] *Doctrina Christiana*, Sermon 5; cf. above, chap. v.1 at nn. 15ff.
[53] Cobo, *Historia* 13.2, p. 149b.
[54] Cobo, *Historia* 13.1, p. 147ab; 13.5, p. 157a.
[55] Cobo, *Historia*, p. 147b.

kinds of animals, or that thunder was the cause of rain.[56] Similarly, Andeans worshipped the mummies of their ayllu's ancestors as the "cause of their being," reasoning that "had my ancestor not existed, neither would I exist," and looking to these ancestors as "the root of their birth."[57]

To feed and care for one's dead ancestors amounted to making provision for the perpetuation of one's lineage, because being thus cherished, these ancestors would continue to foster the growth of their descendants, just as they had done thus far.[58] Here as elsewhere, according to Cobo, God, the cause of all, was hidden in Andean perceptions behind some secondary cause. This flaw in the ordering of the Andean mental universe was matched by a flaw in the order of the social universe. For philosophical and scientific error in the mind was articulated in society by priestly fraud.

> It is quite clear that none of the persons in charge of teaching the reasons for their [religious] opinions believed that dead bodies ate or drank or felt any passion after their souls went out from them. One should take note of these persons and what they say regarding this matter, and not of those who guarded and served the dead bodies. For regarding the [religious teachers], there is no doubt that sustaining themselves from the offerings and provisions that people gave them, they invented great absurdities lest these offerings cease or diminish, saying that the dead bodies complained when they were neglected. . . . And thus, although the entire kin group provided the dead with food and other things, it was not because they believed that the bodies suffered hunger or had need of food. . . . Rather, they provided their dead with food only so as to sustain those who had charge of them, even though the simple folk among them thought differently.[59]

That is, the "simple folk" were convinced that the dead did consume the offerings made to them, but sophisticated Andeans knew better. Like priests of the dead, so Inca diviners and the Inca priests associated with the huacas

> endeavored to take from the public as much as they were able, and with this purpose invented countless fictions, saying that the huacas complained to them at night in their dreams about the disregard in which they were held and that for this reason the huacas sent to the people whatever hardships they were suffering. Those ignorant people were accordingly moved to multiply the very sacrifices and of-

[56] Cobo, *Historia* 13.6–8, pp. 159ab, 160b, 161b.
[57] Cobo, *Historia* 13.10, p. 165a.
[58] Cobo, *Historia* 13.10, p. 165b.
[59] Cobo, *Historia* 13.10, pp. 164bf.

ferings that their priests, motivated by self-interest, were encouraging them to make.[60]

Throughout the Andes, priestly fraud and pious make-believe went hand in hand with the exigencies of Inca statecraft. For the Incas also perpetrated pious frauds, but they did it, according to Cobo, not so much to oblige a priestly class as to enhance their power and authority. Cobo transcribed, apparently from the version of Antonio de Salazar, the speech of Inca Tupa Amaru from the scaffold.[61] In it the Inca declared that the face-to-face converse that he and the Incas of the past had claimed to have enjoyed with their divine father the Sun and with his statue in Coricancha had been of their own invention. Similarly, Cobo described the vision of Inca Viracocha, which he adapted from Garcilaso, as a "fiction" and "fable" fabricated by this Inca, while the pururaucas who helped him in battle were a "fable" he created in his imagination.[62] Cobo, like other historians before him, thus regarded the religious authority claimed by the Incas as a vital aspect of their exercise of political power. But he left his readers no choice but to conclude that this power was based on religious fraud.

The rites and obligations of religion were ubiquitous in the Inca empire, Cobo noted; the shrines of Cuzco were replicated everywhere, and the Inca subjects regarded Cuzco as "the house and dwelling of the gods, the abode of heavenly things."[63]

> All this the Incas corroborated from their imaginations, dreams, and revelations, and from the commandments they pretended to receive from their gods, so as to make simple people understand that they alone and those whom they designated were privileged to worship Viracocha, who was their principal god, and their other idols. . . . Such were the recourses the Incas employed to ensure respect for their religion and by means of it to render their subjects more submissive and obedient.[64]

The authority and might which the Incas gained by resorting to diplomacy and power politics were enhanced, according to Cobo, by the oracles of demons. For, like earlier historians and missionaries, Cobo was aware of the importance of divination in Andean religion and in Inca politics, and like them, he resolved the cognitive problem divination posited by attributing prophecies, whether made by huacas, human beings, the

---

[60] Cobo, *Historia* 13.33, p. 224.
[61] Quoted above, chap. VI at n. 1; Cobo, *Historia* 11.21, p. 106b.
[62] Cobo, *Historia* 12.10, pp. 74b and 75a.
[63] Cobo, *Historia* 12.35, p. 136ab.
[64] Cobo, *Historia* 13.1, p. 146a.

dead, or animals, to demonic intervention.[65] Perhaps, therefore, it was from Cieza that Cobo learned about the devil appearing as an illusion in the guise of deceased lords so as to demand that sacrifices and offerings be made to the dead.[66] Elsewhere he read that the devil made himself useful to the Incas by predicting which of their subjects were planning to rebel.[67] However, despite such similarities between Cobo and earlier writers, Cobo's view of demonic agency was new and different, because he did not need the demons to explain the origin and nature of pagan religion, or, as he would have called it, idolatry. Idolatry arose, according to him, from erroneous thinking and reasoning about causation and from the machinations of priests and potentates. The demons merely augmented the effects of what human beings had initiated. For this reason, Cobo considered the imagination not as the potential locus of demonic illusion, as Cieza and Las Casas had done. Rather, for him as for Acosta, the imagination was an aspect of speculative, creative thinking,[68] a faculty that Indians for the most part lacked. "They are so foolish and lacking in discursive capacity," Cobo wrote,

> that they seem to be walking about in a daze. I thus often . . . ask them in their language, when I see them waiting or sitting, what they are thinking. Normally, they answer that they are not thinking anything. On one occasion, a friend asked a Spanish-speaking and capable Indian whom I also knew and who was a tailor what he thought about while sewing? How could he think of anything, was the reply, while at work? To my mind, the reason why the Indians succeed so well at whatever mechanical trade they set out to learn is that they do not divert and deflect the imagination to anything else, but rather occupy all their faculties and senses only on what they have in hand.[69]

However, instead of praising the Indians' technical skills and their capacity for concentration, as earlier Las Casas had done,[70] Cobo considered the episode he described as demonstrating that "the light of their reason is so clouded and darkened . . . that they have little more capacity than brute animals."[71] Not surprisingly, therefore, their ideas about causation, both primary and secondary, were steeped in error.

Cobo's *History* was not published until the nineteenth century and then

---

[65] Cobo, *Historia* 13.36.

[66] Cobo, *Historia* 13.4, p. 154b; cf. above, chap. III.1.

[67] Cobo, *Historia* 13.36, p. 231a.

[68] Cf. above, chap. VI at nn. 129ff.

[69] Cobo, *Historia* 11.5, p. 18ab.

[70] See, e.g., Las Casas, *Apologética Historia* 63–64, on the celebration of Corpus Christi at Tlascala.

[71] Cobo, *Historia* 11.5.

only from an incomplete manuscript. But his views on Inca and Andean religion were shared by other scholars and clerics of his day. In 1649 Fernando de Avendaño, one of the extirpators who had campaigned with José de Arriaga and who continued later on his own,[72] published a summary of what he had been teaching Andeans in a volume of catechetical sermons in Quechua and Spanish. In these sermons Avendaño presented to Andeans the same arguments regarding the scientific inadequacy of their religious tenets as Cobo formulated in his *History*,[73] and similar arguments had been used by Francisco de Ávila in his posthumous Quechua sermons of 1648.

Avendaño's sermons were published jointly with a pastoral letter against idolatry by Pedro de Villagomez, archbishop of Lima.[74] In this letter Villagomez reproduced most of Arriaga's treatise against idolatry. But also, like Avendaño in his sermons, he approached the issue of divine causation and of the secondary causes that Andeans worshipped as huacas or idols in the light of idolatry as described in the Old Testament. Avendaño mocked the helplessness of the huacas under the onslaught of the extirpator in the language of the Letter of Jeremiah,[75] while Villagomez proclaimed that the huacas lay prostrate just as the idol Dagon of the Philistines had lain prostrate before the ark of the covenant.[76] The Old Testament was thus no longer interpreted in the manner of the sixteenth century, as a repertory of pagan beliefs and rituals useful for elucidating American religions. Rather, the Old Testament provided a set of irrefutable precedents for extirpation. There was no room here for any part of Las Casas' or Garcilaso's opinion of Andean religion as preparatory to Christianity. The records generated by the extirpators enabled them to catalog Andean beliefs and rituals in unparalleled detail. At the same time, after over a century of scholarly debate, Cobo and his contemporaries were convinced they had understood what was at issue in Andean and Inca religion.

Andeans had lived, and many continued to live, in the grip of a double engaño. In theological and scientific terms they were mistaken with regard to causation. This error in turn led to the fraud or pious make-believe whereby the Incas, through claiming kinship with the Sun and proximity to the huacas underpinned their political power. The same error also opened the door to the demons, who misled Andeans in general by manipulating the cult of the dead and the Incas in particular by manipu-

[72] Cf. Acosta in *Runa yndio* (1987), pp. 607f.
[73] Avendaño, *Sermones*, Sermons 4 and 5.
[74] A copy of this publication is in the Biblioteca Nacional of Madrid, Raros 34086.
[75] Avendaño, *Sermones*, Sermon 4. For the Letter of Jeremiah in English, see *New Oxford Annotated Bible with the Apocrypha* (New York, 1965), pp. [205]–[208].
[76] Villagomez, *Carta* (above, n. 24), p. 4.

lating oracles. Cobo and his contemporaries thus crystallized propositions on Andean religion that had been debated for over a hundred years
into a tightly knit and coherent argument.

Encrusted though this argument was with the apparatus of seventeenth-century theology, it also contains some modern components. By
highlighting on the one hand the perceived scientific errors inherent in
Andean religious tenets and on the other the activity of demons in Andean religious practice, Cobo and scholars like him ruled out the possibility of any comparison between Andean religion and Christianity. They
could thus study Andean religion untrammeled by any of the taboos that
conditioned research into the Christian past and the history of Christian
thought. Christian teaching had been canonized as the unalterable truth
that—at least in theory—required no temporal aid for its dissemination.
As a result, it was not possible to investigate freely the social and political
factors that accompanied or abetted Christianity's growth and rise to
power and often made it into a servant of the secular state. But no such
impediments conditioned the study of Andean religion. Without caving
in to "the murderous Machiavel" who had ventured to examine how secular government might avail itself of the support of religion, Spaniards
were thus at liberty to inquire into how the Incas exploited religion for
political purposes.[77] Moreover, by demonstrating that the huacas were at
best a conglomeration of powerless symbols and at worst vehicles for
demonic delusions, the missionaries reinforced their own conviction that
natural science supported Christian theology instead of contradicting it.
For it was by resorting to Christian theology paired with natural science
that the missionaries now evaluated and refuted Andean religious tenets.

Andean religion was studied in seventeenth-century Lima not because
of any theological or cultural merit that might have been perceived in it.
Rather, it was studied, in the manner of Polo de Ondegardo, who remained a much-quoted authority, for purposes of refutation and extirpation. This was also the context from which Cobo approached the religion of the Incas, which required extirpation no more. Polo had already

---

[77] Shakespeare, 3 *Henry VI*, act 3, sc. 2:

> Earl of Gloster: I'll play the orator as well as Nestor;
> Deceive more slily than Ulysses could;
> And, like a Sinon, take another Troy;
> I can add colours to the chameleon;
> Change shapes with Proteus for advantage;
> And set the murderous Machiavel to school.
> Can I do this and cannot get a crown?
> Tut, were it further off, I'll pluck it down.

It was, however, Machiavelli's reputation, rather than personal study of his writing, that
produced such lines; for Shakespeare's predecessors, see E. Meyer, *Machiavelli and the Eliz-
abethan Drama. Inauguraldissertation Heidelberg* (Weimar, 1897).

noted that many Inca religious observances had fallen into desuetude, and by the mid-seventeenth century, nothing was left. What Cobo thus investigated was a species of human error that belonged to the past. Since what was at issue was the Andean past, not the present, Cobo's research was separable from the program of extirpation. This research was undertaken in its own right, without external or practical justification.[78]

Yet extirpation and the presence of alien government in the Andes did leave their mark on Cobo's work. By necessity, missionary discourse must contain the proposition that potential converts are mistaken in their religious opinions, for without this proposition there would be no need for a missionary. From the beginning, missionaries in Peru thus endeavored to convince Andean people of their errors, whether they did it gently, by persuasion, or as happened increasingly, by force and a policy of religious extirpation. In the course of the seventeenth century, the penalties for idolatry became ever more ferocious: public whipping and ignominy, forced labor, perpetual incarceration, the galleys.[79] The missionary discourse that accompanied these brutal punishments was formulated with a new vehemence of logic, designed to overpower the audience by sheer force of reasoning. God, a Prime Mover, must exist, Avendaño said in a sermon, for it is clear to everyone that neither things nor humans make themselves.

> For if things were to make themselves, they would make themselves greater, more beautiful, and stronger. Tell me, my child, if you who are endowed with understanding and willpower were to make yourself, would you make yourself black and a slave? No, but white. And would you make yourself a tributary Indian? No, surely, but an Inca, and rich and powerful. Would you make yourself poor and infirm? Not this either, but strong and healthy. Would you make yourself ugly and blind? No, but beautiful and with good sight. Therefore, you did not make yourself, and you have no being and no life from within yourself, but another gave you the being which you have; you are the creature of another. "It is true, father, I cannot deny it," you will say.[80]

Avendaño here slipped from a theological argument into a political, economic, and even racial one, and so did many of his contemporaries. Idolatry was a "vice that comes with the blood"; it was "drunk in with mother's milk" and clouded rational judgment, so that "the customs of the

[78] For this new direction in historical research, see P. Burke, *The Renaissance Sense of the Past* (New York, 1969), pp. 89ff.; 125 on Paolo Sarpi.
[79] E.g. Peña Montenegro, *Itinerari para parrocos* 2.4.5.
[80] Avendaño, *Sermones*, Sermon

fathers . . . are converted into nature among their descendants."[81] What came to be at stake in discussions of idolatry was not merely the truth of Christianity but the legitimacy of the colonial order of society in which Andeans participated in a subordinate capacity. Their religion matched their political position in society, and was of subordinate value, if indeed any worth at all could be ascribed to it, just as Cobo and others had already demonstrated in the case of Inca religion. For the Indians were, quite simply, prevented by their "short capacity" from grasping what the rational basis of religious practice ought to be.[82]

Ramos Gavilán and Calancha, although they were contemporaries of Ávila, Arriaga, Cobo and Avendaño, took a view of Inca and Andean religion that was more old-fashioned, more moderate, and somewhat contradictory. Ramos Gavilán regarded Andean religion, demonically inspired though it was, as a reflection of true Christian religion. There was, accordingly, a great deal in Andean religion that he thought could be salvaged and assimilated into Christianity. Both the solemnity and splendor of the Inca solar cult and the piety and devotion of simple people that had found expression in confession and in purificatory rituals could be transformed into the worship of the Christian God and the Virgin of Copacabana. Calancha, under the spell of Garcilaso, thought that Andeans had formed a concept of god on which Christianity could build. But at the same time he agreed with Polo de Ondegardo and Arriaga on the necessity of extirpation. These contradictory perceptions of Andean religion— approving, even laudatory, on the one hand, critical on the other—go back to the earliest observers of Inca and Andean religion and culture. Cobo, following closely in the trail laid out by his fellow Jesuit Acosta, was the first to knit these contradictions into a unified and coherent argument in which the negative evaluation of Inca and Andean religion consistently prevailed over the positive.

From the beginning most Spaniards in Peru had studied Andean peoples in order the better to control them. Knowledge was acquired for the sake of wielding power more effectively. At the same time, the possession of power shaped and reshaped Spanish attitudes toward the phenomena they were seeking to understand. For extirpation, which resulted in repeated public destruction of accumulated mummies, huacas, ceremonial textiles, and objects of cult, devalued Andean religious belief and practice quite independently of what might be said about them by scholars. Exponents of the European learned tradition convinced themselves of their cultural superiority over Andeans by resorting not only to argument but also to violence. It was thus indoctrination and reasoning going hand in

---

[81] Peña Montenegro, *Itinerario para parrocos* 4.2.1.

[82] Peña Montenegro ibid.; cf. Cobo, *Historia* 11.7, p. 22a, those who lack the truth lack the capacity for virtue.

hand with the cumulative effect of over a century of gradually intensifying religious coercion and extirpation that knit the arguments of Cobo and his contemporaries into a coherent and consistent whole.

In the course of the seventeenth century, the combined force of reasoning and extirpation also modified Andean religion, which, on the surface at any rate, came to resemble the ancient residual paganism of fifteenth- and sixteenth-century European country people. Beliefs that had once been enacted in the splendid ceremonies of the Inca state lived on in humble countryside rituals.[83] In the Andes, as in Europe, the beliefs that were ratified by public display and spectacle were Christian ones.

Yet ultimately the situation in the Andes was very different from that in Europe and led to very different results. The European country people who lived by beliefs that went far back into the Roman past preserved no memories of the Romans who had once ruled over them. In the Andes, by contrast, the memory of the Incas remained a challenge to Spanish claims of political legitimacy until the wars of independence from Spain and beyond.[84] Furthermore, because the pagan Roman empire constituted no lasting threat to its Christian successor states, the Christian victors looked back to their fallen opponents with pathos and with a sense of the grandeur and beauty of what existed no more.[85] The Christian newcomers to the Andes, however, did not honor the ancient deities of the land in any comparable fashion. For the early colonial missionaries and officials who did their utmost to destroy these deities could not find in them the grandeur and beauty with which the Christian converts of late antiquity and their medieval successors endowed the fallen gods of Greece and Rome. The reason for this difference was that in the Andes extirpation conditioned the cultural values of missionaries and officials as much as it did their theology. As a result, the myths and stories of Andean gods entered metropolitan cultural awareness to a limited extent only. But outside cities, the Andean deities, fractured and metamorphosed though they were in the long course of their coexistence with the Christian god, continued to manifest their power.[86]

[83] See above, chap. I.2 at nn. 2ff. But note *Relación de las fiestas que en el Cuzco se hicieron*, describing celebrations for the beatification of Ignatius Loyola in Cuzco. Here, notwithstanding the urban and officially Christian environment, ceremonies of Andean religious content found a place within the official celebration. Also note the political role of figures from Christian sacred story as reformulated in the Andes: I. Silverblatt, "Political Memories," in *Rethinking History and Myth*, ed. J. D. Hill (1988).

[84] Rowe, "Genealogía y rebelión," *Revista Historica* 33 (1981–1982): 317–336; "Las circunstancias," *Revista Historica* 34 (1983–1984): 119–140.

[85] See T. Gregory, "Julian and the Last Oracle at Delphi," *Greek, Roman and Byzantine Studies* 24 (1983): 355–366.

[86] J. Bastien, *Mountain of the Condor: Metaphor and Ritual in an Andean Ayllu* (1985); M. J. Sallnow, *Pilgrims of the Andes* (1987).

2. ANDEANS IN THEIR LAND

On 12 March 1656 the extirpator of idolatries Bernardo de Noboa initiated a prosecution against Don Alon o Ricari, curaca and priest of Otuco in the central Andean province of Cajatambo. The verbatim transcript of this prosecution has been preserved, along with several dozen similar documents dating mostly from the m id- to the later seventeenth century,[1] in the archive of the archbishopric of Lima. For it was a succession of archbishops of Lima, beginning with Francisco de Ávila's patron, Lobo Guerrero, who sponsored these prosecutions.[2] The transcripts reveal both the extent of Christianization in the Andes and its limitations, while at the same time conveying a uniquely detailed and privileged insight into Andean religious life in the archdiocese.

Almost from the outset, missionaries and officials had imposed on Andean cults and myths, as well as on their exponents, the terminology of contempt that Europeans had long addressed to their perceived cultural and religious inferiors.[3] Arriaga's manual for extirpators provided the definitive demonstration of how this terminology was to be applied in the Andes. The extirpators of the mid-seventeenth century in the central Andes were thus heirs to a method of categorizing Andean religion that had established itself as definitive in the course of missionary experience accumulated during more than a century. Shamans who spoke with the dead and the deities, as well as priests and priestesses were described as *hechiceros* and *hechiceras*, male and female sorcerers who had made compacts with the devil.[4] Religious teachers were called dogmatizers, this being a derogatory term that insinuated that their teaching was false. Other religious specialists were quite simply designated as *embusteros*, impostors. There were also "ministers of idols," wizards, and quacks.[5] Similarly, the objects in which Andean deities dwelt or which represented them were usually referred to as idols. For the sake of clarity, this blanket classification was often supplemented by Andean terms for specific kinds of numinous objects. Among these were the term *conopa*, referring to small domestic deities and talismans presiding over the increase of humans, animals, and plants; *huanca*, a stone guardian of a community's fields;[6] and *mallqui*, the mummified bodies of ancestors.

When speaking in Spanish to Spaniards and criollos, Andean people by

[1] Huertas Vallejos, *La religión* (1981), pp. 121ff.
[2] Duviols, *Lutte* (1971), pp. 153ff.
[3] I. Opelt, "Griechische und lateinische Bezeichnungen der Nichtchristen. Ein terminologischer Versuch," *Vigiliae Christianae* 19 (1965): 1–22; Quiroga, *Coloquios de la Verdad* 4: 115; *Doctrina Christiana*, Sermons 21, 22.
[4] E.g., Duviols, *Cultura andina y represión* (1986), p. 25. Hereafter Duviols (1986).
[5] Wizards, in Spanish, *brujos*; quacks, in Spanish, *curanderos*; Duviols (1986), p. 178.
[6] Duviols (1986), p. 59.

force of necessity used this same terminology, there being no other available in that language. But while this terminology conveyed to its Spanish users a set of negative meanings and values, the same terms when used by Andeans range from being merely descriptive to conveying a positive content. When giving evidence before the extirpators, a shaman might thus refer to himself or herself with the plain term "sorcerer," while describing another shaman as a "great sorcerer," by way of acknowledging that other persons's eminence in a positive sense. Similarly, Andean people referred to their holy objects and deities as idols. In Spanish as spoken by Spaniards, an idol was by definition a false god. Andean people by contrast used the term descriptively and also in a way that implied respect and worship.[7]

Force came in many guises in early colonial Peru, ranging from the intellectual force of reasoning and describing in language to the physical force of imprisonment, forced labor, and beating. Its use had a paradoxical outcome that was not anticipated by those who resorted to it, because it maximized the distance that the fact of conquest had established between Andean conquered and Spanish conquerors, thereby circumscribing the influence that the conquerors were able to exercise on the conquered. Missionaries and their charges might thus speak the same language, but not infrequently that language conveyed to the two sides mutually exclusive meanings. Extirpators might burn Andean "idols" and imprison their priests, but they did not succeed in bringing the worship of these "idols" to an end. This, at any rate, was what Noboa learned as he cross-examined witnesses in Otuco on that day in March 1656.

The first witness whom he called was the priestess Francisca Cochaquillay. Some years earlier, Hernando de Avendaño had scoured the region for mallquis, representations of deities, and objects of cult, all of which had been burned. But they had not been forgotten. In particular, when pressed by the extirpator, Francisca Cochaquillay mentioned Raupoma and Choqueruntu, who were revered by the ayllus Guangry and Otuco respectively. They were two round stones the color of partridge eggs that at night gave off a light like glowworms. On the site where they had been destroyed, Avendaño arranged for a cross to be raised. But the ayllu members continued to worship their old protectors in this same place "and went to them with their needs and asked them for good fortune when they took their turn at forced labor and for their crops. For although the extirpator had burned them, the deities would come down when sacrifice was made to them and would listen to those who made prayer to them." Francisca Cochaquillay likewise was accustomed to sacrifice to the twin deities, and as she did so, she would pray:

[7] E.g., Duviols (1986), pp. 69–72.

Flower of fire, tongue of fire, remnant of fire and leavings of fire, eat this, drink this, Burned Lord, so that there may be good food, so that there may be good water.[8]

Avendaño had also burned Huari, the mythic forebear and protector of the entire community, who had been represented by a stone in the form of a man. This figure along with five conopas, had been revered beneath a willow tree called Ocuncha.[9] The priestess Catalina Guacayllano, who had taught and initiated Francisca Cochaquillay into her sacred office, replaced the destroyed holy beings with ten substitutes and supervised the continuing cult. The prayer she would speak ran thus:

"Burned father, parched father, you who guard the irrigation canal, who guard the water and guard the fields, give me water, give me fields, give me food. Ever since you have been burned, since you have been scorched, we are dying of hunger, we have no food." And they would pour chicha into a great fire they had prepared and burn sacrificial guinea pigs, maize, coca and llama grease until everything was consumed.[10]

Similar prayers were addressed to the burned deities in other places the extirpators had visited. In Santo Domingo de Paria, Carua Roncoy, who was worshiped when the Pleiades reappeared in the sky each June around the time of Corpus Christi, was implored with this prayer:

Burned Father, may there be good fields, may there be good food, good fields and good silver coins, that people may increase and not fall ill, that there may be llamas, that the world may exist.[11]

Although they had been incinerated, these deities still listened to prayers; indeed, they were asked to concern themselves with the very existence of the world. Desecration and destruction of their representations did not seem to stand in the way of their presence in this world. Rather, desecration and destruction provided Andean people with the occasion to restate and to formulate more explicitly and sharply the theological concepts that defined the deities.

One such concept concerned identity and its representation. In the Andes, identity could be conceptualized as continuous even when its expression or representation changed. The *pururaucas* who fought for Pachacuti[12] were recognized as such, even after they had turned to stone. Andean myths pointed to countless other stones that had formerly been

[8] Duviols (1986), p. 7.
[9] Duviols (1986), p. 11 with p. 24.
[10] Duviols (1986), p. 11 with pp. 526f.
[11] Duviols (1986), p. 89 and p. 530.
[12] Above, chap. VII.1 at nn. 15ff.

human beings or animals and that continued to be identified by their human or animal names.[13] Their external appearance had changed, but their identity remained continuous with their previous animate existence. It was for this reason that in Inca Cuzco, the rock Guanacaure, which represented the metamorphosed Inca sibling Ayar Cache, was thought to be watching over the city's welfare and accordingly received sacrifices.[14] In seeing one of these metamorphosed stones, the informed beholder at the same time saw and addressed himself to its inherent but hidden identity. A similar perception of continuing identity also functioned in other aspects of religious expression. In 1609 a Jesuit extirpator in Huarochiri made some tantalizingly brief comments on the use of masks composed of the facial skin and bones of certain eminent deceased individuals as a way of representing their continuing presence in society. "Such a mask would be of some noble, distinguished Indian, and at the time when they were to harvest the maize someone placed this mask on his face, and with this act alone he acquired such authority that people carried him in procession in a litter and made offerings to him as to something divine."[15] The mask thus conferred that continuity of identity, and indeed of existence, that was also operative in myths of metamorphosis into stone. In the central Andes, extirpation resulted in the extension to some of the burned deities of the perception of continuity expressed elsewhere in masks.

In San Pedro de Hacas, Avendaño burned the human-shaped deities Caquiguaca and Caruayacolca, who had belonged to the ayllus Quirca and Yanaqui. But "after the Lord Bishop left," said the witness Alonso Chaupis during the next campaign of extirpation that swept through Hacas,

Anton Pacari, headman of this village of Hacas, and Raucallan, a shaman and religious teacher . . . ordered two wooden masks called *guasac* to be made so that people could adore and worship them in the place and as a representation of the burned idols. After the campaign of extirpation, Domingo Manchapa and Andres Hachamalqui, now deceased, took up their office as ministers of these idols. After they died, Martin Guamancapcha and a certain Libiapoma succeeded them. . . . The mask deities represented the deities Caqueguaca and Caruayacolca, of whom the shamans and ministers said that they were creators of food and of Indians, and that they gave health and life, and for this reason [the masks] have been left in the charge [of their priests] so that people should adore and worship them.[16]

[13] *Runa yndio* 5.68 (ed. Urioste); 5.106f. (ed. Taylor).
[14] Cieza, *Segunda Parte* 7.
[15] C. Romero, "Paliques bibliograficos," *Revista Historica* 10 (1936): 192–228 at p. 206.
[16] Duviols (1986), p. 203; cf. pp. 158, 161, 227.

The masks accordingly took part in the seasonal festivals, in particular the agricultural celebrations in January and June, when, along with other deities and the community's mallquis, they were addressed with prayer and sacrifice for life, health, food, and increase. "Sometimes they placed these masks on litters and paraded them in processions with hayllis and dances in the old village. At other times, they held the masks in their hands and danced with them, and at yet other times they placed them on their faces as masks."[17] These masks, which had large noses and were painted yellow and orange, were kept in a mountain cave, where they received sacrifices of guinea pigs, coca, llama fat, and silver coins. One of them also owned a herd of thirty llamas "of the ancient times," meaning that the herd of llamas had been given a long time ago and that their offspring were maintained for the deity by his ayllu.[18]

While extirpation thus disrupted Andean religious life, fundamental religious concepts remained operative. Indeed, they were reasserted with greater emphasis. This was the case not only regarding Andean concepts of divine identity but also regarding that of the energy or essence inherent in divine, and also in human, beings, which Andean people referred to as camaquen. The extirpators usually translated the term as "soul" or "spirit."[19] Numerous villagers of the central Andes believed that the camaquen of deities whose representations had been destroyed by the extirpators lived on.

In 1656 the extirpators in the village of Otuco stumbled across such an incinerated but living deity. The witness Francisco Poma told how he had watched three designated ministers of religion sacrifice a llama to the deity Macacayan, whose representation had earlier been burned by Avendaño. Poma had asked these three why "they adored and worshiped this idol, seeing that it had been desecrated and burned. And they answered him that although the deity had been burned, his soul lived and came down to the sacrifice and received it."[20] Similarly, in nearby San Pedro de Hacas the soul of the burned deity Corcuicayan was alive and received sacrifices.[21] Moreover, every year as the time arrived for the village to celebrate the festival of its Christian patron, St. Peter, the curaca Don Cristóbal Pomalibia would send priests with a sacrifical llama to obtain the permission of Apu Urauc and Carua Tarpo Urauc, deities whom Avendaño had desecrated and burned, because "although they had been desecrated, their souls were alive."[22] In San Juan de Machaca, Avendaño

[17] Duviols (1986), p. 204; similarly, pp. 182–183, 218.
[18] Duviols (1986), pp. 158, 182, 247.
[19] Duviols (1986), p. 67, el alma o el camaquen; p. 92, camaqueni upani = criador sombra.
[20] Duviols (1986), p. 185.
[21] Duviols (1986), p. 206; see also p. 121.
[22] Duviols (1986), p. 156.

had confiscated and burned a number of dead bodies, mallquis, that the members of different ayllus or kin groups had preserved in their *machayes*, their ancestral burial grounds. A few years later, however, the extirpator Bernardo de Noboa found that some of these mallquis were still revered because "their souls lived, and they were *guanca*, guardians . . . and [people] worshiped them because they represented their ancestors, and for this reason they adored them in the place where they had lived."[23]

Andean deities and ancestors thus proved to be extraordinarily resilient. The reason was twofold. On the one hand, while Andean concepts of deity were anchored in the natural and human environment, they were at the same time capable of being expressed in abstract, indeed in philosophical, terms. The physical destruction of a deity or a mallqui thus did not entail the destruction of the concept thereof. On the other hand, the deities and mallquis proved resilient because their mythic, and sometimes their historical, doings affected the daily concerns of every ayllu and every village.

The members of the ayllu Cotos in the village of San Francisco de Mangas thus remembered its first ancestors as a couple who had come there from the sea. They were Condortocas and his sister-consort, Coya Guarmi, whose name means "Lady Queen." Condortocas was a mallqui that was preserved in his place of burial,[24] while Coya Guarmi was a little pitcher in the shape of a woman. This pitcher, dressed in woman's clothes and jewels, was kept in a "small chapel," whence she would from time to time be taken to visit Condortocas.[25] The journey of these founders to their present abodes and their virtues were sung at festivals and recited in prayers.[26] The two deities were honored in particular at the time of Corpus Christi and whenever a new house was being built. At the roofing ceremony of the curaca Alonso Callampoma's house, the members of his ayllu of Cotos thus danced to the music of a song that narrated the deeds and virtues of the deities.

> The curacas and members of the ayllu Cotos worship and adore [the two deities] because they say that Condortocas is the camaquin and first progenitor of their ayllu and that his pacarina and place of birth is from the sea, and that he came from there with his sister, Coya Guarmi, and rested in the plain of Cusi and in the plain of Lucma and Llaclla and in another place called Pisar Cutam. And later he found his rest in the place where he has his tomb, and this is why

[23] Duviols (1986), p. 271.
[24] Duviols (1986), pp. 325; 334, for Coya Guarmi; 380 for Condortocas.
[25] Duviols (1986), p. 372, the small chapel; pp. 372, 380, 351, the visiting.
[26] See for Greek parallels for singing the virtues of a deity, W. Burkert, *Griechische Religion der archaischen und klassischen Epoche* (Stuttgart, 1977), pp. 167–169; G. Nagy, *The Best of the Achaeans* (Baltimore, 1979), pp. 59–65.

. . . people sing and dance for him and bring him offerings of silver, many-colored wool and cloth, and this is what they say and sing in their dances: "To the village of Cusi, to the village of Llaclla, to Pisarcuta you went forth, with a flower of pacae, with a flower of lucuma, from the sea, with your sister the queen, Father Lord Condortocas."[27]

Coya Guarmi's attendants had meanwhile escorted her from her chapel to stay inside Don Alonso's new house in the place where the chicha was kept, so as to bring him good fortune and prosperity. In her honor, Don Alonso dressed himself in a tunic of cumbi cloth, and on his head he wore an ornament of silver flowers. For three nights, the people who were gathered in Don Alonso's new house danced and sang for their ancestral divine couple and on the third night, at cockcrow, they escorted Coya Guarmi to the abode of her brother and spouse, Condortocas. The inauguration of human domesticity was thereby placed under the protection of the domesticity of the gods.[28]

The roofing ceremony of a new house built for any ayllu member—not only the curaca—was a vehicle for restating the community's mythic history, identity, and purpose, because the songs that were sung and the dances that were danced in the course of the celebrations endowed the mythic past with immediate and tangible relevance. For Cotos ayllu, this amounted to explaining how the founding deities had come from their distant place of origin, their pacarina in the sea to the abode where their descendants still lived. The mythic history of Cotos thus extended from the ayllu's very origins to the present. This history also bonded the life energy of the founders to that of the ayllu, for the founders were the ayllu's camaquin, its soul. This vital link between the divine founders and their descendants was particularly evident in the person of the ayllu's curaca. Again and again, the people of Mangas returned to the point that Condortocas, or Condortocas and Coya Guarmi jointly, were the camaquin of the curaca Don Alonso Callampoma.[29]

The mallqui Condortocas was found and burned by the extirpators who visited Mangas in 1662. But Coya Guarmi, who had disappeared from her "little chapel," was not found. Don Alonso, who apparently knew where she had been hidden, would not reveal the spot and was therefore deprived of his office and sentenced to four years of forced labor in the monastery of the discalced Franciscans in Lima.[30] All the other men and women of Mangas who had served their ayllu's deities were con-

---

[27] Duviols (1986), p. 352 with 535; see also p. 343 with 534.
[28] Duviols (1986), pp. 349, 352, 387.
[29] Duviols (1986), pp. 335, 341, 343, 380, 386, etc.
[30] Duviols (1986), pp. 380, 387.

demned to penalties of greater or lesser severity. The houses that had been used in the cult of these deities were destroyed. Objects of religious significance that had not been destroyed by fire were confiscated, as were the sacred fields on which the crops had been raised that were used for sacrifice and in the cult of the deities. Yet it seems that the old gods lived to see another day after this visitation finally departed from the village. For when the sacred fields were put up for auction, none of the villagers wanted to buy them.[31]

Condortocas and Coya Guarmi were the protectors and souls of people who in the remote past had arrived in Mangas as newcomers, newcomers moreover who had remembered their distinct identity. Similar myths of newcomers, ayllu progenitors who had come from distant parts to the place where their descendants still lived, abounded in the Andes. All these myths share one theme. It is that the lands to which these newcomers of however long ago laid claim had been occupied from time immemorial by yet earlier settlers who traced their origins back to the land itself. As Arriaga had ascertained, throughout the central Andes the newcomers called themselves llacuaz, while the original inhabitants called themselves *huari* or *llactayoc*, "villagers."[32]

In Otuco members of the three ayllus of llacuaces looked back to their mythic ancestor, "the Lord" Apu Libiac Cancharco, "who fell from heaven like lightning." He had three sons, to each of whom he gave a little soil. The sons were to settle in the place where the soil resembled that which their father had given them. In Mangas the people would not receive the three wanderers, and in Guancos the soil was not right. In Otuco, however, the soil was perfectly suited, but the Huari people who lived there killed the young boy whom the three brothers sent as their emissary, along with his llama. Worthy sons of the Lightning, who in Andean thought controls the weather, the brothers sent a dark fog in which the huaris died. Notwithstanding this outcome of the llacuaces' myth of origins, there were two ayllus of huaris in Otuco who had their own view of their beginnings. They recounted having sprung from the snowy peak Yarupaxa above Mangas, which had eight doors giving access to caves. From these the huaris, who were bearded giants, had come forth. The separate origins of huaris and llacuaces were registered not only in myth but also in cult, in that the two groups revered different sets of ancestral mallquis and the huaris in addition revered the mountain lord Yarupaxa as their creator and the Sun as their father.[33]

---

[31] Duviols (1986), p. 391.

[32] Above, sec. 1. at nn. 16–19.

[33] Duviols (1986), pp. 52–55, on different ancestral mallquis; on the Sun, see p. 55, tienen un apo que los crió y estos adoran al sol por su padre; cf. p. 464, the llactas of Ocros adore the Sun as father.

In nearby Santa Catalina de Pimachi, the llacuaces recounted being sons of the Lightning and having come from the Titicaca region. They were herders and had been induced to settle in Pimachi by the huaris of the place, who "went out with drums and gentile dances and brought them down [from the puna] to live with them." Such a myth was also told in Santo Domingo de Pariac,[34] and in San Pedro de Hacas a myth of llacuaz settlement was acted out in an annual ceremonial. In June, around the time of Corpus Christi, the llacuaces fasted for five days before going up to the puna to pair guanucos and tarugas. On returning they were welcomed by the huaris with music and dancing and with hayllis, songs of triumph[35] such as were also sung at the completion of the harvest and of plowing. As in Pimachi, so in Recuay the llacuaces told of their origin in the puna of Lake Titicaca. But in Recuay their advent had led to such friction that "in order to contract a friendship with each other the llactas and llacuaces sacrificed two sons from among their number to the Lightning. They were called Runa Curi and Anco Ripay and were most handsome and perfectly formed, without flaw or wrinkle. . . . They were consulted [for oracles in their] underground [burial places]."[36]

These myths and rituals reiterate themes pervasive throughout the Andes and which also speak through the myths and rituals of the Incas. Like the huaris of Otuco, the Incas had sprung from openings in a mountain, and worshiped the Sun as father. At the same time, the Incas were newcomers to Cuzco, and the myths of their arrival there echo myths about newcomers elsewhere in the Andes. For instance, on the journey to a new abode, the Incas, like the llacuaces of Otuco, had looked for the right soil, good, arable soil into which their golden rod or digging stick would penetrate.[37] They found such soil in the region of Cuzco and settled there, but the people who had originally lived in the area only reconciled themselves to the Inca presence with difficulty. Conflicts between huaris, or llactayocs, and llacuaces elsewhere in the Andes reveal the almost universal nature of these problems of coexistence in the Andean highlands.

Inca expansion beyond the valley of Cuzco added to the intricacy of these problems. For throughout the Andes the presence of the Incas added further strands to an already manifold network of sacred presences and of multiple claims to material resources. During the early decades after the invasion, accordingly, Spanish officials found quite regularly that the Incas were remembered principally for the burdens and strains

[34] Duviols (1986), p. 120, Pimachi; p. 94, Santo Domingo de Pariac.

[35] Duviols (1986), pp. 161, 173.

[36] Duviols (1986), p. 486; Curi means "son of the thunder"; cf. Calancha, *Corónica moralizada* 2.13, p. 869.

[37] Sarmiento, *Historia Indica* 12, p. 214, Manco Capac trajo consigo una estaca de oro para experimentar las tierras; see also above, chap. VIII.1 at n. 24.

they had imposed on local resources.[38] Historians, especially Sarmiento and Cobo, echoed these bitter memories when they wrote of the Incas as tyrants. Inter alia, Cobo drew attention to what he called the Inca "tribute in children," that is, girls and boys who were designated to be sacrificed as capacocha.[39] Similarly, Guaman Poma recorded sundry ritual details of the sacrifice of capacocha and remembered that the parent "who gave his child went about weeping."[40]

However, by the early seventeenth century, and more so as the century wore on, the structure of Andean memories of the Incas changed, at any rate in the central Andean region of which the extirpation documents inform us. Thanks, perhaps, to the infinitely harsher impact of Spanish governance and Christianity, Andean people now recalled the Incas without that sense of opposition and resentment that had characterized many of their earlier memories. Over a century after the Spanish invasion, Andeans had come to treasure the memory of those of their lords who had gone to Cuzco and "talked with the Inca,"[41] thereby enhancing their status. Similarly, even quite minor objects of cult introduced by the Incas continued to be remembered as such, along with offerings they had made to local divinities.[42] Moreover, as the historical Incas receded ever further into the past and mythic Incas took their place,[43] so also the presence of the Incas in Andean communities took on new contours. In many villages, the death of Atahualpa was annually represented in a play that served to crystallize Andean memory around this central incident of the invasion.[44] Elsewhere, relations between Andeans and invaders were formulated in terms of ritual battles for which one party would appear in all the ancient Andean finery as Incas, while the other party dressed as Spaniards. On one such occasion, the participants in the conflict sought to assure the extirpator that the costumes and the fight were "for entertainment" only. But the reality was otherwise, because the memory of the Inca past was the yardstick by which the present could be interpreted and judged.[45]

On several occasions, the extirpators stumbled across burials of per-

---

[38] E.g., *Justicia 413*, ed. M. Rostworowski, pp. 186, 226; above, chap. II.1 at n. 23; chap. IV.1 at nn. 48ff., 101.

[39] Cobo, *Historia* 12.38; above, chap. IV.3 at nn. 110ff.

[40] Guaman Poma, *Nueva Crónica* pp. 250 [252], 228, 247, 262.

[41] Duviols (1986), pp. 271, 467.

[42] Duviols (1986), pp. 95, 345, 370.

[43] See above, chap. VII.

[44] R. Ravines, *Dramas coloniales en el Perú actual* (Lima, 1985); A. Flores Galindo, *Buscando un Inca. Identidad y utopia en los Andes* (Lima, 1987); M. Burga, *Nacimiento de una utopia. Muerte y resurrección de los Incas* (1988).

[45] Duviols (1986), p. 350, ritual battle "for entertainment"; p. 499, memory of the Inca. Further, J. Szeminski, *La Utopia Tupamarista* (Lima, 1984); MacCormack, "Pachacuti," *American Historical Review* 93 (1988): 960–1006.

sons who had been sacrificed as capacocha in Inca times and found that these carefully remembered capacochas continued to play an important religious role.[46] In 1622, for instance, the extirpator Hernández Principe ascertained that the ayllu Chaupis Churi of Recuay remembered very clearly having sent twelve persons as capacochas to Cuzco, to Quito, and to Chile, to Lake Yahuarcocha and to Lake Titicaca.[47] In nearby Ocros, Hernández Principe heard from the old men the story of the girl Tanta Carhua. She had been offered to the Inca as capacocha by her father, the curaca Caque Poma, and after visiting Cuzco was buried alive in her own home province.[48] The old men remembered the occasion in detail, down to the parting comment of the girl. "Finish with me now," she had said, "for the festivals they celebrated for me in Cuzco were quite sufficient."[49] There was not a word of opposition or criticism directed against the Incas who had made the arrangements for these empirewide ceremonies. Quite the contrary: people in Ocros remembered and described these ceremonies to Hernández Principe in loving detail.

From all four parts of Peru the capacochas set forth and it was a sight to behold how people came out to receive them in processions, with their huacas. The capacochas came to Cuzco accompanied by the principal huaca of their land and entered the city with their curacas and attendants, just before the festival of Inti Raimi. Those from Cuzco went out to receive them, and when the Inca and members of his council had made their confessions and had washed in the River Apurimac, they entered into the main square where the Inca sat on his golden stool. The statues of Sun, Lightning, and Thunder and the embalmed Incas with their priests processed round the square twice, bowing before the statues and the Inca. The Inca greeted them with a glad countenance and when they came close to him spoke to the Sun, requesting him to accept these chosen ones for his service. The Inca toasted the Sun with chicha matured over many years for this festival, which the coya, accompanied by the *pallas*,[50] brought in two beakers of gold. The chicha with which the Inca toasted the Sun was emptied by order of the devil to attract the entire kingdom, which was represented there, to the religion of the Sun. The Inca rubbed his body with the lees in order to participate in [the Sun's] deity.[51]

[46] Cf. Zuidema, "Shaft Tombs," *Journal of the Steward Anthropological Society* 9 (1977–1978): 133–178.
[47] Duviols (1986), p. 499.
[48] Duviols (1986), pp. 471ff.; Zuidema (1977; see above, n. 46), pp. 162ff.
[49] Duviols (1986), p. 473.
[50] *Coya*, Quechua, "queen"; *palla*, Quechua, "princess."
[51] Duviols (1986), p. 472, translation slightly condensed.

The gesture of being rubbed or rubbing oneself as a way of absorbing an object's properties was familiar beyond the Inca court from the ritual of confession that was observed throughout the Andes. After the penitent's confession was completed, the Andean confessor would rub him or her with white wool to finalize the purification.[52] Once the Inca had thus identified himself with the Sun, there followed the ceremonies of vowing loyalty to him and of consuming the consecrated sanco.[53] After days of celebration, which Betanzos, Cieza, and Molina had described earlier on the basis of information collected in Cuzco,[54] some of the capacochas were buried alive near Guanacaure and others in Coricancha, while the remainder were sent back to their homes to be sacrificed there. Here, each of them would become "a guardian and protector of the entire province," just as those who had been sacrificed away from home "would counsel the shamans, their descendants, from afar."[55]

Children were perhaps still sacrificed as capacochas in the early seventeenth century,[56] and rituals focusing on capacochas who had been buried in Inca times continued to be observed later in the century and possibly beyond. At the same time, however, some aspects of the accounts of how these children had been sacrificed were in the course of being transformed into myth. Tanta Carhua, for instance, had been buried on land belonging to the Inca, in whose name Caque Poma had brought together a work force to construct a new irrigation canal. When progress was brought to a halt by two insurmountably steep inclines, Caque Poma called upon his shamans for help. "According to [the Indians'] story, two of them became a serpent and the other two became a star, and in one day and the following night they constructed along the inclines an irrigation canal so level that it is marvelous to behold."[57] Tanta Carhua's tomb, a shaft dug deep into the earth, marked a nearby spot on the edge of the Inca's land. Here her brother, and after his death other men of her kin, delivered oracles to the sick and to people in need in the voice of a woman, in the voice, that is, of Tanta Carhua herself.[58]

The initiative regarding Tanta Carhua's sacrifice was taken by her father, who in return received from the Inca the "seat and lordship of a curaca."[59] In San Pedro de Hacas, by contrast, it had been the Inca who initiated such a sacrifice. In 1657 people still remembered that the curaca Ticllaurao, who by that time was himself revered as a mallqui "went to

[52] Huertas Vallejos, *La religión en una sociedad rural* (1981), p. 45; Duviols (1986), p. 58.
[53] Cf. above, chap. VIII.3 at n. 27.
[54] Above, chap. III.2 at nn. 34ff.; chap. IV.2.
[55] Duviols (1986), pp. 473, 499; I translate *hechiceros* as "shamans."
[56] See Romero, "Idolatrias," *Revista Historica* 6 (1918): 188.
[57] Duviols (1986), p. 424.
[58] Duviols (1986), pp. 472–473.
[59] Duviols (1986), p. 473.

speak with the Inca on behalf of his village. The Inca ordered him when he returned to his village to offer there a capacocha . . . to the Sun, the Inca's father. Ticllaurao offered the capacocha in the place called Nabincoto, next to the idol Yanaurau."[60] This location points to the distinguished position the capacocha occupied among the local deities. In 1657 the extirpators found that Yanaurau, a divinatory deity,[61] was still worshiped even though his representation had been destroyed during an earlier campaign of extirpation. His cult went hand in hand with the cults of the divinatory mallqui Guamancama and of the curaca Ticcllaurao's mallqui. The principal times of worship were the annual festivals of Pocoimita, celebrated before sowing in January, and Caruamita, celebrated at the time of Corpus Christi, when the maize was ripening. During these agricultural festivals, sacrifices were made in the "old village" of Yanaurau's ayllu, Chaca.[62] Alongside the cult offered to Yanaurau by his ayllu, he enjoyed the worship of the entire village of Hacas.[63] By interring their capacocha near Yanaurau, the people of Hacas integrated this supernatural presence, generated by association with the Inca, with the divine presences whom they revered in their own agricultural cults.

Yanaurau cared not only for the crops but also had the task of protecting the curacas of the region. Thus, when Don Juan de Mendoza, the curaca of the entire repartimiento of Lampas, wanted to ensure that his son returned safely from the college of El Cercado in Lima and in due course become a curaca beloved of his people, he resorted to Yanaurau. The sacrifice, followed by the customary sacrificial meal, was performed by the region's most respected priest, Hernando Hacaspoma, and was attended by several lords and their followers. The capacocha, at whose burial place the extirpators found offerings of coins and little sheets of silver along with the remains of numerous llama sacrifices,[64] thus stood at the center of the community's political and economic concerns. In Inca times, the capacochas, who, after participating in the celebration of Inti Raimi in Cuzco, returned to be sacrificed at home articulated the imperial presence in every detail of local affairs. With the empire's fall, this network of political patronage collapsed, but the cult of the burial sites continued, both in the central Andes and in Cuzco itself, where such places were called villca.[65]

[60] Duviols (1986), p. 169; cf. 248.
[61] Duviols (1986), p. 158.
[62] Duviols (1986), p. 144; p. 158, Pocoimita and Caruamita; sacrifices in the old village, p. 221.
[63] Duviols (1986), p. 204.
[64] Duviols (1986), pp. 186f.; 232, sacrifice followed by meal; site of burial of capacocha, p. 248; but here the document mentions two individuals as against one, p. 170, the place being the same.
[65] Pérez Bocanegra, Ritual y formulario, pp. 137–138.

The capacocha, a primary sacred obligation of the Inca empire, was directly integrated with the ruling Inca's life, in that this sacrifice was offered not only for Inti Raimi but also for Inca inaugurations and obsequies. Similarly, as Cieza had observed, Andean lords other than the Inca were honored by human sacrifices when they died, for ladies and attendants would frequently follow their masters into death, sometimes voluntarily. This kind of sacrifice, which bore a certain external resemblance to the Inca capacocha,[66] continued into the colonial period and troubled missionaries. The Augustinian friar Alonso Ramos Gavilán knew of at least one young girl who was buried alive in a *chullpa*[67] near Sicasica as a sacrifice "to their vain gods," but survived because a Spanish mining prospector who was passing by heard her weeping.[68] Similarly, in his manual for missionaries of 1631, Juan Pérez Bocanegra, who was cura of Belén in Cuzco before moving to nearby Andahuailillas, advised confessors to ask their Andean penitents whether they had buried any deceased curaca's wife and children with him to serve him in the other world.[69]

Ramos Gavilán contrasted the murderous ferocity of the Andean demonic gods with his own god's mercy and compassion. Yet Andeans were likely to arrive at a somewhat different evaluation of this god's characteristics. For in catechisms and sermons they were regularly informed that the Christian god had consigned their own ancestors and all the Incas to everlasting torment in hell, and that moreover he threatened to unleash the same fate upon themselves for noncompliance with his commands.[70] Such assertions by missionaries and parish clergy jarred with the affective bonds that tied Andean people to their huacas and mallquis and at the same time endowed a set of arguments that had first been used in the Taqui Onqoy three generations earlier with renewed vigor and relevance. Again and again the extirpators of the mid-seventeenth century in the central Andes were told that the Spaniards had their god and "painted saints" or "sticks"[71] to whom they could pray. For Andeans, however, contact with this god and his rituals entailed pollution and was to be avoided if at all possible. On the frequent occasions when avoidance was not possible, Andean people danced for and sacrificed to their deities and mallquis by way of asking their permission to attend mass and Christian

---

[66] Capacocha as ritual obligation, see Gonzalez Holguin, *Vocabulario de la lengua general*, p. 200 and above, chap. III.1 at nn. 45ff. Ladies buried with husbands, above, p. 93; despite the external resemblance to capacocha, this kind of sacrifice was substantially different in nature, because capacochas became divine.

[67] Funerary tower.

[68] Ramos Gavilán, *Historia . . . de Copacabana* 1.19, p. 65.

[69] Pérez Bocanegra, *Ritual y formulario*, p. 131.

[70] Avendaño, *Sermones*, sermon 3, fol. 333; sermon 4, fols. 44vf.

[71] Taqui Onqoy, above, chap. IV.3 at nn. 19–22; "painted saints," Romero, "Paliques bibliograficos," *Revista Historica* 10 (1936): 211; Duviols (1986), p. 227; "sticks," Duviols (1986), pp. 189, 207, 266.

festivals.[72] The rationale was that the Christian god and those "pieces of painted wood" were the camaquenes of the Spaniards, while the huacas and mallquis brought health and abundance to their Andean worshipers.[73]

Often Andeans contrived to construct a compromise or convergence between the two religions, for the two supernatural worlds, jostling each other on a daily basis, could not be kept apart. During the Christian patronal festival in San Pedro de Hacas, the villagers were accustomed to sit in the square drinking and feasting, but they could not begin without first dropping on the ground some coca leaves for the huacas and mallquis and making a small libation to them so that they also could drink. During this same festival, the statue of the patron, St. Peter, stayed in the house of the church's standard-bearer and was there honored with the traditional Andean offerings of coca, chicha, and a guinea pig. Elsewhere, Andean holy objects were hidden in Christian altars so that people could worship their own deities in church.[74] Similarly, the design of the parish church of Andahuailillas, which was built and decorated while Juan Pérez Bocanegra was cura, accommodates Andean reverence for the Sun. In its east gable, a round window admits the rays of the rising sun, which the frescoed decoration interprets as standing for the Holy Spirit at the Annunciation to the Virgin Mary. But for Andean people this round window had a more ancient and more archetypal meaning, for in the central sierra, when roofing a house, people "always leave a piece of the roof uncovered as a window [facing] towards the rising sun, so that through that place sicknesses may depart and good things may enter."[75]

The religious calendar likewise allowed scope for ambiguity. As in Inca Cuzco, so in the central Andean highlands during the seventeenth century, the agricultural festivals marked the times of plowing, planting and harvesting. Often these two seasons were called Pocoimita, the "time when it rains," and Caruamita, "time of yellowing," referring to the ripening maize.[76] The Incas had celebrated this latter festival as Inti Raimi. In the Christian calendar, Caruamita coincided with Corpus Christi in June. A generation after the Spanish invasion, Polo de Ondegardo had already noted that Andeans were observing Corpus Christi as a cover for

[72] Duviols (1986), pp. 164, 167, 176, 196–197, 222, 244, 266f., 277, 281, 284, 298f., etc. Note especially the story on pp. 185–186.

[73] Duviols (1986), p. 180.

[74] Coca leaves and libation to Andean deities, Duviols (1986), p. 160; Andean offerings to St. Peter, p. 235; Andean holy objects in Christian altars, pp. 270, 273, 283.

[75] Duviols (1986), p. 160; similarly, p. 203, For the church of Andahuaillillas, Gisbert, *Iconografía y mitos indígenas en el arte* (1980), pp. 31f.

[76] Gonzalez Holguin, *Vocabulario de la lengua general*, p. 292a, poccuy, poccuypacha, poccuymitta; Santo Tomás, *Lexicon*, s.v. carua, etc., pp. 250f.

their own Inti Raimi, a point later contradicted by Garcilaso.[77] But the central Andean evidence shows that Polo was right, for throughout the seventeenth century, Corpus Christi was used to disguise the manifold observances of Caruamita. Caruamita was the time when the Pleiades reappeared in the sky after being invisible for two months.[78] During this period, frost was liable to spoil the crops, so that the Pleiades were known as Oncoicoillur, "stars of disease." In Andean awareness, Corpus Christi thus marked the time when one must make confession and sacrifice to the huacas and mallquis for the sake of the crops. In some communities, it was also at Corpus Christi that the llacuaces went up to the puna to hunt or pair animals and were then ceremoniously welcomed back by the huaris.[79] Throughout the viceroyalty of Peru, therefore, the festival that in Catholic Europe epitomized the theological position of the post-Tridentine church became encrusted with a variety of Andean associations and accretions—even though from a Hispanic point of view, these were deeply at variance with the significance of that festival.

The opposing deities for whom these festivals were celebrated spoke to Andean people through their representatives: the Christian god through parish clergy, missionaries, and extirpators, and the Andean deities through their shamans, priests, and priestesses. Pérez Bocanegra, drawing on his intimate knowledge of Cuzco and its countryside, perceived these Andean religious specialists as a tightly organized counterclergy who threatened to draw Andean converts away from the church. The Indians, by contrast, described their priests and priestesses as "enlightened elder brothers and elder sisters, dazzled by light."[80] The terms suggest that these individuals had experienced a divine revelation such as convinced Don Cristóbal of Huarochiri to remain a Christian[81]—except that these visionaries from the region of Cuzco were drawn further into Andean spirituality by their experience, not away from it.

Although seventeenth-century Andean religious practice changed under the impact of Catholic rituals and beliefs and of the Catholic emphasis on sin, confession, and absolution, the extent of this impact should not be overestimated. Andeans had practiced confession of sin before the invasion and had entrusted their religious affairs to a variety of specialists whose expertise was not supplanted by that of Catholic priests. While the

[77] Polo de Ondegardo, *Errores* 8.7, fol. 10v; above, chap. IV.3 at n. 90; on Garcilaso, above, chap. VIII.3 at nn. 10ff.

[78] "Zuidema, Catachillay," in *Ethnoastronomy and Archaeoastronomy in the American Tropics*, ed. A. F. Aveni and G. Urton (1982), pp. 203–229.

[79] Confession and sacrifice for the crops, Duviols (1986), pp. 88, 151, cf. 100, 169, 444f.; llacuaces welcomed by huaris, p. 22; cf. above, at n. 35.

[80] I translate Spanish *alumbrados,* as "enlightened" and Spanish *aturdidos,* as "dazzled by light"; Duviols, (1986), p. 111.

[81] Above, chap. VII.1 at nn. 61ff.

imperial religious institutions of the Incas fell prey to the invasion, at a local level the basic organization of Andean religion remained continuous with the past. After the invasion, just as before it, village units, often described as *sapsi* or "community,"[82] were each headed by a curaca and his *segunda persona*, and also by a priest, often called *camachico* or "superior,"[83] and his delegates or representatives. In the mid-seventeenth century, the village of San Pedro de Hacas was thus governed by Don Cristobal Pomalibiac as curaca and by Don Hernando Hacaspoma as camachico. Sometimes, however, the positions of curaca and camachico coincided or overlapped, as they did in the case of Don Alonso Ricari of Otuco, who held both offices.[84] The grandson of a shaman, he was a man of widely acknowledged authority and took a leading part in religious events both in his own Otuco and in nearby Cajamarquilla and Santo Domingo de Pariac.[85]

Don Alonso Ricari and Don Hernando Hacaspoma, like other individuals in corresponding positions elsewhere, had charge of the worship of the deities who were common to the entire community. Beyond these deities, each ayllu revered it's own huacas, mallquis and sometimes capacochas, all of whom were cared for by ayllu members assigned to the task. The cult of the capacocha Tanta Carhua thus fell to her youngest brother and after him to other kinsfolk, all members of her immediate family.[86] While here succession to the office was determined by membership in the capacocha's own family, other religious specialists serving at the ayllu level were appointed by the camachico of the entire community. Within their ayllus they accordingly acted as his delegates, just as the curaca of an ayllu acted as the delegate of the curaca of the entire community.

This structure of authority was particularly clear in San Pedro de Hacas, where Don Hernando Hacaspoma actively supervised and directed the religious affairs of the village's ayllus and on several occasions selected priests for them. Juan Raura thus stated that after his father, who had been priest of his ayllu, died, a certain Francisco Caruanaupan succeeded him. When Caruanaupan died, Don Hernando Hacaspoma and three other men of authority ordered Juan Raura "to take up the office of minister of the idols of his ayllu, because the Indians of his ayllu were wasting away and their fields and food were being lost, and they would soon be eating soil if there was no one to make the sacrifices and offerings to the mallquis and idols."[87] Similarly, to Andres Guaman Pilpi of the ayllu of Carampa, Hacaspoma had said:

[82] Gonzalez Holguin, *Vocabulario de la lengua general*, p. 324; cf. Duviols (1986), pp. 350, 353, 335.
[83] Gonzalez Holguin, p. 47; Santo Tomás, *Lexicon*, fol. 114r.
[84] Duviols (1986), p. 35, curaca; p. 30, sacerdote.
[85] Grandson of a shaman, Duviols (1986), pp. 56f.; religious leader, p. 26.
[86] Duviols (1986), p. 473.
[87] Duviols (1986), p. 191.

The old men of your ayllu, masas, confessors, dogmatizers, attendants of the huacas[88] have vanished away because all have died, and there is no one who takes care to serve the idols. You are the leader[89] and the oldest of your ayllu, and you are responsible for the office of minister of the idols, for if the sacrifices to the mallquis are not made, the people who are still alive in your ayllu will also die away, and you will have neither fields, nor clothes, nor food.

The two men therefore went to the old village of ayllu Carampa, where its mallquis were kept. Nearby, Hacaspoma sacrificed three guinea pigs, scattered about their blood, and then burned them with coca, llama grease, and white and black maize, sprinkling the whole with chicha. As was the custom, the sacrifice also included "*coricallanca*, which are sea shells, greatly prized and esteemed among the Indians." While sprinkling the chicha, Hacaspoma prayed:

> "Lord mallquis, receive and eat this offering that Guaman Pilpi gives you and receive it so he may continue bringing you this same offering and serve you." And then he said to Guaman Pilpi: "Now you are appointed to the office of *malquibilla* and *guacabilla* and *aucachi*," which is to say, he who speaks to the mallquis and idols and makes offerings to them. And *aucachi* is to say confessor, he who hears confessions and absolves.[90]

This sequence of sacrifice and prayer, followed by the words of inducting the candidate into his office, made up the ceremonial that was followed whenever a new ayllu priest was appointed.[91]

Throughout the Andes, men tended to address the Sun as their father and creator, while women looked to the Moon as their creator and mother. Indeed, the Moon was mother not just to women, but also to zaramamas, mothers of the maize, to coca, and to food crops in general, and in Inca myth it was a woman, Mama Huaco, who had sown the first maize. Accordingly, throughout the Andes, while men tended to confess to men, women's confessions were often heard by women. These female confessors also performed women's sacred tasks, such as making the chicha that was used in sacrifice, keeping the ceremonial clothes of zaramamas, and pasturing the llamas belonging to the dead and the deities.[92]

This pattern obtained throughout the Andes. In the course of the campaigns of extirpation of the mid-seventeenth century, a particularly clear

---

[88] Translating Quechua *guacavillas*, p. 173.

[89] Translating Spanish *principal*.

[90] Duviols (1986), pp. 173f.

[91] Duviols (1986), pp. 198, 220.

[92] Moon as mother, Duviols (1986), p. 122 (to crops); also, pp. 151, 189f., 274, 466, etc. Women confessors, p. 215, para confesar a las indias de su aillo; but note p. 51, where a woman also hears men's confessions. Women make chicha, etc., pp. 29, 71, 215. See Silverblatt, *Moon, Sun and Witches* (1987).

example came to light in Ocros. Here the extirpators learned, Catalina Guacayllana had taught Francisca Cochaquilla how to perform a variety of sacred tasks related to the well-being of the crops, and had then, after sacrifice and prayer, inducted her into the office of priestess.[93] When some four years later Catalina Guacayllana died, her body was clothed in cumbi cloth and secretly taken to repose, not in the Christian cemetery, but among the members of her ayllu in the pre-Christian cemetery. Another priestess, Francisca Guacaquillay, niece to Don Alonso Ricari, had been set aside to serve the huacas from infancy. She had not been baptized and never went to mass, thereby avoiding all polluting contact with things Christian and Hispanic.[94] Like the acllas, women consecrated to the Sun in Inca times, she lived as a virgin and had in her charge little girls under the age of ten whom she instructed in the performance of sacred tasks.[95]

The rituals performed by these priests and priestesses met the religious concerns of Andean country folk. But much more was at issue. For an individual's concerns converged with the concerns of ayllu and community, which Andean people expressed as mythic and historical memories projected onto the present. These memories were focused in part on human existence and in part on the natural environment. To perform an Andean religious ritual thus amounted to making a statement about the past, ever-relevant as this was to the present. For abundance and well-being were thought to come from a community's originating deities and from its mallquis.[96]

Relationships between Andean people and their ancestral mummies had been severely disrupted when, in the later sixteenth century, the viceroy Toledo and others resettled or "reduced" Andeans living in scattered hamlets into larger villages, or reducciones. With their main squares overlooked by the church, the corregidor's house, and the prison (cf. fig. 14),[97] these villages were laid out in conformity with Spanish concepts of life in society. Resettlement often entailed moves over significant distances and thus severed a community's links with its mythic origins and its mummies. In time, however, many of these links were reestablished. Not all communities stayed where they had been resettled, and many of those that did stay returned to the "old village" on a regular basis. The

[93] Translating Spanish echicera; Duviols (1986), p. 6; cf. pp. 7, 20.

[94] Buried in Andean cemetery, Duviols (1986), p. 18; no contact with Spanish things, p. 50, "pecados de sacrilegio" from an Andean standpoint; cf. p. 215.

[95] Duviols (1986), pp. 43f., 45, 46; other priestesses in Otuco, pp. 25, 29; Don Alonso Ricari and other echiceros help with instruction, p. 51.

[96] Cf. Duviols (1986), pp. 326, 335, 350, 387, on Domingo Nuna Callam, priest of Coya Guarmi and quipucamayoc, who delivered Coya Guarmi's oracles and supervised the harvesting and storage of her maize. P. 53, mountains, Sun, stars, etc. are informed that ayllu members' confessions have been completed.

[97] Matienzo, Gobierno del Perú 1.14, p. 50.

resettlement village of San Francisco de Otuco, for instance, celebrated three major agricultural festivals every year. For each of these, the ayllu members were accustomed to go to their old villages, where the pre-Hispanic burial places were to be found, to make their confessions. This done, the confessor proclaimed to the mountains, the daylight, the morning star, the Twin Stars, and the Pleiades that running river water was carrying the sins away to the sea.[98] Elsewhere also, festivals were celebrated, whenever possible, in the presence of the deities and mallquis in the old villages, away from Christian clerical supervision.

What was at issue here was the care of the dead and, with that, the maintenance of correct relationships between the dead and the living. Before the reducciones were implemented, ayllu members in the central Andean highlands had taken their dead to rest in *machayes*, mountain caves or "caves the size of a house," as the lexicographer Gonzalez Holguin put it.[99] There, often the corpses were set down "with a *chuspa*, a little bag of cumbi cloth filled with coca leaf hanging from the neck. They were shrouded in the ancient way, seated crouched with their hands on their cheeks and the knees tucked under their tunic, so that the tunic served as a shroud."[100] Some of the more eminent people might be taken to their rest not in a machay but in a separate "house" such as Guaman Poma depicted somewhat schematically when describing burial in Chinchaysuyo (fig. 51).[101] Whether in "house" or machay, the dead were available to receive the attention of the living, initially during the days immediately following their departure from this life, next on the recurrent anniversaries of death, and in due course more intermittently. All this came to an end when the Christian clergy forced Andean people to bury their dead not in the machayes near the old villages but in the Christian fashion under the floor of the church. Don Alonso Ricari, priest and curaca of Otuco, described the outcome:

> In these burials, the dead were much afflicted, for during the three days when [the family and ayllu priest] brought the funerary offerings [to the church], they heard the dead complaining and accusing their kinsfolk, that they were more contented in the machayes because there they did not have earth weighing on them and would be able to shift about. [The villagers] therefore took the dead out [of their graves] and carried them to the machayes, where they celebrated their anniversaries. [At those times] they changed their

[98] Duviols (1986), p. 53, he also addresses yaya hacha, Lord Tree; cf. p. 55, those with few sins go to a little river, those with many to a big one.

[99] Gonzalez Holguin, *Vocabulario de la lengua general*, p. 222; cf. Santo Tomás, *Lexicon*, fol. 147v; Guaman Poma, p. 882 [892]; machayes of parcialidades, Duviols (1974–1976), p. 287.

[100] Duviols (1986), p. 18.

[101] Guaman Poma, *Nueva Crónica*, p. 289 [291]; Duviols (1986), p. 25.

51. Burial in Chinchaysuyo: the deceased is being carried to his burial place on a litter. Tears run down the faces of the dead man's child and his widow, who walks with a stick. Guaman Poma, *Nueva Crónica*, p. 289, Royal Library, Copenhagen. Photo from facsimile, Paris 1936.

clothes, killed llamas for them, offered them chicha and the llamas' blood, and burned llama fat, coca leaf, maize, and guinea pigs. . . . They danced diverse dances for [the dead], and while they did so, the closest kinsman carried the corpse on his shoulders and danced with it a day and a night.[102]

At the Third Council of Lima in 1583, ecclesiastics for the first time objected vigorously to Andeans removing their dead from churches so as to lay them to rest in accord with Andean ritual and belief. Objections led to searching out not only mummies that had been removed from churches but also mummies of pre-Christian times to whom offerings continued to be made. Baptized individuals were often reburied, while the others were burned in those ever-repeated public spectacles of destruction that were pioneered in 1609 by the extirpator Francisco de Ávila.[103] Discovering mummies was thus as central a preoccupation for the extirpators in mid-seventeenth century Cajatambo as concealing them was for Andean people. It was in the course of their search for mummies that the extirpators again and again forced Andeans to describe their beliefs about the afterlife and the rituals they performed for the dead. Generally, the first step in these rituals was to retrieve the corpse after it had been buried under the floor of the church and to take it back home. Here the deceased was placed in the spot where she or he had died and received the blood of a sacrificed llama, while the mourners ate the meat and drank and danced until cockcrow. Then they sallied forth into the streets, where they sprinkled sacrificial blood and chicha while calling on the deceased "to return and to console them, and asking him where he was and how he was faring."[104] This calling by the mourners for the deceased corresponds to the first phase of the funerary ritual of the Incas, when the nobles of Cuzco searched for the dead Inca in his favorite haunts.[105] That the funerary ceremonial of the Incas and of the Central Andes should resemble each other in this respect points to significant continuities in belief and ritual. In Inca times and on into the seventeenth century, people feared that the deceased would blame his death on their own insouciance or might feel vengeful and angry for other reasons. It was as though when someone died he became a malignant power hungry for human resources and human life, a power to which survivors were accountable.[106] Care for the dead was thus designed to deflect this malig-

---

[102] Duviols (1986), p. 72, condensed translation.
[103] Above, p. 389; cf. Romero, "Idolatrias," *Revista Historica* 6 (1918): 191.
[104] Duviols (1986), p. 33.
[105] Betanzos, *Suma* 1.31, p. 145; see above, p. 128.
[106] Duviols (1986), pp. 112, 149, 170; Allen, *The Hold Life Has* (1988), pp. 60f. The documents printed by Duviols seem to imply that the funerary rituals for women were similiar

nance and to demonstrate responsible accountability on the part of the living. In the machayes, year by year the dead were attired in new clothes; year by year they received sacrifice of blood, food, and chicha; and year by year they surveyed the festivities the living celebrated in their honor.[107]

The most perilous period in the passage from this world to the next was the "five days," *piscapunchao*, that is, the first five days after death, when the deceased "suffered many labors in this world before getting to his pacarina." During that time, attendance on the deceased, along with attempts to appease his anger, was at its most intensive. When the five days were over, the family would wash the deceased's good clothes for reuse and burn the older ones, or even burn all the clothes for the deceased's own continued use.[108] But then the tone of the ritual changed. The family would now walk up and down in the house, stepping into all the corners and say: "Let the soul go to its machay and its pacarina, whence his ancestors, vilcas, and mallquis came forth. For this is no longer his house." Meanwhile, the deceased, aided by blood sprinkled on the streets of his village and even on his face, crossed the bridge to the next world. This bridge was called Achacaca and was platted of human hair just as the suspension bridges of the Incas were platted of *ichu* grass.[109]

Pacarina, the term that the family used to refer to the destination of the deceased, also described an ayllu's or a community's place of origin, and this in turn defined who they were in society. Hence, Domingo de Santo Tomás translated the cognate term *pacarisca* as a person's legal status.[110] To perform the rituals of the first five days after a person died amounted to preparing his pacarina, establishing his new status, and enabling him to "rest in the birthplace and pacarina of his ancestors."[111] On occasion, this place was described more closely as "Titicaca, where their mallquis came from," or "*upaimarca*, which was in Titicaca and Yarocaca, the birthplace of the Sun and the Libia, which is the lightning."[112] This link that the people of Cajatambo perceived between human origins and the destination of the dead in the next world had been intuited a century ear-

---

or identical to those for men, although the witnesses, most of whom were men, speak of the deceased as male. For simplicity's sake, I retain this usage.

[107] Duviols (1986), p. 33; similar rituals, pp. 63, 86, 99f., 112; somewhat different ritual if the corpse remains in the church, pp. 149f., 157f., 170f.

[108] Suffering labors on the way to one's pacarina, Duviols (1986), p. 157; disposal of clothes, pp. 170f.; cf. 93, 157.

[109] Sending the soul away, Duviols (1986), p. 92; sprinkled blood, pp. 63, 183; crossing the bridge to the next world, pp. 150, 200, 205, etc.; but cf. 213, 222, the soul labors for a year in this world and then goes to its pacarina.

[110] "Condición por ley," see Santo Tomás, *Lexicon*, fol. 258r.

[111] Establish new status, Duviols (1986), pp. 77, 78, 79, 81, 92, 98, 99, etc. "Rest in the birthplace," p. 212.

[112] Duviols (1986), p. 150.

lier by Cieza de Leon. At his end, man returned to his beginning. Consequently, the Andean cult of the dead articulated a community's awareness of its origins, of its present place in space and time, and of its ultimate destination. To perform the cult of one's community's mallquis thus amounted to laying claim to a specific position in space and time.

Around 1645 the people of San Pedro de Hacas made ready to lay claim to the lands of the village Cochillas, all of whose people had died. As a first step they planned to open a new irrigation canal. Before beginning the work, however, they collected a guinea pig from each household and one *real* from each person, money with which to buy a llama for sacrifice to the mallquis of Cochillas. For without such a sacrifice, these mallquis "would be angry and the villagers would not be able to construct the irrigation canal or sow the fields"; rather, they would all die. But once the people of San Pedro de Hacas had, as it were, adopted the dead who were at home in their new fields, they constructed the canal, tilled the fields, and repeated their sacrifices to the mallquis of Cochillas every year.[113]

The same guidelines applied to the cult of the mallquis of one's own community. When a person died, it was by blood sacrifice that he was aided to reach his pacarina. By leaving this world to the living, by not contaminating it with their own death, the recently deceased shed their menacing quality. But this was not a transaction that could be terminated once and for all when the deceased crossed the bridge Achacaca. Rather, at every anniversary of a person's death, and later, when that person had receded into the anonymous mass of the dead, at every seedtime and harvest, correct relationships—that is, relationships of contact followed by separation and distance—had to be established once more between the living and the dead, between the community and its mythic past.

When a person died, it was a shaman, a priest of ayllu or community, who established communication between him and his living kinsfolk. The purpose of this communication was to learn the cause of death, thereby allowing the kinsfolk to make amends for their transgressions against the deceased, and if there were no such transgressions, somehow to appease his anger.[114] The shaman was the intermediary between the living and the mallquis. Shamans communicated not only with the recently deceased but with mallquis long dead and with a community's mythic founders. Here also Pedro Cieza de León had intuited a process that was central to Andean religious experience. He had sensed that Andean people communed with the dead. But he could only conceptualize such a converse as the outcome of the deception of the human imagina-

[113] Duviols (1986), p. 237; same story told by another witness, p. 162.
[114] E.g., Duviols (1986), p. 273.

tion by demons. It was by placing illusory images of their long-dead ancestors before the eyes of Andean people that the devil was able to lodge
in their imagination the perception that they must make sacrifice to these
ancestors, must bury the living with the dead. This theory of the devil's
manipulation of the Andean imagination had become common currency
by the seventeenth century. The devil spoke through huacas and mallquis;
Andean healers performed cures thanks to having made a compact with
the devil; and by the same means Andean prophets were able to predict
the future.[115] What to Cieza had been a terrifying ethical and theological
dilemma, that the devil should hold such sway in the Andes, was in the
seventeenth century a dilemma no longer but a fact of daily life that Hispanic Peruvians accepted with equanimity. Even Andeans were reduced
to using the conceptual framework of demonic activity when speaking in
Spanish of their religious experience. The documents from Cajatambo
do, however, contain one description of divination that implies a deliberate Andean rejection of this demonic conceptual framework and its significance. Here, a shaman explained to the extirpators how divination,
the aspect of Andean religion that was and remained so problematic to
sixteenth- and seventeenth-century Spaniards and Peruvians, was to be
understood in Andean terms.

The shaman was Hernando Hacaspoma of San Pedro de Hacas. When
the extirpator Hernando de Avendaño visited Hacas, Hernando Hacaspoma's predecessor, the priest and shaman Andrés Chaupis Capcha, was
able to hide the prophetic mallqui Guamancama, son of the Lightning and
progenitor of the ayllu of Chacac. Before dying, Chaupis Capcha "placed
and ordained Hacaspoma in the office and ministry of priest to this
mallqui," having first carefully instructed him. The mallqui Guamancama, Hacaspoma explained,

> raised men and increased them and gave the Indians money and pos-
> sessions and told them what they had to do, and therefore those of
> ayllu Chacac have always adored him. Andrés Chaupis told this wit-
> ness [Hacaspoma] that when they had a lawsuit or a business trans-
> action or it was a bad year for food, they should consult this mallqui
> and offer sacrifice to him. This is what he has done every year at
> Pocoimita before sowing their fields and at Caruamita at the time of
> Corpus Christi, when the maize ripens. The sacrifice was coca,
> guinea pigs, chicha, and some llamas, all contributed by the entire
> village of Hacas. Having made the sacrifice before the mallqui, this
> witness remained there in ecstasy, bereft of his senses, and heard
> within himself that the mallqui spoke to him and told him if it was

[115] For some particularly explicit statements, see Romero, "Idolatrias," *Revista Historica* 6
(1918): 186, 192ff.

going to be an abundant year or not and if there was going to be plague or disease. And it happened just as he had heard it being said in that ecstasy. If the response was favorable he went down to the village and announced it to all the people, and they were glad and danced with drums. But if it was unfavorable, he ordered the entire village to fast by abstaining from salt, aji, and sexual intercourse with their wives for two days and their nights, and then to make renewed sacrifices.[116]

By explaining that he heard the mallqui speak while he was in an ecstasy and bereft of his senses, Hacaspoma made clear that what he heard was not a demonic illusion of his sense perceptions, such as missionaries and others were prone to attributing to Andeans. He drove home this same point by specifying that he heard the voice within himself. His statement, therefore, disposed of all the complicated logistics of demons speaking in dead bodies or idols, thereby deceiving the ignorant. Hacaspoma then went on to describe a specific instance when he went to consult the mallqui Guamancama. This was when the villagers were hoping to avoid having to supply workers for the repair of a nearby bridge, while also ridding themselves of their parish priest, Francisco Morales, and bringing a lawsuit against a certain lawyer Cartaxena. Hacaspoma ordered the entire village and its curacas to fast for two days and keep watch for one night while he made sacrifice and consulted Guamancama.

When he had made the sacrifices, he embraced the mallqui and remained in another ecstasy, and he said the camaquen of the deity Guamancama, the soul of the mallqui, came down into his heart and told him what had to be done regarding the matters on which they had consulted him. And when the mallqui had given him the answer he went down to the village to announce to the curacas and the common people what their Lord and Father had said to him. And they carried it out as he had said,

the upshot being that they did not have to repair the bridge, and successfully ridded themselves of both the priest Morales and the lawyer Cartaxena.[117]

Divinatory knowledge was thus not knowledge acquired by an isolated individual in his own right, knowledge that was then somehow imposed on the community, as Bernabé Cobo, among others, was prone to suppose.[118] For Hernando Hacaspoma acted as priest on behalf of his ayllu and his community. In accord with the time-honored ritual, he had been

[116] Duviols (1986), pp. 142f.
[117] Duviols (1986), pp. 143–144; the episode was also described by others, pp. 158, 165, 176, 178, 219.
[118] Above, sec. 1 at nn. 59–60.

inducted into this office by his predecessor. The villagers, on their side, validated the performance of this ritual by recognizing Hernando Hacaspoma as their priest and acting in accord with his precepts. Thus, when Hacaspoma went up to the machay to consult Guamancama, the village fasted and kept a vigil. Altogether, to consult a mallqui was to act jointly as a community, for in the course of the consultation each member of the community had a task to perform. The community in question could be the small and intimate gathering of kinsfolk who came together to hear a shaman articulate what a recently deceased family member had to say about the cause of death, and it could also be the community of an entire village consulting the mallqui of its first progenitor with regard to the harvest and other matters of common concern.

Hernando Hacaspoma died, apparently in 1658, as a result of the tortures to which the extirpators subjected him in the course of wresting from him information leading to the discovery of his community's mallquis, deities, and holy objects.[119] The majority of his priestly colleagues, both male and female, in San Pedro de Hacas and elsewhere in Cajatambo, met with similar fates. Hundreds of mallquis were incinerated and their ashes were scattered. Stone huacas were hacked to pieces. Fields that had been cultivated and llamas that had been herded as the property of mallquis and huacas, to provide the wherewithal of worship and sacrifice, were confiscated. However much the village people would not, indeed could not, change their convictions to accord with what the extirpators demanded, these measures did meet with a certain success. Prosecutions for idolatry recurred in the later seventeenth and early eighteenth centuries but brought to light a rather different religious world. Andean religion as practiced in Cajatambo down to the mid-seventeenth century, and maybe a little beyond, remained at many levels continuous with the pre-Christian and Inca past. For, missionary intervention notwithstanding, it had remained a public religion. Sacred authority was handed on from one generation to the next in public. The mallquis and huacas owned property that was cared for by village communities in public. And rituals, however much aspects of them were conditioned and curtailed by the presence and activities of Christian priests, continued being performed in public. By contrast, the beliefs and practices that were examined in the course of subsequent prosecutions were for the most part clandestine: rituals of curing and enchantment that had somehow outlasted the conflagrations of the mid-seventeenth century and beliefs that, while continuous with the Inca past, were held without conscious awareness of that fact.[120]

[119] Duviols (1986), pp. 246ff., 311ff.
[120] In some places, however, continuity with the past extended beyond the seventeenth century; see F. Salomon, "Ancestor Cults and Resistance to the State in Arequipa, ca. 1748–

In the sixteenth and seventeenth centuries, Andeans still formulated their beliefs and rituals within a sacred topography that would have been recognizable to their forebears. Shrines and holy places peopled by mallquis and diverse sacred representations abounded, and most of them had not yet been Christianized. In the contemporary Andes, by contrast, most shrines are Christian at least in name, and so are the sacred representations dwelling in them.[121] But that is only one part of disposable space. Jesus, the Virgin Mary, and the saints occupy buildings; theirs is sacred space indoors, which can be assigned and consecrated by human hands. Beyond the reach of extirpation and consecration, however, earth and sky are still inhabited by the ancient powers.

1754," in *Resistance, Rebellion, and Consciousness in the Andean Peasant World. 18th to 20th Centuries*, ed. S. J. Stern (Madison, 1987), pp. 148–165. For the contemporary Andes, cf. R. T. Zuidema and U. Quispe, "A Visit to God," *Bijdragen tot de Taal-, Land-, en Volkenkunde* 124 (1968): 22–39; Platt, "Andean soldiers of Christ," *Journal de la Société des Américanistes* (1987): 131–191.

[121] Randall, "Qoyllur Rit'i," *Bulletin de l'Institut Français des Études Andines* 11 (1982): 37–81; Sallnow, *Pilgrims of the Andes* (1987); Urton, *At the Crossroads of the Earth and the Sky* (1981).

EPILOGUE:
VISION, IMAGINATION, AND SOCIETY

IN JULY 1664, the year when Bernardo de Noboa petitioned the Spanish Crown to reward him for his services in the extirpation of idolatry in Cajatambo,[1] Benedict Spinoza wrote from Voorburg in the Netherlands to console his friend Peter Balling for the death of his child. In Peru, extirpation had run its course, while in Europe, Spinoza was engaged in rethinking the nature and workings of imagination and understanding. The letter Spinoza wrote to Peter Balling provides a glimpse of what was old and what was new in the concept of imagination that was emerging in the later seventeenth century. This glimpse will enable us to locate within their European context the outcomes of the debates we have followed about Inca and Andean religion.

Spinoza wrote to console his friend for the death of his little son. While this son was still in good health and strong, Peter Balling had been troubled at night by groans like those he subsequently heard the sick child utter not long before he died. In his grief, Peter Balling could not rid himself of the memory of those disembodied night-time groans, and therefore wrote about them to Spinoza. Those groans had not been real sounds, Spinoza wrote in reply, but creations of Peter Balling's imagination that arose from his soul's participation in "the ideal essence of the child and his states and their results." Such participation could give rise to a "confused presentiment of the future," so that the noctural groans Peter Balling had heard could be understood as an omen of sorts of the child's death. All effects of the imagination, Spinoza wrote, arose from either bodily or mental causes. Fevers, for example, caused delirious imaginings, while the imaginations of stubborn persons were liable to dwell on quarrels and brawls. Imaginings also occurred in dreams. By way of illustration, Spinoza mentioned a dream of his own involving a "black and leprous Brazilian whom I had never seen before," who kept returning before his inner eye even after he had awakened. This dream helped to define Peter Balling's experience more closely, for "the same thing which occurred with regard to my inward sense of sight occurred with your

[1] Duviols, *Cultura andina y represión* (1986), pp. 421ff.

hearing; but as the causes were very different, yours was an omen and mine was not."[2]

Spinoza's vocabulary and the concepts he utilized in this letter would have been familiar to his friend because they were part of the philosophical culture of the time. Likewise, the habits of thought and the images Spinoza mentioned were anchored in seventeenth-century culture and were therefore shared by even those of his contemporaries whose views he was careful to disown. Spinoza himself was aware of this phenomenon. The same image, he explained in his *Ethics*, had different meanings for different people, depending on their preoccupations. The hoof mark of a horse on the ground spoke to a soldier of war and battle, while a farmer's thoughts would be led by it to the peaceful activity of plowing.[3] Similarly, in Spinoza's view, images such as that of the black Brazilian were simply liable to arise from the almost infinite variety of a person's experiences. Individuals less philosophically inclined than Spinoza, however, were likely to endow such an image with demonic significance. Consider a misadventure that had occurred some sixty years earlier. Two Spanish friars from Guadalupe in rural Extremadura were sent to America to collect alms for their image of the Virgin Mary. Freshly arrived in Puerto Rico, they were greeted in the monastery where they were to stay by a black Caribbean servant. Taken aback by the unfamiliar sight, they reacted as though she were a visitation from the other world, either a devil or else "some lost soul of an Englishman, from among the many who had been killed there." At the very sight of her, they covered themselves with signs of the cross and called noisily on the name of Jesus.[4] But one did not have to be a Spanish friar—nor yet a Peruvian missionary— to believe in devils. One of Spinoza's own acquaintances, having converted to Roman Catholicism, was convinced that Spinoza had allowed himself "to be ensnared and deceived by that most wretched and most proud of beings, the prince of evil spirits."[5]

Even so, the devil was becoming less fashionable in the seventeenth century, and this not only for Spinoza. Demonic manipulation of sense perception and imagination figured less prominently in missionaries' explanations of Andean religious difference. José de Acosta, among others, demonstrated that familiarity with the Andes opened up alternative explanatory strategies. Simultaneously, European conceptions of intellect and imagination were changing profoundly.

[2] Spinoza, *Letter* 17, ed. Gebhardt, p. 77 (Letter 30, transl. Elwes).

[3] Spinoza, *Ethics* 2.18, schol; Funkenstein, *Theology and the Scientific Imagination* (1986), p. 221, n. 18.

[4] Ocaña, *Un viage fascinante*, p. 7.

[5] Spinoza, *Letter* 67 (Letter 73, transl. Elwes); see also *Letters* 51–56 (55–60, transl. Elwes) on ghosts.

Some of these changes are reflected in a set of canvases that in 1638 the friars of Guadalupe commissioned Francisco Zurbarán to paint for their monastery. One of these pictures depicts the temptations Jerome experienced in the Syrian desert and described to a correspondent (fig. 52).[6] His heart filled with bitterness and the fear of hell, Jerome fasted in sackcloth and lived, as he put it, among scorpions and wild beasts. Nonetheless, he could not free himself of the imagination of sensual and sexual enticements, of the dainty dishes and dancing girls of the city of Rome, and accordingly spent night after night combatting his lustful thoughts. In the early sixteenth century, Joachim Patinir had depicted the hermit Anthony in the grip of similar temptations, which came before him as a bevy of demons in the guise of seductive women (fig. 5). Like Patinir's Anthony,

52. Francisco Zurbarán: St. Jerome is tempted, his contemplative concentration is broken by a lovely sight before his eyes and by sweet melodies sounding in his ears. Guadalupe.

[6] Jerome, *Letter* 22.7 in *Select Letters of St. Jerome*, ed. and transl. F. A. Wright (Cambridge, Mass., 1980).

so Zurbarán's Jerome is tempted by women, but Zurbarán interpreted the bitter spiritual warfare Jerome described in his letter in much kindlier terms. In Zurbarán's painting, there is nothing sinister or demonic in the exquisitely poised lady musicians whose melody has taken the saint's attention away from his book. It is simply the choice between two different goods that confronts the aged ascetic, who must reject the melody of feminine beauty in order to remain faithful to his prior commitment to learned chastity. But, so Zurbarán reminded the friars of Guadalupe, this beauty that, in the footsteps of their founder, they had chosen to set aside was indeed beautiful. If Zurbarán read Jerome's letter, he interpreted it to one side of the church father's intended meaning.[7]

Others among Zurbarán's paintings for Guadalupe depict visions perceived by friars who had lived and died in the monastery. Fray Diego de Orgaz confronts the repugnant apparition of a woman he knew when still in the world and is thus confirmed in his vocation (fig. 53).[8] Fray Pedro de Cabañuelas, suffering from doubts about the truth of transubstantiation, regains his faith when he sees the host elevated above the altar after he spoke the words of consecration (fig. 54).[9] Christ, appearing to Friar Andrés de Salmerón in a blaze of glory, announces to him the day of his death, or rather, of his entry into the celestial city (fig. 55).[10] Fray Pedro de Salamanca, pointing to an eerie reddish radiance in the night sky feels dark premonitions of the war against Granada (fig. 56).[11] All these visions are intelligible as perceptions of the Thomist imagination, and this was how, forty years earlier, they had been described by the historian of the Jeronymite order, Fray José de Siguenza, whose work Zurbarán seems to have consulted.[12]

The visions Zurbarán painted illustrate different aspects of imaginative activity. The eucharistic vision, like the appearance of Jesus to Fray Andrés de Salmerón, was, as Aquinas had written, "divinely formed in the eye so as to represent a certain truth."[13] By contrast, the distorted facial expression and clawlike hands of the woman who appeared before

[7] Note also, Jerome wrote the letter in his early maturity, while Zurbarán depicts him as an old man. Zurbarán's vision of holiness was also brought before viewers in the New World; see D. Kinkead, "The Last Sevillian Period of Francisco de Zurbarán," *Art Bulletin* 65 (1983): 305–311.
[8] Cf. Siguenza, *Historia de la Orden de San Jerónimo* 4.6, vol. 8, p. 434.
[9] Siguenza, *Historia* 4.3, vol. 8, p. 421.
[10] Siguenza, *Historia* 2.7. vol. 8, p. 208a.
[11] See M. S. Soria, *The Paintings of Zurbarán* (London, 1955), p. 175. For an analogy to Fray Pedro de Salamanca's vision, see F. Pulgar, *Crónica de Don Fernando y Doña Isabel* 3.41, Biblioteca de autores españoles, vol. 70 (Madrid, 1953), p. 412b: a rainstorm occurs and the Christian host besieging the Muslim stronghold Montefrio "imaginaron que era señal de algun infortunio que les habia de acaecer."
[12] In addition to passages cited above, see on visions Siguenza, *Historia* 2.3, p. 179b, la figura en la fantasia; 2.6, p. 195b, feas imaginaciones.
[13] Aquinas, *Summa Theologica* 3.76.8 resp; see above, chap. 1.1 at n. 14.

53. Francisco Zurbarán: Fray Diego de Orgaz confronts the apparition of a woman he knew when living in the world, but whom now he sees as a demonic being accompanied by animal monsters. In the background, Fray Diego prays to the Virgin of Guadalupe who appears to him in a blaze of light. Guadalupe.

54. Francisco Zurbarán: Fray Pedro Cabañuelas sees the eucharistic host being miraculously elevated from the altar and is thus assured of the real presence of Christ in the sacrament. Guadalupe.

55. Francisco Zurbarán: Christ announces to Fray Andrés de Salmerón the
time of his death. Guadalupe.

56. Francisco Zurbarán: Fray Pedro de Salamanca is forewarned of the war against Granada by a reddish light in the sky. This vision is neither demonic nor divine but is composed of purely natural phenomena that the friar's prophetic insight knows how to interpret.

Fray Diego de Orgaz suggests a demonic presence, and this is confirmed by Siguenza's description of the incident. Jerome's lady musicians, however, were mental images without any demonic interference, and similarly, Fray Pedro de Salamanca's foreboding of war resulted from the autonomous activity of his imagination. Mental images of this latter kind were formed in the imagination on the basis of earlier sense impressions, without interference of God or demon. The quality of such images, as Thomist philosophers were accustomed to point out, depended on the moral stature of the individual experiencing them.[14] This is also what Spinoza wrote to his friend Peter Balling: stubborn people tend to imagine quarrels.

The vision of Fray Andrés de Salmerón—an image of Jesus in his imagination—anticipated his impending death. Here also, Spinoza offers a parallel, for he thought that Peter Balling's auditory imagination of groans had been an omen of his child's death. Spinoza carefully explained to his friend that his had been a noncorporeal experience. It was because the "soul of the father participates ideally in the consequences of his child's essence" that "he may sometimes imagine some of the said consequences as vividly as if they were present with him."[15] This was how Peter Balling had somehow foreseen his child's death. Similarly, Aquinas and his followers had pointed to the exceptional nature and content of certain visions or apprehensions of the imagination. But where Thomists tended to attribute visionary experiences to movement in the physical universe,[16] Spinoza stressed that Peter Balling's apprehension had originated in his own soul.

Nonetheless, Spinoza reflected on understanding and imagination in terms continuous with earlier discussions of these topics and responded to questions raised by his friends and correspondents in those same terms. Most families in the Jewish community to which Spinoza belonged until his expulsion from the synagogue came from Portugal or Spain. Although Spinoza's family was Portuguese,[17] he himself felt more drawn to things Hispanic. Several books in his library were translations into Spanish; he also owned works of Spanish political philosophy and admired the literature of Spain's Golden Age. Indeed, outside Greek and Latin literary classics, the only other literary writings he possessed were the works of Góngora and Quevedo, the *Novelas Exemplares* of Cervantes, and the third volume of Gracían's *Criticon*.[18] In addition, he owned a copy of Co-

[14] Above, chap. I.1 at nn. 31–34.
[15] Spinoza, *Letter* 17 (Letter 30, transl. Elwes).
[16] Above, chap. I.1 at nn. 36, 42–43.
[17] Vaz Dias and Van der Tak, "Spinoza Merchant," *Studia Rosenthaliana* 16 (1982): 109–171.
[18] Servaas van Rooijen, *Inventaire des livres . . . de Benedict Spinoza* (1889), pp. 143f., Quevedo; p. 159, Góngora; p. 189, another copy of Góngora; p. 176, Cervantes; p. 183,

varrubias' *Tesoro de la lengua Castellana.*[19] The meanings assigned in this work to the terms *fantasia, fantasma,* and *imaginación* reflect the traditional Thomist-Aristotelian concepts with which Spinoza repeatedly expressed disagreement.[20] Although the *Tesoro* is not an index of Spinoza's familiarity with the Aristotelian and Thomist tenets that were so pervasive in Spanish thinking,[21] the work does assist in identifying specific aspects of Spinoza's disagreement with these tenets. For example, Covarrubias defined phantasm as "fantastic vision or false imagination. . . . They happen to persons who are neither really awake nor really asleep. . . . At other times they occur because of the great fear that the person has, so that any shadow or body, irrespective of what it is, seems to be that which he fears and carries about in his imagination. Except when, with God's permission, the devil causes these visions." Given that the devil did not exist in Spinoza's universe, he dismissed theories of cognition that included the devil as an explanatory factor.

As Spinoza saw it, exponents of such theories failed to distinguish clear, and therefore true, ideas from false, fictitious and doubtful ones. He undertook to draw this distinction in the treatise *On the Improvement of the Understanding,*[22] pointing out that one would have to question the existence of true ideas if one did not differentiate between waking and sleeping. The issue was that Aristotelians, who held that of necessity thought arose from phantasms, saw a kinship between waking phantasms and those occurring to the imagination in dreams. They would therefore, Spinoza suggested, be unable under any circumstances to conceptualize a clear and true idea. Another obstacle in the path of forming clear and true ideas was the absence of a valid sequence of inquiry.[23]

Spinoza discussed this last issue under the heading of doubtful ideas.[24] To explain what a doubtful idea was, he used an example familiar from Aristotle and Aquinas, namely, the relationship between the apparent size of the sun and its real size.[25] Doubt arose in the mind not through one particular idea, whether this was true or false, but through another idea

Gracián. Gracián was not identified by the editor, but is recognizable from the title *El criticon.*

[19] Servas van Rooijen, *Inventaire,* p. 129, author not identified; see also p. 173, Italian-Spanish dictionary.

[20] The one volume of Aristotle that Spinoza owned contained rhetorical writings; see Servas van Rooijen, pp. 127f.

[21] See Wolfson, *The Philosophy of Spinoza* (1934), 2: 72ff. The medieval Aristotelian of whom Spinoza thought most frequently was of course not Aquinas but Maimonides; see ibid., pp. 98ff.

[22] Spinoza, *De intellectus emendatione* (ed. A. Koyré, under the title *Traité de la réforme de l'entendement* [Paris, 1984]; hereafter *IE*), 50.

[23] Spinoza, *IE* 80.

[24] Spinoza, *IE* 77ff.

[25] Aristotle, *On the Soul* 3.3, 428b; above, p. 25.

that was held concurrently and was indistinct. Country people usually entertained no doubt regarding the size of the sun because they had "never reflected . . . that our senses sometimes deceive us" and were greatly astonished when told of its actual size. Doubt thus arose from the coexistence in the mind of two ideas. To resolve this doubt, the mind, following a valid sequence of inquiry, ought initially to focus not on the sun but on "a true understanding of the senses and how by means of them things at a distance are represented."[26]

What was at issue between Spinoza and earlier philosophers was a subtle but fundamental shift of emphasis. Aristotelians were primarily concerned with replicating the order of things, indeed of the cosmos, by the order of thought. Spinoza's primary concern, by contrast, was to establish clear, distinct, and true ideas.[27] This concern led him to reject as a usable tool of analysis the Aristotelian distinction between substance and accidents that had been so important in earlier theories of cognition.[28] Among the many occasions when he raised the question of clear ideas was an exchange of letters with Hugo Boxel about ghosts, the existence of which Boxel asserted and Spinoza denied.[29] Having considered Boxel's arguments for the existence of ghosts in the light of the perfection of the cosmic order, of the image and likeness of God, and of the existence of body and soul independently of each other,[30] Spinoza defined the real issue as being the differentiation of what was certain and true both from what was probable and from what was false. He concluded that provided this was done, ghosts would be understood to have no intelligible properties, i.e., no clear and distinct ideas could be formed about them. Thus, in effect, they did not exist, irrespective of the opinions of earlier authorities such as Plato and Aristotle. To conclude the matter, Spinoza observed that one of the properties customarily attributed to ghosts, that they were sometimes visible and sometimes not, presented no difficulty to the imagination.[31] The point here was that the imagination might indeed separate what Aristotelians called the accidents of visibility from the substance of ghosts. But Spinoza's intellect could not accept that an object was both visible and invisible, that it both had a body and did not have a body.

Spinoza repeatedly implied that he did not regard intellect, imagination, and sense perceptions in the Aristotelian sense as faculties of the soul jointly engaged in a continuous process of cognition, of rendering sense

[26] Spinoza, *IE* 78.
[27] Cf. R. McKeon, *The Philosophy of Spinoza: The Unity of His Thought* (Woodbridge, 1987), pp. 224f.
[28] Wolfson, *The Philosophy of Spinoza* (1934), 1: 64–72; above, p. 27.
[29] Spinoza *Letters* 51–56 (Letters 55–60, transl. Elwes).
[30] Spinoza *Letters* 53–55 (Letters 57–58, transl. Elwes).
[31] Spinoza *Letter* 56, p. 261, ed. Gebhardt (Letter 60, transl. Elwes).

impressions intelligible.[32] Rather, imagination saw things indistinctly and fortuitously, reflecting the fortuitous manner in which external causes impacted on a person's body and hence on the senses. Although imagination thus made no contribution to the production of clear and distinct ideas, it might represent such ideas in the corporeal and quantitative terms available to it.[33] To Hugo Boxel Spinoza therefore declared that one could not form a correct mental image of God, even though one could understand his attributes as clearly and distinctly as one understood a triangle.[34] But the imagination could make no useful contribution to this understanding.[35]

The convergence we observed earlier between Spinoza's view of imagination and that depicted in Zurbarán's renderings of visionary and prophetic experience is thus only a partial one. Spinoza confronted the same issues as sixteenth- and seventeenth-century Spanish theologians had done before him, but his method of resolving these issues was fundamentally different, and so, therefore, were his results. This becomes yet more apparent if we consider the views on language and prophecy, society and sacred scripture that he expressed in his *Theologico-Political Treatise*. The torrent of embittered disagreement occasioned by this book when it was published anonymously in 1670 highlights its topical content,[36] which reached far beyond the immediate concerns of the Jews and Christians of Amsterdam who were among its first readers.

The message of the Jewish and Christian scriptures, Spinoza argued in the *Treatise*, focused not on the true nature of God but on the pursuit of a virtuous and pious life. Hence, the laws of a wisely constituted commonwealth should foster peace and social harmony but should allow individuals freely to express their own thinking about the deity. These propositions, revolutionary as they were, arose from Spinoza's meticulous and learned analysis of the form and content of biblical, and particularly of prophetic, texts.

Prophecy, as Spinoza understood it, was defined and delimited by the fact that it was communicated in words, which "are only extrinsic denominations of things and are not attributed to things except metaphorically."[37] Put differently, words were "part of the imagination" and were

[32] See for these views, above, chap. I.1 at nn. 17–19.

[33] Spinoza IE 74, 84; *Ethics* 2, proposition 18; proposition 40 scholium 2; proposition 29 corollarium; McKeon, *The Philosophy of Spinoza*, pp. 227ff.; Strauss (1930), pp. 169ff.

[34] Spinoza, *Letter* 56 (Letter 60, transl. Elwes).

[35] See Spinoza, IE 90.

[36] Spinoza, *Letters* 61 (17, transl. Elwes); 68; 71 (19–20, transl. Elwes); 73–75 (21–23 transl. Elwes), 77–78 (24–25 transl. Elwes); 25A, transl. Elwes (not in Gebhardt's edition); further, Spinoza's *Life*, in A. Wolf, *The Oldest Biography* (1927), pp. 60f.

[37] Spinoza, *Expositor of Descartes* 1.246, transl. Curley, in *The Collected Works of Spinoza*, vol. 1.

"confusedly placed in memory from some disposition of the body." As a result,

> we invent many concepts, so that it cannot be doubted that words, like the imagination, can be the cause of many great errors, unless we take careful precautions regarding them. In addition, words are made up randomly, according to popular fancy. Thus they are no more than signs of things as they exist in the imagination, and not as they exist in intellect.[38]

The very shape of words was determined by imagination: the majority of concepts residing in the intellect were described by negatives, such as "infinite" or "immortal" precisely because "their contraries are more easily imagined."[39]

It was thus no wonder that the revelations and prophecies of the Hebrew scriptures were couched in terms accessible not to intellect but to the imaginations of the different biblical authors and their audiences. What the Bible said of God, therefore, did not necessarily correspond to what a seventeenth-century public expected to read. For example:

> As Moses clearly teaches that God is jealous, and nowhere states that God is without passions or emotions, we must evidently infer that Moses held this doctrine himself, or at any rate, that he wished to teach it, nor must we refrain because such a belief seems contrary to reason. For . . . we cannot wrest the meaning of texts to suit the dictates of our reason or our preconceived opinions.[40]

Furthermore, different biblical authors contradicted each other. The prophet Samuel believed that God never repented of anything, while Jeremiah stated the opposite.[41] These features of the Bible became intelligible once it was understood that God accommodated his revelation both to the intellectual capacity and knowledge of the recipients and to their culture and circumstances. The mentality of an author living in a well-ordered society was different from that of one living under oppression.[42] As a result, Spinoza wrote, "God has no particular style in speaking, but according to the learning and capacity of the prophet, is cultivated, compressed, severe, untutored, prolix, or obscure."[43] To understand the Bible therefore entailed the philological study of its different texts and an inquiry into the cultural and political circumstances in which they were

---

[38] Spinoza, *IE* 88–89.
[39] Spinoza, *IE* 89.
[40] Spinoza, *A Theologico-Political Treatise* (hereafter *TrTP*), 7, pp. 102f.
[41] Spinoza *TrTP* 2, p. 39; cf. *TrTP* 7, p. 103, God is jealous.
[42] Spinoza, *TrTP* 7, p. 105.
[43] Spinoza, *TrTP* 2, p. 31.

written.[44] In this way the exegete would avoid confounding the mind of the biblical "prophet or historian with the mind of the Holy Spirit or with the truth of the matter."[45]

The same principles of exegesis were relevant to the Christian scriptures, Spinoza argued. Jesus himself, "acting in this respect the part of God," had accommodated himself to the understanding and the assumptions of his listeners: "For instance, when he said to the Pharisees, 'And if Satan cast out devils, his house is divided against itself, how then shall his kingdom stand?' he only wished to convince the Pharisees according to their own principles, not to teach that there are devils, or any kingdom of devils."[46] The apostle Paul, likewise, spoke "merely humanly," "and it was doubtless in concession to human weakness that he attributed mercy, grace, anger and similar qualities to God, adapting his language to the popular mind, or, as he puts it, to carnal men."[47] The statements of scriptural authors—be they the writers of the Hebrew Bible or of the Christian New Testament—could thus not be universalized or accommodated in disregard of the circumstances in which they had been conceived, because all these authors wrote in the language of humanity. This language, like the concepts it communicated, was anchored not in intellect but in imagination and therefore in particulars.[48] Moses did not formulate the law in philosophically valid terms; Joshua thought that the sun moved round the earth, not vice versa; and contrary to much scholarly speculation,[49] Solomon did not design the Temple according to mathematically sophisticated proportions but rather according to proportions such as any workman would use.[50]

Spinoza arrived at these conclusions regarding scriptural concepts of deity by studying the Hebrew Bible and the New Testament. In Peru, analogous conclusions had earlier been reached by some historians and missionaries who had studied Inca and Andean concepts of deity. It was on the basis of such conclusions that these same historians and missionaries became ever less interested in demonic intervention as a rationale for religious difference and instead turned to cultural and political explanations. In several instances, observations of the characteristics of Inca and Andean concepts of deity were matched precisely by Spinoza's observa-

[44] Spinoza, TrTP 7, pp. 108ff.; cf. 1, pp. 19ff.
[45] Spinoza, TrTP 7, p. 107; see further on accommodation, Funkenstein, *Theology and the Scientific Imagination* (1986), chap. 4, esp. pp. 219ff.
[46] Spinoza, TrTP 2, p. 41.
[47] Spinoza, TrTP 4, p. 65.
[48] Spinoza, IE 88ff.; TrTP 1, p. 25.
[49] For sixteenth-century scholarship on this and related matters, see the short treatise by B. Arias Montano, published along with his polyglot Bible, *Exemplar sive de sacris fabricis liber Benedicto Aria Montano Hispalensi Auctore* (Antwerp, 1572).
[50] Spinoza, TrTP 1, pp. 14, 18; 2, p. 34.

tions of concepts of deity in the Hebrew Bible. Spinoza's reasons for dis-
allowing the explanatory role of the devil were different from those arrived at in Peru. But the convergences between his interpretations of the
religion of Israel and the explanations of Inca and Andean religion put
forward by historians and missionaries point to the beginnings of the
modern study of religion.

At the root of these convergences lies the observation that Israelite and
Andean religion both lacked those abstract concepts that philosophic religion took for granted. José de Acosta thus noted that in Quechua there
existed no general term for *god*,[51] while Spinoza pointed out that the patriarchs "were not cognizant of any attribute of God which expresses his
absolute essence, but only of his deeds and promises, that is, of his power
as manifested in visible things."[52] Similarly, Spinoza mentioned repeatedly that throughout the Bible, God was described by reference to the
human imagination, that is, in physical and spatial terms. Adam, for instance, hid from God, and Jonah thought that he was fleeing from God's
sight.[53] Correspondingly, Abraham imagined that God had told him that
he would go down to Sodom, "to see whether they have done altogether
according to the cry of it which is come unto me; and if not I will
know,"[54] while Moses thought that on top of Mount Sinai he would be
closer to God than in the plains.[55] Garcilaso de la Vega described the divine Sun of the Incas in very similar terms. Inca rulers would inform the
Sun of a victory they had won "as though the Sun had not seen it" and
altogether thought of him in corporeal, human terms, "because their
imagination did not reach beyond what they saw materially with their
eyes."[56]

A generation later, the Jesuit Bernabé Cobo commented on the irratio-
nality of Inca and Andean cults of celestial bodies and atmospheric phenomena, because the celestial bodies and the weather were perceived in
myth and cult contrary to the order of causation described by natural
science.[57] The issue was that Andeans were inordinately preoccupied with
visible secondary causes, thus overlooking the divine and primary cause
of all phenomena. Here also, Spinoza arrived at a parallel conclusion
when he wrote that

> since without God nothing can exist or be conceived, it is evident
> that all natural phenomena involve and express the conception of

[51] Acosta, *HNM* 5.3.
[52] Spinoza, *TrTP* 13, p. 177.
[53] Spinoza, *TrTP* 2, pp. 35, 39.
[54] Spinoza, *TrTP* 2, p. 35, transl. Elwes.
[55] Spinoza, *TrTP* 2, p. 38.
[56] Garcilaso, *CR* 5.19, p. 175 and 2.22, p. 73, respectively. Above, chap. VIII.1 at nn. 41–42.
[57] Cobo, *Historia* 13.6, p. 158; 13.2, p. 149b; see above, p. 396.

God as far as their essence and perfection extend, so that we have greater and more perfect knowledge of God in proportion to our knowledge of natural phenomena. Conversely . . . the greater our knowledge of natural phenomena, the more perfect our knowledge of the essence of God. [58]

At the same time, Spinoza stressed that such an understanding of God was not to be looked for in the Bible, which taught practical ethics and theology but not philosophy and reason. Here Spinoza differed fundamentally from missionaries and historians of the Incas, who were all committed to defending the superiority of the Christian religion and with that the universal applicability of Christian scripture, that is, the idea that in some sense Scripture contained the seeds of all knowledge.

Spinoza rejected this idea. Indeed, the central issue in his criticism of earlier exegetes of Scripture, Maimonides in particular, was that they erroneously explained the biblical texts not in the light of criteria derived from those texts themselves but in the light of the writings of Aristotle. [59] As a result, the prophets had been endowed with the speculative propensities and tranquillity of soul cultivated by Greek philosophers, which according to the biblical texts they clearly did not possess. [60] A case in point was the prophet Daniel, whose visions, according to Thomist theologians, had been filtered through the powerful and lucid imagination of a man of philosophic temper. [61] According to Spinoza, the exact opposite had been the case:

> The visions of Daniel could not be understood by him even after they had been explained, and this obscurity did not arise from the difficulty of the matter revealed (for being merely human affairs, these only transcend human capacity in being future), but solely in the fact that Daniel's imagination was not so capable for prophecy while he was awake as while he was asleep; and this is further evident from the fact that at the very beginning of the vision he was so terrified that he almost despaired of his strength. Thus, on account of the inadequacy of his imagination and his strength, the things revealed were so obscure to him that he could not understand them even after they had been explained. [62]

All this did not make the visions of Daniel and the other prophets valueless, Spinoza argued, although it did reveal that they were misinterpreted when endowed with philosophical significance. Thus, where José de Acosta had complained that the Indians of Peru could not understand

[58] Spinoza, *TrTP* 4, p. 59.
[59] Spinoza, *TrTP*, Preface, p. 7; chap. 1, p. 17; 7, pp. 114ff.
[60] Spinoza, *TrTP* 2, pp. 30f.
[61] Above, chap. 1.2 at n. 43.
[62] Spinoza, *TrTP* 2, p. 32.

"the sublimity of our doctrine,"[63] Spinoza pointed out that the Bible did not teach sublime notions of divinity but piety, moral goodness, and obedience.[64] Put bluntly, "faith does not demand so much that dogmas should be true, as that they should be pious."[65] Philosophy and theology, reason and revelation, thus belonged to different realms; on this ground alone they could not be in conflict with each other. To accommodate revelation as found in the Bible to reason, and reason to the Bible, amounted to discovering in the text what was not in it.[66]

When Garcilaso defended the validity, however limited, of Inca notions of deity as expressed in the cult of the Sun, the implication was that the attainment of religious insight had not been restricted to Europe or to Christianity. Spinoza likewise urged that piety was no one's monopoly, but unlike Garcilaso and other apologists of the Incas, he distinguished the practice of piety and goodness from holding philosophically valid ideas about God. Given that "we are not able to imagine God, though we can understand him,"[67] it was also true that individuals whose concept of God did not reach beyond a confused and inadequate mental image could live a morally good life.[68] The number of these individuals included the prophets of the Hebrew Bible and also devout and pious people the world over. This position of Spinoza's was part and parcel of his view of Scripture as a book not of philosophy but of theology and ethics, and it also lay at the root of his conception of what was meant in Scripture by divine election.

The Hebrew Bible contained the history of God's dealings with Israel and recorded his many declarations of having chosen this people and given them laws. But here also, Spinoza asserted, God had spoken "only according to the understanding of [his] hearers, who . . . knew not true blessedness," seeing that "every man's true happiness and blessedness consists solely in the enjoyment of what is good, not in the pride that he alone is enjoying it, to the exclusion of others."[69] In so far as election by God had regard to blessedness and true virtue, therefore, "we must evidently believe that the true gentile prophets (and every nation . . . possessed such) promised the same to the faithful of their own people, who were thereby comforted. Wherefore this eternal covenant of the knowledge and love of God is universal."[70]

There was, however, another sense in which God could be said to have

---

[63] Acosta, *De procuranda* 2.9, p. 446a; cf. above, p. 280.
[64] Spinoza, *TrTP* 2, p. 40; 4, p. 65; 13, pp. 175ff.
[65] Spinoza, *TrTP* 14, p. 185; cf. 2, pp. 35f., on Abraham.
[66] Spinoza, *TrTP* 13, p. 195.
[67] Spinoza, *Letter* 56 (Letter 56, transl. Elwes).
[68] Spinoza, *TrTP* 2, p. 41.
[69] Spinoza, *TrTP* 2, p. 43.
[70] Spinoza, *TrTP* 3, p. 55.

chosen the Jews, which was with regard to their social organization and political success. This election, however, had nothing to do with their ideas about god, which were, Spinoza pointed out repeatedly, "very ordinary."[71] To think of god as lawgiver and potentate, as Moses had done, amounted to endowing god with human characteristics, to forming of him an image in the imagination that had nothing to do with conceiving a true and distinct idea of god. Nonetheless, the laws that Moses promulgated led to the creation of an ordered polity and to the attainment of temporal security and well-being. In this sense, Spinoza reasoned, god had also chosen other nations, and would in future choose yet others. Indeed, "so changeable are human affairs" that it was not inconceivable that god would in this temporal and secular sense elect the Jews a second time and would "raise up their empire afresh."[72] This very subject had been fervently debated among the Jews of Amsterdam when in 1665 news reached them that the Messiah Sabbatai Sevi had manifested himself in Smyrna, and Spinoza himself had been consulted on the issue by one of his friends.[73]

The possibility of the recreation of a Jewish polity had been considered by the Jews of Amsterdam on an earlier occasion. Spinoza owned a copy of the treatise *Hope of Israel*, which its author Menasseh ben Israel had addressed to the *parnassim*, the elders, of the synagogue and had published in 1650.[74] One of these elders was Spinoza's father, Michael Espinosa, from whom he had perhaps inherited the book. The treatise began with the report, brought to Amsterdam in 1644 by the Portuguese Jew Antonio Montezinos, that descendants of the ten lost tribes of Israel had been found in the upper reaches of the Magdalena River in the northern viceroyalty of Peru. The theory that Amerindians were descendants of the ten lost tribes had been propounded earlier.[75] The report of Montezinos, however, came to be endowed with special urgency thanks to the millennial expectations that were at the time current among both Jews and Christians.[76]

Where Jews anticipated the manifestation of the Messiah and the consequent establishment of a messianic state, many Christians believed that the prophecies of the Hebrew Bible were finding their fulfillment in the framework of Christian states already in existence. The Jesuit missionary Antonio Vieira, whom Menasseh ben Israel met in 1647, thus believed

---

[71] Spinoza, *TrTP* 3, p. 46; cf. 1, p. 21.

[72] Spinoza, *TrTP* 3, p. 56.

[73] Spinoza, *Letter* 16, p. 178, ed. Gebhardt (Letter 33, transl. Elwes). Scholem, *Sabbatai Sevi* (1973), pp. 543ff.

[74] Servas van Rooijen, *Inventaire*, p. 184.

[75] Cf. Acosta, *HNM* 1.13–18; Garcia, *Origen*, bk. 3.

[76] See Menasseh ben Israel, *Espérance d'Israel*, introduction and notes by H. Mechoulan and G. Nahon (Paris, 1979), pp. 51ff., 71ff.

that Daniel's prophecy of the fifth empire was being fulfilled in his own lifetime through the work of the missionaries of his order in Brazil.[77] In Spain also, men of the church were looking to the Americas for the fulfillment of the prophecies of the Hebrew Bible. In a treatise dated 1644, the priest Fernando Montesinos produced scriptural evidence suggesting that Peru had been Solomon's Ophir and had been rediscovered in the fullness of time to become now the Ophir of Spain, the source of gold, silver, and exotic plants and minerals.[78] Moreover, Montesinos argued, the prophet Daniel's predictions about the fifth empire were coming to fruition in Peru thanks to the labor of evangelization being undertaken there by Spanish missionaries.[79] Montesinos' treatise was consulted some years later by the New Christian jurist Antonio León Pinelo, who redeployed some of its arguments to show that the terrestrial Paradise was to be found in the upper Amazon and that Noah's ark had set sail from near Lima.

Throughout Europe and the Americas, Scripture was thus read in the mid-seventeenth century with the purpose of finding in it prophecies that were being fulfilled in contemporary events, events that were in turn understood as signs of the consummation of time. These readings were validated by a venerable exegetical tradition that injoined religious teachers and preachers to extend the significance of a given biblical text beyond its specific historical meaning and accommodate it to their own period and to the immediate concerns of their listeners. Among the advocates of this method of reading the Bible had been the Jesuit missionary José de Acosta, who felt, however, that Indian neophytes in the faith were not endowed with sufficient religious insight to benefit by the accommodation of the scriptures to their experience. Missionary preaching had to be restricted, therefore, to those parts of the Bible that could be satisfactorily explained according to the literal sense alone.[80] But Acosta, like other missionaries, was convinced that in themselves the biblical texts enshrined an absolute and universal validity capable of being accommodated to all times and all circumstances.

---

[77] For Vieira and Menasseh ben Israel, see A. J. Saraiva, "Antonio Vieira, Menasseh ben Israel et le Cinquième Empire," *Studia Rosenthaliana* 6, no. 1 (1972): 25–57; see esp. pp. 47, 52: according to Vieira, Menasseh ben Israel was willing to attribute to Jesus a spiritual redemption of all humanity, while also expecting a temporal redeemer who would lead the Jews out of temporal captivity. Spinoza was thinking along similar lines, see *TrTP* 3, p. 56, transl. Elwes, cited above at n. 71. On Vieira's ideas about the fifth empire, see Tom Cohen, *The Fire of Tongues: Antonio Vieira and the Christian Mission in Brazil* (Dissertation, Department of History, Stanford University, 1990), pp. 236ff.; cf. on similar ideas expounded by Fray Luis de León, Noreña, *Studies in Spanish Renaissance Thought* (1975), p. 159 and the excellent study on Fr. Luis by C. P. Thompson, *The Strife of Tongues: Fray Luis de León and the Golden Age of Spain* (Cambridge, 1988), pp. 94–103.

[78] Fernando de Montesinos, *Ophir* 1, chaps. 17–29.

[79] Fernando de Montesinos, *Ophir* 3, chap. 24.

[80] Above, chap. VI at n. 64.

This was precisely what Spinoza argued could not be done without radically misrepresenting the content and nature of Scripture. Many of his contemporaries therefore accused him of impiety and atheism: he had deprived the Bible of its status as a revealed and privileged text. The physician Lambert de Velthuysen in particular charged him with having attributed to the prophets "untrue arguments accommodated to the preconceived opinions of those whom they addressed," and of having undermined the study of "the true sense of Scripture." As a result, Velthuysen concluded, Spinoza "had placed the Koran on a level with the word of God" and had "no arguments left with which to prove that Mohammed is a false prophet."[81] This last charge was not without foundation. Spinoza saw no useful purpose to be achieved by the pursuit of religious controversy and by assigning privilege or precedence to one religious opinion over another. *Geen ketter sonder letter,* "No heretic without a text," ran the Belgian proverb that he quoted by way of pointing to the futility and sheer subjectivity of sectarian exegesis of the Bible.[82]

But ultimately, as Velthuysen was aware, what was at stake was not so much the exegesis of the Bible as the nature of knowledge and the scope of political authority. Although the governance of the Protestant Netherlands was incomparably more liberal than that of Catholic Spain, there existed nonetheless a few elements that the two political cultures shared. For in both of them, Christanity and the written word as validated by Christian teachers constituted points of reference in relation to which understanding, thought, and imagination, as well as social and political order, were rendered intelligible. When thus, in the early sixteenth century, Pedro Ciruelo endeavored to distinguish true religion from error and superstition, he defined the former by reference to its control over sacred scripture and to the authority of its teachers. In his opinion, therefore, true knowledge was inseparable from its institutional and social context, and knowledge lacking such a context, alleged to have been "infused by God without the need of a teacher's instruction or the study of books," was worthless.[83] Many of Spinoza's Jewish and Christian fellow Dutchmen would have found little to criticize in this statement.[84] A similar insistence on the value and authority of the Christian religious and learned tradition characterized both the study of Inca and Andean religion and the teaching of the missionaries. Spinoza's reasoning, however, placed all these attitudes toward the authority of texts and their exegetes in a very different light.

[81] Spinoza, *Letter* 42, pp. 209, 215, 218 (omitted in the translation by Elwes).
[82] Spinoza, *TrTP* 14, p. 182.
[83] Ciruelo, *Treatise* 3.1, p. 183; cf. above, chap. 1.2, p. 41.
[84] Cf. A. L. Katchen, *Christian Hebraists and Dutch Rabbis: Seventeenth Century Apologetics and the Study of Maimonides' Mishneh Torah* (Cambridge, Mass., 1984).

Of the diverse forms of understanding[85] one can achieve, Spinoza described understanding on the basis of authority, or as he expressed it of "hearsay," as the lowest. Next came understanding on the basis of experience; then understanding on the basis of the inferred cause of the object or phenomenon under consideration; and finally, understanding of that object or phenomenon through its essence.[86] It was this last kind of understanding that Spinoza's friend Peter Balling had possessed with regard to his child. Understanding tempered the imagination, which was why Peter Balling's understanding of, and identification with, his child led to his experiencing in imagination an omen of the child's coming death. Other imaginings arose from states of the body and from the random impact on the body of external objects and from memory.[87] Such images had to be distinguished from ideas if one was to avoid looking on ideas as "silent paintings on a panel," without realizing that ideas as such "involved affirmation or negation."[88] It was ideas involving affirmation and negation, rather than demons or divine interventions in the behavior of material bodies or human sense perceptions, that defined and described the output of imagination. Concurrently, Spinoza considered the traditional theological arguments about the inscrutable but never unjust judgments of God, that permitted demonic activity and its divine counterpart, to be so many appeals to human ignorance, not to divine justice.[89] This theological consideration was accompanied by a philosophical one. In philosophical terms, the cause of error was to be sought not in the order of the cosmos but in the mind, where it could be remedied:

> In order to begin to indicate what error is, I should like you to note that the imaginations of the mind, considered in themselves, contain no error, or that the mind does not err from the fact that it imagines, but only in so far as it is considered to lack an idea that excludes the existence of those things that it imagines to be present to it. For if the mind while it imagines nonexistent things as present to it, at the same time knows that those things do not exist, it attributes this power of imagining to a virtue of its nature, not to a vice—especially if this faculty of imagining depended only on its own nature, i.e., if the mind's faculty of imagining were free.[90]

The freedom Spinoza posits, a freedom from equivocal, unclear, and indistinct ideas, was attainable independently of cultural tradition. His phi-

[85] "Understanding" translates the Latin *perceptio*.
[86] Spinoza, *IE* 19; cf. 23–29, 108; also *Ethics* 2, proposition 40.
[87] Spinoza, *Ethics* 2, proposition 18; cf above, p. 444.
[88] Spinoza, *Ethics* 2, proposition 49 scholium 2.
[89] Spinoza, *Ethics* 1, proposition 36 Appendix, with Las Casas, *Apologética Historia* 92, quoting Augustine; see also above, chap. 1.2 at notes 48–49.
[90] Spinoza, *Ethics* 2, proposition 17 scholium, transl. Curley.

losophy yields no grounds for arguing either that Indians were more prone to vain imaginings than other people or that the religious notions conveyed in their myths and rituals were substantially inferior to equivalents recorded in the Hebrew Bible. Similar arguments had been formulated earlier, although with much less rigor, by Las Casas and Garcilaso. But these arguments did not, for the most part, gain the support of the men who framed policies in viceregal Peru. In the eyes of those of Spinoza's Spanish and Peruvian contemporaries who did frame policies, and in the eyes of their eighteenth-century successors, Indians were no longer opponents in warfare, who for this reason alone had, in one way or another, to be reckoned with. Nor were they perceived as the heirs of the great culture that Cieza and his contemporaries had admired so profoundly, or as the targets of evangelizing rhetoric, resonating with contempt and ferocity. Rather, Indians in their new Enlightenment guise of noble savages figured in quiet and sometimes profound European inquiries into humanity's origin and true nature.[91] But those noble savages had nothing in common with the Incas recently dead, or with the living Andeans whose voices we have heard. The European imagination came to be free of demons, and perhaps of equivocation. What was lost to Europeans of the Enlightenment however, was their ancestors' capacity for passionate engagement with the exponents of another religion and another culture.

[91] See on this shift, M. Ryan, "Assimilating New Worlds in the Sixteenth and Seventeenth Centuries," *Comparative Studies in Society and History* 23 (1981): 519–536, and now A. Pagden, *Spanish Imperialism and the Political Imagination* (New Haven, 1990), especially chap. 4.

GLOSSARY

THE bracketed letter [Q] denotes a Quechua term, and the bracketed letter [S] denotes a term in Spanish. Fuller definitions of many terms may be found in text and notes: consult index.

aclla [Q]: woman chosen for the service of the Sun
acso [Q]: woman's skirt
ají [term from Caribbean]: spicy condiment, Quechua *ucho*
altiplano [S]: the Andean highlands of Bolivia and Peru
alumbrado [S]: "enlightened"; in sixteenth-century Spain, individual with mystical leanings
amaru [Q]: serpent
amauta [Q]: wise man, trickster
anan [Q]: upper, the opposite of *urin*; used of places and moieties in society
apo, apu [Q]: lord
aravi [Q]: song or dance of love
audiencia [S]: royal judicial and administrative council
auqui [Q]: nobleman; lord
ayllu [Q]: kin group
behetría [S]: in medieval Castile, region free to choose its own lord; in the Andes, region lacking political order
bulto [S]: three-dimensional representation. In the Andes, mummified body.
callpa [Q]: power or faculty; divinatory ritual
camachico [Q]: man holding authority over village; priest
camaquen [Q]: soul, life force
camasca [Q]: Andean diviner
capacocha [Q]: solemn obligation or ritual; sacrifical ceremony of the Incas, often involving human sacrifice
caruamita [Q]: "time of yellowing," i.e., of the maize; harvest season
castellano [S]: Spanish gold coin
cay pacha [Q]: "this earth" or "this time" (as distinct from the afterlife or the world of the dead)
ceque [Q]: in Inca Cuzco, sight line marked with shrines, going from Coricancha to points on or beyond the horizon
chacara, chacra [Q]: field
chicha [term from central America]: maize beer, in Quechua *aka*
chullpa [Q]: burial tower
chuquiylla [Q]: lightning, synonym of *illapa*
churi [Q]: son

chuspa [Q]: small pouch carried by a band hanging from shoulder
citua [Q]: Inca celebration of expelling evils
conopa [Q]: domestic holy object
converso [S]: convert from Judaism to Christianity
Coricancha [Q]: "enclosure of gold," the temple of the Sun in Cuzco
corregidor [S]: judicial and administrative official representing the Crown
cumbi [Q]: very fine cloth
curaca [Q]: Andean lord
desengaño [S]: disenchantment, inner tranquillity
doctrina [S]: missionary parish
encomienda [S]: in early colonial Peru, grant by the Spanish crown of Indians and
    land to a Spanish beneficiary
estancia [S]: small settlement usually in remote location
guaoque, guaoqui [Q]: brother
hapiñuñu [Q]: ghost who "snatches" with the "breast"
Haucaypata [Q]: "square of celebration," the main square of Inca Cuzco
haylli [Q]: song of triumph that is also sung at harvest
huaca [Q]: Andean object of veneration, holy place
huacascamayoc [Q]: Inca official keeping record of offerings to huacas
huanca [Q]: holy object protecting a community
huara [Q]: garment of adult men
huari [Q]: person indigenous to a place; dance evocative of the ancient past
illapa [Q]: lightning
inti [Q]: sun
Indicancha [Q]: "enclosure of the sun"
llactayoc [Q]: from *llacta*, village: person indigenous to a place
llacuaz [Q]: newcomer
llijllia, lliquilla [Q]: woman's shawl, carrying cloth
machay [Q]: burial cave
mallqui [Q]: embalmed body; tree
Mamacocha [Q]: "Mother Sea"
mama [Q]: honored matron, in charge of convent of *acclas*; pl. *mamacona*
mazcca paycha [Q]: headband of Inca ruler
molle [Q]: tree indigenous to the Andes
monasterio [S]: monastery, convent
mullo [Q]: spondylus shell, used in sacrifice
napa [Q]: white
ñusta [Q]: princess
oidor [S]: Crown official serving as member of audiencia
orejón [S]: Inca noble, thus named from earlobes enlarged by earspools worn by
    noblemen
pacarimoc [Q]: individual indigenous to a place
pacarina [Q]: place of origin
Pacaritambo, Paccarectampo [Q]: "inn of the dawn," mythic and actual place near
    Cuzco
Pachacamac [Q]: "Maker of the World"

pachacuti [Q]: "turning about of the time"

pacsa [Q]: moon, full moon

palla [Q]: princess

phantasm [in Thomist thought]: mental image formed by imagination on the basis of sense perceptions

pirua [Q]: deposit for foodstuffs

pocoimita [Q]: rainy season

puna [Q]: lands at high altitude

punchao [Q]: day

purucaya [Q]: ritual of mourning for the Inca

purunpacha [Q]: an epoch of Andean history preceding epoch of speaker

pururauca [Q]: in Inca legend, divinely sent warriors to assist Inca Pachacuti; in daily life, "rock projectile thrown from a fort to defend it"

quipu [Q]: knotted cord used by Incas to store numerical and narrative information

quipucamayo [Q]: specialist storing and "reading" quipus

raimi [Q]: dance, festival

real [S]: Spanish coin, usually of silver

reducción [S]: resettlement village organized by Spanish

repartimiento [S]: administrative district

requerimiento [S]: legal document "requiring" native Americans to submit to evangelization and Spanish government

sanco [Q]: mixture of maize flour and blood used in sacrificial ritual

sapsi [Q]: community

suyo [Q]: province

Tahuantinsuyo [Q]: the "four parts" of the Inca empire

tambo [Q]: inn

taqui onqoy [Q]: "dance of disease"

Ticci Viracocha [Q]: "divine foundation," the Andean creator god

topayauri, tupayauri [Q]: the Inca's scepter

topo [Q]: a measure of land

ucupacha [Q]: world inside the earth; the Christian hell

Upaimarca [Q]: world above

urin [Q]: lower, the opposite of *anan*; used of places and moieties in society

ushnu [Q]: pit for sacrificial offerings, Inca throne structure

vecino [S]: householder with voting rights in Spanish town

villca [Q]: Andean holy site

visita [S]: official inquiry

yana [Q]: personal retainer, usually of Inca ruler; pl. *yanacona*.

Zaramama [Q]: "Mother of Maize"

SELECT BIBLIOGRAPHY

I. Ancient, Medieval and Early Modern Sources

Works relating to sixteenth- and seventeenth-century Spain and Peru are cited with the original place and date of publication; where a modern edition is available, I add its particulars. Works not published until modern times are cited with the date, or presumed date, of composition, followed by particulars of the modern edition I used. For works by classical, patristic, and medieval authors, I likewise cite the modern editions I used. Works of uncertain authorship are cited with the name of the presumed author in brackets; anonymous works are listed by title. Works commented upon in general terms or without reference to specific passages have been omitted; works referred to only once or not central to the main themes of this book are cited in full in the relevant footnote but are not cited here.

Acosta, José de. *Obras del P. José de Acosta*. Edited by F. Mateos. Biblioteca de autores españoles, vol. 73. Madrid, 1954.

———. *De Christo revelato libri novem*. Rome, 1590.

———. *Historia natural y moral de las Indias* (Seville, 1590). Edited by E. O'Gorman. Mexico City, 1962.

Albornoz, Cristóbal de. *Las Informaciones de Cristóbal de Albornoz* (1569–1584). In *El retorno de las huacas. Estudios y documentos sobre el Taki Onqoy. Siglo XVI.* Edited by L. Millones. Lima, 1990.

———. *Instrucción para descubrir todas las guacas del Pirú y sus camayos y haziendas* (1581/1585). In C. de Molina and C. de Albornoz, *Fábulas y mitos de los Incas.* Edited by H. Urbano and P. Duviols. Madrid, 1989. For the passage missing at p. 178, see P. Duviols, "Un inédit de Cristóbal de Albornoz: La Instrucción para descubrir todas las guacas del Pirú y sus camayos y haziendas," *Journal de la Société des Américanistes* 56 (1967): 7–39 at 25–26.

Aldrete, Bernardo José de. *Del origen y principio de la lengua Castellana o Romance que oi se usa en España* (Rome, 1606). Edited by L. Nieto Jiménez. Madrid, 1972–1975.

Alfonso X el Sabio. *Las quatro partes enteras de la Crónica de España que mandó componer el serenissimo rey don Alonso llamado el Sabio . . . vista y emendada mucha parte de su impresión por el maestro Florián Docampo: Cronista del emperador rey nr señor.* Zamora, 1541.

Annius of Viterbo. *Antiquitatum variorum volumina XVII.* Venice, 1498.

Aquinas, Thomas. *In Aristotelis librum de anima commentarium.* Edited by A. M. Pirotta. Torino, 1959.

Aquinas, Thomas. *Summa Theologica*. Biblioteca de autores cristianos, vols. 77,80,81,83,87. Madrid, 1961–1965.

Arias Montano, Benito. *Exemplar sive de sacris fabricis liber Benedicto Aria Montano Hispalensi Auctore*. Antwerp, 1572.

Aristotle. *Commentarii Collegii Conimbricensis Societatis Iesu, in libros De Anima Aristotelis Stagiritae*. Coimbra, 1598.

———.*On the Soul, Parva Naturalia, On Breath*. Edited and translated by W. S. Hell. Cambridge, Mass.: 1936.

———. *Politics*. Edited and translated by H. Rackham. Cambridge Mass., 1975.

Arriaga, Pablo Joseph de. *La extirpación de la idolatría en el Perú* (Lima, 1621). Colección de libros y documentos referentes a la historia del Perú, first series, vol. 1. Lima, 1920.

Avendaño, Fernando de. *Sermones de los Misterios de Nuestra Santa Fé Catolica en lengua Castellana y la General del Inca*. Lima, 1649.

Aviso de el modo que havia en el gobierno de los Indios en tiempo del Inga (Aviso de Chincha). In M. Rostworowski de Diez Canseco (1970), 163–173.

Bandera, Damián de la. *Relación general de la disposición y calidad de la provincia de Guamanga . . . 1557*. In *Relaciones geograficas de Indias—Perú*, edited by M. Jiménez de la Espada, Biblioteca de autores españoles, vol. 183, 176–180. Madrid, 1965.

Barrientos, Lope de. *Vida y obras de Fr. Lope de Barrientos, Anales Salmantinos I*. Edited by Luis G. A. Getino. Salamanca, 1927.

Benzoni, Girolamo. *La Historia del Mundo Nuevo de M. Jerónimo Benzoni Milanés* (first edition in Italian; Venice, 1565). Translated by C. Radicati di Primeglio. Lima, 1968.

Berosus. See Annius of Viterbo.

Bertonio, Ludovico. *Vocabulario de la lengua aymara* (Juli, 1612). Cochabamba, 1984.

Betanzos, Juan de. *Suma y narración de los Incas* (1551), book 1, chapters 1–18. Edited by F. Esteve Barba. In *Crónicas Peruanas de intéres indígena*, Biblioteca de autores españoles, vol. 209. Madrid, 1968.

———. *Suma y narración de los Incas* (1551). Edited by M. del Carmen Martin Rubio. Madrid, 1987.

Bodin, Jean. *Los seis libros de la República de Juan Bodino traducidos de lengua Francesa y enmendadas Catholicamente por Gaspar de Anastro Ysunza*. Milan, 1590.

Book of Wisdom. See *Liber Sapientiae Salomonis*.

Borregán, Alonso. *Crónica de la conquista del Perú* (c. 1565). Edited by R. Loredo. Seville, 1948.

Botero, Giovanni. *Le relationi universali di Giovanni Botero Benese, Divise in quattro parti*. Venice, 1597.

Cabello Valboa, Miguel. *Miscelánea antártica* (1586). Lima, 1951.

Calancha, Antonio de la. *Corónica moralizada del Orden de San Augustín en el Perú* (Barcelona, 1639). Edited by I. Prado Pastor. Lima, 1974–1981.

Carabajal, Pedro de. *Descripción fecha de la provincia de Vilcas Guaman . . . año de 1586*. In *Relaciones geograficas de Indias—Perú*, edited by M. Jiménez de la Espada, Biblioteca de autores españoles, vol. 183, 205–219. Madrid, 1965.

Castañega, Martín de. *Tratado de las supersticiones y hechicerías* (Logroño, 1529). Madrid, 1946.

Castro, Cristóbal de, and Ortega Morejón, Diego de. *Relación y declaración del modo que este valle de Chincha y sus comarcanos se governaron. . . .* (1558). In *Quellen zur Kulturgeschichte des präkolumbinischen Amerika*, edited by H. Trimborn, 236–246. Stuttgart, 1938.

Cicero, Marcus Tullius. *De natura deorum*. Edited by A. S. Pease. Cambridge, Mass., 1955; reprint Darmstadt, 1968.

Cieza de León, Pedro. *Parte primera de la Chrónica del Perú* (Seville, 1553). Edited by F. Pease, with the title *Crónica del Perú. Primera parte*. 2d ed., corrected. Lima, 1984.

————. *Parte Primera de la Chrónica del Perú*. Antwerp, 1554.

————. *Crónica del Perú. Segunda Parte* (before 1554). Edited by F. Cantù. Lima, 1985.

————. *Crónica del Perú. Tercera Parte* (before 1554). Edited by F. Cantù. Lima, 1987.

Ciruelo, Pedro. *A treatise reproving all superstitions and forms of witchcraft* (first edition in Spanish; Alcalá, c. 1530). Translated by Eugene A. Maio and D'Orsay W. Pearson. Rutherford, c. 1977.

Cobo, Bernabé. *Historia del nuevo mundo* (1653). Edited by F. Mateos. Biblioteca de autores españoles, vols. 91–92. Madrid, 1964.

————. See J. H. Rowe, "An Account of the Shrines" (1979).

Covarrubias Horozco, Sebastian de. *Tesoro de la lengua castellana o española* (Madrid, 1611). Madrid, 1979.

Cuzco. *Acta de Fundación* (1534). In *Francisco Pizarro. Testimonio. Documentos oficiales, cartas y escritos varios*, edited by G. Lohmann Villena, 163–167. Madrid, 1986.

————. *Libro primero de cabildos*. See R. Rivera Serna (1965).

————. *Relación de las fiestas que en la ciudad del Cuzco se hicieron . . . Año de 1610*. See *Relación de las fiestas. . . .*

Diez de San Miguel, Garci. *Visita hecha a la provincia de Chucuito por Garci Diez de San Miguel en el año 1567*. Edited by W. Espinoza Soriano and J. V. Murra. Lima, 1964.

Doctrina Christiana y Catecismo para Instrucción de los Indios . . . Compuesto por Auctoridad del Concilio Provincial que se celebró en la Ciudad de los Reyes . . . (Lima, 1584). Madrid, 1985.

Domingo de Santo Tomás. *Grammática o arte de la lengua general de los Indios de los Reynos del Perú* (Valladolid, 1560). Lima, 1951.

————. *Lexicon o vocabulario de la lengua general del Perú* (Valladolid, 1560). Lima, 1951.

Esquivel y Navia, Diego de. *Noticias cronológicas de la gran ciudad del Cuzco* (1749). Lima, 1980.

Estete, Miguel de. *Relación del viaje que hizo el señor capitán Hernando Pizarro por mandado de su hermano desde el pueblo de Caxamarca a Parcama y de allí a Xauxa*. In Francisco Xérez, *Verdadera relación* (1534).

[Estete, Miguel de]. *Noticia del Perú* (1535?). Colección de libros y documentos referentes a la historia del Perú, 2d ser., vol. 8. Lima, 1924.

Falcón, Francisco. *Representación hecha por el licenciado Francisco Falcón en el concilio provincial, sobre los daños y molestias que se hacen a los Indios* (1567). Colección de libros y documentos referentes a la historia del Perú, vol. 9, 133–176. Lima, 1918.

Fontes Iudaeorum Regni Castellae. Vol. 2, *El Tribunal de la Inquisición en el Obispado de Soria (1486–1502).* Edited by C. Carrete Parrondo. Salamanca, 1985.

Garcia, Gregorio. *Origen de los Indios de el Nuevo Mundo e Indias Occidentales* (Valencia, 1607; expanded version, Madrid, 1729). Edited by F. Pease. Mexico City, 1981.

———. *Predicación del Santo Evangelio en el Nuevo Mundo, viviendo los Apostoles.* Baeza, 1625.

Garcilaso de la Vega. See Vega, Garcilaso de la.

Gasca, Pedro de la. *Descripción del Perú* (1553). Edited and translated by J. M. Barnadas. Universidad Catolica "Andres Bello," Caracas, 1976.

[Gasca, Pedro de la]. *La Visitación de los Yndios Chupachos* (1549). In Iñigo Ortíz de Zúñiga, *Visita de la Provincia de León de Huanuco en 1562*, vol. 1, 289–310 and in M. Helmer (1955–1956).

Gonzalez Holguin, Diego. *Vocabulario de la lengua general de todo el Perú llamada lengua Qquichua o del Inca* (Lima, 1608). Lima, 1952.

Guaman Poma de Ayala. *Nueva crónica y buen gobierno* (1615). Edited by J. V. Murra, R. Adorno, and J. Urioste. Madrid, 1987.

Hernández Principe, Rodrigo. *Visitas de Idolatrías* (1621–1622). In *Cultura Andina y represión. Procesos y visitas de idolatrías y hechicerías, Cajatambo siglo XVII*, edited by P. Duviols, 461–507. Cuzco, 1986.

Herrera y Tordesillas, Antonio de. *Historia general de los hechos de los Castellanos en las islas y tierra firme del Mar Océano escrita por Antonio de Herrera y Tordesillas, cronista de Castilla y Mayor de las Indias. Decada Quinta.* Madrid, 1615.

Huarochiri. See *Runa yndio.*

Huarte de San Juan, Juan. *Examen de ingenios para las ciencias* (Baeza, 1575). Edited by Estéban Torre. Madrid, 1977.

Idolatrías de los indios huachos y yauyos. See C. Romero (1918).

Información hecha en el Cuzco por orden del Rey y encargo del Virrey Martín Enriquez acerca de las costumbres que tenían los Incas. . . . (1582). In *Gobernantes del Perú, Cartas y Papeles, Siglo XVI . . .* , edited by R. Levillier, vol. 9, 268–288. Madrid, 1929.

John of the Cross, *Vida y obras completas de San Juan de la Cruz.* Biography by Crisogono de Jesús, edited by Matias del Niño Jesus; works edited by Lucinio Ruano. Biblioteca de autores cristianos, vol. 15. Madrid, 1973.

Josephus. *Jewish Antiquities.* Edited and translated by H. St.J. Thackeray. Cambridge, Mass., 1978.

Justicia 413: Conflicts over Coca Fields in XVIth Century Peru (1558–1567). Edited by M. Rostworowski de Diez Canseco. Memoirs of the Museum of Anthropology, University of Michigan, no. 21. Ann Arbor, 1988.

Kramer, Heinrich, and James Sprenger. *The Malleus Maleficarum*. Translated by Montague Summers. London, 1928; reprint New York, 1971.

Las Casas, Bartolomé de. *Del unico modo de atraer a todos los pueblos a la verdadera religión* (c. 1536/1537). Spanish translation introduced by A. Millares Carlo and L. Hanke, Mexico City, 1975.

——. *Apologética Historia* (before 1559). Edited by E. O'Gorman. Mexico City, 1967.

——. *Memorial del obispo Fray Bartolomé de las Casas y Fray Domingo de Santo Tomás, en nombre de los Indios del Perú, contra la perpetuidad* (c. 1560). In *Obras escogidas de Fray Bartolomé de las Casas*, vol. 5, *Opusculos, cartas y memoriales*, edited by J. Pérez de Tudela y Bueso, Biblioteca de autores españoles, vol. 112, 465–468. Madrid, 1958.

——. *Los Tesoros del Perú* (c. 1561). Latin text edited and translated by A. Losada. Madrid, 1958.

——. *Tratado de las doce dudas* (1564). In *Obras escogidas de Fray Bartolomé de las Casas*, vol. 5, *Opusculos, cartas y memoriales*, edited by J. Pérez de Tudela y Bueso, Biblioteca de autores españoles, vol. 112, 478–536. Madrid, 1958.

Leone Ebreo. *La traduzión del Indio de los Tres Dialogos de Amor hecha de Italiano en Español por Garcilaso de la Vega . . .* (Madrid, 1590). Edited by C. Saenz de Santa Maria. Biblioteca de autores españoles, vol. 132. Madrid, 1965.

León Pinelo, Antonio de. *El Paraiso en el Nuevo Mundo. Comentario Apologético, Historia Natural y Peregrina de las Indias Occidentales Islas de Tierra Firme del Mar Océano*. Edited by R. Porras Barrenechea. Lima, 1943.

Liber Sapientiae Salomonis. In *Biblia Sacra iuxta vulgatam versionem*, edited by R. Weber, O.S.B. and others, vol. 2, 1003–1028. Stuttgart, 1969.

Lima. Acts of Provincial Councils. Edited by R. Vargas Ugarte, under the title *Concilios Limenses 1551–1772*. Lima, 1951–1954.

López de Gómara, Francisco. *Hispania Victrix. Primera y segunda parte de la historia general de las Indias* (Medina del Campo, 1553). Edited by P. Guibelalde. Madrid, 1965.

Luis de León, Fr. *The Original Poems*. Edited by E. Sarmiento. Manchester, 1972.

Madrigal, Alfonso de (El Tostado). *Sobre el Eusebio. Libro de las diez questiones vulgares. Libro en respuesta de quatro questiones*. Salamanca, 1506–1507.

Mariana, Juan de. *Historia general de España, compuesta primero en Latín, despues vuelta al Castellano* (Toledo, 1601). Biblioteca de autores españoles, vols. 30–31. Madrid, 1950.

Matienzo, Juan de. *Gobierno del Perú* (1567). Edited by G. Lohmann Villena. Lima, 1967.

Mena, Cristóbal de. See A. Pogo, "The Anonymous *La conquista del Perú*" (1928–1930).

Mena, Juan de. *Laberinto de Fortuna* (1444). Edited by L. Vasvari Fainberg. Madrid, 1976.

Menasseh ben Israel. *Origen de los Americanos, esto es Esperanza de Israel* (Amsterdam, 5410, C.E. 1650). Madrid, 1881.

Molina, Cristóbal de (of Cuzco). *Relación de las fábulas y ritos de los Incas* (1573).

In C. de Molina and C. de Albornoz, *Fábulas y mitos de los incas*, edited by
H. Urbano and P. Duviols. Madrid, 1989.

[Molina, Cristóbal de (of Santiago)]. See Segovia, Bartolomé de.

Montesinos, Fernando de. *Memorias antiguas historiales y políticas del Perú, por el
licenciado D. Fernando Montesinos seguidas de las informaciones acerca del señorío de
los Incas hechas por mandado de D. Francisco de Toledo . . .* (1644 and 1571 respectively). Edited by M. Jiménez de la Espada. Madrid, 1882.

———. *Anales del Perú* (c. 1644). Edited by V. Maurtua. Madrid, 1906.

———. *Ophir de España. Memorias historiales i políticas del Pirú, vaticinios de su descubrimiento y conversión* (1644). Seville, Biblioteca Universitaria MS. 332/35.

Monumenta Peruana. Vols. 1–6. Edited by A. de Engaña. Rome, 1954–1974.

Murúa, Martín de. *Historia del origen y genealogía real de los Reyes Incas del Perú*
(1590). Edited by C. Bayle. Madrid, 1946.

———. *Historia general del Perú, origen y descendencia de los Incas* (c. 1611). Edited
by M. Ballesteros Gaibrois. Madrid, 1962.

Nouvelles certaines des isles du Pérou (Lyon, 1534); known as *Relación francesa.* In
Las relaciones primitivas de la conquista del Perú, ed. R. Porras Barrenechea, 69–
78. Paris, 1937.

Ocampo, Florián de. *Las quatro partes enteras de la crónica de España.* Zamora, 1541.
See Alfonso X el Sabio.

———. *Los quatro libros primeros de la corónica general de España.* Zamora, 1543.

Ocaña, Diego de. *Un viage fascinante por la America Hispana del siglo XVII* (1599–
1605). Edited by Arturo Alvarez. Madrid, 1969.

Oliva, Anello. *Historia del Perú y varones insignes en santidad de la Compañia de Jesús*
(1631). Edited by J. F. Pozos Varela and L. Varela y Orbegoso. Lima, 1895.

Oré, Luis Jerónimo. *Symbolo catolico indiano, en el qual se declaran los misterios de la
Fé. . . .* Lima, 1598.

Ortíz de Zúñiga, Iñigo. *Visita de la provincia de León de Huanuco en 1562.* Edited
by J. V. Murra. Huanuco, 1972.

Osuna, Francisco de. *The Third Spiritual Alphabet* (Toledo, 1527). Translated by
Mary E. Giles. New York, 1981.

Oviedo y Valdés, Gonzalo Fernández de. *Corónica de las Indias. La hystoria general
de las Indias agora nuevamente impressa, corregida y emendada. 1547 con la conquista
del Perú. Primera parte de la hystoria natural y general de las Indias yslas y tierra
firme del mar océano.* Salamanca, 1547.

Pachacuti Yamqui, Joan de Santacruz. *Relación de antiguedades deste Reyno del Pirú*
(early seventeenth century). Biblioteca Nacional, Madrid, MS. 3169, fols.
131–174. In *Tres relaciones de antiguedades peruanas.* Edited by M. Jiménez de la
Espada, 229–328. Madrid, 1879.

*Parecer de Yucay: Copia de una carta . . . donde se trata el verdadero y legitimo dominio
de los Reyes de España sobre el Perú y se impugna la opinión del Padre Fray Bartolomé
de las Casas* (1571). Colección de documentos inéditos para la historia de España, vol. 13, 425–469. Madrid, 1848. See M. Mustapha, "Encore le Parecer
de Yucay" (1977).

Peña Montenegro, Alonso de la. *Itinerario para párrocos de Indios, en que se tratan las materias mas particulares tocantes a ellos, para su buena administración*. Madrid, 1668.

Pérez Bocanegra, Juan. *Ritual, formulario e institución de curas para administrar a los naturales de este Reyno los sanctos sacramentos*. . . . Lima, 1631.

Pizarro, Hernando. *Relación de Hernando Pizarro acerca de la conquista* (1533). Colección de libros y documentos referentes a la historia del Perú, 2d ser., vol. 3, 167–180. Lima, 1920.

Pizarro, Pedro. *Relación del descubrimiento y conquista del Perú* (1572). Edited by G. Lohmann Villena. Lima, 1978.

Polo de Ondegardo, Juan. *Copia de unos capitulos de una carta del licenciado Polo, vecino de la ciudad de La Plata, para el doctor Francisco Hernández de Liébana* (c. 1560). Colección de libros y documentos referentes a la historia del Perú, vol. 4, 153–160. Lima, 1917.

———. *Informe del Licenciado Juan Polo de Ondegardo al Licenciado Briviesca de Muñatones sobre la Perpetuidad de las encomiendas in el Perú* (1561). In *Revista Historica* (Lima) 13 (1940): 124–196.

———. *Notables daños de no guardar a los indios sus fueros* (1571). In Polo de Ondegardo, *El mundo de los incas*, edited by L. González and A. Alonso. Madrid, 1990.

———. *Los errores y supersticiones de los indios sacadas del tratado y averiguación que hizo el Licenciado Polo*. In *Doctrina Christiana y Catecismo para Instrucción de los Indios . . . compuesto por Autoridad del Concilio Provincial que se celebró en la Ciudad de Los Reyes . . .* (Lima, 1584). Madrid, 1985, fols. 7–16.

[Polo de Ondegardo, Juan]. *Del linage de los Incas y como conquistaron* (1571?). Colección de libros y documentos referentes a la historia del Perú, vol. 4, 45–94. Lima, 1917.

———. *Instrucción contra las ceremonias y ritos que usan los Indios*. . . . In *Doctrina Christiana* (Lima, 1584), Madrid, 1985, fols. 1–5.

Quipucamayos de Vaca de Castro: Collapiña, Supno y otros Quipucamayos. *Relación de la descendencia, gobierno y conquista de los Incas* (1542 and later). Edited by J. J. Vega. Lima, 1974.

Quiroga, Pedro de. *Libro intitulado coloquios de la verdad* (c. 1562). Seville, 1922.

Ramos Gavilán, Alonso. *Historia del Santuario de Nuestra Señora de Copacabana* (Lima, 1621). Edited by I. Prado Pastor. Lima, 1988.

Relación de las constumbres antiguas de los naturales del Perú (Relación anónima) (c. 1590). In *Crónicas peruanas de interés indígena*, edited by E. Barba, Biblioteca de autores españoles, vol. 209. Madrid, 1968.

Relación de las fiestas que en el Cuzco se hizieron por la beatificación del . . . Padre Ignacio de Loyola . . . 1610. Edited by C. Romero. In his *Los origenes del Periodismo en el Perú*, 13–21. Lima, 1940.

Relación francesa de la conquista del Perú. See *Nouvelles certaines* (1534).

Relación de las guacas del Cuzco. See J. H. Rowe, "An Account of the Shrines" (1979).

Relación Samano-Xerez. See Joan de Samano.

Religiosos Agustinos. *Relación de la religión y ritos del Perú hecha por los primeros religiosos Agustinos que allí pasaron . . .* (1560). Colección de documentos inéditos relativos al descubrimiento, conquista y colonización de las posesiones españolas en América y Occeania, vol. 3, 5–58. Madrid, 1865.

Ricardo, Antonio. *Vocabulario y phrasis en la lengua general de los Indios del Perú, llamada Quichua y en la lengua española* (Lima, 1586). Lima, 1951.

Román, Jerónimo. *Repúblicas del Mundo, Divididas en XXVII Libros*. Medina del Campo, 1575. Rev. ed., Salamanca, 1595.

Ruiz de Arce, Juan. *Relación de los servicios en Indias de don Juan Ruiz de Arce, conquistador del Perú* (after 1542). Edited by A. del Solar y Taboada and J. de Rujula y Ochotorena, marqués de Ciadoncha. *Boletín de la Real Academia de Historia* (Madrid) 102 (1933): 327–384.

Runa yndio niscap Machoncuna naupa pacha . . . (c. 1608). Edited by G. L. Urioste. *Hijos de Pariya Qaqa: La Tradición Oral de Waru Chiri (Mitología, Ritual y Constumbres)*. Syracuse, 1983.

Runa yndio niscap Machoncuna naupa pacha . . . (c. 1608). Edited by G. Taylor. *Ritos y tradiciones de Huarochiri del siglo XVII. Estudio biografico sobre Francisco de Avila de Antonio Acosta*. Lima, 1987.

Salazar, Antonio. *Relación sobre el periodo de gobierno de los virreyes Don Francisco de Toledo y Don Garcia Hurtado de Mendoza* (1596). Colección de documentos inéditos relativos al descubrimiento, conquista y organizacion de las antiguas posesiones españolas de América y Oceania, vol. 8, 212–421. Madrid, 1867.

Salinas y Cordova, Buenaventura de. *Memorial de las Historias del Nuevo Mundo Pirú* (Lima, 1630). Lima, 1957.

Samano, Joan de. *Relación* (1525?). In *Las relaciones primitivas de la conquista del Perú*, edited by R. Porras Barrenechea, 63–68. Paris, 1937.

Sanchez de Vercial, Clemente. *Libro de los exemplos por a. b. c.* (1421). Edited by J. E. Keller. Madrid, 1961.

Sancho, Pedro. *An account of the conquest of Peru* (1534). Translated (from Ramusio, *Viaggi*) by P. A. Means. New York, 1969.

Santillán, Hernando de. *Relación del origen, descendencia, politica y gobierno de los Incas* (after 1553). In *Crónicas peruanas de intéres indígena*, edited by E. Barba. Biblioteca de autores españoles, vol. 209. Madrid, 1968.

Santillana, Iñigo Lopez de Mendoza, marqués de. *Comedieta de Ponça* (1435). Edited by M.P.A. Kerkhof. Madrid, 1987.

———. *Canciones y Decires*. Edited by V. Garcia de Diego. Madrid, 1968.

Sarmiento de Gamboa, Pedro. *Historia Indica* (1572). Edited by C. Saenz de Santa Maria. Biblioteca de autores españoles, vol. 135, 189–279. Madrid, 1965.

[Segovia, Bartolomé de]. *Relación de muchas cosas acaesidas en el Perú . . . en la conquista y población destos reinos* (1553; formerly attributed to Cristóbal de Molina of Santiago). In *Crónicas peruanas de intéres indígena*, edited by E. Barba, Biblioteca de autores españoles, vol. 209, 57–95. Madrid, 1968.

Señores que sirvieron al Inga Yupangui y a Topainga Yupangui, a Guainacapac y a Huascar Inga. *Relación del Origen e Gobierno que los Ingas tuvieron* (after 1581). In *Informaciones sobre el antiguo Perú*, Colección de libros y documentos referentes a la historia del Perú, 2d ser., vol. 3, 57–86. Lima, 1920.

Siguenza, José de. *Historia de la Orden de San Jerónimo* (1595–1605). Nueva biblioteca de autores españoles, vols. 8 and 12. Madrid, 1907; 1909.

Spinoza, Benedict. *Opera*. Vols. 1–4. Edited by C. Gebhardt. Heidelberg, 1924.
———. *The Collected Works*. Vol. 1. Edited and translated by E. Curley. Princeton, 1985.
———. *A Theologico-Political Treatise* (Original Latin text, Hamburg, 1670) and *Correspondence*. Translated by R.H.M. Elwes. New York, 1951; 1955.
Suarez, Francisco. *Doctoris Francisci Suarez Granatensis e Societate Jesu . . . partis secundae Summae Theologiae tractatus tertius De Anima* (Lyons 1621). Reproduced in *Francisco Suarez de Anima*, edited by S. Castellote, vol. 1. Madrid, 1978.
Titu Cusi Yupanqui. *Relación de la conquista del Perú* (1570). Edited by F. Carillo. Lima, 1973.
Toledo, Francisco de. *Informaciones acerca del señorío de los Incas* (1571). See Fernando Montesinos (1882).
———. *Informaciones sobre los Incas (1570–1572)*. See R. Levillier (1940).
Trujillo, Diego de. *Una relación inédita de la conquista. La crónica de Diego de Trujillo* (1571). Edited by R. Porras Barrenechea. Lima, 1948.
Vega, Garcilaso de la, el Inca. *Primera Parte de los Comentarios reales de los Incas* (Lisbon, 1609) and *Historia general del Perú* (Cordoba, 1617). Edited by C. Saenz de Santa Maria. Biblioteca de autores españoles, vols. 133–135. Madrid, 1960–1965.
Villagomez, Pedro de. *Carta pastoral de exortación e instrucción contra las idolatrias de los Indios del arcobispado de Lima* (Lima, 1649). Colección de libros y documentos referentes a la historia del Perú, vol. 12. Lima, 1919.
Villena, Enrique de. *Tratado de la consolación*. Edited by D. C. Carr. Madrid, 1976.
Vitoria, Francisco de. *Relectio de Indis o libertad de los Indios* (1539; first ed. Lyon, 1557). Edited and translated by L. Pereña and J. M. Perez Prendes. Madrid, 1967.
Xérez, Francisco de. *Verdadera relación de la conquista del Perú y provincia del Cuzco llamada Nueva Castilla* (Seville, 1534). Edited by C. Bravo. Madrid, 1985.
Zárate, Agustín de. *Historia del descubrimiento y conquista del Perú con las cosas naturales que señaladamente allí se hallan y los sucessos que ha avido* (Antwerp, 1555). Biblioteca de autores españoles, vol. 26. Madrid, 1947. See also M. Bataillon (1963).

II. Secondary Works

Works referred to only once or not central to the main themes of this book are cited in full in the relevant footnotes but not here.

Acosta, A. "Francisco de Avila, Cuzco 1573 (?)—Lima 1647." In *Runa yndio* (1987): 551–616.
Adorno, R. "Las otras fuentes de Guaman Poma: sus lecturas Castellanas." *Historica* (Lima) 2, no. 2 (1978): 137–158.
———. *Guaman Poma: Writing and Resistance in Colonial Peru*. Austin, 1986.
Adorno, R., ed. *From Oral to Written Expression: Native Andean Chronicles of the Early Colonial Period*. Syracuse, 1982.

Allen, C. J. *The Hold Life Has: Coca and Cultural Identity in an Andean Community*. Washington, D.C., 1988.

Allen, D. C. *The Legend of Noah: Renaissance Rationalism in Art, Science and Letters*. Urbana, 1949.

Andersson, T. M. "Lore and Literature in a Scandinavian Conversion Episode: King Olav and Dala-Guthbrand in Snorri's *Heimskringla*." In *Idee, Gestalt, Geschichte. Festschrift für Klaus von See*, edited by G. W. Weber, 261–284. 1989.

Araníbar, C. "Notas sobre la necropompa entre los Incas." *Revista del Museo Nacional* (Lima) 36 (1969–1970): 108–142.

Arguedas, José Maria. *Relatos completos*. Madrid, 1983.

Assadourian, C. S. "Las rentas reales, el buen gobierno y la hacienda de Dios: el parecer de 1568 de Fray Francisco Morales sobre la reformacion de las Indias temporal y espiritual." *Historica* (Lima) 9 (1985): 75–130.

Aveni, A., and G. Urton, eds. *Ethnoastronomy and Archaeoastronomy in the American Tropics*. Annals of the New York Academy of Sciences, vol. 385. New York, 1982.

Bandelier, A. F. *The Islands of Titicaca and Koati*. New York, 1910.

Baron, S. W. *A Social and Religious History of the Jews: Late Middle Ages and Era of European Expansion, 1200–1650*. Volume 10, *On the Empire's Periphery*. New York, 1965.

Bastien, J. *Mountain of the Condor: Metaphor and Ritual in an Andean Ayllu*. Prospect Heights, 1985.

Bataillon, M. *Erasmo y España*. Mexico City, 1950.

———. "Zárate ou Lozano? Pages retrouvées sur la religion péruvienne." *Caravelle* 1 (1963): 1–28.

———. *Estudios sobre Bartolomé de Las Casas*. Madrid, 1976.

Beinart, H. "Jewish Witnesses for the Prosecution of the Spanish Inquisition." In *Essays in Honour of Ben Beinart*, vol. 1, 37–46. Cape Town, 1978.

———. "The Spanish Inquisition and a *Converso* Community in Extremadura." *Medieval Studies* (Toronto) 43 (1981): 445–71.

Bermejo-Martínez, E. *La pintura de los primitivos Flamencos en España*. Madrid, 1980.

Berthelot, J. "L'exploitation des métaux précieux au temps des Incas." *Annales. Économies, sociétés, civilisations* (Paris) 33, nos. 5–6 (1978): 948–966.

Borchgrave d'Altena, J. de. "La messe de Saint Grégoire." *Bulletin des Musées Royaux des Beaux Arts* (May–June 1959): 3–34.

Bosque, A. de. *Quentin Metsys*. Brussels, 1975.

Bouysse-Cassagne, T. *La identidad aymara. Approximación histórica, siglo XV, siglo XVI*. La Paz, 1987.

———. "Le jeu des hommes et des dieux: les Colla et le contrôle de l'île Titicaca." *Cahiers des Amériques Latines* (Paris) 6 (1987): 61–91.

Bouysse-Cassagne, T., with P. Bouysse. *Lluvias y Cenizas. Dos Pachacuti en la Historia*. La Paz, 1988.

Brading, D. A. "The Incas and the Renaissance: The *Royal Commentaries* of Inca Garcilaso de la Vega." *Journal of Latin American Studies* 18 (1986): 1–23.

Brennan, R. E. "The Thomist concept of Imagination." *New Scholasticism* 15 (1941): 149–161.

Bundy, M. W. *The Theory of Imagination in Classical and Medieval Thought*. University of Illinois Studies in Language and Literature, no. 12. Urbana, 1927.

Burkert, W. "Air-Imprints or Eidola: Democritus' Aetiology of Vision." *Illinois Classical Studies* 2 (1977): 97–109.

Busto Duthuburu, J. A. del. "Tres conversos en la captura de Atahualpa." *Revista de Indias* 27 (1967): 427–442.

Camille, M. *The Gothic Idol: Ideology and Image-Making in Medieval Art*. Cambridge, 1989.

Caro Baroja, J. *The World of the Witches*. Chicago, 1965.

Carrete Parrondo, C. See *Fontes Judaeorum* (1985).

Chang-Rodriguez, R. "Writing as Resistance: Peruvian History and the *Relación* of Titu Cusi Yupanqui." In *From Oral to Written Expression: Native Andean Chronicles of the Early Colonial Period*, edited by R. Adorno, 41–64.

Christian, W., Jr. *Apparitions in Late Medieval and Renaissance Spain*. Princeton, 1981.

———. *Local Religion in Sixteenth Century Spain*. Princeton, 1981.

Cirac Estopañán, S. *Los procesos de hechicerías en la Inquisición de Castilla la Nueva: Tribunales de Toledo y Cuenca*. Madrid, 1942.

Condori, B. and Gow, R. *Kay Pacha*. Cuzco, 1982.

Cooke, J. D. "Euhemerism: A Medieval Interpretation of Classical Paganism." *Speculum* 2 (1927): 396–410.

Cotarelo y Mori, E. *Don Enrique de Villena. Su vida y obras*. Madrid, 1896.

Dearborn, D. S. and K. J. Schreiber. "Houses of the Rising Sun." In *Time and Calendars in the Inca Empire*, edited by M. S. Ziolkowski and R. M. Sadowski, 49–76. Oxford, 1989.

De Dieu, J.-P. "The Inquisition and Popular Culure in New Castile." In *Inquisition and Society in Early Modern Europe*, edited by S. Haliczer, 129–146. London, 1987.

Dillehay, T. D. "Tawantinsuyu. Integration of the Chillon Valley, Peru. A case of Inca geo-political mastery." *Journal of Field Archeology* 4 (1977): 397–405.

Dillon, M. and T. Abercrombie. "The Destroying Christ: An Aymara Myth of Conquest." In *Rethinking History and Myth: Indigenous South American Perspectives on the Past*, edited by J. D. Hill, 50–77. Urbana, 1988.

Domínguez Ortiz, A., and B. Vincent. *Historia de los moriscos. Vida y tragedia de una minoría*. Madrid, 1978.

Dronke, P. *Dante and Medieval Latin Traditions*. Cambridge, 1986.

Durand, J. "La biblioteca del Inca." *Nueva Revista de Filología Hispánica* 2 (1948): 239–264.

———. "Sobre la biblioteca del Inca." *Nueva Revista de Filología Hispánica* 3 (1949): 166–170.

———. "Garcilaso between the World of the Incas and That of Renaissance Concepts." *Diogenes* 43 (1969): 14–21.

———. "Perú y Ophir en Garcilaso Inca, el Jesuita Pineda y Gregorio Garcia." *Historica* (Lima) 3, no. 2 (1979): 35–55.

Duviols, P. "Les sources religieuses du chroniqueur péruvien Fray Martín de Murúa." *Annales de la Faculté des Lettres d'Aix* 36 (1962): 267–277.

――――. "La visite des idolatries de Concepción de Chupas (Pérou 1614)." *Journal de la Société des Américanistes* 55 (1966): 497–510.

――――. *La lutte contre les religions autochtones dans le Pérou colonial. L'extirpacion de l'idolatrie entre 1532 et 1660.* Lima, 1971.

――――. "La represión del paganismo andino y la expulsión de los moriscos." *Anuario de Estudios Americanos* 28 (1971): 201–207.

――――. "Huari y llacuaz, agricultores y pastores. Un dualismo prehispanico de oposición y complementaridad." *Revista del Museo Nacional* (Lima) 39 (1973): 153–191.

――――. "Une petite chronique retrouvée. Errores, ritos, supersticiones y ceremonias de los Indios de la provincia de Chinchaycocha." *Journal de la Société des Américanistes* 63 (1974–1976): 275–296.

――――. "La capacocha." *Allpanchis* (Cuzco) 9 (1976): 11–58.

――――. "Punchao, idolo mayor del Coricancha. Historia y tipología." *Antropología Andina* (Cuzco) no. 1–2 (1976): 156–183.

――――. "Camaquen upani: un concept animiste des anciens Péruviens." In *Amerikanistische Studien. Festschrift für Hermann Trimborn*, edited by R. Hartmann and U. Oberem, vol. 1, 132–144. St. Augustin, 1978.

――――. *Cultura andina y represión. Procesos y visitas de idolatrías y hechicerías, Cajatambo siglo XVII.* Cuzco, 1986.

――――. "Las cinco edades primitivas del Perú segun Guaman Poma de Ayala." In *Time and Calendars in the Inca Empire*, edited by M. S. Ziolkowski and R. M. Sadowski. Oxford, 1989.

Earls, J., and I. Silverblatt. "La realidad fisica y social en la cosmologia andina." *Proceedings of the 42nd International Congress of Americanists* 4 (1976): 299–325.

Edwards, J. "Elijah and the Inquisition: Messianic Prophecy among *Conversos* in Spain, c. 1500." *Nottingham Medieval Studies* 28 (1984): 79–94.

――――. "Religious Faith and Doubt in Late Medieval Spain: Soria *circa* 1450–1500." *Past and Present* 120 (1988): 3–25.

Elliott, J. H. *The Old World and the New.* Cambridge, 1970.

Engl, L. "La aparición del Sol al joven Inca Pachacutec en la fuente Susurpuquio." *Revista Española de Antropología Americana* (Madrid) 5 (1970): 123–134.

Espinoza Soriano, W. "La guaranga y la reducción de Huancayo: tres documentos inéditos de 1571 para la etnohistoria del Perú." *Revista del Museo Nacional* (Lima) 32 (1963): 8–90.

――――. "El primer informe etnologico sobre Cajamarca, ano de 1540." *Revista Peruana de Cultura* 11–12 (1967): 5–41.

――――. "Alonso Ramos Gavilán. Vida y obra del cronista de Copacabana." *Historia y Cultura* (Lima) 6 (1972): 121–194.

――――. "Copacabana del Collao. Un documento de 1548 para la etnohistoria andina." *Bulletin de l'Institut Français des Études Andines* (Lima) 1, no. 1 (1972): 1–15.

Fraker, C. F. "Abraham in the 'General Estoria.'" In *Alfonso X of Castile, the Learned King (1221–1284): An International Symposium-Harvard University, 17*

November 1984, edited by F. Marquez-Villanueva and C. A. Vega, Harvard Studies in Romance Languages, no. 43, 17–29. Cambridge, 1990.

Funkenstein, A. *Theology and the Scientific Imagination from the Middle Ages to the Seventeenth Century*. Princeton, 1986.

Gade, D. W. "Lightning in the Folklife and Religion of the Central Andes." *Anthropos. International Review of Anthropology and Linguistics* 78, (1983): 770–788. St. Augustin.

Gasparini, G., and L. Margolies. *Inca Architecture*. Bloomington, Ind., 1980.

Gilly, C. *Spanien und der Basler Buchdruck bis 1600. Ein Querschnitt durch die spanische Geistesgeschichte aus der Sicht einer europäischen Buchdruckerstadt*. Basel, 1985.

Ginzburg, C. *The Night Battles. Witchcraft and Agrarian Cults in the Sixteenth and Seventeenth Centuries*. New York, 1985.

———. *Ecstasies. Deciphering the Witches' Sabbath*. New York, 1991.

Gisbert, T. *Iconografía y mitos indígenas en el arte*. La Paz, 1980.

———. "Pachacamac y los dioses del Collao," *Historia y Cultura* (La Paz) 17 (1990): 105–121.

Goldberg, H. "The Dream Report as a Literary Device in Medieval Hispanic Literature." *Hispania* (Cincinnati) 66, (1983): 21–31.

Gonzalez Carré, E., and F. Rivera Pineda. "La muerte del Inca en Santa Ana de Tusi." *Bulletin de l'Institut Français des Études Andines* (Lima) 11, nos. 1–2 (1982), 19–36.

González, J. *La idea de Roma en la Historiografía Indiana*. Madrid, 1981.

Green, Otis H. *The Literary Mind of Medieval and Renaissance Spain*. Lexington, 1970.

Gregory, T. "Julian and the Last Oracle at Delphi." *Greek, Roman and Byzantine Studies* 24 (1983): 355–366.

Guillén, E. *Versión Inca de la Conquista*. Lima, 1974.

Hadot, P. "L'image de la Trinité dans l'âme chez Victorinus et chez Saint Augustin." *Studia Patristica* 6 (Texte und Untersuchungen 81), Berlin (1962): 409–442.

Haliczer, S., ed. *Inquisition and Society in Early Modern Europe*. London, 1987.

Hampe Martínez, T. "Lecturas de un jurista del siglo XVI." *Atenea. Revista de Ciencia, Arte y Literatura* (Concepcion, Chile) 455 (1987): 237–251.

———. *Don Pedro de la Gasca. Su obra política en España y América*. Lima, 1989.

Hanke, L. U. "The *Requerimiento* and Its Interpreters." *Revista de historia de America* 1 (1938): 25–34.

———. *Aristotle and the American Indians: A study in Race Prejudice in the Modern World*. Chicago, 1959.

Harrison, R. "Modes of Discourse: The *Relación de antiguedades deste reyno del Pirú* by Joan de Santacruz Pachacuti Yamqui Salcamaygua." In R. Adorno (1982), 65–99.

Helmer, M. "La *Visitación de los Yndios Chupachos*. Inka et encomendero." *Travaux de l'Institut Français des Études Andines* (Lima) 5 (1955–1956): 3–50.

Hemming, J. *The Conquest of the Incas*. New York, 1970.

Hemming, J., and E. Ranney. *Monuments of the Incas*. New York, 1982.

Hernández, M., M. Lemlij, L. Millones, A. Pendola, and M. Rostworowski. *Entre el mito y la historia. Psicoanalisis y pasado andino.* Lima, 1987.

Huertas Vallejos, L. *La religión en una sociedad rural andina. Siglo XVII.* Ayacucho, 1981.

Hyslop, J. *Inka Settlement Planning.* Austin, 1990.

Imbelloni, J. "La tradición peruana de las cuatro edades del mundo en una obra rarisima impresa en Lima en el año 1630." *Anales del Instituto de Etnografía* 5 (1944): 55–94.

Jiménez Borja, A. *Paracas.* Colección arte y tesoros del Perú, edited by J. A. de Lavallé and W. Lang. Lima, 1983.

Kenny, A. "Intellect and Imagination in Aquinas." In *The Anatomy of the Soul: Historical Essays in the Philosophy of Mind,* 62–80. Oxford, 1973.

Klein, R. "L'imagination comme vêtement de l'âme chez Marsile Ficin et Giordano Bruno." *Revue de métaphysique et de morale* 61 (1956): 18–39.

Kriegel, M. "La prise d'une décision: l'expulsion des Juifs d'Espagne en 1442." *Revue Historique* 260 (1978): 49–90.

Leonard, I. A. "On the Lima Book Trade." *Hispanic American Historical Review* 33 (1953): 511–525.

Levack, B. P. *The Witch-Hunt in Early Modern Europe.* New York, 1987.

Levillier, R. *Don Francisco de Toledo. Supremo organizador del Perú, 1515–1582.* Vol. 1, *Su vida, su obra.* Madrid, 1935. Vol. 2, *Sus informaciones sobre los Incas (1570–1572).* Buenos Aires, 1940.

Lida de Malkiel, M. R. *Juan de Mena. Poeta del prerenacimiento español.* Mexico City, 1950.

Lohmann Villena, G. "Juan de Matienzo, autor del *Gobierno del Perú.* Su personalidad y su obra." *Anuario de Estudios Americanos* 22 (1965): 767–886.

———. "La restitución por conquistadores y encomenderos: un aspecto de la incidencia Lascasiana en el Perú." *Anuario de Estudios Americanos* 23 (1966): 21–89.

———. "El licenciado Francisco Falcón (1521–1587). Vida, escritos y actuación de un procurador de los Indios." *Anuario de Estudios Americanos* 27 (1970): 131–194.

Lothrop, S. K. *The Inca Treasure as Depicted by Spanish Historians.* Los Angeles, 1938.

MacCormack, S. "Roma, Constantinopolis, the Emperor and his Genius." *Classical Quarterly* 25 (1975): 131–150.

———. "Antonio de la Calancha. Un Agustino del siglo XVII en el nuevo mundo." *Bulletin Hispanique* 84 (1982): 60–94.

———. "From the Sun of the Incas to the Virgin of Copacabana." *Representations* 8 (1984): 30–60.

———. "The Fall of the Incas: A Historiographical Dilemma." *History of European Ideas* 6 (1985): 421–445.

———. "The Heart Has Its Reasons: Predicaments of Missionary Christianity in Early Colonial Peru." *Hispanic American Historical Review* 65 (1985): 443–466.

———. "Atahualpa y el libro." *Revista de Indias* 48 (1988): 693–714.

———. "Pachacuti: Miracles, Punishments and Last Judgment. Visionary Past and Prophetic Future in Early Colonial Peru." *American Historical Review* 93 (1988): 960–1006.

———. *"Loca Sancta*: The Organization of Sacred Topography in Late Antiquity." In *The Blessings of Pilgrimage*, edited by R. Ousterhout, 7–40. Champaign, Ill., 1990.

McCown, C. C. *The Testament of Solomon, Edited from Manuscripts at Mount Athos, Bologna, Holkham Hall, Jerusalem, London, Milan, Paris and Vienna, with Introduction.* Leipzig, 1922.

MacKay, A. "Popular Movements and Pogroms in Fifteenth Century Castile." *Past and Present* 55 (1972): 33–67. Reprinted as No. 10 in MacKay, *Society, Economy and Religion in Late Medieval Castile.* London, 1987.

McKeon, R. *The Philosophy of Spinoza: The Unity of His Thought.* New York, 1928.

Mahoney, E. P. "Sense, Intellect and Imagination in Albert, Thomas and Siger." In *The Cambridge History of Later Medieval Philosophy*, edited by N. Kretzmann and others, 602–622. Cambridge, 1982.

Mannheim, B. "Poetic Form in Guaman Poma's Wariqsa Arawi." Postscript by R. T. Zuidema. *Amerindia* 11 (1986): 41–64.

———. *The Language of the Inca since the European Invasion.* Austin, 1990.

Marcus, R. "Las Casas Pérouaniste." *Caravelle* 7 (1966): 25–41.

Martin, L. "La biblioteca del Colegio de San Pablo (1568–1767), antecedente de la Biblioteca Nacional." *Fenix. Revista de la Biblioteca Nacional* (Lima) 21 (1971): 25–36.

Marzal, M. M. *Historia de la antropología indigenista: Mexico y Perú.* Lima, 1981

Masferer Kan, E. R. "Criterios de organización andina. Recuay siglo XVII." *Bulletin de l'Institut Français des Études Andines* 13, nos. 1–2 (1984): 47–61.

Maticorena Estrada, M. "Cieza de León en Sevilla y su muerte in 1554. Documentos." *Anuario de Estudios Americanos* 12 (1955): 615–672.

Mechoulan, H. *Menasseh ben Israel, Espérance d'Israel. Introduction, traduction et notes par Henri Mechoulan et Gerard Nahon.* Paris, 1979.

———. "Un révélateur de l'hispanité des juives d'Amsterdam au temps de Spinoza: *L'espejo de la vanidad del mundo* d'Abraham Pereyra (1671)." *Revue des Études Juives* 144 (1985): 81–92.

Mendizabal Losack, E. "Las dos versiones de Murua." *Revista del Museo Nacional* (Lima) 32 (1963): 153–185.

Menzel, D., and J. Rowe. "The Role of Chincha in Late Pre-Spanish Peru." *Nawpa Pacha* 4 (1966): 63–77.

Millas Vallicrosa, J. M. "El libro de Astrologia de Don Enrique de Villena." *Revista de Filologia Española* 27 (1943): 1–29.

Miro Quesada, A. *El Inca Garcilaso y otros estudios garcilasistas.* Madrid, 1971.

Momigliano, A. *Alien Wisdom: The Limits of Hellenization.* Cambridge, 1975.

Morris, C., and D. Thompson. *Huanuco Pampa: An Inca City and Its Hinterland.* New York, 1985.

Murra, J. V. "Rite and Crop in the Inca State," In *Culture in History. Essays in Honor of Paul Radin*, edited by S. Diamond, 393–407. New York, 1960.

———. *Formaciones económicas y politicas del mundo andino.* Lima, 1975.

Murra, J. V. "Aymara Lords and Their European Agents at Potosi." *Nova Americana* (Torino) 1 (1978): 231–243.

———. *The Economic Organization of the Inca State*. Greenwich, Conn., 1980.

Mustapha, M. "Encore le *Parecer de Yucay*. Essai d'attribution." *Ibero-Amerikanisches Archiv* 3, no. 2 (1977): 215–231.

Nader, H. *The Mendoza Family in the Spanish Renaissance, 1350–1550*. New Brunswick, N.J., 1979.

Nalle, S. "Popular religion in Cuenca on the Eve of the Catholic Reformation," In *Inquisition and Society*, ed. S. Haliczer (1987), 67–87.

Napoli, G. di. *L'immortalità dell'anima nel rinascimiento*. Turin, 1963.

Niles, S. *Callachaca: Style and Status in an Inca Community*. Iowa City, 1987.

Noreña, C. *Studies in Spanish Renaissance Thought*. The Hague, 1975.

Norton, F. J. *A Descriptive Catalogue of Printing in Spain and Portugal, 1501–1520*. Cambridge, 1978.

Olmos, E.M.A. *Santa Maria de los Inocentes y Desamaparados*. Valencia, 1968.

Opelt, I. "Griechische und Lateinische Bezeichnungen der Nicht-Christen. Ein terminologischer Versuch." *Vigiliae Christianae* 19 (1965): 1–22.

Ortiz Rescaniere, A. *De Adaneva a Inkarrí. Una vision indígena del Perú*. Lima, 1973.

Pagden, A. *The Fall of Natural Man: The American Indian and the Origins of Comparative Ethnology*. Cambridge, 1982.

———. *Spanish Imperialism and the Political Imagination*. New Haven, 1990.

Pease, F. *El Dios Creador Andino*. Lima, 1973.

———. "Garcilaso Andino." *Revista Historica* (Lima) 34 (1983–1984): 41–52.

Peritore, C. C. "La conoscenza e lo studio di Dante alla Corte Aragonese di Alfonso il Magnanimo e dei suoi successori." In *Dante nel Pensiero e nella Esegesi dei Secoli XIV e XV*, Atti del III Congresso Nazionale di Studi Danteschi, Melfi, 27 Settembre–2 Ottobre 1970, 423–432. Florence, 1975.

Peters, E. *Inquisition*. New York, 1988.

Pino Diaz, F. del. "Culturas clásicas y americanas en la obra del Padre Acosta." In *America y la España del Siglo XVI*, 327–362. Madrid, 1982.

Platt, T. "Acerca del sistema tributario pre-Toledano en el Alto Peru." *Avances* 1 (1978): 33–46.

———. "The Andean Soldiers of Christ. Confraternity Organisation, the Mass of the Sun and Regenerative Warfare in Rural Potosi (18th–20th Centuries)." *Journal de la Societé des Américanistes* 73 (1987): 139–191.

Pogo, A. "The Anonymous *La conquista del Perú* (Seville, April 1534) and the *Libro Ultimo del Sumario delle Indie Occidentali* (Venice, October 1534)." *Proceedings of the American Academy of Arts and Sciences* 64 (1928–1930): 177–286.

Porras Barrenechea, R. *Las relaciones primitivas de la conquista del Perú*. Paris, 1937.

———. "Crónicas perdidas, presuntas y olvidadas sobre la conquista del Perú." *Documenta* 2, no. 1 (1951): 179–243. Reprinted in Porras Barrenechea, *Los Cronistas del Perú*, (1986), 689–734.

———. *El Inca Garcilaso en Montilla, 1561–1614*. Lima, 1955.

———. *Los cronistas del Perú y otros ensayos*. Edited by F. Pease. Lima, 1986.

Post, C. R. *A History of Spanish Painting*. Vol. 14, *The Later Renaissance in Castile*. Cambridge, Mass., 1966.

Prado, Museo del. *Catálogo de las pinturas*. Introduction by A. E. Perez Sanchez. Madrid, 1986.

Quiroz, A. "The Expropriation of Portuguese New Christians in Spanish America, 1635–1649." *Ibero-Amerikanisches Archiv*, n.s. 11, no. 4 (1985): 407–465.

Randall, R. "Qoyllur Rit'i, an Inca Fiesta of the Pleiades: Reflections on Time and Space in the Andean World." *Bulletin de l'Institut Français des Études Andines* 11, nos. 1–2 (1982): 37–81.

Redmond, W. "Juan Espinoza Medrano: Prefacio al lector de la *Logica*." *Fenix. Revista de la Biblioteca Nacional* (Lima) 20 (1970): 74–80.

Redondi, P. *Galileo Heretic*. Princeton, 1987.

Rico, F. *Alfonso el Sabio y la "General Estoria."* Barcelona, 1984.

Rivera Serna, R. "Libro primero de cabildos de la ciudad del Cuzco." *Documenta* 4 (1965): 441–480.

Romero, C. "Idolatrías de los Indios Huachos y Yauyos." *Revista Histórica* (Lima) 6 (1918): 180–197.

Rostworowski de Diez Canseco, M. "Succession, Cooption to Kingship and Royal Incest among the Inca." *Southwestern Journal of Anthropology* 16, no. 4 (1960): 417–427.

———. "Los Ayarmaca." *Revista del Museo Nacional* (Lima) 36 (1969–1970): 58–101.

———. "Mercaderes del valle de Chincha en la época prehispanica. Un documento y unos comentarios." *Revista Española de Antropología Americana* 5 (1970): 135–177.

———. "El sitio arqueologico de Concon en el valle de Chillón: derrotero etnohistórico." *Revista del Museo Nacional* (Lima) 38 (1972): 315–326.

———. *Estructuras andinas de poder*. Lima, 1983.

———. *Historia del Tahuantinsuyu*. Lima, 1987.

———. 1988. See *Justicia 413*.

Round, N. G. "Renaissance Culture and Its Opponents in Fifteenth Century Castile." *Modern Language Review* 57 (1962): 204–215.

———. "Five Magicians, or the Uses of Literacy." *Modern Language Review* 64 (1969): 793–805.

Rowe, J. H. "Absolute Chronology in the Andean Area." *American Antiquity* 10 (1944–1945): 265–284.

———. *An Introduction to the Archaeology of Cuzco*. Papers of the Peabody Museum of American Archaeology and Ethnology, vol. 27, no.2. Cambridge, 1944.

———. "Eleven Inca Prayers from the Zithuwa Ritual." *Kroeber Anthropological Society Papers* 8–9 (1953): 82–99.

———. "The Origins of Creator Worship among the Incas." In *Culture in History: Essays in Honor of Paul Radin*, 408–429. New York, 1981. Orig. pub. 1960.

———. "Un memorial del gobierno de los Incas del año 1551." *Revista Peruana de Cultura* 9–10 (1966): 27–39.

Rowe, J. H. "An Account of the Shrines of Ancient Cuzco." *Ñawpa Pacha* 17 (1979): 1–80.

———. "Genealogia y rebelión en el siglo XVIII." *Revista Histórica* (Lima) 33 (1981–1982): 317–336.

———. "Las Circunstancias de la rebelión de Thupa Amaro en 1780." *Revista Histórica* (Lima) 34 (1983–1984): 119–140.

———. "La constitución Inca del Cuzco." *Histórica* (Lima) 9 (1985): 35–73.

———. "Probanza de los Incas nietos de conquistadores." *Histórica* (Lima) 9 (1985): 193–245.

———. "La mentira literaria en la obra de Martín de Murua." In *Libro de homenaje a Aurelio Miro Quesada Sosa*, vol. 2, 753–761. Lima, 1987.

Ryan, M. T. "Assimilating New Worlds in the Sixteenth and Seventeenth Centuries." *Comparative Studies in Society and History* 23 (1981): 519–538.

Sallnow, M. J. *Pilgrims of the Andes. Regional Cults in Cuzco*. Washington, D.C., 1987.

Salomon, F. "Chronicles of the Impossible: Notes on Three Peruvian Indigenous Historians." In *From Oral to Written Expression*, ed. R. Adorno (1982), 9–39.

———. *Native Lords of Quito in the Age of the Incas: The Political Economy of North Andean Chiefdoms*. Cambridge, 1986.

Schiff, M. "La première traduction espagnole de la Divine Comédie." In *Homenaje a Don Marcelino Menendez y Pelayo*, vol. 1, 268–307. Madrid, 1899.

———. *La bibliothèque du Marquis de Santillane*. Paris, 1905.

Scholem, G. *Sabbatai Sevi: The Mystical Messiah*. Princeton, 1973.

Servaas van Rooijen, A. J. *Inventaire des livres formant la bibliothèque de Benedict Spinoza, publié d'après un document inédit*. The Hague, 1889.

Seznec, J. *The Survival of the Pagan Gods: The Mythological Tradition and Its Place in Renaissance Humanism and Art*. Princeton, 1953.

Sherbondy, J. "El regadío, los lagos y los mitos de origen." *Allpanchis* (Cuzco) 20 (1982): 3–32.

———. *Mallqui: ancestros y cultivo de arboles en los Andes*. Proyecto FAO-Holanda/ INFOR GCP/PER/027/NET, Apoyo a las plantaciones forestales . . . , Documento de trabajo no. 5. Lima, 1986.

Sicroff, A. A. *Los estatutos de limpieza de sangre. Controversias entre los siglos XV y XVII*. Madrid, 1985.

Silverblatt, I. M. *Moon, Sun, and Witches: Gender Ideologies and Class in Inca and Colonial Peru*. Princeton, 1987.

———. "Political Memories and Colonizing Symbols: Santiago and the Mountain Gods of Colonial Peru." In *Rethinking History and Myth: Indigenous South American Perspectives on the Past*, edited by J. D. Hill, 174–194. Urbana, 1988.

Spalding, K. "Social Climbers: Changing Patterns of Mobility among the Indians of Colonial Peru." *Hispanic American Historical Review* 50 (1970): 645–664.

———. *De Indio a campesino. Cambios en la estructura social del Perú colonial*. Lima, 1974.

———. *Huarochiri: An Andean Society under Inca and Spanish Rule*. Stanford, 1984.

Stern, S. *Peru's Indian Peoples and the Challenge of Spanish Conquest. Huamanga to 1640*. Madison, Wis., 1982.

Szeminski, J. "Las generaciones del mundo segun Don Felipe Guaman Poma de Ayala." *Historica* (Lima) 7 (1983): 69–109.

———. "De la imagen de Wiraqucan segun las oraciones recogidas por Joan de Santacruz Pachacuti Yamqui Salcamaygua." *Histórica* (Lima) 9 (1985): 247–264.

———. *Un kuraka, un dios y una historia.* San Salvador de Jujuy, Argentina, 1987.

Tate, R. B. *Ensayos sobre la historiografía peninsular del siglo XV.* Madrid, 1970.

Taylor, G. "Camay, camac et camasca dans le manuscrit Quechua de Huarochiri." *Journal de la Société des Américanistes* 63 (1974–1976): 231–244.

———. "Supay." *Amerindia* 5 (1980): 47–63.

———. 1987. See *Runa yndio* (1987).

Taylor, R. *El Arte de la memoria en el Nuevo Mundo.* San Lorenzo de el Escorial, 1987.

Tello, J. C. "Idolatrías de los Indios Wancas." *Inca* 1, no. 3 (1932): 651–667.

Tibesar, A. *Franciscan Beginnings in Colonial Peru.* Washington, D.C., 1953.

Trexler, R. C. "Aztec Priests for Christian Altars: The Theory and Practice of Reverence in New Spain." In *Church and Community, 1200–1600: Studies in the History of Florence and New Spain,* 469–492. Rome, 1987.

Uhle, M. *Pachacamac. Report of the William Pepper M.D., Ll.D. Peruvian Expedition of 1896.* Philadelphia, 1903.

Urioste, J. See *Runa yndio* (1983).

Urton, G. *At the Crossroads of the Earth and the Sky.* Austin, 1981.

———. "La historia de un mito: Pacariqtambo y el origen de los Incas." *Revista Andina* 7, no. 1 (1989): 129–216.

———. *The History of a Myth. Pacaritambo and the Origin of the Inkas.* Austin, 1990.

Varón Gabai, R. "El Taki Onqoy: las raíces andinas de un fenómeno colonial." In *El retorno de las huacas. Estudios y documentos Sobre el Taki Onqoy. Siglo XVI,* edited by L. Millones, 331–405. Lima, 1990.

Vaz Dias, A. M., and W. G. van der Tak. "Spinoza, Merchant and Autodidact." *Studia Rosenthaliana* 16 (1982): 109–171.

Vigneras, L.-A. "Saint Thomas, Apostle of America." *Hispanic American Historical Review* 57 (1977): 82–90.

Villanueva Urteaga, H. "Documentos sobre Yucay en el siglo XVI." *Revista del Archivo Historico del Cuzco* 13 (1970): 1–148.

Wachtel, N. "Structuralisme et histoire: à propos de l'organisation sociale de Cuzco." *Annales. Économies, Sociétés, Civilisations* 21 (1966): 71–94.

———. *La vision des vaincus. Les indiens du Pérou devant la conqûete espagnole.* Paris, 1971.

———. *Sociedad e ideología. Ensayos de historia y antropología andinas.* Lima, 1973.

Walker, D. P. *Spiritual and Demonic Magic from Ficino to Campanella.* London, 1958.

Wedin, A. *El concepto de lo Incaico y las fuentes.* Studia historica Gothoburgensia. Upsala, 1966.

Wolf, A. *The Oldest Biography of Spinoza. Edited, with translation, introduction, annotations, etc., by —.* London, 1927.

Wolfson, H. A. *The Philosophy of Spinoza: Unfolding the Latent Processes of His Reasoning.* Cambridge, Mass., 1934.

――――. "The Internal Senses in Latin, Arabic and Hebrew Philosophic Texts." *Harvard Theological Review* 28 (1935): 69–133.

――――. "The Problem of the Souls of the Spheres from the Byzantine Commentaries on Aristotle through the Arabs and St. Thomas to Kepler." *Dumbarton Oaks Papers* 16 (1962): 65–93.

Yaranga Valderrama, A. "Taki Onqo ou la vision des vaincus au XVIe siecle." In *Les mentalités dans la Péninsule Ibérique et en Amérique Latine aux XVIè et XVIIè siècle. Actes du XIIIè Congres de la Société des Hispanistes Français . . . Tours 1977,* 119–179. Tours, 1978.

Yerushalmi, Y. H. *From Spanish Court to Italian Ghetto; Isaac Cardoso; A Study in Seventeenth Century Marranism and Jewish Apologetics.* Seattle, 1971.

Ziolkowski, M. S. "El calendario metropolitano Inca." In *Time and Calendars,* ed. M. S. Ziolkowski and R. M. Sadowski (1989), 129–166.

Ziolkowski, M. S., and R. M. Sadowski. "The Reconstruction of the Metropolitan Calendar of the Incas in the Period 1500–1571 A.D." In *Time and Calendars,* ed. M. S. Ziolkowski and R. M. Sadowski (1989), 167–196.

Ziolkowski, M. S., and R. M. Sadowski. eds. *Time and Calendars in the Inca Empire.* BAR International Series, vol. 479. Oxford, 1989.

Zuidema, R. T. *The Ceque System of Cuzco: The Social Organisation of the Capital of the Inca.* Leiden, 1964.

――――. "La parenté et le culte des ancêtres dans trois communautés péruviennes. Un compte rendu de 1622 par Hernandez Principe." *Signes et Lagages des Amériques. Recherches Amérindinnes au Quebec* 3, nos. 1–2 (1973): 129–145.

――――. "Shaft Tombs in the Inca Empire." *Journal of the Steward Anthropological Society* 9 (1977): 133–178.

――――. "El puente del rio Apurimac y el origen mitico de la villca." In *Amerikanistische Studien. Festschrift für Hermann Trimborn,* vol. 2, 322–334. St. Augustin, 1979.

――――. "El ushnu." *Revista de la Universidad Complutense* 28, no. 117 (1979): 317–362.

――――. "Catachillay: The Role of the Pleiades and of the Southern Cross and α and β Centauri in the Calendar of the Incas." In *Ethnoastronomy and Archaeoastronomy in the American Tropics,* edited by A. F. Aveni and G. Urton, 203–229. New York, 1982.

――――. "The Lion in the City: Symbols of Transition in Cuzco." *Journal of Latin American Lore* 9 (1983): 39–100.

――――. *La civilisation inca au Cuzco.* Paris, 1986. Transl. and rev. ed., *Inca Civilisation in Cuzco.* Austin, 1990.

Zuidema, R. T., and M. U. Quispe. "A Visit to God." *Bijdragen tot de Taal-, Land-, en Voldenkunde* (Leiden) 124 (1968): 22–39.

INDEX

accommodation, principle of, 261–263, 271f., 452–453

aclla (chosen woman of the Sun and the Inca), 65f. and n. 12, 66 n. 14, 78 n. 70, 112 n. 94, 149, 157, 424; acllahuasi, in Cuzco, 65 n. 12

Acosta, José de, on accommodation principle, 261–263; on barbarians, 266–267; and Bernabé Cobo, 394–396, 404; on cult of the dead, 29f.; demons and cultural inferiority, 276–277; and Garcilaso de la Vega, 336, 340 and n. 32, 359, 362, 373; on idolatry, 265–267; on imagination, 277–279; on Inca and Andean religion, 264ff.; on Jesuit church in Cuzco, 252; in Peru, 11; on Quechua language, 264; on supay, 255; writings of, 261

afterlife, Andean belief in, 89, 367

Albornoz, Cristóbal de: and Guaman Poma, 318–319; his list of shrines, 189; in Taqui Onqoy, 185

amauta, in Garcilaso, 335, 341, 344, 387

anan and urin (upper and lower), 120, 171–173, figs. 19–20, 197, 291, 310. See also llacuaz

Anthony (Saint), tempted, 30f., figs. 5–6, 87 and n. 10, 239, 436–437

apostle: in America, 52, 285, 285 n. 18, in Guaman Poma, 314, fig. 41, 318, 354–355, fig. 45, 364; image at Cacha, 312–313

Apurimac, 58, 74, 84, 103, 416

aravi (love and harvest song), 168 and n. 41, 175, 179, 319

Aristotle: on barbarians, 266; on sensation, reason, imagination, 16f., 24ff., 277, 280, 443–444; on society, 211; on virtue, 209, 209 n. 14

arpa (sacrificial food), 114; and arpay (to sacrifice), 112

Arriaga, José de, 384–388, 389, 406

Atahualpa: and Betanzos, 108, 130; in Cajamarca, 55, 309; and Catequil, 143; death of, 3, 6, 50, 65; inauguration of, 129–130, 132; lineage of, 352; and Pacha-

camac, 62–63; play about, 415; successors, 137–138; his treasure, 80

Augustine of Hippo, 380; and City of God, 230, 378; on conversion of Rome, 376; on soul and body, 17 n. 9, 134 and n. 73; on soul and city, 235; on witch of Endor, 229

Ausangate, creator at, 96

Avendaño, Fernando de, on causation, 403; on extirpation, 407, 408–409; sermons of, 375, 401

Avila, Francisco de, 284, 319, 389–390

Ayar brothers, 101, 110, 146 n. 18, 193

ayllu, 390–392, 407, 411, 413, 422–423, 429

Barrientos, Lope de, 36, 37, 39

Bartholomew. See apostle

behetría, in the Andes, 100, 102, 107

Betanzos, Juan de, 10; chronology, 114–115; on Coricancha and Cuzco, 112–114; creation myth, 108–112; in Cuzco, 81; Inca informants and, 108, 130; and initiation of young men, 115–117; and inauguration of Inca rulers, 120–131; vision of Inca Pachacuti, 287ff.

Bible, the: as history, 101; on religious evolution, 214; in Spinoza, 445–450

bulto, 68, 77–78, 77–78 nn. 67–70, 124, 124 nn. 21–22, 133. See also effigy; mummy

Cabello Valboa, Miguel: 281, 303f.; and image of Mama Ocllo, 134; and Las Casas, 312

Cacha, 100f., 312, 354, 364

Calancha, Antonio de la, 383, 386; allegory, 378–379; on Andean religion, 404; and Garcilaso, 375–377; and the Inquisition, 389; and Pachacamac, 375, 378–379

callpa, 303

capacocha, 94, 103 n. 36, 104 and n. 38, 112, 150, 151ff., 192, 199–200, 415–418, 419 and n. 66, 422; procession, 200–202; and redistribution, 201–202. See also human sacrifice

divination: in the Andes, 302–306, 399–400; in Chincha, 155; in Huamachuco, 141, 144; in Inca Cuzco, 104, 106, 197–198; in Peru, 58–59, 61; witch of Endor, 29, 229. *See also* devil; Hacaspoma; oracle; Pachacamac

Domingo de Santo Tomás: and Cieza, 80, 86; and Guaman Poma, 316; and Las Casas, 206; and Polo de Ondegardo, 186–187; on Quechua language, 263; and supay, 254

dream: in Aristotle and Aquinas, 25f.; prophetic, 15, 43 cf. 155, 434–435, 443

dynasty: of Incas, 118 n. 1, 120 and n. 7; of kings in Spain, 133

effigy, of deceased's nails and hair, 70, 130, 367

Euhemerus, 107 n. 57, 219 n. 34, 220

Eusebius: and Cieza, 107 n. 57; and Garcilaso, 362; and Las Casas, 207 n. 13, 213, 214, 218

evangelization, 92, 139–141; Andean reception of and resistance to, 183–185, 202–203, 257–258, 322, 410–411, 419–422; in Europe and Peru, compared, 404–405; by example, 267; in Huamachuco, 144–145, 149; limits of effectiveness, 241, 284–285; political aspects, 377–382; and research, 402. *See also* conversion; extirpation

exorcism, 42, 233, 378

extirpation: of Andean religion, 5, 12f., 185–188, 248, 253–254, 263, 302, 373f., 385–388, 401–403, 405, 406–411, 421, 432; in Guaman Poma, 318–319; procedure of, 389–392

fasting, in Andean religion, 146, 185, 347, 431

fraud, by priests, 57–58, 251, 398–399

free will: in Acosta, 280; and habit in Las Casas, 232–234, 244. *See also* soul

friars, 141–147, 154, 379, 383

Garcia, Gregorio, 313, 349 n. 75, 355–357, 374

Garcilaso. *See* Vega, Garcilaso de la

Gasca, Pedro de la, 80, 88; *visita*, 140, 149

Genesis, Book of: and Andean myth and history, 83f., 100, 219, 372; in Leone Ebreo, 339. *See also* Noah

God: aniconic in the Andes, 328–329 cf. 193; Christian, protects Spaniards, 57, 182; inscrutable judgments, 44, 89, 228, 240, 347; how known, 214–215, 221–222, 223–225, 236; how known in the Andes, 264, 318, 320, 323, 324–331, 367,

370; Quechua term for, 264, 345 and n. 63, 396, 448. *See also* demon(s); devil; Sun

Guamancama, 418, 430–431

Guaman Poma de Ayala: on Andean knowledge of God, 247; on Andean priests, 303; his *Crónica*, 282, 317; on extirpation and Andean culture, 319–320; on Incas, 317–319; in Lima, 386–387; sources, 316; supay, 255, fig. 28; time, 12, 317f.

Guanacaure: capacocha, 105, 199; Citua, 197–198; idolatry and, 322; in Inca myth, 101, 105, 106, 110f., 193, 338; in initiation, 116; myth and cult, 173, 191–193, 409; namesake, 149

guaoque, 269, 292–293 and n. 46

Guaribilca, 84, 95–96

Guascar Inca, 108, 129–130, 132

Guayna Capac: cults under, 321; cults of Huamachuco, 141, 148; Cuni Raya and, 310; death of, 62, 129, 130; descendants of, 81; huaca of Chacalla and, 61; huacas and, 158; inauguration, 127 n. 32, 128; mother's statue, 134; mummy, 65 and n. 10, 71, 129, 149, 339; predicts Spaniards, 308–309, 311

Hacaspoma, Hernando, 418, 422–423, 430–432

Hammer of Witches, 39, 227

harvest: in Inca festival cycle, 117, 159; of maize, in Cuzco, 74ff., 102–103, 106, 162, 168; of potatoes, 87; in provinces, 179–180. *See also* haylli; Inti Raimi; plowing

Haucaypata, 66, 68, 103, 113, 161 n. 9; capacocha, 416; Citua, 197–198; initiation, 117; napa llama, 173; people's place of worship, 113–114

haylli, 168 and n. 44, 175, 319, 368. *See also* aravi

Hernandez Principe, 94, 416

Herrera, Antonio de, 279, 374

huacas: as animate nature, figs. 19–20, 144, 147; Christian sacred objects and, 180–181, 184, 419–420; in Cobo, 396; and the dead, 95; fight Spaniards, 182–184; in Garcilaso, 335–339, 348–349, 349 n. 75; hostile to Incas, 61–63, 85 n. 31, 96, 143 cf. 151; of Huamachuco, 147; myths, cults, possessions, 96, 103f., 156, 392; network in Cuzco, 128, 159–161; offerings, 189–190; petrified human beings, 61; resurrect in Taqui Onqoy, 182; silenced by Christians, 57, fig. 8, 308, 309; speak, 301, 302; speak to Inca rul-